HOW TO PREPARE FOR

LSAT

LAW SCHOOL ADMISSION TEST

SEVENTH EDITON

BY

Jerry Bobrow, Ph.D.

Executive Director
Bobrow Test Preparation Services

Programs at major universities, colleges, and law schools throughout California
Lecturer, consultant, author of over 20 nationally known test preparation books

Dr. Bobrow personally instructs over 2,000 LSAT test takers each year

IN COLLABORATION WITH

William A. Covino, Ph.D
Associate Professor
Department of English
University of Illinois, Chicago

David A. Kay, M.S.
Computer Analyst, Professor
Moorpark College, California

Brian N. Siegel, J.D.
Bar Review Specialist
Author/Legal Study Aids

Daniel C. Spencer, M.S.
Management Services Officer
University of California at Los Angeles (UCLA)

Merritt L. Weisinger, J.D.
Attorney at Law, Lecturer
Weisinger and Associates (Los Angeles)

BARRON'S EDUCATIONAL SERIES, INC.

All inquiries should be addressed to:
Barron's Educational Series, Inc.
250 Wireless Boulevard
Hauppauge, New York 11788

Paper Edition
International Standard Book No. 0-8120-1681-5
International Standard Serial No. 1066-5803

Library of Congress Cataloging-in-Publication Data

Bobrow, Jerry.
    Barron's how to prepare for the LSAT, law school admission test /
  by Jerry Bobrow, in collaboration with William A. Covino … [et
  al.]. — 7th ed.
      p.   cm.
    ISBN 0-8120-1681-5
    1. Law schools—United States—Entrance examinations.   2. Law
  School Admission Test.   3. Law schools—United States—Directories.
  I. Title.   II. Title: How to prepare for the LSAT, law school
  admission test.
  KF285.Z9B6   1993
  340'.076—dc20   90-27729
                                                          CIP

PRINTED IN THE UNITED STATES OF AMERICA
3456   100   98765432

Contents

Preface

YOU CAN PREPARE YOURSELF FOR THE LSAT!

Regardless of your background and your fears about test taking, there are strategies, techniques, and practice exercises that can improve your test taking in general and your LSAT score in particular.

The LSAT measures some of the reading, reasoning, and analyzing skills that are necessary to do well your first year in law school, but it also measures another important skill: your test-taking skill. To strengthen this skill you must (1) know as much about the test as possible before taking the actual exam; (2) understand the thinking processes involved in the question types; and (3) practice using techniques and strategies under time pressure. Getting used to working under time constraints takes lots of practice. But mastering the skill of test taking will help you maximize your score by more effectively and efficiently applying your reading, reasoning, and analyzing skills.

In this book we have gathered the expertise and materials developed in over 20 years of successful LSAT, GMAT, GRE, NTE, CBEST, and SAT preparation courses that are currently offered at 30 universities, colleges, and law schools. By thoroughly analyzing each of the sections on the LSAT and reviewing the thinking processes and the skills necessary for top performance, this text aims at complete preparation. It is up to date with the most recent forms of the latest test. The staff of writers and consultants includes specialists in problem solving, reading, writing, law, logic, and test psychology. All these authors have been teaching prelaw students in LSAT preparation programs for many years.

The most successful overall systems of objective test taking—"Understanding the Thinking Process," "The One-Check, Two-Check System," and "The Elimination Strategy"—are described in detail (see page 8). They provide you with strategies for assessing every question on the LSAT, eliminating wrong answers, and answering correctly all the questions that you should get right. To supplement this overall strategy, we show you a variety of specific techniques for each section of the test, including extensive charting and diagram techniques for the Analytical Reasoning section and a newly updated and expanded comprehensive analysis of the Logical Reasoning sections.

An introductory mini-exam will both acquaint you with the format of the LSAT and help you spot any of your test-taking weaknesses. Then a series of chapters on the most recent sections of the test will pinpoint specific test-taking strategies and include additional practice. Six full-length practice tests will allow you to get the feel of the real thing while you begin applying new skills and techniques. Your answer sheet will resemble the machine-graded LSAT answer sheet, and an analysis chart will enable you to assess your strengths and weaknesses. The answers to each practice test are fully explained.

Altogether, this book combines complete analysis, thorough instruction, extensive practice, and up-to-date examples. The test-taking strategies and approaches we've included have been proved effective for over 500,000 graduate and undergraduate students and teachers whom we've assisted in preparing for these important exams.

REMEMBER: Success is finally up to you. To assure the best preparation possible, work through the book using the Five-Week Study Program, which begins on page 6. You'll be glad you did!

Jerry Bobrow, Ph.D.

May 1993

ACKNOWLEDGMENTS

I gratefully acknowledge the following sources for granting permission to use materials from their publications:

Wesley Barnes, *Existentialism,* © 1968 by Barron's Educational Series, Inc., Hauppauge, N.Y.

Barron's Guide to Law Schools, © 1990 by Barron's Educational Series, Inc., Hauppauge, N.Y.

Arthur Doerr and J. L. Guernsey, *Principles of Geography,* © 1975 by Barron's Educational Series, Inc., Hauppauge, N.Y.

Ann Fagan Ginger, *The Law, the Supreme Court and the People's Rights,* © 1977 by Barron's Educational Series, Inc., Hauppauge, N.Y.

Donald Heiney and Lenthiel H. Downs, *Recent American Literature After 1930,* Vol. 4, © 1974 by Barron's Educational Series, Inc., Hauppauge, N.Y.

Donald Heiney and Lenthiel H. Downs, *Contemporary British Literature,* Vol. 2, © 1974 by Barron's Educational Series, Inc., Hauppauge, N.Y.

John Hollister Hedley, *Harry S Truman—The Little Man from Missouri,* © 1979 by Barron's Educational Series, Inc., Hauppauge, N.Y.

Nicholas Horvath, *Essentials of Philosophy,* © 1974 by Barron's Educational Series, Inc., Hauppauge, N.Y.

George E. Riggs, publisher; news articles and editorials from *The Herald News,* Fontana, Calif.

C. Leland Rodgers, *Essentials of Biology,* © 1974 by Barron's Educational Series, Inc., Hauppauge, N.Y.

Erwin Rosenfeld and Harriet Geller, *Afro-Asian Culture Studies,* © 1979 by Barron's Educational Series, Inc., Hauppauge, N.Y.

Ernst B. Schultz, *Democracy,* 2nd ed., © 1977 by Barron's Educational Series, Inc., Hauppauge, N.Y.

Roger-Gérard Schwartzenberg, *The Superstar Show of Government,* © 1980 by Barron's Educational Series, Inc., Hauppauge, N.Y. © Flammarion, 1977, solely with respect to the French language edition.

Dr. Albert Upton, *Design for Thinking,* Stanford University Press, Stanford, Calif.

Dean Seymour Greitzer, Law Reviews from Glendale University College of Law.

Law Reviews from the University of California at Los Angeles (UCLA) Law School—Comment, "United States Tax Treaty Policy Toward Developing Countries: The China Example," 35 UCLA L. Rev. 369 (1987).

Law Reviews from Western State University College of Law—*United States v. Stanley: A Soldier's Story of Injustice—An Argument for Establishment of a New Standard for Government Liability to Military Servicemen. Author Patricia A. Smith.*

(Note: Some of the Law Reviews have been edited, including changes in names, places, and dates.)

My thanks also to James Zinger, President, Hypmovation, for the use of excerpts from his writings; to Stacey Baum and Joy Mondragon, for their assistance in assembling the manuscript; to Lynn Turner, Dana Lind, Brenda Clodfelter, and Jennifer Johnson for typing the manuscript; and to Linda Turner for manuscript editing and final preparation.

And finally, thanks to my wife, Susan Bobrow, for critical analysis and moral support; and to my three children, Jennifer Lynn, 15, Adam Michael, 12, and Jonathan Matthew, 8, for comic relief.

Jerry Bobrow

PART ONE

INTRODUCTION

Getting Acquainted
with the Test

Introduction to the LSAT

ANSWERS TO SOME COMMONLY ASKED QUESTIONS

What does the LSAT measure?

The LSAT is designed to measure a range of mental abilities related to the study of law; therefore it is used by most law schools to evaluate their applicants.

Will any special knowledge of the law raise my score on the LSAT?

The LSAT is designed so that candidates from a particular academic background are given no advantage. The questions measure reading comprehension, logical reasoning, and analytical reasoning, drawing from a variety of verbal and analytical material.

Does a high score on the LSAT predict success in law school or in the practice of law?

Success on the LSAT demonstrates your ability to read with understanding and to reason clearly under pressure; surely these strengths are important to both the study and the practice of law, as is the ability to write well, measured by the LSAT Writing Sample. To say that success on the LSAT *predicts* success in law school may overstate the case, however, because success in law school also involves skills that are not measured by the LSAT.

When is the LSAT administered?

The regular administration of the test occurs nationwide four times each year, around the beginning of the fall, winter, spring, and summer seasons. Except for the summer month, the test is usually administered on a Saturday morning from 8:30 A.M. to about 1:00 P.M. For the past few years, the *summer exam* has been given on a Monday afternoon. Dates are announced annually by the Law School Admission Council in Newtown, PA.

What if I cannot take the test on a Saturday?

Some special arrangements are possible: check the LSAS General Information Booklet in your registration packet. Those who must take the exam at a time when the regular administration occurs on Saturday, but who cannot participate on Saturday for religious reasons, may arrange for a special Monday administration.

How early should I register?

Regular registration closes about one month prior to the exam date. Late registration is available up to three weeks prior to the exam date. There is an additional fee for late registration.

Is walk-in registration available?

Walk-in registration will be permitted only for students who telephone the Law School Admission Services (LSAS) in advance. Students who do not telephone the LSAS will not be permitted to be walk-ins the day of the test. If you must be a walk-in, be sure to very carefully read the General Information Booklet section on "walk-in registration at test centers."

What is the LSDAS?

The LSDAS (Law School Data Assembly Service) compiles a report about each subscribing applicant. The report contains LSAT results, a summary of the applicant's academic work, and copies of college transcripts. A report is sent to each law school that the applicant designates. Thus, if you register for the LSDAS, you will not need to mail a separate transcript to each of your prospective law schools. REMINDER: You can register for the Candidate Referral Service *only* at the same time you register for the LSDAS.

How is the LSAT used?

Your LSAT score is one common denominator by which a law school compares you to other applicants. Other factors also determine your acceptance to law school: a law school may consider your personal qualities, grade-point average, extracurricular achievements, and letters of recommendation. Requirements for admission vary widely from school to school, so you are wise to contact the law school of your choice for specific information.

How do I obtain registration forms?

The registration form covering both the LSAT and the LSDAS is available in the LSAT/LSDAS REGISTRATION PACKET. Copies of the packet are available at the admissions offices of most law schools and the testing offices at most undergraduate universities and colleges. You may also obtain the packet by writing to LAW SCHOOL ADMISSION SERVICES, Box 2000, Newtown, Pennsylvania 18940.

What is the structure of the LSAT?

The LSAT contains five 35-minute multiple-choice sections followed by a 30-minute Writing Sample. The Writing Sample does not count as part of your LSAT score. The common question types that do count toward your score are Logical Reasoning (two sections), Analytical Reasoning (one section), and Reading Comprehension (one section). In addition to these four sections, one experimental or pretest section will appear. This experimental or pretest section, which will probably be a repeat of one of the common question types, will not count in your score.

How is the LSAT scored?

The score for the objective portion of the test ranges from 120 to 180, and there is no penalty for wrong answers. The Writing Sample is unscored, but copies are sent to the law schools of your choice for evaluation.

What about question structure and value?

All LSAT questions, apart from the Writing Sample, are multiple-choice with five choices. All questions within a section are of equal value, regardless of difficulty.

Should I guess?

There is no penalty for guessing on the LSAT. Therefore, before you move on to the next question, at least take a guess. You should fill in guess answers for those you have left blank or did not get to, before time is called for that section. If you can eliminate one or more choices as incorrect, your chances for a correct guess increase.

How often can I take the LSAT?

You may take the LSAT more than once if you wish. But keep in mind that any report sent to you or to law schools will contain scores for any exams taken over the past few years, along with an average score for those exams. The law school receiving your scores will decide which score is the best estimate of your ability; many law schools rely on the average score as a reliable figure.

Is it at all possible to cancel my LSAT score?

You may cancel your score only within 5 days after taking the test.

How early should I arrive at the test center, and what should I bring?

Arrive at the test center 15 to 30 minutes before the time designated on your admission ticket. Bring three or four sharpened No. 2 pencils, an eraser, and a watch, as well as your LSAT Admission Ticket and proper identification as described in the LSAT Registration/Information Booklet.

Can I prepare for the LSAT?

Yes. Reading skills and test-taking strategies should be the focus of your preparation for the test as a whole. Success on the more specialized analytical sections of the test depends on your thorough familiarity with the types of problems you are likely to encounter and the reasoning process involved. For maximum preparation, work through this book and practice the strategies and techniques outlined in each section.

NOTE: For your convenience, this Barron's text labels each section of the practice tests (e.g., Reading Comprehension, Logical Reasoning, etc.). In contrast, sections of the actual LSAT exam are not usually labeled.

BASIC FORMAT OF THE LSAT AND SCORING

THE *ORDER* OF THE FOLLOWING MULTIPLE-CHOICE SECTIONS *WILL* VARY.

Section	Number of Questions	Minutes
I. Logical Reasoning	24–26	35
II. Logical Reasoning	24–26	35
III. Reading Comprehension	26–28 (4 passages)	35
IV. Analytical Reasoning	22–24 (4 sets)	35
V. Experimental Section	varies	35
Writing Sample	1 essay	30
TOTALS	118–132 questions (only 96–104 count toward your score)	205 minutes or 3 hours 25 minutes

A Breakdown of the Timing

3 multiple-choice sections (35 minutes each)
short break
2 multiple-choice sections (35 minutes each)
1 unscored writing sample (30 minutes)

Important Notes

AT LEAST HALF OF YOUR TEST WILL CONTAIN LOGICAL REASONING QUESTIONS. PREPARE ACCORDINGLY.

The experimental or pretest section will usually repeat other sections and can appear in different places on the exam. At the time of the exam, you will not know which section is experimental.

Scoring will be from 120 to 180, with all questions having equal value.

There is NO PENALTY for guessing.

The 30-minute Writing Sample will not be scored, but copies will be forwarded to the law schools to which you apply. Scratch paper will be provided for the Writing Sample only. A 5- to 10-minute break will probably be given between Sections III and IV.

A Sampling of Formats

Logical Reasoning	Analytical Reasoning	Reading Comp.	Logical Reasoning	Analytical Reasoning	Reading Comp.
Analytical Reasoning	Reading Comp.	Logical Reasoning	Logical Reasoning	Logical Reasoning	Reading Comp.
Reading Comp.	Logical Reasoning	Logical Reasoning	Analytical Reasoning	Analytical Reasoning	Logical Reasoning
Logical Reasoning	Analytical Reasoning	Analytical Reasoning	Reading Comp.	Logical Reasoning	Analytical Reasoning
Reading Comp.	Logical Reasoning	Logical Reasoning	Logical Reasoning	Reading Comp.	Logical Reasoning
Writing Sample	Writing Sample	Writing Sample	Writing Sample	Writing Sample	Writing Sample

IT IS EVIDENT THAT MANY ADDITIONAL COMBINATIONS ARE POSSIBLE. But remember: regardless of the format, two sections of Logical Reasoning, one section of Analytical Reasoning, and one section of Reading Comprehension always count toward your score.

An Effective Study Program— Some Words to the Wise

A FIVE-WEEK LSAT STUDY PLAN

Many students don't even bother to read the LSAT bulletin, let alone do any thorough preparation for the test. You, however, should begin your LSAT preparation by reading the LSAT bulletin (book) carefully; information about how to obtain one is on page 4. The bulletin is filled with information about registration and score reporting. Also provided with the registration packet is an "official" practice test. You should also send for copies of old exams (good practice).

Check with the law schools to which you are applying to find out what score each requires for admission. Requirements vary widely and are often influenced by your grade-point average and other achievements.

With these preliminaries out of the way, begin working through this book. If you have the time, the following study plan is ideal and is used in many LSAT preparation programs at major universities and colleges. However, if you have a shorter time to prepare, simply adjust the following five-week plan to meet your needs (remember, lots of *practice* and *analysis*). You will find the techniques, strategies, practice, and analyses in this book invaluable to your preparation, either with the ideal five-week plan or with the shorter study plan.

Most people can keep up with the following study sequence by devoting about 7 to 10 hours a week. It is most important that you review and practice *daily,* for about an hour or two each day. Don't "save up" your practice for one long session each week. Shorter, regular practice sessions will allow you to assimilate skills and strategies more effectively and efficiently.

Always spend some extra time reviewing "why" you made your mistakes. Watch for repeated or consistent errors. These errors are often the easiest to correct. As you review, focus on the thinking process involved in reaching the credited response, and note specifically where you made the error.

If you have reviewed an explanation, and still do not understand where you made an error, mark the problem in your book and go on. Return to review this problem later, after you have had an opportunity to review other problems that use similar thinking processes. Don't get stuck on reviewing one problem.

Week 1

- Read the section "Answers to Some Commonly Asked Questions" (p. 3).
- Complete, correct, and analyze the Diagnostic Mini-Exam (p. 11).
- Read carefully "Before You Begin" (p.7), paying special attention to the "One-Check, Two-Check System" and the "Elimination Strategy." Applying these techniques confidently should make quite a difference in your test taking.
- Read carefully the chapters on Reading Comprehension, Logical Reasoning, Analytical Reasoning, and the Writing Sample.
- Spend some extra time reviewing the chapter on Logical Reasoning. Remember: Logical Reasoning will comprise two of the four scored sections of your exam.

Week 2

- Review the chapter on Reading Comprehension. Do the Reading Comprehension problems in the chapter, the ones in the LSAT sample test, and those in Model Test One (p. 161). Correct and analyze your performance.

  Note: Do not time yourself on these practice tests. Your task at present is to familiarize yourself with strategies and techniques, a task that is best done slowly, working back and forth between the introductory chapter and the practice problems. You may get an uncomfortable number of problems wrong at this stage, but, instead of being discouraged, you should

attempt to understand clearly the reasons for your errors. Such understanding will become a plus in the future.
- Review the chapter on the Writing Sample, and write an essay about one of the given topics. Ask a friend with good writing skills to read your essay and offer constructive criticism.
- Review the chapter on Logical Reasoning. Do the Logical Reasoning problems in the chapter, those in the LSAT practice test, and the ones in Model Test One (pp.173 and 183). Correct and analyze your performance.

Week 3

- Review the chapter on Analytical Reasoning. Do the Analytical Reasoning problems in the chapter, those in the LSAT practice test, and those in Model Test One (p. 169). Correct and analyze your performance.

  Note: At this point you have introduced yourself to the whole test, and have tried some effective strategies. Now you should begin timing each of your practice tests.
- Do the Reading Comprehension problems in Model Test Two (p. 215), and the Logical Reasoning problems in Model Test Two (pp 209 and 227). Correct and analyze your performance.
- Do the Analytical Reasoning problems in Model Test Two (p. 222). Correct and analyze your performance.
- Write another essay about one of the topics given in the Writing Sample chapter, and have a friend read and respond to your effort.

Week 4

- Do all of Model Test Three; practice and review two or three sections each day. For each section, time yourself (always short yourself on time during practice by about 10–15 percent), then correct and analyze your performance.
- Do all of Model Test Four. Start with the first three sections. After a sufficient break, correct and analyze your performance. On the next day, take the next three sections (two multiple-choice sections and the Writing Sample) in one sitting. Correct and analyze your performance. Have a friend read and respond to your Writing Sample.

  Note: This long practice testing will familiarize you with some of the difficulties you will encounter on the actual test—maintaining focus and concentration, dealing with fatigue, pacing, etc. It will also help you build your endurance. Remember, as you analyze your mistakes, to watch for repeated errors. Sometimes these are the easiest to eliminate.

Week 5

- Early in the week, do all of Model Test Five; practice and review three sections each day. For each section, time yourself, then correct and analyze your performance. Again, have a friend read and respond to your efforts on the Writing Sample.
- If you have time early in the week, you may wish to do Model Test Six for extra practice. You can follow the procedure used for Model Test Five, or simply take and review individual sections as needed.
- A few days before your exam, review some of the problems you have already completed—focus on the thinking processes. You may wish to reread chapters that gave you the most difficulty.
- Finally, carefully read the review of test-taking strategies at the end of the book (p. 462). It will recap the highlights of the book, and supply a variety of tips for putting yourself into an effective state of mind before the LSAT.

BEFORE YOU BEGIN
UNDERSTANDING THE THINKING PROCESS

One of the key factors in your success on the LSAT is your mastery of the LSAT "thinking process." There is no question that this will take lots of practice, but it will also take a carefully focused analysis of that practice.

As you read each introductory chapter, keep in mind the thinking process involved as it is explained. You are not trying to learn or memorize any actual problem; rather, you are trying to learn the process behind solving each problem type so that you will be able to apply that process to new problems.

Notice that each section is designed to analyze this thinking process and to help you understand what the test maker had in mind when constructing the question. Learn to understand the reasoning behind the construction of each question.

If you focus on this reasoning as you prepare, the techniques carefully explained in each chapter will be easier to apply and will become even more effective. Remember that it is the mastery of this thinking process within the time constraints that will yield success on the LSAT.

THE ONE-CHECK, TWO-CHECK SYSTEM

Many people score lower than they should on the LSAT simply because they do not get to many of the easier problems. They puzzle over difficult questions and use up the time that could be spent answering easy ones. In fact, the easy questions are worth exactly the same as the difficult ones, so it makes sense not to do the hard problems until you have answered all the easy ones.

To maximize your correct answers by focusing on the easier problems, use the following system:

1. Attempt the first question. If it is answerable quickly and easily, work the problem, circle the answer in the question booklet, and then mark that answer on the answer sheet. The mark on the answer sheet should be a complete mark, not merely a dot, because you may not be given time at the end of the test to darken marks.
2. If a question seems impossible, place two checks ($\sqrt{}$ $\sqrt{}$) on or next to the question number in the question booklet and mark the answer you guess on the answer sheet. Again, the mark on the answer sheet should be a complete mark, not merely a dot.
3. If you're in the midst of a question that seems to be taking too much time, or if you immediately spot that a question is answerable but time-consuming (that is, it will require more than two minutes to answer), place one check ($\sqrt{}$) next to the question number, mark an answer you guess on the answer sheet, and continue with the next question.
   NOTE THAT NO QUESTIONS ARE LEFT BLANK. AN ANSWER CHOICE IS *ALWAYS* FILLED IN BEFORE LEAVING THAT QUESTION.
4. When all the problems in a section have been attempted in this manner, there may still be time left. If so, return to the single-check ($\sqrt{}$) questions, working as many as possible, changing each guessed answer to a worked-out answer, if necessary.
5. If time remains after all the single-check ($\sqrt{}$) questions are completed, you can choose between
   a. attempting those "impossible" double-check ($\sqrt{}$ $\sqrt{}$) questions (sometimes a question later on in the test may trigger one's memory to allow once-impossible questions to be solved);

   or

   b. spending time checking and reworking the easier questions to eliminate any careless errors.
6. Remember: use *all* the allotted time as effectively as possible.

You should use this system as you work through the practice tests in this book; such practice will allow you to make "one-check, two-check" judgments quickly when you actually take the LSAT. As our extensive research has shown, use of this system results in less wasted time on the LSAT.

THE ELIMINATION STRATEGY

Faced with five answer choices, you will work more efficiently and effectively if you *eliminate unreasonable or irrelevant answers immediately.* In most cases, two or three choices in every set will stand out as obviously incorrect. Many test takers don't perceive this because they painstakingly analyze every choice, even the obviously ridiculous ones.

Consider the following Logical Reasoning problem:

According to the theory of aerodynamics, the bumblebee is unable to fly. This is because the size, weight, and shape of its body in relationship to the total wingspan make flying impossible. The bumblebee, being ignorant of this "scientific truth," flies anyway.

The author's statement would be strengthened by pointing out that   Ⓐ Ⓑ Ⓒ Ⓓ Ⓔ

(A) the theory of aerodynamics may be readily tested
(B) the bumblebee does not actually fly but glides instead
(C) bumblebees cannot fly in strong winds
(D) bumblebees are ignorant of other things but can't do all of them
(E) nothing is impossible

A student who does not immediately eliminate the unreasonable choices here, and instead tries to analyze every choice, will find herself becoming confused and anxious as she tries to decide how even silly choices might be correct. Her thinking goes something like this: "I wonder if bumblebees do glide; I've never looked that closely—maybe the test has me on this one…come to think of it, I've never seen a bumblebee in a strong wind; (C) is tricky, but it just might be right…I can't understand (D); it seems irrelevant but that just might be a trick…"
On and on she goes, becoming more and more uncertain.

Using the elimination strategy, a confident test taker proceeds as follows:

"(A)?   Possible choice.
(B)?   Ridiculous. Both false and irrelevant. Cross it out.
(C)?   Another ridiculous, irrelevant one. Cross it out.
(D)?   Incomprehensible! Eliminate it.
(E)?   Too *general* to be the best choice."

This test taker, aware that most answer choices can be easily eliminated, does so without complicating the process by considering unreasonable possibilities.
To summarize the elimination strategy:

- Look for unreasonable or incorrect answer choices first. Expect to find at least two or three of these with every problem.
- When a choice seems wrong, cross it out in your test booklet *immediately,* so that you will not be tempted to reconsider it.

Eliminating choices in this fashion will lead you to correct answers more quickly, and will increase your overall confidence.

MARKING IN THE TEST BOOKLET

Many test takers don't take full advantage of opportunities to mark key words and draw diagrams in the test booklet. Remember that, in the Reading Comprehension and Logical Reasoning sections, *marking key words and phrases will significantly increase your comprehension and lead you to a correct answer.* Marking also helps to keep you focused and alert. In the Analytical Reasoning section, *drawing diagrams is absolutely essential.*

Further, more specific hints about marking are given in the introductory chapters that follow. The important general point to stress here is that active, successful test taking entails marking and drawing, and that passive, weak test takers make little use of this technique.

THE COMMON MISTAKE—THE MISREAD

The most common mistake for many test takers is the MISREAD. The MISREAD occurs when you read the question incorrectly. For example, "Which of the following *must* be true?" is often read as "Which of the following *could* be true?" and "All of the following must be true EXCEPT" often loses the word "except."

If you MISREAD the question, you will be looking for the wrong answer.

To help eliminate the MISREAD, always underline or circle what you are looking for in the question. This will also help you focus on the main point of the question.

By the way, the MISREAD also occurs while reading answer choices. You may wish to underline or circle key words in the answers to help you avoid the MISREAD.

THE "MULTIPLE-MULTIPLE-CHOICE" ITEM (Not appeared recently)

Although the "Multiple-Multiple-Choice" Item has not appeared in the last few years, we have included a few samples with some excellent strategies in the event that any do reappear on a future exam.

Example

According to the theory of aerodynamics, the bumblebee should be unable to fly. But it flies anyway.

Which of the following can be logically inferred from the above statement?   Ⓐ Ⓑ Ⓒ Ⓓ Ⓔ

   I.   The bumblebee's behavior contradicts scientific theory.
  II. The bumblebee is not really able to fly.
 III. Some theories don't hold true in all cases.
(A) I only   (B) II only   (C) I and II only   (D) I and III only   (E) I, II, and III

When faced with a problem of this structure, first try to quickly answer each of the roman numerals as true or false and label them accordingly. They would therefore be labeled as follows:

T   I.   The bumblebee's behavior contradicts scientific theory.
F   II. The bumblebee is not really able to fly.
T   III. Some theories don't hold true in all cases.
(A) I only   (B) II only   (C) I and II only   (D) I and III only   (E) I, II, and III

Therefore since I and III are true, the answer is (D).

Quite frequently, however, determining each of the roman numerals as true or false is not a quick or easy proposition. In such a case it may be effective (and possibly less time consuming) to skip the difficult roman numerals, solve the easy ones, and then eliminate the final choices, as follows:

?   I.   The bumblebee's behavior contradicts scientific theory.
F   II. The bumblebee is not really able to fly.
T   III. Some theories don't hold true in all cases.
(A̶) I only   (B̶) II only   (C̶) I and II only   (D) I and III only   (E̶) I, II, and III

Notice that, since II is false, any choice containing a false II may be eliminated. Thus (B), (C), and (E) should be crossed out. Continuing, since III is true, any remaining choice must contain a true III for it to be correct. Thus choice (A) may be eliminated as it does not contain a true III. This leaves only choice (D) as the correct answer.

In some cases you will be able to eliminate all but the correct answer, as above. In other cases you may find several possible choices remaining, and thus have a more educated guess.

Becoming familiar with this technique will often save you time and allow you to take better educated guesses in those cases when you have partial information, when parts of the problem appear too difficult, or when the question itself does not appear to give enough direction.

Chapter

1

A Diagnostic Mini-Exam

The purpose of this mini-exam is to familiarize you with the common areas on the LSAT by giving you a sampling of typical problems. It is designed to introduce the testing areas. The chapters to follow on each exam area will give you a much more complete range of the problem types and difficulties.

This mini-exam should be taken under strict test conditions with each section timed as follows:

Section	Description	Number of Questions	Time Allowed
I	Logical Reasoning	9	10 minutes
II	Reading Comprehension	8	10 minutes
III	Analytical Reasoning	7	10 minutes
IV	Logical Reasoning	9	10 minutes
	Writing Sample		30 minutes
TOTALS:		33	70 minutes

The actual LSAT contains five 35-minute sections plus a 30-minute Writing Sample for a total of almost 3½ hours of testing. Note that one section will be experimental and will be a duplication of one of the above sections. Also note that it may appear anywhere in the test. Thus only four sections will count toward your score—two Logical Reasonings, one Analytical Reasoning, and one Reading Comprehension.

After correcting the mini-exam and assessing your strengths and weaknesses, you should start your area analysis with Chapters 2 through 5.

Now tear out your answer sheet from this book, turn to the next page, and begin the mini-exam.

ANSWER SHEET—PRACTICE MINI-EXAM
LAW SCHOOL ADMISSION TEST (LSAT)
Note: The actual LSAT has five sections, plus a Writing Sample.

Section I:
Logical Reasoning

1. Ⓐ Ⓑ Ⓒ Ⓓ Ⓔ
2. Ⓐ Ⓑ Ⓒ Ⓓ Ⓔ
3. Ⓐ Ⓑ Ⓒ Ⓓ Ⓔ
4. Ⓐ Ⓑ Ⓒ Ⓓ Ⓔ
5. Ⓐ Ⓑ Ⓒ Ⓓ Ⓔ
6. Ⓐ Ⓑ Ⓒ Ⓓ Ⓔ
7. Ⓐ Ⓑ Ⓒ Ⓓ Ⓔ
8. Ⓐ Ⓑ Ⓒ Ⓓ Ⓔ
9. Ⓐ Ⓑ Ⓒ Ⓓ Ⓔ

Section III:
Analytical Reasoning

1. Ⓐ Ⓑ Ⓒ Ⓓ Ⓔ
2. Ⓐ Ⓑ Ⓒ Ⓓ Ⓔ
3. Ⓐ Ⓑ Ⓒ Ⓓ Ⓔ
4. Ⓐ Ⓑ Ⓒ Ⓓ Ⓔ
5. Ⓐ Ⓑ Ⓒ Ⓓ Ⓔ
6. Ⓐ Ⓑ Ⓒ Ⓓ Ⓔ
7. Ⓐ Ⓑ Ⓒ Ⓓ Ⓔ

Section II:
Reading Comprehension

1. Ⓐ Ⓑ Ⓒ Ⓓ Ⓔ
2. Ⓐ Ⓑ Ⓒ Ⓓ Ⓔ
3. Ⓐ Ⓑ Ⓒ Ⓓ Ⓔ
4. Ⓐ Ⓑ Ⓒ Ⓓ Ⓔ
5. Ⓐ Ⓑ Ⓒ Ⓓ Ⓔ
6. Ⓐ Ⓑ Ⓒ Ⓓ Ⓔ
7. Ⓐ Ⓑ Ⓒ Ⓓ Ⓔ
8. Ⓐ Ⓑ Ⓒ Ⓓ Ⓔ

Section IV:
Logical Reasoning

1. Ⓐ Ⓑ Ⓒ Ⓓ Ⓔ
2. Ⓐ Ⓑ Ⓒ Ⓓ Ⓔ
3. Ⓐ Ⓑ Ⓒ Ⓓ Ⓔ
4. Ⓐ Ⓑ Ⓒ Ⓓ Ⓔ
5. Ⓐ Ⓑ Ⓒ Ⓓ Ⓔ
6. Ⓐ Ⓑ Ⓒ Ⓓ Ⓔ
7. Ⓐ Ⓑ Ⓒ Ⓓ Ⓔ
8. Ⓐ Ⓑ Ⓒ Ⓓ Ⓔ
9. Ⓐ Ⓑ Ⓒ Ⓓ Ⓔ

SECTION I
LOGICAL REASONING

Directions:

In this section you will be given brief statements or passages and will be required to evaluate the reasoning involved. In some instances, more than one choice will appear to be a possible answer. You are to choose the *best* answer. Use common sense and reasonableness in making your selection; then mark the proper space on the answer sheet.

1. The theory that the subconscious is simply the unsymbolized suggests the desirability of adequate verbalization at the earliest possible stage of emotional development. It is the nameless fears and frustrations that defy analysis.

   The author of this passage would most likely agree that
   (A)   there is nothing to fear but fear itself
   (B)   emotional development starts at birth
   (C)   verbalization is the key to complete emotional development
   (D)   unsymbolized thoughts and emotions cannot be analyzed
   (E)   the subconscious initiates only nameless fears and frustrations

2. Anyone who thinks that ignorance is no excuse isn't paying attention. Therefore
   (A)   ignorance is an excuse
   (B)   not paying attention is no excuse
   (C)   ignorance comes from not paying attention
   (D)   no one is ignorant
   (E)   ignorance is no excuse

3. The most serious threat to modern man, it would seem, is not physical annihilation but the alleged meaninglessness of life. This latent vacuum becomes manifest in a state of boredom. Automation will lead to more and more free time and many will not know how to use their leisure hours. This is evidenced today by what Dr. Frankl refers to as Sunday Neurosis, the depression which afflicts people who become conscious of the lack of content in their lives when the rush of the busy week stops. Nothing in the world helps man to keep healthy so much as the knowledge of a life task. Nietzsche wisely said, "He who knows a Why of living surmounts every How."

   Which of the following is the best refutation of the above argument?
   (A)   The availability of free time does not afford people more opportunity to enjoy their blessings.
   (B)   Nuclear annihilation would vastly transcend the issue of personal meaningfulness.
   (C)   Automation may actually result in more people working in such fields as computer science and technology.
   (D)   The problem of personal meaning has existed since the beginning of modern times.
   (E)   Most people actually enjoy their weekends when their work week ends on Friday.

4. Reading is an activity involving the use of the visual apparatus by means of which printed words are recognized.

   The above definition would be weakened most by pointing out that
   (A)   skimming is a form of reading
   (B)   a "nonreader" can recognize words
   (C)   some printed words can be difficult to interpret
   (D)   seeing is necessary for reading
   (E)   lengthy printed words are not easily recognized

Questions 5–6 refer to the following passage.

Juan said, "It takes a good swing to be a good golfer. It takes practice to develop a good swing. Thus, it takes practice to be a good golfer."

5. Which of the following most closely parallels the logic of this statement?
  - (A) Betsy can bake a good cake if she wants to. Betsy baked a good cake. Thus she must have wanted to bake a good cake.
  - (B) A vote for Senator Cobb is a vote for peace. I voted for Senator Cobb. Thus, I want peace.
  - (C) You must work to earn money. You need money to pay the rent. Thus, you must work to pay the rent.
  - (D) It costs $200 to buy the TV. It costs $50 to buy the radio. Thus, the TV costs more than the radio.
  - (E) It is important to be alert when you take an exam. If you take a cold shower, you will be alert. Thus, you should take a cold shower before you take your exam.

6. Which of the following would weaken Juan's argument the most?
  - (A) It takes more than a good swing to be a good golfer.
  - (B) Some good golfers have average swings.
  - (C) Some people are born with a good golf swing.
  - (D) It takes strong forearms to have a good golf swing.
  - (E) Many good golfers lift weights.

Questions 7–8 require you to complete missing portions of the following passage by selecting from the five alternatives the one that best fits the context of the passage.

We suggest making a distinction between a highly developed or complex culture and a civilization. Culture may be defined in passing as the relatively rigid and unreasoned type of social behavior found in hives, lodges, and sometimes even in pentagons. It may be impressive and its achievements marvelous. We suggest a meaning for "(7) —————————————————" that would make it rather a special sort of complex culture in which the constituent parts have developed linguistic, that is to say, parliamentary, techniques for resolving the "(8) ————————————" that arise from the conflicts of interest, real or apparent.

7. (A) culture   (B) behavior   (C) civilization   (D) parliamentary   (E) life

8. (A) inevitable disputes   (B) unfortunate circumstances   (C) complex situations
  (D) meaningless subsidies   (E) total carelessness

9. Many people believe that capital punishment acts as a deterrent to crime. This belief would be most weakened by
  - (A) examination of the number of murders before and after the abolition of the death penalty in a number of areas
  - (B) supplying statistics explaining the number of occurrences of crimes that are punishable by death
  - (C) a study of which crimes occur most and when they occur
  - (D) the fact that most crimes are not punishable by death
  - (E) the fact that the death penalty has not been enforced in 10 years

STOP

IF YOU FINISH BEFORE TIME IS UP, CHECK YOUR WORK ON THIS SECTION OF THE TEST ONLY. DO NOT GO ON TO THE NEXT SECTION OF THE TEST UNTIL TIME IS UP FOR THIS SECTION.

SECTION II
READING COMPREHENSION

Time—10 Minutes
8 Questions

Directions:
Read the passages and answer the questions following each passage by blackening the appro-priate space on the answer sheet. You may refer back to the passages when answering the questions. Answer all questions on the basis of what is stated or implied.

Passage

    In 1957, Congress passed the Price-Anderson Act, which provides a current limitation of $665 million on the liability of nuclear power companies in the event of a "nuclear incident." The dual purpose of the Act is to "protect the public and encourage the development of the atomic energy industry." While the objective of encouraging the development of atomic energy has been achieved, it is not yet known if
(5) Price-Anderson would fully compensate the public in the event of a serious nuclear accident.

    In the event that a major accident does occur in this country, would the victims be adequately compensated for their injuries? The nuclear industry is promoted under Price-Anderson by having a limit on potential liability even if the accident was the result of gross negligence or willful misconduct. Victims are protected by having an asset pool of at least $665 million in which to recover for damages.
(10) This amount will undoubtedly be raised when Price-Anderson is renewed. Victims are also protected if an accident is deemed to be an "extraordinary nuclear occurrence" by the requirement that certain defenses be waived by the utility company. However, the victims would still substantially bear the risk because of the uncertainty of recovery for radiation injuries. This is contrary to the tort (wrongful act) concept that "he who breaks must pay."
(15) The Price-Anderson Act does not disturb the common law rule of causation. A person injured in a nuclear incident has the burden of proving a causal relationship between the incident and his alleged injury. While the plaintiff does not have to show that the conduct of the defendant was the sole cause of the injury, the plaintiff must prove that it is more likely than not that the conduct of the defendant was a substantial factor in bringing about the injury. The plaintiff has the burden of showing that there is a high
(20) probability (i.e., 51 percent or more) that the defendant's conduct caused his alleged injury. A mere possibility of such causation is not enough; and when the matter remains one of pure speculation or conjecture, or the probabilities are at least evenly balanced, it becomes the duty of the court to direct a verdict for the defendant. In the event of a nuclear incident involving a large release of radioactive material, such as Chernobyl, it would probably not be difficult for immediate victims to demonstrate a
(25) causal link between the accident and their injuries. Scientists are able to detect approximately how much radiation was released into the atmosphere, and how surrounding areas are affected by it.

    An argument in favor of Price-Anderson is that it ensures that claimants have an asset pool of at least $665 million in which to recover for damages. Without Price-Anderson, the possibility is very real that the utility company would be unable to pay claims arising out of a major accident. If the claims were
(30) sufficiently large or numerous, a private company could well choose bankruptcy over paying the claims. For example, the Planex Corporation, a defendant in thousands of asbestos cases, filed for reorganization under Chapter 11 of the Bankruptcy Code in 1982.

    Furthermore, as the ceiling on liability will undoubtedly be raised when Price-Anderson is renewed, the limit on liability will be more commensurate with the amount of damages that could result from a
(35) nuclear accident. Therefore, it is more likely that there will be adequate funds to compensate victims with acute, or immediate, injuries. However, victims with delayed, or latent, injuries, would still face a major obstacle in proving that their injuries were caused by the nuclear accident. Furthermore, even if causation could be proved, it is still possible that latent injuries would not be manifest until after the twenty-year statute of limitations under Price-Anderson. Therefore, Congress should consider imple-

(40)   menting a more relaxed standard of proving causation than under the common law and should extend the statute of limitations to at least forty years after the date of the nuclear accident. Furthermore, Congress should expressly state whether or not punitive damages would be allowed in the event that the conduct of the licensee was reckless or seriously indifferent to the rights of others. As it currently stands, there is uncertainty as to whether a licensee would be shielded from having to pay punitive

(45)   damages. As we all benefit from nuclear power, the victims of a nuclear accident should not bear the burden of uncertainty in recovering for their injuries.

1. The primary purpose of the passage is to
  (A)   describe the Price-Anderson Act
  (B)   criticize the Price-Anderson Act
  (C)   support the Price-Anderson Act
  (D)   analyze and then condemn the Price-Anderson Act
  (E)   present the advantages and disadvantages of the Price-Anderson Act

2. The advantages to the nuclear industry in the United States of the Price-Anderson Act include all of the following EXCEPT
  (A)   the limitation of the liability to $665 million
  (B)   some injuries may not be apparent until after the statute of limitations has expired
  (C)   the potential liability far exceeds the limit fixed
  (D)   the plaintiff must show the high probability that the defendant's conduct caused the injury
  (E)   the ceiling on liability will probably be raised when Price-Anderson is renewed

3. If there were a major nuclear accident in the United States equal in size to the Chernobyl incident, we can infer that under the rules of the Price-Anderson Act
  (A)   there would be difficulty in proving causation
  (B)   the asset pool would be exhausted
  (C)   victims with latent injuries would be able to collect damages
  (D)   the liability would not apply if the accident was caused by provable negligence
  (E)   the concept of "he who breaks must pay" would be applied

4. Which of the following is an advantage of the Price-Anderson Act to the general public?
  (A)   The liability pool of $665 million would pay many victims of a nuclear accident.
  (B)   A utility company responsible for a nuclear accident would not need to file for bankruptcy if the claim exceeded the $665 million in the asset pool.
  (C)   A claim against a company responsible for a nuclear accident could be filed under relaxed common law rules of causation.
  (D)   Injuries caused by nuclear exposure might not be apparent for many years.
  (E)   Victims of an accident could collect punitive damages if an accident is caused by industry negligence.

5. According to the passage, the Price-Anderson Act does NOT make clear
  (A)   what standard of causation will apply
  (B)   what length of statute of limitations will apply
  (C)   whether or not a company is liable for punitive damages
  (D)   whether or not a company is liable for delayed or latent injuries
  (E)   what, if any, is the ceiling on liability

6. Under the terms of Price-Anderson, in the case of a minor nuclear accident a successful plaintiff would have to show that the defendant's conduct was the
  (A)   sole cause of his injury
  (B)   probable cause of his injury
  (C)   possible cause of his injury
  (D)   contributing cause of his injury
  (E)   cause of his injury through negligence

7. According to the passage, the Planex Corporation (line 31) filed for bankruptcy
   (A) after paying damages in a nuclear accident case
   (B) after paying damages in a toxic waste case
   (C) after paying damages in an asbestos case
   (D) to avoid paying damages in a toxic waste case
   (E) to avoid paying damages in an asbestos case

8. With which of the following statements would the author of the passage be most likely to disagree?
   (A) Attitudes toward nuclear energy have changed dramatically since the incidents at Three Mile Island and Chernobyl.
   (B) The radioactive contamination from Chernobyl may result in thousands of cancer deaths in the next fifty years.
   (C) Congress should disallow any expansion of the nuclear power industry.
   (D) The size of the asset pool under Price-Anderson should be increased.
   (E) The twenty-year statute of limitations under Price-Anderson is too short.

STOP

IF YOU FINISH BEFORE TIME IS UP, CHECK YOUR WORK ON THIS SECTION OF THE TEST ONLY.
DO NOT GO ON TO THE NEXT SECTION OF THE TEST UNTIL TIME IS UP FOR THIS SECTION.

SECTION III
ANALYTICAL REASONING

Time—10 Minutes
7 Questions

Directions:
In this section you will be given a group of questions based on a specific set of conditions. Drawing a simple diagram may be helpful in answering some of the questions. You are to choose the best answer and mark the corresponding space on your answer sheet.

Eight students, A, B, C, D, E, F, G, and H, are standing in a straight line, not necessarily in order.

The first and last people in line are the two tallest.
The 4th, 5th, and 6th students in line are the only girls.
C is always third in line.
E is always next to F, and they are not girls.
H is a boy.
A and D are sisters, but will not stand next to each other.

1. If G is a girl, then which of the following must be true?
   (A) D is in the 4th place.
   (B) A is next to C.
   (C) D is in the 5th place.
   (D) G is in the 5th place.
   (E) G is next to C.

2. If H is one of the two tallest, then H could be next to
   (A) F   (B) B   (C) C   (D) D   (E) E

3. If G is a girl and H is last in line, then
   (A) E must be the other tallest student
   (B) E may be next to a girl
   (C) D must be next to C
   (D) G may be next to C
   (E) B must be next to H

4. If F is 2nd in line, which of the following must be true?
   (A) E is the shortest.
   (B) B is either 7th or 8th in line.
   (C) H is either 7th or 8th in line.
   (D) C is 4th in line.
   (E) F is one of the two tallest.

5. If E and B are the two tallest students, then the correct order in line could be:
   (A) E F C D H A G B
   (B) E H C A G D F B
   (C) B H C A G D F E
   (D) B G C D H A F E
   (E) E F C G A D H B

6. If H is last in line, which of the following could be true?
- (A)   E is one of the tallest.
- (B)   G is next to C.
- (C)   B is one of the tallest.
- (D)   D is one of the tallest.
- (E)   B is next to G.

7. If E and G are the two tallest, then the order in line could be:
- (A)   G   F   C   A   B   D   H   E
- (B)   G   B   C   A   H   D   F   E
- (C)   E   H   C   D   B   A   F   G
- (D)   E   F   C   D   B   A   H   G
- (E)   E   F   C   D   H   A   B   G

STOP

IF YOU FINISH BEFORE TIME IS UP, CHECK YOUR WORK ON THIS SECTION OF THE TEST ONLY.
DO NOT GO ON TO THE NEXT SECTION OF THE TEST UNTIL TIME IS UP FOR THIS SECTION.

SECTION IV
LOGICAL REASONING

Time—10 Minutes
9 Questions

Directions:
In this section you will be given brief statements or passages and will be required to evaluate the reasoning involved. In some instances, more than one choice will appear to be a possible answer. You are to choose the *best* answer. Use common sense and reasonableness in making your selection; then mark the proper space on the answer sheet.

1.   Although man is thinking constantly during the course of every day, he is usually not aware of his thoughts. Just walking a few steps entails a number of mental choices and activities that are performed more or less unconsciously. To become conscious of everything going on in the mind would be immobilizing.

Which of the following best supports the passage above?
(A)   Researchers have concluded that driving an automobile for only one minute entails over one thousand separate unconscious decisions.
(B)   Thinking is such a complex process that it cannot be adequately defined.
(C)   People have difficulty remembering more than three diverse concepts.
(D)   Most individuals can perform more than one task simultaneously.
(E)   The unconscious mind is still a mystery even to most psychologists.

2. During the last 50 years, the majority of individuals receiving awards for their humanitarian works have been blonde. Therefore, having blonde hair is the cause of humanitarianism.

Each of the following, if true, *weakens* the preceding conclusion EXCEPT
(A)   these people who received such honors are not representative of all humanitarians
(B)   a physical condition not caused by having blonde hair, but more prevalent among blondes than among others, causes humanitarian behavior
(C)   during the last 100 years fewer blondes than others received humanitarian honors
(D)   the total population contains a higher percentage of blondes than others at any given time
(E)   the total population contains a far smaller percentage of blondes than does the subpopulation consisting of those individuals having received honors for humanitarian endeavors

Questions 3–4 refer to the following passage.

   Lotteries are a socially expensive form of generating revenues. They attract those least able to afford it, and thus become a form of regressive taxation. A six-month study conducted in 1979 in New Castle County, Delaware, found that poor persons bet three times as much on a regular basis as did those from upper-middle income areas. In fact, most lottery machines were located in the poorest areas of the county, areas where unemployment is highest and the standard of living lowest. By contrast, not a single lottery machine was located in the high-income neighborhood of the county. Maryland's instant lottery came under such severe criticism that it was soaking the poor that the government finally scrapped it several weeks ago.

3. Which of the following facts would be most useful in judging the effectiveness of the details offered to support the author's criticism of lotteries?
(A)   The name of the group that conducted the six-month survey.
(B)   A comparison of the amounts bet by the poor, the middle class, and the upper class.

   (C)   A discussion of the gambling activity of upper-class citizens.

   (D)   The rationale for locating the lottery machines in poor neighborhoods.

   (E)   A discussion of the revenue-generating programs that preceded the lottery in Delaware.

4. Which of the following, if true, would be the best refutation of the argument above?

   (A)   Many of the poor have enjoyed the opportunity to gamble.

   (B)   The high-income neighborhood is exclusively residential.

   (C)   Money from the lottery is generated more from the middle-class areas.

   (D)   The study conducted in New Castle has been duplicated elsewhere, but other lotteries continue to operate.

   (E)   The upper-class citizens shoulder 10 percent of the tax burden.

5. Every movie star I have read about lives in an expensive home. They must all live in such places.

Which of the following most nearly parallels the logic of the foregoing argument?

   (A)   All movie producers must be demanding, probably because of the stresses placed upon them.

   (B)   This piece of matter must be a rock, since it does not fit any other description in the textbook.

   (C)   All the paintings by Visson in the library are bright. Every one of his works must be bright.

   (D)   All paint has noxious odor. This liquid has such an odor and, therefore, must be paint.

   (E)   Inasmuch as all pine trees are evergreen and this tree has not lost its needles, it is likely to be a pine.

6. Smith, Klingle, and Smith, a well-known national polling firm, surveyed one thousand registered voters in Kentucky to determine their positions on the No-Fault Insurance Initiative, Ballot Proposition No. 106. Their survey included the following results regarding Proposition No. 106: Given that the foregoing are true, which of the following must be FALSE?

Strongly support	43%
Support	18%
Oppose	21%
Strongly oppose	11%
Undecided	7%

Which of the conclusions below can be best supported by the results of the survey above?

   (A)   Most Kentucky voters strongly oppose Ballot Proposition No. 106.

   (B)   Most Kentucky voters are not well aware of Ballot Proposition No. 106.

   (C)   A majority of Kentucky voters are not in favor of Ballot Proposition No. 106.

   (D)   A majority of Kentucky voters will probably vote for the Ballot Proposition No. 106.

   (E)   The Kentucky voters who are undecided will change the outcome of the vote.

7. All medications are habit forming.
Everything habit forming soothes pain.
Nothing nonaddictive soothes pain.

Given that the foregoing are true, which of the following must be FALSE?

   (A)   All medications soothe pain.

   (B)   Some medications are nonaddictive.

   (C)   Aspirins are habit forming and addictive.

   (D)   Addictive medications soothe pain.

   (E)   No medications are not habit forming.

Questions 8–9 refer to the following passage.

With so many opportunities for true reform that would save the taxpayers' money, there is reason to look askance at proposals by legislators that would make life easier for them with public funds. Only last year, the Assembly, after a considerable public outcry, finally ruled out a bill whereby only 25 percent of campaign spending reports filed by legislative candidates would be audited instead of 50 percent under current law.

8. Which of the following is the most logical continuation of this passage?
   (A) Clearly, it is through increased auditing of campaign spending that we will secure honest representation.
   (B) Must we consider every "gift" the legislator offers us as a Trojan horse, filled with traitors bent on destroying the state?
   (C) Who are they trying to kid?
   (D) We must bemoan the fact that there are no opportunities for true reform, only for white-collar fraud.
   (E) Is it any wonder, then, that citizens should be as wary of legislators bearing election reforms as the adage warns one to be of Greeks bearing gifts?

9. The author is arguing that
   (A) legislators often act in their own best interests
   (B) public outcry is more effective than the ballot box
   (C) more than half of campaign expenditures are unwarranted
   (D) legislators are not aware of opportunities for true reform
   (E) this year, reform is more possible than it was last year

STOP

END OF MULTIPLE-CHOICE EXAMINATION. IF YOU FINISH BEFORE TIME IS UP, CHECK YOUR WORK ON THIS SECTION OF THE TEST ONLY. DO NOT GO BACK TO ANY OTHER SECTION OF THE EXAMINATION.

EXAMINATION

WRITING SAMPLE

Time—30 Minutes

Directions:
You have 30 minutes to write an essay in response to a given topic. Take a few minutes to plan your work before you begin writing. DO NOT WRITE ON A TOPIC OF YOUR OWN CHOICE. ESSAYS THAT DO NOT ADDRESS THE GIVEN TOPIC ARE UNACCEPTABLE.

The quality of your writing is more important than the length of your response or the content. Pay attention to organization, appropriate diction, and correct usage. You will not be expected to display any specialized knowledge in your response, nor will you be expected to write a "perfect" essay; law schools understand that you are writing under a time constraint, and will allow for the minor lapses in writing ability that might occur under this circumstance.

Only the lined area in your booklet will be reproduced for the law schools, so do not write outside this space. *Do not* skip lines or use wide margins. These precautions, along with careful planning and legible handwriting that is not unduly large, will keep you within the allowed space.

SAMPLE TOPIC:

Read the following descriptions of Bergquist and Kretchmer, applicants for the job of Assistant Director on a major motion picture. *Then, in the space provided, write an argument for hiring either Bergquist or Kretchmer.* The following criteria are relevant to your decision:

- In addition to working closely with and advising the Director on creative decisions, the Assistant Director must work with all types of individuals—from stars to Teamster truck drivers—and elicit the best from every cast and crew member for the good of the motion picture.
- The Assistant Director is responsible for all the planning and organization—including paperwork, travel itinerary, meals, etc.—of the entire film project. He/she lays the groundwork for a successful "shoot."

BERGQUIST began her career in films as an Administrative Assistant to the president of a major film studio. As such, she often accompanied her employer in his wining and dining of stars, or to the set when problems arose. She doublechecked contracts, shooting schedules, cast and crew checks, and kept a close eye on the budget of several multimillion-dollar films. When her boss was subsequently fired due to a poor season of films, Bergquist was able to secure a position as Assistant Editor at the studio, helping several highly respected film editors "cut" feature films. It was here that she learned about the creative end of the business, and soon after became the chief editor of an hour-long studio documentary, which won several awards. After two years, Bergquist was accepted into the Assistant Directors Training Program, and is presently a candidate for Assistant Director of this new $15,000,000 motion picture.

KRETCHMER was a principal/teacher for 12 years before embarking on a film career. Not only did she teach math at the New York School for the Creative Arts, but she worked with parents in the community, the board of education, and local government representatives in securing financing for the $20,000,000 school building. As Chairperson of the New Building Committee, she worked closely with architects, townspeople, contractors, and even children to understand their needs for the building. Today the building stands as a model for such schools everywhere. Eight years ago Kretchmer came to Hollywood and, through persistence and charm, secured a studio position and worked her way up to Chief Auditor, where she oversaw budgets on several multimillion-dollar films. She enrolled in the Assistant Directors Training Program, which she recently completed, and is now the other candidate being considered for the position of Assistant Director of this new film.

ANSWER KEY

Section I:
Logical Reasoning

1. **D**	4. **B**	7. **C**
2. **A**	5. **C**	8. **A**
3. **B**	6. **B**	9. **D**

Section III:
Analytical Reasoning

1. **D**	4. **C**	7. **D**
2. **B**	5. **C**	
3. **E**	6. **A**	

Section II:
Reading Comprehension

1. **E**	4. **A**	7. **E**
2. **E**	5. **C**	8. **C**
3. **B**	6. **B**	

Section IV:
Logical Reasoning

1. **A**	4. **C**	7. **B**
2. **E**	5. **C**	8. **E**
3. **B**	6. **D**	9. **A**

MINI-TEST ANALYSIS

Section	Total Number of Questions	Number Correct	Number Incorrect	Number Unanswered*
I: Logical Reasoning	9			
II: Reading Comprehension	8			
III: Analytical Reasoning	7			
IV: Logical Reasoning	9			
TOTAL:	33			

*Since there is no penalty for incorrect answers on the LSAT, you should leave no question unanswered. Even if you don't have time to answer a question, at least fill in the answer space with a guess.

EXPLANATIONS OF ANSWERS

Section I

1. **D** The passage states that nameless fears and frustrations defy analysis and implies that unsymbolized thoughts and emotions constitute nameless fears and frustrations. (C) and (E) are close, but note the absolute words "complete" and "only" in each.

2. **A** If anyone who thinks that ignorance is no excuse isn't paying attention, then those who are paying attention will know that ignorance is an excuse.

3. **B** The consequences of nuclear annihilation—namely the end of human life—would include the disappearance of all other human questions. Thus, the author's contention that the most serious threat to modern man may be the alleged meaninglessness of life is seriously challenged by the magnitude of nuclear annihilation.

4. **B** If a "nonreader" (one who cannot read) can recognize words, then reading cannot be defined as the act of recognizing words.

5. **C** Good swing implies good golfer and practice implies good swing; therefore practice implies good golfer. (X implies Y and Y implies Z; therefore X implies Z.) This is most closely paralleled by (C), even though the terms are in slightly different order, or not exactly parallel. (B) is wrong since voting for peace and wanting peace are two different things. Betsy may have baked a good cake (A) even if she did not want to. (E), although in proper form, brings in excess subjectivity.

6. **B** This is the only answer that refutes the premise that you need a good swing. (A) talks about what else you need, and (C) says nothing about the need for a good swing.

7. **C** None of the other choices is a "special sort of culture."

8. **A** "Disputes" are the most specific and logical results of "conflicts."

9. **D** If most crimes are not punishable by death, then, even if capital punishment were reinstated, most criminals would not be deterred by it. (A) would be a good answer, except that it might strengthen the belief, depending on the outcome of the statistics.

Section II

1. **E** Though the author has reservations about the Price-Anderson Act, the passage presents both the advantages and suggestions to rectify what the author sees as disadvantages.

2. **E** All of the first four items are advantageous financially to the industry. The rise in the ceiling on liability will raise the potential costs to the industry in the event of an "incident."

3. **B** The number of deaths, injuries, and damages caused by the accident at Chernobyl would surely cost more than $665 million in the asset pool. The other four answers are false.

4. **A** Only (A) is true and an advantage to the public. (B) is an advantage to the company, not to the public. (C) and (E) are untrue. (D) is true, but because the injuries might be slow to be recognized, the victim might not be able to qualify for reparations before the statute of limitations expired.

5. **C** The Act does not make clear whether or not a company will be liable for punitive damages. The other four statements are defined by the Act.

6. **B** The plaintiff under common law rules of causation would have to show a probability of 51 percent or more.

7. **E** The passage asserts that Planex declared bankruptcy to avoid the damages in a large number of suits involving asbestos.

8. **C** Though the author points to faults in Price-Anderson, he never suggests that the nuclear power industry's growth should be restricted. All of the other statements are either factual or opinions specifically supported in the passage.

Section III

From the information given, a "position" diagram may be drawn as follows:

		C	A/D		D/A		
1	2	3	4	5	6	7	8
tallest			girl	girl	girl		tallest

Now notice that, since E and F are always adjacent, they may be in positions 1 and 2, or in positions 7 and 8. And, for instance, if they are in 7 and 8, then H (a boy) must be in 1 or 2 (and vice versa).

1. **D** If G is a girl, then she must be in 5th place, since the sisters (A and D) will not stand next to each other.

2. **B** if H is one of the two tallest, then H will be on one end. Thus at the other end must be E and F. Therefore, H could be next to either B or G, depending upon who is the boy.

3. **E** If G is a girl, and H is last in line, your diagram must look like this:

E/F	F/E	C	A/D	G	D/A	B	H

Thus, the only true statement is (E), B must be next to H.

4. **C** If F is second in line, then your diagram should look like this:

E	F	C	A/D		D/A	H?	H?

From the diagram, H is 7th or 8th in line. Notice that B could possibly be 5th in line, so (B) is not true.

5. **C** If E and B are the two tallest, then two diagrams are possible:

E	F	C	A/D	G	D/A	H	B

and

B	H	C	A/D	G	D/A	F	E

Notice that (A) and (D) are incorrect because H, a boy, cannot be in the 5th place. (B) is incorrect because E and F must be adjacent. Finally, (E) is incorrect because A and D will not stand next to each other in line.

6. **A** If H is last in line, then your diagram should look like this:

E/F	F/E	C	A/D		D/A		H

Notice that B and G must go in the 5th and 7th spots, but we cannot tell which one goes where. Therefore, the only statement that may possibly be true is III: E is one of the tallest.

7. **D** If E and G are the two tallest, your diagram is either

E	F	C	A/D	B	D/A	H	G

or

G	H	C	A/D	B	D/A	F	E

Notice that, since H is a boy, he must be next to G. Therefore, (D) is the only possible correct order of the students.

Section IV

1. **A** This statement lends even more support to the passage that normal activities are conducted through constant thought processes, many of which are done more or less unconsciously.

2. **E** (E) may be restated: "The group consisting of humanitarians who received honors contains a much higher proportion of blondes than that which exists in the total population." Such a condition increases the credibility of the conclusion. (A), (B), (C), and (D) all reduce the probability of the conclusion.

3. **B** The author's criticism of lotteries is based on the contention that poor persons are spending more than they can afford. However, the details he offers in support of this contention mention the frequency of betting without specifying the amount gambled. The effectiveness of the *frequency* detail could be better judged if the *amount* were given. None of the other choices is closely related to the author's central criticism, the costliness of the lotteries.

4. **C** This fact severely weakens the author's contention that most of the revenue from the lottery comes from the lower class or poor.

5. **C** The given argument may be reduced to:
   Some stars (those the speaker has read about) have expensive homes.
   All stars (they) have expensive homes (such places).

   (C) is the only choice that both parallels the faulty logic of the original and retains the pattern, specific to general:
   Some movie stars → All movie stars. Note the structure of (C):
   Some paintings (those in the library) are bright.
   All paintings (every one) are bright.

6. **D** Because 43 percent strongly support the ballot and 18 percent support the ballot, a total of 61 percent are in favor of the ballot and will probably vote for it. This is the only conclusion of the five given that can be plausibly supported.

7. **B** Since all medications are habit forming and everything habit forming soothes pain, then all medications make one feel better; therefore, (A) is true. Since nothing nonaddictive soothes pain and all medications soothe pain, then no medications can be nonaddictive; therefore, (B) is false.

8. **E** (A) is a *non sequitur*; the passage does not align honesty with auditing. (B) is weaker than (E) because it mentions destroying the state, an extreme not expressed or implied in the passage. (C) is too vague. (D) introduces a new subject, fraud.

9. **A** The author explicitly opposes legislative proposals that would "make life easier for them [the legislators]."

PART TWO
<u>ANALYSIS</u>
Understanding the Sections and the Key Strategies

Chapter

2

Reading Comprehension

INTRODUCTION TO QUESTION TYPE

The entire LSAT is, generally speaking, a test of reading comprehension. However, the Reading Comprehension section itself is a test of general reading skills rather than the more particular analytical skills stressed in the Analytical Reasoning section.

Each Reading Comprehension section usually consists of four passages, each ranging in length from 400 to 700 words. Each passage is followed by six to eight questions relating to the passage. These 26 to 28 questions are to be answered in 35 minutes.

The passages are drawn from many topics, including ethics, philosophy, humanities, physical science, social science, and the law. No specialized knowledge is necessary to answer any of the questions. All of the questions can be answered by referring to the passage. Because law-related articles are less familiar to many of our readers, we have inserted additional law-related passages in some of our sample exams.

Some of the common types of Reading Comprehension questions that follow a passage include questions about:

- the main point of the passage or the passage's primary purpose;
- the meaning of specific words or phrases in the context of the passage;
- the author's method of presenting his or her points;
- information that is explicitly stated in the passage;
- inferences and implications related to the passage;
- the author's tone or attitude.

ACTIVE READING

The Reading Comprehension section presents long passages demanding your steady concentration. Because such passages are complex, you must approach them *actively,* focusing in with a specific plan of attack.

Suppose that midway through the first paragraph of a passage you encounter a sentence like this:

Ordinarily, of course, we are invited only to criticize the current neglect of government programs; politicians cling to their own fringe benefits while the strife in our inner cities is only nominally contained with a plethora of half-baked local projects whose actual effect is the gradual erosion of trust in the beneficence of the republic.

Different students may respond in different ways:

"What? Let me read that again" (and again and again).
"I used to know what *beneficence* meant; uh . . . ."
"Boy, am I tired."
"I should have eaten a better breakfast; my head aches."
"I wonder what I'll wear tonight . . . ."
"This writer is screwy; I was a Senator's aide and I know he's wrong."
"How can I read this!? It's written so poorly; that word *plethora* is a terrible choice."

These typical responses—getting stuck, getting distracted, getting angry—all work against your purpose: using the passage to increase your LSAT score. The techniques described below should help you avoid some common reading test pitfalls.

Essentially, active reading consists of marking as you read. But the marking you do must be strategic and efficient. To present some effective active reading techniques, we will consider a sample reading passage and seven typical LSAT questions.

SAMPLE PASSAGE AND QUESTIONS

With the possible exception of equal rights, perhaps the most controversial issue across the United States today is the death penalty. Many argue that it is an effective deterrent to murder, while others maintain there is no conclusive evidence that the death penalty reduces the number of murders.

(5)　　The principal argument advanced by those opposed to the death penalty, basically, is that it is cruel and inhuman punishment, that it is the mark of a brutal society, and finally that it is of questionable effectiveness as a deterrent to crime anyway.

In our opinion, the death penalty is a necessary evil. Throughout recorded history there have always been those extreme individuals in every society who were capable of terribly violent crimes such as murder. But some are more extreme, more diabolical than others.

(10)

For example, it is one thing to take the life of another in a momentary fit of blind rage, but quite another to coldly plot and carry out the murder of one or more people in the style of an executioner. Thus, murder, like all other crimes, is a matter of relative degree. While it could be argued with some conviction that the criminal in the first instance should be merely isolated from society, such should not be the fate of the latter type murderer. To quote Moshe Dayan, "Unfortunately, we must kill them."

(15)

The value of the death penalty as a deterrent to crime may be open to debate, but there remains one irrefutable fact: Gary Gilmore will never commit another murder. Charles Manson and his followers, were they to escape, or—God forbid—be paroled, very well might.

(20)　　The overwhelming majority of citizens believe that the death penalty protects them. Their belief is reinforced by evidence which shows that the death penalty deters murder. For example, the Attorney General points out that from 1954 to 1963, when the death penalty was consistently imposed in California, the murder rate remained between three and four murders for each 100,000 population. Since 1964 the death penalty has been imposed only once (in 1967), and the murder rate has

(25)　　skyrocketed to 10.4 murders for each 100,000 population. The sharp climb in the state's murder rate, which commenced when executions stopped, is no coincidence. It is convincing evidence that the death penalty does deter many murderers.

If the Governor's veto of the bill reestablishing the death penalty is upheld, an initiative will surely follow. However, an initiative cannot restore the death penalty for six months. In the interim, innocent

(30)　　people will be murdered—some whose lives may have been saved if the death penalty were in effect.

This is literally a life or death matter. The lives of hundreds of innocent people must be protected. The Governor's veto must be overridden.

1. The primary purpose of the passage is to   Ⓐ Ⓑ Ⓒ Ⓓ Ⓔ
- (A) criticize the governor
- (B) argue for the value of the death penalty
- (C) initiate a veto
- (D) speak for the majority
- (E) impose a six-month moratorium on the death penalty

2. The passage attempts to establish a relationship between   Ⓐ Ⓑ Ⓒ Ⓓ Ⓔ
- (A) Gary Gilmore and Charles Manson
- (B) the importance of both equal rights and the death penalty
- (C) the murder rate and the imposition of the death penalty
- (D) executions and murders
- (E) the effects of parole and the effects of isolation

3. It can be inferred that the author assumes which of the following about the Governor's veto of the death penalty legislation?   Ⓐ Ⓑ Ⓒ Ⓓ Ⓔ
- (A) It might be upheld.
- (B) It will certainly be overridden.
- (C) It represents consultation with a majority of citizens.
- (D) The veto is important, but not crucial.
- (E) It is based on the principle of equal protection for accused murderers.

4. The author's response to those who urge the death penalty for all degrees of murder would most likely be   Ⓐ Ⓑ Ⓒ Ⓓ Ⓔ
- (A) strongly supportive
- (B) noncommittal
- (C) negative
- (D) supportive
- (E) uncomprehending

5. In the passage the author is primarily concerned with   Ⓐ Ⓑ Ⓒ Ⓓ Ⓔ
- (A) supporting a position
- (B) describing an occurrence
- (C) citing authorities
- (D) analyzing a problem objectively
- (E) settling a dispute

6. In lines 28–29, "initiative" refers to   Ⓐ Ⓑ Ⓒ Ⓓ Ⓔ
- (A) a demonstration against the Governor's action
- (B) a rise in the murder rate
- (C) a more vocal response by the majority of citizens
- (D) the introduction of legislation to reinstate the death penalty
- (E) overriding the Governor's veto

7. The passage provides answers to all of the following questions EXCEPT   Ⓐ Ⓑ Ⓒ Ⓓ Ⓔ
- (A) Are all murders equally diabolical?
- (B) Does the public believe the death penalty deters murder?
- (C) What happened to Gary Gilmore?
- (D) Will Charles Manson be paroled?
- (E) Does the Governor support the death penalty?

FOUR-STEP APPROACH

STEP ONE: SKIM THE QUESTIONS.

Before reading the passage, spend a short time familiarizing yourself with the questions. You should preread or "skim" the questions for two reasons: (1) to learn what *types* of questions are being asked; and (2) to learn what specific *information* to look for when you do read the passage. In order to skim efficiently and effectively, you should read over only the portion of each question that *precedes* the multiple choices, and you should mark *key words* as you do so.

A *key word* or phrase is any segment that suggests what you should look for when you read the passage. Marking these key words will help you remember them as you read (luckily, the questions will be printed directly below and alongside the passage, so that as you read the passage you will be able to glance at the questions and remind yourself about what you've marked). In order to further explain and clarify these tips on skimming, let's examine the questions that follow the preceding passage.

The key words for each of them are circled.

1. The (primary purpose) of the passage is to . . . .

This is a "main idea" or "primary purpose" question; most LSAT reading passages are followed by at least one of these. You are asked what the passage is trying to *do* or *express*, as a whole. Here is a list of possible purposes that may be embodied in a reading passage:

to inform	to criticize	to show
to persuade	to argue for or against	to question
to analyze	to illustrate	to explain
to change	to represent	to prove
to restore	to parody	to describe

This list is by no means exhaustive; the possible purposes are almost endless, and you might try thinking of some yourself.

The main idea or primary purpose of a passage is usually stated or implied in the *thesis sentence* of one or more of the paragraphs. A thesis sentence tells what the paragraph as a whole is about; it states a main idea or primary purpose. For example, the second sentence of paragraph 6 in the passage is the thesis sentence; it sums up the evidence of that paragraph into a single statement.

A primary purpose or main idea question should direct your attention to the thesis sentences in the passage, that is, the *general statements* that sum up the specific details.

2. The passage attempts to (establish a relationship) between . . . .

This question requires that you locate *explicit* (established) *information* in the passage, information that defines a relationship. The question allows you to anticipate the mention of at least one relationship in the passage, and warns you through its wording that the relationship is not "hidden," but is instead one that the author deliberately attempts to establish.

3. It can be (inferred) that the author assumes which of the following about the (veto of the Governor's death penalty legislation?)

This question requires that you locate *implicit,* rather than explicit, information; you are asked to draw an *inference* (a conclusion based on reasoning), not just to locate obvious material. It is more difficult than question 2. When you read about the Governor's veto in the passage, you should take mental note of any unstated assumptions that seem to lie behind the author's commentary.

4. The (author's response) to those who urge the (death penalty for all degrees of murder) would most likely be . . . .

This question type, usually more difficult than the types previously discussed, requires you to *apply* the information in the passage itself. As you read the passage, you should pay special attention to the author's attitude toward types, or degrees, of murder; applying this attitude to the situation described in the question should lead toward the answer.

5. In the passage the author is (primarily concerned) with . . . .
This is another variety of the "primary purpose" or "main idea" question.

6. In lines 28-29, "initiative" refers to . . . .
The question requires you to focus on specific language in the passage and define it in context. Such a question is relatively easy insofar as it specifies just where to look for an answer; its difficulty varies according to the difficulty of the word or phrase you are asked to consider.

7. The passage provides answers to all of the following questions EXCEPT . . . .
Although many questions that you skim will lead you to useful information in the passage, some like this one, do not. It is still important, however, to circle key words in the question to avoid the <u>misread.</u>

In general, spend only a few seconds skimming the questions. Read each question, mark key words, and move on.
DO NOT:
- dwell on a question and analyze it extensively.
- be concerned with whether you are marking the "right" words (trust your intuition).
- read the multiple choices (this wastes time).

STEP TWO (OPTIONAL): SKIM THE PASSAGE.

Some students find skimming the passage helpful. Skimming the passage consists of quickly reading the first sentence of each paragraph, and marking key words and phrases. This will give you an idea of what the paragraph as a whole is about. The first sentence is often a general statement or thesis sentence that gives the gist of the paragraph.

Consider the passage given above. Reading the first sentence of each paragraph, we mark the key words and phrases, and may draw the following conclusions:

Paragraph 1: "With the possible exception of equal rights, perhaps the most controversial issue across the United States today is the death penalty." This sentence suggests that the passage will be about the death penalty, and the word "controversial" suggests that the author is about to take a stand on the controversy.

Paragraph 2: "The principal argument advanced by those opposed to the death penalty, basically, is that it is cruel and inhuman punishment, that it is the mark of a brutal society, and finally that it is of questionable effectiveness as a deterrent to crime anyway." This sentence (which is also the whole paragraph) presents opposition arguments, and because those arguments are presented as the views of others, not the views of the author, we begin to suspect that he does not align himself with the opposition.

Paragraph 3: "In our opinion, the death penalty is a necessary evil." This confirms our suspicion; the author is beginning an argument *in favor of* the death penalty.

Paragraph 4: "For example, it is one thing to take the life of another in a momentary fit of blind rage, but quite another to coldly plot and carry out the murder of one or more people in the style of an executioner." Here the author is distinguishing between *degrees* of murder, and you may at this point recall question 4; this information seems relevant to that question.

Paragraph 5: "The value of the death penalty as a deterrent to crime may be open to debate, but there remains one irrefutable fact: Gary Gilmore will never commit another murder." The most significant feature of this sentence is that the author's tone is so absolute, indicating his strong belief in his own position.

Paragraph 6: "The overwhelming majority of citizens believe that the death penalty protects them." This sentence points toward statistical evidence in favor of the author's view.

Paragraph 7: "If the Governor's veto of the bill reestablishing the death penalty is upheld, an initiative will surely follow." Coincidently with the author's faith in the will of the majority, here he suggests that the death penalty will be upheld one way or another, by overriding a veto or through initiative.

Paragraph 8: "This is literally a life or death matter." The author here reemphasizes the seriousness and importance of this question.

Do not expect your own skimming of the passage to necessarily yield a series of conclusions such as those expressed above. Most of the knowledge you gather as you skim will "happen" without a deliberate effort on your part to translate your intuitions into sentences. Just read and mark the sentences, without slowing yourself down by analyzing each sentence. The preceding analysis suggests some possible conclusions that may occur to a reader, but drawing such full conclusions from sentence clues will take both practice and a relaxed attitude; don't push yourself to make sense out of everything, and don't reread sentences (skimming the passage should take only a few seconds). Some sentences you read may be too difficult to make sense of immediately; just leave these alone and move along. Remember that getting stuck wastes time and raises anxiety.

STEP THREE: READ AND MARK THE PASSAGE.

Now you are ready to read the entire passage. To read quickly, carefully, and efficiently, you must be *marking* important words and phrases while you read. At least such marking will keep you alert and focused. At most it will locate the answers to many questions.

Skimming the questions will have helped you decide what to mark. If a question refers to a specific line, sentence, or quotation from the passage, you will want to mark this reference and pay special attention to it. Whenever a key word from a question corresponds with a spot in the passage, mark the spot. In the scheme for marking a passage, these spots are called, simply, ANSWER SPOTS. There are two other kinds of "spots" that you should mark as you read: REPEAT SPOTS and INTUITION SPOTS. Repeat spots are sections of the passage in which the same type of information is repeated.

Consider the following excerpt from a passage:

Proposed cutbacks in the Human Resources Agency are scheduled for hearing 9 A.M. on the 17th. Included in possible program reductions are cutbacks in the veterans' affairs program, including closure of the local office; in potential support for the county's Commission on the Status of Women; and in payments provided by the county for foster home care, which are not being adjusted for cost-of-living increases this year.

Programs in the Environmental Improvement Agency will be examined by the board beginning 9 A.M. Friday, August 18. The milk and dairy inspection program has been recommended by County Administrative Officer Fred Higgins for transfer to state administration. In addition, budget recommendations do not include funds for numerous community general plans which have been discussed previously by the board of supervisors. Such areas as Joshua Tree, Crestline, Lytle Creek, and Yucaipa are not included in the Planning Department's program for the upcoming year.

A special session to discuss proposed budget cuts in the county's General Services Agency will be conducted at 9 A.M. Saturday, August 19. A number of county branch libraries have been proposed for closure next year, including the Adelanto, Bloomington, Crestline, Joshua Tree, Mentone, Morongo, Muscoy, and Running Springs locations. A rollback in hours of operation will also be considered. Branches now open 60 hours a week will be cut to 52 hours. Other 50-hour-a-week branches will be reduced to 32 hours a week. Testimony will be heard on cutbacks in various agricultural service programs, including the county trapper program in the Yucaipa region and support for 4-H activities.

Generally, this excerpt stresses information about times, dates, and locations; we are conscious of repeated numbers and repeated place names. Marking the spots in which such information is found will help you to sort out the information, and also to answer more efficiently a question that addresses such information, a question such as "Which of the following cities are (is) *not* included in the Planning Department's program and *are* (is) liable to lose a branch library?" Having marked the REPEAT SPOTS that contain location names, you may be better able to focus on the appropriate information quickly.

INTUITION SPOTS are any spots that strike you as significant, for whatever reason. As we read, we tend to pay special attention to certain information; marking those spots that your intuition perceives as important will help increase your comprehension and will therefore contribute to correct answers.

You may notice that ANSWER SPOTS, REPEAT SPOTS, and INTUITION SPOTS are not necessarily different spots. An answer spot may also be a spot that contains repeat information AND appeals to your intuition.

Don't overmark. Some students, fearing that they will miss an important point, underline everything. Such misplaced thoroughness makes it impossible to find any specific word or phrase. Just mark the main idea of each paragraph and several important words or phrases. And vary your marks. You may want to underline main ideas, use circles or brackets or stars to indicate other important spots, and jot some notes to yourself in the margin. Here is how you might mark the death penalty passage:

With the possible exception of equal rights, perhaps the most (controversial issue) across the United States today is the (death penalty.) Many argue that it is an effective deterrent to murder, while others maintain there is no conclusive evidence that the death penalty reduces the number of murders. *[contrast]*

The (principal argument) advanced by those opposed to the death penalty, basically, is that it is cruel and inhuman punishment, that it is the mark of a brutal society, and finally that it is of questionable effectiveness as a deterrent to crime anyway. *[opposition points]*

* (In our opinion, the death penalty is a necessary evil.) Throughout recorded history there have always been those extreme individuals in every society who were capable of terribly violent crimes such as murder. But some are more extreme, more diabolical than others.

For example, it is one thing to take the life of another in a momentary fit of blind rage, but quite another to coldly plot and carry out the murder of one or more people in the style of an executioner. Thus, murder, like all other crimes, is a matter of (relative degree.) While it could be argued with some conviction that the criminal in the first instance should be merely isolated from society, such should not be the fate of the latter type murderer. To quote Moshe Dayan, "Unfortunately, we must kill them." *[degrees of murder penalty]*

The value of the death penalty as a deterrent to crime may be open to debate, but there remains one <u>irrefutable fact</u>: Gary Gilmore will never commit another murder. Charles Manson and his followers, were they to escape, or—God forbid—be paroled, very well might. ←

[The overwhelming majority of citizens believe that the death penalty protects them.] Their belief is reinforced by evidence which shows that the death penalty deters murder. For example, the Attorney General points out that from 1954 to 1963, when the death penalty was consistently imposed in California, the murder rate remained between three and four murders for each 100,000 population. Since 1964 the death penalty has been imposed only once (in 1967), and the murder rate has skyrocketed to 10.4 murders for each 100,000 population. The sharp climb in the state's murder rate, which commenced when executions stopped, is no coincidence. It is convincing evidence that the death penalty <u>does deter many murderers.</u> *[STATS]*

If the (Governor's veto) of the bill reestablishing the death penalty is upheld, an initiative will surely follow. However, an initiative cannot restore the death penalty for six months. In the interim, innocent people will be murdered—some whose lives may have been saved if the death penalty was in effect. *[veto effects]*

<u>This is literally a life or death matter.</u> The lives of hundreds of innocent people must be protected. <u>The Governor's veto must be overridden.</u>

Your marking method should be active, playful, and personal. While you are marking, don't worry about whether you are doing it correctly. You may notice that, in the discussion of skimming the passage, some sentences are marked differently than they are here, in order to stress that there is no single, "correct" method.

Remember not to react subjectively to the passage, or add to it. Your own background may have you disagreeing with the passage, or you may be tempted to supply information from your own experience in order to answer a question. You must use only the information you are given, and you must accept it as true.

Avoid wasting time with very difficult or technical sentences. Concentrating on the sentences and ideas you do understand will often supply you with enough material to answer the questions. Rereading difficult sentences takes time, and usually does not bring greater clarity.

STEP FOUR: ANSWER THE QUESTIONS.

As you attempt to answer each question, follow these steps: (1) assess the level of difficulty, and skip the question if necessary; (2) eliminate unreasonable and incorrect answer choices; (3) make certain that information in the passage supports your answer. We will follow this procedure, using the questions on the "death penalty" passage above as examples.

ANSWERS AND EXPLANATIONS

1. **B** Remember that this sort of question asks for the *primary* purpose, not a subsidiary purpose. Often the incorrect answer choices will express minor or subsidiary purposes; this is true of (A) and (D). Another type of incorrect answer choice *contradicts* the information in the passage. So it is with (C) and (E). Both contradict the author's expressed support of the death penalty. Having marked thesis sentences in the passage, you should be aware of the author's repeated arguments for the value of the death penalty, and choose (B).

2. **C** "Equal rights" is mentioned only in passing, and a relationship between parole and isolation is scarcely even implied; therefore (B) and (E) should be eliminated. (A) is not a good answer because, strictly speaking, Gary Gilmore and Charles Manson are not compared; their *sentences* are. (D) is a true answer, but not the best one because it is more vague and general than the best choice, (C); paragraph 6 makes this specific comparison.

3. **A** We are looking for information that is (1) assumed but not explicit, and (2) relevant to the Governor's veto. Having marked the appropriate section of the passage, you are able to return immediately to the final two paragraphs, which discuss the veto. (B), (C), and (D) contradict passage information: (C) contradicts the author's earlier explanations that most citizens approve of the death penalty, and (D) contradicts the author's emphatic final statement. (B) contradicts the author's acknowledgment that the veto might be upheld (first sentence of paragraph 7). (E) is irrelevant to the veto issue. (A) is correct because the assumption that the veto might be upheld would certainly underlie an argument against it.

4. **C** Having marked the section that refers to different degrees of murder, you are once again able to focus on the appropriate section. In paragraph 4, the author argues that unpremeditated murder may not warrant the death penalty. This argument suggests his negative attitude toward someone who urges the death penalty for all murderers.

5. **A** With your general knowledge of the passage, you should immediately eliminate (B) and (D), because the author is *argumentative* throughout, never merely descriptive or objective. Citing authorities (C) is a *subsidiary* rather than a primary concern; the author does so in paragraph 5. (E) is incorrect because it is the author himself who is *creating* a dispute over the death penalty. A review of the thesis sentences alone shows that the author is consistently supporting a position; (A) is certainly the best answer.

6. **D** Skimming this question has allowed you to pay special attention to "initiative" as you read the passage. The sentence suggests that the initiative is a response to the Governor's veto of the death penalty; and it is a *certain* response, as indicated by "surely." It is also an action that can eventually restore the death penalty; this fact especially signals (D) as the answer. (B) states information mentioned apart from the initiative; the murder rate will rise "in the interim." Demonstrations (A) or vocal responses (C) are not suggested as possibilities anywhere. (E) is eliminated because the last sentence of the passage urges an override, thus distinguishing this action from an initiative.

7. **D** The passage answers all of these questions except the question of Manson's parole, which remains a possibility.

ACTIVE READING, A SUMMARY CHART

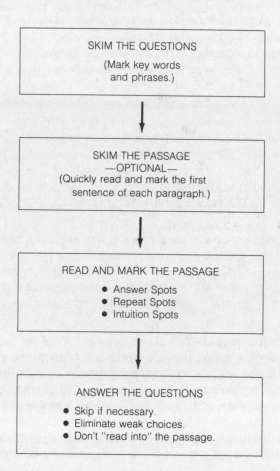

SKIM THE QUESTIONS

(Mark key words
and phrases.)

SKIM THE PASSAGE
—OPTIONAL—
(Quickly read and mark the first
sentence of each paragraph.)

READ AND MARK THE PASSAGE

- Answer Spots
- Repeat Spots
- Intuition Spots

ANSWER THE QUESTIONS

- Skip if necessary.
- Eliminate weak choices.
- Don't "read into" the passage.

AN ALTERNATIVE GENERAL APPROACH

Some students, regardless of how much they review, analyze, and practice, cannot seem to finish the Reading Comprehension section. They simply cannot work fast enough and continue to maintain a high level of comprehension. If you find that you consistently have a problem getting to or into the fourth passage, you may wish to try this alternative approach: Focus your time on three of the four passages. That is, try to do well on the three passages and the questions that follow, and simply guess at the questions for the remaining passage. You can skip a passage and still receive a good score. The idea is to significantly raise your percentage of correct answers on the passages and questions you <u>are</u> completing. Remember, this is an alternative approach that you may wish to try if you are having a real problem getting to all four passages and maintaining a good level of comprehension.

BASIC TRAINING: EXTRA, EFFECTIVE PRACTICE

The following procedure, *practiced daily*, should strengthen precisely the kinds of skills that you will need for the Reading Comprehension section of the LSAT:

1. Locate the editorial page in your daily newspaper. There you will probably find three or four editorials on different subjects.

2. Read several editorials at your normal reading speed, marking them, if possible.

3. Set the editorials aside, and try to write a summary sentence describing each editorial. Make your summary as precise as possible. Do not write, "This editorial was about the economy." Instead, try to write something like this: "This editorial argued against the value of supply-side economics by referring to rising unemployment and interest rates."

    You may not be able to write so precise a summary right away, but after a few days of practicing this technique, you will find yourself better able to spot and remember main ideas and specific details, and to anticipate and understand the author's point of view.

    It is most important that you *write down* your summary statements. This takes more time and effort than silently "telling" yourself what the editorial means, but the time and effort pay off.

4. Every few days, create some of your own multiple-choice questions about an editorial. What would you ask if you were a test maker? Putting yourself in the test maker's shoes can be very instructive. You will realize, for instance, how weak or incorrect answer choices are constructed, and that realization will help you to eliminate such choices when you take the LSAT.

EXTRA PRACTICE: READING COMPREHENSION

Passage 1 (Written in 1982)

A recent Harris Survey revealed that a majority of Americans say the price of gasoline would have to go to $1.50 a gallon before they would cut back on the use of their automobiles for pleasure driving. The survey, conducted among 1517 adults nationwide, also found that gasoline prices would have to go to $1.85 per gallon before adults would cease to use their own cars to go to work and would turn to public transportation and car pooling.

In fact, the price of gasoline is presently going *down* rather than up. Major oil companies have announced plans to reduce wholesale prices by as much as eight cents a gallon. As a result, those drivers who insisted that only rising gasoline costs would cut their consumption will now probably begin to drive more rather than less. Already, according to the Highway Patrol, highways are becoming more crowded with cars carrying only one passenger, and with gas-guzzling recreational vehicles.

These results are interesting when one considers that we are presently at the height of the smog season. As most of us know by now, the majority of our smog problem is caused by exhaust emissions from cars. Yet how many of us have actually made an effort to drive less? In fact, how many of us have even made an effort to drive more slowly to help conserve gasoline? Unfortunately, the answer to both questions is: not very many. Even though we all are aware—or certainly should be by now—that there is a desperate need both to conserve fuel and to clean up our air, far too few of us are willing to make even a small sacrifice to help.

Recently we read that a small group of botanists is busily attempting to develop a strain of pine tree that can resist the smog. It seems that as the smog has gotten worse each year it has taken an increasingly greater toll on the pines in mountain areas. Now the situation is becoming critical; either we develop a hardier tree or they will all die. It's sad to think that in a country which professes so much love for nature, and where so much natural beauty abounds, we have to develop a breed of "supertrees" which can cope with the polluted air we create.

The solution to our smog problem lies not in eliminating the steel industry's coke oven emissions, or any other industrial emissions, but in convincing the millions of people who traverse our freeways daily to try at least to drive less. Obviously it's necessary to drive in order to get to and from work, but if each of us could at least reduce the pleasure driving a little, drive the speed limit, and have our automobile engines tuned regularly, the improvement would be immediately noticeable. If we make these small sacrifices we won't have to worry about eventually paying $1.85 per gallon for gasoline. The reduced consumption will keep prices low because there will be enough for everyone without having to increase prices to "force" us to use less.

1. The primary purpose of this passage is to   Ⓐ Ⓑ Ⓒ Ⓓ Ⓔ
   (A) convince smog producers to reduce emissions
   (B) convince drivers to reduce smog
   (C) convince drivers to drive less
   (D) describe an instance of the supply/demand phenomenon
   (E) argue against higher gasoline prices

2. The author puts the blame for air pollution on   Ⓐ Ⓑ Ⓒ Ⓓ Ⓔ
   (A) individuals   (B) institutions   (C) corporations   (D) botanists
   (E) pollsters

3. With which of the following statements about the effects of smog would the author be most likely to agree?   Ⓐ Ⓑ Ⓒ Ⓓ Ⓔ
   (A) A greater number of vans and campers at our national parks threatens the parks' beauty.
   (B) Smog encourages the survival of hardy vegetation.
   (C) The price of gasoline may rise in the future.
   (D) People who drive alone have no respect for nature.
   (E) Smog will gradually become something we can live with.

4. Who of the following would be most likely to object to the author's argument?   Ⓐ Ⓑ Ⓒ Ⓓ Ⓔ
   (A) an industrialist
   (B) an auto mechanic
   (C) a botanist
   (D) a Highway Patrol officer
   (E) a manufacturer of recreational vehicles

5. The author implies which of the following in his argument?   Ⓐ Ⓑ Ⓒ Ⓓ Ⓔ
   (A) Industrial emissions are uncontrollable.
   (B) Reduced driving will occur even if drivers do not follow his advice.
   (C) Reduced driving will not inconvenience drivers.
   (D) The diminishing supply of fuel is not a problem.
   (E) Gasoline prices should not go down.

6. The author's tone in this passage is   Ⓐ Ⓑ Ⓒ Ⓓ Ⓔ
   (A) cynical   (B) analytical   (C) satirical   (D) urgent
   (E) objective

7. To accept the author's argument, we must assume which of the following about the Harris Survey?   Ⓐ Ⓑ Ⓒ Ⓓ Ⓔ
   (A) The people conducting the survey were opposed to pleasure driving.
   (B) The people conducting the survey were not drivers.
   (C) The survey was conducted recently.
   (D) The 1517 adults actually represent a majority of Americans.
   (E) The people conducting the survey were not employed by the steel industry.

Passage 2

In their study, Kalven and Zeisel (hereafter referred to as "Kalven") surveyed 3576 trials in two reporting samples. Over 500 judges cooperated in the study. The survey was conducted using judges as reporters for jury trials. Two major questions were explored in the survey, "First, what is the magnitude and direction of the disagreement between judge and jury? And, second, what are the sources and explanations of such disagreement?"

The study found that judges and juries agree (would decide the same case the same way) in 75.4 percent of the cases. If cases in which the jury hung are eliminated, the overall agreement rate rises to 78 percent. Thus at the outset, whatever the defects of the jury system, it can be seen that the jury at least arrives at the same result as the judge in over three-fourths of the cases.

The direction of disagreement is clearly toward a more lenient jury than judge. The trend was not isolated to any particular type of offense but was spread throughout crime categories. Additionally the pattern found was that in convictions, juries tended to be more lenient as far as counts, degrees, and sentencing.

For civil cases the percentage of agreement and disagreement was about the same except that there did not appear to be any strong sentiment in favor of plaintiff over defendant (or vice versa) by the jury.

In cases decided differently because the judge had facts the jury did not, generally, these facts related to suppressed evidence, personal knowledge of the defendant's prior record, etc. The factors that made the difference between judge and jury in these cases, then, were all facts that we as a society purposefully keep from juries because the information is irrelevant or because it is highly prejudicial. From the study it can be assumed that the judge, hearing the information, did not disregard it but, quite the contrary, used it in reaching his (harsher) judgment.

The overwhelming number of cases in which judge and jury agree argue for the jury's understanding of the evidence because it is not to be expected that a jury deciding cases it does not understand and a judge deciding cases he does understand (we presume) would not agree in their results so often. Also, judges themselves generally did not identify "jury misunderstood the facts" as the reason for disagreement.

The level of sympathy that the jury had with the defendant did make some difference. Although generally the jury was neutral, in about 36 percent of the cases the jury had some reaction (positive or negative) because of the personal characteristics, occupation, family, or court appearance. These factors affected juries differently depending on the age, race, or sex of the defendant. Through various statistical evaluations Kalven is able to state that "the sympathetic defendant causes disagreement in . . . 4 percent of all cases." Similar figures apply for the unsympathetic defendant.

8. This passage was probably written in response to an argument for ⒶⒷⒸⒹⒺ
(A) the appointment rather than the election of judges
(B) the election rather than the appointment of judges
(C) the wider use of the trial by jury
(D) the reduced use of the trial by jury
(E) the increased use of statistics in the courts

9. According to the passage, judge and jury are likely to reach the same verdict in
(A) criminal cases rather than in civil cases ⒶⒷⒸⒹⒺ
(B) civil cases rather than in criminal cases
(C) cases where the judge has facts denied to the jury
(D) cases in which the jury hung
(E) roughly three-quarters of the cases

10. The results of Kalven's study suggest that, when there is disagreement between a judge and a jury, the judgments of the judge are   Ⓐ Ⓑ Ⓒ Ⓓ Ⓔ
- (A) harsher than those of juries
- (B) less harsh than those of juries
- (C) very nearly the same as those of juries
- (D) less likely to be influenced by irrelevant or prejudicial information
- (E) less harsh than those of juries in criminal cases only

11. From the results of the study we can infer that withholding from a jury information that is irrelevant or prejudicial to a defendant   Ⓐ Ⓑ Ⓒ Ⓓ Ⓔ
- (A) has no significant effect on the results of a trial
- (B) works to the disadvantage of most defendants
- (C) works to the advantage of most defendants
- (D) works to increase the objectivity of the judge
- (E) works to decrease the objectivity of the jury

12. The author's argument for the jury's understanding of the evidence presented in trial is based upon
- (A) his assumption that the judge understands the evidence
- (B) his assumption that evidence too complex for the jury to understand would not be admitted
- (C) the fact that evidence is rarely complex   Ⓐ Ⓑ Ⓒ Ⓓ Ⓔ
- (D) the fact that juries are able to reach verdicts
- (E) the fact that no judges have accused juries of misunderstanding

13. With which of the following statements would the author be most likely to disagree?
- (A) Juries are likely to be influenced by the personal characteristics, occupation, family, or court appearance of defendants.
- (B) Juries are influenced by the age, race, or sex of the defendant.   Ⓐ Ⓑ Ⓒ Ⓓ Ⓔ
- (C) The judge's misunderstanding the evidence is not a likely cause of judge-jury disagreements.
- (D) The jury's misunderstanding the evidence is not a likely cause of judge-jury disagreements.
- (E) The jury's sympathy with a defendant is a major cause of judge-jury disagreements.

14. By including the information in the final paragraph about the effect of sympathy with the defendant upon the jury, the author of the passage   Ⓐ Ⓑ Ⓒ Ⓓ Ⓔ
- (A) unfairly denigrates the opposing argument
- (B) undermines the case he has presented
- (C) suggests that his arguments are objective
- (D) conceals a weakness in his case
- (E) underscores the lack of objectivity in judges

15. The author includes statistical information in the passage chiefly in order to   Ⓐ Ⓑ Ⓒ Ⓓ Ⓔ
- (A) demonstrate his familiarity with social science research methods
- (B) support his case for the use of juries
- (C) make what is really a hypothesis appear to be factual
- (D) give an appearance of objectivity to a subjective view
- (E) support a case against the use of juries

Passage 3

Although different plants have varying environmental requirements because of physiological differences, there are certain plant species that are found associated with relatively extensive geographical areas. The distribution of plants depends upon a number of factors among which are (1) length of daylight and darkness, (2) temperature means and extremes, (3) length of growing season, and (4) precipitation amounts, types, and distribution.

Daylight and darkness are the keys by which a plant regulates its cycle. It is not always obvious how the triggering factor works, but experiments have shown day length to be a key. A case in point is that many greenhouse plants bloom only in the spring without being influenced by outside conditions other than light. Normally, the plants keyed to daylight and darkness phenomena are restricted to particular latitudes.

In one way or another, every plant is affected by temperature. Some species are killed by frost; others require frost and cold conditions to fruit. Orange blossoms are killed by frost, but cherry blossoms will develop only if the buds have been adequately chilled for an appropriate time. Often the accumulation of degrees or the direction of temperatures above or below a specific figure critically affects plants. Plant distributions are often compared with isotherms to suggest the temperature limits and ranges for different species. The world's great vegetation zones are closely aligned with temperature belts.

Different plant species adjust to seasonal changes in different ways. Some make the adjustment by retarding growth and arresting vital functions during winter. This may result in the leaf fall of middle latitude deciduous trees. Other plants disappear entirely at the end of the growing season and only reappear through their seeds. These are the *annuals*, and they form a striking contrast to the *perennials*, which live from one season to another.

Precipitation supplies the necessary soil water for plants, which take it in at the roots. All plants have some limiting moisture stress level beyond which they must become inactive or die. Drought-resistant plants have a variety of defenses against moisture deficiencies, but *hygrophytes*, which also are adapted to humid environments, have hardly any defense against a water shortage.

16. According to the passage, the temperature belts aligned with the world's great vegetation zones may be characterized by Ⓐ Ⓑ Ⓒ Ⓓ Ⓔ
    (A)   extreme frost
    (B)   either frost or warmth
    (C)   extreme cold, but not frost
    (D)   the accumulation of degrees
    (E)   directed temperatures

17. From this passage we must conclude that a long drought striking a humid environment must inevitably Ⓐ Ⓑ Ⓒ Ⓓ Ⓔ
    (A)   render most plants inactive
    (B)   result in legislation aimed at building new canals
    (C)   reduce or extinguish the hygrophytes
    (D)   affect the plant's responses to daylight and darkness
    (E)   produce a corresponding change in drainage conditions

18. The passage implies that plants affected by length of day are normally located in
    (A)   random locations Ⓐ Ⓑ Ⓒ Ⓓ Ⓔ
    (B)   regions where nights are longer
    (C)   regions where days are longer
    (D)   certain regions east or west of the prime meridian
    (E)   certain regions north or south of the equator

19. The behavior of annuals may be compared to Ⓐ Ⓑ Ⓒ Ⓓ Ⓔ
    (A)   senility   (B) eternal life   (C) reincarnation   (D) exfoliation   (E) hibernation

20. According to the passage, the phrase "distribution of plants" (paragraph 1) refers to   Ⓐ Ⓑ Ⓒ Ⓓ Ⓔ
   (A)   factors too numerous to be listed in this brief passage
   (B)   the marketing of plants in areas conducive to further germination and reproduction
   (C)   the varieties of size, shape, and color among plants
   (D)   the locations in which plants grow and thrive
   (E)   certain species only

21. As the author discusses each of the factors affecting the distribution of plants, the overall implication that he does not stress is that   Ⓐ Ⓑ Ⓒ Ⓓ Ⓔ
   (A)   each of the factors produces notable effects
   (B)   no one of these factors operates independently of the others
   (C)   soil conditions have one of the most pronounced effects upon plant life
   (D)   environmental factors either promote or retard growth
   (E)   isotherms affect every factor surveyed

Passage 4

No sooner had the British forces in June 1944 carried out their part in the Allied invasion of Germany than they were faced with the fact that among the prisoners of war captured there were Russians in German uniforms. By the time the war in Europe ended, between two and three million Soviet citizens had passed through Allied hands. This extraordinary situation, certainly never before known in the history of war, was the consequence of the policy of both the Soviet and the German regimes. On the Soviet side, the very existence of prisoners of war was not recognized: the Soviet government refused to adhere to the Geneva Convention, and washed its hands of the millions who fell into German power.

The Germans, in turn, treated their Soviet prisoners with such callous brutality that only a relatively small number of them survived. For a Soviet prisoner in German hands to enlist in the German armed forces was about the only way open to him of saving his life. There were also Soviet citizens whose hatred of the Communist regime was so strong that they were prepared to fight alongside the Germans in order to overthrow Stalin: nominally headed by General Andrey Vlasov, they saw little combat until the end of the war, largely because of Hitler's suspicion of Vlasov's claims to maintain his political independence of the National Socialist regime even as a prisoner of war. There were also some other combat units composed of Russians, some of them noted for their savagery. Then there were hordes of civilians in German hands—some compulsorily swept into the German labor mobilization drive, many more borne along the wave of the German retreat from Russia and thereafter drafted for labor duties. These civilians included many women and children.

The problem facing the British government from the outset was what policy to adopt toward this mass of humanity that did not fall into any of the accepted categories thrown up by war. Quite apart from the logistic problems, there existed a well-established tradition in Britain which refused to repatriate against their will people who found themselves in British hands and the nature of whose reception by their own government was, to say the least, dubious. The first inclination of the Cabinet—to send all captured Russians back to the Soviet Union—was challenged by the minister of economic warfare, Lord Selborne, who was moved by the fact that the Russians in British hands had only volunteered to serve in German uniforms as an alternative to certain death; and that it would therefore be inhuman to send them back to be shot or to suffer long periods of forced labor. Winston Churchill was also swayed by this argument.

22. The primary purpose of this passage is to   Ⓐ Ⓑ Ⓒ Ⓓ Ⓔ
   (A)   explain one of the problems facing British forces near the end of World War II
   (B)   reveal the savagery of both the German and the Russian forces
   (C)   stress America's noninvolvement
   (D)   detail a "war within a war"
   (E)   give evidence for Churchill's position

23. "Repatriate" in paragraph 3 means to   Ⓐ Ⓑ Ⓒ Ⓓ Ⓔ
- (A) send back to the country of birth
- (B) send back to the country of allegiance
- (C) send back to the victorious country
- (D) reinstill patriotism
- (E) reinstill British patriotism

24. The author's position is   Ⓐ Ⓑ Ⓒ Ⓓ Ⓔ
- (A) pro-Russian   (B) anti-Russian   (C) pro-British   (D) pro-German   (E) neutral

25. The problem in World War II concerning the disposition of Soviet prisoners of war was very similar to
- (A) the plight of Armenian refugees   Ⓐ Ⓑ Ⓒ Ⓓ Ⓔ
- (B) Hitler's own loss of identity after 1944
- (C) the plight of British prisoners of war
- (D) no previous situation
- (E) several instances in the history of war

26. Lord Selborne's opinion disregards which of the following facts?   Ⓐ Ⓑ Ⓒ Ⓓ Ⓔ
- (A) The Soviet Union posed a nuclear threat to the United States.
- (B) Traditionally, repatriation was not imposed by Great Britain.
- (C) Certain Soviet citizens wanted to overthrow Stalin.
- (D) General Andrey Vlasov was politically independent.
- (E) Soviet prisoners were treated brutally.

27. The German labor mobilization drive consisted partly of   Ⓐ Ⓑ Ⓒ Ⓓ Ⓔ
- (A) women and children
- (B) retreating German soldiers
- (C) followers of General Andrey Vlasov
- (D) savage combat units
- (F) those born during the retreat

28. The Soviet policy toward their prisoners of war was one of   Ⓐ Ⓑ Ⓒ Ⓓ Ⓔ
- (A) nonrecognition   (B) nonaggression   (C) nonproliferation   (D) noncontempt
- (E) nonadherence

Passage 5

     The right to an unbiased jury is an inseparable part of the right to trial by jury as guaranteed by the Seventh Amendment of the United States Constitution. This right guarantees that twelve impartial jurors will hear and "truly try" the cause before them.

(5)   In September 1982, the California Supreme Court upheld a lower court's $9.2 million verdict against Ford Motor Company despite the fact that three jurors had been working crossword puzzles and one juror had been reading a novel during the presentation of testimony. Four of the twelve jurors hearing the case were admittedly participating in the activities charged and were clearly guilty of misconduct, yet the California Supreme Court found no resultant prejudice against Ford's position.

(10)   In the United States, citizens are called upon by the government to serve as jurors. Only under extraordinary circumstances may a citizen be excused from such service. Juries are therefore not necessarily comprised of willing volunteers, but instead, are sometimes made up of individuals who are serving against their will. J. P. Reichert's article, "Juror's Attitudes Toward Jury Service," is illustrative of how justice is adversely affected when citizens are "forced" to

(15) serve on juries. In R. L. Schott's article, "Reflections of a Juror," some additional insight is revealed by the author who, while serving as a juror himself, recognized two distinct perspectives shared among jurors. Some jurors had a very positive attitude about their being asked to

serve on a jury. Their perspective was that of rendering a public service by fulfilling their jury duties. On the other hand, some jurors viewed their obligation as just that, a burdensome
(20) obligation, and nothing more. Their attitude was one of getting through with the ordeal as soon as possible, a let's-get-out-of-here-by-this-afternoon approach.

A study conducted with mock juries, concerned specifically with the issue of juror prejudgment, revealed that 25 percent of the jurors polled reached their decision early in the trial. The jurors in the study who admitted to having made up their minds before having heard all the
(25) evidence also stated that they generally held to their first-impression assessments. By prejudging the outcome of the case the jurors had, in effect, breached their sworn duty.

From a reading of the California Supreme Court's opinion, it appears that the Court itself has committed the one form of conduct universally prohibited, that of prejudgment. Ford's battle was lost before it had even begun to present its case. In the first place, Ford is a multibillion dollar
(30) international corporation with "pockets" deeper than most. Secondly, Ford had experienced a great deal of negative publicity resulting from recent jury verdicts awarding large sums of money to victims of Pinto automobile accidents wherein it was determined that Ford had defectively designed the Pinto's gasoline tank so that it was prone to explode upon rear end impacts. Finally, the plaintiff was a nineteen-year-old college freshman whose pursuit of a medical career was
(35) abruptly ended when he suffered extensive brain damage after the brakes on his 1966 Lincoln failed, causing him to crash into a fountain after careening down a steeply curving hillside street. Ford presented a considerable amount of evidence in an attempt to prove that the cause of the accident was driver error and faulty maintenance and not defective design. The Supreme Court responded to Ford's arguments by stating that the jury was responsible for judging the credibility
(40) of witnesses and it would be wholly improper for the Court to usurp that function by reweighing the evidence. How ironic that the Court should so gallantly refuse to upset the decision of the jury, a jury wherein four members admittedly were engaging in extraneous activities when they were supposed to be "judging the credibility of witnesses." It would appear from the misconduct of the jury and the conclusionary statements of the California Supreme Court that Ford's liability was
(45) indeed a predetermined, prejudged fact.

If the decision has any impact upon our present system of justice, it will regretfully be a negative one. The California Supreme Court has, in effect, approved a standard of jury conduct so unconscionable as to, in the words of dissenting Justice Richardson, "countenance such a complete erosion of a constitutional command," namely, the right to a fair and impartial jury trial.

29. Which of the following best states the central idea of the passage? Ⓐ Ⓑ Ⓒ Ⓓ Ⓔ
- (A) By not questioning the decision in the Ford case, the California Supreme Court, like the jury, was guilty of prejudgment.
- (B) There are serious defects in the system of trial by jury.
- (C) The jury in the case of *Hasson* v. *Ford* was guilty of prejudging the case.
- (D) The Supreme Court's handling of *Hasson* v. *Ford* may lead to an erosion of the constitutional right to a fair and impartial jury trial.
- (E) Studies suggest that a large number of the men and women serving on juries fail to "truly try" the cases they hear.

30. All of the following data from the passage could be used to argue against the jury system EXCEPT
- (A) in the Ford case, three jurors were working crossword puzzles and one was reading a novel during the presentation of testimony Ⓐ Ⓑ Ⓒ Ⓓ Ⓔ
- (B) juries are likely to include individuals who are serving against their will
- (C) in a study of mock jurors, 25 percent reached a decision early in the trial
- (D) pre-trial publicity about Ford Pintos resulting in large jury verdicts to victims influenced the Supreme Court's decision
- (E) some jurors view their service as an ordeal to be ended as quickly as possible

31. The author's belief that Ford was denied a fair trial in the lower court is best supported by the fact that   Ⓐ Ⓑ Ⓒ Ⓓ Ⓔ
- (A) the jury was unduly sympathetic to the nineteen-year-old accident victim who suffered extensive brain damage
- (B) the jury was influenced by unfavorable publicity about the defective gas tanks on the Ford Pinto
- (C) three of the jurors were admittedly working crossword puzzles during the testimony
- (D) the California Supreme Court refused to reverse the decision of the jury
- (E) the California Supreme Court refused to judge the credibility of the witnesses

32. An argument in favor of the Supreme Court decision in the Ford case might include all of the following EXCEPT   Ⓐ Ⓑ Ⓒ Ⓓ Ⓔ
- (A) if the case were retried, the jury would probably include jurors who were serving against their will
- (B) it is probable that the jurors working puzzles and reading were also paying attention to the testimony
- (C) if the case were retried, some members of the jury are likely to come to a decision early in the trial
- (D) if the case were retried, those jurors who made up their minds early would be unlikely to alter their verdicts later in the trial
- (E) the jury at the original trial is in a better position to judge the credibility of the witnesses than the Supreme Court

33. The author suggests that the California Supreme Court reached its decision in the Ford case for all of the following reasons EXCEPT   Ⓐ Ⓑ Ⓒ Ⓓ Ⓔ
- (A) a prejudice against Ford because of its wealth
- (B) a prejudice against Ford because of recent negative publicity
- (C) an agreement with the lower court's evaluation of the credibility of the witnesses
- (D) a bias in favor of the young accident victim
- (E) a refusal to find fault with deplorable jury conduct

34. In the next to last paragraph of the passage, the author uses irony when he writes
- (A) "Ford's battle was lost before it had even begun to present its case."   Ⓐ Ⓑ Ⓒ Ⓓ Ⓔ
- (B) "Ford is a multibillion dollar international corporation with 'pockets' deeper than most."
- (C) The plaintiff's "pursuit of a medical career was abruptly ended when he suffered extensive brain damage . . . ."
- (D) ". . . the Court should so gallantly refuse to upset the decision of the jury . . . ."
- (E) ". . . Ford's liability was indeed a predetermined, prejudged fact."

35. From information given in lines 46–49, it is clear that the Supreme Court decision
- (A) was unanimous   Ⓐ Ⓑ Ⓒ Ⓓ Ⓔ
- (B) was not unanimous
- (C) will have a significant impact on the justice system
- (D) reverses that of the lower court
- (E) will be appealed

Passage 6

At the heart of Anglo-American jurisprudence is the "adversary" system. This is a device by which justice and truth are to emerge from the clash of two opposing viewpoints. As stated by Monroe H. Freedman:

> (The adversary) system proceeds on the assumption that the best way to ascertain the truth is to present to an impartial judge or jury a confrontation between the proponents of conflicting views, assigning to each the task of marshalling and presenting the evidence in as thorough and persuasive a way as possible . . . . Thus, the judge or jury is given the

strongest possible view of each side, and is put in the best possible position to make an accurate and fair judgment.

Though Judge Marvin E. Frankel does not doubt the superiority of the adversary process over any other, he emphatically proclaims that "our adversary system rates truth too low among the values that institutions of justice are meant to serve."

> We proclaim to each other and to the world that the clash of adversaries is a powerful means for hammering out the truth . . . (yet) we know that many of the rules and devices of adversary litigation as we conduct it are not geared for, but are often aptly suited to defeat the development of the truth . . . . Employed by interested parties, the process often achieves truth only as a convenience, a byproduct, or an accidental approximation.

Judge Frankel goes on to say that "the business of the advocate, simply stated, is to win if possible without violating the law . . . . His is not the search for truth as such."

New York City attorney Abraham Pomerantz held nothing back in his criticism of the adversary system, saying:

> We boast about it, but it's a very mischievous system designed not to achieve but to frustrate the truth . . . . Each side pulls out the facts that help and ignores those that do not. Out of that come confusion and distortion, and the clever guy wins.

Though criticism runs high, the system is defended as the best of available alternatives. Such reasoning is rooted in the nature of our system of criminal justice and in the fundamentals of our system of government. As stated by Freedman:

> Before we will permit the state to deprive any person of life, liberty or property, we require that certain processes be duly followed which ensure regard for the dignity of the individual, irrespective of the impact of those processes upon the determination of truth.

Thus, it is easier to understand the basis upon which an individual, known by the state to have committed a heinous offense, is accorded the rights to trial by jury, due process, counsel, and the privilege against self-incrimination. Freedman stresses that:

> . . . a trial is far more than a search for truth, and the constitutional rights that are provided by our system of justice may well outweigh the truth-seeking value—a fact which is manifest when we consider that those rights and others guaranteed by the Constitution may well impede the search for truth rather than further it.

Freedman contrasts the emphasis in a free society, wherein the dignity of the individual is paramount to the interests of the state, with that of a totalitarian state, wherein the interests of the state are absolute. In totalitarian governments, an individual's guilt or innocence is to be determined by everyone involved—judge, prosecutor, and defense counsel. This implies that if defense counsel ascertained his client's guilt, such would be brought to the state's attention. In an adversary system of justice, however, a defendant is presumed innocent, placing the burden of proving guilt upon the prosecution alone.

36. Which of the following best summarizes the content of the passage? Ⓐ Ⓑ Ⓒ Ⓓ Ⓔ
   (A) how the truth is determined in the adversary system
   (B) Freedman's defense of the adversary system
   (C) the strengths of the adversary system
   (D) the adversary system
   (E) the strengths and weaknesses of the adversary system

37. The passage suggests that the adversary system works to preserve all of the following rights EXCEPT the right Ⓐ Ⓑ Ⓒ Ⓓ Ⓔ
   (A) to trial by jury
   (B) against self-incrimination
   (C) to due process
   (D) to self-incrimination
   (E) to counsel

38. The adversary system trial is based upon all of the following assumptions EXCEPT

    (A)   though imperfect, the adversary system is better than any other   Ⓐ Ⓑ Ⓒ Ⓓ Ⓔ

    (B)   the best way to find the truth is to present two strongly opposed viewpoints

    (C)   a jury is able to recognize which one of two versions is true

    (D)   a judge will be impartial

    (E)   a trial is best conducted using both judge and jury

39. The adversary system may be said to be an enemy of truth because   Ⓐ Ⓑ Ⓒ Ⓓ Ⓔ

    (A)   the object is to present evidence as persuasively as possible

    (B)   the prosecuting attorney may conceal facts that do not support his case

    (C)   the judge or jury may be victims of unconscious prejudice

    (D)   the determination of truth is seldom straightforward

    (E)   the defense attorney may not know all the facts about the person he is defending

40. The obligation of an attorney to preserve the confidence and secrets of a client can easily be used to support the argument that in the adversary system   Ⓐ Ⓑ Ⓒ Ⓓ Ⓔ

    (A)   the interests of the defendant are less important than the interests of the state

    (B)   ascertaining the truth is more important than ascertaining justice

    (C)   the right to counsel should guarantee the defendant a counselor he can trust

    (D)   the purpose is to win if possible without violating the law

    (E)   each side ignores the facts that do not support the case

41. Critics of the adversary system can support their case by citing all of the following arguments EXCEPT

    (A)   a randomly selected jury is likely to be ill informed on both the legal issues and the factual background information   Ⓐ Ⓑ Ⓒ Ⓓ Ⓔ

    (B)   one side may use some facts but ignore others in order to strengthen its case

    (C)   both sides may use some facts but ignore others in order to strengthen their cases

    (D)   the object of the lawyer is to win his case, not to find the truth

    (E)   if the more clever lawyer is more likely to win, the side with more money to hire a clever lawyer is at an advantage

42. By using quotations from Freedman, Frankel, and Pomerantz, the author of the passage   Ⓐ Ⓑ Ⓒ Ⓓ Ⓔ

    (A)   imitates the way in which the adversary system works

    (B)   presents a one-sided case for the adversary system

    (C)   gives a chronological organization to the passage

    (D)   presents the case against the adversary system first

    (E)   develops his argument from the specific to the general

Answers and Explanations

Passage 1

1. **C** This purpose is stated most explicitly in paragraph 5, although there are several other points in the passage where the author urges drivers to drive less. (A) is weak because it is too general and inclusive; (B) is vague about the means of reducing smog; (D) and (E) are very minor points.

2. **A** This is stated explicitly in paragraph 5, where the author blames individual drivers rather than industry.

3. **A** The second paragraph implies that recreational vehicles create more smog, and the fourth paragraph describes smog's effects on nature; therefore, we may conclude that gas-guzzling vacation vehicles help to damage the natural beauty of vacation spots. The author *might* also agree with (D), but the evidence in the passage itself points more substantially to (A).

4. **E** The author criticizes the increased use of recreational vehicles (see explanation for question 3).

5. **B** The final sentence in the passage implies that we will be "forced" to conserve if we do not do so voluntarily. (A) is neither stated nor implied; the author does imply that industrial emissions *should not be controlled*, but this is not the same as suggesting that they are *uncontrollable*.

6. **D** The author is almost pleading that drivers make immediate changes in their habits; the urgency of his purpose coincides with the urgency of his tone.

7. **D** The author begins the passage by claiming that the Harris Survey represents a "majority of Americans"; we must share that assumption in order to accept the importance of his argument. All other choices are irrelevant.

Passage 2

8. **D** The passage is part of a longer essay written to refute the arguments of Judge Jerome Frank, who holds that a judge alone is likely to be more reliable than a jury.

9. **E** The second paragraph says that judges and juries agree in 75.4 percent of the cases, according to the Kalven study.

10. **A** The third paragraph discusses the greater harshness of judges in all categories of crime—in counts, degrees, and sentencing.

11. **C** Because the effect of this information upon judges is to make their judgments harsher, we can infer it would have the same effect on juries and the withholding of this information is, predictably, to the defendant's advantage.

12. **A** The author assumes the judge understands the evidence and because the juries agree with the judge so often, he argues the juries must also have understood the evidence to come to the same conclusion as the judge.

13. **E** The passage supports each of the first four statements, but the jury's sympathy with a defendant according to the last paragraph leads to judge-jury differences in only 4 percent of all the cases studied and so could not be called a "major" cause of disagreement.

14. **C** By admitting frankly that juries are not always fully objective the author demonstrates a willingness to discuss facts that may not advance his case. All of the four other options are false.

15. **B** The statistics are used to support the author's case for the use of juries. Because the statistics are the result of other writers' research, and are based upon a large sample, they give more than an "appearance" of objectivity.

Passage 3

16. **B** Paragraph 3 states, "Some species are killed by frost; others require frost and cold conditions to fruit."

17. **C** Paragraph 5 tells that hygrophytes have little defense against a water shortage.

18. **E** The final sentence in paragraph 2 aligns plants affected by light and darkness with "particular latitudes," that is, particular regions north or south of the equator.

19. **C**   Reincarnation (C) might be associated with *annuals*, which disappear and reappear again through new seeds ("new life").

20. **D**   The factors that account for distribution are all related to geographic location, and all affect the plant's growth and sustenance; this becomes more obvious through the remainder of the passage. (A) must be eliminated because, although the author may have left other factors unmentioned, she does not acknowledge their existence within the passage.

21. **B**   Each of the factors is accorded a separate paragraph, and although we must reasonably suppose that such factors must coexist, the author does not express interrelationships among factors. (E) is not stressed in the passage, but neither is it implied. Each of the other choices is an expressed fact.

Passage 4

22. **A**   The passage discusses the past and present facts contributing to the British problem with captured Russians.

23. **A**   The final paragraph discusses at length the question of whether to send Russians back to Russia despite their lack of allegiance to Russia. This is the repatriation question and is consistent with the dictionary definition of *repatriate*—to send back to the country of birth.

24. **E**   The author does not himself argue for or against a particular position or nationality. He simply presents facts and the arguments of others. His comments in paragraph 2 might be called anti-German, but this attitude is not one of the choices.

25. **D**   Paragraph 1 states, "This extraordinary situation [was] . . . never before known in the history of war."

26. **C**   Selborne argued that Russians served the Germans only "as an alternative to certain death" (paragraph 3). But paragraph 2 states that some Russians fought with the Germans "in order to overthrow Stalin."

27. **A**   Paragraph 2 says that "the German labor mobilization drive . . . included many women and children."

28. **A**   Paragraph 1 states, "On the Soviet side, the very existence of prisoners of war was not recognized."

Passage 5

29. **A**   The author wishes to criticize both the jury, which was inattentive, and the Supreme Court, which allowed the jury's decision to stand. Some of the other options are stated or implied ideas of the passage but not its central idea.

30. **D**   (D) is relevant to the Supreme Court decision but not to the jury system. (A), (B), (C), and (E) all expose deficiencies in the jury system.

31. **C**   The inattentiveness of four jurors is explicit support for a charge that Ford's case was not fairly heard. We don't know for certain if (A) or (B) is true. (D) and (E) are true but do not support the author's belief in the unfairness of the trial.

32. **B** The limitations of all juries discussed in the passage would apply as well to the jury retrying the case as to the jury who reached a decision already. The Supreme Court's argument that the original jury was in a better position to judge the credibility of the witnesses is surely correct; the Supreme Court did not see the witnesses who testified. Though (B) is remotely possible, it is not a point one would wish to use in support of the Supreme Court decision.

33. **C** Though the Supreme Court agreed with the lower court jury, it specifically asserted the impropriety of its attempting to reweigh the evidence and the credibility of the witnesses.

34. **D** A case could be made that (B), an understatement, is ironic but a clearer instance is the sarcasm of "gallantly"; the author does not believe the Supreme Court acted gallantly.

35. **B** Because Justice Richardson dissented, the decision cannot have been unanimous.

Passage 6

36. **E** Though all five options are possible answers, the last, which refers to the strengths and weaknesses of the adversary system, gives the best idea of what the passage contains.

37. **D** The right against, not the right to, self-incrimination is one of the rights guaranteed to Americans on trial.

38. **E** The passage presents the system using a judge or a jury, and does not insist on using both. Choices (A), (B), (C), and (D) are assumptions upon which the adversary system is based.

39. **B** Both (A) and (B) are plausible answers. (B) is better because it refers specifically to suppression of truth. It might be that the most persuasive way to present evidence in a trial would be simply to tell the truth.

40. **C** (C) is the only point that attorney confidentiality supports. (A) is untrue. (B) is debatable, and in any case, is not supported by confidentiality. (D) and (E) are charges against the adversary system with no real connection to attorney-client confidentiality.

41. **A** Though the statement in (A) may be true, it is an argument against trial by jury rather than the adversary system. (B), (C), (D), and (E) are all points that critics of the adversary system have made.

42. **A** The passage, by presenting a defender (Freedman) and two critics (Frankel, Pomerantz) of the adversary system, imitates the way in which the system works.

Chapter

3

Analytical Reasoning

INTRODUCTION TO QUESTION TYPE

The Analytical Reasoning section is designed to measure your ability to analyze, understand, and draw conclusions from a group of conditions and relationships. This section is 35 minutes long and contains from 22 to 24 questions (usually four sets of conditions, statements, or rules). Each set is followed by four to seven questions.

The Analytical Reasoning type of question first appeared officially on the LSAT in June of 1982, but a similar form of Analytical Reasoning has been used on the Graduate Record Exam since 1977.

Analytical reasoning situations can take many forms, but you should be aware of some general things before reviewing the problem types.

WHEN YOU START A SET:

1. Read each statement carefully and actively, marking important words.

2. Learn to flow with the information given, looking for relationships between items.

3. Remember that making *simple* charts, diagrams, or simply displaying information is essential on most sets.

4. Because you will probably be drawing some sort of diagram or display, place a check mark next to each statement or condition as you read it or use it in the diagram. This will help you avoid skipping a statement or condition as you work back and forth in setting up your diagram.

5. Put a star or an asterisk next to big, general, and important statements. Sometimes these statements will affect a group, category, or placement. (Examples are, "No two people of the same sex are sitting in adjacent seats," and "All of the members of a department cannot take the same day off." Two other examples might include: "At least two graduate students must be on the team," and "People with pets with them must stay in hotel room 1 or 8.")

6. Put a star or an asterisk by statements that are difficult to understand. Try to rephrase these statements to yourself for better understanding.

7. If you wish to read through all of the conditions of a set before starting a diagram, begin your diagram on the second reading.

8. If no diagram seems apparent or conducive to the information given, look at a few of the questions. Sometimes the questions can give you some good hints on how to display the information.

9. Keep in mind that any information given to you in a specific question (If..., Assume that..., Suppose..., etc.) can be used only for that question and not for any others.

10. Remember: No formal logic is required.

WHEN YOU START DRAWING A CHART OR DISPLAYING INFORMATION, KEEP THE FOLLOWING TECHNIQUES IN MIND:

1. Keep the chart simple. Don't complicate the issue.

2. Look for the setup, frame, or framework. Sometimes this is given in the first statement, but in other cases you may need to read a number of conditions before constructing the type of drawing that will be most effective.

3. If you discover the frame or framework, fill in as much of the diagram as possible, but do not spend a great deal of time trying to complete it. This may not be possible or necessary to answer the questions.

4. Be aware that you may have to redraw all or part of your diagram several times (typically, a few times for each set) as different conditional information is given for specific questions.

5. If a framework is not given, see if the information can be grouped by similarities or differences.

6. As you read each statement, look for concrete information that you can enter into your chart or that you can simply display. (For example, "Tom sits in seat 4," or "Cheryl is Elma's mother.")

7. Locate off to the side any information that you cannot place directly into your chart. (Whatever you can't put in, goes out; for example, "Jill will not sit next to Helen," or "A biology book must be next to a science book.")

8. Some very important statements may not fit into your chart. Remember to put a star or an asterisk by these big, general, and important statements.

9. If some statements are not immediately placeable in your chart (and they are not the big, general statements), you may have to return to them for later placing, after you have placed other statements. Remember to mark such statements with an arrow or some other symbol so you don't forget to return to them.

10. As you place information, use question marks (?) to mark information that is variable or could be placed in a number of different places in the diagram.

11. Apply evidence in both directions. For instance, if a statement tells you that a condition must be true, consider whether this means that certain other conditions must not be true. (For example: "All blue cars are fast" tells you that a slow car is *not* blue.)

12. Notice what information is used, and what is left to use. (For example, "Bob, Carl, Don, Ed, and Fred are riding the school bus home. Don, Ed, and Fred are sitting in seats one, two, and three, respectively." You should realize that Bob and Carl are left to be placed.)

13. Watch for actions and the subsequent reactions in initial conditions or from information given in the questions. (For example, "Dale, Ralph, and Art cannot be on the same team. Dale is on Team A." Your action is that Dale is on Team A; your immediate reaction is that Ralph and Art cannot be on Team A.)

14. Understand the distinction between *must be* and *could be*:

MUST BE	COULD BE
No exceptions	May be, but doesn't
All the time	necessarily have to be
Always	

15. Watch the number of items, places, and people (males to females, adults to children, etc.) you are working with. Sometimes these numbers are the basis for correct answers, and they can even tip off how to construct a diagram.

16. If the diagram you construct shows positions or specific dates or other limits, watch for items that will force you off the end or out of the limits. (For example, "There are five houses in a row on the

north side of the street numbered 1, 2, 3, 4, 5 consecutively. There is one yellow house that is between two blue houses." Therefore, the yellow house cannot be in place 1 or 5, because there would be no room for the blue house. It would be forced off the end or out of bounds.)

17. If, as is true in many cases, no standard type of chart will apply to the problem, be aware that you can merely pull out information in a simple display or through simple notes. Remember to flow with the information given, looking for relationships between items.

AND A FINAL REMINDER:
KEEP THE DRAWING SIMPLE; DON'T COMPLICATE YOUR THINKING.

The following sections provide some detailed examples of typical problem types and charts. These samples are intended to give you insight into the methods of charting that are possible. REMEMBER: Different students may prefer different types of charts. Use what is effective and efficient for you!

SOME TYPES OF CHARTING
THE CONNECTION CHART

One of the many types of charts is the *connection chart*. In constructing such a chart, your first step is usually to group or align items into *general* categories. Then the second step is to draw connections according to relationships between *specific* items. Remember to take information forward and backward (what can and can't happen) and to watch for actions and reactions.

Example

Sales manager Tom Forrester is trying to put together a sales team to cover the Los Angeles area. His team will consist of four members—two experienced and two new salesmen.

(1) Sam, Fred, Harry, and Jim are the experienced salesmen.
(2) John, Tim, and Tom are new.
(3) Sam and Fred do not work together.
(4) Tim and Sam refuse to work together.
(5) Harry and Tom cannot work together.

1. If Sam is made part of the team, the following must be the other members: Ⓐ Ⓑ Ⓒ Ⓓ Ⓔ
(A) John, Tim, Tom
(B) John, Tom, Jim
(C) Tim, Harry, Jim
(D) Tom, John, Fred
(E) John, Tom, Harry

2. If Sam is not chosen as part of the sales team and Tim is, then which of the following must be true?
(A) Tom and Harry are on the team. Ⓐ Ⓑ Ⓒ Ⓓ Ⓔ
(B) Jim and John are on the team.
(C) Harry and Fred are on the team.
(D) John or Tom is not on the team.
(E) Fred or Jim is not on the team.

3. Which of the following must be true? Ⓐ Ⓑ Ⓒ Ⓓ Ⓔ
(A) Fred and Sam always work together.
(B) Jim and Tom never work together.
(C) Jim and Fred always work together.
(D) If John works, then Jim doesn't work.
(E) If Sam works, then Tom works.

4. If Tom is chosen as part of the sales team, but John is not, then the other three members must be

(A) Fred, Tim, and Harry   Ⓐ Ⓑ Ⓒ Ⓓ Ⓔ

(B) Fred, Tim, and Jim

(C) Harry, John, and Tim

(D) Tim, Tom, and Jim

(E) Sam, Fred, and Harry

5. Which of the following must be true?   Ⓐ Ⓑ Ⓒ Ⓓ Ⓔ

(A) If Harry works, then John works.

(B) If Jim works, then John works.

(C) If John works, then Tom works.

(D) If Tom works, then John works.

(E) If John works, then Jim works.

ANSWERS AND EXPLANATIONS

When drawing a connection chart, always prefer fewer connections to many connections. In this case, drawing connections between the workers who can work together will result in a complicated system of intersecting lines. Connecting those who *do not* or *cannot* work together results in a simple, clear chart:

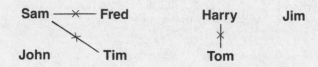

This chart encourages you to use information in both directions, recognizing that, because connected workers *cannot* work together, unconnected workers *can* work together.

Notice that the conditions gave initial information about those who cannot work together, helping you to formulate the most efficient method of connecting the diagram. If the conditions had stated that some salesmen always work together and some never work together, you would have used a different type of marking to denote each type of connection.

1. **B** The team must consist of two experienced and two new salesmen. Sam is experienced, so the rest of the team must include one experienced and two new salesmen. (C) should be eliminated both because it contains two experienced salesmen and because Sam does not work with Tim; also eliminate (A) because it includes Tim. Eliminate (D) because Sam does not work with Fred, and eliminate (E) because Tom does not work with Harry.

2. **D** With Tim on the team, there is room for one other new salesman. Therefore, *either* John *or* Tom is on the team, but not both.

3. **E** The key word in this question is <u>must</u>, which excludes possible but not necessary combinations. (A) is false, as the chart reveals. (B) is false because they <u>could</u> work together if Harry does not work. (C) is false because Jim and Fred do not have to work together. You could have the team of Jim, Sam, John, and Tom. This also eliminates (D). (E) must be true since Sam and Tim never work together; Sam must always work with Tom and John.

4. **B** If Tom is chosen as part of the team, and John is not, then Tim must be the other inexperienced member. So, if Tom and Tim both are chosen, then Sam and Harry are not chosen. The team now consists of Tom, Tim, Fred, and Jim.

5. **A** Since Harry will not work with Tom, then John must be one of the other inexperienced members in the group when Harry works. The other combinations (Jim and John, John and Tom) do not always work together.

THE POSITION CHARTS

Another type of diagram is the *position chart*. This type is very common on the LSAT and appears in a variety of forms. Often a framework will be given in the first condition or in a statement preceding the conditions. Look for concrete information first, but remember to mark large, general, and important statements. Keep in mind: whatever won't go in the diagram immediately, goes out to the side for possible placement later (whatever won't go in, goes out).

Example 1

John, Paul, George, and Herman sit around a square table with eight chairs, which are equally distributed.

Bob, Carol, Ted, and Alice join them at the table.
The two women (Carol and Alice) cannot sit next to each other.
John and Herman are seated on either side of George and are next to him.
Ted is seated next to Herman.
Carol is seated next to John, but not directly across from George.
John is directly across from Alice.

1. Which men could switch positions without contradicting the seating arrangement? Ⓐ Ⓑ Ⓒ Ⓓ Ⓔ
   (A) George and Herman
   (B) John and George
   (C) Paul and Ted
   (D) Bob and Paul
   (E) Bob and George

2. Which of the following must be FALSE? Ⓐ Ⓑ Ⓒ Ⓓ Ⓔ
   (A) George is not next to Ted.
   (B) Alice is not next to Carol.
   (C) Herman is next to Carol.
   (D) George is across from Paul.
   (E) Bob is not next to Paul.

3. Which of the following could be true? Ⓐ Ⓑ Ⓒ Ⓓ Ⓔ
   (A) Herman sits next to Carol.
   (B) Herman sits next to John.
   (C) Ted sits next to Paul.
   (D) John sits next to Paul.
   (E) George sits next to Alice.

4. Which of the following must be true? Ⓐ Ⓑ Ⓒ Ⓓ Ⓔ
   (A) Ted sits next to Paul.
   (B) Alice sits next to Paul.
   (C) George sits next to Carol.
   (D) Ted sits next to Bob.
   (E) Bob sits next to John.

5. If Arnold were now to take Ted's seat, then Arnold Ⓐ Ⓑ Ⓒ Ⓓ Ⓔ
   (A) must now be next to Bob
   (B) must be next to Alice
   (C) must be across from Bob
   (D) is either next to or across from Paul
   (E) is either next to or across from George

ANSWERS AND EXPLANATIONS

Note that the statement preceding the six conditions immediately suggests that you draw a square table with two spaces on each side. The first piece of concrete information is condition 3, which tells you to seat John, George, and Herman in that order. Next, seat Ted next to Herman (#4), seat Carol next to John (#5), and seat Alice across from John (#6). Note that Carol and Alice are not sitting next to each other (#2), and that Paul and Bob are in *variable* positions on either side of Alice. The resulting chart is as follows:

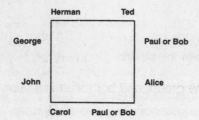

1. **D** As the chart points out, only Bob and Paul are in variable positions and, thus, interchangeable.

2. **C** Working from the answer choices and inspecting the chart, you see that (C) *must* be false in any case, and that (D) *may* be false, depending upon where Paul is seated.

3. **C** From the diagram you can see that Paul could be in the seat next to Ted. None of the other choices are possible.

4. **B** Since the two seats next to Alice are taken by Paul and Bob, then Alice must sit next to Paul.

5. **D** If Arnold takes Ted's seat, then either he is seated next to Paul, or else Paul is seated across from him.

Example 2

A graphic artist is designing a modern type style for the alphabet. This type style is based on artistic design and relative sizes of the letters. At this point, the relative sizes among the letters that the artist has designed are as follows:

A is taller than B but shorter than C.
B is shorter than D but taller than E.
F is shorter than A but taller than B.
G is taller than D but shorter than F.
H is shorter than B.

1. Which of the following could be FALSE, but is not necessarily false? Ⓐ Ⓑ Ⓒ Ⓓ Ⓔ
    (A) E is shorter than D.
    (B) C is taller than E.
    (C) D is taller than F.
    (D) H is taller than E.
    (E) E is shorter than A.

2. Which of the following could be true? Ⓐ Ⓑ Ⓒ Ⓓ Ⓔ
    (A) D is taller than most of the others.
    (B) A is the tallest
    (C) H is the shortest
    (D) D is not shorter than G.
    (E) H is taller than F.

3. Which of the following must be true?   Ⓐ Ⓑ Ⓒ Ⓓ Ⓔ
- (A)   F is taller than D.
- (B)   H is the shortest of all.
- (C)   H is taller than D.
- (D)   E is the shortest of all.
- (E)   E is taller than H.

4. If Q is added to the group and Q is taller than B but shorter than G, then Q must be
- (A)   taller than F   Ⓐ Ⓑ Ⓒ Ⓓ Ⓔ
- (B)   shorter than D
- (C)   between D and F
- (D)   taller than only three of the others
- (E)   shorter than at least three of the others

5. If Q and Z are both added to the group, and both are taller than H, then   Ⓐ Ⓑ Ⓒ Ⓓ Ⓔ
- (A)   H is the shortest of all
- (B)   E is the shortest of all
- (C)   C is the tallest of all
- (D)   either Q or Z is the tallest of all
- (E)   either H or E is the shortest of all

ANSWERS AND EXPLANATIONS

From the information given, a simple chart may be constructed using the following steps:

The first statement reads, "A is taller than B but shorter than C." Using a position chart where the top is the tallest and the bottom is the shortest, you have:

C

A

B

The first part of the second statement reads, "B is shorter than D...." Notice that D can be *anywhere* taller than B, so a "range" for D has to be drawn:

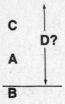

Adding the second part of the second statement gives "B is shorter than D but taller than E." Since B is taller than E, E will be placed under B:

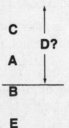

The third statement reads, "F is shorter than A but taller than B." Therefore F must fit between A and B:

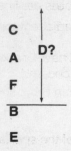

C
A
    D?
F

B

E

According to the fourth statement, "G is taller than D but shorter than F." Therefore G is above D, but since it's below F, both G and D must fit between F and B:

C

A

F

G

D

B

E

The fifth statement reads, "H is shorter than B," so H must have a possible range anywhere under B:

C

A

F

G

D

B

E   H?

Note that H is in a variable position.

1. **D** H may be taller than E, or it may be shorter than E. This is the only part of the chart that isn't definitely resolved.

2. **C** H may be the shortest, because it could possibly be shorter than E.

3. **A** Inspection of the chart reveals that F is taller than D. It also reveals that H cannot be taller than D and that H or E <u>could</u> be the shortest of all, since H is in a relatively variable position.

4. **E** If Q is added to the group, it may be either taller or shorter than D. Therefore, only (E) is true.

5. **E** If Q and Z are added, and both are taller than H, we know little more except that H or E must still be the smallest. Q or Z could possibly be the tallest, but not necessarily so. Only (E) *must* be true.

Example 3

In a parking lot, seven company automobiles are lined up in a row in seven parking spots.

(1)   There are two vans, which are both adjacent to the same sports car.
(2)   There is one station wagon.
(3)   There are two limousines, which are never parked adjacent to each other.
(4)   One of the sports cars is always on one end.

1. If the station wagon is on one end, one of the sports cars must be in the   Ⓐ Ⓑ Ⓒ Ⓓ Ⓔ
   (A)   2nd spot
   (B)   3rd spot
   (C)   4th spot
   (D)   5th spot
   (E)   7th spot

2. If one of the vans is on one end, then the station wagon must be   Ⓐ Ⓑ Ⓒ Ⓓ Ⓔ
   (A)   only in the 4th spot
   (B)   either in the 2nd or the 6th spot
   (C)   only in the 3rd spot
   (D)   either in the 3rd or the 5th spot
   (E)   only in the 6th spot

3. If a limousine is in the 7th spot, then the station wagon could be in   Ⓐ Ⓑ Ⓒ Ⓓ Ⓔ
   (A)   the 2nd spot
   (B)   the 3rd spot
   (C)   the 6th spot
   (D)   either the 2nd or 6th spot
   (E)   either the 2nd, 3rd, or 6th spot

4. If one of the sports cars is in the 2nd spot, then the station wagon   Ⓐ Ⓑ Ⓒ Ⓓ Ⓔ
   (A)   could be in the 5th spot
   (B)   could be in the 6th spot
   (C)   must be in the 5th spot
   (D)   must be in the 6th spot
   (E)   must be in the 3rd spot

5. If both sports cars are adjacent to a van, the station wagon must be in   Ⓐ Ⓑ Ⓒ Ⓓ Ⓔ
   (A)   the 2nd spot
   (B)   the 4th spot
   (C)   the 6th spot
   (D)   either the 2nd or 4th spot
   (E)   either the 2nd or 6th spot

6. If an eighth car (a limousine) is added, and another parking spot is also added, then in order not to violate any of the original statements EXCEPT the number of limousines in statement 3
   (A)   a limousine must be parked in the 2nd spot   Ⓐ Ⓑ Ⓒ Ⓓ Ⓔ
   (B)   the station wagon must be parked in the 2nd spot
   (C)   the station wagon must be parked in the 6th spot
   (D)   a limousine must be parked on one end
   (E)   a limousine cannot be parked on either end

ANALYTICAL REASONING

ANSWERS AND EXPLANATIONS

1. **C** In this question, two charts are possible:

   `__S__ _____ _____ _____ _____ _____ __SW__`

   and

   `__SW__ _____ _____ _____ _____ _____ __S__`

   Now notice that for *both* of the vans to be adjacent to the same sports car, there must be another sports car, and they must always be in the order V S V. Thus, the only way to place V S V in either of the above diagrams so that two limousines are never adjacent is to place V, S, and V in spots 3, 4, and 5, as follows:

   `__S__ _____ __V__ __S__ __V__ _____ __SW__`

   or

   `__SW__ _____ __V__ __S__ __V__ _____ __S__`

   Thus, the limousines will not be adjacent if one of the sports cars is in the 4th spot.

2. **D** Again there are two possible diagrams for this question:

   `__V__ __S__ __V__ _____ _____ _____ __S__`

   and

   `__S__ _____ _____ _____ __V__ __S__ __V__`

   Now notice that, in order that the limousines not be adjacent, the station wagon must be in either the 5th spot or the 3rd spot.

3. **E** If a limousine is in the 7th spot, then a sports car, to be on an end, must be in the 1st spot:

   `__S__ _____ _____ _____ _____ _____ __L__`

   Notice that the station wagon could now be in the 6th spot:

   `__S__ __L__ __V__ __S__ __V__ __SW__ __L__`
   (with V, S, V, L above L, V, S, V, SW respectively)

   or else in either the 2nd or the 3rd spot:

   `__S__ __SW__ __L__ __V__ __S__ __V__ __L__`
   (with L, SW above SW, L respectively)

   So the station wagon could be in either the 2nd, the 3rd, or the 6th spot.

4. **C** If one of the sports cars is in the 2nd spot, the other sports car must be in the 7th spot:

   `__V__ __S__ __V__ _____ _____ _____ __S__`

   Thus, in order for the limousines not to be adjacent, the station wagon must be in the 5th spot.

5. **E** Two diagrams are necessary for this problem. If both sports cars are adjacent to a van, your diagrams will be:

   `__S__ __V__ __S__ __V__ _____ _____ _____`

   and

   `_____ _____ _____ __V__ __S__ __V__ __S__`

   Thus, in order for the limousines not to be adjacent, the station wagon must be in either the 2nd spot or the 6th spot.

6.   **D**   If another limousine is added along with an eighth parking spot, all the original statements can be obeyed ONLY if a limousine is parked on one end. For example:

S   L   V   S   V   L   SW   L

POSITION CHART WITH THE DIAGRAM PROVIDED

On occasion, the LSAT will contain Analytical Reasoning problems with the diagram provided. For example,

Nine guests—A, B, C, D, E, F, G, H, I—attend a formal dinner party. Ten chairs are arranged around the rectangular dining room table as follows:

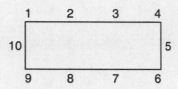

Seat 1 is directly across from seat 9.
Seat 2 is directly across from seat 8.
Seat 3 is directly across from seat 7.
Seat 4 is directly across from seat 6.
Seats 5 and 10 are at the ends of the table and are directly across from each other.
A, B, C, and D are females.
E, F, G, H, and I are males.
A and E are a married couple.
B and F are a married couple.
C and G are engaged to each other.
Each married couple always sits next to his or her spouse on one side of the table.
Members of the same sex never sit in adjacent seats.
Guests in end seats 5 and 10 are considered adjacent to seats on each side of them.
If G is in seat 10, then C is not in seat 5.
I is never in seat 6.
A is always in seat 1.

1. Which of the following could sit in seat 10?
  (A) A
  (B) C
  (C) D
  (D) F
  (E) H

2. Which of the following is a complete and accurate list of guests who could sit in seat 3?
  (A) A, B, C, D, E, F, G
  (B) B, C, D, E, F
  (C) B, C, D, E
  (D) B, C, D
  (E) B, C

3. If seat 9 is empty and G sits in seat 10, which of the following could sit in seat 5?
(A) B
(B) D
(C) C
(D) H
(E) I

4. If C sits in seat 5, and F sits in seat 4, which of the following could be the arrangement of seats from 1 to 10 respectively?

1, 2, 3, 4, 5, 6, 7, 8, 9, 10
(A) A, B, E, F, C, G, _, I, D, H
(B) A, E, B, G, C, F, D, H, _, I
(C) A, E, B, F, C, I, D, _, G, H
(D) A, E, B, F, C, H, D, I, _, G
(E) A, E, B, F, C, G, D, H, _, I

5. If D sits in seat 5, and the engaged couple sits together in seats 7 and 8, which of the following seats must be empty?
(A) 3
(B) 4
(C) 6
(D) 9
(E) 10

6. Which of the following is a complete and accurate list of guests who could sit in seat 5?
(A) C
(B) D
(C) C, D
(D) B, C, D
(E) C, D, G

7. If a female sits directly across from A, which of the following must be true?
(A) Seat 3 is empty.
(B) Seat 4 is empty.
(C) Seat 6 is a female.
(D) Seat 7 is a female.
(E) Seat 8 is a male.

ANSWERS AND EXPLANATIONS

From the initial conditions, the diagram would look like this:

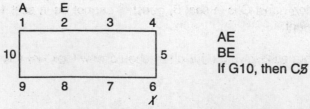

1. **E** Since guest A sits in seat 1, a male must sit in seat 10 if it is not empty. This eliminates (A), (B), and (C) since guests A, C, and D are females (A is in seat 1 anyway). Since guests B and F are a married couple, they must sit next to each other on a side. This eliminates (D). Guest H is a male and could sit in seat 10.

2. **D** Since guest E is in seat 2, only a female could sit in seat 3. Since guest A is in seat 1, the remaining females are guests B, C, and D.

3. **B** From the information given in the question and the initial conditions, the diagram should look like this:

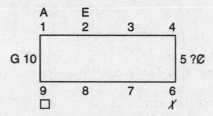

It can now be determined that seat 3 is a female, seat 4 is a male, and seat 5 is a female. You may have added to your diagram so it would now look like this:

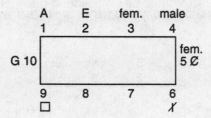

Seat 5 cannot be guest B, since guest B cannot be on the end. Guest H and I are males, so (D) and (E) are eliminated. Since guest G is in seat 10, then guest C cannot be in seat 5 (from initial conditions), so only guest D is left.

4. **E** From the information given, the diagram should look like this:

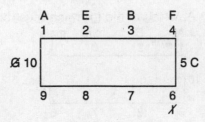

You could eliminate (A) because guest B cannot be in seat 2. Since guest F is in seat 4, guest B is in seat 3. This eliminates (B). (C) can be eliminated since male guests G and H cannot be seated next to each other. Since guest C is in seat 5, guest G cannot be in seat 10, so (D) is eliminated. (E) is a possible arrangement.

5. **D** From the information given, your chart should now look like this:

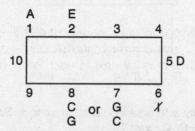

You should also be able to fill in seats 3 and 4 and determine that seats 6 and 10, if not empty, must be males. Your diagram should now have this information:

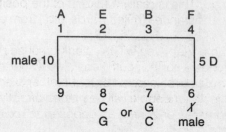

Since only male guests H and I are not seated, guest H must be in seat 6 and guest I in seat 10. This leaves seat 9 empty. In any other arrangement, two males are next to each other.

6. **C** First eliminate (D) since guest B must be on a side. If guest G is in seat 5, then the diagram would look like this:

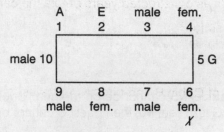

This requires two males to be next to each other, so seat 5 must be a female, either guest C or D.

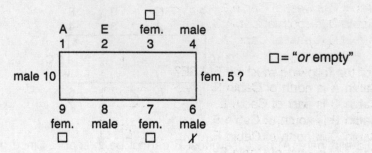

7. **E** If a female sits across from guest A, your diagram would now have the following information:

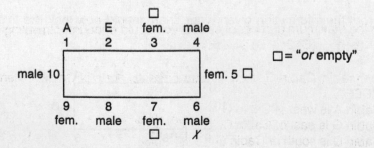

Since seats 3, 5, or 7 could be empty, only (E), a male is in seat 8, must be true.

THE MAP

Another type of diagram is the *map*. This is really a takeoff of the position diagram with some more possibilities. Maps can include actual distances (miles, yards, etc.) from one place to another, or simply relative alignments.

In many cases, while constructing a map, you will be placing houses, cities, objects, or people, in general areas, limited areas, or zones—north, south, east, west, northeast, southwest, etc. These placements will often be relative to a central location or to the other placements.

Sometimes the houses, cities, objects, or people will be placed *directly* north (*due* north), or *directly* southeast, etc. Watching for limited areas or zones, as opposed to exact locations, can take careful reading, reasoning, and placement.

Example

Six cabins—A, B, C, D, E, and F—were constructed on a small flat area in the mountains. The focal point of the area was a statue that was constructed years before the cabins were constructed.

Cabin A is directly north of the statue.
Cabin C is directly west of the statue.
Cabin D is south of Cabin C.
Cabin E is west of Cabin A.
The statue is directly southeast of Cabin B and directly northwest of Cabin F.

1. Which of the following must be true?   Ⓐ Ⓑ Ⓒ Ⓓ Ⓔ
  (A) Cabin B is east of Cabin C.
  (B) Cabin B is west of Cabin C.
  (C) Cabin F is west of Cabin E.
  (D) Cabin D is south of Cabin B.
  (E) Cabin D is east of Cabin A.

2. Which of the following must be FALSE?   Ⓐ Ⓑ Ⓒ Ⓓ Ⓔ
  (A) Cabin A is north of Cabin E.
  (B) Cabin C is east of Cabin E.
  (C) Cabin B is south of Cabin F.
  (D) Cabin D is north of Cabin F.
  (E) Cabin D is east of Cabin E.

3. How many cabins must be west of Cabin A?   Ⓐ Ⓑ Ⓒ Ⓓ Ⓔ
  (A) 0   (B) 1   (C) 2   (D) 3   (E) 4

4. What is the maximum number of cabins you could encounter traveling directly east from Cabin C?
  (A) 0   (B) 1   (C) 2   D) 3   (E) 4   Ⓐ Ⓑ Ⓒ Ⓓ Ⓔ

5. If another cabin, Cabin G, is constructed directly north of Cabin F, then all of the following must be true EXCEPT   Ⓐ Ⓑ Ⓒ Ⓓ Ⓔ
  (A) Cabin A is west of Cabin G
  (B) Cabin G is east of Cabin C
  (C) Cabin D is south of Cabin G
  (D) Cabin G is east of Cabin A
  (E) Cabin B is west of Cabin G

6. If Cabins H and J are constructed so that H is directly east of J, and H is directly north of A, then which of the following must be true? Ⓐ Ⓑ Ⓒ Ⓓ Ⓔ

(A) Cabin H is north of Cabin B.

(B) Cabin C is west of Cabin J.

(C) Cabin H is south of Cabin D.

(D) Cabin E is south of Cabin H.

(E) Cabin F is east of Cabin J.

7. If Cabin M is constructed west of Cabin A, which of the following is a possible order of cabins a traveler could encounter while traveling directly northwest from F? Ⓐ Ⓑ Ⓒ Ⓓ Ⓔ

(A) BEDM   (B) DMBE   (C) MDEBC   (D) DMCBE   (E) MDABE

ANSWERS AND EXPLANATIONS

From the information given, a simple chart may be constructed as follows (possible ranges are denoted with arrows):

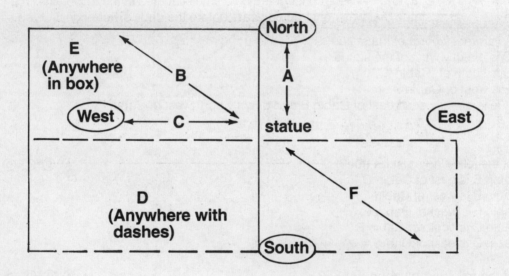

Or an even simpler map (if you can remember the zones) is possible:

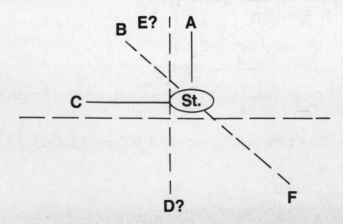

1. **D** Statements (A), (B), and (E) *could* be true, but do not necessarily have to be true. (C) is false. Only (D) must be true.

2. **C** Choices (A), (B), (D), and (E) *could* be true, but (C) *must* be false.

3. **D** Cabins E, B, and C must be west of A. Cabin D does not have to be west of Cabin A.

4. **B** Traveling directly east from Cabin C, you could encounter Cabin E.

5. **C** Adding Cabin G to the chart results in:

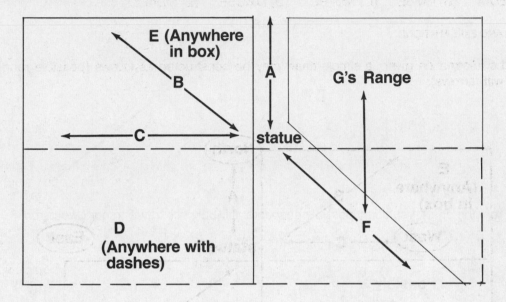

Statements (A), (B), (D), and (F) must be true. Statement (C) could be true, but does not necessarily have to be true.

6. **E** Adding Cabins H and J to the chart results in:

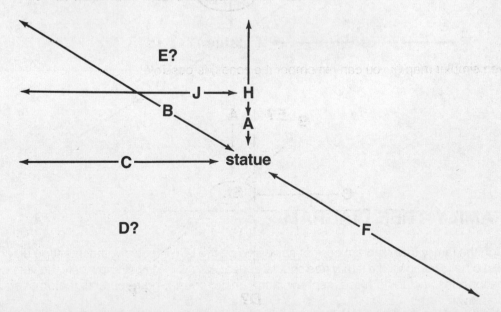

From the chart, Cabin F must be east of Cabin J. Choices (A), (B), and (D) could be true, but do not necessarily have to be true. Choice (C) must be false.

7. **B** Adding Cabin M to the chart results in:

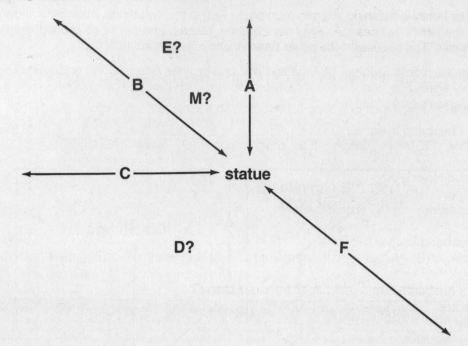

From the chart, you could possibly encounter DMBE while traveling northwest from F.

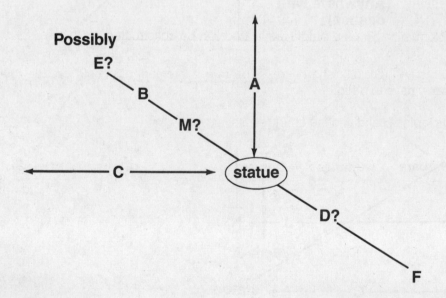

THE FAMILY TREE DIAGRAM

Although the family tree diagram has not appeared on the LSAT recently, the tree-type diagram can be useful in other situations. If a family tree should appear, you will need to know only the very common family relationships, including niece, nephew, aunt, uncle, cousin, grandparents (paternal and maternal), and in-laws.

As you set up the following examples, you will notice that some diagrams work down, some up, and some in both directions.

Example 1

The Mindez family is planning a family reunion. In writing the invitations, Alice Swill, the oldest living member of the family, notices that all of her children, nieces, and nephews are still married to their original spouses. The spouses have never been previously married.

Barbara is the oldest daughter of Alice and has one brother, Charles, and one sister, Denise.
Alice's only sister, Frances Martins, has two children: son George, and daughter Helene.
Edna is Denise's only daughter.

1. Barbara's husband is Edna's   Ⓐ Ⓑ Ⓒ Ⓓ Ⓔ
   (A) father   (B) stepfather   (C) grandfather   (D) aunt   (E) uncle

2. Denise and Helene are   Ⓐ Ⓑ Ⓒ Ⓓ Ⓔ
   (A) sisters   (B) first cousins   (C) second cousins
   (D) stepsisters   (E) sisters-in-law

3. Alice's husband Darnell is Edna's   Ⓐ Ⓑ Ⓒ Ⓓ Ⓔ
   (A) uncle   (B) father   (C) stepfather   (D) grandfather   (E) great-grandfather

4. Frances's husband, Sam, could NOT be older than   Ⓐ Ⓑ Ⓒ Ⓓ Ⓔ
   (A) Frances
   (B) Alice
   (C) Alice's husband Darnell
   (D) Denise
   (E) George

ANSWERS AND EXPLANATIONS

Using the information given, a simple family tree can be constructed, as follows:

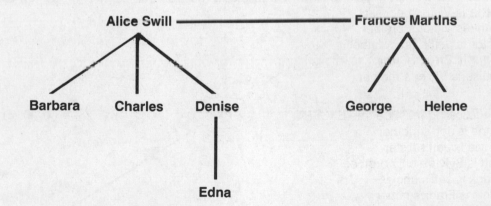

1. **E**   Edna's mother is Denise. Barbara is Denise's sister and therefore is Edna's aunt. Barbara's husband is therefore Edna's uncle.

2. **B**   Because Denise and Helene are each children of sisters, they are considered first cousins.

3. **D**   Alice's husband Darnell is Denise's father. Because Edna is Denise's daughter, Darnell is Edna's grandfather.

4. **B**   Sam could not be older than Alice if Alice is the oldest living member of the family, as stated in the information.

Example 2

Jeff Alton has located his few remaining relatives in Altontown, South Dakota. He has discovered that all of the remaining relatives who were married are still married to their original spouses. Ernie Alton, Tim Alton, Frank Alton, Anna Alton, Sylvia Alton, and Louise Daly are his only living relatives in the small South Dakota town. The town is named after the founder, Jeff's grandfather, Ernie Alton. Jeff's notes show the following relationships between the relatives:

Jeff's father, Tim, has only one sibling, a brother, Frank, who is not married and has no children.
Anna is Tim's wife.
Louise Daly, Anna's mother, still lives with Anna.
Ernie Alton has one granddaughter, Sylvia, and two grandsons, only one of whom lives in Altontown.

1. Louise is Sylvia's   Ⓐ Ⓑ Ⓒ Ⓓ Ⓔ
   (A) mother   (B) aunt   (C) paternal grandmother
   (D) maternal grandmother   (E) great-grandmother

2. Frank is Jeff's   Ⓐ Ⓑ Ⓒ Ⓓ Ⓔ
   (A) brother   (B) uncle   (C) cousin   (D) maternal grandfather   (E) father

3. Ernie's deceased wife, Zina, would be Sylvia's   Ⓐ Ⓑ Ⓒ Ⓓ Ⓔ
   (A) aunt   (B) mother   (C) mother-in-law
   (D) paternal grandmother   (E) maternal grandmother

4. If Louise's brother, Manny, were still alive, which of the following would be true? Ⓐ Ⓑ Ⓒ Ⓓ Ⓔ
   (A)   Manny would be Anna's uncle.
   (B)   Manny would be Frank's uncle.
   (C)   Manny would be Jeff's cousin.
   (D)   Manny would be Ernie's uncle.
   (E)   Manny would be Sylvia's cousin.

5. If Anna has one brother, Victor, which of the following must be true?   Ⓐ Ⓑ Ⓒ Ⓓ Ⓔ
   (A)   Sylvia is Victor's cousin.
   (B)   Frank is Victor's brother.
   (C)   Victor is Jeff's grandfather.
   (D)   Victor is Ernie's uncle.
   (E)   Louise is Victor's mother.

6. All of the following must be true EXCEPT   Ⓐ Ⓑ Ⓒ Ⓓ Ⓔ
   (A)   Anna is Jeff's mother
   (B)   Sylvia is Jeff's sister
   (C)   Jeff is Sylvia's only brother
   (D)   Frank is Jeff's uncle
   (E)   Ernie is Frank's father

ANSWERS AND EXPLANATIONS

From the information given, a family tree diagram similar to this can be constructed:

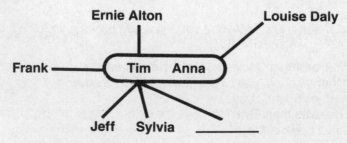

1. **D** From the diagram, Louise is Anna's mother; therefore, she is Sylvia's maternal grandmother.

2. **B** From the diagram, because Frank is Tim's brother, he is Jeff's uncle.

3. **D** From the diagram, Ernie is Sylvia's paternal grandfather; therefore, his deceased wife, Zina, would be the paternal grandmother.

4. **A** With this information you could add to the diagram as follows (but remember: you are making this addition for only this one question):

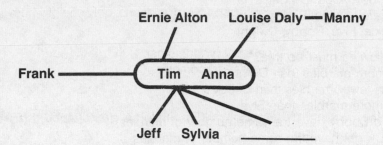

Because Manny is Louise's brother, he would be Anna's uncle.

5. **E** With this information, you could add to the diagram as follows (again, remember: you are making this addition for only this one question):

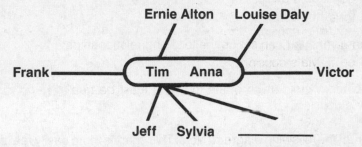

Because Victor is Anna's brother, Louise is Victor's mother (E).

6. **C** From the original statements, Ernie Alton has one granddaughter, Sylvia, and two grandsons. Therefore, Sylvia has two brothers.

NUMERICAL DISPLAYS OR NUMERICAL POSITION DIAGRAMS

This type of display or diagram deals with *numerical* relationships—lengths, heights, scores, etc. Often, when these relationships are displayed or after they are listed, they can be converted into a sort of position diagram.

Example 1

Alice, Bobby, Carole, Dwight, and Elva were playing a game with marbles. When the game ended, Alice wrote down the following information:

Carole has more marbles than Alice and Bobby together.
Alice's total is the same as the total of Dwight and Elva together.
Alice has more marbles than Bobby.
Bobby has more marbles than Elva.
Everyone has at least one marble.

1. Who ended the game with the most marbles?
(A) Alice   (B) Bobby   (C) Carole   (D) Dwight   (E) Elva   Ⓐ Ⓑ Ⓒ Ⓓ Ⓔ

2. If Dwight has more marbles than Bobby, who ended the game with the least marbles?
(A) Alice   (B) Bobby   (C) Carole   (D) Dwight   (E) Elva   Ⓐ Ⓑ Ⓒ Ⓓ Ⓔ

3. Which of the following is a possible order of children going from most marbles to least?
(A)   Alice, Bobby, Carole, Dwight, Elva   Ⓐ Ⓑ Ⓒ Ⓓ Ⓔ
(B)   Carole, Alice, Bobby, Elva, Dwight
(C)   Carole, Bobby, Alice, Dwight, Elva
(D)   Dwight, Carole, Alice, Bobby, Elva
(E)   Carole, Alice, Elva, Bobby, Dwight

4. Which of the following must be true?
(A)   Elva has more marbles than Dwight.   Ⓐ Ⓑ Ⓒ Ⓓ Ⓔ
(B)   Dwight has fewer marbles than Bobby.
(C)   Alice has more marbles than Elva.
(D)   Dwight and Bobby have the same number of marbles.
(E)   Elva and Dwight have the same number of marbles.

5. If Elva has 3 marbles and everyone has a different number of marbles, which of the following could NOT be the number of marbles that Alice could have?   Ⓐ Ⓑ Ⓒ Ⓓ Ⓔ
(A) 5   (B) 6   (C) 7   (D) 8   (E) 9

ANSWERS AND EXPLANATIONS

From the information given, you can set up the following relationships:

    C > A + B
    A = D + E
    A > B
    B > E

Then you can construct the following diagram (Note: This chart is more easily realized by starting with the last condition and working up.):

MOST

C

A

B   **D?**

E

LEAST

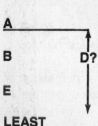

1. **C** Carole has more marbles than Alice and Bobby together. Because Alice has more marbles than Dwight, Elva, or Bobby each have alone, Carole must have most of all.

2. **E** If Dwight has more marbles than Bobby, then Elva must have the least number of marbles. See preceding chart.

3. **B** From the chart, we can see that Carole must have most of all, followed by Alice. Because Bobby has more marbles than Elva, only answer (B) can be a possible correct order.

4. **C** Only (C) *must* be true. In (A) and (E) Elva *could* have more marbles than Dwight, but not necessarily. She could have less *or the same*. Notice the possible range of placement for Dwight on the chart. Again, in (B) and (D) Dwight's placement is uncertain: Dwight could have fewer, *the same*, or more marbles than Bobby.

5. **B** If Elva has 3 marbles, then Dwight can have any number *but* 3. Because Alice's total equals Dwight's and Elva's total together, Alice cannot have 3 + 3, or 6.

Example 2

Five students, A, E, I, O, and U, were comparing the scores each received on a test and a quiz. The following was discovered:

A's quiz score was 80.
A's test score equals U's quiz score.
U's test score equals A's quiz score.
A's quiz score is 15 less than U's quiz score.
O's test score is 20 more than his quiz score and is 20 more than I's test score.
O's test score is 40 more than E's quiz score.
I's quiz score is 10 less than E's quiz score.

1. If E's quiz score is 60, what is O's quiz score?   Ⓐ Ⓑ Ⓒ Ⓓ Ⓔ
    (A) 80   (B) 70   (C) 60   (D) 50   (E) 40

2. Which of the following must be true?   Ⓐ Ⓑ Ⓒ Ⓓ Ⓔ
    (A) I's quiz score equals O's test score.
    (B) E's quiz score equals U's quiz score.
    (C) A's quiz score equals U's test score.
    (D) E's quiz score equals O's quiz score.
    (E) I's quiz score equals I's test score.

3. What is U's test score?   Ⓐ Ⓑ Ⓒ Ⓓ Ⓔ
    (A) 55   (B) 65   (C) 80   (D) 95   (E) 100

4. If I's test score is 45, what is O's test score?   Ⓐ Ⓑ Ⓒ Ⓓ Ⓔ
    (A) 25   (B) 35   (C) 45   (D) 55   (E) 65

5. If E's quiz score is 50, which of the following must be true?   Ⓐ Ⓑ Ⓒ Ⓓ Ⓔ
    (A) I's test score is 70.
    (B) O's test score is 100.
    (C) I's quiz score is 30.
    (D) O's quiz score is 60.
    (E) O's test score is 70.

6. If O's quiz score is the same as U's quiz score, which of the following must be true?
    (A) I's test score is 90.   Ⓐ Ⓑ Ⓒ Ⓓ Ⓔ
    (B) O's test score is 110.
    (C) I's quiz score is 70.
    (D) E's quiz score is 75.
    (E) O's quiz score is 80.

ANSWERS AND EXPLANATIONS

You could have set up the following relationships from the information given:

$$Aq = 80$$
$$At = Uq$$
$$Ut = Aq$$
$$Aq = Uq - 15$$
$$Ot = Oq + 20$$
$$Ot = It + 20$$
$$Ot = Eq + 40$$
$$Iq = Eq - 10$$

and you could have discovered that $Ut = 80$ (since $Aq = Ut$), $Uq = 95$ (since $Aq = Uq - 15$), $At = 95$ (since $At = Uq$), and $Oq = It$ (since $Ot = Oq + 20$ and $Ot = It + 20$).

You might have used the following diagram to help visualize the solutions to these problems:

Quiz	A	U	
------------------------------ 80 -------------- 95 ---
Test	U	A	
Quiz	I <- - - - 10 - - - -> E <- - - - 20 - - - -> O		

Test		I <- - - - 20 - - - -> O	

1. **A** From the preceding information we can see that O's quiz score is 20 greater than E's quiz score. Thus, 80 is the correct answer.

2. **C** From the diagram, A's quiz score equals U's test score. We do not have a relationship between E's quiz scores and A's or U's scores.

3. **C** Because U's test score equals A's quiz score, and that is 80, the answer must be C.

4. **E** Because O's test score is 20 greater than I's test score, and I's test score is 45, O's test score must be 65.

5. **A** From the diagram, I's test score is 70. Using the relationships gives $Oh = 50 + 40 = 90$, $Oh = It + 20$; therefore $It = 70$.

6. **D** This problem relates the two groups of scores together. Because A's quiz score is 80, U's quiz score is 95. Therefore, O's quiz score is 95. Thus, I's test score is 95. E's quiz score is 20 less than O's quiz score, thus it is 75, making (D) true.

THE INFORMATION CHART

The *information* chart is helpful for spotting specific information and making deductions quickly.

Example

Unless otherwise stated, each workman must work alone in the store.
Unless otherwise stated, each workman is able to complete his own job in half a day.

(1) In order to open a new furniture store the following week, Mr. Worble hired a painter, a carpet layer, an electrician, and a carpenter.
(2) The painter is available only on Tuesday morning, Wednesday afternoon, and all day Friday.
(3) The carpet layer is available only on Monday, Wednesday, and Friday mornings.
(4) The electrician is available only on Tuesday morning and Friday afternoon.
(5) The carpenter is available only on Monday morning, Tuesday all day, and Wednesday afternoon.

1. If the carpenter and the electrician must work on the same day to coordinate their efforts, but cannot work at the same time, who of the following will NOT be able to start work until Wednesday, at the earliest?　　　　　　　　　　　　　　　　　Ⓐ Ⓑ Ⓒ Ⓓ Ⓔ
(A) painter
(B) carpet layer
(C) electrician
(D) carpenter
(E) carpet layer and electrician

2. If the painter needs the whole day on Friday to complete his job, the　Ⓐ Ⓑ Ⓒ Ⓓ Ⓔ
(A) carpenter must work on Thursday
(B) electrician and carpet layer must work on the same day
(C) total job cannot be completed in one week
(D) electrician must work on Tuesday
(E) carpet layer and carpenter must work on the same day

3. Mr. Worble is expecting a supply of furniture on Thursday morning. Which of the following must be true?　　　　　　　　　　　　　　　　Ⓐ Ⓑ Ⓒ Ⓓ Ⓔ
(A) The carpenter will be the only one finished before the merchandise arrrives.
(B) Before the merchandise arrives, the painter will be finished, but the electrician will have to work Wednesday night.
(C) The carpet layer, the carpenter, and the electrician will be the only ones finished before the merchandise arrives.
(D) The carpet layer will have to work on the Tuesday before the merchandise arrives.
(E) All of the workers could have their jobs completed before the merchandise arrives.

4. If the store must be closed Monday and Tuesday and no worker may enter on those days, then, for all the work to be completed by the end of the week,　　　　Ⓐ Ⓑ Ⓒ Ⓓ Ⓔ
(A) the carpet layer must work Friday morning
(B) the painter must work Friday morning
(C) the painter must work Wednesday afternoon
(D) the painter must work Friday afternoon
(E) the carpet layer must work Friday afternoon

5. If the store must be painted before any of the other work may begin, then, for all the work to be completed, all the following are true EXCEPT　　　　　Ⓐ Ⓑ Ⓒ Ⓓ Ⓔ
(A) the carpenter may work Tuesday or Wednesday afternoon
(B) the electrician must work Friday afternoon
(C) the carpet layer must work Wednesday or Friday morning
(D) the electrician and the carpet layer may work the same day
(E) the painter and the electrician may work the same day

ANSWERS AND EXPLANATIONS

An information chart is suggested whenever you are trying to determine the points at which two sets of facts coincide. In this case, we chart the daily schedule of each worker, simply following the explicit information given in conditions 2–5:

	M	T	W	T	F
Painter		Morning	Afternoon		All day
Carpet layer	Morning		Morning		Morning
Electrician		Morning			Afternoon
Carpenter	Morning	All day	Afternoon		

Although we have written out "morning," "afternoon," and "all day," you may wish to abbreviate such terms.

The chart reveals that:

1. **A** The carpet layer may work on Monday, and the carpenter and the electrician *must* work Tuesday (the only day they are available together). In this case, the painter (A) may not begin until Wednesday.

2. **D** The electrician *must* work Tuesday, because his only other working day, Friday, interferes with the painter's work.

3. **E** One possible plan is this: The carpet layer works Monday morning, the electrician works Tuesday morning, the carpenter works Tuesday afternoon, and the painter works Wednesday afternoon.

4. **B** If the store must be closed on Monday and Tuesday, then the carpenter must work Wednesday afternoon, and the electrician must work Friday afternoon, as these workers have no other available days to work. Since the painter cannot work Wednesday afternoon (the carpenter is already working then), he must work Friday morning. This leaves the carpet layer Wednesday morning to complete his work.

5. **E** If the store must be painted first, then the painter could do his work Tuesday morning. All of the choices then are true, except (E). The painter and electrician may not work the same day, because if it's Tuesday, then they both would work in the morning, which is not allowed. The only other day they could both work is Friday, but that wouldn't allow all the work to be completed if the painter first works Friday morning.

THE ELIMINATION GRID

This type of chart will assist you in eliminating many possibilities, thus narrowing your answer choices and simplifying the reasoning process.

Example

Two boys (Tom and Sal) and two girls (Lisa and Molly) each receive a different one of four different passing grades (A,B,C,D) on an exam.

(1) Both boys receive lower grades than Lisa.
(2) Sal did not get a B.
(3) Tom got a B.
(4) Molly did not get an A.

1. Which statement(s) may be deduced from only one of the other statements?　Ⓐ Ⓑ Ⓒ Ⓓ Ⓔ
(A)　statement 1　　　(B)　statement 2　　　(C)　statement 3
(D)　statement 4　　　(E)　statements 1 and 3

2. If Molly received the lowest grade, then Sal must have received　Ⓐ Ⓑ Ⓒ Ⓓ Ⓔ
(A)　the A　(B)　the B　(C)　the C　(D)　the D　(E)　either the A or the B

3. Which of the following is a complete and accurate list of the grades that Sal could have received?
(A)　A　　　　　　　　　　　　　　　　　　　　　　　　Ⓐ Ⓑ Ⓒ Ⓓ Ⓔ
(B)　A, C
(C)　B, D
(D)　C, D
(E)　B, C, D

4. Which of the following is a complete and accurate list of the grades that Molly could NOT have
received?　　　　　　　　　　　　　　　　　　　　　　　　Ⓐ Ⓑ Ⓒ Ⓓ Ⓔ
(A)　A
(B)　B
(C)　B, C
(D)　C, D
(E)　A, B

5. If Sal received the D, then Molly received　　　　　　　　　Ⓐ Ⓑ Ⓒ Ⓓ Ⓔ
(A)　the A　(B)　the B　(C)　the C　(D)　the D　(E)　either the A or the D

6. If the grades that Sal and Lisa received were reversed, then which of the
original statements would no longer be true?　　　　　　　　　Ⓐ Ⓑ Ⓒ Ⓓ Ⓔ
(A)　statement 1　　　(B)　statement 2　　　(C)　statement 3
(D)　statement 4　　　(E)　statements 2 and 3

ANSWERS AND EXPLANATIONS

1.　**B**　Statement 2 may be deduced from statement 3. If Tom got the B, it must be true that Sal did
　　　not get the B.

2.　**C**　This question requires you to complete a chart, using the information from the statements. First,
　　　since both boys received lower grades than Lisa, we know that Lisa could not have gotten the C
　　　or D, and that neither of the boys could have gotten the A. Thus, your chart will look like this:

	A	B	C	D
Tom	X			
Sal	X			
Lisa			X	X
Molly				

From statements 2 and 3, we can fill in that Tom received the B (and thus the others didn't):

	A	B	C	D
Tom	X	√	X	X
Sal	X	X		
Lisa		X	X	X
Molly		X		

Statement 4 allows us to indicate on our chart that Molly didn't get an A. Thus, we can see from our chart that Lisa *must* have gotten the A:

	A	B	C	D
Tom	X	√	X	X
Sal	X	X		
Lisa		X	X	X
Molly	X	X	·	

Notice that we could have deduced that even without statement 4, as there was no other grade Lisa could possibly receive.

Now we know that Lisa received the A, and Tom received the B. But we cannot deduce Sal's or Molly's grade. Be aware that, on many problems like this, you will have to proceed to the questions with an incomplete chart. We can, however, now answer the rest of the questions: If Molly received the lowest grade (D), then Sal must have gotten the C.

3. **D** From our chart we can easily see that Sal could have received either the C or the D.

4. **E** From our chart we can easily see that Molly could not have received either the A or the B. We could also have determined this from statements 3 and 4.

5. **C** From our chart we can easily see that, if Sal received the D, then Molly must have received the C.

6. **A** If Sal and Lisa reversed their grades, then

> Sal would get the A.
> Tom would get the B.
> Lisa received either the C or the D.
> Molly received either the C or the D.

Therefore, only statement 1 ("Both boys receive lower grades than Lisa") would no longer be true.

PULLING OUT INFORMATION

In some instances, no chart appears to fit the situation. If this is the case, then simply pull out whatever information seems important to you.

Example

One left-handed tongo player (Sandy) and two right-handed tongo players (Arnie and Betsy) are the only entrants in a tongo tournament.

Tongo is a sport where, in each game, three players oppose each other.

The winner of each game receives 5 points; the second place finisher gets 3 points; and the third place finisher gets 1 point.

There are no tie games.

The one player with the most game points at the end of the tournament is the grand winner.

If, at the end of the tournament, two or more players have the same total number of points, there will be a playoff.

1. Which of the following must be true? Ⓐ Ⓑ Ⓒ Ⓓ Ⓔ
   (A) Betsy plays only right-handed opponents.
   (B) Arnie never plays a right-handed opponent.
   (C) Arnie plays just right-handed opponents.
   (D) Sandy never plays right-handed opponents.
   (E) Sandy always plays right-handed opponents.

2. If, after three games, both right-handed players have each scored 9 points, which of the
   following could be true? Ⓐ Ⓑ Ⓒ Ⓓ Ⓔ
   (A) One of the right-handed players finished first twice.
   (B) At least one of the right-handed players finished second three times.
   (C) Both right-handed players each finished first, second, and third.
   (D) The left-handed player finished first twice.
   (E) The left-handed player was ahead after three games.

3. Which of the following must be true? Ⓐ Ⓑ Ⓒ Ⓓ Ⓔ
   (A) A player with no first-place game points cannot win the tournament.
   (B) A player with only second-place game points can win the tournament.
   (C) A player with no first-place game points can win the tournament.
   (D) A player with no third-place game points must win the tournament.
   (E) A player with no second-place game points cannot come in second.

4. If, after three games, Arnie has 11 points, Betsy has 9 points, and Sandy Ⓐ Ⓑ Ⓒ Ⓓ Ⓔ
   has 7 points, which of the following must be false?
   (A) After four games, there is a three-way tie.
   (B) After four games, Betsy is alone in first place.
   (C) After four games, Betsy is alone in third place.
   (D) After four games, Sandy is alone in first place.
   (E) After four games, Sandy is alone in third place.

5. If, just before the last game, it is discovered that the left-handed player has
   finished first in every even-numbered game, then Ⓐ Ⓑ Ⓒ Ⓓ Ⓔ
   (A) Sandy must win the tournament
   (B) Sandy cannot win the tournament
   (C) Arnie may win the tournament
   (D) Betsy can't win the tournament
   (E) Betsy must win the tournament

ANSWERS AND EXPLANATIONS

You probably found that this set of conditions was not conducive to constructing any standard chart. As soon as this was evident, you should have simply pulled out information as follows:

L—Sandy	1st—5 pts.
R—Arnie	2nd—3 pts.
R—Betsy	3rd—1 pt.

Sometimes just pulling out information can be very helpful. Now let's look at the answers.

1. **E** Since Sandy is the only left-handed player, then she must play only right-handed opponents.

2. **C** Only (C) may be true. (A) is blatantly false, since two first-place wins would result in 10 points. (B) is incorrect because, if one player finished second in all three games, then there is no way a second player could score exactly 9 points in three games. (D) and (E) are incorrect since there must be 27 points scored during the three games with each player scoring 9 points.

3. **A** Only (A) is true. With no first-place game points, the most a player could score per game is 3 points. The best that that player could hope for would be that the other two players would split first place and third place on all the games. But even then, the other two players would average 3 points per game. At best a playoff would be necessary, and the player without a first-place finish would thus lose the tournament. (D) and (E) are false by example.

4. **D** The only statement that could not be true is (D). Since the most Sandy could score after four games would be 12 points, Betsy and/or Arnie will at least tie her for first place.

5. **C** Even though Sandy may have scored 5 points in every even-numbered game, she may not necessarily win the tournament. For instance, if, say, Arnie scores 5 points in every odd-numbered game, and if the tournament consists of an odd number of games, then Arnie will win the tournament. Sandy *can* win the tournament, but not necessarily *must* win the tournament. Betsy, also, could possibly win the tournament, if she scores first-place wins in every odd-numbered game.

THE DEPENDENT CONNECTION CHART

This type of chart is usually more complex than the linear position chart, because the conditions create a dynamic rather than a static relationship between interdependent factors in a sequence.

Example

(1) To enter the bar, you need a blue ticket and a yellow card.
(2) To get a blue ticket, you need an orange hat or a green bicycle.
(3) To get a yellow card, you need a blue card and a yellow hat.
(4) If you have a red ticket, you can get a green bicycle and a yellow hat.
(5) A blue hat will get you a red ticket.

1. Which of the following will allow you to enter the bar? Ⓐ Ⓑ Ⓒ Ⓓ Ⓔ
   (A) an orange hat and a blue card
   (B) a red ticket and a green bicycle
   (C) a green bicycle and a yellow hat
   (D) a yellow hat and a blue card
   (E) a blue card and a red ticket

2. What will get you a blue ticket? Ⓐ Ⓑ Ⓒ Ⓓ Ⓔ
   (A) a yellow card
   (B) a blue card
   (C) a blue hat
   (D) a yellow hat
   (E) an orange bicycle

3. If a purple card will get you a yellow hat, what is also needed to get a
yellow card? Ⓐ Ⓑ Ⓒ Ⓓ Ⓔ
- (A) a purple hat
- (B) a blue card
- (C) a green bicycle
- (D) an orange hat
- (E) a blue ticket

4. If you have a blue ticket and a blue card, which of the following will get
you into the bar? Ⓐ Ⓑ Ⓒ Ⓓ Ⓔ
- (A) a yellow hat
- (B) a red ticket
- (C) a blue hat
- (D) a yellow card
- (E) an orange hat

ANSWERS AND EXPLANATIONS

The following diagram results from the given conditions:

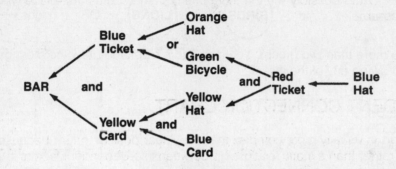

You can begin constructing this diagram by working backwards from the endpoint or goal (BAR); note
that when you get to condition 4 you may want to switch from thinking backwards through the sequence
to thinking forwards.

1. **E** A red ticket will get you a green bicycle and a yellow hat. A green bicycle, a yellow hat, and a
blue card will get you a yellow card and a blue ticket, and you may then enter the bar.

2. **C** Since a blue hat gets a red ticket, and a red ticket gets a green bicycle, and a green bicycle
gets a blue ticket, then a blue hat ultimately gets a blue ticket.

3. **B** To get a yellow card you need *both* a yellow hat and a blue card.

4. **E** If you have a blue ticket and a blue card, then a yellow hat (with the blue card) will get you
a yellow card, and that yellow card (with the blue ticket) will get you into the bar. A red ticket
will also get you that yellow hat, which will start the whole process rolling until you get into
the bar. A blue hat will also get you a red ticket, which will again begin the process that gets
you into the bar. A yellow card will obviously get you in. Only (E), the orange hat, will not get
you the required yellow card.

VENN DIAGRAMS/GROUPING ARROWS

Another type of charting (also mentioned in Chapter 4; Logical Reasoning) is the *Venn diagram/ grouping arrow*. This type of diagram can be useful when information is given that shows relationships between sets or groups of sets. Venn diagrams should be used *only* in *very simple situations* involving a small number of items. Grouping arrows seem to be more effective and simpler to work with, especially in complex situations.

Some very basic Venn diagrams and grouping arrows look like this:

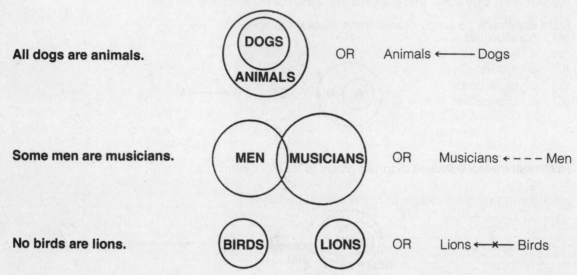

All dogs are animals.   OR   Animals ⟵——— Dogs

Some men are musicians.   OR   Musicians ⟵ – – – Men

No birds are lions.   OR   Lions ⟵—✗— Birds

In diagramming more than two groups, you may find it helpful to draw the most general or largest category before drawing any of the others.

Example

(1) All A's are B's.
(2) All B's are C's.
(3) Some, but not all, D's are A's.
(4) All D's are B's.
(5) No E's are C's.

1. Which of the following must be true?   Ⓐ Ⓑ Ⓒ Ⓓ Ⓔ
  (A) All C's are A's.
  (B) Some E's are B's.
  (C) All A's are D's.
  (D) No B's are E's.
  (E) Some E's are A's.

2. Which of the following must be FALSE?   Ⓐ Ⓑ Ⓒ Ⓓ Ⓔ
  (A) All D's are A's.
  (B) No A's are E's.
  (C) Some A's are D's.
  (D) Some C's are D's.
  (E) No B's are E's.

3. If all E's are F's, then which of the following must be true?   Ⓐ Ⓑ Ⓒ Ⓓ Ⓔ
  (A) All F's are E's.
  (B) Some F's are E's.
  (C) All A's are F's.
  (D) Some B's are F's.
  (E) No F's are C's.

4. If some G's are A's, then   Ⓐ Ⓑ Ⓒ Ⓓ Ⓔ
  - (A)   some G's are D's
  - (B)   all D's are G's
  - (C)   all B's are G's
  - (D)   some E's are G's
  - (E)   some G's are C's

ANSWERS AND EXPLANATIONS

From statement 1 we may draw a Venn diagram as follows:

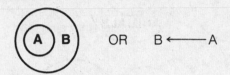

From statement 2 our Venn diagram grows to look like this:

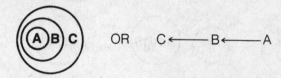

Now statements 3 and 4 add another circle (note that we need the fourth statement in order to "contain" the D circle within the B circle) as follows:

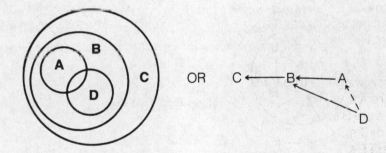

And, finally, from statement 5 we get:

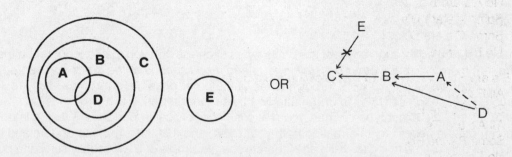

Now it will be relatively simple to answer the questions simply by referring to our final Venn diagram.

1. **D**
2. **A**
3. **B** Note that this problem requires us to add another circle to our Venn diagram, as follows:

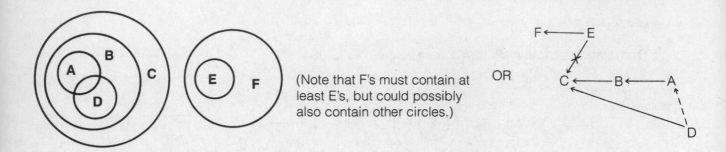

(Note that F's must contain at least E's, but could possibly also contain other circles.)   OR

4. **E** This problem, too, requires us to add to our original Venn diagram. If some G's are A's, our Venn diagram must *at least* contain some G's in the A circle (x notes location of some G's):

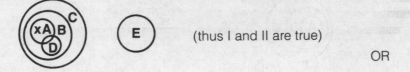

(thus I and II are true)

OR

but it *could* also look like this:

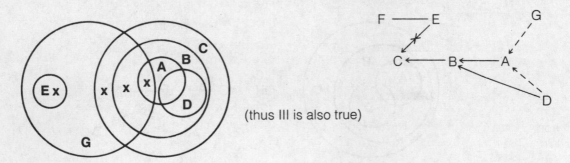

(thus III is also true)

IN CONCLUSION

You have just worked through some of the basic types of charts that you may encounter on the LSAT. Be aware that there are *many other possible charts and modifications of the charts presented*. In the following practice tests, as you work through some of the other possible charts, carefully review the explanations of each to assist you in understanding these other types.

Remember that the exact type of chart you make is not of critical importance. What is important is that you can get the necessary information from your chart, and that it is simple to understand. Do not spend a great deal of time trying to make an elaborate chart; a simple one will usually serve the purpose.

AN ALTERNATIVE GENERAL APPROACH

Some students, regardless of how much they review, analyze, and practice, cannot seem to finish the Analytical Reasoning section. They simply cannot work fast enough or make displays or rough diagrams quickly enough to see relationships and maintain a high level of correct answers. If you find that you consistently have a problem getting to or into the fourth set, you may wish to try this alternative approach: Focus your time on only three of the four sets. That is, try to set up and do well on the three sets and the questions that follow, and simply guess at the questions to the remaining set. You can skip one of the four sets and still receive a good score. The idea is to significantly raise your percentage of correct answers on the questions you <u>are</u> attempting. Remember, this is an alternative approach that you may wish to try if you are having a real problem getting to all four sets and maintaining a good level of correct answers. In using this method, you may wish to decide which set of questions you are going to skip after you have read the conditions and realize that the set is going to be problematic and difficult to complete.

EXTRA PRACTICE, ANALYTICAL REASONING

Questions 1–4

(1) Four books are standing next to each other on a shelf in order from left to right. One of the books is red, one is yellow, one is blue, and one is orange.
(2) The red book is between the yellow and blue books.
(3) The blue book is between the orange and red books.
(4) The orange book is not fourth.

1. If the orange book could be fourth, then which of the following can be deduced?
   (A) The red book is fourth.
   (B) The blue book is not third.
   (C) The red book is next to the orange book.
   (D) The blue book is next to the yellow book.
   (E) The yellow book is not second.

   Ⓐ Ⓑ Ⓒ Ⓓ Ⓔ

2. If a white book is added to the shelf, and the fourth book is not necessarily an orange book, then which of the following is a possible order of the books?
   (A) yellow, red, orange, blue, white
   (B) white, yellow, blue, red, orange
   (C) yellow, red, blue, white, orange
   (D) orange, blue, red, yellow, white
   (E) blue, red, yellow, orange, white

   Ⓐ Ⓑ Ⓒ Ⓓ Ⓔ

3. Which of the following pairs are next to each other on the shelf?
   (A) yellow and blue
   (B) blue and orange
   (C) yellow and orange
   (D) red and orange
   (E) No books are next to each other on the shelf.

   Ⓐ Ⓑ Ⓒ Ⓓ Ⓔ

4. If a green book were placed just to the left of the blue book, what position would it be in (counting from the left)?
   (A) first   (B) second   (C) third   (D) fourth   (E) fifth

   Ⓐ Ⓑ Ⓒ Ⓓ Ⓔ

Questions 5–8

Note: Questions 6, 7, and 8 are multiple-multiple choice questions that have not appeared on the LSAT recently.

Disease J is always communicable; its symptoms are red splotches, which appear the day after infection.

Disease K is only communicable the day after infection; its symptoms are blue lips or red splotches, which appear the day of infection.

Disease L only infects concurrently with Disease J; its symptoms—swollen ears, which appear the day after infection—are negated by Disease K.

These are the only diseases possible.

Peter had lunch with Paul on Tuesday.

Paul had dinner with Mary on Wednesday.

Symptoms appear for only one day.

5. If Peter broke out in red splotches on Tuesday, which of the following must be true?　　　　　　　　　　　　　　　　　Ⓐ Ⓑ Ⓒ Ⓓ Ⓔ
   - (A)　Peter was infected with Disease K.
   - (B)　Peter was infected with Disease J.
   - (C)　Peter was infected with Disease L.
   - (D)　Peter could have given Disease K to Paul on Tuesday.
   - (E)　Peter didn't give Paul Disease K on Tuesday.

6. Which of the following pairs of symptoms are possible?　　Ⓐ Ⓑ Ⓒ Ⓓ Ⓔ
   - I.　blue lips and swollen ears
   - II.　swollen ears and red splotches
   - III.　blue lips and red splotches
   - (A) I only　　(B) II only　　(C) III only　　(D) II and III only　　(E) I and III only

7. If Paul had red splotches on Tuesday, then he could have　Ⓐ Ⓑ Ⓒ Ⓓ Ⓔ
   - I.　given Peter Disease J
   - II.　given Peter Disease K
   - III.　given Mary Disease J
   - IV.　given Mary Disease K
   - (A) I and III only　　(B) I and IV only　　(C) II and III only　　(D) I, III and IV only
   - (E) I, II, and IV only

8. If on Monday Peter was only infected with Disease K, then which of the following could be true on Wednesday only because of Peter's passing Disease K on?　　　　　　　　　　　　　　　　　　　Ⓐ Ⓑ Ⓒ Ⓓ Ⓔ
   - I.　Mary's lips were blue.
   - II.　Mary's ears were swollen.
   - III.　Mary had red splotches.
   - (A) I only　　(B) II only　　(C) III only　　(D) I and II only　　(E) I and III only

Questions 9–17

A head counselor is choosing people to go on a hiking trip. The head counselor must choose from among 3 adult counselors (A, B, C) and 9 campers (boys D, E, F, G, H, and girls J, K, L, M).

At least two adult counselors must go on the hike.

Camper D will not go without friends E and F.

Campers J and L will not hike together.

Camper M will not hike with counselor C.

There can never be more boy campers than girl campers.

9. If camper D is chosen for the hike   Ⓐ Ⓑ Ⓒ Ⓓ Ⓔ
    (A)   camper L must be chosen
    (B)   camper J cannot be chosen
    (C)   camper L cannot be chosen
    (D)   ·camper G cannot be chosen
    (E)   camper H must be chosen

10. If camper K is NOT chosen for the hike   Ⓐ Ⓑ Ⓒ Ⓓ Ⓔ
    (A)   camper G cannot be chosen
    (B)   camper H cannot be chosen
    (C)   camper E cannot be chosen
    (D)   camper D cannot be chosen
    (E)   camper L cannot be chosen

11. If camper D is chosen for the hike, which of the following
CANNOT be true?   Ⓐ Ⓑ Ⓒ Ⓓ Ⓔ
    (A)   Camper H goes on the hike.
    (B)   Camper K goes on the hike.
    (C)   Counselor A goes on the hike.
    (D)   Counselor B goes on the hike.
    (E)   Camper M goes on the hike.

12. An acceptable combination of campers and counselors is   Ⓐ Ⓑ Ⓒ Ⓓ Ⓔ
    (A)   ABCDEFJKM
    (B)   ABDEFJLM
    (C)   ABGHJKM
    (D)   ACDEFJK
    (E)   ACEFGKLM

13. If counselor A is NOT chosen for the hike, then   Ⓐ Ⓑ Ⓒ Ⓓ Ⓔ
    (A)   camper D must be chosen
    (B)   camper D cannot be chosen
    (C)   camper J must be chosen
    (D)   camper L cannot be chosen
    (E)   camper F cannot be chosen

14. If counselor A is NOT chosen for the hike, then which of the following must be true?
    (A)   If camper E is chosen, camper K must be chosen.   Ⓐ Ⓑ Ⓒ Ⓓ Ⓔ
    (B)   If camper F is chosen, camper K must be chosen.
    (C)   Camper J cannot be chosen.
    (D)   Camper D cannot be chosen.
    (E)   If camper L is chosen, camper F must be chosen.

15. If camper D is chosen for the hike, which of the following could represent the other hikers?
    (A)   ACEFJKM   Ⓐ Ⓑ Ⓒ Ⓓ Ⓔ
    (B)   ABGHKML
    (C)   ABEFJKM
    (D)   ABFGJKL
    (E)   ACEFGKLM

16. What is the largest number of hikers that can go on the hike?
    (A) 5   (B) 6   (C) 7   (D) 8   (E) 9   Ⓐ Ⓑ Ⓒ Ⓓ Ⓔ

17. Which of the following must be true?　　　Ⓐ Ⓑ Ⓒ Ⓓ Ⓔ
  (A) Campers K and M never hike together.
  (B) Campers E and G never hike together.
  (C) Campers D and G never hike together.
  (D) Campers J and M never hike together.
  (E) Campers D and M never hike together.

Questions 18–23

Four people, Q, R, S, and T, compete in a round robin tournament, playing one game against each of the other three.

Each player scores only when a player that he defeats beats another player. (For example, A beats B, and B beats C and D. A receives 2 points because B won two games. Note that A does not get a point for beating B.)

  (1) No one won all three of his games.
  (2) No one lost all three of his games.
  (3) Q won the tournament by scoring the most points.
  (4) S came in last by scoring 1 point and winning the smallest number of games.
  (5) T beat Q.
  (6) The most points scored was 3.

18. How many points did Q score?　　　Ⓐ Ⓑ Ⓒ Ⓓ Ⓔ
  (A) 1　(B) 2　(C) 3　(D) 4　(E) 5

19. Who beat T?　　　Ⓐ Ⓑ Ⓒ Ⓓ Ⓔ
  (A) Q and R　(B) R and S　(C) Q and S　(D) R only　(E) S only

20. Who won two games?　　　Ⓐ Ⓑ Ⓒ Ⓓ Ⓔ
  (A) Q and R　(B) R and S　(C) Q and T　(D) Q only　(E) R only

21. How many points did T score?　　　Ⓐ Ⓑ Ⓒ Ⓓ Ⓔ
  (A) 1　(B) 2　(C) 3　(D) 4　(E) 5

22. A tie in total points scored occurred between which players?　　　Ⓐ Ⓑ Ⓒ Ⓓ Ⓔ
  (A) R and S　(B) S and T　(C) R and T　(D) R, S, and T　(E) Q, R, and S

23. If one player had won all three of his games, how many points would he
have scored?　　　Ⓐ Ⓑ Ⓒ Ⓓ Ⓔ
  (A) 3　(B) 4　(C) 5　(D) 6　(E) 7

Questions 24–27
Do, Rey, Mi, Fa, and So are children who are planning to sing at the annual holiday festival.

  Do is Rey's brother.
  Rey is Mi's sister.
  Mi is Fa's brother.
  So is Rey's sister.

24. Which of the following must be true?　　　Ⓐ Ⓑ Ⓒ Ⓓ Ⓔ
  (A) Do is a boy.
  (B) Fa is a girl.
  (C) Rey is a boy.
  (D) Mi is a girl.
  (E) So is a boy.

25. Which of the following could be FALSE?   Ⓐ Ⓑ Ⓒ Ⓓ Ⓔ
  (A) Fa is Rey's brother.
  (B) Do is Mi's brother.
  (C) So is Fa's sister.
  (D) Rey is Fa's sister.
  (E) Mi is Rey's brother.

26. Which of the following could be true?   Ⓐ Ⓑ Ⓒ Ⓓ Ⓔ
  (A) Do is So's sister.
  (B) Mi is not Do's brother.
  (C) Rey is Mi's brother.
  (D) Fa is Rey's brother.
  (E) So is Do's brother.

27. If Fa is a girl, from the information given which of the following must be true? Ⓐ Ⓑ Ⓒ Ⓓ Ⓔ
  (A) There are more brothers than sisters.
  (B) Fa is So's sister.
  (C) Do is older than Fa.
  (D) Mi is younger than So.
  (E) Rey is Fa's brother.

Questions 28–35

Four men, A, B, C, and D, and three women, E, F, and G, are auditioning for a new TV pilot. The director is deciding the order in which they should audition. Since many of the actors have other auditions to attend at different locations, the director must observe the following restrictions:

A must audition first or last.
D and E must audition consecutively, but not necessarily in that order.
Neither F nor G can audition last.
E cannot audition until B has auditioned.

28. Which of the following must be true?   Ⓐ Ⓑ Ⓒ Ⓓ Ⓔ
  (A) F cannot audition first.
  (B) D cannot audition first.
  (C) B cannot audition first or second.
  (D) A must audition before D auditions.
  (E) G must audition second.

29. If A auditions first, which of the following CANNOT be true?   Ⓐ Ⓑ Ⓒ Ⓓ Ⓔ
  (A) G auditions second.
  (B) F auditions before B auditions.
  (C) D auditions second.
  (D) B auditions fifth.
  (E) G auditions before B auditions.

30. If F and G audition first and second respectively, then which of the following must be FALSE? Ⓐ Ⓑ Ⓒ Ⓓ Ⓔ
  (A) C auditions fourth.
  (B) B auditions fourth.
  (C) E auditions sixth.
  (D) D auditions fifth.
  (E) B auditions fifth.

31. Assume that B auditions first, and that F and G audition second and third   Ⓐ Ⓑ Ⓒ Ⓓ Ⓔ
    respectively. Which of the following must be FALSE?
    (A) E auditions sixth.
    (B) C auditions fifth.
    (C) D auditions fourth.
    (D) C auditions sixth.
    (E) E auditions fifth.

32. Suppose that D auditions ahead of E. If A auditions first and B auditions fifth,
    who must audition sixth?   Ⓐ Ⓑ Ⓒ Ⓓ Ⓔ
    (A) D   (B) E   (C) F   (D) G   (E) C

33. Which of the following is a possible order of auditions?   Ⓐ Ⓑ Ⓒ Ⓓ Ⓔ
    (A) A, E, B, D, F, G, C
    (B) A, B, D, E, C, F, G
    (C) C, B, G, F, E, A, D
    (D) B, F, G, D, E, C, A
    (E) F, B, E, G, D, A, C

34. If the director decides NOT to audition two men consecutively, and if C
    auditions first, which of the following must be true?   Ⓐ Ⓑ Ⓒ Ⓓ Ⓔ
    (A) F auditions second.
    (B) G auditions second.
    (C) E auditions fifth.
    (D) D auditions fourth.
    (E) B auditions third.

35. Assume that all the women must audition consecutively. If F auditions third and
    G does NOT audition second, then which of the following must be true?   Ⓐ Ⓑ Ⓒ Ⓓ Ⓔ
    (A) A auditions first.
    (B) B auditions second.
    (C) C auditions seventh.
    (D) G auditions fifth.
    (E) D auditions sixth.

Questions 36–41

Aaron, Clifford, Bryan, Jason, Logan, Prescott, David, and Ellen are weight lifters.

No two lift the same weight.
Ellen lifts more than Aaron.
Bryan lifts less than Logan but more than Prescott.
David lifts more than Logan.
Jason lifts less than Aaron but more than Clifford.
Logan lifts more than Jason.

36. Which of the following statements must be true?   Ⓐ Ⓑ Ⓒ Ⓓ Ⓔ
    (A) David lifts more than Jason.
    (B) Jason lifts more than Prescott.
    (C) Ellen lifts more than Bryan.
    (D) Clifford lifts more than Ellen.
    (E) Bryan lifts more than David.

37. If Prescott lifts more than Aaron, then which of the following must be true? Ⓐ Ⓑ Ⓒ Ⓓ Ⓔ
(A) Logan lifts more than Aaron.
(B) Aaron lifts more than Bryan.
(C) Ellen lifts more than Bryan.
(D) David lifts more than Ellen.
(E) Clifford lifts more than Logan.

38. If Aaron lifts more than David, what is the maximum number that can lift more than Logan?
(A) 0   (B) 1   (C) 2   (D) 3   (E) 4   Ⓐ Ⓑ Ⓒ Ⓓ Ⓔ

39. If 5 people lift less than Logan, then which of the following must be true? Ⓐ Ⓑ Ⓒ Ⓓ Ⓔ
(A) Bryan lifts more than Aaron.
(B) Prescott lifts more than Aaron.
(C) Clifford lifts more than Prescott.
(D) Jason lifts more than David.
(E) David lifts more than Aaron.

40. If Bryan lifts more than Aaron and Jason lifts more than Prescott, then who can lift more than Ellen?
(A) Prescott, Bryan, Logan.   Ⓐ Ⓑ Ⓒ Ⓓ Ⓔ
(B) David, Prescott, Clifford.
(C) Logan, Bryan, Prescott.
(D) David, Logan, Jason.
(E) Logan, David, Bryan.

41. If Prescott lifts more than Jason, then which of the following must be false? Ⓐ Ⓑ Ⓒ Ⓓ Ⓔ
(A) Bryan lifts more than Aaron.
(B) Prescott lifts more than Ellen.
(C) Ellen lifts more than David.
(D) Aaron lifts more than Logan.
(E) Bryan lifts more than David.

Questions 42–47

There are nine cans of soft drinks lined up on a shelf and numbered from 1 to 9, from left to right.

The first and fourth are different brands of cola.
The sixth and eighth are different brands of root beer.
The second, fifth, sixth, seventh, and ninth are the only caffeine-free soft drinks.
The second, third, fifth, seventh, and ninth cans contain unflavored beverages.

42. How many of the cans contain unflavored beverages that contain caffeine? Ⓐ Ⓑ Ⓒ Ⓓ Ⓔ
(A) 0   (B) 1   (C) 2   (D) 3   (E) 4

43. In which of the following places is a beverage that contains caffeine? Ⓐ Ⓑ Ⓒ Ⓓ Ⓔ
(A) second   (B) fourth   (C) fifth   (D) sixth   (E) ninth

44. Which place contains a caffeine-free beverage that is not unflavored? Ⓐ Ⓑ Ⓒ Ⓓ Ⓔ
(A) first   (B) third   (C) fourth   (D) sixth   (E) seventh

45. If the two root beers were replaced with two cans of orange flavored beverage containing caffeine, how many cans would contain either cola or caffeine but not both? Ⓐ Ⓑ Ⓒ Ⓓ Ⓔ
(A) 0   (B) 1   (C) 2   (D) 3   (E) 4

46. If someone randomly chose two cans of caffeine-free beverage, which places could they be?
(A) second and third   (B) fourth and fifth   (C) third and seventh
(D) sixth and ninth   (E) eighth and ninth

Ⓐ Ⓑ Ⓒ Ⓓ Ⓔ

47. How many cans of flavored beverage are next to at least one can of caffeine-free beverage?
(A) 0   (B) 1   (C) 2   (D) 3   (E) 4

Ⓐ Ⓑ Ⓒ Ⓓ Ⓔ

Questions 48–51

The National Domino League is planning to expand by adding one more team. All of the players for the new team will be chosen from the existing teams. Each team must make three players eligible to be chosen for the new team.

(1) The players eligible to be chosen from Team 1 are A, B, and C.
(2) The players eligible to be chosen from Team 2 are D, E, and F.
(3) The players eligible to be chosen from Team 3 are G, H, and K.
(4) The new team must choose two players from each of the three teams.
(5) B refuses to play with D.
(6) If C is chosen, then K must be chosen.
(7) G and H refuse to play together.

48. If A is not chosen, then how many members of the new team are determined?   Ⓐ Ⓑ Ⓒ Ⓓ Ⓔ
(A) 2   (B) 3   (C) 4   (D) 5   (E) 6

49. If D is chosen, then which of the following groups of three players could NOT be chosen?
(A) A, G, K   (D) A, E, G

Ⓐ Ⓑ Ⓒ Ⓓ Ⓔ

(B) B, C, G   (E) E, H, K
(C) C, E, K

50. Which of the following is (are) true?
(A) C must be chosen.

Ⓐ Ⓑ Ⓒ Ⓓ Ⓔ

(B) If A is chosen, then F must be chosen.
(C) If B is chosen, then E must be chosen.
(D) E must be chosen.
(E) If G is chosen, then K is not chosen.

51. In addition to facts (1), (2), (3), and (4), which of the facts lead(s) to the conclusion that K must be chosen?
(A) (5)   (B) (6)   (C) (7)   (D) (6) and (7)   (E) (5), (6), and (7)

Ⓐ Ⓑ Ⓒ Ⓓ Ⓔ

Questions 52–55

Eight people—A, B, C, D, E, F, G, H—are to be seated at a square table, two people on each side.

B must sit directly across from H.
A must sit between and next to F and G.
C cannot sit next to F.

52. Which of the following must be true?
(A) C sits next to either B or H.

Ⓐ Ⓑ Ⓒ Ⓓ Ⓔ

(B) H must sit next to G.
(C) F sits next to D or E.
(D) A sits directly across from B.
(E) F sits directly across from C or D.

53. If B does not sit next to G, then which of the following is NOT possible? ⒶⒷⒸⒹⒺ
   (A)   If C sits next to B, then D could sit directly across from F.
   (B)   If C sits next to D, then E could sit directly across from G.
   (C)   C could sit next to G.
   (D)   If C sits next to H, then B could sit between D and E.
   (E)   If C sits next to B, then A could sit next to H.

54. If C sits directly across from F, who could NOT sit next to H? ⒶⒷⒸⒹⒺ
   (A) C   (B) D   (C) E   (D) G   (E) A

55. How many different people could be seated directly across from A? ⒶⒷⒸⒹⒺ
   (A) 1   (B) 2   (C) 3   (D) 4   (E) 5

Answers and Explanations

Answers 1–4

By following statements 1–3, you could have made these two possible orders:

Y R B O   or   O B R Y

but statement 4 eliminates the first order, Y R B O.

1. **E**   From statements 2 and 3, the red and blue books are between other books; thus, they cannot be first or fourth. Therefore, they are second and third. This leaves first and fourth positions for the orange and yellow books.

2. **D**   Orange, blue, red, yellow, white is a possible order. Notice that each of the other orders could have been eliminated because each broke an initial statement:
   (A)   Orange and blue are switched.
   (B)   Blue and red are switched.
   (C)   White must be on an end since the other four must be next to each other.
   (D)   Blue cannot be on an end.

3. **B**   This follows the order discovered from the initial conditions, YRBO.

4. **B**   Because the blue book was in the second position, it will move to the third position, and the green book will take the second.

Answers 5–8

The following simple chart may be helpful in answering the questions:

Disease	When Communicable	Symptom
J	Always	Red splotches appear DAY AFTER INF.
K	Day after infection	Blue lips OR red splotches appear DAY OF INF.
L	Only with J	Swollen ears appear DAY AFTER INF. NEGATED BY DISEASE K

Tuesday	Wednesday
Peter and Paul	Paul and Mary

5. **E** Either (A) or (B) may be true, but neither necessarily *must* be true. (C) could be true if Disease L is concurrent with Disease J, but it doesn't necessarily have to be true. Choice (D) is false, since Disease K wouldn't be communicable until the day after, Wednesday. Thus (E) *is* true: Peter did not give Paul Disease K, because Disease K isn't communicable until a day later, on Wednesday.

6. **D** I. Blue lips and swollen ears are not possible together: Disease L's symptoms are negated by Disease K. FALSE
   II. Swollen ears and red splotches will both appear the day after infection with Diseases J and L. TRUE
   III. Blue lips and red splotches will appear together if a person is infected with Disease K a day after infection by Disease J. TRUE

7. **D** If Paul had red splotches on Tuesday, then he either was infected with Disease J on Monday or was infected with Disease K on Tuesday. Therefore:
   I. he could have given Peter Disease J because J is always communicable. TRUE
   II. Paul could *not* have given Peter Disease K on Tuesday, because Disease K isn't communicable until the day after (Wednesday). FALSE
   III. Paul could have given Mary Disease J because Disease J is always communicable. TRUE
   IV. Paul could have given Mary Disease K because Disease K is communicable a day after infection (Wednesday). TRUE

8. **E** If Peter was infected with Disease K on Monday, then:
   I. he could have infected Paul with Disease K on Tuesday (one day later); Paul in turn could have infected Mary on Wednesday. Thus, Mary could have blue lips. TRUE
   II. Mary's ears could not have been swollen because simply passing on Disease K would not manifest such a symptom. FALSE
   III. Peter could have given Paul Disease K on Tuesday; Paul in turn could have given it to Mary on Wednesday. Red splotches are also a symptom of Disease K, which Mary could have shown on Wednesday. TRUE

Answers 9–17

Drawing the simple diagram, below, will help answer the questions.

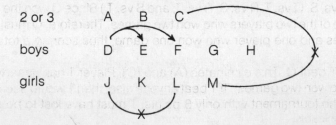

9. **D** If camper D is chosen, then campers E and F are also chosen. Thus three boys have been picked to go on the hike. Note that three girls, at most, can go on the hike. Since boys cannot outnumber girls, no other boys can be chosen.

10. **D** If camper K is not chosen, the maximum number of girls chosen can be two. Therefore, since boys cannot outnumber girls, D cannot be chosen, since selecting D means also selecting two more boys, E and F.

11. **A** If camper D is chosen, then boys E and F are also chosen. Since the maximum number of girls chosen can be three, no other boys may be chosen, since boys may not outnumber girls.

12. **C** Choices (A) and (E) include both C and M, which is not permitted. Choice (B) includes J and L, who will not hike together. In choice (D), boys outnumber girls, which is not permitted. Only choice (C) is an acceptable combination of campers and counselors.

13. **B** If counselor A is not chosen for the hike, then counselors B and C are chosen as there must be at least two counselors on the hike. Since counselor C is chosen, camper M (a girl) cannot be chosen. Therefore, the maximum number of girls on the hike can be two. Since boys cannot outnumber girls, D cannot be chosen, since selecting D would mean also selecting E and F, a total of three boys.

14. **D** If counselor A is not chosen, then counselors B and C will be chosen as there must be at least two counselors on the hike. If counselor C is chosen, camper M cannot be chosen, leaving the maximum number of girls possible on the hike at two. Therefore, since boys may not out-number girls, D cannot be chosen as choosing D would mean also selecting E and F, thus outnumbering the girls.

15. **C** Choices (A) and (E) included both C and M, which is not permitted. Choices (B) and (D) do not include camper E, who must accompany camper D. Only choice (C) includes acceptable companions for a hike with camper D.

16. **D** The largest number of hikers that can go on the hike is eight, as follows: three boys, three girls, and counselors A and B. (Example: A, B, D, E, F, J, K, M)

17. **C** The maximum number of girls possible for the hike is three. Therefore, since choosing camper D means also choosing campers E and F, no other boys (for instance, G) can be chosen, as boys would then outnumber girls.

Answers 18–23

18. **C** Since no player won all three games and no player lost all three games, it is apparent that two players won two games each and two players won one game each. (Six games were played in all: Q vs. R, Q vs. S, Q vs. T, R vs. S, R vs. T, and S vs. T.) Since Q won the tournament, he must have been one of the two players who won two games. Therefore, Q must beat one player who won two games and one player who won one game, thus scoring a total of 3 points.

19. **B** We know that T beat Q. This eliminates (A) and (C). Player T has already earned 2 points by beating Q (who won two games). If T beat anyone else, then T would score more than 2 points. Since Q won the tournament with only 3 points, T must have lost to both R and S.

20. **A** Since Q won two games, the answer must be (A), (C), or (D). We also know that T won only one game. That eliminates (C). We know that R or S must have won two games, since Q won two games, T won one game, and two players won two games each. This eliminates (D). Thus the answer is (A).

21. **B** Since T beat only player Q, and since Q won two games, T must score 2 points.

22. **C** Since Q scored 3 points and won the tournament, and since S lost the tournament by winning only one game, S must have scored 1 point. Thus R and T must have scored 2 points each.

23. **A** Since six games are played, and if one player wins three of them, the other players must have won a total of three games. Thus 3 points is the maximum. The final chart is as follows:

Opponent

		Q	R	S	T		
	Q		W	W	L	=	3 points (R won 2; S won 1)
Player	**R**	L		W	W	=	2 points
	S	L	L		W	=	1 point
	T	W	L	L		=	2 points

KEY
——
W = won; L = lost.

Answers 24–27

Constructing the following chart would be helpful in answering the questions:

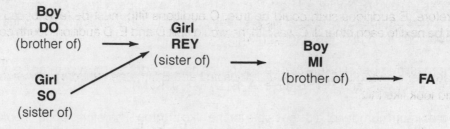

24. **A** Only statement (A) must be true. Because Do is Rey's brother, then Do is a boy. Because Rey is Mi's sister, then Rey is a girl. We do not know if Fa is a boy or a girl.

25. **A** Only statement (A) could be false, because we don't know if Fa is a boy or a girl.

26. **D** We do not know if Fa is a boy or a girl. Thus, (D) could be true. The others are false.

27. **B** We are not given any information about their ages. If Fa is a girl, then we have three sisters and two brothers.

Answers 28–35

From the information given, you could have constructed a diagram similar to this:

```
                                    D–E
                              F̶     B ? E
                              G̶
              A?             A?
          1   2   3   4   5   6   7
```

Notice the information listed off to the side of the diagram.

28. **B** D cannot audition first since D and E have to audition consecutively, and B must audition before E.

29. **C** If A auditions first, then D cannot audition second because B must audition before E, and therefore also before D.

30. **E** If F and G audition first and second respectively, then A must audition last and the diagram for this question would look like this:

```
F G                   A
1 2  3  4  5  6  7
```

Therefore, A must audition last and B cannot audition fifth (no room for D and E to follow B). C could possibly audition fourth.

31. **B** If B auditions first, and F and G audition second and third respectively, then A must audition last and the diagram for this question would look like this:

```
B F G                 A
1 2 3  4  5  6  7
```

Therefore, E auditions sixth could be true. C auditions fifth must be false because D and E must be next to each other. If C was fifth, he would split D and E. D auditions fourth could be true.

32. **A** If D auditions ahead of E, and if A auditions first and B fifth, then the diagram for this question would look like this:

```
A             B D E
1 2  3  4  5  6  7
```

Since B auditions fifth, then D must be sixth and E seventh.

33. **D** This question is most easily answered by eliminating the orders that are not possible. Choice (A) can be eliminated because E is ahead of B and not next to D. Choice (B) can be eliminated because G cannot audition last. Choices (C) and (A) can be eliminated because A is not first or last.

34. **E** From the new information given, men cannot audition consecutively; the diagram for this question would now look like this:

```
C    B    D    A
1 2  3  4  5  6  7
```

Therefore, B must audition third.

35. **E** If F auditions third and all the women must audition consecutively, then G must audition next to F, since E must be next to D. The diagram for this question would now look like this:

```
      F G E D
1 2  3  4  5  6  7
     D̸
     E̸
```

Therefore, D must audition sixth.

Answers 36–41

The following diagram may prove helpful:

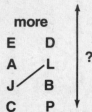

36. **A** Because David lifts more than Logan and Logan lifts more than Jason, David lifts more than Jason. Prescott and Bryan lift less than Logan, but we cannot say anything about their relationship to Jason. It is possible for Prescott to lift more than Ellen.

37. **A** Logan lifts more than Prescott. If Prescott lifts more than Aaron, so must Logan.

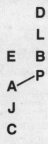

38. **D** If Aaron lifts more than David, then Aaron, Ellen, and David each lift more than Logan.

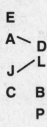

39. **E** If 5 people lift less than Logan, they must be Bryan, Prescott, Clifford, Jason, and Aaron. Thus, David and Ellen lift more than Logan, therefore, David lifts more than Aaron. Answer (C) may be true, but doesn't have to be.

40. **E** Given these additional facts, we can redraw the diagram as follows:

Thus, Logan, David, and Bryan can each lift more than Ellen.

41. **E** From the diagram, all of the following could be true:

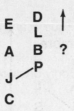

Answers 42–47

This diagram shows these relationships:

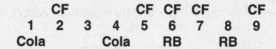

42. **B** Can 3 is the only one.

43. **B** Of the cans listed, only the fourth place (can 4) contains caffeine.

44. **D** The sixth place (can 6) is the can that meets the requirements.

45. **D** For this question, you should use the following diagram:

		CF		CF		CF		CF
1	2	3	4	5	6	7	8	9
Cola			Cola		O		O	

After the replacement, the cans that meet the conditions are 3, 6, and 8.

46. **D** The five caffeine-free cans are 2, 5, 6, 7, and 9. Therefore choice (D), the sixth and ninth places, is the only valid one.

47. **E** All four flavored beverages are next to caffeine-free beverages.

Answers 48–51

From the information given, it would be helpful to construct the following chart to answer the questions:

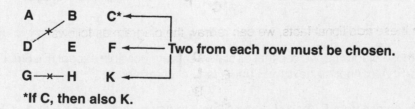

48. **D** If A is not chosen, then B and C are chosen. Since C is chosen, K is chosen too. Since B is chosen, D is not chosen. Thus, E and F are chosen. So, if A is not chosen, B, C, E, F, and K must be chosen.

49. **B** If D is chosen, then B is not chosen. Therefore (B) could NOT be chosen. Also, A and C must be chosen. If C is chosen, then so is K. E or F is chosen. G or H is chosen.

50. **C** If B is chosen, then D is not chosen. Thus, E and F are chosen. Notice that statement 6 is not two-directional.

51. **C** Since G and H do not play together, only one will be chosen. Thus, K must be chosen.

Answers 52–55

From the information given, it would be helpful to construct a diagram to answer the questions.
NOTE: When more than one letter appears at a seat, those letters represent all the possible occupants of that seat.

52. **A** From the diagram, C must sit next to B or H; therefore (A) is true. Taking a second look at the diagram, we can see that H doesn't have to sit next to G, and F doesn't have to sit next to D or E. Therefore, (B) and (C) are not necessarily true. Also, (D) is false since H sits directly across from B. Statement (E) is false since F could sit across from E.

53. **E** If B does not sit next to G, then we should adjust the diagram as follows:

From these diagrams, we see that all statements are possible except (E). Since A sits between G and F, A cannot sit next to H under any circumstances.

54. **E** If C sits across from F, then H could sit next to any of these four (C, D, E, G) depending on the positions of B and H. A cannot sit next to H since A sits between G and F.

55. **C** B and H can't, since they must sit opposite each other. F and G can't, since they must sit next to A. That leaves only C, D, and E.

Chapter

4

Logical Reasoning

INTRODUCTION TO QUESTION TYPE

The LSAT will contain *two* Logical Reasoning sections that will count toward your score. The unscored experimental section could also be Logical Reasoning. Each Logical Reasoning section is 35 minutes in length and contains from 24 to 26 questions. *Since approximately half of your exam consists of Logical Reasoning questions, you should spend additional time reviewing, understanding, and practicing this question type.*

Logical Reasoning questions, which require you to apply your reading and reasoning skills, measure your aptitude for understanding, analyzing, utilizing, and criticizing various short passages and types of arguments. Your ability to reason logically and critically is tested by questions that require you to do the following:

1. Recognize a point.
2. Follow a chain of reasoning.
3. Draw conclusions.
4. Infer missing material.
5. Apply principles from an argument.
6. Identify methods.
7. Evaluate arguments.
8. Differentiate between fact and opinion.
9. Analyze evidence.
10. Assess claims critically.

Logical reasoning questions may take many forms. In analyzing these forms, consider their basic component parts:

1. A *passage, argument,* or *discussion*
   followed by
2. A *question* based upon the preceding text
   followed by
3. The five *answer choices* (A, B, C, D, and E)

The following discussion offers some tips for each of these parts.

1. The Passage, Argument, or Discussion

For the passage, read *actively;* that is, as you read you should mark the important parts with circles, exclamation points, etc., directly on the page of your question booklet. Reading actively helps you stay involved in the passage, it keeps you an active participant in the testing process, and it helps you note and highlight the important points mentioned, should you need to refer to the passage.

As you read you should also note the major issue being discussed, along with the few supporting points, if any.

2. The Question

For the question, it may be helpful to *preread actively;* that is, to read the question first, *before* reading the passage. That way you have an idea of what to look for as you read the passage. This is an effective technique only if the question is short. If the question is as long as (or longer than) the passage, this technique may not be helpful. Use your judgment.

As you read the question, note the key words and *circle* them, in the same manner as you mark the passage. Also note the *reference* of the question. Is it positive or negative? Is it asking what would strengthen the author's argument or what would weaken the author's argument? Is it asking what the author would agree or disagree with? Is it asking what the author believes, or what his critics would believe? Finally, be aware that questions often refer to *unstated* ideas: assumptions (a supposition or a truth taken for granted); implications/inferences (what would logically follow from a previous statement); and conclusions (the necessary consequence or result of the ideas in the passage). Assumptions and implications/inferences are usually not directly mentioned in the passage. Conclusions may or may not be mentioned. You must arrive at all three through logical thinking.

3. The Choices

For the choices, note that you must select the *best* of the five alternatives. Therefore, there may not be a perfect choice. There may also be two good choices. You are to pick the best of the five. Therefore, the elimination strategy (p. 9) is an effective way to approach the answer choices. Eliminate choices that are irrelevant (have nothing to do with the particular topic or issue), off-topic, or not addressed by the passage. Note that often a choice will be incorrect simply because one word in that choice is off-topic. Learn to look for and mark these off-topic key words.

Finally, be very careful, as you read the passage, question, and choices, to watch for words that have very special meanings. The following words, for instance, are frequently used:

except   some   all   none   only   one

few   no   could   must   each

These types of words will often be the key to finding the best answer. Therefore, make sure to underline or circle them in your reading.

DISCUSSION OF QUESTION CATEGORIES

The following sections give detailed examples of the most common types of Logical Reasoning questions, complete with important techniques and strategies. You should not try to memorize the different categories presented here, but rather use them as an aid in identifying strategies needed and in practicing techniques.

AUTHOR'S MAIN POINT OR MAIN IDEA

A very common Logical Reasoning question type will ask you to identify or understand the main point or main idea of the passage. This is also a common question type in the Reading Comprehension section.

As you read the short passage, focus on what the author is trying to say—his major issue. Each paragraph usually contains only one main idea, often stated in the first sentence.

Let's analyze the following passage:

Example 1

As the legal profession becomes more specialized and complex, clerical assistance must become more specialized as well. One legal secretary might be an expert in bankruptcy law, another an expert in criminal justice.

Which of the following is the main point of the passage? Ⓐ Ⓑ Ⓒ Ⓓ Ⓔ
(A) A legal secretary may understand subjects other than law.
(B) A legal secretary should have special training in a particular branch of law.
(C) A legal secretary must be an expert in several types of law.
(D) Attorneys will hire only secretaries without legal experience so they can be trained on the job.
(E) Attorneys will still need legal secretaries with a very general background.

The first sentence of the passage, a general statement about increasing specialization in the legal profession, states the main idea. It is followed by a more specific statement, which gives you additional information.

To help you focus on the main point, you may wish to use the following technique when practicing this question type. As you finish reading each paragraph, try to mentally summarize the paragraph in a few words. For example, after reading the sample above, you might summarize it by saying to yourself, "Legal secretaries should specialize in different types of law."

Next, note whether the paragraph states a particular attitude toward the subject. Typically the author will either approve or disapprove of the main point, or remain neutral. In the sample passage above, the author takes no position pro or con, but delivers the additional information in a matter-of-fact way.

ANSWER AND EXPLANATION

The correct answer is (B). In this case, the main point is that legal secretaries must become more specialized, and the correct answer emphasizes "special training." Notice also that the correct answer here refers as well to the second sentence, which contains additional information about particular branches of law.

(A) is irrelevant. Although particular types of law are mentioned, subjects other than law are not. Note that this statement may certainly be true for some legal secretaries, but receives no support from the paragraph. (C) contradicts information in the passage; the passage discusses legal secretaries who specialize in one type of law, not several. (D) and (E) are not addressed in the passage. The passage does not discuss attorneys' hiring requirements or the need for legal secretaries with a very general background.

Remember, when asked for a main point, be sure to differentiate the main point from secondary or minor points.

Example 2

The belief that positive thinking is the key to success can lead to laziness. It encourages some people to engage in slipshod work, in the hope that an optimistic mental attitude will take the place of hard, careful, dedicated work.

Which of the following is the main idea of this passage?   Ⓐ Ⓑ Ⓒ Ⓓ Ⓔ
(A)   Laziness is always the result of positive thinking.
(B)   Laziness is practiced by successful people.
(C)   Laziness is only permissible after one has completed a hard day's work.
(D)   Laziness may result from a reliance on positive thinking.
(E)   Laziness may result from an assortment of mental attitudes.

ANSWER AND EXPLANATION

The correct choice is (D), which restates the opening statement that "positive thinking . . . can lead to laziness." However, the paragraph does not say that laziness is <u>always</u> the result; therefore (A) is incorrect. (B) is unreasonable and is contradicted by the paragraph. (C) is irrelevant; the paragraph does not discuss <u>when</u> laziness is permissible. (E) brings in an <u>assortment of mental attitudes</u> that are not addressed.

Example 3

Few people understand poetry, and few prefer to read it. Although English professors speak in glowing terms about the greatness of Pope's *Rape of the Lock* and Tennyson's *Ulysses*, it seems that only other professors share their enthusiasm. To appreciate the greatness of difficult poetry, readers must exercise great patience and concentration, and must tolerate the unusual, compressed language of rhythm and rhyme; with so many urgent issues demanding our attention almost every hour of the day, choosing to figure out a poem seems an unlikely possibility.

In the passage above, the writer makes which of the following arguments?   Ⓐ Ⓑ Ⓒ Ⓓ Ⓔ
(A)   English professors pay lip service to great poetry, but, in fact, rarely read it for pleasure.
(B)   Even English professors may not really understand difficult poetry.
(C)   Few laypeople will spend the time necessary to read difficult poetry.
(D)   Simple poetry may continue to be popular, but only English teachers now read difficult poetry.
(E)   To read difficult poetry requires patience, concentration, and tolerance.

ANSWER AND EXPLANATION

The correct answer is (C). The passage does not suggest that the English professors' enthusiasm is insincere (A) nor that they may fail to understand difficult poems (B). It argues that only English professors have the skills, time, and interest in poetry to deal with its difficulties, that laypeople are now unlikely to do so (C). The passage does not allude to simple poetry. (E) is tempting at first, but the argument of the passage is that understanding or appreciating poetry requires these skills, not simply reading it, so (C) is the best of the five choices.

AUTHOR INFORMATION OR AUTHOR'S PURPOSE

Another common Logical Reasoning question refers to a reading passage or paragraph and asks you to understand some things about the author. You may be asked to interpret what the author is trying to accomplish by this statement, or to <u>predict</u> the action and feeling of the author on similar or unrelated subject matter (tell whether the author would agree or disagree with some idea).

To answer this type of question, first look for the values and attitudes of the author. (Ask yourself, "Where is the author coming from?") Second, watch for word connotation: the author's choice of words can be very important. Third, decide the author's purpose and point of view, but don't OVERREAD. Keep within the context of the passage. Sometimes it will be advantageous to skim some of the questions (not the answer choices) before reading the short passage, so that you will know what to expect.

Remember while reading to mark the passage and look for *who, what, when, where, why,* and *how.*
(See the section on "Active Reading" that begins on page 32).

Example 1

Recent studies show that the general public is unaware of most new legislation and doesn't understand 99% of the remaining legislation. This is mainly because of the public's inattention and lack of interest.

The author of this argument would most likely be   Ⓐ Ⓑ Ⓒ Ⓓ Ⓔ
(A)   in favor in new legislation
(B)   against new legislation
(C)   advocating public participation in legislation
(D)   advocating the simplifying of the language of new legislation
(E)   advocating more interesting legislation

ANSWER AND EXPLANATION

The correct answer is (C). The statement does not imply that an increase or decrease in legislation would change the public awareness; therefore (A) and (B) are incorrect. (C) follows in the tenor of the argument because the author's purpose appears to be centered around involvement. He points out that the general public is unaware because of inattention and lack of interest. (D) would be possible, *but* the author is not focusing his criticism on the complex wording of legislation and does not mention it as a reason for unawareness. Remember (1) *whom* the author is talking about—the general public, (2) *what* he mentions—their unawareness of most new legislation, and (3) *why* they are unaware—because of inattention and lack of interest. The author is not advocating more interesting legislation.

Example 2

Writing Teacher: There are advantages and disadvantages to clear, simple writing. Sentences that are easy to understand are processed more quickly and efficiently by readers; those who can express themselves in simple terms are rarely misunderstood. However, prose that is crystal clear often lacks both complexity and imagination. Whether one chooses a style that is simple and clear or complex and unusual often depends upon the tolerance of one's readers.

Ⓐ Ⓑ Ⓒ Ⓓ Ⓔ

The purpose of the writing teacher who makes this statement to a class is probably to
(A)   encourage students to write more simply
(B)   encourage students to imitate in their own pure style the points the teacher is making about pure style
(C)   encourage students to be more imaginative in their writing
(D)   remind students of the importance of the audience to a piece of writing
(E)   urge students to combine simplicity and complexity, clarity and imagination in all their writing

ANSWER AND EXPLANATION

The correct answer is (D). The passage points out the disadvantages and advantages of both simple and complex prose and concludes with the reminder that the readers will determine which is appropriate. The passage does not favor one style over another as in (A) and (C), nor does it say that all writing should be both simple and complex (E). It argues for a style suitable to the audience.

FORM OF ARGUMENTATION

In this type of question, you are asked to decide what type of argument, logic, or reasoning the author is using (example, exaggeration, deduction, induction, etc.).

To answer this type of question, carefully follow the author's line of reasoning while focusing on his or her intent or purpose. Notice how the author starts and finishes the argument. Consider what the author has concluded or proved, or what point has been made or argued. Watch "if" and "how" specific points or examples are used in relation to more general statements.

Example 1

Once again, refer to the argument used earlier concerning legislation.

Recent studies show that the general public is unaware of most new legislation and doesn't understand 99% of the remaining legislation. This is mainly because of the public's inattention and lack of interest.

To make the point, the author of this statement   Ⓐ Ⓑ Ⓒ Ⓓ Ⓔ
(A) gives a general statement followed by supporting facts
(B) argues by pointing out the effects and then the cause
(C) uses specific examples to disprove an argument
(D) infers an outcome and then attempts to support that outcome
(E) assumes the conclusion is true and uses circular reasoning to state the premise

ANSWER AND EXPLANATION

The correct answer is (B). The author starts by making specific points about the general public. It is "unaware of most new legislation and doesn't understand 99% of the remaining legislation." This is followed by a statement of the cause: "This is mainly because of the public's inattention and lack of interest."

Example 2

In the twelfth century, people used the abacus (a simple device made of beads strung on wire) to perform complex calculations. Today we use electronic calculators, and the abacus has become obsolete. In fifty or one hundred years, the calculator will be as quaint and outmoded as the abacus. Every invention of man, every breakthrough of science will, if we wait long enough, be out of date and used no longer.

Which of the following is a questionable technique used in the argument in this passage?
(A) It ignores the fact that the abacus is still in use in Asia.   Ⓐ Ⓑ Ⓒ Ⓓ Ⓔ
(B) It generalizes from a single instance of obsolescence.
(C) It makes a prediction without specifying exactly when the prediction will come true.
(D) It mistakes a minor premise for a major premise and so deduces erroneously.
(E) It considers only scientific advances, but some inventions are not related to science.

ANSWER AND EXPLANATION

The correct answer is (B). The question calls for a questionable technique. The error here is the hasty generalization, based on a single instance of obsolescence. (A), (C), and (E) may be true but they do not point to a technique of argument. (D) is irrelevant and not true of this argument, which is not a syllogism.

STRENGTHENING OR WEAKENING THE AUTHOR'S STATEMENT OR CONCLUSION

This question type is very common on the LSAT. Here you are given a short reading passage or paragraph followed by the question "Which of the following would strengthen the author's statement the most?" or "Which of the following would most weaken the author's statement?" (Both of these questions may be asked. There are many possible varieties of this question type: "least likely to weaken," "strongest criticism of," etc.).

You may find it helpful to preread, or read the question before reading the short paragraph. Focus on the major point of the statement and "how" or "if" it is supported. Be aware of the strength of the statement or argument. Is it a harsh criticism of a certain system? Is it a mildly persuasive paragraph? What point is the author trying to make in supporting this cause?

Remember to always read actively, marking key words or phrases.

Example 1

Psychiatrists and laypeople agree that the best sort of adjustment is founded upon an acceptance of reality, rather than an escape from it.

Which of the following would probably most weaken the author's point? Ⓐ Ⓑ Ⓒ Ⓓ Ⓔ
(A)   Psychiatrists and laypeople do not often agree.
(B)   Reality is difficult to define.
(C)   Escaping reality has worked for many.
(D)   Accepting reality is often traumatic.
(E)   Psychiatrists' definition of reality and laypeople's definition of reality are different.

ANSWER AND EXPLANATION

The correct answer is (C). If escaping reality has worked for many, then it becomes more difficult to defend the acceptance of reality theory. (A) would probably strengthen the point being made. (B) could strengthen or weaken the point. (D) and (E) are irrelevant.

Example 2

The likelihood of America's exhausting her natural resources is growing less. All kinds of waste are being reworked and new uses are constantly being found for almost everything. We are getting more use out of our goods and are making many new by-products out of what was formerly thrown away. It is, therefore, unnecessary to continue to ban logging in national parks, nature reserves, or areas inhabited by endangered species of animals.

Ⓐ Ⓑ Ⓒ Ⓓ Ⓔ
Which of the following most seriously undermines the conclusion of this argument?
(A)   The increasing amount of recycled material made available each year is equal to one-tenth of the increasing amount of natural material consumed annually.
(B)   Recent studies have shown that the number of endangered animals throughout the world fluctuates sharply and is chiefly determined by changes in weather conditions.
(C)   The logging industry contributes huge sums of money to the political campaigns in states where it has a financial interest.
(D)   The techniques that make recycling possible are constantly improved so that more is reclaimed for lower costs each year.
(E)   Political contributions by the recycling industry are now greater than those of the logging or animal protection interests.

ANSWER AND EXPLANATION

The correct answer is (A). First, remember to circle the words underlined undermines and conclusion to help you focus on what you're looking for. Now let's look at the choices. (D) would support rather than undermine the conclusion. (B), (C), and (E) neither support nor weaken the argument, though with more information (C) and (E) might be relevant. If the recycled materials are equal to only one-tenth of the natural materials lost each year, the argument is seriously injured.

Example 3

Some scientists have proposed that, over two hundred million years ago, one giant land mass—rather than various continents and islands—covered one-third of the earth. Long before there was any human life, and over vast periods of time, islands and continents drifted apart. Australia was the first to separate, while South America and Africa were late in splitting apart. Some islands, of course, were formed by volcanoes and were never part of the great land mass.

All the following would support the author's claim EXCEPT ⒶⒷⒸⒹⒺ
(A) Many of the plants of the South American rain forests are markedly similar to those of the African rain forest.
(B) Australia has more animals that are not found on any other continent than have several of the much larger continents.
(C) Volcanic islands like Hawaii have ecosystems very different from those of continental lands with the same average temperature.
(D) The plants of similar conditions in South America have less in common with those of Australia than with those of Asia, Africa, or Europe.
(E) The primitive languages of Australia are unlike those of Africa, which resemble those of South Africa.

ANSWER AND EXPLANATION

The correct answer is (E). If Australia was the first continent to separate, it would follow that its flora and fauna would develop in isolation over a longer period of time. Similarly, we may expect the plants and animals of South America and Africa that separated later to be more alike. (A), (B), and (D) support these ideas. That the separately developed islands are different is also in accord with the passage. However, the languages of all the continents would have developed in isolation, since man did not evolve until after the break-up of the land mass and it is surprising that African and South American languages are similar. Human likeness or difference are irrelevant to the claims of the passage.

Example 4

In America, a baseball game should be described as a series of solo performances: at any given moment, attention is focused on one player and one play. On the other hand, soccer involves all of the team most of the time: each player interacts with others constantly, so that no single individual seems responsible for success or failure. It is because spectators prefer concentrating on individual personalities that baseball remains a much more popular spectator sport than soccer.

Which of the following, if true, can best be used to undermine the conclusion of this argument?
(A) Soccer is more popular with spectators in France than baseball. ⒶⒷⒸⒹⒺ
(B) Among the ten most televised sports in America, by far the most watched is football, and the least watched are tennis and bowling.
(C) Many people watch only the baseball teams of the city in which they live and for whom they root.
(D) Compared to football and basketball, baseball games are much cheaper to attend.
(E) In some sections of the United States, soccer leagues for children under fifteen are more popular than Little League baseball.

ANSWER AND EXPLANATION

The correct answer is (B). The weakness of this argument is not its claim that baseball is more popular than soccer with spectators in America. This is true from the passage. The weakness is its claim that the reason for baseball's greater popularity is that it is an individual performance rather than a team sport. (B) cites a team sport that is more watched than baseball and two solo performance sports that are not very popular. (A) makes a good point, but the passage is concerned with spectators "in America." Even if (C) is true, it may be that these people watch the teams to see individual performances. (D) is true, but not as powerful a criticism as (B). (E) does not necessarily deal with spectators; popularity could refer to the number of participants.

AUTHOR ASSUMPTIONS, PRESUPPOSITIONS, UNDERLYING PRINCIPLES

This is another very common question type in the Logical Reasoning section. Here you are again given a short reading passage or paragraph followed by questions asking about the author's possible assumptions, presuppositions, or underlying principles.

To answer this question type, you may wish to first read the question actively. Make a careful note of what part of the paragraph the question refers to. Is the question asking about the conclusion of the passage? (Which of the following assumptions must be made for the author to reasonably arrive at the stated conclusion?) Or about the opening statement? Or about the complete paragraph? (The complete paragraph may be only one or two sentences.)

Keep in mind that assumptions and presuppositions are things taken for granted, or supposed as facts. In the same sense, an underlying principle is the basis for the original statement. It is necessary for the conclusion to be logical. There may be a number of assumptions possible, but in most cases you are looking for the major assumption, not a minor one. In some cases the major assumption will be evident; you will know what the author is assuming before you even get to the answer choices. In other cases, the assumptions are more subtle, and the answer choices will be helpful by stating them for you.

Example 1

Use the statement in Example 1 on page 111:

Psychiatrists and laypeople agree that the best sort of adjustment is founded upon acceptance of reality, rather than an escape from it.

The author of this statement assumes that   (A) (B) (C) (D) (E)
- (A) there is only one sort of adjustment
- (B) escaping reality is possible
- (C) psychiatrists and laypeople disagree on most things
- (D) psychiatrists never escape reality
- (E) laypeople need many sorts of adjustments

ANSWER AND EXPLANATION

The correct answer is (B). In stating "rather than an escape from it [reality]," the author is assuming that escaping reality is possible.

Example 2

It has been said that a weed is a flower whose virtue has not yet been discovered. As if to prove this point, a homeowner who was tired of constantly maintaining a pretty lawn and shrubbery decided to let weeds run wild in his yard. The result, so far, has been an array of lively shapes and colors. If everyone in the neighborhood would follow this leader, we could save time, effort, money, and water, and soon have one of the most unusual neighborhoods in the city.

Which of the following is a basic assumption on which this argument depends? Ⓐ Ⓑ Ⓒ Ⓓ Ⓔ
(A)   The neighborhood values convenience more than maintaining an attractive environment.
(B)   All the other yards will look like the first homeowner's if the weeds are allowed to run wild.
(C)   Allowing the weeds to take over will save money spent on maintaining a lawn.
(D)   Other neighborhoods in the city will not follow the example of this neighborhood.
(E)   The loss of jobs or revenue to gardeners and garden supply businesses is not so important as the time and money that will be saved.

ANSWER AND EXPLANATION

The correct answer is (A). Although all five of the propositions here may well be true, it is (A) that is the basic assumption of the argument. No one who highly values an attractive lawn and yard will want to let weeds take over, so for the argument to have any validity, its speaker must assume that an audience willing to allow the gain in convenience outweighs the loss in appearance of the neighborhood.

Example 3

Four of the candidates for reelection in this state had been named among those who had more than 100 overdrafts on the House Bank. Two were Democrats, one was a Republican and one an Independent. One other Republican incumbent candidate had bounced over 50 checks. All of the Democrats favored increased federal spending on education and increased government regulation of firearms, while the Republicans opposed these measures. Of the five incumbents, only the Independent candidate was reelected.

Which of the following is the most likely principle upon which the majority of voters cast their votes in the elections?   Ⓐ Ⓑ Ⓒ Ⓓ Ⓔ
(A)   The voters opposed any candidate who had more than 49 overdrafts on the House Bank.
(B)   The voters opposed any candidates who favored increased federal spending.
(C)   The voters opposed reelection of any members of the two major parties who bounced 50 or more checks.
(D)   The voters opposed any candidate who favored increased firearms control.
(E)   The voters opposed any candidate who opposed firearms legislation.

ANSWER AND EXPLANATION

The correct answer is (C). Since the Independent also bounced more than 100 checks, that cannot be the reason for the defeat of the other four candidates. Since we do not know how the Independent candidate stands on spending for education or on firearms regulation, the only factor to explain his victory is his not belonging to one of the two major parties.

Example 4

Time and again studies have shown that 85% of the young adults sent to special juvenile prison farms lead productive lives when they are released. On the other hand, 85% of young adults of the same age who are sent to prisons for adults later return to prisons. The bad influence of the older inmates is permanent. We must expand the number of special juvenile prison farms so that all young adults convicted of crimes can be sent to a penal institution that will not maim them for life.

Which of the following principles most helps to justify this argument?　　ⒶⒷⒸⒹⒺ
(A)　It is more expensive to house adult prisoners in prisons than to house young adults on prison farms.
(B)　Young adults exposed to bad role models will imitate these models.
(C)　Some young adults who are sent to prison farms later become criminals who are sent to prisons for adults.
(D)　Some of the young adults who are sent to prisons for adults become productive members of society and never return to prison.
(E)　Young adults who have been sent to prison farms on two occasions are more likely to return to prison than young adults who have been sent to prison farms only once.

ANSWER AND EXPLANATION

The correct answer is (B). This principle is the basis of the argument to prevent young adults from being exposed to adult felons. If the hope of penologists is to reintegrate young adults into society, these young adults must be kept away from bad models they are likely to imitate. (C) and (D) may be true, but they do not justify the argument. (A) is a practical matter, not a principle to justify the case. (E) would not justify the argument, and might, in fact, be used against it.

Example 5

Drunken drivers in our state kill or maim people every day. I understand that only one out of 500 drunken drivers on the highway is flagged down by the police. Also, 50% of these arrests are made on four holiday weekends when the policing of highways is greatly increased. With these odds, I can afford to drink heavily and drive, so long as I am careful not to do so on holiday weekends.

Which of the following is a necessary premise for the speaker's conclusion in the paragraph above?
(A)　The odds against being arrested from drunken driving are greater on weekends than on weekdays.
　　　　　　　　　　　　　　　　　　　　　　　　ⒶⒷⒸⒹⒺ
(B)　Fear of arrest is a good reason not to drink and drive.
(C)　All that drunken drivers need to fear is being arrested.
(D)　The chances of being arrested for drunken driving are greatest on four holiday weekends.
(E)　The penalties for drunken driving are often incommensurate with the dangers to the public.

ANSWER AND EXPLANATION

The correct answer is (C). The speaker of this passage notes that drunk driving can kill and maim, but his concern is solely with the chances of his being arrested. His conclusion is based on the assumption that no other consequence of drunk driving need trouble him. (A), (B), (D), and (E) are not untrue, but they are not the underlying principle in the speaker's conclusion.

INFERENCES AND IMPLICATIONS

In this very common question type you are asked to "read between the lines." Inferences and implications are not expressed in words in the passage, but may be fairly understood from the passage. If you draw or infer something from a passage, it is called an <u>inference</u>. From the author's point of view, if he or she imparts or implies something, it is called an <u>implication</u>. For the purposes of your exam, you should not be concerned with the differences in the terms, but in understanding what unstated information is in the passage. As you read the passage, focus on the main idea, what the author is suggesting but not actually saying, and what information you can be drawing.

As you approach the choices in inference and implication questions, look for the most direct answer that is not explicitly stated. That is the one that most directly ties back into the passage. Remember that your inference is NOT directly stated in the passage, but is implied by the passage.

Example 1

Since 1890, the federal government and the individual states have passed a number of laws against corrupt political practices. But today many feel that political corruption is a regular occurrence, and deeply distrust their public leaders.

Each of the following can be reasonably inferred from the passage EXCEPT   Ⓐ Ⓑ Ⓒ Ⓓ Ⓔ
(A)   Corrupt political practices have been going on for many years.
(B)   The laws against corrupt political practices have not been effective.
(C)   The federal government and the individual states are against corrupt political practices.
(D)   Many public leaders may be distrusted even though they are not corrupt.
(E)   Leaders in private industry are also involved in corrupt political practices.

ANSWER AND EXPLANATION

The correct answer is (E). Since the passage does not address leaders in private industry, you could not reasonably make an inference regarding their practices. Though (A), (B), (C), and (D) are not stated, all of them are reasonable inferences from the passage.

Example 2

The ability to recognize grammar and usage errors in the writing of others is not the same as the ability to see such errors in one's own writing.

The author of this statement implies that   Ⓐ Ⓑ Ⓒ Ⓓ Ⓔ
(A)   a writer may not be aware of his own errors
(B)   grammar and usage errors are difficult to correct
(C)   grammar and usage errors are very common
(D)   one often has many abilities
(E)   recognizing grammar and usage errors and writing correctly use two different abilities

ANSWER AND EXPLANATION

The correct answer is (A). The author's statement points out that recognizing errors in others' work involves a different ability than recognizing errors in one's own work. Since these abilities are different, writers may not possess both abilities and therefore may not be aware of their own errors. (B) is irrelevant because its focus is "difficulty to correct," which is not addressed. (C) and (D) are incorrect because they are too general, addressing items that are not specific to the statement. (E), which is a common mistake, simply restates information in the statement.

Example 3

A poll of journalists who were involved in the Senate campaign revealed that 80% believed Senator Smith's campaign was damaged by press reports about his record during his last six years in office. His opponent, the recently narrowly elected Senator Jones, believes he was benefited by press coverage of his campaign. Journalists believe the election was covered without bias, and the Senator was defeated because of his record, not, as he insists, because of unfair press coverage. Ninety percent of the voters who supported Senator Smith believe the press was unfair in this election, while 85% of the voters who supported Senator Jones thought the coverage free of any bias.

Which of the following can be inferred from this passage? Ⓐ Ⓑ Ⓒ Ⓓ Ⓔ
(A) The press coverage of the Senate election was free from bias.
(B) Senator Smith lost the election because the press reported his record accurately.
(C) The public's view of the objectivity of the press is likely to be influenced by the election results.
(D) The election was close because of different perceptions of the bias of the press.
(E) Journalists are probably the best judges of bias in political campaign reportage.

ANSWER AND EXPLANATION

The correct answer is (C). We cannot be sure whether or not the reporting of the press was biased since the election was close and the pros and cons are nearly equal. The press cannot be counted on to be objective, so (A), (B), and (E) are not reasonable inferences. The large percentage of each candidate's supporters, whose views of the press coincide with the success or defeat of their candidates, strongly support the inference of (C). Whether or not (D) is true, we cannot tell.

DEDUCTIONS

You may be asked to deduce information from a passage. Deductions are arrived at or attained from general premises—drawing information to a specific piece of information—from general laws to specific cases. In a deduction, if the general premises are true, then the deduction is necessarily true.

To answer this question type you may wish to first actively read the question. Focus on the general premises to see where they lead. As you continue reading, try to follow the logic as it narrows the possibilities of what must be true.

Example 1

Years ago, a nationwide poll concluded that there are more televisions than there are bathtubs in American homes. No doubt that fact remains today, especially in light of the growing popularity of home computers. Now, in addition to owning televisions for entertainment, more and more families are purchasing TV monitors for use with a personal computer. We can safely guess that there are still many more people staring at a picture tube than singing in the shower.

Which of the following statements can be deduced from this passage? Ⓐ Ⓑ Ⓒ Ⓓ Ⓔ
(A) Personal computers probably cost less than installing a shower or a bathtub.
(B) People can wash themselves without a tub or shower, but they cannot watch television unless they own a television set.
(C) TV monitors will work with personal computers in place of regular computer monitors.
(D) As many computers are sold today as television sets a few years ago.
(E) More television monitors are now used with personal computers than are used to watch commercial television broadcasts.

ANSWER AND EXPLANATION

The correct answer is (C). Though (A) and (B) may well be true, they are not deductions that we can make from the information in the passage. But (C) can be deduced since, "more and more families are purchasing TV monitors for use with a personal computer," TV monitors must work with these computers. Otherwise, people would not buy them for that purpose. (D) and (E) may or may not be true, but they are not deductions from the passage, simply additional information.

Example 2

Antifreeze lowers the melting point of any liquid to which it is added so that the liquid will not freeze in cold weather. It is commonly used to maintain the cooling system in automobile radiators. Of course, the weather may become so cold that even antifreeze is not effective, but such a severe climatic condition rarely occurs in well-traveled places.

Which of the following can be deduced from the passage? Ⓐ Ⓑ Ⓒ Ⓓ Ⓔ
(A)   Well-traveled places have means of transportation other than automobiles.
(B)   Antifreeze does not lower the melting point of certain liquids in extreme conditions.
(C)   Severe climatic conditions rarely occur.
(D)   It is not often that many travelers who use antifreeze have their cooling systems freeze.
(E)   Antifreeze raises the melting point of some liquids.

ANSWER AND EXPLANATION

The correct answer is (D). Since severe climatic conditions rarely occur in well-traveled places, it is necessarily true that "It is not often that many travelers who use antifreeze have their cooling systems freeze." (A) mentions other means of transportation, which is not addressed in the passage. (B) refers to "certain" liquids, which again are not addressed. You cannot deduce that "severe climatic conditions rarely occur" (C), because the passage alludes to only well-traveled places. (E) discusses raising the melting point, which is irrelevant to the passage.

Example 3

Sociologists have noted that children today are less "childish" than ever; when they are still very young, perhaps only six or seven years old, children are already mimicking adult fashions and leading relatively independent lives. Dressed in designer jeans, an elementary school child is likely to spend much of every day fending for herself, taking charge of her own life while waiting for her working parents to arrive home. Children become less dependent on adults for their day-to-day decisions.

From the passage above, since children are less dependent on adults for their day-to-day decisions, it must be true that Ⓐ Ⓑ Ⓒ Ⓓ Ⓔ
(A)   children need more supervision
(B)   children are growing up faster
(C)   children should be completely independent
(D)   parents should not leave children home alone
(E)   parents need to spend more "quality time" with their children

ANSWER AND EXPLANATION

The correct answer is (B). Since children today are "less childish than ever," and since they are "less dependent on adults for their day-to-day decisions," they must be "growing up" faster. Although (A), (D), and (E) are probably true, they are not necessarily true and therefore cannot be deduced from the passage.

PARALLEL REASONING OR SIMILARITY OF LOGIC

In this type you will be given a statement or statements and asked to select the statements that most nearly parallel the originals or use similar logic. First, you should decide whether the original statement is valid. (But don't take too much time on this first step because some of the others may tip you off to the correct choice.) If the statement is valid, your choice must be a valid statement. If the statement is invalid, your choice must be an invalid one. Your choice must preserve the same relationship or comparison.

Second, the direction of connections is important—general to specific (deduction), specific to general (induction), quality to thing, thing to quality, and so on.

Third, the tone of the argument should be the same. If the original has a negative slant, has a positive slant, or changes from negative to positive, then so must your choice.

Fourth, the order of each element is important. Remember: Corresponding elements must be in the same order as the original.

It may be helpful to substitute letters for complex terms or phrases, to simplify confusing situations and help you avoid getting lost in the wording. Direction and order are usually more easily followed by letter substitution.

Remember: Don't correct or alter the original; just reproduce the reasoning.

Example 1

Alex said, "All lemons I have tasted are sour; therefore all lemons are sour."

Which of the following most closely parallels the logic of the above statement? Ⓐ Ⓑ Ⓒ Ⓓ Ⓔ
(A) I have eaten pickles four times and I got sick each time; therefore, if I eat another pickle, I will get sick.
(B) My income has increased each year for the past four years; therefore, it will increase again next year.
(C) I sped to work every day last week and I did not get a ticket; therefore they do not give tickets for speeding around here any more.
(D) All flormids are green. This moncle is red; therefore it is not a flormid.
(E) Every teacher I had in school was mean; therefore, all teachers are mean.

ANSWER AND EXPLANATION

The correct answer is (E). First, the logic of the original is faulty; therefore, the correct choice must also be faulty, eliminating (D). Next, notice the direction of connections: generalization form a *few* experiences → generalization about *all* similar experiences. (A) and (B) each project the result of a few past experiences to only ONE similar experience. (C) starts from a few experiences, but finishes with a result that implies a change in a specific area. You could assume that "they" used to give tickets here.

Example 2

Some serious novelists prefer scientific studies to literary studies. All science fiction writers are more interested in science than in literature. Therefore, some serious novelists are science fiction writers.

Ⓐ Ⓑ Ⓒ Ⓓ Ⓔ

Which of the following is most closely parallel to the flawed reasoning in the argument above?
(A) All trees have leaves. Some cactuses have leaves. Therefore all trees are cactuses.
(B) All orchestras include violins and all chamber groups include violins. Therefore, some chamber groups are orchestras.
(C) Some animals sleep through the winter and some animals sleep through the summer. Therefore, all animals sleep through either the summer or the winter.
(D) All hotels have restaurants. Some shopping malls have restaurants. Therefore some shopping malls are hotels.
(E) Some sweaters in this store are made of cotton. All shirts in this store are made of cotton. Therefore all the wearing apparel in this store is made of cotton.

ANSWER AND EXPLANATION

The correct answer is (D). The stem asserts that all science fiction writers prefer science to literature and so do some serious novelists. It then concludes that some serious novelists must be science fiction writers. The "some serious novelists" who prefer science do not have to be science fiction writers, though they share a preference with them. The stem would have to say <u>only</u> science fiction writers prefer science to make this conclusion certain. The two terms used in the stem are "all" and "some," so we can exclude (B) and (C), which use "all" and "all" and "some" and "some." (D), though it gives the "some" term first and the "all" term second, is parallel to the passage.

Example 3 (with a slight twist)

Why do you want to stop smoking?　Ⓐ Ⓑ Ⓒ Ⓓ Ⓔ

Which of the following most closely parallels the reasoning of this question?
(A)　Why do you want to go to Italy?
(B)　When will you decide on the offer?
(C)　Will you ever play cards again?
(D)　When do you want to learn to play tennis?
(E)　Which desk do you like better?

ANSWER AND EXPLANATION

The correct answer is (C). This response is the only one that implies that the *action has already taken place*, as in the original question. To stop smoking, one must have been smoking *before*. To stop playing cards, one must have been playing cards *before*. (A) appears to be the closest, but this is only true regarding sentence structure, not reasoning. (B) and (D) are asking about future plans without implying anything about past actions. (D) does imply past lack of action. (E) merely asks for a comparison.

ARGUMENT EXCHANGE

In this question type, two or more speakers are exchanging arguments or merely discussing a situation. You will then be asked to choose the statement that most strengthens or weakens either argument. Or you may be asked to find the inconsistency or flaw in an argument, or to identify the form of argument. In some instances you will be asked to interpret what one speaker might have thought the other meant by his response.

To answer these questions, you should first evaluate the strength and completeness of the statements. Are they general or specific? Do they use absolutes? Are they consistent?

Second, evaluate the relationship between responses. What kind of response did the first statement elicit from the second speaker?

Third, evaluate the intentions of the author in making his remarks. What was his purpose?

Example 1

Tom: It is impossible to hit off the Yankee pitcher Turley.
Jim: You're just saying that because he struck you out three times yesterday.

Which of the following would strengthen Tom's argument most?　Ⓐ Ⓑ Ⓒ Ⓓ Ⓔ
(A)　Tom is a good hitter.
(B)　Turley pitched a no-hitter yesterday.
(C)　Tom has not struck out three times in a game all season.
(D)　Tom has not struck out all season.
(E)　Turley has not given up a hit to Jim or Tom all season.

ANSWER AND EXPLANATION

The correct answer is (B). Tom's is a general statement about Turley's relationship to all hitters. All choices except (B) mention only Tom or Jim, not hitters in general.

Example 2

Sid: The recent popularity of hot-air ballooning and bungee-jumping are instances of the latest quest for new types of adventure in the modern world.

Phil: That's ridiculous! Certainly these brightly colored floating globes of air are not modern inventions; rather, they recall the spectacle of county fairs and carnivals from the turn of the century.

Sid: Well, bungee-jumping wasn't around at the turn of the century.

Phil's best counter to Sid's last statement would be   Ⓐ Ⓑ Ⓒ Ⓓ Ⓔ

(A) But bungee-jumping is used in fairs and carnivals.

(B) No, bungee-jumping is merely a newer version of a Polynesian ritual hundreds of years old.

(C) You do know that bungee-jumping is more dangerous than hot-air ballooning.

(D) Yes, but hot-air ballooning is more popular than bungee-jumping.

(E) No, but lots of other inventions are adventurous.

ANSWER AND EXPLANATION

The correct answer is (B). Sid's point is that these modern adventures are with modern inventions. His last statement is trying to say that bungee-jumping is modern. Phil's best counter would be to point out that bungee-jumping is not new.

Example 3

Al: To be a good parent, one must be patient.

Bill: That's not so. It takes much more than patience to be a good parent.

Bill has understood Al's statement to mean that   Ⓐ Ⓑ Ⓒ Ⓓ Ⓔ

(A) if a person is a good parent, he or she will be patient

(B) if a person is patient, he or she will make a good parent

(C) some patient people make good parents

(D) some good parents are patient

(E) a person cannot be a good parent unless he or she is patient

ANSWER AND EXPLANATION

The correct answer is (B). This is a problem in grasping an understanding of necessary and sufficient conditions. Al states that if one is a good parent then one is patient. Patience is necessary to be a good parent. However, Bill's response shows that he (Bill) has inferred that Al considers patience to be sufficient to be a good parent, not just a necessary condition. (B) reflects Bill's mistaken inference. (A) is incorrect because it accurately describes Al's statement. (C) and (D) are incorrect because Al's statement concerns "any" or "all" persons and not "some." (E) is incorrect because it is equivalent to (A) and thus accurately describes Al's statement.

SYLLOGISTIC REASONING

Syllogistic reasoning is a slightly more formal type of reasoning. It deals with an argument that has two premises and a conclusion. This type of question gives you short propositions (premises) and asks you to draw conclusions, valid or invalid. You may be expected to evaluate assumptions—information that is or is not assumed.

First, if possible, simplify the propositions to assist your understanding.

Second, draw diagrams (Venn diagrams; see p.86 in Chapter 3) if possible.

Third, replace phrases or words with letters to help yourself follow the logic.

Example 1

All couples who have children are happy.
All couples either have children or are happy.

Assuming the above to be true, which of the following CANNOT be true?　　ⓐ ⓑ ⓒ ⓓ ⓔ
(A)　All couples are happy.
(B)　Some couples who are happy have children.
(C)　Some couples who have children are not happy.
(D)　Some couples have happy children.
(E)　Children of happy couples are happy.

ANSWER AND EXPLANATION

The correct answer is (C). If all couples who have children are happy, and if all couples who don't have children are happy, then all couples are happy. Simplifying the two statements to "all couples are happy" makes this question much more direct and easier to handle. Thus (C) is false, since it contradicts the first statement; we have no information about children.

Example 2

All A's are B's.
Some C's are A's.

Which of the following is warranted based upon the above?　　ⓐ ⓑ ⓒ ⓓ ⓔ
(A)　All B's are A's.
(B)　Some C's are B's.
(C)　All B's are C's
(D)　No B's are A's.
(E)　All C's are B's.

ANSWER AND EXPLANATION

The correct choice is (B). Here is a diagram of the original information:

With this diagram, the following is evident:　　ⓐ ⓑ ⓒ ⓓ ⓔ
(A)　"All B's are A's" is false.
(B)　"Some C's are B's" is true.
(C)　"All B's are C's" is false.
(D)　"No B's are A's" is false. If all A's are B's, then some B's must be A's.
(E)　"All C's are B's" is false.

Example 3

In this question, the second premise shows up in the actual question.

If the Dodgers do not finally win a championship for their fans this season, the team's manager will definitely not return to guide the club next year.

It follows logically from the statement above that, if the Dodgers win a championship this season, then next year the team's manager   Ⓐ Ⓑ Ⓒ Ⓓ Ⓔ
(A) will definitely not return
(B) will probably not return
(C) will probably return
(D) will definitely return
(E) may or may not return

ANSWER AND EXPLANATION

The correct answer is (E). The passage states, "if the Dodgers do not win the championship [condition A], then the manager will not return [condition B]. Thus we have if A then B. The question then asks, what follows if they *do* win the championship [a negation of condition A]? If A implies B, the negation of A [if the Dodgers do win the championship] does *not* imply the negation of B [the manager will return]. Hence, condition A or not A (win or lose) may be the case; the manager may or may not return. (C) is possible, but he may also not return. All we know for sure is that if he loses, he positively won't return.

CHAIN REASONING OR CONCLUSION VALIDITY

Here you will be given a list of conditionals, statements, or a short paragraph, and asked to follow the logic to reach a valid conclusion.

In this type, you will first want to underline key terms to eliminate looking at excess wording.

Second, mark the direction of each statement. Where does it start and end? What connection is it making?

Third, look for the "kicker" statement. That's the one that starts the chain reaction; it gives you the information to work with other statements.

If there is no "kicker" statement, carefully check how the information given in one statement is relative to the information given in the next statement. This relationship may be enough to help you understand the reasoning.

In checking the validity of a conclusion, you should be looking for a key statement that leads you as directly as possible to that conclusion. Sometimes, if the choices don't start with the word "therefore," you may wish to insert the word "therefore" before the answer choices to help you see which one follows logically.

Example 1

Senator Jones will vote for the Pork bill if he is reelected. If the Pork bill passes, then Senator Jones was not reelected. Senator Jones was reelected.

Which of the following can be concluded from these statements?   Ⓐ Ⓑ Ⓒ Ⓓ Ⓔ
(A) Senator Jones assisted in the passage of the Pork bill.
(B) The passage of the Pork bill carried Senator Jones to victory.
(C) Senator Jones voted against the Pork bill, but it passed anyway.
(D) The Pork bill didn't pass, even though Senator Jones voted for it.
(E) The Pork bill was defeated by a large majority.

ANSWER AND EXPLANATION

The correct answer is (D). Notice that the "kicker" statement that started the chain reaction is "Senator Jones was reelected." From this, we know that he voted for the Pork bill. But the Pork bill could not have passed; otherwise he could not have been reelected.

Example 2

Meteorology may qualify as a science, but there is a great deal of guesswork involved as well. Even with increased knowledge about wind currents and weather patterns, and the most sophisticated equipment, forecasters' predictions are often wrong. Even the movement of a phenomenon as prominent as a hurricane cannot be determined very far in advance.

Which of the following is the best conclusion to the passage? Ⓐ Ⓑ Ⓒ Ⓓ Ⓔ
(A)   Therefore, we should be especially skeptical of weather predictions for the distant future.
(B)   Therefore, we cannot control the weather, but we can predict it.
(C)   Therefore, even though we cannot accurately predict the weather now, it will be possible in the near future.
(D)   Therefore, since we cannot predict the weather, our aim should be to control it.
(E)   Therefore, meteorology is a worthless science.

ANSWER AND EXPLANATION

The correct answer is (A). The passage points out that, although we can to some extent predict the weather, we are often wrong. This leads us to the conclusion that we cannot predict far in advance. (A) is the best answer. (B) and (D) do not follow since the passage does not mention controlling the weather. (C) does not follow since the passage does not address our gaining additional knowledge or more sophisticated equipment to help us in the future. The passage does not condemn meteorology, so (E) can be eliminated.

LOGICAL FLAWS

This common question type gives you a passage, statement, or argument, and asks you to find, understand, analyze, or name the type of flaw in the reasoning.

As you watch for logical flaws, notice that some are very evident especially if the passage or argument seems nonsensical. Others are very subtle, and need a second look. If you don't spot the flaw immediately upon reading the passage, let the choices help. Remember, the choices are showing you some possibilities.

Also, reading the question first will stop you from trying to make complete sense from a nonsensical passage, or trying to follow the logic or reasoning when, by design of the question, it does not follow. You see that the question itself warned you that there was a flaw in the reasoning.

Example 1

The new American revolution is an electronic one. Advances in sophisticated circuitry have yielded more gadgets than anyone could have imagined only a few years ago: calculators as small as a wristwatch and automobile dashboards full of digital readouts are two of the many products that have enhanced the quality of life. But we may become so dependent on solid-state circuits to do our thinking that we may forget how to do it ourselves. Certain birds living on islands where there were no predators have, in time, lost their ability to fly. We may just as easily lose the ability to perform even the simplest mathematical calculation without the aid of an electronic gadget.

Which of the following best describes the flaw in the reasoning in this passage?
(A)   It assumes that a temporal sequence implies a causal relation.   Ⓐ Ⓑ Ⓒ Ⓓ Ⓔ
(B)   It generalizes from one instance to every other instance of the same type.
(C)   It draws an analogy between two very different situations.
(D)   It wrongly assumes that no new and better electronic devices will be invented.
(E)   It assumes that what happens in America also happens in the rest of the world.

ANSWER AND EXPLANATION

The correct answer is (C). The flaw in the reasoning here is the comparison of two wholly unlike situations. The analogy compares men and birds and compares an event in the evolutionary history of certain birds that happened under unique circumstances over vast periods of time to what is supposed to be similar situations in the modern world, but which has in fact no real similarity.

Example 2

With the continued water shortage in our area, the Water Department has had to restrict the use of water during daylight hours and to increase the cost of water to consumers. An average water bill has risen twenty-four dollars a year for three years in a row. Three years from now, our water costs will be astronomical.

A major flag in the reasoning is that it   Ⓐ Ⓑ Ⓒ Ⓓ Ⓔ
- (A) relies upon figures that are imprecise to support a conclusion
- (B) fails to indicate exactly how high expenses will be in three years
- (C) assumes the conditions of the past three years will continue
- (D) overlooks the possibility that conservation methods may improve in the next five years.
- (E) ignores the likelihood of the high cost driving down the water usage

ANSWER AND EXPLANATION

The correct answer is (C). To follow the author's line of reasoning, the author must assume that "the conditions of the past three years will continue." This assumption is flawed since the conditions could change. The conclusion is therefore based on a faulty assumption.

Example 3

In 1982 and 1983, when the limit on class size in grades 7, 8, and 9 was 25, our junior high school students had an average reading score of 79 and an average math score of 75 in the state tests administered at the end of grade 9. But, in 1984 and 1985, when the limit on class size was raised to 28, our junior high school students had average scores of 75 in the state reading tests and 75 in the state math tests. The increase in class size limitations has brought about the decline in state test scores.

Which of the following is a major flaw in the reasoning in this passage?   Ⓐ Ⓑ Ⓒ Ⓓ Ⓔ
- (A) The author believes that test scores are accurate.
- (B) The author fails to realize that some students' math test scores have not declined, though the average has.
- (C) The author regards scores in math tests more important than scores in reading.
- (D) The author assumes class size has caused the variation in test scores.
- (E) The author does not know whether or not class size actually increased.

ANSWER AND EXPLANATION

The correct answer is (D). Since the class size limitations were increased and only the reading scores decreased, the author came to the conclusion that class size limitations caused the decline. But the math scores did not decrease, which would lead one to believe other factors are involved in the scores' decline. Also, because there were different class size limitations does not mean the sizes of the classes were different. The author's reasoning is flawed by his assumption that class size caused the variation. (E) is a fact, but is not the flaw in the author's reasoning.

PASSAGE COMPLETION OR FILL-IN

This question type requires you to fill in a word or words in a passage or to choose a phrase or sentence that best completes the passage.

It is initially important that you preserve the meaning of the passage, completing or maintaining the same thought. Unity (same subject) and coherence (order of thoughts) should be carefully noted. Second, it is important that the words you choose fit stylistically, use the same vocabulary, and are from the same context. Many times you will be able to eliminate some choices that "just don't sound good."

Example 1

English, with its insatiable and omnivorous appetite for imported food, has eaten until it has become linguistically unbuttoned. And the glutton has cloaked his paunch with the pride of the gourmet. We would not imply that a large vocabulary is bad, but rather that it is self-destructive if uncontrolled by _____ .

Choose the completion that is best according to the context of this passage.   Ⓐ Ⓑ Ⓒ Ⓓ Ⓔ
(A)   a smattering of slang
(B)   a fine sense of distinction
(C)   the removal of all but Anglo-Saxon derivatives
(D)   a professor who knows the limits of good usage
(E)   an unbuttoned tongue

ANSWER AND EXPLANATION

The correct answer is (B). The passage describes the English language itself; therefore, references to individuals, (D) and (E), are inappropriate. They do not maintain the same general level of thought. Since the author does not condemn a large and distinguished vocabulary, (A) and (C), which do, are both poor choices. (B) preserves the meaning of the passage and fits stylistically.

Example 2

In a reversal of past trends, last year more lawyers left courtroom practice to go into the teaching of law than vice versa. Since courtroom practice on average yields a much higher annual income, this shift discredits the theory that _____ .

Ⓐ Ⓑ Ⓒ Ⓓ Ⓔ
Which of the following best completes the last sentence in the passage above?
(A)   incomes in the teaching of law will at some future time match those of courtroom practice
(B)   the change in profession by those lawyers who are likely to increase their incomes can be predicted in advance
(C)   more lawyers have remained in the teaching of law in the past few years than previously was the case
(D)   lawyers under 40 years of age are more likely to change professions for financial rather than other reasons
(E)   lawyers are likely to move into those professions in which the income is highest

ANSWER AND EXPLANATION

The correct answer is (E). The passage argues a connection between lawyers, profession changes, and income. Any answer choice that does not address those items cannot be a logical conclusion. (E) addresses the three key items and offers a conclusion that is logically consistent with the apparent change from higher to lower paying professions. (A) is irrelevant because the passage does not address the "future." (B) is irrelevant because the passage does not address "prediction." (C) is irrelevant because the passage does not address "remained" in a profession, only changing. (D) is irrelevant because the passage does not address the "age" of lawyers.

GROUP QUESTIONS

In some instances, you may be presented with five choices first, and then two or three questions that refer to these five choices.

Reading the questions first will clue you as to what to look for when reading the choices, and may save you time.

Example

(A) Man cannot fly; therefore man was not meant to fly.
(B) Jogging is good for you unless you have flat feet.
(C) The homeowner doesn't need to pay the tax because he doesn't own a home.
(D) The witness's testimony was truthful because he said he was telling the truth.
(E) The car stalled because of lack of fuel.

1. Which of the statements uses circular reasoning? Ⓐ Ⓑ Ⓒ Ⓓ Ⓔ

2. Which of the statements is internally inconsistent? Ⓐ Ⓑ Ⓒ Ⓓ Ⓔ

3. Which of the statements uses an example to make a point? Ⓐ Ⓑ Ⓒ Ⓓ Ⓔ

ANSWER AND EXPLANATION

1. **D** Circular reasoning is the use of a statement to support itself. Thus, (D) is circular.

2. **C** Statement (C) is internally inconsistent because a homeowner, by definition, is someone who owns a home. Thus, stating that the homeowner doesn't own a home is inconsistent.

3. **A** Statement (A) posits an argument or statement that man is not meant to fly. To support this point, it uses an example: man cannot fly.

Notice that reading the questions first pinpointed what to look for in the preceding answer choices. Because this method may make you observe answers out of order, be careful that you are answering the right question number.

WORD REFERENCE

Here a word, or group of words, is taken out of context, and you are asked either what the word or words mean or what they refer to. In this type of question, first consider the passage as a whole; then carefully examine the key word or words surrounding the selected ones.

Example

English, with its insatiable and omnivorous appetite for imported food, has eaten until it has become linguistically unbuttoned. And the glutton has cloaked his paunch with the pride of the gourmet. We would not imply that a large vocabulary is bad, but rather that it is self-destructive if uncontrolled by a fine sense of distinction.

As used here, the word "glutton" refers to

(A) an English language with a lack of Anglo-Saxon derivation
(B) one who never stops talking about foreign food
(C) an English language bursting with pride
(D) one who is bilingual
(E) an English language bursting with derivatives from foreign languages

Ⓐ Ⓑ Ⓒ Ⓓ Ⓔ

ANSWER AND EXPLANATION

The correct answer is (E). The passage, as a whole, is commenting on the English language, and (E) is the only choice that equates "glutton" with the subject of the passage.

AMBIGUITY OF STATEMENTS

This question type, which has not appeared recently, gives you a statement, argument, proverb, or cliché, and asks you to deal with the possible meanings, either identifying them or applying them.

First you should make sure that you understand the statement; simplify it to make sense if necessary. Take the simplest, most straightforward meaning first. Consider all other possible meanings from all angles only after you have read the choices.

Second, evaluate the strength and completeness of the statement. (Is it general? Specific? Absolute?)

Example

"One may go wrong in many directions, but right in only one," stated Aristotle.

This statement has many meanings. Which of the following could NOT be one of the meanings?

(A) Right has an absolute direction.
(B) Going wrong is more possible than going right.
(C) One may go right more than once.
(D) The right directions are more accessible.
(E) One may go wrong more than once.

Ⓐ Ⓑ Ⓒ Ⓓ Ⓔ

ANSWER AND EXPLANATION

The correct choice is (D). Since statement (D) says the right "directions," it actually contradicts the statement by mentioning more than one right direction. Also the original statement could not mean that the right directions are more accessible because it implies they are less accessible. (A), (B), (C), and (E) are all either stated or can be easily inferred as one of the meanings.

QUESTIONS FROM CHARTS

This question type asks you to use the information given in a chart to make deductions, inferences, evaluations, or analyses of the reasoning involved.

First, make sure that you understand the chart and the information it contains.

Second, see where the question leads you (to a part of the chart, to a specific detail, or to the whole chart).

Example

Teams Alpha and Beta are competing in a game of hockey. There are only three periods and the scores noted in the chart indicate the total number of goals scored by the end of that particular period only. The final score is the total of all three periods. The winning team is the one with the most goals.

Team	1	2	3	Final Score
Alpha	0	2	3	5
Beta	1	3	3	7

According to the information given in the chart, all of the following could be true EXCEPT

Ⓐ Ⓑ Ⓒ Ⓓ Ⓔ

(A) the score was tied during the second period
(B) the Alphas were winning in the third period
(C) the Betas did not score for most of the first period
(D) the Betas were behind in the second period
(E) the Alphas were winning until the last goal

ANSWER AND EXPLANATION

The correct choice is (E). Because the Betas won by 2 goals, the Alphas could not have been winning until the last goal. Also, if the Alphas were winning until the last goal, and the Betas made the last goal, it would be a tie. Notice that (A), (B), (C), and (D) could be true, because we don't know when the goals were scored within a period. For example, (B) could be true: if the Alphas scored the first three goals in period 3, they would be leading 5 to 4.

IN CONCLUSION

As you have seen, Logical Reasoning includes a potpourri of problem types all requiring common sense and reasonableness in the answers. You should take care in underlining what is being asked so that you do not (for example) accidentally look for the valid conclusion when the invalid one is asked for. Because of the nature of the Logical Reasoning problems, it is very easy to get tangled in a problem and lose your original thought, spending too much time on the question. If you feel that you have become trapped or struck, take a guess and come back later if you have time. Remember that you must work within the context of the question, so do not bring in outside experiences or otherwise complicate a problem. The Logical Reasoning question is looking not for training in formal logic, but just for common sense and reasonableness.

Remember: Logical Reasoning accounts for 50% of your LSAT score.

REVIEW OF SOME GENERAL STRATEGIES FOR LOGICAL REASONING

THE PASSAGE
Read *actively,* circling key words.
Note major issue and supporting points.

THE QUESTION
Preread (before reading the passage) *actively.*
Note its reference.
Watch out for *unstated* ideas:
assumptions, implications/inferences, and sometimes conclusions.

ANSWER CHOICES
Sometimes there may not be a *perfect* answer; thus choose the *best* of the five choices.
Use the elimination strategy.
Note that "wrong" words in a choice make that choice incorrect.
Watch for those off-topic key words.

EXTRA PRACTICE: LOGICAL REASONING

In this section you will be given brief statements or passages and be required to evaluate the reasoning involved. In some instances, more than one choice will appear to be a possible answer. You are to choose the *best* answer. Use common sense and reasonableness in making your selection; then mark the correct answer.

Questions 1–3 refer to the following passage.

Robots have the ability to exhibit programmed behavior. Their performance can range from the simplest activity to the most complex group of activities. They not only can build other robots, but also can rebuild themselves. Physically they can resemble humans, yet mentally they cannot. Even the most highly advanced robot does not have the capacity to be creative, have emotions, or think independently.

1. From the passage above, which of the following must be true?   Ⓐ Ⓑ Ⓒ Ⓓ Ⓔ
   (A) Robots could eventually take over the world.
   (B) The most complex group of activities involves being creative.
   (C) A robot should last forever.
   (D) Emotions, creativity, and independent thought can be written as
       programs.
   (E) Building other robots involves independent thinking.

2. The author of this passage would agree that   Ⓐ Ⓑ Ⓒ Ⓓ Ⓔ
   (A) robots would eventually be impossible to control
   (B) in the near future, robots will be able to think independently
   (C) robots have reached their peak of development
   (D) there are dangers in robots that think for themselves
   (E) there are some tasks that are better done by robots than by humans

3. The author's assertions would be weakened by pointing out that   Ⓐ Ⓑ Ⓒ Ⓓ Ⓔ
   (A) humans exhibit programmed behavior for the first few years of life
   (B) robots' behavior is not always predictable
   (C) building other robots requires independent training
   (D) internal feeling is not always exhibited
   (E) the most complex group of activities necessitates independent
       thinking

4. Life is like a parachute jump—you had better get it right the first time.

   The author of this statement assumes that   Ⓐ Ⓑ Ⓒ Ⓓ Ⓔ
   (A) if nothing is ventured, nothing is gained
   (B) risk-taking is foolish
   (C) you only live once
   (D) starting over is possible but difficult
   (E) a second try is usually no better than the first

5. Man is free because he is rational.

   This statement has many possible meanings. All of the following could be possible meanings EXCEPT
   (A) Man's being rational makes him free   Ⓐ Ⓑ Ⓒ Ⓓ Ⓔ
   (B) Man is rational
   (C) Man is free
   (D) Man's freedom is a consequence of his being rational
   (E) all who are free are rational

6. The simplest conceivable situation in which one human being may communicate with another is one in which structurally complementary communicants have been conditioned to associate the same words with the same things.

The sentence that would best complete this thought is: Ⓐ Ⓑ Ⓒ Ⓓ Ⓔ
(A) Therefore, dictionaries are of little value to foreigners.
(B) Therefore, man cannot communicate effectively with animals.
(C) Therefore, communication is a matter of relation.
(D) Therefore, communication is simplest following a common experience.
(E) Therefore, communication is dependent on complementary structures.

7. In a nationwide survey, four out of five dentists questioned recommended sugarless gum for their patients who chew gum.

Which of the following would most weaken the above endorsement for sugarless gum? Ⓐ Ⓑ Ⓒ Ⓓ Ⓔ
(A) Only five dentists were questioned.
(B) The dentists were not paid for their endorsements.
(C) Only one of the dentists questioned chewed sugarless gum.
(D) Patients do not do what their dentists tell them to do.
(E) Sugarless gum costs much more than regular gum.

8. In Tom and Angie's class, everyone likes drawing or painting or both, but Angie does not like painting.

Which of the following statements cannot be true? Ⓐ Ⓑ Ⓒ Ⓓ Ⓔ
(A) Angie likes drawing.
(B) Tom likes drawing and painting.
(C) Everyone in the class who does not like drawing likes painting.
(D) No one in the class likes painting.
(E) Tom dislikes drawing and painting.

9. *Mark:* The big test is tomorrow and I didn't study. I suppose I'll just have to cheat. I know it is wrong, but I have to get a good grade on the test.
Amy: I don't think that's a good idea. Just go to the teacher, tell the truth, and maybe you can get a postponement.

Amy attacks Mark's argument by Ⓐ Ⓑ Ⓒ Ⓓ Ⓔ
(A) attacking his reasoning
(B) applying personal pressure
(C) implying that good triumphs over evil
(D) presenting another alternative
(E) suggesting a positive approach

Questions 10–11 refer to the following passage.

The microwave oven has become a standard appliance in many kitchens, mainly because it offers a fast way of cooking food. Yet, some homeowners believe that the ovens are still not completely safe. Microwaves therefore should not be standard appliances until they are more carefully researched and tested.

10. Which of the following, if true, would most weaken the conclusion of the passage above?
   (A)   Homeowners often purchase items despite knowing they may be unsafe.
   (B)   Those homeowners in doubt about microwave safety ought not to purchase microwaves.
   (C)   Research and testing of home appliances seldom reveal safety hazards.
   (D)   Microwaves are not as dangerous as steam irons, which are used in almost every home.
   (E)   Homeowners often purchase items that they do not need.

11. Which of the following, if true, would most strengthen the conclusion of the passage above?
   (A)   Homeowners often doubt the advertised safety of all new appliances.
   (B)   Speed of food preparation is not the only concern of today's homeowner.
   (C)   Modern homeowners have more free time than ever before.
   (D)   Food preparation has become almost a science, with more complicated and involved recipes.
   (E)   Many microwave ovens have been found to leak radioactive elements.

12. A few mimes are sad.
   All mimes are always funny.
   Children cannot be sad and funny at the same time.

   Given that the foregoing are true, which of the following must be true?   Ⓐ Ⓑ Ⓒ Ⓓ Ⓔ
   (A)   There are no sad children.
   (B)   No child is funny.
   (C)   No sad mimes are children.
   (D)   Mimes cannot be sad and funny simultaneously.
   (E)   All funny mimes are sad.

13. I.   Everyone who is a slow runner either does not engage in any track and field event or does poorly in such events.
   II.   Everyone who does not engage in any track and field event is a slow runner.

   Which of the following best indicates the relationship between the two statements above?
   (A)   If II is true, then I is true.   Ⓐ Ⓑ Ⓒ Ⓓ Ⓔ
   (B)   If II is true, then I is most likely false.
   (C)   If II is true, then I can be either true or false.
   (D)   If I is true, then II is true.
   (E)   If I is false, then II is most likely false.

14. Given that this rock is white in color, it must be quartz.

   The foregoing conclusion can be properly drawn if it is true that   Ⓐ Ⓑ Ⓒ Ⓓ Ⓔ
   (A)   only quartz rocks are white in color
   (B)   quartz rocks are generally white in color
   (C)   other white rocks have proved to be quartz
   (D)   few other types of rocks are white in color
   (E)   all quartz rocks are white in color

Questions 15–16 refer to the following passage.

A special group of enzymes, when occurring together in the blood, causes the breakdown of any serum cholesterol that is present in the blood. In ten experiments, enzymes V, W, X, Y, and Z were combined in various groups. Certain combinations resulted in a breakdown of serum cholesterol, and others did not result in a breakdown phenomenon.

Experiment	Combination	Breakdown
1	V W Y	NO
2	V X Y Z	YES
3	X Y	NO
4	V X Z	YES
5	W Y	NO
6	V W X Z	YES
7	W Y Z	NO
8	W X Y	NO
9	X Y Z	YES
10	V W Z	NO

15. Which of the following is a complete and accurate list of the enzymes that are necessary to cause the breakdown of serum cholesterol? Ⓐ Ⓑ Ⓒ Ⓓ Ⓔ
   (A) V and W only   (B) W and Y only   (C) X and Z only
   (D) V, W, and Z only   (E) W, X, and Z only

16. All of the following can be deduced from the information given above EXCEPT
   (A) fewer breakdowns occurred during experiments than nonbreakdowns   Ⓐ Ⓑ Ⓒ Ⓓ Ⓔ
   (B) the presence of Z does not guarantee a breakdown
   (C) whenever four enzymes were used, a breakdown occurred
   (D) when enzyme W was used, no breakdown occurred
   (E) the presence of Y is not necessary for a breakdown

Questions 17–18 refer to the following passage.

   Some American auto factories are beginning to resemble their Japanese counterparts. In many Japanese factories, the workers enjoy the same status and privileges as their bosses. Everyone works in harmony, and there is much less of the tension and anger that results when one group dominates another.

17. With which of the following would the author of the above passage most likely agree?
   (A) American work environments ought to emulate Japanese auto factories.   Ⓐ Ⓑ Ⓒ Ⓓ Ⓔ
   (B) Japanese automobiles are better built than American automobiles.
   (C) Tension in the workplace enhances worker productivity.
   (D) Japanese culture differs so much from American culture that it precludes any overlap of styles.
   (E) Striving for managerial status induces worker productivity.

18. The argument gives logically relevant support for which of the following conclusions?
   (A) Some American auto factories are experiencing changes in their work environments.
   (B) American auto workers envy their Japanese counterparts.   Ⓐ Ⓑ Ⓒ Ⓓ Ⓔ
   (C) There is no tension or anger in Japanese factories.
   (D) Decrease in tension leads to higher productivity.
   (E) There is no tension or anger in American factories that follow Japanese models.

19. When we approach land, we usually sight birds. The lookout has just sighted birds.

   Which of the following represents the most logical conclusion based upon the foregoing statements?   Ⓐ Ⓑ Ⓒ Ⓓ Ⓔ
   (A) The conjecture that we are approaching land is strengthened.
   (B) Land is closer than it was before the sighting of the birds.
   (C) We are approaching land.
   (D) We may or may not be approaching land.
   (E) We may not be approaching land.

20. The presence of the gas Nexon is a necessary condition, but not a sufficient condition, for the existence of life on the planet Plex.

On the basis of the foregoing, which of the following would also be true?   Ⓐ Ⓑ Ⓒ Ⓓ Ⓔ
(A)   If life exists on Plex, then only the gas Nexon is present.
(B)   If life exists on Plex, then the gas Nexon may or may not be present.
(C)   If life exists on Plex, then the gas Nexon is present.
(D)   If no life exists on Plex, Nexon cannot be present.
(E)   If no life exists on Plex, Nexon is the only gas present.

21. The absence of the liquid Flennel is a sufficient condition for the cessation of life on the planet Fluke, but it is not a necessary condition.

On the basis of the foregoing, which of the following would also be true?   Ⓐ Ⓑ Ⓒ Ⓓ Ⓔ
(A)   If life on Fluke ceased to exist, there would have to have been an absence of the liquid Flennel.
(B)   If all liquid Flennel were removed from Fluke, life there would surely perish.
(C)   If all liquid Flennel were removed from Fluke, life there might or might not cease.
(D)   If all liquid Flennel were removed from Fluke, the cessation of life would depend upon other conditions.
(E)   Life on Fluke cannot cease so long as Flennel is present.

22. None but fools would do that.

All of the following have the same meaning as the preceding statement EXCEPT
(A)   all of those who would do that are fools   Ⓐ Ⓑ Ⓒ Ⓓ Ⓔ
(B)   everyone who would do that is a fool
(C)   all fools do that
(D)   only fools would do that
(E)   nobody except a fool would do that

23. If the poodle was reared at Prince Charming Kennels, then it is a purebred.

The foregoing statement can be deduced logically from which of the following statements?
Ⓐ Ⓑ Ⓒ Ⓓ Ⓔ
(A)   Every purebred poodle is reared at Prince Charming Kennels or at another AKC approved kennel.
(B)   The poodle in question was bred at either Prince Charming Kennels or at another AKC approved kennel.
(C)   The poodle in question either is a purebred or looks remarkably like a purebred.
(D)   The majority of poodles reared at Prince Charming Kennels are purebred.
(E)   There are no dogs reared at Prince Charming Kennels that are not purebred.

24. There is no reason to eliminate the possibility of an oil field existing beneath the Great Salt Lake. Therefore, we must undertake the exploration of the Salt Lake's bottom.

The foregoing argument assumes which of the following?   Ⓐ Ⓑ Ⓒ Ⓓ Ⓔ
(A)   Exploration of the Salt Lake's bottom has not been previously proposed.
(B)   An oil field located beneath the lake would be easy to identify.
(C)   The Great Salt Lake is the only large inland body of water beneath which an oil field may lie.
(D)   The quest for oil is a sufficient motive to undertake exploration of the Salt Lake's bottom.
(E)   An oil field exists beneath the Great Salt Lake.

Questions 25–26 refer to the following passage.

My course of study had led me to believe that all mental and moral feelings and qualities, whether of a good or of a bad kind, were the results of association; that we love one thing, and hate another, take pleasure in one sort of action or contemplation, and pain in another sort, through the clinging of pleasurable or painful ideas to those things, from the effect of education or of experience. As a corollary from this, I was convinced, that the object of education should be to form the strongest possible associations of the salutary class; associations of pleasure with all things beneficial to the great whole. It now seemed to me, on retrospect, that my teachers had occupied themselves but superficially with the means of forming and keeping up these salutary associations. They seemed to have trusted altogether to the old familiar instruments, praise and blame, reward and punishment. I did not doubt that by these means, begun early, and applied unremittingly, intense associations of pain and pleasure, especially of pain, might be created, and might produce desires and aversions capable of lasting undiminished to the end of life. But there must always be something artificial and casual in associations thus produced.

25. By "salutary" the author means   Ⓐ Ⓑ Ⓒ Ⓓ Ⓔ
    (A) "the strongest possible associations"
    (B) ideas that "salute" one's mind
    (C) capable of giving pain
    (D) promoting some good purpose
    (E) those earning a middle-class income or better

26. All of the following questions are answered in the passage EXCEPT   Ⓐ Ⓑ Ⓒ Ⓓ Ⓔ
    (A) Is there any sort of thinking that is not associational?
    (B) Is schooling the only cause of our lifelong "desires and aversions"?
    (C) What else besides education causes these associations?
    (D) What do teachers praise and what do they blame?
    (E) How long would the desires and aversions last?

27. The San Diego Chargers practice expertly for long hours every day and keep a written log of their errors.

    The above statement is an example of which of the following assumptions?   Ⓐ Ⓑ Ⓒ Ⓓ Ⓔ
    (A) Practice makes perfect.
    (B) To err is human.
    (C) People make mistakes; that's why they put erasers on pencils.
    (D) Practice is what you know, and it will help to make clear what now you do not know.
    (E) Writing is a mode of learning.

28. I.   Pine trees may be taller than any other tree.
     II. Pines are never shorter than the shortest palms, and some palms may exceed the height of some pines.
     III. Peppertrees are always taller than palm trees.
     IV. Peach trees are shorter than peppertrees but not shorter than all palms.

    Given the foregoing, which of the following would be true?   Ⓐ Ⓑ Ⓒ Ⓓ Ⓔ
    (A) Peach trees may be shorter than pine trees.
    (B) Peppertrees may be shorter than some peach trees.
    (C) Every pine is taller than every palm.
    (D) A particular palm could not be taller than a particular pine.
    (E) Now and then a peach tree may be taller than a pepper.

29. Most popular paperback novels are of low intellectual quality; therefore, *Splendor Behind the Billboard,* an unpopular paperback novel, is probably of high intellectual quality.

The foregoing argument is most like which of the following?   Ⓐ Ⓑ Ⓒ Ⓓ Ⓔ
- (A) Most locusts inhabit arid places; therefore, locusts are probably found in all deserts.
- (B) Most acts of criminal violence have declined in number during the past few years; therefore, law enforcement during this period has improved.
- (C) Most people who stop drinking gain weight; therefore, if Carl does not cease drinking, he will probably not gain weight.
- (D) Most nations run by autocratic governments do not permit a free press; therefore the country of Endorff, which is run by an autocratic government, probably does not have a free press.
- (E) Most new motor homes are equipped with air conditioning; therefore, Jim's new motor home may not be equipped with air conditioning.

Questions 30–31 refer to the following statement.

Jane states, "All mammals have hair. This creature possesses no hair. Therefore, it is not a mammal."

30. Which of the following most closely parallels the logic of Jane's statement?   Ⓐ Ⓑ Ⓒ Ⓓ Ⓔ
- (A) All reptiles have scales. This creature possesses scales. Therefore, it is a reptile.
- (B) All physics tests are difficult. This is not a physics test. Therefore, it is not difficult.
- (C) All American cars are poorly constructed. Every car sold by Fred was poorly constructed. Therefore, Fred sells only American cars.
- (D) All mammals do not have hair. This creature possesses hair. Therefore, it may be a mammal.
- (E) All lubricants smell. This liquid does not have an odor. Therefore, it is not a lubricant.

31. Which of the following, if true, would most weaken Jane's argument?   Ⓐ Ⓑ Ⓒ Ⓓ Ⓔ
- (A) Animals other than mammals have hair.
- (B) Some mammals do not have hair.
- (C) Mammals have more hair than nonmammals.
- (D) One could remove the hair from a mammal.
- (E) Reptiles may have hair.

Questions 32–34 refer to the missing portions of the following passage. For each question, select the insertion that best fits the meaning of the passage.

Psychoanalytical theory asserts that by attributing (projecting) his own consciously unacceptable motivations to those around him, the individual is able to avoid recognizing them as being his own. Inasmuch as social prejudices involve the ascription of undesirable traits and motives to various groups or classes, they would seem to be particularly attractive to those individuals who employ projection as a technique for (32) _____ their perception of their own consciously unacceptable motivations. The fact that the undesirable traits ascribed to groups or classes in which the target of prejudice often includes motives of greed and mistrust (motives commonly (33) _____ by those who have them) supports the theory that these attributions of traits are, in fact, projections by individuals who (34) _____ their own motivations of the same nature.

32. (A) validating   (B) strengthening   (C) proving   (D) avoiding   (E) clarifying

   Ⓐ Ⓑ Ⓒ Ⓓ Ⓔ

33. (A) desired   (B) rejected   (C) held   (D) projected   (E) accepted

   Ⓐ Ⓑ Ⓒ Ⓓ Ⓔ

34. (A) repress   (B) reject   (C) accept   (D) project   (E) recognize

   Ⓐ Ⓑ Ⓒ Ⓓ Ⓔ

35. Scientific studies have shown that second-hand tobacco smoke in the workplace greatly increases the number of workers who take more than fifteen days of sick-leave and the number of workers who suffer serious respiratory ailments. It has also been shown that the number of workers who die of lung cancer is twice as high in workplaces that permit smoking than in workplaces that do not. Therefore, the state must pass laws that require all companies to forbid smoking in the workplace.

Which of the following is the underlying principle in this argument?   Ⓐ Ⓑ Ⓒ Ⓓ Ⓔ
(A) Every individual has a responsibility for the well-being of every other individual with whom he or she comes into daily contact.
(B) Employers who do not take care of the health of their workers risk increasing losses from absenteeism each year.
(C) States must be permitted to outlaw any dangerous substances or implements.
(D) States must be responsible for the safety of the workplace of all businesses in their jurisdiction.
(E) Workers must be permitted to make their own decisions about their workplace.

36. For the post-election festivities, no athlete was invited to the White House unless he or she was more than 35 years old. No one older than 35 was both an athlete and invited to the White House.

Ⓐ Ⓑ Ⓒ Ⓓ Ⓔ

Which of the following conclusions can be logically drawn from the statements above?
(A) No one but athletes were invited to the White House.
(B) No athlete was invited to the White House.
(C) Only persons older than 35 were invited to the White House.
(D) No one over 35 was invited to the White House.
(E) Some athletes over 35 were invited to the White House.

Answers and Explanations

1. **C** The passage states that robots not only can build other robots but also can rebuild themselves; therefore, they should last forever. (B) is probably true, but (C) must be true. According to the passage, (A) and (E) are not implied, and (D) is probably not true.

2. **E** There are tasks that robots can do better than humans. Any task in which not being able to think independently or not having emotions would be advantageous might be better done by robots. Tasks that require exposure to dangerous chemicals or radioactivity are also suitable for robots.

3. **E** The author states that the robot can do the most complex group of activities, but "does not have the capacity to . . . think independently." If the most complex group of activities necessitates independent thinking, then the author's assertions are in *direct* contradiction. (C) would be a good choice if it mentioned independent thinking, not training, as training is not mentioned in the passage.

4. **C** Only position (C) is a clear assumption; if you only live once, you had better get it right the first time. (D) contradicts the statement. (A), (B), and (E) may be true but they are not assumptions behind this statement.

5. **E** (A), (B), and (C) are all implied meanings. "Man as rational is free," could imply (A). "Man is rational," implies (B). "Man is free," is (C). (D) restates the original thesis. (E) is not what the statement claims. It does not refer to "all" the free but to "Man."

6. **D** (A) and (B) are irrelevant, and (C) and (E) are not as effective as (D) because they are just restatements of the thought, rather than a clarification.

7. **A** The phrase "four out of five" implies 80% of a large sample (nationwide). If only five dentists were in the sample, the reliability would certainly be in question. (B) would strengthen the endorsement, while (D) and (E) are irrelevant. (C) could weaken it, but not nearly as much.

8. **E** (A) must be true by the first statement because everybody in the class likes drawing or painting or both, so if Angie does not like painting, she must like drawing. This same logic holds for (C). "Everyone in the class who does not like drawing," must like painting. And (D), it is possible that no one in the class likes painting. But (E) cannot be true if everyone likes drawing or painting or both.

9. **D** (A) is incorrect since there is no attack on Mark's reasoning. (B) is incorrect because personal pressure is not implied. (C) is incorrect since it is heresay. (E) is incorrect, since who is to say what a "positive" approach is? (E) could have been the correct choice if (D) were not a possibility.

10. **C** The conclusion of the passage is that, because of safety concerns, more research and testing ought to be done before microwaves become standard household appliances. If, however, research and testing are ineffective means of discerning safety problems, then research and testing would be irrelevant. This criticism seriously weakens the conclusion.

11. **E** If many microwave ovens have been found to leak radioactive elements, then the conclusion—that microwaves should not be standard appliances until they are more carefully researched and tested—is further strengthened because more safety concerns needed to be addressed.

12. **C** On the basis of the first and second statements, all sad mimes are also funny. From the third statement, we conclude that no child can be both sad and funny; therefore (D) is false. (C) must be true; that is, no sad mimes are children. (A), (B), and (E) need not be true.

13. **C** Statement I, whether true or false, tells only about slow runners. If everyone who does not engage in track and field is *slow*, then the converse (implied by part of I) *may* also be true. In other words, "all nontrack competitors are slow" does not guarantee that "all slow runners are nontrack competitors," but does not exclude this possibility. Because there is no certain or likely relationship between the two converse statements, the other choices (which require certainty or likelihood) are weak.

14. **A** The conclusion can be properly drawn only if the condition, "*being white*," is sufficient to rule out all but quartz. (A) allows the conclusion, "*must* be quartz," to be reached.

15. **C** By carefully reviewing the information, you will notice that X and Z are the only two enzymes that appear each time there is a breakdown.

16. **D** Again, by reviewing the information, (A) and (C) can be deduced. Notice that during the experiments there were four breakdowns and six nonbreakdowns (A). Whenever four enzymes were used—experiments 2 and 6—a breakdown occurred. (D) is false; a breakdown occurred in experiment 6 with W. (B) is true (experiments 7 and 10), as is (E) (experiments 4 and 6).

17. **A** The tone of the passage is positive: workers "enjoy" the same status; "harmony"; less "tension and anger." One can therefore conclude that the author approves of the work environment of the Japanese auto factory for the workers' well-being, and any resemblance of American factories to those of the Japanese ought to be encouraged. Note that there is no indication at all regarding the quality of the goods produced (B).

18. **A** Only (A) is logically supported by the passage. There is no direct support regarding worker envy for (B). There may be less tension and anger in Japanese auto factories; however, to

conclude that there is <u>no</u> tension or anger is not logically sound. Nothing in the passage describes the relation of tension to productivity (D).

19. **A** The key word in the statements given is "usually." "Usually" suggests a frequent or regular phenomenon. It implies that an event may be normally expected and allows one to draw a conclusion *stronger than* those contained in (D) and (E). "Usually" does not mean "with certainty." Therefore, the categorical conclusions of (B) and (C) are not appropriate.

20. **C** (A) is not true, since Nexon is not a <u>sufficient condition</u> for life; that is, Nexon alone is not enough. (B) is not true because Nexon must be present if there is life (<u>necessary condition</u>). (C) is true; Nexon must be present (it is a necessary condition). (C) does not suggest the absence of things other than Nexon and, therefore, does not contradict the original statement. (D) is untrue since Nexon alone is not a sufficient condition.

21. **B** (A) need not be true, because the absence of Flennel is not a <u>necessary condition;</u> that is, there can be other conditions that result in the end of life. (C) is not true, because the absence of Flennel <u>is sufficient</u> to end life (one cannot say life may "not cease"). (B) is true, given the absence of Flennel is sufficient to end life. Both (D) and (E) are untrue. Absence of Flennel is sufficient cause (D) but there might be other causes as well (E).

22. **C** The statement means that only fools would do that. This is the same as (A), (B), (D), and (E). It does not mean, however, that all fools would do that (C), only fools.

23. **E** The statement presented can be logically made only if being reared at Prince Charming Kennels assures that a poodle is purebred. (E) provides such assurance. (A) does not state that only purebreds are reared and, therefore, does not assure that any given poodle from the kennels is pure.

24. **D** (A) may be eliminated because the argument does not rule out a possible previous proposal. (B) may be eliminated as no suggestion of easy identification or the necessity of easy identification is presupposed. (C) may be eliminated because the argument is independent of any comparison between the Great Salt Lake and any other body of water. (E) can be eliminated because the argument presents the weaker claim of the *possibility* of oil. (D) allows, if true, the *possibility* of oil to be sufficient cause for exploration.

25. **D** The context suggests that salutary associations are positive ones, and the phrase *associations of pleasure* immediately following the first mention of *salutary* certifies (D) as the best choice.

26. **D** (A) is answered in the first sentence, as are (B) and (C). In the first sentence we are told that all thinking is associational, and in the second, that both education and experience promote accusations. Nowhere, however, does the author mention just what teachers blame and praise.

27. **D** Only this choice addresses both parts of the statement, which implies that expert practice helps identify errors. (B) and (C) stress error only; (A) stresses practice only; and (E) stresses writing only.

28. **A** Refer to the following diagram:

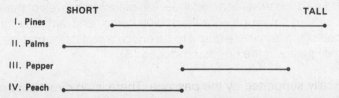

On the basis of the foregoing diagram, (B), (C), (D), and (E) are false.

29. **C** The structure of the given argument may be simplified:
Most are <u>popular</u> and <u>low</u>.
Splendor is <u>not</u> popular and high (<u>not low</u>).

(C) parallels this structure:
Most who <u>stop</u> do <u>gain</u>.
Carl does <u>not stop</u> and will <u>not gain</u>

30. **E** The statement given can be simplified:
<u>All</u> <u>have</u> <u>hair</u> (mammal).
<u>This</u> does <u>not</u> have <u>hair</u>.
<u>It</u> is <u>not</u> (mammal).

Only (E) can be reduced to this same form:
<u>All</u> <u>have</u> <u>smell</u> (lubricants).
<u>This</u> does <u>not</u> have <u>smell</u>.
<u>It</u> is <u>not</u> (lubricant).

31. **B** (A) has no bearing because the argument is concerned only with mammals. (C) is not relevant; the argument does not address the amount of hair. (E) is likewise outside the argument's subject. (D) is a possible answer because the claim is that the absence of hair indicates a nonmammal. However, (B) is a better choice. (D) is a possibility—"One *could* remove." (B) points out that, without any other intervention, there *are* creatures with no hair that are also mammals.

32. **D** The first portion of the passage discusses projection as a method for avoiding the personal recognition of unacceptable motivations. (A), (B), (C), and (E) are inappropriate conclusions because they suggest the employment of projections as a technique for substantiating unacceptable motivations.

33. **B** (A) and (E) illogically condone greed and mistrust. (D) is poor given the balance of the sentence, which stresses repression. (C) is poor because "held" is vague and does not contribute to the final meaning of the sentence. (B) is consistent with the beginning of the discussion and supports the conclusion drawn.

34. **A** (B) does not fit the sentence structure. (C) and (E) are inconsistent with the discussion. (D) would be redundant. (A) is the logical and appropriate insertion.

35. **D** Since the argument concerns state laws to be passed, the best choices must be those that refer to the responsibility of the state, (C) and (D). Of the two, (D) is clearly the more specific and directly relevant to the situation described in the paragraph.

36. **B** The first proposition states that if an athlete and invited, then over 35. The second proposition states that if over 35, then not both an athlete and invited. The propositions contradict each other. Therefore, no person can be both an athlete and invited.

Chapter

5

Writing Sample

INTRODUCTION

The LSAT will include a 30-minute writing sample. You will be asked to respond to a general essay topic that requires no specialized knowledge, but does require you to write an argument for selecting one of two candidates or items based on given criteria. You should express yourself clearly and effectively.

The essay will *not* be scored, but will be forwarded to the law schools to which you apply. Different law schools have adopted different approaches to evaluating and weighing the quality of the essay.

You will write the essay in a "Writing Sample booklet," a paper folder with general directions on the outside, and the essay topic plus space for your response on the inside. A sheet of scratch paper is provided for organizing and/or outlining your ideas. A pen Is also provided for the essay. The essay booklet restricts the length of your response to about *30 lines, each line about seven inches long*. Anything you write outside this restricted space will not be evaluated. Therefore, for practice purposes, restrict yourself to the same space that you will be given on the LSAT to become more comfortable with writing under these restricted conditions.

Following are general directions for the writing sample, a careful analysis of this essay requirement, and a series of steps you may want to follow as you compose your essay. Next, you will examine two completed essays, each written from a different perspective. The chapter concludes with a review of general tips for the writing sample and nine suggested topics for writing your own essays.

GENERAL DIRECTIONS

You have 30 minutes to write an essay in response to a given topic. Take a few minutes to plan your work before you begin writing. DO NOT WRITE ON A TOPIC OF YOUR OWN CHOICE. ESSAYS THAT DO NOT ADDRESS THE GIVEN TOPIC ARE UNACCEPTABLE.

The quality of your writing is more important than the length of your response and content. There is no "right" or "wrong" answer to the question. Pay attention to organization, appropriate diction, and correct usage. You will not be expected to display any specialized knowledge in your response, nor will you be expected to write a "perfect" essay; law schools understand that you are writing under a time constraint and pressured circumstances.

Only the lined area in your booklet will be reproduced for the law schools, so do not write outside this space. *Do not* skip lines or use wide margins. These precautions, along with careful planning and legible handwriting that is not unduly large, will keep you within the allowed space.

ANALYSIS

You will be asked to write an argument for hiring, promoting, selecting, etc., one of two candidates or items based on two or more criteria and two brief sketches of the candidates or items.

Some recent topics have included writing arguments in support of:

"Purchasing one of two films for a public television station"

"Selecting one of two designs submitted for a commemorative sculpture"

"Selecting one of two retirement communities for a retiree"

"Selecting one of two ways of investing money inherited from an uncle"

"Deciding which one of two schools to enter for an undergraduate business degree"

"Selecting one of two proposals for an introductory course in computer training"

In each case, the initial introductory statement was followed by two criteria, and then the background of each candidate, or a description of each film, or a description of each school, or a description of each option.

Let's take a closer look. A recent topic gave us its two criteria for hiring a mathematics teacher: (1) the high school's increased concern with computers and (2) its wish to develop the mathematics program at the school to incorporate work-study projects in the business community. The first candidate had a solid educational background, high school teaching and minor administrative experience, good references, and recent training in computers. The second candidate had a slightly different but equally good educational background and no high school teaching experience, but had worked as a teaching assistant in college and a tutor in community programs, as well as having solid credentials in computers and experience as an employee in financial work for a retail store and a bank.

What should be apparent is that it does *NOT* matter which candidate you choose. The principles and qualifications will be written in such a way that you can write in favor of *EITHER* candidate. Make your choice, and stick to it. Don't worry about the other candidate. What your readers will be looking for are clarity, consistency, relevance, and correctness of grammar and usage. Since you have only one-half hour to read the topic and to plan and write your essay, you will not be expected to produce a long or a subtle essay. But you must write on the topic clearly and correctly.

The questions will make clear the sort of audience you are writing for, and you can be sure that this audience is literate and informed about the issues in your paper. In the math teacher topic, for example, the assumed audience is whoever is to hire the math teacher. You do not need to tell this audience what she already knows, but you do want to make her focus upon the issues that support your case. Let us assume you are making the case for the experienced teacher with some computer training. Your essay should stress the obvious qualifications—his teaching experience and computer training. Where you have no direct evidence of expertise, you can invent, so long as you do so plausibly and work from details that are given in the question. You could, for example, argue that, although there are two criteria, the computer issue is really the more important since the students will not be able to find good work-study projects in the community until they have a greater knowledge of computers.

Assume you have chosen the second candidate. Your essay should focus upon her strengths (for example, her experience in business will help her in setting up a business-related program for the students). Where her qualifications are weaker (her lack of high school teaching experience), your essay can emphasize the other kind of teaching experience she has had. Do not be afraid to introduce details to support your argument that are your own ideas. Just be sure that, when you do present additional information, it is consistent with and arises plausibly from the information on the test.

So far, the writing topics have used two slightly different forms. The first (the math teachers) used two sentences, one for each of two equally weighted criteria, and then described the two equally qualified candidates. Another sample topic type also uses two sentences to describe the principles, but the first contains the two criteria, and the second sentence elaborates on one of them. For example, the two principles might be (1) lifeguards are promoted on the basis of years of service and community activities; and (2) community activities include lifesaving clinics, talks to school children, waterfront safety seminars, and high school swimming-team coaching. The biographies would then describe two candidates whose years of service differ slightly, and each of whom has some strength in the areas listed under (2). Since you are not told which of the two criteria is the more important, or which of the various sorts of community service is most important, you can decide for yourself how to weigh these factors, as long as you do so plausibly. You cannot contradict the question—for example, by saying length of service is not important—but you can argue that, although your candidate's length of service is slightly less than that of her competition, her overwhelming superiority in community service is more important.

Here is a suggested plan for approaching any writing sample of this sort.

Phase 1 — Prewriting

1. Read the two statements of policy or criteria at least twice, *actively*. (Circle or mark the essential points of the topic.) Are they equally weighted? If not, clarify the difference.
2. Read the biographies or descriptions at least twice, *actively*. Test them carefully against the policy or criteria statements.
3. Choose your candidate or item. Again set the qualifications or qualities beside those of the statements. Decide exactly what your choice's greatest strengths are. What are the limitations? Think about how these limitations can be invalidated or turned into strengths.
4. Outline your essay. It should be two or three paragraphs long. If you are selecting a candidate, paragraph 1 might focus on his or her obvious strengths that meet the given criteria. Paragraph 2, or paragraphs 2 and 3, might deal with how the candidate also shows promise of fulfilling the other requirements.

Phase 2 — Writing

1. Do *not* waste time with a fancy opening paragraph on an irrelevant topic like the importance of math teachers or lifeguards in this complex modern world.
2. Start with a direction. Your first sentence should serve a purpose.
3. Support your argument with examples or other specifics.
4. Do *not* write a closing paragraph that simply repeats what you have already said.
5. Write legibly. Write clearly. Write naturally. Do *not* use big words for their own sake. Do not try to be cute or ironic or funny.
6. Remember that the assumed purpose of this paper is to convince a reader to prefer one candidate or item to another. Your real purpose, of course, is to show a law school that you can follow instructions and write an essay that is well organized, adheres to the point, and is grammatically correct.

Phase 3 — Reading

1. Allow sufficient time to proofread your essay. At this point, add any information that is vital, and delete any information that seems confusing or out of place.
2. Don't make extensive changes that will make your writing less readable.
3. Check each sentence for mechanical errors (spelling, punctuation, grammar). Some common types of errors are these:
   - using pronouns with no clear antecedents;
   - lack of agreement between subject and verb;
   - using the wrong verb tense;
   - faulty parallelism in a series of items;
   - misplaced or dangling modifiers;
   - adjective-adverb confusion;
   - misuse of comparative terms or comparisons.

TWO COMPLETED WRITING SAMPLES

Following are two handwritten "model" essays, written on LSAT Writing Sample booklet-type pages. These samples are based on the topic given in the Diagnostic Mini-Exam on page 26. Notice that each of the two sample essays is written from a different perspective.

SAMPLE TOPIC:

Read the following descriptions of Bergquist and Kretchmer, applicants for the job of Assistant Director on a major motion picture. *Then, in the space provided, write an argument for hiring either Bergquist or Kretchmer.* The following criteria are relevant to your decision:

- In addition to working closely with and advising the Director on creative decisions, the Assistant Director must work with all types of individuals—from stars to Teamster truck drivers—and elicit the best from every cast and crew member for the good of the motion picture.
- The Assistant Director is responsible for all the planning and organization—including paperwork, travel itinerary, meals, etc.—of the entire film project. He/she lays the groundwork for a successful "shoot."

BERGQUIST began her career in films as an Administrative Assistant to the president of a major film studio. As such, she often accompanied her employer in his wining and dining of stars, or to the set when problems arose. She doublechecked contracts, shooting schedules, cast and crew checks, and kept a close eye on the budget of several multimillion-dollar films. When her boss was subsequently fired due to a poor season of films, Bergquist was able to secure a position as Assistant Editor at the studio, helping several highly respected film editors "cut" feature films. It was here that she learned about the creative end of the business, and soon after became the chief editor of an hour-long studio documentary, which won several awards. After two years, Bergquist was accepted into the Assistant Directors Training Program, and is presently a candidate for Assistant Director of this new $15,000,000 motion picture.

KRETCHMER was a principal/teacher for 12 years before embarking on a film career. Not only did she teach math at the New York School for the Creative Arts, but she worked with parents in the community, the board of education, and local government representatives in securing financing for the $20,000,000 school building. As Chairperson of the New Building Committee, she worked closely with architects, townspeople, contractors, and even children to understand their needs for the building. Today the building stands as a model for such schools everywhere. Eight years ago Kretchmer came to Hollywood and, through persistence and charm, secured a studio position and worked her way up to Chief Auditor, where she oversaw budgets on several multimillion-dollar films. She enrolled in the Assistant Directors Training Program, which she recently completed, and is now the other candidate being considered for the position of Assistant Director of this new film.

What sets Bergquist apart from Kretchmer is her understanding of, and experience in, the creative elements of filmmaking.

An assistant Director (AD) advises the Director in key creative decisions: how to best structure and order the shooting schedule, how to begin and end scenes, and how best to shoot a scene or sequence. While the ultimate decision rests with the Director, the AD's input is vital. Like a caddy advising a golfer of the distance and terrain of the course, the AD's knowledge of the creative elements of filmmaking enhances her abilities in these tasks. Since a film's success often hinges on these creative decisions, the AD's contributions can be critical.

As an editor, Bergquist learned how a film is cut together and how the pieces must fit coherently. She cut her own films and won numerous awards, thus reflecting her understanding of the good creative choices. This special knowledge of film (which Kretchmer lacks)—how shots must match, how moods and sequences build upon each other—is an essential component in insuring the final success of any film.

ANOTHER APPROACH:

Read the following descriptions of Bergquist and Kretchmer, applicants for the job of Assistant Director on a major motion picture. *Then, in the space provided, write an argument for hiring either Bergquist or Kretchmer.* The following criteria are relevant to your decision:

- In addition to working closely with and advising the Director on creative decisions, the Assistant Director must work with all types of individuals—from stars to Teamster truck drivers—and elicit the best from every cast and crew member for the good of the motion picture.
- The Assistant Director is responsible for all the planning and organization—including paperwork, travel itinerary, meals, etc.—of the entire film project. He/she lays the groundwork for a successful "shoot."

BERGQUIST began her career in films as an Administrative Assistant to the president of a major film studio. As such, she often accompanied her employer in his wining and dining of stars, or to the set when problems arose. She doublechecked contracts, shooting schedules, cast and crew checks, and kept a close eye on the budget of several multimillion-dollar films. When her boss was subsequently fired due to a poor season of films, Bergquist was able to secure a position as Assistant Editor at the studio, helping several highly respected film editors "cut" feature films. It was here that she learned about the creative end of the business, and soon after became the chief editor of an hour-long studio documentary, which won several awards. After two years, Bergquist was accepted into the Assistant Directors Training Program, and is presently a candidate for Assistant Director of this new $15,000,000 motion picture.

KRETCHMER was a principal/teacher for 12 years before embarking on a film career. Not only did she teach math at the New York School for the Creative Arts, but she worked with parents in the community, the board of education, and local government representatives in securing financing for the $20,000,000 school building. As Chairperson of the New Building Committee, she worked closely with architects, townspeople, contractors, and even children to understand their needs for the building. Today the building stands as a model for such schools everywhere. Eight years ago Kretchmer came to Hollywood and, through persistence and charm, secured a studio position and worked her way up to Chief Auditor, where she oversaw budgets on several multimillion-dollar films. She enrolled in the Assistant Directors Training Program, which she recently completed, and is now the other candidate being considered for the position of Assistant Director of this new film.

Kretchmer has what Bergquist seriously lacks: the experience and ability to work well with all kinds of people—a crucial skill in the collaborative art/business of filmmaking.

Any film's lengthy end-credits attest to the huge number of people contributing talent—technicians, laborers, performing artists and others. As the Director's right-hand person, the Assistant Director (AD) must help orchestrate that effort. She must "read" the personalities of different individuals and know how to appeal to each ego to garner the best from each.

As Chairperson of a Building Committee, Kretchmer worked successfully with dozens of different personalities in pursuit of a common goal, not unlike a film project. In working with diverse personalities (parents, administrators, children, teachers, architects and builders), each with different goals, Kretchmer had to have a keen understanding of people and be able to know their strengths and limitations. This is precisely her most important task as a motion picture AD.

Working on the set with hundreds of different personalities requires a specially skilled individual: Kretchmer is that person.

REVIEW OF GENERAL TIPS

1. Read the topic question at least twice, *actively:* circle or mark the essential points of the question. Note the main question or parts to be discussed, the audience you are addressing, and the persona or position from which you are writing.

2. Remember to *prewrite,* or plan before you write. Spend at least five minutes organizing your thoughts by jotting notes, outlining, brainstorming, clustering, etc.

3. As you write, keep the flow of your writing going. Don't stop your train of thought to worry about the spelling of a word. You can fix little things later.

4. Leave a few minutes to reread and edit your paper after you finish writing. A careful rereading will often catch careless mistakes and errors in punctuation, spelling, etc., that you didn't have time to worry about as you wrote.

5. Remember that a good essay will be
- on topic,
- well organized,
- well developed with examples,
- grammatically sound with few errors,
- interesting to read, with a variety of sentence types,
- clear, neat, and easy to read.

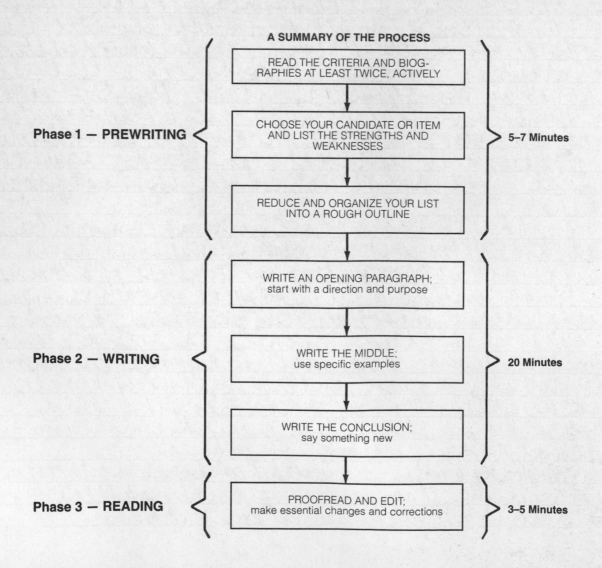

A SUMMARY OF THE PROCESS

Phase 1 — PREWRITING

READ THE CRITERIA AND BIOGRAPHIES AT LEAST TWICE, ACTIVELY

CHOOSE YOUR CANDIDATE OR ITEM AND LIST THE STRENGTHS AND WEAKNESSES

REDUCE AND ORGANIZE YOUR LIST INTO A ROUGH OUTLINE

5–7 Minutes

Phase 2 — WRITING

WRITE AN OPENING PARAGRAPH; start with a direction and purpose

WRITE THE MIDDLE; use specific examples

WRITE THE CONCLUSION; say something new

20 Minutes

Phase 3 — READING

PROOFREAD AND EDIT; make essential changes and corrections

3–5 Minutes

PRACTICE: WRITING SAMPLE

After reviewing the completed essays, try some practice on your own. We have provided sample questions and booklet-type pages.

Try following the steps we have suggested, varying them slightly, if necessary, to suit your personal style. Have an honest critic read and respond to each practice essay you complete.

WRITING SAMPLE TOPIC 1

Read the following description of Arbit and Blatas, candidates for your party's nomination to the city council. *Then, in the space provided, write an argument for nominating either Arbit or Blatas.* Use the information in this description and assume that two general policies guide your party's decision on nomination:

- Nominations are based upon a combination of the probable success in the election and party service.
- Party service includes seniority, committee work, and fund-raising.

Arbit, a Rumanian-American, has lived in the district and worked for the party for fifteen years. He is chairman of two key party committees and a member of two others. His fund-raising picnic, begun ten years ago, now raises at least $10,000 every year. Arbit is 47, a trial lawyer, with no prior experience in elective office. Twenty percent of the district is Rumanian-American, almost all of whom support the party in every election.

Blatas, of Hungarian background, moved to the district seven years ago. She has worked for the party for seven years as a member of several party committees, and as Arbit's assistant in arranging the fund-raising picnic. A graduate of law school, she is 35, and was recently promoted to director of the city's real estate research office. She narrowly lost an election for city assessor two years ago. Thirty-five percent of the voters in the district are Hungarian-American.

WRITING SAMPLE TOPIC 2

Read the following descriptions of Arnot and Brecht, applicants for the position of head chef at *Chez Moi*, a highly successful New York restaurant. *Then, in the space provided, write an argument for hiring either Arnot or Brecht*. The following criteria are relevant to your decision:

- The chef at *Chez Moi* must be able to socialize freely and to discuss each day's menu with the patrons.
- *Chez Moi's* reputation depends upon the remarkable range and originality of its seafood and its desserts.

Chef ARNOT was born in Normandy and trained in Paris. For fifteen years he has been the head chef at major international restaurants in Paris and Marseilles. While in Paris, he won competition among the city's pastry chefs four times. In Marseilles, his specialty was Mediterranean seafood. He is among the most respected chefs in the world, known equally for his inventive recipes for fish and his short temper. His English is competent, but slow and heavily accented. He has, for the first time, agreed to accept a position outside of France.

Chef BRECHT was born in Berlin and trained in Paris, London, and Rome. For the last five years, she has been the head chef in one of Chicago's most successful restaurants. Through her books and her television cooking programs, she has become the most widely known and most popular chef in America. She is especially renowned for her recipes for ice creams and sherbets. She has agreed to apply for the position at *Chez Moi* because of the restaurant's reputation and because it is located in New York, a center of the publishing and television industries.

WRITING SAMPLE TOPIC 3

Read the following descriptions of Selig and Druck, two applicants for the position of receptionist for the medical offices of four physicians (general practitioners). *Then, in the space provided, write an argument for hiring either Selig or Druck.* The following criteria are relevant to your decision:

- The receptionist must answer the phone, schedule appointments for each of the physicians, and relay messages from the physicians to their patients when necessary.
- The receptionist must screen patients over the phone, in order to decide whether to schedule an immediate appointment.

Selig has worked as a registered nurse for ten years and in the emergency room at City Hospital for the last eighteen months. Before this, she was the head nurse in a small suburban hospital staffed by twelve physicians and twenty nurses and aides. She recently decided to leave her position as an emergency room nurse and seek a job with more regular hours and duties. Since high school, Selig has spent two evenings each week counseling the distraught people who phone the free, state-supported "crisis hot line" for help. She has prevented a number of suicides by encouraging the caller to reveal his location and wait for help.

Druck recently moved into the area, leaving his position as office manager for a busy medical corporation in another state. He has long been involved in medical work, having completed two years of medical school before deciding that he was most interested in the business and personnel decisions associated with enhanced patient care. After a series of jobs manning the front office for various private practices, Druck accepted the managerial position only to discover that it kept him more out of touch with the patients themselves than he would like. Druck is a regular subscriber to the major medical journals.

WRITING SAMPLE TOPIC 4

The *Times-Herald*, a large metropolitan newspaper, is about to add a new strip to its comic page. The editorial board must decide between two features that do not now appear in any of the city's other newspapers. *In the space provided, write an argument to be presented to the editorial board in support of one of the two following comic strips.* Two considerations should guide your decision:

- The newspaper wishes to improve its reputation for serious journalism.
- The newspaper wishes to increase its circulation.

Described by *Time* magazine as "America's most beloved comic strip," *Tom Jordan, M.D.* is a serial that depicts the life of a handsome young doctor at a large New York hospital. It appears in more newspapers in the United States than any other comic. Its stories combine medical information, romance, and moral uplift. Each story takes thirty-two weeks to complete. An especially popular recent episode dealt with Tom Jordan's saving the life of an orphaned leukemia victim; others in the recent past have dealt with drug addiction among the very rich, kidney transplants, and anorexia. *Tom Jordan, M.D.* is the work of a group of four cartoonists.

Bart Pollard's comic, *D.C.*, was the first strip cartoon to win a Pulitzer Prize. Its satiric treatment of Democrats and Republicans, of clergymen, doctors, lawyers, and athletes, has at one time or another given such offense that a number of newspapers that had contracted to run the feature have refused to print it. In Washington, Pollard's *D.C.* is called the "comic strip that everyone hates, but everyone reads." A cabinet officer who closely resembled a character pilloried in the comic has recently filed a libel suit against Pollard. Readership of the strip is especially high on college campuses.

WRITING SAMPLE TOPIC 5

The Animal Protection Society must decide on a speaker to address its annual fund-raising dinner. *In the space provided, write an argument in support of one of the two following choices.* Two considerations guide your decision:

- The society must immediately raise as much money as possible to support an emergency airlift to save an endangered species of crane.
- The society wishes to increase the number of life members, subscribers who can be counted on to give money every year.

Jan Gilbert is a comedienne and the star of a popular television talk show. On her program, she frequently invites keepers from the San Diego Zoo, who bring with them lion cubs, talking mynah birds, lemurs, and other small animals that appeal to large audiences. A dog lover, she often appears in public and on television with her miniature poodle, which travels with her wherever she goes. She is an active fund-raiser for conservative political causes. Because of her love of animals, she has agreed to waive half of her usual personal appearance fee of $12,000.

Katrina Nelson is a distinguished zoologist. She is an adjunct research professor at Cambridge University and has spent fourteen years in Africa observing the behavior of packs of Cape hunting dogs, jackals, and hyenas. A film she made on the scavengers and predators of Africa has been shown on educational television stations. She is the author of five books, including one on the animals of Africa that have become extinct in this century. She is an experienced and skillful public speaker. Her lecture fee is $500.

WRITING SAMPLE TOPIC 6

Read the following descriptions of two 1-hour television series, *Love 'Em and Leave 'Em* and *Down and Out*, that are competing for a spot in the network lineup. *Then, in the space provided, write an argument for deciding which of the two the network should choose*. The following criteria are relevant to your decision:

- The only available time slot for the chosen series is 10 P.M. on a weeknight.
- Network executives prefer a series that can deal with controversial issues while providing action and adventure.

Love 'Em and Leave 'Em deals with a metropolitan newspaper columnist who writes a daily "advice to the lovelorn" column and often gets involved in the private lives and problems of those who write her letters. Her father is a criminal attorney, and her sister is a police lieutenant. The columnist holds a degree in psychology and provides free counseling a few hours a week at a halfway house for rehabilitated drug addicts. She is always arguing with the managing editor of the newspaper, who wants a column that is entertaining but not controversial.

Down and Out portrays the week-to-week lives of a minor league baseball team. Two members of the team work as private detectives during the off season and are always alert to "shady" situations. The owner of the team is a former U.S. senator who always preferred baseball to politics but still acts as a presidential advisor at times. The team players are an ethnic and racial mix; some are as young as eighteen and some in their early thirties; the private life and personal background of each individual player remain to be developed. The team manager, a former All-Star, has two sons on the team.

WRITING SAMPLE TOPIC 7

The Sundown Realty Company has purchased a large parcel of land for development in Date City. The company must decide between two building plans. *In the space provided, write an argument in support of one of the two plans.* Base your decision on the following considerations:

- The design of the development must be approved by an environmental commission that is likely to be unsympathetic to radical changes in the landscape.
- The construction must be completed, and at least half of the units sold, within eighteen months. All of the units must be sold within two years.

Plan One calls for the building of fifty free-standing one-story units distributed along the fairways of a newly constructed nine-hole golf course. Three of the nine holes will have small water hazards. Buyer studies of the area have shown clearly that the highest demand for new homes is for those on golf courses. The fifty houses will be well within the density limit set by the environmental committee, and none of the houses would be visible from outside the development. The units will be built of local wood and stone. Each will cost $200,000.

Plan Two calls for five multi-storied buildings, each containing twenty units built around an activities building, tennis courts, and pool. The five buildings will be placed far apart in natural wooded areas on the property. Only the top stories will be visible above the trees, and only a few trees on the property will have to be removed for the construction. The units will sell for $100,000 or $150,000 each, and will be constructed from aged brick.

WRITING SAMPLE TOPIC 8

Southwest Pacific University is facing a severe budget crisis and must make up for a short-fall of $1,000,000 in the next fiscal year. *In the space provided, write an argument for Plan A or Plan B.* Keep in mind that the Board of Trustees has determined that the savings must be made under the following conditions:

- Direct and indirect costs to the students should be avoided as much as possible.
- The quality of academic instruction at the school must in no way be compromised.

Plan A would discontinue several campus services that are now running at a loss, including all the food services on campus that are now subsidized by the university. Any student activities such as band, debate, drama, and men's and women's athletics, which are now financially dependent on the university, must become self-supporting, and student admission fees will be charged for all activities that are not operating at a profit. A fund-raising drive among parents and alumni is the first priority of the administration.

Plan B would freeze all faculty and staff salaries, and cancel all paid sabbatical leaves for two years. Throughout the university, a 10% reduction in non-academic staff will take place at once. Tuition fees will remain unchanged, but student users' fees will be assessed for laboratory equipment, printing costs, and computer time. Obtaining state and federal grants is the first priority of the administration.

WRITING SAMPLE TOPIC 9

The Black Hills County Art Museum, a small, well-run institution, must decide how to spend a large state grant. The money was given with the understanding that the museum would accomplish two objectives. *In the space provided, write an argument in favor of Plan A or Plan B.* Keep these objectives in mind:

- The museum will open an area for the display of Native American artifacts.
- The museum will substantially increase its revenues from memberships, contributions, and sales.

Plan A: The museum will use all of the money to construct a display space large and secure enough to attract several of the major popular traveling art exhibits each year. At present, the display space at the museum is too small to be used to present the art exhibits that attract attention in the national media. With the large university population in the area, there is a local audience for such shows, and with the new galleries, the museum could become the most important exhibition space in a six-state area. A leading modern architect has expressed interest in designing the new gallery at a greatly reduced fee. By selling some of the museum's permanent collection, space could be made available for Native American art exhibits.

Plan B: The museum will use the money to construct a new, small gallery for the display of Native American art, and to construct classrooms, a sculpture garden, a museum shop, and a restaurant. The museum has never sponsored a program of art education for either its adult supporters or local schoolchildren, but the many college teachers, along with the museum staff, would provide a fine core of instructors. The museum has never had a shop or a restaurant, though many of its wealthiest supporters have encouraged these additions. The sculpture garden would also serve as an ideal place to display the large Native American carvings that are too tall to be shown inside the buildings.

PART THREE

PRACTICE
Mastering Problem Types
and Time Pressures

Chapter

6

Model Test One

This chapter contains full-length Model Test One. It is geared to the format of the LSAT, and it is complete with answers and explanations. It is equivalent to the LSAT in question structure, number of questions, level of difficulty, and time allotments. (The questions used are not taken directly from the LSAT, as those questions are copyrighted and may not be reproduced.)

Model Test One should be taken under strict test conditions. The test ends with a 30-minute Writing Sample, which is not scored.

Section	Description	Number of Questions	Time Allowed
I	Reading Comprehension	28	35 minutes
II	Analytical Reasoning	24	35 minutes
III	Logical Reasoning	26	35 minutes
IV	Analytical Reasoning	24	35 minutes
V	Logical Reasoning	25	35 minutes
	Writing Sample		30 minutes
TOTALS:		127	3 hours 25 minutes

Now please turn to the next page, remove your answer sheets, and begin Model Test One.

ANSWER SHEET—MODEL TEST ONE
LAW SCHOOL ADMISSION TEST (LSAT)

Section I:
Reading Comprehension

1. Ⓐ Ⓑ Ⓒ Ⓓ Ⓔ
2. Ⓐ Ⓑ Ⓒ Ⓓ Ⓔ
3. Ⓐ Ⓑ Ⓒ Ⓓ Ⓔ
4. Ⓐ Ⓑ Ⓒ Ⓓ Ⓔ
5. Ⓐ Ⓑ Ⓒ Ⓓ Ⓔ
6. Ⓐ Ⓑ Ⓒ Ⓓ Ⓔ
7. Ⓐ Ⓑ Ⓒ Ⓓ Ⓔ
8. Ⓐ Ⓑ Ⓒ Ⓓ Ⓔ
9. Ⓐ Ⓑ Ⓒ Ⓓ Ⓔ
10. Ⓐ Ⓑ Ⓒ Ⓓ Ⓔ
11. Ⓐ Ⓑ Ⓒ Ⓓ Ⓔ
12. Ⓐ Ⓑ Ⓒ Ⓓ Ⓔ
13. Ⓐ Ⓑ Ⓒ Ⓓ Ⓔ
14. Ⓐ Ⓑ Ⓒ Ⓓ Ⓔ
15. Ⓐ Ⓑ Ⓒ Ⓓ Ⓔ
16. Ⓐ Ⓑ Ⓒ Ⓓ Ⓔ
17. Ⓐ Ⓑ Ⓒ Ⓓ Ⓔ
18. Ⓐ Ⓑ Ⓒ Ⓓ Ⓔ
19. Ⓐ Ⓑ Ⓒ Ⓓ Ⓔ
20. Ⓐ Ⓑ Ⓒ Ⓓ Ⓔ
21. Ⓐ Ⓑ Ⓒ Ⓓ Ⓔ
22. Ⓐ Ⓑ Ⓒ Ⓓ Ⓔ
23. Ⓐ Ⓑ Ⓒ Ⓓ Ⓔ
24. Ⓐ Ⓑ Ⓒ Ⓓ Ⓔ
25. Ⓐ Ⓑ Ⓒ Ⓓ Ⓔ
26. Ⓐ Ⓑ Ⓒ Ⓓ Ⓔ
27. Ⓐ Ⓑ Ⓒ Ⓓ Ⓔ
28. Ⓐ Ⓑ Ⓒ Ⓓ Ⓔ

Section II:
Analytical Reasoning

1. Ⓐ Ⓑ Ⓒ Ⓓ Ⓔ
2. Ⓐ Ⓑ Ⓒ Ⓓ Ⓔ
3. Ⓐ Ⓑ Ⓒ Ⓓ Ⓔ
4. Ⓐ Ⓑ Ⓒ Ⓓ Ⓔ
5. Ⓐ Ⓑ Ⓒ Ⓓ Ⓔ
6. Ⓐ Ⓑ Ⓒ Ⓓ Ⓔ
7. Ⓐ Ⓑ Ⓒ Ⓓ Ⓔ
8. Ⓐ Ⓑ Ⓒ Ⓓ Ⓔ
9. Ⓐ Ⓑ Ⓒ Ⓓ Ⓔ
10. Ⓐ Ⓑ Ⓒ Ⓓ Ⓔ
11. Ⓐ Ⓑ Ⓒ Ⓓ Ⓔ
12. Ⓐ Ⓑ Ⓒ Ⓓ Ⓔ
13. Ⓐ Ⓑ Ⓒ Ⓓ Ⓔ
14. Ⓐ Ⓑ Ⓒ Ⓓ Ⓔ
15. Ⓐ Ⓑ Ⓒ Ⓓ Ⓔ
16. Ⓐ Ⓑ Ⓒ Ⓓ Ⓔ
17. Ⓐ Ⓑ Ⓒ Ⓓ Ⓔ
18. Ⓐ Ⓑ Ⓒ Ⓓ Ⓔ
19. Ⓐ Ⓑ Ⓒ Ⓓ Ⓔ
20. Ⓐ Ⓑ Ⓒ Ⓓ Ⓔ
21. Ⓐ Ⓑ Ⓒ Ⓓ Ⓔ
22. Ⓐ Ⓑ Ⓒ Ⓓ Ⓔ
23. Ⓐ Ⓑ Ⓒ Ⓓ Ⓔ
24. Ⓐ Ⓑ Ⓒ Ⓓ Ⓔ

Section III:
Logical Reasoning

1. Ⓐ Ⓑ Ⓒ Ⓓ Ⓔ
2. Ⓐ Ⓑ Ⓒ Ⓓ Ⓔ
3. Ⓐ Ⓑ Ⓒ Ⓓ Ⓔ
4. Ⓐ Ⓑ Ⓒ Ⓓ Ⓔ
5. Ⓐ Ⓑ Ⓒ Ⓓ Ⓔ
6. Ⓐ Ⓑ Ⓒ Ⓓ Ⓔ
7. Ⓐ Ⓑ Ⓒ Ⓓ Ⓔ
8. Ⓐ Ⓑ Ⓒ Ⓓ Ⓔ
9. Ⓐ Ⓑ Ⓒ Ⓓ Ⓔ
10. Ⓐ Ⓑ Ⓒ Ⓓ Ⓔ
11. Ⓐ Ⓑ Ⓒ Ⓓ Ⓔ
12. Ⓐ Ⓑ Ⓒ Ⓓ Ⓔ
13. Ⓐ Ⓑ Ⓒ Ⓓ Ⓔ
14. Ⓐ Ⓑ Ⓒ Ⓓ Ⓔ
15. Ⓐ Ⓑ Ⓒ Ⓓ Ⓔ
16. Ⓐ Ⓑ Ⓒ Ⓓ Ⓔ
17. Ⓐ Ⓑ Ⓒ Ⓓ Ⓔ
18. Ⓐ Ⓑ Ⓒ Ⓓ Ⓔ
19. Ⓐ Ⓑ Ⓒ Ⓓ Ⓔ
20. Ⓐ Ⓑ Ⓒ Ⓓ Ⓔ
21. Ⓐ Ⓑ Ⓒ Ⓓ Ⓔ
22. Ⓐ Ⓑ Ⓒ Ⓓ Ⓔ
23. Ⓐ Ⓑ Ⓒ Ⓓ Ⓔ
24. Ⓐ Ⓑ Ⓒ Ⓓ Ⓔ
25. Ⓐ Ⓑ Ⓒ Ⓓ Ⓔ
26. Ⓐ Ⓑ Ⓒ Ⓓ Ⓔ

ANSWER SHEET—MODEL TEST ONE
LAW SCHOOL ADMISSION TEST (LSAT)

Section IV:
Analytical Reasoning

1. (A) (B) (C) (D) (E)
2. (A) (B) (C) (D) (E)
3. (A) (B) (C) (D) (E)
4. (A) (B) (C) (D) (E)
5. (A) (B) (C) (D) (E)
6. (A) (B) (C) (D) (E)
7. (A) (B) (C) (D) (E)
8. (A) (B) (C) (D) (E)
9. (A) (B) (C) (D) (E)
10. (A) (B) (C) (D) (E)
11. (A) (B) (C) (D) (E)
12. (A) (B) (C) (D) (E)
13. (A) (B) (C) (D) (E)
14. (A) (B) (C) (D) (E)
15. (A) (B) (C) (D) (E)
16. (A) (B) (C) (D) (E)
17. (A) (B) (C) (D) (E)
18. (A) (B) (C) (D) (E)
19. (A) (B) (C) (D) (E)
20. (A) (B) (C) (D) (E)
21. (A) (B) (C) (D) (E)
22. (A) (B) (C) (D) (E)
23. (A) (B) (C) (D) (E)
24. (A) (B) (C) (D) (E)

Section V:
Logical Reasoning

1. (A) (B) (C) (D) (E)
2. (A) (B) (C) (D) (E)
3. (A) (B) (C) (D) (E)
4. (A) (B) (C) (D) (E)
5. (A) (B) (C) (D) (E)
6. (A) (B) (C) (D) (E)
7. (A) (B) (C) (D) (E)
8. (A) (B) (C) (D) (E)
9. (A) (B) (C) (D) (E)
10. (A) (B) (C) (D) (E)
11. (A) (B) (C) (D) (E)
12. (A) (B) (C) (D) (E)
13. (A) (B) (C) (D) (E)
14. (A) (B) (C) (D) (E)
15. (A) (B) (C) (D) (E)
16. (A) (B) (C) (D) (E)
17. (A) (B) (C) (D) (E)
18. (A) (B) (C) (D) (E)
19. (A) (B) (C) (D) (E)
20. (A) (B) (C) (D) (E)
21. (A) (B) (C) (D) (E)
22. (A) (B) (C) (D) (E)
23. (A) (B) (C) (D) (E)
24. (A) (B) (C) (D) (E)
25. (A) (B) (C) (D) (E)

SECTION I
READING COMPREHENSION

Time—35 Minutes
28 Questions

Directions:
Read the passages and answer the questions following each passage by blackening the appropriate space on the answer sheet. You may refer back to the passages when answering the questions. Answer all questions on the basis of what is stated or implied.

Passage 1

Although statutory law (a law enacted by the legislature) expressly forbids strikes by government workers, the constitutional validity of these laws as well as their interpretative applications have been under attack in various cases, the most recent and most publicized case being that of the federal government air traffic controllers.

(5) The First Amendment to the United States Constitution guarantees the right of free speech. The constitutional issue to be resolved therefore is whether strikes are a form of "symbolic speech" or "symbolic conduct" that should be accorded the same degree of First Amendment protection as verbal communications. In a case that involved private rather than public employees, a Texas Court held that picketing as an incident to a labor dispute is a proper exercise of freedom of speech. The court went on

(10) to say that only a "clear and present danger of substantive evil will justify an abridgement of the right to picket." Later, the New Jersey state court concluded that even though picketing is protected by freedom of speech, this does not mean that statutes prohibiting strikes are constitutionally invalid. This case involved a constitutional interpretation of the New Jersey statute. The court stated that the justification of this statute is based on the ground of "clear and present danger" that would result to the

(15) state if the performance of functions of a public utility was ceased or impaired by a strike. Those in favor of no-strike clauses seem to concede that strikes are a form of symbolic speech that should be accorded the same degree of First Amendment protection as verbal speech. Their justification for upholding these clauses, is the "clear and present danger" doctrine. They tend to believe that strikes by government employees automatically present a "clear and present danger of substantive evil."

(20) However, according to the U.S. Supreme Court, legislatures cannot be relied upon to make a determination of what constitutes a "clear and present danger." In effect this is what happened when President Reagan ordered the firing of the air traffic controllers, based on the antistrike clause pronounced by Congress. The Supreme Court held that courts themselves must determine what constitutes a clear and present danger. The Supreme Court went on to say that mere public

(25) inconvenience or annoyance is not enough to constitute a clear and present danger. Thus, the public inconvenience and annoyance created by the curtailment of air traffic as a result of the controllers' strike may not be sufficient to constitute such a danger. The argument that a clear and present danger resulted from the emergency staffing of control towers by military and supervisory personnel is invalidated by the fact that the airlines have run safely since the strike.

(30) This is not to suggest that every employee should automatically have the right to strike. However, constitutional consideration of due process and freedom of speech should bar denying government workers, as a class, the right to strike. A close look should be taken at what actually constitutes a "clear and present danger of substantive evil." It is an evasion for courts to allow legislatures to prejudge all government services to be different for "strike" purposes than those provided by the private sector. The

(35) court itself should look at such factors as the nature of the service in determining whether particular no-strike clauses are constitutionally valid. The nature of the provider of the service (i.e., government v. private) is not a compelling justification for upholding no-strike clauses. Whereas it may be argued that it is in the public interest to deny government workers the right to strike because of the potential danger to our national security and safety, it should also be noted that they may be even more impaired as a

(40) result of having such prejudicial requirements as no-strike clauses. These clauses are likely to discourage some of the more intelligent and highly qualified individuals from seeking government

employment. However, as Judge Wright said, "If the right of public employees to strike, with all its political and social ramifications, is to be recognized and protected by the judiciary, it should be done by the Supreme Court, which has the power to reject established principles of law and the authority to (45) enforce such a sweeping rule."

The "abnormally dangerous working conditions" argument may be one way of getting around a no-strike clause. However, in using this argument, it is imperative to have well-documented evidence of such conditions. Employees may be properly discharged in accordance with a no-strike clause if later proof fails to support their good faith contentions that they walked off their jobs believing that their (50) working conditions were abnormally dangerous.

1. According to the passage, strikes by government workers are
   (A) constitutionally invalid
   (B) forbidden by statutory law
   (C) permissible when there is no danger of substantial evil
   (D) permissible when there is no public inconvenience or annoyance
   (E) permissible when there is no danger to national security and safety

2. If government workers as a class are denied the right to strike, it can be argued that they have been denied all of the following EXCEPT
   (A) due process
   (B) freedom of speech
   (C) the clear and present danger doctrine
   (D) redress from abnormally dangerous working conditions
   (E) an abridgment of the right to picket

3. According to the passage, the "clear and present danger" justification of forbidding a strike has been misapplied for all of the following reasons EXCEPT
   (A) the dangers should be determined by the executive branch
   (B) the dangers are often merely inconveniences
   (C) the danger should be determined by the courts
   (D) strikes by government workers do not automatically present dangers
   (E) the inconvenience caused by the air traffic controllers may not have been a danger

4. The fact that there was no rise in the number of airline accidents in the first six months after the firing and replacement of the striking air traffic controllers undermines the
   (A) government's argument that a strike would present a danger to the public
   (B) argument that the no-strike clause violates first amendment rights
   (C) argument that a strike is a form of symbolic speech
   (D) air traffic controllers' argument that they left their jobs because of dangerous working conditions
   (E) argument that no-strike clauses discourage more highly qualified individuals from applying for positions

5. Which of the following would strengthen the case of the dismissed air traffic controllers who claimed that they were subject to "abnormally dangerous working conditions" mentioned in line 46?

   (A) Since the replacement of the air traffic controllers, the number of airline accidents is virtually unchanged.
   (B) Since the replacement of the air traffic controllers, the number of flights that fail to leave or to arrive on time has increased by 40 percent.
   (C) Illness rates for the new employees are no different from the rates of the dismissed air traffic controllers.
   (D) Absences due to stress-related illness are 30 percent higher among air traffic controllers than any other group in the air transportation field.
   (E) Since the replacement of the air traffic controllers, the number of airline fatalities increased slightly.

6. The author of the passage objects to the current situation in which
   (A) all employees do not equally have the right to strike
   (B) the government regards national security more important than an individual's freedom
   (C) the Supreme Court avoids taking a position in its dealing with regret-to-strike cases
   (D) an unfair burden of proof is placed upon workers who leave jobs they believe to have unsafe working conditions
   (E) a false distinction is made between workers doing similar jobs for the government and private employees

7. According to the author, one of the harmful effects of the no-strike rule may be that
   (A) it deters the highly skilled from taking government jobs
   (B) it can be used as a precedent in the private sector
   (C) it places too much power in the hands of the executive and legislative branches of the government
   (D) it prevents the courts from determining whether or not particular no-strike clauses are valid
   (E) it forces some workers to suffer abnormally dangerous working conditions with no means of redress

Passage 2

In ancient Rome "orient" meant the direction toward the rising sun because "orient" means "rising" in Latin. For us it may mean as much as to tell what we are, where we are, whither we would go, and how we propose to get there. Here, then, is our orientation: we are English-speaking human beings; we live in a world full of conflict and distrust; we go in pursuit of the good life, which is liberty and happiness; and we set forth believing that the best way to do it is to use our heads, and to use them as a competent engineer might use a delicate instrument with appropriate care and skill. If you proposed to be a mechanical engineer, you would accept the challenge of the mathematical discipline as a matter of course; you would acknowledge the extreme utility of the slide rule and all it represents. The principles and procedures we invite you to consider stand in the same vital relationship to you if you would be civilized and free. They appear to us to offer the only solid ground upon which free men may ultimately stand between their loved homes and war's desolation—be the war within these homes or on distant shores or hilltops.

We have commented thus emphatically upon what seems to us the desperately important connection between freedom and language because we wish to make it clear at the start that this connection presents a philosophy of life as well as a system for controlling the most characteristically human activity in it.

Now as language is the most characteristic sort of human behavior, so it is the most imitative, the most conventional, of all behavior. We might, therefore, study it as a social discipline. Of words we might ask many questions: "What do other people do with them?" "How do others arrange them—particularly the 'best people'?" "What is 'correct'?" "What are the 'rules'?" This is etiquette. It is critically important sometimes and has to do with such things as usage and grammar, "split" infinitives and the agreement of nouns and verbs; it frowns upon comma faults and misspellings. People call it "composition-rhetoric." You scorn it at your peril.

But in a democracy science is more vital than etiquette. Progress takes precedence over protocol. We shall leave important tasks undone or even unattempted if we dally overlong in getting democrats to say "pre-SEED-ence" instead of "PRESS-a-dence." We believe that the psychological approach to language study is more worthy than the conventional one, but we also know that if you become genuinely interested in the wonderful phenomena of linguistic behavior, much knowledge of the etiquette will come to you.

Be this as it may, our approach is the engineer's approach. We study not rhetoric or philology but linguistic engineering. We shall not be content with the mere description of language behavior or even the fascinating story of its historical development; we seek rather to make our language behave. Our study is really a branch of applied psychology; and like most other practical activities, it is an art which calls for a sound working knowledge of the anatomy and physiology of the subject. In our case, that subject is the conscious mind, which we here define as the highest function of the brain.

8. The primary purpose of this passage is to
   - (A) establish psychological rules for language
   - (B) develop the connection between freedom and language
   - (C) establish the author's orientation
   - (D) set aside the rules of grammar and usage
   - (E) replace mechanical engineering with language study

9. The author believes that the ability most essential for attaining the "good life" is
   - (A) intellectual ability
   - (B) skill in elocution
   - (C) familiarity with the principles and procedures of one's chosen field
   - (D) the ability to remain free
   - (E) scientific ability

10. Which of the following is consistent with the statement in the second paragraph?
    - (A) Speaking freely is related to speaking philosophically.
    - (B) Understanding how language works helps one to attain liberty and to think philosophically.
    - (C) Those who are most adept at language are most free.
    - (D) Those who can control the language of others are most free.
    - (E) Wars are based on ignorance.

11. The author creates an analogy between
    - (A) psychology and linguistics
    - (B) freedom and language
    - (C) correctness and pronunciation
    - (D) the mechanical engineer and the linguistic engineer
    - (E) etiquette and democracy

12. We may infer from the passage that the study of language is related to the
    - (A) study of the brain
    - (B) study of diverse practical activities
    - (C) study of politics
    - (D) study of ancient cultures
    - (E) study of liberty and happiness

13. The author concludes that learning the etiquette of language is a result of
    - (A) imitating others
    - (B) accepting social discipline
    - (C) becoming interested in linguistic behavior
    - (D) studying the practice of the "best people"
    - (E) taking a course in composition-rhetoric

14. One of the reasons for taking a psychological rather than a conventional approach to language study is that
    - (A) the psychological approach is an art rather than a skill
    - (B) the conventional approach is not interesting
    - (C) correct usage is unrelated to utility
    - (D) conventions are always changing
    - (E) conventional study concentrates on correctness at the expense of progress

Passage 3

Video display terminals (VDTs), those ubiquitous cathode-ray tube devices used with word processors, computers, radar screens, and even many video games, are clearly hazardous to the health of a certain, substantial number of operators unless adequate precautions are taken. Frequent, prolonged use of these devices without such protection produces a curiously varied assortment of
(5) symptoms, most of which initially appear to be minor, but can become progressively more serious with time spent operating VDTs.

Moreover, video terminal environments are also suspected of causing gestation problems at certain stages of pregnancy, and of contributing to the formation of irreversible cataracts in the lens of the eye. These latter suspicions are based on very suggestive statistical evidence, which, to my knowledge, has
(10) not yet been verified under laboratory conditions to the satisfaction of federal health authorities. Yet, in view of the statistical evidence, the authorities cannot deny the possibility; until the cause-and-effect relationship has been established in accordance with the standards of scientific methodology (i.e., double-blind tests on sufficient number of controlled subjects under rigid protocols), they can only state that they have not seen sufficient evidence—and reject such evidence as does not meet official
(15) standards without weighing it.

So the issue of employer liability in the case of Workers' Compensation claims may well rest on the weight and acceptability of existing evidence in the minds of a judge or jurors, who must form their own opinions with or without the benefit of a firm position by the constituted authorities.

The following factors bear on the question of liability when a video display operator claims to have
(20) been damaged by these occupational hazards:

—The National Institute of Occupational Safety and Health (NIOSH) has repeatedly sanctioned or issued statements to the effect that there is no evidence of health hazards arising from video display technology, and any symptoms developed in using these devices can be attributed to other factors such as job stress, posture, furniture, and lighting.

(25) —The Occupational Safety and Health Administration (OSHA), a regulatory agency, is unable to initiate regulatory action without recommendations from NIOSH or other responsible agencies.

—VDT manufacturers understandably deny the existence of intrinsic health hazards on the basis of the position adopted by NIOSH.

—Affected workers and their labor organizations insist that VDT health hazards exist and they are
(30) suffering in consequence.

—The statistical evidence, unrecognized by federal health authorities, is so strong that a number of state legislatures are contemplating severe regulatory measures for the protection of operators— palliative, unproven measures modeled after those adopted in other countries to deal with these problems.

(35) —American employers deny liability on the basis of the current federal government position, and strenuously object to state government moves to legislate constraints on working conditions that would have an immediate adverse impact on employee productivity. They are more vocal on the latter problem, because the liability issue falls on their Workers' Compensation insurers.

—Lastly, but very significantly, there are inexpensive devices on the market that effectively protect
(40) VDT operators from the consequences of these real, but unacknowledged hazards. Most employers are not aware of the existence of either the hazards or the protective devices, and therein lies an essential issue of jurisprudence: willful negligence.

The official position of "insufficient evidence" must be taken as ambiguous or indeterminate; after all, the government has some good legal counselors, too. So the flat denial of VDT hazards by employers,
(45) insurers, manufacturers, and other interested parties, when made, is based on a reaching and imprecise interpretation of the official position of the federal government. Therefore, presumably those who make such an interpretation should be liable for the consequences—at least in my legally unqualified view.

15. The best title for this passage would be
- (A) Employer Liability in Video Display Operators' Health Complaints
- (B) The Dangers to Health of Video Display Environments
- (C) Governmental Sanctions and Video Display Health Hazards
- (D) Video Display Environments and Employer Liability
- (E) Are Video Display Terminals Hazardous to Your Health?

16. The author of the passage believes that unprotected exposure to video display terminals
- (A) is clearly dangerous to the health of all people
- (B) is clearly dangerous to the health of some people
- (C) might prove not to be dangerous to health
- (D) is not dangerous to health
- (E) has been proven to be dangerous to health

17. That video terminal environments cause irreversible cataracts in humans
- (A) is contradicted by potent statistical evidence
- (B) has been verified to the satisfaction of the National Institute of Occupational Safety and Health
- (C) has not yet been verified by double-blind tests on a large sample
- (D) is attested to by federal health authorities
- (E) is affirmed by the Occupational Safety and Health Administration

18. We can infer from the passage that the position of the National Institute of Occupational Safety and Health on the hazards of video display terminals is firmly supported by
- (A) the Occupational Safety and Health Administration
- (B) video display terminal manufacturers
- (C) the labor organizations of workers in video display terminal environments
- (D) manufacturers of devices to protect VDT operators
- (E) state legislatures considering controls on VDT working conditions

19. The author argues in lines 37–38 that "They [employers] are more vocal on the latter problem, because the liability issue falls on their Workers' Compensation insurers" because
- (A) the employers deny liability on the basis of the federal government's position on the absence of hazard
- (B) the employers believe federal laws should preempt state regulations
- (C) the employers believe the state should have the power to regulate an industry within its borders
- (D) the employers are more concerned with productivity than with the possibility of lawsuits
- (E) there is no likelihood of losing a worker's compensation case so long as the government denies that a hazard exists

20. The passage suggests that the author believes the government's handling of the potential dangers of the video display terminals has been
- (A) illegal
- (B) correct
- (C) judicious
- (D) unscientific
- (E) evasive

21. Of which of the following possible actions would the author of the passage probably disapprove?
  (A)   the immediate distribution of information about the hazards of video display terminals
  (B)   the immediate distribution of information about the protective devices
  (C)   strict state regulatory measures
  (D)   OSHA regulatory actions on video display terminals
  (E)   wider distribution of the NIOSH views of the health hazards

Passage 4

In science, as elsewhere, we meet the assumptions of convenience and expedience, such as equations that assume frictionless machines or chemicals in a pure state. But by far the most important function of langugage in the development of scientific understanding and control of the world about us is the use of a kind of assumption called *hypothesis* at first, *theory* in a more developed state, and *law* when its implications have been extensively corroborated. A hypothesis resembles other assumptions in that it may be either true or false and may be used as the premise of rational action; otherwise it differs radically as to function and purpose. Hypotheses are employed experimentally in the search for truth. Without them the so-called scientific method is not possible. The reason for this is not always readily grasped and will now be illustrated in some detail.

Suppose, for example, that you are about to prepare an account of some fairly complex subject, such as the history of marriage. As soon as you have arrived at a clear working definition of your topic, you begin the collection of data. Now a *datum* is an item of some sort regarded as relevant to your problem. But everything is in some way related to everything else, and since you cannot possibly consider all the facts related to marriage, you must limit the field of relevance in some practical, arbitrary manner. Let us assume that you are at work on the status of marriage in modern urban society; perhaps you may attempt to discover to what extent the institution persists because it is biologically useful, economically expedient, socially convenient, religiously compulsory, or merely psychologically traditional. To proceed thus is to set up a fivefold hypothesis that enables you to gather from the innumerable items cast up by the sea of experience upon the shores of your observation only the limited number of relevant data—relevant, that is, to one or more of the five factors of your hypothesis. The hypothesis (the reference of the symbol *hypothesis*) is like a light by means of which we search for truth; but it is a colored light that may render invisible the very object we seek. That is why, after a fair trial, we must not hesitate to abandon one color for another. When our hypothesis possesses the proper color and intensity, it will reveal some of the facts as data, which may then be further studied and verified as signs of truth.

As the evidence in favor of a hypothesis (the thing again, not the word) accumulates to a convincing degree, we frequently symbolize the fact with the term *theory*. Thus, semantically, a theory is the name of a hypothesis that has outgrown its experimental short pants. With Charles Darwin, *biological evolution* was a hypothesis; in contemporary science it is a theory that no rational observer, however cautious, hesitates to accept.

When predictions based on the implications of a theory are continually borne out by observation, the relation symbolized is still further elevated to the status of a *law or natural law*. The abstraction "law" is a dangerous one to employ because it implies that the mind has finally arrived at the truth, ultimate and eternal. Thus, the eyes of science become myopic and lose the power to discover old errors and discern new truths.

22. The author's primary purpose is to
  (A)   note the progress in understanding since Darwin's time
  (B)   define and discuss some basic scientific terms
  (C)   develop a hypothesis
  (D)   argue for the value of scientific truth
  (E)   criticize the scientific method

23. We may infer that the author would have difficulty accepting which of the following statements?
    (A)   The discovery of old errors may lead to new truths.
    (B)   The Darwinian theory was once a hypothesis.
    (C)   The establishment of natural laws is the final goal of science.
    (D)   It is sometimes advisable to abandon a hypothesis.
    (E)   A hypothesis may be either true or false.

24. On two occasions, the author follows the word "hypothesis" with a parenthetical remark that serves to
    (A)   diminish the value of scientific hypotheses
    (B)   stress the value of symbolism in science
    (C)   demonstrate that the term presents semantic problems
    (D)   stress the difference between a hypothesis and a theory
    (E)   stress the difference between the term and what it stands for

25. According to the passage, the factor that distinguishes a hypothesis from a theory is the
    (A)   passage of time
    (B)   goal of the scientist
    (C)   method of the scientist
    (D)   relevance of the investigation
    (E)   convincingness of the evidence

26. The author would agree with which of the following statements?
    (A)   Hypotheses and truth are mutually exclusive.
    (B)   "Hypothesis," "theory," and "law" are synonymous terms.
    (C)   Language hinders the development of scientific understanding.
    (D)   Hypotheses are more important for science than are equations.
    (E)   Most people understand the importance of hypotheses to the scientific method.

27. We may infer from the passage that a hypothesis is always
    (A) objective   (B) subjective   (C) the wrong color   (D) fivefold   (E) useful

28. The author assumes that the relationship between hypotheses and the scientific method is
    (A)   only a theory
    (B)   not commonly understood
    (C)   not significant
    (D)   a product of evolution
    (E)   apparent to most people

STOP

IF YOU FINISH BEFORE TIME IS UP, CHECK YOUR WORK ON THIS SECTION OF THE TEST ONLY. DO NOT GO TO THE NEXT SECTION OF THE TEST UNTIL TIME IS UP FOR THIS SECTION.

SECTION II
ANALYTICAL REASONING

Time—35 Minutes
24 Questions

Directions:
In this section you will be given groups of questions based on different sets of conditions. Drawing a simple diagram may be helpful in answering some of the questions. You are to choose the best answer and mark the corresponding space on your answer sheet.

Questions 1–6

The Bell Canyon Condominium is a four-story building with a single penthouse apartment on the fourth floor. There are two apartments on each of the three other floors. The apartments are owned by A, B, C, D, E, F, and G.

A's apartment is on one of the floors higher than B's.
C's apartment is on one of the floors lower than D's.
C's apartment is on one of the floors lower than E's.
F and G's apartments are on the same floor.

1. Which of the following could be the owner of the penthouse?
    (A) B   (B) C   (C) E   (D) F   (E) G

2. If F's apartment is on the second floor, which of the following must be true?
    (A)   C's apartment is on the first floor.
    (B)   D's apartment is on the third floor.
    (C)   A's apartment is on the fourth floor.
    (D)   G's apartment is on the first floor.
    (E)   B's apartment is on the third floor.

3. If D owns the penthouse apartment, on which floor or floors could G's apartment be located?
    (A)   the first floor only
    (B)   the second floor only
    (C)   the third floor only
    (D)   the second or the third floor
    (E)   the first, second, or third floor

4. If D's and E's apartments are on the same floor, which of the following must be true?
    (A)   D and E are on the third floor.
    (B)   D and E are on the second floor.
    (C)   A is on the fourth floor.
    (D)   B and C are on the first floor.
    (E)   F and G are on the second floor.

5. If C's apartment is on the first floor, and A is the owner of the penthouse, which of the following must be true?
    (A)   G's apartment is on the third floor.
    (B)   D's apartment is on the second floor.
    (C)   E's apartment is on the second floor.
    (D)   B's apartment is on the first floor.
    (E)   F's apartment is on the second floor.

6. Which of the following is possible?
(A) A and C are on the same floor.
(B) A and E are on the same floor.
(C) A is on the first floor.
(D) D is on the first floor.
(E) C is on the fourth floor.

Questions 7–12

A scientist starts experimenting with four chemicals—Alpha, Beta, Theta, and Zeta. These chemicals combine in the following ways:

(1) Alpha combines with Beta, giving Zeta.
(2) Theta combines with Zeta, giving Beta.
(3) Zeta combines with Beta, giving Alpha.
(4) Beta combines with Theta, giving Omega.
(5) Theta is formed only when Alpha and Zeta combine.
(6) Alpha combines with Theta, giving Zeta.
(7) The order of the combinations makes no difference in their outcome.

7. Omega may be formed from a combination of
(A) Theta and Beta   (B) Alpha and Beta   (C) Beta and Zeta
(D) Theta and Zeta   (E) Alpha and Theta

8. Beta may be involved in the combination if the outcome is
(A) Alpha or Theta   (B) Alpha, Omega, or Zeta   (C) Beta
(D) Beta, Theta, or Zeta   (E) Alpha, Beta, or Theta

9. If Omega combines with Zeta, the outcome is
(A) Alpha   (B) Beta   (C) Theta   (D) Zeta   (E) cannot be determined

10. Which of the following must be true?
(A) Zeta and Theta combine to give Beta.
(B) Beta and Zeta combine to give Omega.
(C) Alpha and Beta combine to give Theta.
(D) Theta and Alpha combine to give Beta.
(E) Alpha and Zeta combine to give Omega.

11. If the outcome of Alpha and Beta combine with the outcome of Alpha and Zeta, the result is
(A) Alpha   (B) Beta   (C) Omega   (D) Theta   (E) Zeta

12. If Omega combines with Theta, the outcome is Zeta or Theta. Then the outcome of a combination of Omega and Theta is similar to the outcome of
(A) Alpha with any other
(B) Beta with any other
(C) Theta with any other
(D) Zeta with any other
(E) Beta with Zeta

Questions 13–19

Three division office managers, Fred, Al, and Cynthia, draw office assistants each day from the clerical and typing pools available to them. The clerical pool consists of Lyndia, Jim, Dennis, and Sylvia. The typing pool consists of Edra, Gene, and Helen. The office assistants are selected according to the following conditions:

Fred always needs at least one typist, but never more than two assistants.
Al always needs at least two assistants, but never more than three.
Sylvia or Gene and one other assistant always work for Cynthia.
Gene and Lyndia always work together.
Dennis and Edra will not work together.
No more than two typists work for the same manager, but all three typists must work each day.

13. If Gene works for Fred and all of the assistants work, then which of the following must be FALSE?
  (A)   Jim works for Cynthia.
  (B)   Sylvia works for Cynthia.
  (C)   Lyndia works for Fred.
  (D)   Dennis works for Al.
  (E)   Edra works for Al.

14. If Sylvia doesn't work for Cynthia, then which of the following must be true?
  (A)   Edra works for Fred.
  (B)   Gene works for Al.
  (C)   Lyndia works for Cynthia.
  (D)   Dennis works for Al.
  (E)   Helen works for Cynthia.

15. Assume that Lyndia and Jim work for Al. Which of the following must be true?
  (A)   Gene works for Al.
  (B)   Edra works for Cynthia.
  (C)   Helen works for Fred.
  (D)   Edra words for Fred.
  (E)   Helen works for Cynthia.

16. Assume that Sylvia and Jim work for Al. If all of the assistants work, then which of the following must be true?
  (A)   Edra works for Al.
  (B)   Gene works for Fred.
  (C)   Lyndia works for Al.
  (D)   Helen works for Fred.
  (E)   Dennis works for Fred.

17. Which of the following must be FALSE?
  (A)   Helen and Edra never work for Cynthia on the same day.
  (B)   Edra can work for Cynthia.
  (C)   Dennis and Gene never work for Fred on the same day.
  (D)   Jim and Sylvia never work for Fred on the same day.
  (E)   Lyndia and Sylvia can work for Al on the same day.

18. If Jim works for Cynthia and all of the assistants work, then
  (A)   Dennis works for Al.
  (B)   Edra works for Al.
  (C)   Helen works for Al.
  (D)   Lyndia works for Al.
  (E)   Sylvia works for Fred.

19. Assume that Al needs only two assistants and Fred needs only one assistant. If Helen works for Fred, then which of the following must be true?
  (A)   Jim works for Al.
  (B)   Sylvia doesn't work.
  (C)   Dennis doesn't work.
  (D)   Edra works for Al.
  (E)   Edra works for Cynthia.

Questions 20–24

In a certain culture, people have either blue eyes or green eyes; also, they have either red hair or brown hair.

All males have either blue eyes or brown hair, or both.

All females have either green eyes or red hair, or both.

Male children always retain both of the father's characteristics for eyes and hair.

All female children retain only one of their father's traits and the other of their mother's traits for eyes and hair.

20. If all the children born of a blue-eyed, brown-haired male each have blue eyes and red hair, then which of the following must be true?
(A)   Their mother has green eyes.
(B)   None of the children are girls.
(C)   Their mother has blue eyes.
(D)   They have a red-haired mother.
(E)   They have a brown-haired mother.

21. A blue-eyed, brown-haired male and a blue-eyed, red-haired female marry (first generation) and many years later are blessed with one grandchild. This grandchild (third generation) has red hair and green eyes. Which of the following must be true?
(A)   The child of the first generation is a male.
(B)   The grandchild is a male.
(C)   If the child of the first generation is female, she has brown hair.
(D)   The grandchild's father has red hair.
(E)   The father from the second generation has green eyes.

22. A blue-eyed, brown-haired male and a green-eyed, red-haired female have a child. All of the following are possible characteristics of the child EXCEPT
(A)   green eyes, brown hair
(B)   red hair, blue eyes
(C)   green eyes, red hair
(D)   blue eyes, brown hair
(E)   all are possible

23. A green-eyed male
(A)   may have red hair
(B)   may have brown hair
(C)   must have red hair
(D)   must have brown hair
(E)   has the same hair color as his mother

24. Two blue-eyed people get married. If their child has red hair, it must be true that
(A)   the child has brown eyes
(B)   the mother has red hair
(C)   the child is a male
(D)   the child is a female
(E)   the father has brown hair

STOP

IF YOU FINISH BEFORE TIME IS UP, CHECK YOUR WORK ON THIS SECTION OF THE TEST ONLY.
DO NOT GO ON TO THE NEXT SECTION OF THE TEST UNTIL TIME IS UP FOR THIS SECTION.

SECTION III
LOGICAL REASONING

Time—35 Minutes
26 Questions

Directions:
In this section you will be given brief statements or passages and will be required to evaluate the reasoning involved. In some instances, more than one choice will appear to be a possible answer. You are to choose the *best* answer. Use common sense and reasonableness in making your selection; then mark the proper space on the answer sheet.

Questions 1–2 refer to the following passage.

Chariots of Fire may have caught some professional critics off guard in 1982 as the Motion Picture Academy's choice for an Oscar as the year's best film, but it won wide audience approval as superb entertainment.

Refreshingly, *Chariots of Fire* features an exciting story, enchanting English and Scottish scenery, a beautiful musical score, and appropriate costumes.

All of these attractions are added to a theme that extols traditional religious values—without a shred of offensive sex, violence, or profanity.

Too good to be true? See *Chariots of Fire* and judge for yourself.

Those who condemn the motion picture industry for producing so many objectionable films can do their part by patronizing wholesome ones, thereby encouraging future Academy Award judges to recognize and reward decency.

1. The author of the above passage implicitly defines which of the following terms?
(A) objectionable   (B) appropriate   (C) patronizing   (D) Oscar   (E) professional

2. Which of the following is a basic assumption underlying the final sentence of the passage?
(A) Academy judges are not decent people.
(B) The popularity of a film influences academy judges.
(C) Future academy judges will be better than past ones.
(D) There are those who condemn the motion picture industry.
(E) *Chariots of Fire* is a patronizing film.

3. *Andy*: All teachers are mean.
Bob: That is not true. I know some doctors who are mean too.

Bob's answer demonstrates that he thought Andy to mean that
(A) all teachers are mean
(B) some teachers are mean
(C) doctors are meaner than teachers
(D) teachers are meaner than doctors
(E) only teachers are mean

4. Theodore Roosevelt was a great hunter. He was the mighty Nimrod of his generation. He had the physical aptitude and adventurous spirit of the true frontiersman. "There is delight," he said, "in the hardy life of the open; in long rides, rifle in hand; in the thrill of the fight with dangerous game." But he was more than a marksman and tracker of beasts, for he brought to his sport the intellectual curiosity and patient observation of the natural scientist.

Which of the following would most weaken the author's concluding contention?
(A) Theodore Roosevelt never studied natural science.
(B) Actually, Theodore Roosevelt's sharpshooting prowess was highly exaggerated.

(C)   Theodore Roosevelt always used native guides when tracking game.
(D)   Theodore Roosevelt was known to leave safaris if their first few days were unproductive.
(E)   Theodore Roosevelt's powers of observation were significantly hampered by his near-sightedness.

5. The following is an excerpt from a letter sent to a law school applicant:

"Thank you for considering our school to further your education. Your application for admission was received well before the deadline and was processed with your admission test score and undergraduate grade report.

"We regret to inform you that you cannot be admitted for the fall semester. We have had to refuse admission to many outstanding candidates because of the recent cut in state funding of our program.

"Thank you for your interest in our school and we wish you success in your future endeavors."

Which of the following can be deduced from the above letter?
(A)   The recipient of the letter did not have a sufficiently high grade point average to warrant admission to this graduate program.
(B)   The recipient of the letter was being seriously considered for a place in the evening class.
(C)   The law school sending the letter could not fill all the places in its entering class due to a funding problem.
(D)   Criteria other than test scores and grade reports were used in determining the size of the entering class.
(E)   The school sending the letter is suffering severe financial difficulties.

Questions 6–7 refer to the following passage.

At birth we have no self-image. We cannot distinguish anything from the confusion of light and sound around us. From this beginning of no-dimension, we gradually begin to differentiate our body from our environment and develop a sense of identity, with the realization that we are a separate and independent human being. We then begin to develop a conscience, the sense of right and wrong. Further, we develop social consciousness, where we become aware that we live with other people. Finally, we develop a sense of values, which is our overall estimation of our worth in the world.

6. Which of the following would be the best completion of this passage?
(A)   The sum total of all these developments we call the self-image or the self-concept.
(B)   This estimation of worth is only relative to our value system.
(C)   Therefore, our social consciousness is dependent on our sense of values.
(D)   Therefore, our conscience keeps our sense of values in perspective.
(E)   The sum total of living with other people and developing a sense of values makes us a total person.

7. The author of this passage would most likely agree with which of the following?
(A)   Children have no self-dimension.
(B)   Having a conscience necessitates the ability to differentiate between right and wrong.
(C)   Social consciousness is our most important awareness.
(D)   Heredity is predominant over environment in development.
(E)   The ability to distinguish the difference between moral issues depends on the overall dimension of self-development.

8. Opportunity makes the thief.
Without thieves there would be no crime.
Without opportunity there would be no crime.

Which of the following most weakens the statements above?
(A)   Thieves wait for opportunities.
(B)   Without crime there would be no opportunity.
(C)   Thieves are not the only criminals.
(D)   Some crimes carry greater penalties.
(E)   Many thieves are not caught.

Questions 9–10 refer to the following passage.

In a report released last week, a government-funded institute concluded that there is "over-whelming" evidence that violence on television leads to criminal behavior by children and teenagers.
The report based on an extensive review of several hundred research studies conducted during the 1970s, is an update of a 1972 Surgeon General's report that came to similar conclusions.

9. Which of the following is the most convincing statement in support of the argument in the first paragraph above?
(A)   A 50-state survey of the viewing habits of prison inmates concluded that every inmate watches at least 2 hours of violent programming each day.
(B)   A 50-state survey of the viewing habits of convicted adolescents shows that each of them had watched at least 2 hours of violent programming daily since the age of 5.
(C)   One juvenile committed a murder that closely resembled a crime portrayed on a network series.
(D)   The 1972 Surgeon General's report was not nearly as extensive as this more recent study.
(E)   Ghetto residents who are burglarized most often report the theft of a television set.

10. The argument above is most weakened by its vague use of the word
(A) violence   (B) government   (C) extensive   (D) update   (E) overwhelming

Questions 11–12 require you to complete the missing portions of the following passage by selecting from five alternatives the one that best fits the context of the passage.

It may be that sensation is the most primitive nervous activity, that in the evolutionary process certain sensations or combinations of sensations may develop the intensities which we know as affects and that those affects when connected with observed causes, or more properly with observations that are taken to be causes, become in the higher animals the complex patterns we know as (11) _____. If such is the case, then an emotion is simply an intense sensation complex with a logical component. This would imply that only a symbol-using animal can have emotions. Of course, his symbols may be private symbols and even (12) _____.

11. This sentence would be best completed with the words
(A) emotional intentions   (B) emotional behavior   (C) unintentional reactions
(D) unconquerable fears   (E) emotional sensation

12. This sentence would be best completed with the word
(A) unintelligible   (B) illogical   (C) nonlingual   (D) irrational   (E) nonsensical

13.   The study of village communities has become one of the fundamental methods of discussing the ancient history of institutions. It would be out of the question here to range over the whole field of

human society in search for communal arrangements of rural life. It will be sufficient to confine the present inquiry to the varieties presented by nations of Aryan race, not because greater importance is to be attached to these nations than to other branches of humankind, although this view might also be reasonably urged, but principally because the Aryan race in its history has gone through all sorts of experiences, and the data gathered from its historical life can be tolerably well ascertained. Should the road be sufficiently cleared in this particular direction, it will not be difficult to connect the results with similar researches in other racial surroundings.

Which of the following, if true, most weakens the author's conclusion?
(A)   Information about the Aryan race is no more conclusive than information about any other ethnic group.
(B)   The experiences and lifestyle of Aryans are uniquely different from those of other cultures.
(C)   The Aryan race is no more important than any other race.
(D)   The historical life of the Aryans dates back only 12 centuries.
(E)   Aryans lived predominantly in villages, while today 90 percent of the world population live predominantly in or around major cities.

14. Although any reasonable modern citizen of the world must abhor war and condemn senseless killing, we must also agree that honor is more valuable than life. Life, after all, is transient, but honor is _____.

Which of the following most logically completes the passage above?
(A) sensible   (B) real   (C) eternal   (D) of present value   (E) priceless

Questions 15–16 refer to the following statements.

Bill said, "All dogs bark. This animal does not bark. Therefore, it is not a dog."

15. Which of the following most closely parallels the logic of this statement?
(A)   All rocks are hard. This lump is hard. Therefore, it may be a rock.
(B)   All foreign language tests are difficult. This is not a foreign language test. Therefore, it is not difficult.
(C)   All Blunder automobiles are poorly built. Every auto sold by Joe was poorly built. Therefore, Joe sells Blunder automobiles.
(D)   Rocks beat scissors, scissors beat paper, and paper beats rocks. Therefore, it is best to choose paper.
(E)   All paint smells. This liquid does not smell. Therefore, it is not paint.

16. Which of the following would weaken Bill's argument the most?
(A)   Animals other than dogs bark.
(B)   Some dogs cannot bark.
(C)   Dogs bark more than cockatiels.
(D)   You can train a dog not to bark.
(E)   You can train birds to bark.

17. No one cheats on all the exams he takes. Some people cheat on most of the exams they take. Most cheat on some of the exams they take. Everyone has cheated on at least one exam he has taken. Cheating is wrong.

Which of the following is inconsistent with the preceding facts?
(A)   Joe has never been caught cheating.
(B)   Cheating is an acceptable procedure.
(C)   Jack is never wrong.

(D)　More people cheat on none of the exams they have taken than cheat on all of the exams they have taken.

(E)　More people cheat on some of the exams they have taken than cheat on most of the exams they have taken.

Questions 18–19 refer to the following sentence.

Everyone is ignorant, only on different subjects.

18. This sentence can have more than one meaning. In which of the following is at least one of its meanings implied?

(A)　Everybody is ignorant.

(B)　No one knows all subjects.

(C)　Frank is not ignorant about life.

(D)　Frank and Hal cannot be ignorant on the same subject.

(E)　Hal can be ignorant on more than one subject.

19. The author of this sentence would most likely be a

(A) politician　(B) merchant　(C) satirist　(D) actor　(E) attorney

20. The law of parsimony urges a strict economy upon us; it requires that we can never make a guess with two or three assumptions in it if we can make sense with one.

Which of the following is the main point of the author's statement?

(A)　Complications arise from economy.

(B)　Simplify terminology whenever possible.

(C)　Don't complicate a simple issue.

(D)　Assumptions are necessarily simple in nature.

(E)　Excess assumptions never clarify the situation.

21. You can use a bottle opener to open the new beer bottles.
You do not need to use a bottle opener to open the new beer bottles.

Which of the following most closely parallels the logic of these statements?

(A)　You must turn on the switch to light the lamp. If you turn on the switch, the lamp may not light.

(B)　A cornered rattlesnake will strike, so do not corner a rattlesnake.

(C)　If you do not study you will fail the test. If you do study, you may fail the test.

(D)　Every candidate I voted for in the election lost his race. I must learn to vote better.

(E)　I can move the sofa with my brother's help. If my brother is not available, I'll get a neighbor to help me.

22. To be admitted to Bigshot University, you must have a 3.5 grade-point average (GPA) and a score of 800 on the admissions test, a 3.0 GPA and a score of 1000 on the admissions test, or a 2.5 GPA and a score of 1200 on the admissions test. A sliding scale exists for other scores and GPAs.

Which of the following is inconsistent with the above?

(A)　The higher the GPA, the lower the admissions test score needed for admission.

(B)　Joe was admitted with a 2.7 GPA and a score of 1100 on the admissions test.

(C)　No student with a score of less than 800 on the admissions test and a 3.4 GPA will be admitted.

(D)　More applicants had a GPA of 3.5 than had a GPA of 2.5.

(E)　Some students with a score of less than 1200 on the admissions test and a GPA of less than 2.5 were admitted.

23. The Census Bureau's family portrait of America may remind us of the problems we face as a nation, but it also gives us reason to take heart in our ability to solve them in an enlightened way. The 1980 census was the first in history to show that the majority of the population in every state has completed high school. And the percentage of our people with at least 4 years of college rose from 11 percent in 1970 to 16.3 percent in 1980. That's progress—where it really counts.

Which of the following assumptions underlies the author's conclusion in the above passage?
(A) Greater numbers of high school and college degrees coincide with other firsts in the 1980 census.
(B) Greater numbers of high school and college degrees coincide with greater numbers of well-educated people.
(C) Greater numbers of high school and college degrees coincide with a great commitment to social progress.
(D) Greater numbers of high school and college degrees coincide with a better chance to avoid national catastrophe.
(E) Greater numbers of high school and college degrees coincide with the 1980 census.

24. Add No-NOCK to your car and watch its performance soar. No-NOCK will give it more get-up-and-go and keep it running longer. Ask for No-NOCK when you want better mileage!

According to the advertisement above, No-NOCK claims to do everything EXCEPT
(A) improve your car's performance
(B) increase your car's life
(C) improve your car's miles per gallon
(D) cause fewer breakdowns
(E) stop the engine from knocking

25. So many arrogant and ill-tempered young men have dominated the tennis courts of late that we had begun to fear those characteristics were prerequisites for championship tennis.
    Tennis used to be a gentleman's game. What is sad is not just that the game has changed. With so much importance placed on success, it may be that something has gone out of the American character—such things as gentleness and graciousness.

Which of the following statements, if true, would most weaken the above argument?
(A) The American character is a result of American goals.
(B) Tennis has only recently become a professional sport.
(C) Some ill-tempered tennis players are unsuccessful.
(D) The "gentlemen" of early tennis often dueled to the death off the court.
(E) Some even-tempered tennis players are successful.

26. *Dolores:* To preserve the peace, we must be prepared to go to war with any nation at any time, using either conventional or nuclear weapons.
Fran: Which shall it be, conventional weapons or nuclear weapons?

Fran mistakenly concludes that the "either…or" phrase in Dolores's statement indicates
(A) fear   (B) indecision   (C) a choice   (D) a question   (E) a refusal

STOP

IF YOU FINISH BEFORE TIME IS UP, CHECK YOUR WORK ON THIS SECTION OF THE TEST ONLY.
DO NOT GO ON TO THE NEXT SECTION OF THE TEST UNTIL TIME IS UP FOR THIS SECTION.

SECTION IV
ANALYTICAL REASONING

Time—35 Minutes
24 Questions

Directions:
In this section you will be given groups of questions based on different sets of conditions. Drawing a simple diagram may be helpful in answering some of the questions. You are to choose the best answer and mark the corresponding space on your answer sheet.

Questions 1–6

A group of tourists is planning to visit a cluster of islands— U,V,W,X,Y, and Z, connected by bridges. The tourists must stay on each island visited for exactly three days and three nights. Each bridge takes one hour to cross, may be crossed in either direction, and can be crossed only in the morning to give the tourists a full day on the island.

The islands are connected by bridges only as indicated below:

U is connected to W, X, and Y
V is connected to Y and Z
X is connected to Z and W
Y is connected to X and Z

1. If the group visits island W first, eight days later it could NOT be at which of the following islands?
   (A) U   (B) V   (C) X   (D) Y   (E) Z

2. If the group stays on island X for three nights, it CANNOT spend the next three days and nights on island
   (A) U   (B) V   (C) W   (D) Y   (E) Z

3. Which of the following is a possible order of Islands visited in 12 days and nights?
   (A) UWYZ   (B) UVYZ   (C) UYVX   (D) UXZV   (E) UWYX

4. If the group visits island W first and can visit an island more than once, but does not use a bridge more than once, what is the greatest number of visits it can make?
   (A) 4   (B) 5   (C) 6   (D) 7   (E) 8

5. Assume the group visits island X first, and does not use a bridge more than once. Assume also that the group does stay at island Y twice. What is the greatest number of different islands the group can visit?
   (A) 3   (B) 4   (C) 5   (D) 6   (E) 7

6. Assume another island, T, is added to the tour. Assume also that T is connected only to U. Which of the following statements must be true?
   (A)   On the eighth day of a tour, starting its visit at island T, the group could be on island V.
   (B)   On the fifth day of a tour, starting its visit at island T, the group could be on island X.
   (C)   On the seventh day of a tour, starting its visit at island T, the group could be on island U.
   (D)   On the eighth day of a tour, starting its visit at island V, the group could be on island T.
   (E)   On the tenth day of a tour, starting its visit at island Z, the tour group could be on island T.

Questions 7–13

Teams A and B play a series of 9 games. To win the series, a team must win the most games, but must also win a minimum of 3 games.

There are no ties in the first 3 games.
Team A wins more of the last 3 games than team B.
Team B wins more of the last 5 games than team A.
The last game is a tie.
Games 1 and 3 are won by the same team.

7. Which of the following must be true?
  (A)   One team must win 5 games to win the series.
  (B)   There are no ties.
  (C)   One team wins at least 2 of the first 3 games.
  (D)   The same team wins the last 5 games.
  (E)   The last three games are won by one team.

8. Considering all of the conditions mentioned above, game 6
  (A)   could be won by team A
  (B)   could be won by team B
  (C)   could be a tie
  (D)   must be won by team A
  (E)   must be won by team B

9. If game 7 is won by team A, then
  (A)   game 8 is a tie
  (B)   game 2 is a tie
  (C)   game 4 is won by team A
  (D)   game 5 is a tie
  (E)   game 6 is won by team A

10. Which of the following must be true?
  (A)   There is only 1 tie in the last 5 games.
  (B)   Team A wins 2 of the first 3 games.
  (C)   Team B can win 3 of the last 5 games.
  (D)   Game 4 is a tie.
  (E)   Team A can win only 1 of the last 5 games.

11. If team A wins game 1 and game 4, then which of the following must be FALSE?
  (A)   Team A wins game 3.
  (B)   Team A wins game 2.
  (C)   Team B wins game 2.
  (D)   Team A wins the series.
  (E)   Team B wins the series.

12. Assume that game 4 is won by the winner of game 5. If game 2 is not won by the winner of game 3, then which of the following must be true?
  (A)   Team A wins game 7.
  (B)   Team B is the winner of the series.
  (C)   Team A wins game 2.
  (D)   Team B wins game 1.
  (E)   Team A wins game 3.

13. Which of the following must be true?
  (A)   For team A to win the series, team A must win exactly two of the first four games.
  (B)   For team B to win the series, team B must win exactly one of the first four games.

(C) For team A to win the series, team A must win only three of the first seven games.
(D) For team B to win the series, team B must win at least three of the first four games.
(E) For team A to win the series, team A must win two consecutive games.

Questions 14–18

Eight busts of American Presidents are to be arranged on two shelves, left to right. Each shelf accommodates exactly four busts. One shelf is directly above the other shelf. The busts are of John Adams, George Washington, Abraham Lincoln, Thomas Jefferson, James Monroe, John Kennedy, Theodore Roosevelt and Franklin Delano Roosevelt.

The Roosevelt busts may not be directly one above the other.
The bust of Kennedy must be adjacent to the bust of a Roosevelt.
The bust of Jefferson must be directly above the bust of John Adams.
The busts of Monroe, Adams, Kennedy and Franklin Delano Roosevelt must be on the bottom shelf.
The bust of Monroe must be third from the left.

14. If the bust of Theodore Roosevelt is second from the left on one shelf, which of the following must be true?
    (A) The bust of Adams must be first on a shelf.
    (B) The bust of Adams must be third on a shelf.
    (C) The bust of Kennedy must be first on a shelf.
    (D) The bust of Kennedy must be second on a shelf.
    (E) The bust of Kennedy must be third on a shelf.

15. Which of the following must be true about the bust of Monroe?
    (A) It is next to the bust of Adams.
    (B) It is next to the bust of Kennedy.
    (C) It is next to the bust of Franklin Delano Roosevelt.
    (D) It is directly under the bust of Lincoln.
    (E) It is directly under the bust of Theodore Roosevelt.

16. If the bust of Washington is first, directly above Kennedy's, all of the following must be true EXCEPT
    (A) the bust of Jefferson is fourth
    (B) the bust of Theodore Roosevelt is third
    (C) the bust of Franklin Delano Roosevelt is second
    (D) the bust of Lincoln is third
    (E) the bust of Adams is fourth

17. Which of the following is not a possible order for the busts on either shelf?
    (A) Washington, Lincoln, Theodore Roosevelt, Jefferson
    (B) Franklin Delano Roosevelt, Kennedy, Monroe, Adams
    (C) Theodore Roosevelt, Lincoln, Washington, Jefferson
    (D) Lincoln, Theodore Roosevelt, Washington, Jefferson
    (E) Kennedy, Adams, Monroe, Franklin Delano Roosevelt

18. If the bust of Lincoln is next to the bust of Jefferson, all of the following are true EXCEPT
    (A) if the bust of Kennedy is first, the bust of Theodore Roosevelt is also first
    (B) if the bust of Washington is first, the bust of Franklin Delano Roosevelt is also first
    (C) if the bust of Washington is second, the bust of Kennedy is also second
    (D) if the bust of Kennedy is second, the bust of Theodore Roosevelt is also second
    (E) if the bust of Washington is second, the bust of Franklin Delano Roosevelt is also second

Questions 19–24

For a dinner party, a hostess needs several different three-bean salads.

Each salad is to contain three types of beans, chosen from garbanzos, chili beans, wax beans, lima beans, and kidney beans.
Chili beans and lima beans do not taste good together and therefore are never used in the same salad.
Lima beans and kidney beans do not look good together and therefore are never used in the same salad.

19. How many different salads (using the above ingredients) could the hostess serve that contain lima beans?
(A) 0   (B) 1   (C) 2   (D) 3   (E) 4

20. How many different salads could she serve that do not contain chili beans?
(A) 0   (B) 1   (C) 2   (D) 3   (E) 4

21. How many different salad combinations could she serve at the party?
(A) 4   (B) 5   (C) 6   (D) 7   (E) 8

22. Which beans will occur most often in the salad combinations that could be served at the party?
(A)   chili and garbanzos
(B)   chili and limas
(C)   limas and wax beans
(D)   kidney and limas
(E)   garbanzos and wax beans

23. If there are only enough wax beans to go into two salads, what is the total number of salads that can be served?
(A) 1   (B) 2   (C) 3   (D) 4   (E) 5

24. If the hostess discovers the garbanzos have gone bad, how many three-bean combinations can she serve without using the rotten garbanzos?
(A) 0   (B) 1   (C) 2   (D) 3   (E) 4

STOP

IF YOU FINISH BEFORE TIME IS UP, CHECK YOUR WORK ON THIS SECTION OF THE TEST ONLY.
DO NOT GO ON TO THE NEXT SECTION OF THE TEST UNTIL TIME IS UP FOR THIS SECTION.

SECTION V
LOGICAL REASONING

Time—35 Minutes
25 Questions

Directions:
In this section you will be given brief statements or passages and will be required to evaluate the reasoning involved. In some instances, more than one choice will appear to be a possible answer. You are to choose the *best* answer. Use common sense and reasonableness in making your selection; then mark the proper space on the answer sheet.

1. Chrysanthemums that have not been fertilized in July will normally not blossom in October. In October, the chrysanthemums did not blossom.

   With the premises given above, which of the following would logically complete an argument?
   (A) Therefore, the chrysanthemums were not fertilized in July.
   (B) Therefore, the chrysanthemums may not have been fertilized in July.
   (C) Therefore, the chrysanthemums may blossom later in the fall.
   (D) Therefore, the chrysanthemums will blossom in the fall.
   (E) Therefore, the chrysanthemums will not blossom later in the fall.

2. When asked about the danger to public health from the spraying of pesticides by helicopters throughout the county, the County Supervisor replied, "The real danger to the public is the possibility of an infestation of harmful fruit-flies, which this spraying will prevent. Such an infestation would drive up the cost of fruits and vegetables by 15 percent."

   Which of the following is the most serious weakness in the Supervisor's reply to the question?
   (A) He depends upon the ambiguity in the word "danger."
   (B) His response contains a self-contradiction.
   (C) He fails to support his argument concretely.
   (D) He fails to answer the question that has been asked.
   (E) His chief concern is the economic consequences of spraying.

3. So far this year researchers have reported the following:

   Heavy coffee consumption can increase the risk of heart attacks.
   Drinking a cup of coffee in the morning increases feelings of well-being and alertness.
   Boiled coffee increases blood cholesterol levels.
   Coffee may protect against cancer of the colon.

   If all these statements are true, which of the following conclusions can be drawn from this information?

   (A) Reducing coffee consumption will make people healthier.
   (B) Reducing coffee consumption will make people feel better.
   (C) People at risk for heart attack should limit their coffee drinking.
   (D) Percolated coffee will not affect cholesterol levels.
   (E) People at risk for cancer should reduce their coffee consumption.

4. Compared with children in other states, infants born in California weigh more, survive the first years in greater numbers, and live longer. The hysteria about the danger of pesticides in California has attracted attention simply because a few Hollywood stars have appeared on television talk shows. Pesticides are the responsibility of the California Department of Food and Agriculture, and we can be sure its members are doing their job.

The argument of this paragraph would be weakened if all of the following were shown to be true EXCEPT

(A) rates of melanoma and some forms of leukemia in California are above national norms.

(B) the three highest positions at the California Department of Food and Agriculture are held by farm owners

(C) synthetic pesticide residues in food cause more cancer than do "natural pesticides" that the plants themselves produce

(D) more Californians suffer the consequences of air pollution than do the citizens in any other state

(E) children of farm workers are three times more likely to suffer childhood cancers than children of urban parents

5. Should we allow the Fire Department to continue to underpay its women officers by using policies of promotion that favor men?

The question above most closely resembles which of the following in terms of its logical features?

(A) Should the excessive tax on cigarettes, liquor, and luxury goods be unfairly increased again this year?

(B) Should corrupt politicians be subject to the same sentencing laws as blue-collar felons?

(C) Should the police chief be chosen by examination score regardless of gender or seniority?

(D) Should the religious right be allowed to determine the censorship laws for all of society?

(E) Are liberal political values an appropriate basis for all of the social values in this state?

6. If airline fares have risen, then either the cost of fuel has risen or there are no fare wars among competing companies. If there are no fare wars among competing companies, the number of airline passengers is larger than it was last year.

According to the passage above, if there has been a rise in airline fares this month, which of the following CANNOT be true?

(A) There are no fare wars among competing airlines.

(B) The cost of fuel has risen, and the number of passengers is the same as last year.

(C) The cost of fuel has risen, there are no fare wars, and the number of passengers is larger than it was last year.

(D) There are no fare wars, and the number of passengers is larger than it was last year.

(E) The cost of fuel has risen, there are no fare wars, and the number of passengers is smaller than it was last year.

7. The cost of fresh swordfish is $6.00 per pound. The cost of fresh clams is $1.50 per pound. Therefore, it will be cheaper to serve clams for dinner than to serve swordfish.

Which of the following, if true, would make the conclusion above a logical one?

(A) There are more calories in four pounds of clams than in one pound of swordfish.

(B) One pound of swordfish or three pounds of clams will make an adequate meal for two adults.

(C) Eighty-five percent of the weight of a clam is an inedible shell.

(D) The cost of preparing swordfish is no higher than the cost of preparing clams.

(E) Even a small swordfish weighs many times as much as several bushels of clams.

8. A cigarette advertisement in a magazine asks, "What do gremlins, the Loch Ness monster, and a filter cigarette claiming 'great taste' have in common?" The answer is "You've heard of all of them, but don't really believe they exist."

The advertisement contains no pictures, and no additional text except the words Gold Star Cigarettes and the Surgeon General's warning in a box in the lower corner.

Which of the following conclusions can be drawn from the information given above?

(A) Cigarette advertising depends upon visual appeal to create images for specific brands.

(B) All cigarette advertising depends on praising a specific brand.

(C) Gold Star Cigarettes are non-filters.

(D) The writers of this advertisement do not believe in advertising.

(E) The writers of this advertisement do not believe the Surgeon General's warning is true.

9. While some cities impose tough, clear restrictions on demolitions of older buildings, our city has no protection for cultural landmarks. Designation as a landmark by the Cultural Heritage Commission can delay a demolition for only one year. This delay can be avoided easily by an owner's demonstrating an economic hardship. Developers who simply ignore designations and tear down buildings receive only small fines. Therefore, _____.

Which of the following best completes the passage above?
(A) the number of buildings protected by Cultural Heritage Commission designation must be increased
(B) developers must be encouraged to help preserve our older buildings
(C) the designation as landmark must be changed to delay demolition for more than one year
(D) developers who ignore designations to protect building must be subject to higher fines
(E) if our older buildings are to be saved, we need clearer and more rigorously enforced laws

10. Despite the very large increase in the federal tax on luxury items, the value of the stock of Harry Evans, Inc., seller of the world's most expensive jewelry, continues to rise. Six months after the introduction of the tax, Evans's stock is at an all-time high. Moreover, sales in the United States continue to increase. In other countries, where Evans does 30 percent of its business, there have been no rises in excise taxes and the company will open new stores in Tokyo, Monte Carlo, and Singapore. According to a company spokesperson, _____.

Which of the following most logically completes this paragraph?
(A) American customers who can afford to shop at Evans are not likely to be deterred by a rise in luxury taxes
(B) American customers are expected to spend far less at Evans because of the tax rise
(C) American sales are not significant enough to affect the overall profits of the firm
(D) the company will probably be forced to close most of its stores in America
(E) state taxes are more likely to influence jewelry sales than federal taxes

11. A recent study of cigarette smokers has shown that, of cancer patients who are heavy smokers of unfiltered cigarettes, 40 percent will die of the disease. For cancer patients who are light smokers of filter cigarettes, the percentage is 25 percent.

Which of the following conclusions can be drawn from the information above?
(A) There are more heavy smokers of unfiltered cigarettes than light smokers of filter cigarettes.
(B) More heavy smokers of unfiltered cigarettes die of cancer than light smokers of filter cigarettes.
(C) A heavy smoker of unfiltered cigarettes who has cancer is more likely to die than a light smoker of unfiltered cigarettes.
(D) A heavy smoker of unfiltered cigarettes who has cancer may be more likely to die than a light smoker of unfiltered cigarettes.
(E) A heavy smoker of unfiltered cigarettes who has cancer is more likely to die than a light smoker of filtered cigarettes who has cancer.

Questions 12–13 refer to the following passage.

Archeologists have come to the support of Arctic anthropologists. A small minority of anthropologists assert that Stone-Age tribes of the Arctic domesticated wolves and trained them to haul sleds. Excavations have recently found evidence to support this claim. Archeologists have found wolf bones near the site of a Stone-Age village. They have also found walrus bones that might have been used on primitive sleds. The small minority of anthropologists believe that their theories have been proved.

12. Which of the following is true of the evidence cited in the paragraph above?
   (A)   It is not relevant to the anthropologists' conclusions.
   (B)   It conclusively contradicts the anthropologists' conclusions.
   (C)   It neither supports nor refutes the anthropologists' conclusions positively.
   (D)   It supports the anthropologists' conclusions authoritatively.
   (E)   It conclusively supports only a part of the anthropologists' conclusions.

13. Which of the following, if true, would best support the theory of the anthropologists?
   (A)   Wolves are known to have fed upon the garbage of villages in northern Europe.
   (B)   Wolves as a species are easily domesticated and trained.
   (C)   Almost all Stone-Age Arctic tools were made of walrus bone.
   (D)   Stone-Age villages were located on the migration routes of the caribou herds upon which wolves preyed.
   (E)   The earliest sled part found in the Arctic was made one thousand years after the Stone Age.

Questions 14–15 refer to the following passage.

   The following criticism of a self-portrait by Vincent van Gogh appeared in a magazine in 1917:

   "Here we have a work of art which is so self-evidently a degenerate work by a degenerate artist that we need not say anything about the inept creation. It is safe to say that if we were to meet in our dreams such a villainous looking jailbird with such a deformed Neanderthal skull, degenerate ears, hobo beard and insane glare, it would certainly give us a nightmare."

14. The author of this passage makes his point by using
   (A) invective   (B) analogy   (C) citation of authority   (D) paradox   (E) example

15. In relation to the first sentence of the quotation, the second sentence is
   (A)   an example of an effect following a cause
   (B)   a specific derived from a general principle
   (C)   a logical conclusion
   (D)   a contradiction
   (E)   a personal experience in support of a generalization

16. A company called Popcorn Packaging is promoting the use of popcorn as a cushioning material in packing. Unlike the commonly used Styrofoam beads or chips, popcorn can be recycled as a food for birds or squirrels and can serve as a garden mulch. Used out of doors, popcorn disappears almost overnight, while the Styrofoam beads may be in the environment for centuries. Even before we became ecology conscious, popcorn was used in packing in the 1940s. Since it now costs less to produce than Styrofoam, there is every reason to return to wide-scale use of packaging by popcorn.

   Which of the following, if true, would most seriously weaken the author's argument?
   (A)   A package using popcorn as a cushioning material will weigh less than a package using Styrofoam beads.
   (B)   Popcorn may attract rodents and insects.
   (C)   A large number of squirrels can damage a garden by consuming flowering bulbs.
   (D)   Less than 1 percent of the material now used for package cushioning is recycled.
   (E)   Styrofoam replaced popcorn in the early 1950s because it was cheaper to produce.

17. This produce stand sells fruits and vegetables. All fruits are delicious, and all vegetables are rich in vitamins. Every food that is vitamin-rich is delicious, so everything sold at this stand is delicious. Which of the following assumptions is necessary to make the conclusion in the argument above logically correct?
   (A)   The stand sells many fruits and vegetables.
   (B)   This produce stand sells only fruits and vegetables.
   (C)   Something cannot be both vitamin-rich and delicious.
   (D)   Some stands sell fruits that are not delicious.
   (E)   Some vegetables are delicious.

18. Voter turnout in primary elections has declined steadily from 1982 to 1990. In 1990, more than 80 percent of the Americans eligible to vote failed to do so. Only 11.9 percent of the Democrats and 7.7 percent of the Republicans went to the polls. The largest number of voters turned out for elections in the District of Columbia (28 percent) and in Massachusetts, where the 32 percent total was the highest since 1962. In each of the twenty-four other states holding elections, the number of voters was smaller than it had been in 1986 and 1982.

Based on the information in this passage, which of the following must be true?
(A) The turnout in the District of Columbia was affected by favorable weather conditions.
(B) Fewer than 20 percent of the eligible major-party voters voted in the 24 states other than Massachusetts.
(C) The voter turnout in Massachusetts is always higher than the turnouts in other states.
(D) The voter turnout decline is a signal of a nationwide voter rebellion.
(E) More voters cast their votes in general elections than in primary elections.

19. Each year the number of schools that no longer allow smoking on school property grows larger. Four states, New Jersey, Kansas, Utah, and New Hampshire, now require tobacco-free schools. The Tobacco Institute has fought against regulations restricting smoking everywhere from airlines to restaurants on the grounds that they trample on the rights of smokers, but is conspicuously absent from school board lobbyists. Tobacco industry spokesmen have denounced the rules treating teachers like children, but have said they will not go on record to defend policies that affect children.

Which of the following, if true, best accounts for the Tobacco Institute's behavior?
(A) The tobacco industry is presently fighting the charge that it attempts to recruit new smokers among minors.
(B) The tobacco industry can depend on continued high profits from overseas operations, where restrictions do not exist.
(C) Most tobacco companies are highly diversified corporations whose profits no longer depend wholly on tobacco products.
(D) The tobacco industry believes the rights of children to be equal to the rights of adults.
(E) The tobacco industry agrees with the schools that have rules against tobacco.

Questions 20–21 refer to the following passage.

A number of lawsuits have been brought against popular singing groups charging that suicidal themes in their songs have led to teenage suicides. So far, the courts have found that the lyrics are protected by the First Amendment. But what if this should change, and a court decides that suicidal themes in popular songs are dangerous? In fact, the songs that have been charged so far are antisuicide; they present sardonically the self-destructive behavior of drinking, drugs, and escape by death. They describe a pitiful state of mind, but they do not endorse it.

Blaming suicide on the arts is nothing new. In the late eighteenth century, Goethe's popular novel *Werther* was said to be the cause of a rash of suicides in imitation of the novel's hero. If we begin to hold suicide in books or music responsible for suicides in real life, the operas of Verdi and Puccini will have to go, and *Romeo and Juliet* and *Julius Caesar* will disappear from high school reading lists.

20. The author of this passage argues by
(A) providing examples to support two opposing positions
(B) using an observation to undermine a theoretical principle
(C) disputing an interpretation of evidence cited by those with an opposing view
(D) predicting personal experience from a general principle
(E) accusing the opposing side of using inaccurate statistical information

21. Which of the following is an assumption necessary to the author's argument?
(A) A lyric presenting suicide in a favorable light should not have First Amendment protection.
(B) Literature or music cannot directly influence human behavior.
(C) Many record albums already carry labels warning purchasers of their dangerous contents.

(D)   The audience, not the performer, is responsible for the audience's actions.

(E)   Freedom of speech is the most threatened of our personal freedoms.

22. Haven't you at some time had a favorite song or book or film that was not well known but later became popular? And didn't you feel somehow betrayed and resentful when what you had thought was unique became commonplace? On a larger scale, the same thing happens to novelists or film makers who have enjoyed critical esteem without popular success. Let them become public sensations, and the critics who praised their work will attack them virulently.

This paragraph most likely introduces an article on a film maker who has made a

(A)   series of commercially successful films

(B)   series of commercially unsuccessful films

(C)   single film, a commercial success

(D)   single film, a commercial failure

(E)   critical success and a commercial success

23. Studies of the effects of drinking four or more cups of coffee per day have shown that coffee consumption increases work efficiency by improving the ability to process information. People who drink two cups of coffee in the morning are more alert and feel better than those who do not. But there are other factors to be considered.

Which of the following sentences would provide the most logical continuation of this paragraph?

(A)   Contrary to popular belief, drinking coffee cannot erase the effect of alcohol.

(B)   Some studies suggest that coffee drinking will protect against cancer of the colon.

(C)   Combined with the stress of heavy exercise, coffee drinking may be the cause of higher blood pressure.

(D)   Drinking two or more cups of coffee per day increases the risk of heart attacks in men.

(E)   Many people cannot distinguish between the taste of decaffeinated and that of regular coffee.

24. All of the members of the chorus will sing in the performance of the oratorio *Messiah*. Some of these are highly trained professionals, some are gifted amateurs, and some are singers of mediocre ability.

If the statements above are true, which of the following must also be true?

(A)   *Messiah* will be performed by highly trained professionals, gifted amateurs, and some singers of mediocre ability.

(B)   Some of the members of the chorus are not highly trained professionals, gifted amateurs, or singers of mediocre ability.

(C)   *Messiah* will be performed by some highly trained professionals, but not all of them are in the chorus.

(D)   Not all of those in the chorus who are gifted amateurs will perform in the oratorio.

(E)   All of those who will perform *Messiah* are members of the chorus.

25. The passage of laws that limit elected officials to one or two terms in office is an admission that voters are civic fools, unable to tell good lawmakers from bad ones. To ban all the politicians when the real intention is to get rid of the corrupt ones is to burn the house down to get rid of the vermin.

The author of this passage makes his point chiefly by

(A)   defining a key term

(B)   exposing a self-contradiction

(C)   drawing an analogy

(D)   questioning the evidence of his opponents

(E)   citing an example

STOP

END OF MULTIPLE-CHOICE EXAMINATION. IF YOU FINISH BEFORE TIME IS UP, CHECK YOUR WORK ON THIS SECTION ONLY. DO NOT GO BACK TO ANY OTHER SECTION OF THE EXAMINATION.

EXAMINATION

WRITING SAMPLE

Directions:
You have 30 minutes to write an essay in response to a given topic. Take a few minutes to plan your work before you begin writing. DO NOT WRITE ON A TOPIC OF YOUR OWN CHOICE. ESSAYS THAT DO NOT ADDRESS THE GIVEN TOPIC ARE UNACCEPTABLE.

The quality of your writing is more important than the length of your response or the content. Pay attention to organization, appropriate diction, and correct usage. You will not be expected to display any specialized knowledge in your response, nor will you be expected to write a "perfect" essay; law schools understand that you are writing under a time constraint, and will allow for the minor lapses in writing ability that might occur under this circumstance.

Only the lined area in your booklet will be reproduced for the law schools, so do not write outside this space. *Do not* skip lines or use wide margins. These precautions, along with careful planning and legible handwriting that is not unduly large, will keep you within the allowed space.

SAMPLE TOPIC

Read the following descriptions of Jackson and Brown. *Then, in the space provided, write an argument for deciding which of the two should be assigned the responsibility of hiring teachers for the Hapsville School System.* The following criteria are relevant to your decision:

- The taxpayers want educators who can instill in students the desire to learn and an excitement for knowledge, something that has been lacking in their schools.
- A majority of students' parents believe that their children should be equipped, upon graduation, to earn a living, and thus favor a more trade-oriented (rather than academic) approach to schooling.

JACKSON was appointed as Superintendent of Schools by the Hapsville School Board, which was elected by the community's taxpayers. As a 30-year resident of Hapsville (population 45,000), Jackson is unique in that he holds not only a doctorate in administration, but also a master's degree in education. He taught in the Hapsville schools for 16 years until he served on the state Commission on Education. He has always favored a progressive approach to education, although it may not always have been popular with the town's population. Through the years he has brought many fine teachers to the faculty, because of his willingness to encourage new classroom techniques.

BROWN is a 52-year resident of Hapsville, having been born in the same house in which he now lives. He was elected to the School Board 13 years ago, and continues to win nearly unanimous reelection every two years. As the foremost developer in the Four Counties area, Mr. Brown has had the opportunity to build hundreds of new homes in the six housing developments he's planned and actualized, and, in the interim, has employed hundreds of Hapsville residents as carpenters, electricians, plumbers, architects, landscapers, groundskeepers, etc. As such, he is held in high esteem by most of the town, not only for his providing livelihoods for many, but also for his fair and realistic outlook on life. Mr. Brown feels strongly that the key to life is having a marketable skill.

ANSWER KEY

Section I: Reading Comprehension	Section II: Analytical Reasoning	Section III: Logical Reasoning	Section IV: Analytical Reasoning	Section V: Logical Reasoning
1. B	1. C	1. A	1. B	1. B
2. C	2. A	2. B	2. B	2. D
3. A	3. E	3. E	3. D	3. C
4. A	4. C	4. D	4. E	4. D
5. D	5. D	5. D	5. D	5. A
6. E	6. B	6. A	6. E	6. E
7. A	7. A	7. B	7. C	7. B
8. C	8. B	8. C	8. E	8. C
9. A	9. E	9. B	9. A	9. E
10. B	10. A	10. E	10. E	10. A
11. D	11. B	11. B	11. E	11. E
12. A	12. A	12. C	12. B	12. C
13. C	13. A	13. B	13. E	13. B
14. E	14. C	14. C	14. D	14. A
15. A	15. A	15. E	15. A	15. D
16. B	16. D	16. B	16. D	16. B
17. C	17. E	17. D	17. E	17. B
18. B	18. D	18. C	18. C	18. B
19. D	19. C	19. C	19. B	19. A
20. E	20. D	20. C	20. C	20. C
21. E	21. E	21. E	21. B	21. D
22. B	22. C	22. E	22. E	22. E
23. C	23. D	23. B	23. C	23. D
24. E	24. B	24. E	24. B	24. A
25. E		25. D		25. C
26. D		26. B		
27. B				
28. B				

MODEL TEST ANALYSIS

Doing model exams and understanding the explanations afterwards are of course important in acquainting you with typical LSAT question types and successful approaches to the questions. However, another benefit of carefully analyzing these model tests is to understand the kinds of errors you are making and thus work to minimize them. For instance, if a very high percentage of your incorrect answers is due to "careless error" or "misread problem," then perhaps you are working much too fast and should slow your pace accordingly. If your incorrect answers are due primarily to "lack of knowledge," then a careful rereading and reworking of the appropriate question-type chapter may be in order. Or if you find that you aren't completing a large number of questions because of lack of time, you may need to either increase your speed or learn to use the "one-check, two-check" technique more effectively.

This kind of analysis of the model tests will enable you to identify your particular weaknesses and thus remedy them.

Model Test One Analysis

Section	Total Number of Questions	Number Correct	Number Incorrect	Number Unanswered*
I: Reading Comprehension	28			
II: Analytical Reasoning	24			
III: Logical Reasoning	26			
IV: Analytical Reasoning	24			
V: Logical Reasoning	25			
TOTALS:	127			

*At this stage in your preparation, you should not be leaving any blank answer spaces. At least fill in a guess, as there is no penalty for a wrong answer.

Reasons for Incorrect Answers

You may wish to evaluate the explanations before completing this chart.

Section	Total Number Incorrect	Lack of Knowledge	Misread Problem	Careless Error	Unanswered or Wrong Guess
I: Reading Comprehension					
II: Analytical Reasoning					
III: Logical Reasoning					
IV: Analytical Reasoning					
V: Logical Reasoning					
TOTALS:					

EXPLANATIONS OF ANSWERS

Section I

Passage 1

1. **B** Government workers are forbidden to strike by statutory law.

2. **C** If strikers are a form of symbolic speech, the denial of the right to strike is arguably a denial of free speech. It also can be argued that it denies due process, the right to picket, and the right to avoid abnormally dangerous working conditions.

3. **A** The courts, not the legislative or the executive branches, should determine the "clear and present danger."

4. **A** Because the firing of the controllers had the same effect as a strike, it appears that there was no danger to the public.

5. **D** A higher rate of stress-related illness would support the contention that the working conditions were dangerous.

6. **E** The author points out that workers in government who do the same job as workers in private industry cannot strike. The passage argues that the nature of the service should determine the right to strike not the employer.

7. **A** The passage contends that some of the more "highly qualified" may seek employment outside of government, because of the no-strike clause.

Passage 2

8. **C** The author begins with several definitions of "orient" and "orientation," and then goes on to discuss the orientation (direction and purpose) of his own study. (A), (B), and (D) are mentioned in the passage, but constitute subsidiary points rather than a primary purpose. (E) contradicts the analogy between engineering and language study made explicit in the final paragraph.

9. **A** In the first paragraph, the author proposes that we believe that the good life will result from "using our heads." He joins in this belief by associating his own (intellectual) study with freedom and happiness during the course of the passage. (E) is not as strong a choice because it is not as comprehensive as (A).

10. **B** The second paragraph emphasizes the connection between freedom and language and a "philosophy of life." All other choices draw conclusions that are neither explicitly nor implicitly supported in the paragraph: to pick one of these choices requires "reading into" the paragraph, a poor test-taking strategy.

11. **D** In the final paragraph, the author calls his approach "linguistic engineering," thus creating an analogy by recalling the mechanical engineer he introduced in the first paragraph. None of the other choices is, strictly speaking, an analogy.

12. **A** The final two sentences stress the connection between the author's study, applied psychology, the conscious mind, and the brain. The other choices are not so explicitly relevant as this one, and therefore are weaker.

13. **C** In the fourth paragraph the author states that interest in linguistic behavior will result in knowledge of language "etiquette."

14. **E** The fourth paragraph stresses that concentration on the rules of language will cause us to "leave important tasks undone," and that in a democracy "progress" is preferred to "protocol."

Passage 3

15. **A** Only choice (A) includes both of the major issues of the passage: employers' liability and video display health hazards.

16. **B** Unlike the government, the author has no doubt about the health hazard to some persons, though he does not claim proof of his views.

17. **C** Though some statistics suggest these results, there has not yet been laboratory verification.

18. **B** Both the NIOSH and the manufacturers deny any evidence of health hazards. The passage gives no information to make an inference about the view of OSHA. Manufacturers of protective devices and state legislatures considering controls must both believe that health hazards do exist.

19. **D** The "latter problem" is employee productivity, which determines the profits. Liability lawsuits would be the insurance companies' expense.

20. **E** One of the five choices, the best is evasive. It is clear that the author regards the danger as real and the government's refusal to recognize the statistical evidence as evasive.

21. **E** (A), (B), (C), and (D) are all actions of which the author would approve. Since the NIOSH believes there are no health hazards in video display terminals, the author would not support an even wider distribution of these views.

Passage 4

22. **B** The passage discusses the terms *hypothesis, theory, law,* and, to a lesser extent, *datum,* all to examine the function of language "in the development of scientific understanding." The second paragraph discusses the method of developing a hypothesis, but does not itself develop one, so (C) is not a good answer.

23. **C** Toward the end of the passage, the author expresses his skepticism about *natural law:* it is a term "dangerous . . . to employ." All other choices are agreeable to the author.

24. **E** The author's parenthetical remarks in paragraphs 2 and 3 emphasize that hypothesis is a *word,* a *symbol,* which stands for (in reference to) an action. He is pointing out the difference between language and what it stands for.

25. **E** In the third paragraph we learn that "As the evidence in favor of a hypothesis . . . accumulates to a convincing degree," it often becomes a theory.

26. **D** All other choices are explicitly refuted in the passage. The author begins the passage by mentioning scientific assumptions such as equations, and then states that the hypothesis is a much more important function.

27. **B** The long second paragraph describing the development of a hypothesis stresses that a hypothesis is a "colored light," that is, subjective and subject to question. The author's claim that a hypothesis may be abandoned suggests that not all hypotheses are useful (E).

28. **B** This is stated at the end of the first paragraph: hypotheses are "not always readily grasped."

Section II
Answers 1–6

From the information given, you could have made the following diagram:

Higher	A	D	E		Pent.	4	___	
	?	?	?	FG		3	___	___
						2	___	___
Lower	B	C	C			1	___	___

1. **C** Since F and G are on the same floor, they can't be on 4. Since B and C are below A or D/E, they can't be on 4; therefore only A, D, or E can be on 4.

2. **A** If F's apartment is on 2, so is G's. For B and C to be below A, D, and E, B and C must be on 1 and A, D, and E on 3 and 4, but we don't know exactly where on 3/4.

3. **E** If D is on 4, G (and F) *can* be on 3, 2, or 1.

D	D	D
FG	AE	AE
AE	FG	BC
BC	BC	FG

4. **C** If D and E are on the same floor, A must be on 4. All the other answers are possible but *not* certain.

5. **D** If A is on 4 or C on 1, the arrangement must be either

A		A
FG	or	DE
DE		FG
BC		BC

6. **B** A and E can be on the same floor if D is on 4.

D		D
AE	or	AE
FG		BC
BC		FG

	A	**B**	**T**	**Z**
A	?	Z	Z	T
B	Z	?	O	A
T	Z	O	?	B
Z	T	A	B	?

7. **A** This answer may be derived directly from statement 4: Beta combines with Theta, giving Omega.

8. **B** From our chart we can see that, if Beta is involved, then the outcome may be Alpha, Omega, or Zeta.

9. **E** We have no information about the results if Omega combines with anything.

10. **A** From the chart we can see that Zeta and Theta combine to give Beta.

11. **B** The outcome of Alpha and Beta is Zeta. The outcome of Alpha and Zeta is Theta. Thus, if the two outcomes (Zeta and Theta) combine, the result will then be Beta.

12. **A** Alpha with any other (with the exception of Omega, which we do not know) produces either Zeta or Theta, which is similar to the outcome of Omega with Theta.

Answers 13–19

From the information given, you could have constructed the following simple diagram and display of information:

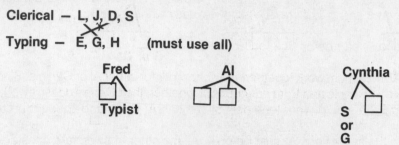

Clerical — L, J, D, S

Typing — E, G, H   (must use all)

13. **A** From the diagram and information above, if Gene works for Fred, then Lyndia also works for Fred, and Sylvia must work for Cynthia. Since Dennis and Edra will not work together, one of them must work for Cynthia; therefore choice (A) must be false. Jim cannot work for Cynthia.

14. **C** Using the diagram, if Sylvia doesn't work for Cynthia, then Gene must work for Cynthia. If Gene works for Cynthia, then Lyndia must also work for Cynthia, since Gene and Lyndia always work together.

15. **A** If Lyndia and Jim work for Al, then Gene must also work for Al, and Sylvia must work for Cynthia. The diagram would look like this:

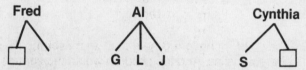

First, (A) is true since Gene and Linda always work together. Stop there. Go no further. Edra could work for Cynthia or Fred, and also Helen could work for Cynthia or Fred.

16. **D** If Sylvia and Jim work for Al, then Gene and Lyndia must work for Cynthia. Since Dennis and Edra cannot work together, one of them must work for Fred and the other for Al. The diagram would now look like this:

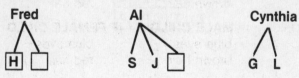

Therefore, only (D) is true.

17. **E** From the diagram, if Lyndia and Sylvia work for Al, then Gene also must work for Al. But either Sylvia or Gene must work for Cynthia. Therefore (E) must be false.

18. **D** From the diagram, if Jim works for Cynthia, then Sylvia must also work for Cynthia, since Gene and Lyndia must work together. Gene and Lyndia cannot work for Fred, because then Dennis and Edra (who cannot work together) would work for Al. Therefore, Lyndia must work for Al. The diagram would look like this:

19. **C** If Al needs only two assistants and Fred needs only one, and if Helen works for Fred, then the diagram would look like this:

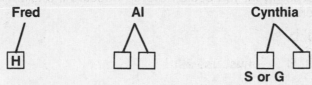

Since Gene and Lyndia must work together, they can work for either Al or Cynthia. Since Edra (typist) must work and Dennis and Edra cannot work together, then Dennis doesn't work. Otherwise, Dennis and Edra would work together. Statemens A, B, D, and E <u>could</u> be true.

Answers 20–24

A simple chart may help to answer each question.

20. **D** For this question your chart may look like this:

First, note that, if all the children have red hair, then all must be girls, since a boy would take both of the father's characteristics. And the children would thus have to get their red hair from their mother. Statement C is not necessarily true as their red-haired mother could have blue eyes.

21. **E** This is a difficult problem. Your chart should look like this:

1ST GENERATION: **FATHER**   **MOTHER**
                        blue eyes   blue eyes
                        brown hair   red hair

2ND GENERATION: **IF MALE CHILD** **IF FEMALE CHILD**   **CHILD'S SPOUSE**
                        blue eyes   blue eyes   ?
                        brown hair   red hair

3RD GENERATION: **GRANDCHILD**
                                           red hair
                                           green eyes

Since the grandchild has red hair and green eyes, she must be a girl. And since she is a girl, she must get one characteristic from each of her parents (the second generation). Therefore, the only person from whom she could get green eyes would be the other spouse of the second generation. The red hair must thus come from the second generation female.

22. **C** Only girls can have both green eyes and red hair. But any girl from a blue-eyed, brown-haired father must have at least one of his characteristics. Therefore, green eyes and red hair are not possible characteristics of his child.

23. **D** Every male must have *at least one* of the following characteristics: blue eyes, brown hair. Therefore, a green-eyed male *must* have brown hair.

24. **B** If two blue-eyed people get married, the female *must* have red hair because all females have *at least one* of the following characteristics: green eyes and/or red hair. Note that the father could also have blue eyes and red hair; therefore, the child could be either a boy or girl.

Section III

1. **A** By criticizing "offensive sex, violence, or profanity" in the third paragraph, the author implicitly defines "objectionable" as used in the fifth paragraph. (C), (D), and (E) are common enough terms so that no explicit or implicit definition is required here, and (B), "appropriate," is left largely undefined in the passage.

2. **B** By urging moviegoers to patronize films *in order to* influence academy judges, the author reveals his assumption that the academy will be influenced by the number of people paying to see a movie.

3. **E** Bob's answer shows that he thinks that people other than teachers are mean. His thought was that Andy meant otherwise.

4. **D** The author's concluding contention is that Roosevelt was not only a good marksman, but also an intellectually curious and patient man. If Roosevelt was known to leave safaris which were not immediately productive, this fact would substantially weaken the author's contention about Roosevelt's "patient observation."

5. **D** The words "because of a recent cut in state funding of our program" indicate that another criterion was used in determining entering class size besides candidates' scores and grades, namely, the financial situation of the college. The words *seriously* in choice (B) and *severe* in choice (E) are not necessarily supported by the passage, and thus make those choices incorrect. Since grade point average is only one of several criteria for admission, we cannot deduce (A) with certainty.

6. **A** This sentence not only fits well stylistically but completes the thought of the passage by tying it into the opening statement.

7. **B** The author of this passage actually defines conscience as the ability to sense right and wrong.

8. **C** "Without opportunity there would be no crime" fails to consider that thievery is not the only type of crime.

9. **B** This choice offers the most thorough and comprehensive evidence that the viewing of violent television precedes criminal behavior. (A) is not the best choice because it describes viewing habits that follow rather than precede criminal behavior.

10. **E** The use of "overwhelming" leaves the evidence unspecified, thus opening to challenge the extent and nature of the report's data.

11. **B** The mention of "emotion" in two of the sentences following (11) narrows your choices to (A), (B), or (E). Since the passage is about the "affects" of sensations, (A) or (E) would be inaccurate.

12. **C** An emotion has a *logical* component, so the passage says. All choices except (C) are "illogical" terms.

13. **B** If the experiences and lifestyle of the Aryan race are uniquely different from those of other cultures, it would seriously weaken the author's conclusion that studying the Aryan race will be helpful in understanding the experiences and life styles of other races. That its communal arrangements are *unique* would make comparison between the Aryan race and other cultures impossible.

14. **C** The author presents a *contrast* between life and honor: in particular, the final sentence suggests that life and honor have opposite qualities. Of the choices, the only opposite of *transient* is *eternal*.

15. **E** The logic of this statement goes from the general absolute ("all") to the specific ("this animal"), concluding with specific to specific. Symbolically, if *P* implies *Q*, then *not Q* implies *not P*. (E) goes from general absolute ("all") to specific ("this liquid"), concluding with specific to specific. Notice how and where the inverse ("not") is inserted. Using symbols, we have that, if *P* implies *Q*, then *not Q* implies *not P*.

16. **B** This is a close one. (B) and (D) both weaken the argument by pointing out that all dogs do not always bark, but (B) is absolute. (D) is tentative, since a dog trained not to bark might do so by accident.

17. **D** (D) is the correct answer, since it states "cheat on *none* of the exams," while the passage states, "Everyone has cheated on *at least* one exam." (A) is incorrect, since it says nothing about what Joe actually did. (B) is incorrect, since, although we are told that cheating is "wrong," we do not know what is "acceptable" and what is not. Do not make subjective answers. (C) is not a good choice, since Jack may never have taken an exam. (E) is incorrect, since it just restates two of the given conditions.

18. **C** Statements (A) and (B) repeat the first part of the sentence—ignorance of <u>different</u> subjects. But since the sentence singles out no one subject, (C) is correct.

19. **C** The sentence criticizes people, and a satirist is such a critic.

20. **C** (A) contradicts the statement's urging of economy. (B) introduces an irrelevant word, "terminology." (D) and (E) are *absolute* statements about assumptions, but the statement itself is *relative*, urging us only to simplify our assumptions *if one such simplification is possible; in other words, "If an issue is simple, don't complicate it."*

21. **E** The question demonstrates a solution and the fact that an alternative exists.

22. **E** (A) is obviously true. (B) also satisfies the conditions. (C) is correct, since 3.5 was required with a score of 800. (D) is correct, since we do not know anything about numbers of applicants. (E) is inconsistent, since a score of 1200 is required with a GPA of 2.5. (E) specifies a score *less than* 1200. Therefore, a GPA greater than (*not less than*) 2.5 would be required for admittance.

23. **B** To speak in positive terms about the increase in school degrees, the author must assume that the degrees indicate what they are supposed to indicate, that is, well-educated individuals. (A) and (E) are empty statements; (C) and (D) are altogether unsubstantiated by either expressed or implied information.

24. **E** Although the brand name is No-NOCK, the advertisement makes no claim to stop the engine from knocking. All the other claims are contained in the advertisement.

25. **D** The choice repudiates the suggestion that gentleness and graciousness were once part of the American character. (B), another choice worth considering, is not best because it does not address the temperament of tennis players as directly as does (D).

26. **B** By asking Dolores to choose between conventional and nuclear weapons, Fran has concluded that Dolores's statement calls for a decision. (C), worth considering, is not best because Fran supposes that Dolores has *not* made a choice—hence her question.

Section IV

Answers 1–6

From the information given, you should have constructed a diagram similar to this:

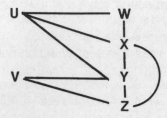

1. **B** From the diagram, if the group begins on island W, it could not reach island V in the eight days. Remember three days would have to be spent on W and three on X.

2. **B** From the diagram, if the group stays on island X for three nights, then the group cannot get to island V on the next visit.

3. **D** To answer this question, you must try each answer choice and eliminate the ones that do not connect. From the diagram, the only possible order listed would be U X Z V.

4. **E** From the diagram, if the group visits island W first, it could go to U to X to Y to V to Z, back to X, and back to W. A total of 8 visits. You could work from the choices, but remember to start from the highest number.

5. **D** From the diagram, the group could go from X to W to U to Y to V to Z to Y. This would be 6 different islands.

6. **E** Adding island T to the diagram connected only to V could look like this:

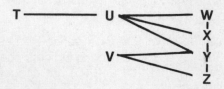

From this revised diagram, only (E) must be true. On the tenth day of a tour starting on Z, the tour group could be on island T. It would go from Z to Y to U to T or Z to X to U to T.

Answers 7–13

From the information given, you could have constructed the following diagram:

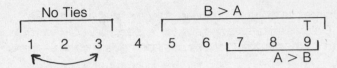

Notice the simple markings to show:

There are no ties in the first 3 games.
Team A wins more of the last 3 games than team B.
Team B wins more of the last 5 games than team A.
The last game is a tie.
Games 1 and 3 are won by the same team.

From this information you could deduce that team A wins either game 7 or 8, but not both, and team B cannot win any of the last 3 games. (If team A won both, team B could not win more of the last 5 games.) If team A wins game 7, then 8 is a tie, and if team A wins game 8, then 7 is a tie.

You could also deduce that team B must win games 5 and 6. Your diagram now looks like this:

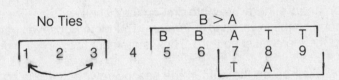

7. **C** From the information given, since games 1 and 3 are won by the same team, then one team wins at least 2 of the first 3 games.

8. **E** From the diagram, game 6 must be won by team B.

9. **A** From the diagram, if game 7 is won by team A, then game 8 must be a tie.

10. **E** From the diagram, you can see that (E) must be true.

11. **E** If team A wins games 1 and 4, then it must also win game 3. This would give team A four wins total, and team B could only win three, therefore team B could not win the series. For this question, the diagram would now look like this:

$$\begin{array}{ccccccccc} A & A & A & B & B & A & & T \\ 1 & 2 & 3 & 4 & 5 & 6 & 7 & 8 & 9 \end{array}$$

12. **B** If game 4 is won by the winner of game 5, then team B wins game 4. If game 2 is not won by the winner of game 3, then team B wins either game 2 or 3. This gives team B at least four wins and team A only a possible three wins, therefore B is the winner of the series.

13. **E** From the original diagram, team A must win either games 1, 2, and 3, or games 1, 3, and 4 to win the series. [This also eliminates choice (A).] If team B wins exactly one of the first four games [choice (B)], then team B cannot win the series as team A will win at least three games. If team A wins only three of the first seven games [choice (C)], then team A could still lose the series as team B could win games 2, 4, 5, and 6, with team A winning only games 1, 3, and 7. Team B could win the series by winning two of the first four games, eliminating choice (D).

Answers 14–18

Drawing a simple diagram, below, will help answer the questions.

```
                                                      TR
                                                       *
_____ _____ _____  __J__           FDR

M, A, K, FDR  →  _____ _____ __M__ __A__   K - FDR or FDR - K
```

Note that, once Madison is placed in position 3 on the bottom, Adams must go in position 4 in order to leave spots for Kennedy to be adjacent to Franklin Delano Roosevelt.

14. **D** If Theodore Roosevelt is second from the left (on top), then Franklin Delano Roosevelt must be first on the bottom since one Roosevelt may not be above the other. Therefore, Kennedy must be second on the bottom.

15. **A** Adams must go to the far right on the bottom to allow Kennedy to be adjacent to Franklin Delano Roosevelt.

16. **D** If Washington and Kennedy are both first on their shelves, then Franklin Delano Roosevelt must be second on the lower shelf. Therefore, Theodore Roosevelt cannot be second on the top shelf and therefore must be third. Thus, statement D cannot be true.

17. **E** Since Adams must be on the right in the second row, only (E) is not possible.

18. **C** If Lincoln is next to Jefferson, that leaves Theodore Roosevelt and Washington for the first two positions on the top shelf. All of the choices are therefore true except (C) because that choice would place one Roosevelt above the other, which is not permitted.

Answers 19–24

19. **B** Since lima beans will not go with kidney beans or chili beans, they can go only with wax beans and garbanzos. Therefore, there is only one salad (limas + wax + garbanzos) that contains limas and that may be served at the party.

20. **C** The combinations of salads without chili beans are as follows:

1. garbanzos + wax + limas
2. garbanzos + limas + kidneys
3. garbanzos + wax + kidneys
4. wax + limas + kidneys

But remember that the *servable* salads may not include limas with kidneys or chili beans, thus reducing the number to two: garbanzos + wax + kidneys, and garbanzos + wax + limas.

21. **B** Without any restrictions there are 10 possible ways to choose three ingredients from a total of five:

```
CGW   GWL   WLK
CGL   GLK
CGK   GWK
CWL
CWK
CLK
```

However, the imposed restrictions (lima beans do not go with kidney beans or chili beans) narrow the servable salads down to five:

CGW	GWL	~~WLK~~
~~CGL~~	~~GLK~~	
CGK	GWK	
~~CWL~~		
CWK		
~~CLK~~		

22. **E** From the chart above, we can see that garbanzos and wax beans appear more times in the servable salads. The other ingredients do not appear as often.

23. **C** From our chart we can see that having only enough wax beans for two salads will eliminate two of the four wax bean salads. Therefore, instead of five servable salads, there will now be only three.

24. **B** Again from our chart, if we eliminate the servable salads with garbanzos, we are left with only one servable salad: chili + wax + kidneys.

Section V

1. **B** The correct answer must use both premises. The first qualifies the assertion with "normally," so (A) will not follow, but (B) (with the qualifier "may") will. (C) may or may not be true, but it is not a logical conclusion based on the two premises. (D) and (E), like (A), do not use both premises.

2. **D** The question asked concerns the danger to public health, but the reply does not deal with this issue at all. It changes the subject.

3. **C** Reducing coffee consumption in general will not guarantee a healthier population (A) if "heavy" consumers do not reduce their coffee intake. Reducing coffee consumption would make those who drink a morning cup of coffee feel less well (B). (C) is a logical conclusion since heavy consumption increases heart attack risk. There is no information in the passage to justify the assertion about percolated coffee (D). If coffee may protect against colon cancer, (E) is not true.

4. **D** The issue of the danger of pesticides is addressed by (A), (C), and (E), while (B) calls into question the objectivity of the Food and Agriculture Department. But (D) deals with a different issue: air pollution. And if air pollution is a cause of illness, pesticides may be less to blame.

5. **A** The question contains its own prior judgment (underpay, unfair promotion policies) on what it asks, regardless of a "yes" or "no" answer. Similarly, the adjective "excessive" and the adverb "unfairly" prejudge any answer in choice (A).

6. **E** Since fares have risen, the cost of fuel has risen or there are no fare wars. And if there are no fare wars, the number of passengers is larger. Only (E) cannot be true. (B) is possible if fuel costs have risen, and there are fare wars.

7. **B** What must be known is the weight of each commodity that is needed. Choice (B) tells us three pounds of clams is equal to one of swordfish, so the cost would be $4.50 for clams versus $6.00 for swordfish.

8. **C** The advertisement asserts filter cigarettes cannot have great taste. A reasonable inference is that Gold Star is not a filter cigarette. (A) is contradicted by this ad without visual appeal. (B) is contradicted by this ad, which does not specifically praise a brand. (D) is illogical given the existence of this ad. Nothing in the ad supports (E).

9. **E**   Though all of the choices are plausible, (E) deals with all three of the problems mentioned in the paragraph. Each of the other choices deals only with one.

10. **A**   There is nothing in the paragraph to support (E), and there are details that contradict (B), (C), and (D). That "sales in the United States continue to increase" supports (A).

11. **E**   The passage does not give the information that would lead to the conclusion in (A), (B), or (C). (E) is a better answer than (D), the odds against the heavy smoker being 40 in 100 as opposed to 25 in 100 for the light smoker.

12. **C**   The presence of wolf bones and walrus bones near a village is not evidence that wolves were trained to haul sleds; it does not disprove the theory, however.

13. **B**   Choices (A), (C), (D), and (E) would undermine the theory. But if wolves were easily domesticated and trained, it would make the theory of their domestication by Stone-Age tribes more plausible.

14. **A**   The author makes his point by invective, an abrasive verbal attack.

15. **D**   The first sentence asserts the needlessness of commenting on the picture; the second nonetheless makes a detailed criticism.

16. **B**   If popcorn attracts rodents and insects, warehouses where packages using popcorn are stored would have vermin problems.

17. **B**   Only (B) is a necessary assumption. It must be assumed that no other items (for example dressings, recipes, spices, etc.) are sold at the stand in order to conclude definitively that everything sold there is delicious.

18. **B**   Though (E) is probably true, it is not a conclusion based on the information in the passage. But the passage does assert that only 19.67 percent (11.9 plus 7.7) of the eligible voters in the Democratic and Republican parties went to the polls.

19. **A**   Choices (B) and (C), although true, are not relevant, while (D) and (E) are probably untrue. That it is only in the schools that the tobacco spokesmen are silent supports the inference of (A).

20. **C**   In both paragraphs, the author disputes the interpretations of his opponents.

21. **D**   The author assumes that an audience is able to evaluate a work and determine its own course of action.

22. **E**   The opening lines describe esteem without popularity, later followed by popular success.

23. **D**   The "But" introducing the last sentence suggests that a contrast, a disadvantage of coffee, is to follow. Either (C) or (D) is possible, but since exercise has not been an issue, (D) is the better choice.

24. **A**   Only choice (A) must be true. There may be other performers as well as the chorus members (the orchestra, for example) in the performance, so (E) is incorrect.

25. **C**   The passage draws an analogy comparing corrupt politicians to vermin.

Chapter

7

Model Test Two

This chapter contains full-length Model Test Two. It is geared to the format of the LSAT, and it is complete with answers and explanations. It is equivalent to the LSAT in question structure, number of questions, level of difficulty, and time allotments. (The questions used are not taken directly from the LSAT, as those questions are copyrighted and may not be reproduced.)

Model Test Two should be taken under strict test conditions. The test ends with a 30-minute Writing Sample, which is not scored.

Section	Description	Number of Questions	Time Allowed
I	Logical Reasoning	26	35 minutes
II	Reading Comprehension	27	35 minutes
III	Analytical Reasoning	24	35 minutes
IV	Logical Reasoning	26	35 minutes
V	Reading Comprehension	27	35 minutes
	Writing Sample		30 minutes
TOTALS:		130	3 hours 25 minutes

Now please turn to the next page, remove your answer sheet, and begin Model Test Two.

ANSWER SHEET—MODEL TEST TWO
LAW SCHOOL ADMISSION TEST (LSAT)

Section I: Logical Reasoning	Section II: Reading Comprehension	Section III: Analytical Reasoning
1. Ⓐ Ⓑ Ⓒ Ⓓ Ⓔ	1. Ⓐ Ⓑ Ⓒ Ⓓ Ⓔ	1. Ⓐ Ⓑ Ⓒ Ⓓ Ⓔ
2. Ⓐ Ⓑ Ⓒ Ⓓ Ⓔ	2. Ⓐ Ⓑ Ⓒ Ⓓ Ⓔ	2. Ⓐ Ⓑ Ⓒ Ⓓ Ⓔ
3. Ⓐ Ⓑ Ⓒ Ⓓ Ⓔ	3. Ⓐ Ⓑ Ⓒ Ⓓ Ⓔ	3. Ⓐ Ⓑ Ⓒ Ⓓ Ⓔ
4. Ⓐ Ⓑ Ⓒ Ⓓ Ⓔ	4. Ⓐ Ⓑ Ⓒ Ⓓ Ⓔ	4. Ⓐ Ⓑ Ⓒ Ⓓ Ⓔ
5. Ⓐ Ⓑ Ⓒ Ⓓ Ⓔ	5. Ⓐ Ⓑ Ⓒ Ⓓ Ⓔ	5. Ⓐ Ⓑ Ⓒ Ⓓ Ⓔ
6. Ⓐ Ⓑ Ⓒ Ⓓ Ⓔ	6. Ⓐ Ⓑ Ⓒ Ⓓ Ⓔ	6. Ⓐ Ⓑ Ⓒ Ⓓ Ⓔ
7. Ⓐ Ⓑ Ⓒ Ⓓ Ⓔ	7. Ⓐ Ⓑ Ⓒ Ⓓ Ⓔ	7. Ⓐ Ⓑ Ⓒ Ⓓ Ⓔ
8. Ⓐ Ⓑ Ⓒ Ⓓ Ⓔ	8. Ⓐ Ⓑ Ⓒ Ⓓ Ⓔ	8. Ⓐ Ⓑ Ⓒ Ⓓ Ⓔ
9. Ⓐ Ⓑ Ⓒ Ⓓ Ⓔ	9. Ⓐ Ⓑ Ⓒ Ⓓ Ⓔ	9. Ⓐ Ⓑ Ⓒ Ⓓ Ⓔ
10. Ⓐ Ⓑ Ⓒ Ⓓ Ⓔ	10. Ⓐ Ⓑ Ⓒ Ⓓ Ⓔ	10. Ⓐ Ⓑ Ⓒ Ⓓ Ⓔ
11. Ⓐ Ⓑ Ⓒ Ⓓ Ⓔ	11. Ⓐ Ⓑ Ⓒ Ⓓ Ⓔ	11. Ⓐ Ⓑ Ⓒ Ⓓ Ⓔ
12. Ⓐ Ⓑ Ⓒ Ⓓ Ⓔ	12. Ⓐ Ⓑ Ⓒ Ⓓ Ⓔ	12. Ⓐ Ⓑ Ⓒ Ⓓ Ⓔ
13. Ⓐ Ⓑ Ⓒ Ⓓ Ⓔ	13. Ⓐ Ⓑ Ⓒ Ⓓ Ⓔ	13. Ⓐ Ⓑ Ⓒ Ⓓ Ⓔ
14. Ⓐ Ⓑ Ⓒ Ⓓ Ⓔ	14. Ⓐ Ⓑ Ⓒ Ⓓ Ⓔ	14. Ⓐ Ⓑ Ⓒ Ⓓ Ⓔ
15. Ⓐ Ⓑ Ⓒ Ⓓ Ⓔ	15. Ⓐ Ⓑ Ⓒ Ⓓ Ⓔ	15. Ⓐ Ⓑ Ⓒ Ⓓ Ⓔ
16. Ⓐ Ⓑ Ⓒ Ⓓ Ⓔ	16. Ⓐ Ⓑ Ⓒ Ⓓ Ⓔ	16. Ⓐ Ⓑ Ⓒ Ⓓ Ⓔ
17. Ⓐ Ⓑ Ⓒ Ⓓ Ⓔ	17. Ⓐ Ⓑ Ⓒ Ⓓ Ⓔ	17. Ⓐ Ⓑ Ⓒ Ⓓ Ⓔ
18. Ⓐ Ⓑ Ⓒ Ⓓ Ⓔ	18. Ⓐ Ⓑ Ⓒ Ⓓ Ⓔ	18. Ⓐ Ⓑ Ⓒ Ⓓ Ⓔ
19. Ⓐ Ⓑ Ⓒ Ⓓ Ⓔ	19. Ⓐ Ⓑ Ⓒ Ⓓ Ⓔ	19. Ⓐ Ⓑ Ⓒ Ⓓ Ⓔ
20. Ⓐ Ⓑ Ⓒ Ⓓ Ⓔ	20. Ⓐ Ⓑ Ⓒ Ⓓ Ⓔ	20. Ⓐ Ⓑ Ⓒ Ⓓ Ⓔ
21. Ⓐ Ⓑ Ⓒ Ⓓ Ⓔ	21. Ⓐ Ⓑ Ⓒ Ⓓ Ⓔ	21. Ⓐ Ⓑ Ⓒ Ⓓ Ⓔ
22. Ⓐ Ⓑ Ⓒ Ⓓ Ⓔ	22. Ⓐ Ⓑ Ⓒ Ⓓ Ⓔ	22. Ⓐ Ⓑ Ⓒ Ⓓ Ⓔ
23. Ⓐ Ⓑ Ⓒ Ⓓ Ⓔ	23. Ⓐ Ⓑ Ⓒ Ⓓ Ⓔ	23. Ⓐ Ⓑ Ⓒ Ⓓ Ⓔ
24. Ⓐ Ⓑ Ⓒ Ⓓ Ⓔ	24. Ⓐ Ⓑ Ⓒ Ⓓ Ⓔ	24. Ⓐ Ⓑ Ⓒ Ⓓ Ⓔ
25. Ⓐ Ⓑ Ⓒ Ⓓ Ⓔ	25. Ⓐ Ⓑ Ⓒ Ⓓ Ⓔ	
26. Ⓐ Ⓑ Ⓒ Ⓓ Ⓔ	26. Ⓐ Ⓑ Ⓒ Ⓓ Ⓔ	
	27. Ⓐ Ⓑ Ⓒ Ⓓ Ⓔ	

ANSWER SHEET—MODEL TEST TWO
LAW SCHOOL ADMISSION TEST (LSAT)

Section IV:
Logical Reasoning

1. (A) (B) (C) (D) (E)
2. (A) (B) (C) (D) (E)
3. (A) (B) (C) (D) (E)
4. (A) (B) (C) (D) (E)
5. (A) (B) (C) (D) (E)
6. (A) (B) (C) (D) (E)
7. (A) (B) (C) (D) (E)
8. (A) (B) (C) (D) (E)
9. (A) (B) (C) (D) (E)
10. (A) (B) (C) (D) (E)
11. (A) (B) (C) (D) (E)
12. (A) (B) (C) (D) (E)
13. (A) (B) (C) (D) (E)
14. (A) (B) (C) (D) (E)
15. (A) (B) (C) (D) (E)
16. (A) (B) (C) (D) (E)
17. (A) (B) (C) (D) (E)
18. (A) (B) (C) (D) (E)
19. (A) (B) (C) (D) (E)
20. (A) (B) (C) (D) (E)
21. (A) (B) (C) (D) (E)
22. (A) (B) (C) (D) (E)
23. (A) (B) (C) (D) (E)
24. (A) (B) (C) (D) (E)
25. (A) (B) (C) (D) (E)
26. (A) (B) (C) (D) (E)

Section V:
Reading Comprehension

1. (A) (B) (C) (D) (E)
2. (A) (B) (C) (D) (E)
3. (A) (B) (C) (D) (E)
4. (A) (B) (C) (D) (E)
5. (A) (B) (C) (D) (E)
6. (A) (B) (C) (D) (E)
7. (A) (B) (C) (D) (E)
8. (A) (B) (C) (D) (E)
9. (A) (B) (C) (D) (E)
10. (A) (B) (C) (D) (E)
11. (A) (B) (C) (D) (E)
12. (A) (B) (C) (D) (E)
13. (A) (B) (C) (D) (E)
14. (A) (B) (C) (D) (E)
15. (A) (B) (C) (D) (E)
16. (A) (B) (C) (D) (E)
17. (A) (B) (C) (D) (E)
18. (A) (B) (C) (D) (E)
19. (A) (B) (C) (D) (E)
20. (A) (B) (C) (D) (E)
21. (A) (B) (C) (D) (E)
22. (A) (B) (C) (D) (E)
23. (A) (B) (C) (D) (E)
24. (A) (B) (C) (D) (E)
25. (A) (B) (C) (D) (E)
26. (A) (B) (C) (D) (E)
27. (A) (B) (C) (D) (E)

SECTION I:
LOGICAL REASONING

Time—35 Minutes
26 Questions

Directions:

In this section you will be given brief statements or passages and will be required to evaluate the reasoning involved. In some instances, more than one choice will appear to be a possible answer. You are to choose the *best* answer. Use common sense and reasonableness in making your selection; then mark the proper space on the answer sheet.

Questions 1–2 refer to the following passage.

Probability is a curiously unstable concept. Semantically speaking, it is an assumption, a pure artifice, a concept that may or may not be true, but nevertheless facilitates a logical process. It is not a hypothesis because, by its very nature, it cannot be proved. Suppose we flip a coin that has a distinguishable head and tail. In our ignorance of the coming result, we say that the coin has one chance in two of falling heads up, or that the probability of a head turning up is one-to-two. Here it must be understood that the one-to-two is not "true" but is merely a species of the genus probability.

1. The author of this passage assumes that
   (A) nothing about our coin influences its fall in favor of either side or that all influences are counterbalanced by equal and opposite influences
   (B) probability can be dealt with without the use of logic
   (C) an assumption must be plausible
   (D) the probability of the coin's landing on an edge is counterbalanced by the probability of its not landing on an edge
   (E) probability can be precisely calculated

2. The last sentence implies that
   (A) probability is not absolute
   (B) one-to-two is merely a guess
   (C) one-to-two is a worthless ratio
   (D) truth is not important
   (E) genus is a category of species

3. Self-confidence is a big factor in success. The person who thinks he can, will master most of the things he attempts. The person who thinks he can't, may not try.

   The author of these statements would agree that
   (A) nothing is impossible
   (B) no task is too large
   (C) success relies on effort
   (D) self-confidence is of most importance
   (E) trying is half the battle

4. Booker T. Washington was criticized by members of his own race for rationalizing the fate of African-American people with the following assertion: "No race shall prosper 'til it learns there is as much dignity in tilling a field as in writing a poem."

Which of the following, if true, would strengthen the criticism of Washington's assertion?
(A) Most African-American people during Washington's time were denied access to a liberal arts education.
(B) African-American landowners who worked hard running a farm were often able to pay for the artistic or professional education of their children.
(C) White people had respect for both African-American poets and African-American farmers.
(D) The economically dominant countries of the world are mainly agricultural.
(E) Most of Washington's critics had never tilled a field.

5. If no test has no easy questions, then all of the following must be true EXCEPT
(A) every test has some easy questions
(B) some tests have some easy questions
(C) no test has all hard questions
(D) easy tests have easy questions
(E) every test has some hard questions

Questions 6–7 require you to complete the missing portions of the following passage by selecting from the five alternatives the one that best fits the context of the passage.

Relations are spiritual or mental things that inhabit the world of consciousness. We may call them holy ghosts if they have to do with the relation between the finite and infinite, the limited and the limitless, the conceivable and the inconceivable. Thus it is the very contrary of stupidity to say that you cannot be (6) _____ of one thing and one only. In order to have one, you must have three: a thing, a relation, and another thing. The meaning of one of them is determined by your (7) _____.

6. (A) unaware   (B) considerate   (C) conscious   (D) knowledgeable   (E) stupid

7. (A) momentary awareness of the other two
(B) momentary unawareness of the other two
(C) overall knowledge of the other relation
(D) complete mastery of the relationship
(E) identification of the ambiguity of the statement

Questions 8–10 refer to the following statements.

(A) The President is not well. He must therefore miss his appointment.
(B) Imagine what would happen if you tried to raise geraniums in a dark room. Plants must have light to survive.
(C) His tardiness was probably the key factor in his failure to be prompt, according to his supervisor.
(D) Arnold's disability was apparent. He winced during the examination of his knee.
(E) Kermit and I kept a dozen trophies; otherwise we would have nothing to show for our years of playing sports.

8. Which of the above statements is an example of the use of *specific instance* to support a point?

9. Which of the above statements is an example of *circular reasoning* to support a point?

10. Which of the above statements uses *hypothetical example* to support a point?

Questions 11–13 refer to the following passage.

Sixty percent of the American people, according to the latest polls, now believe that inflation is the nation's most important problem. This problem of inflation is closely related to rising prices.

The inflation rate has been 10 percent or more most of this year. Undoubtedly, our gluttonous appetite for high-priced foreign oil has been a major factor. We have been shipping billions of dollars overseas, more than foreigners can spend or invest here. Dollars are selling cheaply and this has forced the value of the dollar down. Government programs now being inaugurated to slow this trend are at best weak, but deserve our support, as they appear to be the best our government can produce. Hopefully, they won't fail as they have in the past.

11. The author of this passage implies that
    (A) inflation cannot be stopped or slowed, because of a weak government
    (B) the fear of inflation is not only unwarranted, but also detrimental
    (C) 40 percent of non-Americans believe inflation is not the most important problem
    (D) foreign oil is the sole reason for the sudden increase in inflation
    (E) the present programs will probably not slow inflation.

12. Which of the following contradicts something in the preceding passage?
    (A) Foreign oil is actually underpriced.
    (B) The inflation rate has not risen for most of this year.
    (C) Overseas investors are few and far between.
    (D) Our government is trying a new approach to end inflation.
    (E) The weakness of the programs stems from lack of support.

13. The author of this passage would agree that
    (A) American goods are selling well in foreign markets
    (B) government programs will reduce inflation
    (C) our government is giving its utmost
    (D) the latest polls are giving false information
    (E) oil independence could help slow the trend

14. No one reads *Weight-Off* magazine unless he is fat. Everyone reads *Weight-Off* magazine unless he eats chocolate.

    Which of the following is inconsistent with the above?
    (A) No one is fat and only some people eat chocolate.
    (B) Some people are fat and no one eats chocolate.
    (C) Everyone is fat.
    (D) No one is fat and no one reads *Weight-Off*.
    (E) No one who is fat eats chocolate.

15. *Jerry*: Every meal my wife cooks is fantastic.
    Dave: I disagree. Most of my wife's meals are fantastic, too.

    Dave's response shows that he understood Jerry to mean that
    (A) Dave's wife does not cook fantastic meals
    (B) only Jerry's wife cooks fantastic meals
    (C) every one of Jerry's wife's meals is fantastic
    (D) not every one of Jerry's wife's meals is fantastic
    (E) no one cooks fantastic meals all the time

Questions 16–17 refer to the following quotation.

"Before a man can be in any capacity to speak on the subject, it is necessary he be acquainted with it; or else it is as foolish to set him to discourse of it as to set a blind man to talk of colors, or a deaf man of music."—*Dewey*

16. This passage is discussing
    (A) scientific methods
    (B) biological behavior
    (C) sociological foundations

    (D)   education practices
    (E)   legal implications

17. The author of this passage is most likely a
    (A) lawyer   (B) chemist   (C) philosopher   (D) poet   (E) minister

18. Mike will talk to Joe if Joe will talk to Henry.
If Henry does not talk to Dave, then Mike will not talk to Joe.

All of the following are true based on the above conditions EXCEPT
    (A)   if Mike won't talk to Joe, then Joe won't talk to Henry
    (B)   if Joe talks to Henry, Mike will talk to Joe
    (C)   if Henry talks to Dave, then Mike will talk to Joe
    (D)   if Mike talks to Joe, then Henry will talk to Dave
    (E)   Mike will not talk to Joe if Dave and Henry do not talk to each other

19. X: "We discover new knowledge by the syllogistic process when we say, for example, 'All men are mortal; Socrates is a man; therefore Socrates is mortal.'"

    Y: "Yes, but the fact is that if all men are mortal we cannot tell whether Socrates is a man until we have determined his mortality—in other words, until we find him dead. Of course, it's a great convenience to assume that Socrates is a man because he looks like one, but that's just a deduction. If we examine its formulation—'Objects that resemble men in most respects are men; Socrates resembles men in most respects; therefore Socrates is a man'—it's obvious that if he is a man, he resembles men in *all* necessary respects. So it's obvious we're right back where we started."

    X: "Yes, we must know all the characteristics of men, and that Socrates has all of them, before we can be sure."

Which of the following best expresses X's concluding observation?
    (A)   In deductive thinking we are simply reminding ourselves of the implications of our generalizations.
    (B)   It is often too convenient to arrive at conclusions simply by deduction instead of induction.
    (C)   Socrates' mortality is not the issue; the issue is critical thinking.
    (D)   Socrates' characteristics do not necessarily define his mortality.
    (E)   The key to the syllogistic process is using theoretical, rather than practical, issues of logic.

20. It takes a good telescope to see the moons of Neptune. I can't see the moons of Neptune with my telescope. Therefore, I do not have a good telescope.

Which of the following most closely parallels the logic of this statement?
    (A)   It takes two to tango. You are doing the tango. Therefore, you have a partner.
    (B)   If you have a surfboard, you can surf. You do not have a surfboard. Therefore, you cannot surf.
    (C)   You need gin and vermouth to make a martini. You do not have any gin. Therefore, you cannot make a martini.
    (D)   If you know the area of a circle, you can find its circumference. You cannot figure out the circumference. Therefore, you do not know the area.
    (E)   You can write a letter to your friend with a pencil. You do not have a pencil. Therefore, you cannot write the letter.

Questions 21–22 refer to the following passage.

Over 90 percent of our waking life depends on habits which for the most part we are unconscious of, from brushing our teeth in the morning, to the time and manner in which we go to sleep at night. Habits are tools which serve the important function of relieving the conscious mind for more important activities. Habits are stored patterns of behavior which are found to serve the needs of the individual that has them and are formed from what once was conscious behavior which over years of repetition can become an automatic behavior pattern of the unconscious mind.

21. It can be inferred that the author bases his beliefs on
    (A) the testimony of a controlled group of students
    (B) biblical passages referring to the unconscious state
    (C) an intense psychological research
    (D) extensive psychological research
    (E) recent findings of clinical psychologists

22. The last sentence implies that
    (A) all repetitious patterns become unconscious behavior
    (B) conscious behavior eventually becomes habit
    (C) the unconscious mind causes repetitive behavior
    (D) automatic behavior patterns of the conscious mind are not possible
    (E) habits can be good or bad

Questions 23–24 refer to the following passage.

It should be emphasized that only one person in a thousand who is bitten by a disease-carrying mosquito develops symptoms that require hospitalization, according to Dr. Reeves. But it is a potentially serious disease that requires close collaboration by citizens and local government to prevent it from reaching epidemic proportions.

Citizens should fill or drain puddles where mosquitoes breed. They should repair leaking swamp coolers and be sure swimming pools have a good circulating system. Make sure drain gutters aren't clogged and holding rainwater. Keep barrels and other water-storage containers tightly covered. Use good window screens.

23. Which of the following statements, if true, would most strengthen the advice given in the second paragraph above?
    (A) Leaking swamp coolers are the primary cause of mosquito infestation.
    (B) It is possible to completely eliminate mosquitoes from a neighborhood.
    (C) No one can completely protect herself from being bitten by a mosquito.
    (D) Tightly covered water containers do not ensure the purity of the water in all cases.
    (E) Window screens seldom need to be replaced.

24. What additional information would strengthen the clarity of the second sentence above?
    (A) The names of some local governments that have fought against disease.
    (B) The name of the disease under discussion.
    (C) The names of those bitten by disease-carrying mosquitoes.
    (D) The full name of Dr. Reeves.
    (E) A description of the symptoms that a bitten person might develop.

25. That which is rare is always more valuable than that which is abundant. And so we are continually frustrated in our attempts to teach young people how to use time wisely; they have too much of it to appreciate its value.

Which of the following statements, if true, would most weaken the argument above?
    (A) Appreciation is not the same as obedience.
    (B) "Abundant" is a term whose definition varies widely.
    (C) Currency that is based on rare metals is more valuable than currency that is not.
    (D) Many young people possess an intuitive knowledge of what time is, a knowledge they lose around middle age.
    (E) The leisure time of people aged 18–24 has decreased by 80 percent over the last 10 years.

26.   Many theorists now believe that people cannot learn to write if they are constantly worrying about whether their prose is correct or not. When a would-be writer worries about correctness, his ability for fluency is frozen.

With which of the following statements would the author of the above passage probably agree?
(A)   Writing theorists are probably wrong.
(B)   Writing prose is different from writing poetry.
(C)   Literacy is a function of relaxation.
(D)   Fear blocks action.
(E)   Most good writers are careless.

STOP

IF YOU FINISH BEFORE TIME IS UP, CHECK YOUR WORK ON THIS SECTION OF THE TEST ONLY. DO NOT GO ON TO THE NEXT SECTION OF THE TEST UNTIL TIME IS UP FOR THIS SECTION.

SECTION II
READING COMPREHENSION

Time—35 Minutes
27 Questions

Directions:
Read the passages and answer the questions following each passage by blackening the appropriate space on the answer sheet. You may refer back to the passages when answering the questions. Answer all questions on the basis of what is stated or implied.

Passage 1

The Sixth Amendment's right to the "assistance of counsel" has been the subject of considerable litigation in twentieth century American courts. The emphasis has traditionally centered on the degree to which a criminal defendant can demand the assistance of counsel in various courts and at different hierarchical stages of the criminal proceeding. Although past courts have
(5)   alluded to the idea that a defendant has a converse right to proceed without counsel, the issue had not been squarely addressed by the United States Supreme Court until late in its 1974–75 term. At that time, the Court held that within the Sixth Amendment rests an implied right of self-representation.

As early as 1964, Justice Hugo Black wrote that "the Sixth Amendment withholds from federal
(10)   courts, in all criminal proceedings, the power and authority to deprive an accused of his life or liberty unless he has or waives the assistance of counsel." However, recognizing that the Sixth Amendment does not require representation by counsel, it is quite another thing to say that the defendant has a constitutional right to reject professional assistance and proceed on his own.

Notwithstanding such a logical and legal fallacy, the Court has, by way of opinion, spoken of a
(15)   Sixth Amendment "correlative right" to dispense with a lawyer's help. Many lower federal courts have seized upon this and supported their holdings on it, in whole or in part.

The basic motivation behind this proffered right of self-representation is that "respect for individual autonomy requires that (the defendant) be allowed to go to jail under his own banner if he so desires" and that he should not be forced to accept counsel in whom he has no confidence.
(20)   Courts have ruled that neither due process nor progressive standards of criminal justice require that the defendant be represented at trial by counsel.

The Supreme Court, in its 1975 decision, held that a defendant in a state criminal trial has a constitutional right to waive counsel and carry on his own case *in propria persona*. In raising this obscure privilege to a constitutional level, the Court stated that, so long as the defendant is made
(25)   aware of the dangers and disadvantages of self-representation, his lack of technical legal knowledge will not deprive him of the right to defend himself personally.

The Court conceded that the long line of right to counsel cases have alluded to the idea that the assistance of counsel is a prerequisite to the realization of a fair trial. However, the Court noted that the presence of counsel is of minor significance when a stubborn, self-reliant defendant
(30)   prohibits the lawyer from employing his knowledge and skills. This line of reasoning is concluded with the observation that "the defendant, and not his lawyer or the state, will bear the personal consequences of a conviction." The logical extension of this premise brings the Court to its decision that, recognizing the traditional American respect for the individual, the defendant "must be free personally to decide whether in his particular case counsel is to his advantage."
(35)   In his dissenting opinion, Justice Harry Blackmun pointed out various procedural problems that were raised but left unanswered by the Court:

Must every defendant be advised of his right to proceed by himself? If so, when must that notice be given? Since the right to assistance of counsel and the right to self-representation are mutually exclusive, how is the waiver of each right to be
(40)   measured? If a defendant has elected to exercise his right to proceed by himself, does he still have a constitutional right to the assistance of standby counsel? How

soon in the criminal proceeding must a defendant decide between proceeding by counsel or by himself? Must he be allowed to switch in mid trial? May a violation of the right to self-representation ever be harmless error? Must the trial court treat the self

(45)   defendant differently than it would professional counsel?

In keeping with its traditional practice of limiting its opinions to as few, narrow issues as possible it seems the Court created many more questions than it answered. Aside from those issues enumerated by Justice Blackmun, there are several basic matters to be considered in order to evaluate the Court's new position on the rights of an accused.

1. According to the passage, the chief purpose of the Sixth Amendment is to
  (A)   assure a defendant the assistance of counsel in capital cases
  (B)   assure a defendant the assistance of counsel in civil cases
  (C)   assure a defendant the assistance of counsel in criminal cases
  (D)   allow a defendant to represent himself in a criminal trial
  (E)   allow a defendant to represent himself in a civil trial

2. The "logical and legal fallacy" referred to in line 14 is probably
  (A)   the ability to waive a right does not automatically give rise to a replacement of that right by another
  (B)   the right to reject implies a correlative right to refuse to reject
  (C)   the right to dispense with a lawyer's help
  (D)   the right to legal assistance
  (E)   the defendant who chooses to go to jail is free to do so

3. From the passage, the phrase *"in propria persona"* in line 23 means
  (A)   in his own person
  (B)   by an appropriate person
  (C)   in place of another person
  (D)   improperly
  (E)   by using a stand-in

4. In allowing a defendant to refuse counsel, the Supreme Court may have reasoned all of the following EXCEPT
  (A)   a defendant who objected to a court-appointed attorney would prevent the lawyer from defending him effectively
  (B)   the assistance of counsel is necessary to the realization of a fair trial
  (C)   in the event of an unfavorable verdict, the defendant will suffer the consequences
  (D)   American tradition recognizes the individual's freedom to make decisions that will affect him
  (E)   it is possible that a defendant might defend himself more effectively than a court-appointed lawyer

5. A defendant who is acting as counsel in his own defense must be
  (A)   given additional legal assistance
  (B)   allowed to give up his own defense if he chooses to do so before the trial has concluded
  (C)   warned of the disadvantages of self-representation
  (D)   assisted by the judge in areas where the defendant's lack of knowledge of technical legal terms is deficient
  (E)   tried before a jury

6. All of the following are objections that might be raised to self-representation EXCEPT
  (A)   by accepting the right to self-representation, a defendant must waive his right to assistance of counsel
  (B)   a defendant determined to convict himself can do so more easily
  (C)   if the right to self-representation is not asserted before the trial begins, it is lost
  (D)   self-representation has a tradition in American law that dates back to the colonial period
  (E)   a self-representation defendant may be unruly or disruptive

7. The author's attitude to the Supreme Court's 1975 decision is
  (A)   strong approval
  (B)   mild approval
  (C)   indifference
  (D)   unclear
  (E)   disapproval

Passage 2

More than two thousand years ago, Aristotle utilized two major criteria in classifying governments. One was the *number of persons* in which governing authority is vested; the other, the *primary purpose* toward which the exercise of governmental powers is directed.

In terms of the first criterion Aristotle distinguished three forms of government, viz., government by the one, by the few, and by the many. The second basis of classification, i.e, purpose, led him to differentiate "true" from "perverted" forms. True forms of government are characterized by the exercise of governmental authority for the benefit of all members of the body politic, whereas *perverted* types are featured by the use of governing power to promote the special and selfish interests of the ruling personnel. Government by the one for the benefit of all is *kingship* or *royalty;* government by the one for his private advantage is *tyranny.* Government by the few, if conducted for the purpose of promoting the common welfare, constitutes *aristocracy.* If the few rule in furtherance of their own selfish interests, the government is an *oligarchy.* The dominant few are likely to be men of property interested in increasing their wealth. Finally, government by the many (the citizens at large) for the benefit of all was identified as *polity* or *constitutional government,* whereas government by the many, usually the poor or the needy, for the purpose of promoting their selfish interests, was named *democracy,* a perverted form of government.

Unlike Aristotle, contemporary political scientists usually classify forms of government without introducing a test of purpose or motivation with respect to the use of governmental powers. Definitions of democracy, for instance, seldom include stipulations concerning the objectives to be attained by a government of the democratic type. However, an underlying assumption, even though unstated, seems to be that democratic processes of government probably will result in promotion of the common welfare.

Aristotle conceived of government by the many, whether of the true or perverted variety, as involving direct action by the body of qualified citizens in the formulation and adoption of policies. Hamilton and Madison, in their comments about democracy in the Federalist Papers, revealed a like conception of the nature of democracy. Thus Madison distinguished between a republic (representative government) and pure democracy. In his words a pure democracy is "a society consisting of a small number of citizens, who assemble and administer the government in person." A distinction is still drawn between direct and indirect democracy, but emphasis now is placed on the latter form, that is, democracy of the representative variety. Although direct democracy survives in a few small communities, e.g., New England towns and some of the cantons of Switzerland, representative democracy prevails in communities of large size. Consequently, the term *democracy* as used today almost always signifies a democratic government of the indirect or representative type.

8. According to the author's understanding of Aristotle, democracy is a "perverted" form of government because
  (A)   the poor comprise a special interest group
  (B)   the needs of the poor are sought through perverted behavior
  (C)   the poor comprise a larger group than the citizens at large
  (D)   the needs of the poor are less pure than those of other groups
  (E)   excessive poverty is the prelude to tyranny

9. In his discussion of pure democracy, the author is not explicit about
(A) Madison's conception of pure democracy
(B) the typical modern definition of democracy
(C) why pure democracy on a large scale is unwieldy
(D) the distinction between direct and indirect democracy
(E) why the views of Hamilton and Madison are similar to those of Aristotle

10. The author's primary purpose in this passage is to
(A) compare American and Greek philosophies
(B) judge the relative worth of various forms of government
(C) discuss the relationship of Aristotle's conception to later theory and practice
(D) praise the foresight of Aristotle
(E) develop an absolute definition of democracy

11. The author says that a modern democracy would regard the promotion of the common welfare as a
(A) partial result
(B) probable result
(C) certain result
(D) questionable result
(E) unique result

12. The author seems to presume that Aristotle
(A) would have supported the American Revolution
(B) utilized more than two major criteria in classifying governments
(C) is the one figure from antiquity whose political analyses are especially relevant to a discussion of modern government
(D) was studied by Hamilton and Madison
(E) was a philosopher who scarcely recognized the human potential for democratic government

13. The author's reliance on conceptions of government which are many centuries old suggests his belief that
(A) governments since antiquity have been obeying Aristotle's classification scheme
(B) conceptions of government change little through the ages
(C) political scientists have no need for new definitions
(D) later political theorists had read Aristotle before formulating their theories
(E) ancient definitions of government are analogous but not identical to current conceptions

Passage 3

(This passage was written in 1982.)

The largest manufacturing belt in the world is within the quadrilateral bounded by Baltimore, Boston, Minneapolis-St. Paul, and Kansas City. In the United States a number of manufacturing regions of considerable significance are located outside this quadrilateral. Centers such as those focused in southern California, the San Francisco Bay region, the Seattle-Portland axis, Dallas-Ft. Worth, the Galveston Bay area, and the Atlanta region are of considerable importance.

The principal advantages of the manufacturing belt are: (1) the principal market for commodities in the country; (2) a great variety and abundance of raw materials; (3) large quantities of high quality, low cost bituminous coal; (4) access to large quantities of electric power; (5) access to supplies of petroleum and natural gas; (6) excellent transportation facilities; (7) a large and skilled labor supply.

Just across the border in Canada in the Ontario Peninsula and St. Lawrence River Valley is an extension of the American manufacturing belt. The principal advantages of this region are essentially the same as those on the American side of the border. The accident of international boundaries separates what is essentially a single region with great significance in manufacturing.

Another major manufacturing region is located in western and northwestern Europe. This region served as a focus for the Industrial Revolution, and the advantages of an early start have persisted. Manufacturing was assisted early by the presence of important coal and iron deposits. Several districts in the United Kingdom, the Saar Basin, the Sambre-Meuse coal districts, and the Ruhr Valley all spawned coal demanding industries. The presence of ore in several areas of the United Kingdom and the Lorraine deposits of France and Luxembourg were additional spurs to early industrial development. Heavy industries, such as iron and steel, chemicals, rolling mills, metal fabrication plants, and others, developed and flourished. The United Kingdom, the Federal Republic of Germany (West Germany), the Benelux (Belgium, Netherlands, and Luxembourg) nations, and France were involved in these early developments. Expansion of industrial activities into most other urbanized areas of Europe has accelerated in the interval after World War II.

The population of Europe enjoys a stimulating climate, and is, in itself, a huge market. Excellent transportation facilities, availability of power, and coal are significant advantages of the region. Exploration for, and development of, oil and natural gas in the North Sea has been an added benefit and spur to industry in countries which rim it. This region rivals the industrial might of North America and is one of the great manufacturing regions of the world.

The Soviet Union has become a massive industrial power, and her wealth of resources has contributed mightily to her industrial might. She has become a leading producer of coal, and her production of oil exceeds national needs. Clusters of industrial facilities, such as those in the Ukraine, around Moscow, in the Urals, and in Soviet middle Asia have typically had a major local resource and power base. Strategic considerations along with governmental considerations have obviously been of major concern in plant location. It's clear that recent thaws in relationships with the West have come to open the door for the infusion of new technologies and equipment from capitalist states.

14. The author provides information to answer which of the following questions?
    (A)   Are there manufacturing belts in Asian countries south of Russia?
    (B)   Did the Industrial Revolution influence the growth of manufacturing belts?
    (C)   What is manufactured in the large American "quadrilateral" belt?
    (D)   What is the second largest manufacturing belt?
    (E)   What minerals have been found in the manufacturing belt in Canada?

15. "Strategic considerations," mentioned in the final paragraph, probably refers to which of the following?
    (A)   the relationship of a plant to the West
    (B)   the vulnerability of a plant to military attack
    (C)   the receptivity of a plant to new technologies
    (D)   the efficiency of a plant's facilities
    (E)   the marketing of excess oil

16. Which of the following is the most appropriate substitute for "spurs to" (fourth paragraph)?
    (A)   impulses over   (B) cleats on   (C) reasons of   (D) matters for
    (E)   motivators of

17. The primary purpose of the passage is to
    (A)   compare North America, Europe, and the Soviet Union
    (B)   reveal the advantages of manufacturing
    (C)   argue for the dominance of the United States as a manufacturer
    (D)   survey the locations and characteristics of manufacturing belts
    (E)   describe the influence of the Industrial Revolution on manufacturing

18. The author believes which of the following about the Industrial Revolution?
  (A) It created manufacturing belts.
  (B) Its effects on the United States were negligible.
  (C) It afforded western Europe a head start in manufacturing.
  (D) It did not take effect in Europe until after World War II.
  (E) It encouraged the presence of coal and iron deposits.

19. Which of the following is NOT a principal advantage of a manufacturing belt?
  (A) availability of energy
  (B) good highways
  (C) a temperate climate
  (D) availability of trained workers
  (E) a market for the manufactured goods

20. In general, this passage discusses the relationship between manufacturing and
  (A) geography   (B) history   (C) energy   (D) political pressure   (E) capitalism

Passage 4

"A sad spectacle!" exclaimed Thomas Carlyle, contemplating the possibility that millions of planets circle other suns. "If they be inhabited, what a scope for pain and folly; and if they be not inhabited, what a waste of space!"

Much more is now known about the universe than in Carlyle's time, but the question of whether ETI (a fashionable new acronym for Extraterrestrial Intelligence) exists is as open as it ever was. However, one incredible new fact has entered the picture. For the first time in history we have the technology for maybe answering the question. This mere possibility is so overwhelming in its implications that a new science called "exobiology" has already been named even though its entire subject matter may not exist.

We do know that our Milky Way galaxy contains more than 200 billion suns, and that there are billions of other galaxies. Are there other planets? Fifty years ago the two most popular theories about the origin of the solar system each made such planetary systems so unlikely that top astronomers believed that ours was the only one in the galaxy. After flaws were found in both theories, astronomers returned to a model proposed by Immanuel Kant (later by Laplace) in which solar systems are so likely that most of the Milky Way's stars must have them. The wobblings of a few nearby suns suggest big planets close to them, but no one really knows.

If solar systems are plentiful, our galaxy could contain billions of planets earthlike enough to support carbon-based life. Biologists have a strong case for confining life to carbon compounds (silicon and boron are the next best bets), but no one has any notion of how earthlike a planet must be to permit carbon life to arise. Our two nearest neighbors, Venus and Mars, were probably formed the same time the earth was; yet their atmospheres are strikingly different from each other and from ours. Even if a planet goes through an early history exactly like our earth's, no one knows the probability that life on its surface can get started. If it does start, no one knows the probability that it will evolve anything as intelligent as a fish.

Our probes of Mars have been great disappointments in SETI (Search for ETI). I can still recall the tingling of my spine when as a boy I read on the first page of H. G. Wells' *War of the Worlds*:

> Yet across the gulf of space, minds that are to our minds as ours are to those of the beasts that perish, intellects vast and cool and unsympathetic, regarded this earth with envious eyes, and slowly and surely drew their plans against us.

Not even Wells guessed how quickly the Martians would vanish from science fiction.

21. The primary purpose of this passage is to
    (A)   describe the space program
    (B)   disprove the existence of Martians
    (C)   discuss the possibility of ETI
    (D)   provide conclusive evidence about ETI
    (E)   point out the folly of Carlyle and Wells

22. Thomas Carlyle was probably H. G. Well's
    (A)   contemporary   (B) predecessor   (C) colleague   (D) nemesis   (E) friend

23. ETI is an acronym for
    (A)   something fashionable and new
    (B)   exobiology
    (C)   a model proposed by Immanuel Kant
    (D)   Extraterrestrial Intelligence
    (E)   the situation described in *War of the Worlds*

24. The quotation from H.G. Wells suggests that
    (A)   the Martians would vanish from science fiction
    (B)   we were being scrutinized by superior aliens
    (C)   an intergalactic war would be imminent
    (D)   our intellect is comparatively similar to beasts
    (E)   it would take a long time for earth to be invaded

25. The passage implies that the intelligence of a fish is
    (A) equal to man's   (B) equal to that on Venus and Mars   (C) carbon-based
    (D) small   (E) confined to water

26. The naming of a new science, exobiology, contradicts the fact that
    (A)   its subject matter may not exist
    (B)   the name is probably inappropriate
    (C)   the name fits no corresponding acronym
    (D)   carbon-based life is not necessarily biological
    (E)   there is no literary precedent for the name

27. The question "Are there other planets?" refers only to
    (A)   planets outside our own solar system
    (B)   planets outside our own galaxy
    (C)   planets within our own solar system and outside our own galaxy
    (D)   planets outside our own solar system and within our own galaxy
    (E)   nongalactic planets

STOP

IF YOU FINISH BEFORE TIME IS UP, CHECK YOUR WORK ON THIS SECTION OF THE TEST ONLY.
DO NOT GO ON TO THE NEXT SECTION OF THE TEST UNTIL TIME IS UP FOR THIS SECTION.

SECTION III
ANALYTICAL REASONING

Time—35 Minutes
24 Questions

Directions:

In this section you will be given groups of questions based on different sets of conditions. Drawing a simple diagram may be helpful in answering some of the questions. You are to choose the best answer and mark the corresponding space on your answer sheet.

Questions 1–6

There are five flagpoles lined up next to each other in a straight row in front of a school.

Each flagpole flies one flag and one pennant.
The flags are either red, white, or blue.
The pennants are either green, white, or blue.
On a given flagpole, the pennant and the flag cannot be the same color.
Two adjacent flagpoles cannot fly the same color flags.
Two adjacent flagpoles cannot fly the same color pennants.
No more than two of any color flag or pennant may fly at one time.

1. If the 2nd and 5th pennants are blue, the 2nd and 5th flags are red, and the 3rd flag is white, then which of the following must be true?
   (A)   Two of the flags are white.
   (B)   Two of the pennants are white.
   (C)   The 4th pennant is green.
   (D)   If the 1st pennant is green, then the 1st flag is blue.
   (E)   If the 1st flag is white, then the 1st pennant is green.

2. If the 1st flag is red and the 2nd pennant is blue, then which of the following is NOT necessarily true?
   (A)   The 2nd flag is white.
   (B)   If the 5th flag is red, then the 3rd flag is blue.
   (C)   If the 4th pennant is green, then the 1st pennant is white.
   (D)   If the 1st and 5th flags are the same color, then the 3rd flag is blue.
   (E)   If the 4th pennant is green and the 5th pennant is white, then the 1st and 3rd pennants are different colors.

3. If the 1st and 3rd flags are white and the 2nd and 4th pennants are blue, then which of the following is FALSE?
   (A)   The 4th flag is red.
   (B)   The 1st pennant is green.
   (C)   The 3rd pennant is not red.
   (D)   The 5th pennant is green.
   (E)   There is one blue flag.

4. If the 1st and 4th flags are blue and the 3rd pennant is white, then which of the following must be true?
   (A)   If the 1st pennant is green, then the 5th pennant is white.
   (B)   If the 5th pennant is white, then the 1st pennant is green.
   (C)   The 2nd flag is red.
   (D)   The 5th flag is red.
   (E)   The 1st pennant is green.

5. If the 2nd flag is red and the 3rd flag is white, and the 4th pennant is blue, then which of the following must be true?
   (A)   If the 5th flat is white, then two of the pennants are blue.
   (B)   If the 1st flag is white, then the 2nd flag is white.
   (C)   If the 1st pennant is blue, then the 5th pennant is green.
   (D)   If the 1st pennant is green, then the 5th flag is not blue.
   (E)   If the 1st and 5th flags are the same color, then the 1st and 5th pennants are not the same color.

6. If the 1st flag and the 2nd pennant are the same color, the 2nd flag and the 3rd pennant are the same color, the 3rd flag and the 4th pennant are the same color, and the 4th flag and the 5th pennant are the same color, then which of the following must be true?

   (A)   The 1st pennant is white.
   (B)   The 2nd flag is not white.
   (C)   The 5th flag is red.
   (D)   The 3rd pennant is blue.
   (E)   The 4th flag is white.

Questions 7–13

   There are 10 books standing next to each other on a shelf.

   There are two math books, two science books, three English books, and three poetry books.
   There is a math book on one end and an English book on the other end.
   The two math books are never next to each other.
   The two science books are always next to each other.
   The three English books are always next to each other

7. If the 8th book is a math book, then which of the following must be true?
   (A)   The 5th book is a science book.
   (B)   The 7th is an English book.
   (C)   The 6th book is not a poetry book.
   (D)   The 4th book is next to an English book.
   (E)   The 9th book is a science book.

8. If the 9th book is an English book and the 5th and 6th books are poetry books, then which of the following must be true?
   (A)   There is a math book next to a poetry book.
   (B)   The 2nd book is a science book.
   (C)   The 3 poetry books are all next to one another.
   (D)   The 7th book is a math book.
   (E)   The 4th book is not a poetry book.

9. If the 1st book is a math book and the 7th book is a science book, then which of the following could be FALSE?
   (A)   Both math books are next to poetry books.
   (B)   All three poetry books are next to each other.
   (C)   The 2nd book is a poetry book.
   (D)   The 10th book is an English book.
   (E)   The 6th book is a science book.

10. If the 4th book is a math book and the 5th book is a science book, then which of the following must be true?
  (A)   An English book is next to a science book.
  (B)   If the 7th book is a poetry book, then the 3rd book is an English book.
  (C)   If the 8th book is an English book, then the 2nd book is a poetry book.
  (D)   If the 10th book is a math book, then a poetry book is next to an English book.
  (E)   The three poetry books are next to each other.

11. If no two poetry books are next to each other, then which of the following must be true?
  (A)   A science book is next to a math book.
  (B)   The 7th book is a poetry book.
  (C)   The 8th book is an English book.
  (D)   An English book is next to a science book.
  (E)   A poetry book is next to an English book.

12. If a science book is next to an English book, but not next to a poetry book, then which of the following must be true?
  (A)   The 7th book is a poetry book.
  (B)   The 3rd book is an English book or a math book.
  (C)   The 5th or the 6th book is a math book.
  (D)   The three poetry books are not next to each other.
  (E)   The 7th or the 10th book is a math book.

13. If the 7th and 8th books are poetry books, how many different arrangements are there for the 10 books?
  (A)   1   (B) 2   (C) 3   (D) 4   (E) 5

Questions 14–19

The following restrictions apply to freshmen taking courses at State College:

Each freshman must take either Latin or Greek, or both.
Enrollment in the Sex Lab requires concurrent enrollment in Marriage/Family Relations.
Enrollment in Marriage/Family Relations does not require concurrent enrollment in the Sex Lab.
Freshmen may not enroll in American History and Latin at the same time.
Anyone enrolled in Roman History must also be enrolled in Greek.
A freshman must enroll in at least three classes.
The above-listed courses are the only ones offered to freshmen.

14. What is the maximum number of courses that a freshman can take?
  (A)   3   (B) 4   (C) 5   (D) 6   (E) 7

15. If a freshman wishes to enroll in American History and the Sex Lab, then which of the following is true?
  (A)   She must enroll in at least four classes.
  (B)   She cannot enroll in Marriage/Family Relations.
  (C)   She may enroll in Latin.
  (D)   She cannot enroll in Roman History.
  (E)   She must enroll in Roman History.

16. If a freshman does not enroll in Greek, what is the maximum number of classes he can take?
  (A)   1   (B) 2   (C) 3   (D) 4   (E) 5

17. If a freshman enrolls in Latin, which of the following classes must be taken in addition to Latin?
    (A)   Marriage/Family Relations or Sex Lab
    (B)   Greek or American History
    (C)   Roman History or Greek
    (D)   Roman History or Sex Lab
    (E)   Greek or Marriage/Family Relations

18. If a freshman does not wish to take American History or Greek, what is the maximum number of classes he can take?
    (A) 1   (B) 3   (C) 4   (D) 5   (E) 6

19. If a freshman enrolls in Latin, which of the following must be true?
    (A)   He enrolls in only three classes.
    (B)   He enrolls in Sex Lab.
    (C)   He may choose from four classes.
    (D)   He enrolls in Marriage/Family Relations.
    (E)   He cannot enroll in Marriage/Family Relations.

Questions 20–24

Four teams (Red, Blue, Green, and Yellow) participate in the Junior Olympics, in which there are five events. In each event participants place either 1st, 2nd, 3rd, or 4th. First place is awarded a gold medal, 2nd place is awarded a silver medal, and 3rd place is awarded a bronze medal. There are no ties and each team enters one contestant in each event. All contestants finish each event.

The results of the Junior Olympics are:

No team wins gold medals in two consecutive events.
No team fails to win a medal within two consecutive events.
The Blue team wins only two medals, neither of them gold.
The Red team only wins three gold medals, and no other medals.

20. If the green team wins only one gold medal, then which of the following must be true?
    (A)   The yellow team wins two gold medals.
    (B)   The red team wins only two bronze medals.
    (C)   The yellow team wins only one gold medal.
    (D)   The yellow team wins only silver medals.
    (E)   The green team wins only bronze medals.

21. Which of the following must be true?
    (A)   The yellow team wins only bronze and gold medals.
    (B)   The yellow team wins five medals.
    (C)   The green team cannot win a silver medal.
    (D)   The yellow team cannot win a bronze medal.
    (E)   The green team wins exactly three medals.

22. If the yellow team wins five silver medals, then the green team must win
    (A)   more silver than gold
    (B)   more gold than bronze
    (C)   two gold, two bronze, one silver
    (D)   two gold, three bronze
    (E)   six medals

23. All of the following must be true EXCEPT
   (A) the green team wins five medals
   (B) the yellow team wins five medals
   (C) if the green team wins one gold medal, the yellow team wins one gold medal
   (D) if the green team wins only one silver medal, the yellow team wins only one silver medal
   (E) if the yellow team wins only silver medals, the green team cannot win a silver medal

24. If a fifth team, Orange, enters all events and wins only three consecutive silver medals, which of the following must be true?
   (A) If green wins a gold in the 2nd event, it also wins a bronze in the 3rd event.
   (B) If green wins a gold in the 2nd event, it also wins a silver in the 4th event.
   (C) If yellow wins a gold in the 2nd event, green wins a bronze in the 3rd event.
   (D) If yellow wins a gold in the 2nd event, blue wins a silver in the 3rd event.
   (E) If red wins a gold in the 1st event, orange wins a silver in the last event.

STOP

IF YOU FINISH BEFORE TIME IS UP, CHECK YOUR WORK ON THIS SECTION OF THE TEST ONLY.
DO NOT GO ON TO THE NEXT SECTION OF THE TEST UNTIL TIME IS UP FOR THIS SECTION.

SECTION IV
LOGICAL REASONING

Time—35 Minutes
26 Questions

Directions:
In this section you will be given brief statements or passages and will be required to evaluate the reasoning involved. In some instances, more than one choice will appear to be a possible answer. You are to choose the *best* answer. Use common sense and reasonableness in making your selection; then mark the proper space on the answer sheet.

Questions 1–2 refer to the following passage.

The spate of bills in the legislature dealing with utility regulation shows that our lawmakers recognize a good political issue when they see one. Among the least worthy is a proposal to establish a new "Consumers Utility Board" to fight proposed increases in gas and electric rates.

It is hardly a novel idea that consumers need representation when rates are set for utilities which operate as monopolies in their communities. That's exactly why we have a state Public Utilities Commission.

Supporters of the proposed consumer board point out that utility companies have the benefit of lawyers and accountants on their payrolls to argue the case for rate increases before the PUC. That's true. Well, the PUC has the benefit of a $40 million annual budget and a staff of 900—all paid at taxpayer expense—to find fault with these rate proposals if there is fault to be found.

1. Which of the following is the best example to offer in support of this argument against a Consumers Utility Board?
   (A) the percentage of taxpayer dollars supporting the PUC
   (B) the number of lawyers working for the Consumers Utility Board
   (C) the number of concerned consumers
   (D) a PUC readjustment of rates downward
   (E) the voting record of lawmakers supporting the board

2. Which of the following would most seriously weaken the above argument?
   (A) Private firms are taking an increasing share of the energy business.
   (B) Water rates are also increasing.
   (C) The PUC budget will be cut slightly, along with other state agencies.
   (D) Half of the PUC lawyers and accountants are also retained by utilities.
   (E) More tax money goes to education than to the PUC.

3. Most of those who enjoy music play a musical instrument; therefore, if Maria enjoys music, she probably plays a musical instrument.

   Which of the following most closely parallels the reasoning in the statement above?
   (A) The majority of those who voted for Smith in the last election oppose abortion; therefore, if the residents of University City all voted for Smith, they probably oppose abortion.
   (B) If you appreciate portrait painting you are probably a painter yourself; therefore, your own experience is probably the cause of your appreciation.
   (C) Most of those who join the army are male; therefore, if Jones did not join the army, Jones is probably female.
   (D) Over 50% of the high school students polled admitted hating homework; therefore, a majority of high school students do not like homework.
   (E) If most workers drive to work, and Sam drives to work, then Sam must be a worker.

4. "To be a good teacher, one must be patient. Some good teachers are good administrators."

Which of the following can be concluded from the above statement?
(A) Some good teachers are not patient.
(B) All good administrators are patient.
(C) Some good administrators are patient.
(D) Only good administrators are patient.
(E) Many good administrators are patient.

5. "Good personnel relations of an organization depend upon mutual confidence, trust, and good will. The basis of confidence is understanding. Most troubles start with people who do not understand each other. When the organization's intentions or motives are misunderstood, or when reasons for actions, practices, or policies are misconstrued, complete cooperation from individuals is not forthcoming. If management expects full cooperation from employees, it has a responsibility of sharing with them the information which is the foundation of proper understanding, confidence, and trust. Personnel management has long since outgrown the days when it was the vogue to 'treat them rough and tell them nothing.' Up-to-date personnel management provides all possible information about the activities, aims, and purposes of the organization. It seems altogether creditable that a desire should exist among employees for such information which the best-intentioned executive might think would not interest them and which the worst-intentioned would think was none of their business."

The above paragraph implies that one of the causes of the difficulty that an organization might have with its personnel relations is that its employees
(A) have not expressed interest in the activities, aims, and purposes of the organization
(B) do not believe in the good faith of the organization
(C) have not been able to give full cooperation to the organization
(D) do not recommend improvements in the practices and policies of the organization
(E) can afford little time to establish good relations with their organization

6. Of all psychiatric disorders, depression is the most common; yet, research on its causes and cures is still far from complete. As a matter of fact, very few facilities offer assistance to those suffering from this disorder.

The author would probably agree that
(A) depression needs further study
(B) further research will make possible further assistance to those suffering from depression
(C) most facilities are staffed by psychiatrists whose speciality is not depression
(D) those suffering from depression need to know its causes and cures
(E) depression and ignorance go hand in hand

7. No brown-eyed people have red hair. Some short people have red hair.

Based on the foregoing information, all of the following must also be true EXCEPT
(A) there are short people who do not have brown eyes
(B) there are people without brown eyes who are short
(C) there are people with red hair who do not have brown eyes
(D) some brown-eyed people are short
(E) there are people with red hair who are not short

8. *Ivan:* What the Church says is true because the Church is an authority.
Mike: What grounds do you have for holding that the Church is a genuine authority?
Ivan: The authority of the Church is implied in the Bible.
Mike: And why do you hold that the Bible is true?
Ivan: Because the Church holds that it is true.

The argument present in the foregoing dialogue is best described as
(A) vague   (B) pointed   (C) undeniable   (D) taboo   (E) circular

9. *Mary:*   All Italians are great lovers.
   Kathy: That is not so. I have met some Spaniards who were magnificent lovers.

   Kathy's reply to Mary indicates that she has misunderstood Mary's remark to mean that
   (A)   every great lover is an Italian
   (B)   Italians are best at the art of love
   (C)   Spaniards are inferior to Italians
   (D)   Italians are more likely to be great lovers than are Spaniards
   (E)   there is a relationship between nationality and love

Questions 10–11 refer to the following passage.

Mr. Dimple: Mrs. Wilson's qualifications are ideal for the position. She is intelligent, forceful, determined, and trustworthy. I suggest we hire her immediately.

10. Which of the following, if true, would most weaken Mr. Dimple's statement?
    (A)   Mrs. Wilson is not interested in being hired.
    (B)   There are two other applicants whose qualifications are identical to Mrs. Wilson's.
    (C)   Mrs. Wilson is currently working for a rival company.
    (D)   Mr. Dimple is not speaking directly to the hiring committee.
    (E)   Mrs. Wilson is older than many of the other applicants.

11. Which of the following, if true, offers the strongest support of Mr. Dimple's statement?
    (A)   All the members of the hiring committee have agreed that intelligence, trustworthiness, determination, and forcefulness are important qualifications for the job.
    (B)   Mr. Dimple holds exclusive responsibility for hiring new employees.
    (C)   Mr. Dimple has known Mrs. Wilson longer than he has known any of the other applicants.
    (D)   Mrs. Wilson is a member of Mr. Dimple's family.
    (E)   Mrs. Dimple is intelligent, forceful, determined, and trustworthy.

12. American publisher Horace Greeley said, "The illusion that times that were are better than those that are has probably pervaded all ages."

    Which of the following expresses at least one of the meanings of Greeley's words?
    (A)   The grass is always greener on the other side.
    (B)   Life is full of sound and fury, signifying nothing.
    (C)   Beauty is in the eyes of the beholder.
    (D)   Live for today.
    (E)   All ages look at the world through rose-colored glasses.

13.   When a dental hygienist cleans your teeth, you may not see much evidence that she is supervised by a dentist. Hygienists often work pretty much on their own, even though they are employed by dentists. Then why can't hygienists practice independently, perhaps saving patients a lot of money in the process? The patients would not have to pay the steep profit that many dentists make on the hygienists' labors.

    Which of the following statements weakens the argument above?
    (A)   Some patients might get their teeth cleaned more often if it costs less.
    (B)   Some dentists do not employ dental hygienists.
    (C)   Hygienists must be certified by state examinations.
    (D)   A dentist should be on hand to inspect a hygienist's work to make sure the patient has no problems that the hygienist is unable to detect.
    (E)   In some states, there are more female hygienists than male.

14.   There are those of us who, determined to be happy, are discouraged repeatedly by social and economic forces that cause us nothing but trouble. And there are those of us who are blessed with health and wealth and still grumble and complain about almost everything.
    To which of the following points can the author be leading?
    (A)   Happiness is both a state of mind and a state of affairs.
    (B)   Both personal and public conditions can make happiness difficult to attain.
    (C)   Happiness may be influenced by economic forces and by health considerations.
    (D)   No one can be truly happy.
    (E)   Exterior forces and personal views determine happiness.

15.   "Keep true, never be ashamed of doing right; decide on what you think is right and stick to it."—*George Eliot*
    If one were to follow Eliot's advice, one
    (A)   would never change one's mind
    (B)   would do what is right
    (C)   might never know what is right
    (D)   would never be tempted to do wrong
    (E)   would not discriminate between right and wrong

16.   To paraphrase Oliver Wendell Holmes, taxes keep us civilized. Just look around you, at well-paved superhighways, air-conditioned schools, and modernized prisons, and you cannot help but agree with Holmes.

    Which of the following is the strongest criticism of the statement above?
    (A)   The author never actually met Holmes.
    (B)   The author does not acknowledge those of us who do not live near highways, schools, and prisons.
    (C)   The author does not assure us that he has been in a modernized prison.
    (D)   The author does not offer a biographical sketch of Holmes.
    (E)   The author does not define "civilized."

Questions 17–18 refer to the following passage.

    Information that is published is part of the public record. But information that a reporter collects, and sources that he contacts, must be protected in order for our free press to function free of fear.

17.   The above argument is most severely weakened by which of the following statements?
    (A)   Public information is usually reliable.
    (B)   Undocumented evidence may be used to convict an innocent person.
    (C)   Members of the press act ethically in most cases.
    (D)   The sources that a reporter contacts are usually willing to divulge their identity.
    (E)   Our press has never been altogether free.

18.   Which of the following statements is consistent with the argument above?
    (A)   Privileged information has long been an important and necessary aspect of investigative reporting.
    (B)   Not all the information a reporter collects becomes part of the public record.
    (C)   Tape-recorded information is not always reliable.
    (D)   The victim of a crime must be protected at all costs.
    (E)   The perpetrator of a crime must be protected at all costs.

Questions 19–21 refer to the following passage.

A federal court ruling that San Diego County can't sue the government for the cost of medical care of illegal aliens is based upon a legal technicality that ducks the larger moral question. But the U.S. Supreme Court's refusal to review this decision has closed the last avenue of legal appeal.

The medical expenses of indigent citizens or legally resident aliens are covered by state and federal assistance programs. The question of who is to pay when an undocumented alien falls ill remains unresolved, however, leaving California counties to bear this unfair and growing burden.

19. The author implies that
(A)   the U.S. Supreme Court has refused to review the federal court ruling
(B)   the burden of medical expenses for aliens is growing
(C)   the larger moral question involves no legal technicalities
(D)   San Diego should find another avenue of appeal
(E)   the federal government is dodging the moral issue

20. Which of the following arguments, if true, would most seriously weaken the argument above?
(A)   There are many cases of undocumented aliens being denied medical aid at state hospitals.
(B)   A private philanthropic organization has funded medical aid programs that have so far provided adequate assistance to illegal aliens nationwide.
(C)   Illegal aliens do not wish federal or state aid, because those accepting aid risk detection of their illegal status and deportation.
(D)   Undocumented aliens stay in California only a short time before moving east.
(E)   Judges on the Supreme Court have pledged privately to assist illegal aliens with a favorable ruling once immigration laws are strengthened.

21. Which of the following changes in the above passage could strengthen the author's argument?
(A)   adding interviews with illegal aliens
(B)   a description of the stages that led to a rejection by the Supreme Court
(C)   a clarification with numbers of the rate at which the burden of medical expenses is growing
(D)   the naming of those state and federal assistance programs that aid indigent citizens
(E)   the naming of those California counties that do not participate in medical aid to illegal aliens

22.   History is strewn with the wreckage of experiments in communal living, often organized around farms and inspired by religious or philosophical ideals. To the more noble failures can now be added Mao Tse-tung's notorious Chinese communes. The current rulers of China, still undoing the mistakes of the late Chairman, are quietly allowing their agricultural communes to _____.

Which of the following is the most logical completion of the passage above?
(A) evolve   (B) increase   (C) recycle   (D) disintegrate   (E) organize

23. *Sal:* Herb is my financial planner.

Keith: I'm sure he's good; he's my cousin.

Which of the following facts is Keith ignoring in his response?

(A) Financial planning is a professional, not a personal, matter.

(B) Sal is probably flattering Keith.

(C) Professional competence is not necessarily a family trait.

(D) "Good" is a term with many meanings.

(E) Sal's financial planner is no one's cousin.

24. Many very effective prescription drugs are available to patients on a "one time only" basis. Suspicious of drug abuse, physicians will not renew a prescription for a medicine that has worked effectively for a patient. This practice denies a patient her right to health.

Which of the following is a basic assumption made by the author?

(A) A new type of medicine is likely to be more expensive.

(B) Physicians are not concerned with a patient's health.

(C) Most of the patients who need prescription renewals are female.

(D) Most physicians prescribe inadequate amounts of medicine.

(E) Patients are liable to suffer the same ailment repeatedly.

Questions 25–26 refer to the following passage.

Forty years ago, hardly anybody thought about going to court to sue somebody. A person could bump a pedestrian with his Chrysler Airflow and the victim would say something like, "No harm done," and walk away. Ipso facto. No filing of codicils, taking of depositions or polling the jury. Attorneys need not apply.

25. Which of the following sentences most logically continues the above passage?

(A) The Chrysler Airflow is no longer the harmless machine it used to be.

(B) Fortunately, this is still the case.

(C) Unfortunately, times have changed.

(D) New legislation affecting the necessity for codicils is a sign of the times.

(E) But now, as we know, law schools are full of eager young people.

26. Which of the following details, if true, would most strengthen the above statement?

(A) There were fewer courthouses then than now.

(B) The marked increase in pedestrian accidents is a relatively recent occurrence.

(C) Most citizens of 40 years ago were not familiar with their legal rights.

(D) The number of lawsuits filed during World War II was extremely low.

(E) Most young attorneys were in the armed forces 40 years ago.

STOP

IF YOU FINISH BEFORE TIME IS UP, CHECK YOUR WORK ON THIS SECTION OF THE TEST ONLY. DO NOT GO ON TO THE NEXT SECTION OF THE TEST UNTIL TIME IS UP FOR THIS SECTION.

SECTION V
READING COMPREHENSION

Time—35 Minutes
27 Questions

Directions:
Read the passages and answer the questions following each passage by blackening the appropriate space on the answer sheet. You may refer back to the passages when answering the questions. Answer all questions on the basis of what is stated or implied.

Passage 1

Article I, Section 4, of the Constitution provides: "The Times, Places and Manner of holding Elections for Senators and Representatives shall be prescribed in each State by the Legislature thereof; but the Congress may at any time by Law make or alter such Regulations, except as to the Places of chusing Senators."

(5) At first Congress exercised its power to supervise apportionment by simply specifying in the statutes how many representatives each state was to have. From 1842 until the 1920s, it went further and required that the districts be relatively compact (not scattered areas) and relatively equal in voting population.

Major shifts in population occurred in the twentieth century: large numbers of farmers could

(10) no longer maintain small farms and moved to the cities to find employment; rapidly growing industries, organized in factory systems, attracted rural workers; and many blacks who could no longer find work in southern agriculture moved to the North to get better jobs and get away from strict Jim Crow living conditions. The rural areas of the country became more sparsely populated while the city populations swelled.

(15) As these changes were occurring, Congress took less interest in its reapportionment power, and after 1929 did not reenact the requirements. In 1946, voters in Illinois asked the Supreme Court to remedy the serious malapportionment of their state congressional districts. Justice Frankfurter, writing for the Court in *Colegrove* v. *Groon,* said the federal courts should stay out of "this political thicket." Reapportionment was a "political question" outside the jurisdiction of

(20) these courts. Following the *Colgrove* holding, malapportionment grew more severe and widespread in the United States.

In the Warren Court era, voters again asked the Court to pass on issues concerning the size and shape of electoral districts, partly out of desperation because no other branch of government offered relief, and partly out of hope that the Court would reexamine old decisions in this

(25) area as it had in others, looking at basic constitutional principles in the light of modern living conditions.

Once again the Court had to work through the problem of separation of powers, which had stood in the way of court action concerning representation. In this area, too, the Court's rulings were greeted by some as shockingly radical departures from "the American way," while others

(30) saw them as a reversion to the democratic processes established by the Constitution, applied to an urbanized setting.

1. The primary purpose of the passage is to
(A) criticize public apathy concerning apportionment
(B) describe in general the history of political apportionment
(C) argue for the power of the Supreme Court
(D) describe the role of the Warren Court
(E) stress that reapportionment is essentially a congressional concern

2. The author implies which of the following opinions about federal supervision of apportionment?
(A)   Federal supervision is unnecessary.
(B)   Federal supervision is necessary.
(C)   Apportionment should be regulated by the Court.
(D)   Apportionment should be regulated by Congress.
(E)   Court rulings on apportionment violate "the American way."

3. In lines 17 and 20, "malapportionment" refers to the
(A)   influx of farmers into the city
(B)   Jim Crow phenomenon
(C)   shift from rural to urban populations
(D)   distribution of voters in Illinois
(E)   unfair size and shape of congressional districts

4. We may infer that during the Warren Court era
(A)   the most dissatisfied voters lived in cities
(B)   the constituency was dissatisfied
(C)   the separation of powers became important for the first time
(D)   the public turned its attention away from issues of apportionment
(E)   a ballot issue concerning electoral apportionment passed

5. The passage answers which of the following questions?
(A)   Does the Constitution delegate authority for supervising apportionment?
(B)   Do population shifts intensify racism?
(C)   Should the Constitution still be consulted, even though times have changed?
(D)   Why did the Warren Court agree to undertake the issue of representation?
(E)   How did the Warren Court rule on the separation of powers issue?

6. We may conclude that Justice Frankfurter was
(A)   a member of the Warren Court
(B)   not a member of the Warren Court
(C)   opposed to reapportionment
(D)   skeptical about the separation of powers
(E)   too attached to outmoded interpretations of the Constitution

7. In the passage the author is primarily concerned with
(A)   summarizing history
(B)   provoking a controversy
(C)   suggesting a new attitude
(D)   reevaluating old decisions
(E)   challenging constitutional principles

Passage 2

Alain Robbe-Grillet is not as cerebral a writer as Nathalie Sarraute or Michel Butor. But he has been more popular, particularly in America. Perhaps that is one reason. There are others. He relies even more heavily than his fellow novelists on the *roman policier* for basic structure, and detective stories have a built-in popular fascination. Most of his characters, so far as we can determine, seem to be psychopathological. He is therefore a kind of Alfred Hitchcock of the novel. He has also devoted himself to film writing and film making in association with the *Nouvelle Vague*. His cinema-novels as he called them, rather than film-scripts, *L'Année Dernière à Marienbad* (1961) and *L'Immortelle* (1963), have certainly brought him a wider public exposure than would have been possible with the novels alone. Furthermore his novels have had wide paperback distribution in English translation. But he is an authentic New Novelist and therefore disturbing but not easy. He is reported to have said that he *wants* his readers to feel disappointed (in their expectation of clarification, presumably), that if they feel disappointed he knows he has succeeded in what he was trying to do. At least one critic has placed Robbe-Grillet at "the most advanced point of evolution of the twentieth-century novel and film."

LIFE: Alain Robbe-Grillet was born August 18, 1922, in Brest on the seacoast of Brittany, the son of Gaston and Yvonne Robbe-Grillet, who had moved there from the Jura. As a child he was intrigued by the lichens and rock plants of the coast (perhaps observing their tropisms while Nathalie Sarraute was writing in these terms) and by the gulls on the cliffs of Finistère (which may reappear in *The Voyeur*). Educated at the Lycée Buffon, the Lycée St. Louis, and the Institut National Agronomique in Paris, he became a professional agronomic engineer in the years 1949 to 1951 at the Institute des Fruits Tropicaux in Guinea, Morocco, Martinique, and Guadaloupe; but his interests turned increasingly toward writing, which eventually became his full-time career. The banana plantations, verandas, and fronds of Martinique return in *La Jalousie*. Robbe-Grillet's first novel, *Les Gommes* (*The Erasers*), appeared in 1953; his second, *Le Voyeur*, in 1955; and his career was well launched. In 1957 he married Catherine Rstakian and published his third novel, *La Jalousie*, followed two years later by a fourth, *Dans le Labyrinthe* (*In the Labyrinth*).

His attention then turned to the cinema, at first in collaboration with the film director Alain Resnais. In 1961 *L'Année Dernière à Marienbad* hit the movie world with an originality that for a time usurped the attention customarily given to the Italian films of Fellini or the Swedish films of Bergman. *Last Year at Marienbad* played long runs in the art film houses in New York and across the United States. Bruce Morrissette in a critique of the film pointed out to less perceptive critics that it represented a continuation of techniques established in the earlier novels: "False scenes and objectified hypothesis as in *The Voyeur*, a subjective universe converted into objective perceptions as in *Jealousy*—with its detemporalization of mental states, its mixture of memories (true and false), of desire images and affective projections—the 'dissolves' found in *The Labyrinth*: all these reach a high point in Marienbad. . . . The spectator's work, like that of the reader, becomes an integral part of the cinematic or novelistic creation." The viewer like the reader was expected to collaborate in creating meaning. *Marienbad* takes place at an ornate Bavarian palace; the action is circular (like *Finnegans Wake*, says Morrissette) beginning with "Once more" as the camera moves through Freudian corridors, empty rooms and a formal garden (with a return at the end); characters emerge as a young woman, A, and older man, M (presumably her jealous husband), and a persistent lover, X. Fantasies of seduction, resistance, desire, fear, rape, and even murder are projected; but whose they are, A's or M's or X's, is never clear. You take your choice.

8. We may assume that the plot of a *roman policier* involves
   (A) French characters
   (B) a crime
   (C) psychopathological characters
   (D) an omniscient narrator
   (E) the collaboration of other novelists

9. According to the passage, the viewer of *Last Year at Marienbad* is a
   (A) participant in the clearly delineated fantasy
   (B) fan of triangular love relationships
   (C) detached spectator
   (D) reader as well
   (E) partner in constructing the plot

10. According to the passage, one might finish a successful Robbe-Grillet novel feeling
- (A) more intelligent
- (B) in the mood to read the novel
- (C) as if he had seen an Alfred Hitchcock film
- (D) wondering "Who dunnit?"
- (E) disappointed

11. According to the passage, Robbe-Grillet's literary work indicated his familiarity with
- (A) the habits of gulls   (B) jealousy   (C) farming   (D) French life
- (E) insoluble problems

12. The "that" in line 2 refers to which of the following?
- (A) the cerebral quality of most French fiction
- (B) the contention that Robbe-Grillet's work does not appeal to the intellect
- (C) the brainlessness of Robbe-Grillet's work
- (D) Robbe-Grillet's reliance on emotional effects
- (E) a fact apparently discussed elsewhere

13. A prominent stylistic feature of the first sentence of the second paragraph is
- (A) the factuality of its terms
- (B) the realization that Robbe-Grillet is no longer a young man
- (C) its discontinuity with the first paragraph, because of the absence of transitional terms
- (D) the colon following *LIFE*
- (E) the naming of Robbe-Grillet's parents

14. We may conclude that Nathalie Sarraute and Michel Butor are
- (A) interested in Robbe-Grillet
- (B) masters of detective fiction
- (C) contemporaries of Robbe-Grillet
- (D) antagonistic to Robbe-Grillet
- (E) comparable to Robbe-Grillet

Passage 3

The American philosophy has always been one in favor of promoting private enterprise. In terms of a process, private enterprise means producing goods and selling them. The catalyst of this process is competition, which is manifested through the policy of business priorities, i.e., produce the most goods at the cheapest expense to make the most money. The aftermath of this process in operation is an avalanche of products in the consumer market.

Not all products that reach the marketplace are worthy of consumer purchase, but items that are dangerous to the user are bought daily. The unwary consumer, relying on the onslaught of advertising assurances attesting to the product's advantages, often learns too late that the item purchased was unsafe for use. When a consumer is injured however, there is a legal remedy available by bringing a cause of action commonly referred to as "products liability." The theory behind this action is based on the principle that "the law should at least enforce the promise of the messages that propel consumer goods into society." Because the manufacturers are in a better financial position than the individual consumer to insure the costs of injustices from a faulty product, they are subject to a legal standard of care, which requires producers to exert reasonable diligence to market reasonably safe products. The manufacturer will be liable however, only if the product that caused the injury is defective and the particular defect is within those sought to be prevented by imposing the duty. Consequently, categorizing the defect is crucial and may determine the success of the lawsuit.

There are two opposing views as to whether crashworthiness is a defect included in the duty imposed on manufacturers of automobiles. They are called the restrictive view and the expansive view. The restrictive view is premised on the intended use doctrine. Because automobiles are not intended to be in collisions, the manufacturer is not held to a duty of providing a crashworthy vehicle. In the landmark case supporting this view, the decedent (deceased person) purchased an automobile that had an X frame chassis. It did not have side frame rails to protect the driver from direct side impact. The decedent had been killed when his vehicle was struck in the side by another vehicle, causing the decedent's car to collapse. In the lawsuit, the complaint alleged that the X chassis was a design defect, but the court held that the manufacturer's duty was to provide a vehicle frame that is safe for its intended purpose, capable of supporting the body weight of the automobile plus that of the passengers. The court added that the duty is not inclusive of providing an automobile that is safe in every situation, as for example, the possibility of driving a car into water does not create the duty of equipping every vehicle with pontoons.

This restrictive view relies on the rationale that manufacturers should only be liable for their products when the product is defective in its normal and proper use. The defect must do more than just add to the seriousness of the injury; it must be the direct cause of the injury. The argument is that crashworthiness is concerned with the second collision, but the primary collision is the direct cause of the injury and collisions are not the normal and proper use of automobiles. Thus, there is no liability for manufacturing an uncrashworthy vehicle under this view.

The expansive view is premised on the reasonable foreseeability doctrine. Because it is reasonably foreseeable that automobiles will be involved in collisions, manufacturers are subject to a duty for providing a crashworthy vehicle. In the most frequently cited case for this position, the plaintiff alleged that his injury was due to the defect in design of the vehicle in having the steering shaft extended beyond the front axle of the car. The defendant disavowed any duty of care to design a collision safe automobile, and the district court supported this contention with an immediate decision. The Eighth Circuit Court reversed the ruling:

> [There is] no rational basis [that] exists for limiting recovery to situations where the defect in design or manufacture was the causative factor of the accident and the resulting injury, usually caused by the so-called 'second collision' of the passenger with the interior part of the automobile, all are foreseeable.

The expansionists contend that automobile makers should not be exempt from the ordinary negligence principle that a known risk of harm gives rise to a duty of commensurate care. They say that manufacturers should consider the traffic conditions in which the product is used and recognize that collisions, with or without fault of the product user, are statistically inevitable. Thus, the duty to provide a safe product must extend to include a design that protects against excessive preventable danger.

15. According to the author of the passage, the primary purpose of private enterprise in America is
    (A) economic growth
    (B) competition
    (C) higher profits
    (D) higher sales
    (E) to overwhelm the consumer

16. We can infer from the passage that the author is critical of all of the following EXCEPT
    (A) advertising
    (B) many consumer products
    (C) product liability laws
    (D) the X frame chassis
    (E) the legal system

17. In a products liability action against a manufacturer the manufacturer will be held liable
  (A) if a consumer is injured
  (B) if a consumer is injured by using the manufacturer's product
  (C) if a consumer is injured by using the manufacturer's product as it was intended to be used
  (D) for injury caused by a defect in the product
  (E) for injury caused by a defect in the product that the manufacturer sought to eliminate

18. Of the following, a supporter of the restrictive view of automobile manufacturers' duty would be likely to endorse all EXCEPT
  (A) defects in automobiles should be defined by automotive experts, not by juries
  (B) if stricter standards are to be imposed upon an industry, the standards should be imposed by the legislature not by courts
  (C) lawsuits against manufacturers are a means of improving standards of safety
  (D) a manufacturer should be liable for a defect when it is the direct cause of injury
  (E) a collision is not a normal or proper use of an automobile

19. A comparison of the legal decisions mentioned in the passage suggests that the duty of the manufacturers to design a crashworthy vehicle is
  (A) legally unsettled
  (B) leaning toward the expansionist viewpoint
  (C) leaning toward the restrictive viewpoint
  (D) a practical, not a legal, issue
  (E) resolved under product liability laws

20. In an automobile accident, the "second collision" is the
  (A) collision that occurs when the body of the automobile, not the bumper, strikes another vehicle
  (B) collision of the passenger and the inside of the vehicle
  (C) coming together of any two cars, both of which are in motion
  (D) coming together of any two or more cars, all of which are in motion
  (E) coming together of any two cars, only one of which is in motion

21. According to the passage, which of the following statements is FALSE?
  (A) The law should at least enforce the promise of messages that propel consumer goods into society.
  (B) Manufacturers, rather than the consumer, should be responsible for the costs of injuries from a defective product.
  (C) The restrictive view of the crashworthiness issue holds that manufacturers should be liable only when a defect occurs in normal use of the vehicle.
  (D) The expansive view of the crashworthiness issue holds that though collisions are statistically inevitable, the fault is that of the driver.
  (E) Collisions are not the normal and proper use of automobiles.

Passage 4

The nomads who inhabit the deserts of the Middle East make up about five percent of the people of the area. They are known as *bedouins* and they live in tribes. Their time is spent moving through the desert in search of water and grass for their herds of sheep, goats, and camels.
Because he is always on the move, the nomad has few goods besides his cooking pots, his loose, flowing clothes, his rugs, and his blankets. He lives in a tent and sleeps and eats on rugs. The men and boys live in one half of the tent, and the women and girls live in the other half.

The animals provide the nomad with most of his needs. Goat's milk and cheese are his main foods. He rarely eats meat. His blankets, his tent, and most of his clothes are woven from the hair of goats and camels. Leather from the hides of the animals is used to make baskets and sandals.

Whatever his animals do not supply, the nomad buys when he reaches an *oasis*. (An oasis is a place in the desert where there is water and vegetation. The water comes from underground streams.) In this way the nomads are dependent on the farms and cities that lie beyond the desert. Part of the nomad's diet consists of flour, dates, and fruits that come from the farms and groves. From the towns and cities he obtains his utensils, cloth, coffee, tea, and sugar. The bedouins in turn provide the farmers and city people with animals and animal products.

Duties and responsibilities among the bedouins have always been divided according to sex. It is the man's duty to fight and look after the camels, while the woman takes care of the other animals, the household, and the children, and sees to it that the family has enough water.

The bedouins are very proud individuals who believe in equality and do not like to be ruled by other people. Nevertheless, the family, clan, and tribe (which is composed of clans) claim the loyalty of individual members.

Since humans are so helpless in the desert, there is complete dependence of man upon other men. Generosity is an important quality among bedouins. A guest is treated as well as or better than one's own family. No bedouin may refuse another man protection from an enemy. He must admit the pursued man to his tent and offer him food and a place to sleep for three days, even though he is a stranger. The enemy cannot attack the person during the time that he is being sheltered in someone's tent.

In the past, the herders of the desert were the rulers of the Middle East. They crossed and recrossed borders as they pleased. They were able to attack the village swiftly on their horses and camels. The bedouins policed the desert and protected the caravans that crossed it. Today, as a result of changes in transportation and communication, the bedouins have come under the control of the governments in the cities. As a result, their whole way of life has changed. Thousands have left the desert to take jobs in the oil industry—especially in Iraq and Saudi Arabia. Others have become soldiers. Large numbers have settled down on the oases and in the cities. Many of the tribal chiefs are now rich landowners. Those living on land where oil has been discovered have adopted a way of life that is totally different from that of their fellow bedouins in the desert.

22. Just as "duties and responsibilities among the bedouins have always been divided according to sex" (paragraph 5), so has (have)
   (A) weapons   (B) water   (C) food   (D) living space   (E) sleeping space

23. The tendency of nomads to protect visitors may be compared to the Medieval European practice of
   (A) Catholicism   (B) sanctuary   (C) treachery   (D) barter   (E) agrarian reform

24. We may infer that ninety-five percent of the Middle East populace
   (A)   is not dependent upon an oasis
   (B)   disdains life in tents
   (C)   does not live in tribes
   (D)   has established nonmobile residencies
   (E)   opposes the practice of the nomads

25. We may infer that the total number of bedouin clans in the Middle East
   (A)   is larger than the number of tribes
   (B)   is equal to the number of families
   (C)   is more significant than the number of tribes
   (D)   is proportional to the number of tribes
   (E)   includes families that are not members of tribes

26. According to the passage, the nomad's diet almost never includes

    (A) fruit   (B) milk   (C) cheese   (D) meat   (E) coffee

27. The author's purpose in this passage is to provide

    (A)   a narrative of events
    (B)   an argument
    (C)   a controversial viewpoint
    (D)   an innovative point of view
    (E)   simple information

STOP

END OF MULTIPLE-CHOICE EXAMINATION. IF YOU FINISH BEFORE TIME IS UP, CHECK YOUR WORK ON THIS SECTION ONLY. DO NOT GO BACK TO ANY OTHER SECTION OF THE EXAMINATION.

EXAMINATION

WRITING SAMPLE

Time—30 Minutes

Directions:
You have 30 minutes to write an essay in response to a given topic. Take a few minutes to plan your work before you begin writing. DO NOT WRITE ON A TOPIC OF YOUR OWN CHOICE. ESSAYS THAT DO NOT ADDRESS THE GIVEN TOPIC ARE UNACCEPTABLE.

The quality of your writing is more important than the length of your response or the content. Pay attention to organization, appropriate diction, and correct usage. You will not be expected to display any specialized knowledge in your response, nor will you be expected to write a "perfect" essay; law schools understand that you are writing under a time constraint, and will allow for the minor lapses in writing ability that might occur under this circumstance.

Only the lined area in your booklet will be reproduced for the law schools, so do not write outside this space. *Do not* skip lines or use wide margins. These precautions, along with careful planning and legible handwriting that is not unduly large, will keep you within the allowed space.

SAMPLE TOPIC:

Read the following descriptions of Thomas and Peters, candidates for the position of head coach of the Ventura Vultures professional football team. *Then, in the space provided, write an argument for appointing either Thomas or Peters.* Use the information in this description and assume that the two general policies below equally guide the Vultures' decision on the appointment:

- The head coach should possess the ability to work with players and coaching staff toward achieving a championship season.
- The head coach should successfully manage the behind-the-scenes activities of recruiting, analyzing scouting reports, and handling the media and fans in order to enhance the public relations and image of the team.

THOMAS has been General Manager of the Vultures for the past ten years. A physical education major with a masters in psychology, he knows the player personnel as well as anyone, including the coaching staff. His on-target assessment of player skills and weaknesses has been instrumental in building a more balanced team over the past decade, through his skillful trading and recruitment of college athletes. As the chief managing officer, he has also enhanced the team's image by his careful press relationship and understated approach when negotiations with star players reached an impasse. He rarely alienates players, coaches, press, or fans with his even-handed (though sometimes unemotional) attitude, and the Vultures' owners feel fortunate that they were able to entice him away from his high school coaching position, which he left 10 years ago. Although he has never played either pro or college ball, he is one candidate for the head coach position.

PETERS, the other candidate for head coach, is presently a wide receiver amd defensive end for the Vultures. A one-time star, Peters has played both offense and defense for the Vultures since their inception in the league 14 years ago, a remarkable feat equalled by few in the game. He was elected captain of the team the past five years because of his charisma, although he occasionally angers management and fellow players with his strong comments about his philosophy of the game. His only experience in the front office was leading a player charity benefit for the Vultures, which raised more than $2,000,000 for abused Ventura County children. Although a high school dropout, Peters is a self-made man who firmly believes the key to life is having a strong educational background, even though he sometimes feels uncomfortable around college-educated athletes. The Vulture owners believe Peters may provide the emotional charge the team needs at its helm to win its first championship.

ANSWER KEY

Section I: Logical Reasoning	Section II: Reading Comprehension	Section III: Analytical Reasoning	Section IV: Logical Reasoning	Section V: Reading Comprehension
1. A	1. C	1. E	1. D	1. B
2. A	2. A	2. C	2. D	2. B
3. D	3. A	3. D	3. A	3. E
4. A	4. B	4. B	4. C	4. E
5. E	5. C	5. A	5. B	5. A
6. C	6. D	6. C	6. B	6. B
7. A	7. E	7. D	7. D	7. A
8. D	8. A	8. A	8. E	8. B
9. C	9. C	9. B	9. A	9. E
10. B	10. C	10. C	10. B	10. E
11. E	11. B	11. E	11. A	11. C
12. D	12. C	12. C	12. A	12. B
13. E	13. E	13. B	13. D	13. C
14. A	14. B	14. C	14. D	14. E
15. B	15. B	15. A	15. B	15. C
16. D	16. E	16. C	16. E	16. E
17. C	17. D	17. E	17. B	17. E
18. C	18. C	18. B	18. A	18. C
19. A	19. C	19. C	19. E	19. A
20. D	20. A	20. C	20. B	20. B
21. D	21. C	21. B	21. C	21. D
22. B	22. B	22. D	22. D	22. D
23. B	23. D	23. D	23. C	23. B
24. B	24. B	24. C	24. E	24. D
25. E	25. D		25. C	25. A
26. D	26. A		26. D	26. D
	27. A			27. E

MODEL TEST ANALYSIS

Doing model exams and understanding the explanations afterwards are of course important in acquainting you with typical LSAT question types and successful approaches to the questions. However, another benefit of carefully analyzing these model tests is to understand the kinds of errors you are making and thus work to minimize them. For instance, if a very high percentage of your incorrect answers is due to "careless error" or "misread problem," then perhaps you are working much too fast and should slow your pace accordingly. If your incorrect answers are due primarily to "lack of knowledge," then a careful rereading and reworking of the appropriate question-type chapter may be in order. Or if you find that you aren't completing a large number of questions because of lack of time, you may need to either increase your speed or learn to use the "one-check, two-check" technique more effectively.

This kind of analysis of the model tests will enable you to identify your particular weaknesses and thus remedy them.

Model Test Two Analysis

Section	Total Number of Questions	Number Correct	Number Incorrect	Number Unanswered*
I: Logical Reasoning	26			
II: Reading Comprehension	27			
III: Analytical Reasoning	24			
IV: Logical Reasoning	26			
V: Reading Comprehension	27			
TOTALS:	130			

*At this stage in your preparation, you should not be leaving any blank answer spaces. At least fill in a guess, as there is no penalty for a wrong answer.

Reasons for Incorrect Answers

You may wish to evaluate the explanations before completing this chart.

Section	Total Number Incorrect	Lack of Knowledge	Misread Problem	Careless Error	Unanswered or Wrong Guess
I: Logical Reasoning					
II: Reading Comprehension					
III: Analytical Reasoning					
IV: Logical Reasoning					
V: Reading Comprehension					
TOTALS:					

EXPLANATIONS OF ANSWERS

Section I

1. **A** The author must assume that "nothing about our coin influences its fall in favor of either side or that all influences are counterbalanced by equal and opposite influences"; otherwise "our ignorance of the coming result" is untrue. Also, he mentions that the chances are one out of two that the coin will fall heads up; this could not be correct if the coin had been weighted or tampered with.

2. **A** (A) is implied by the author's statement that one-to-two is not "true." (B), (C), (D), and (E) are not implied and would not follow from the passage.

3. **D** The author is actually pointing out that self-confidence is of most importance. (C) and (E) focus on behavior, while the author is focusing on mental attitude.

4. **A** (A) stresses that farmwork is a fate rather than a privilege, and therefore strengthens the criticism of Washington's positive attitude toward labor. (B), (C), and (D) weaken the criticism, and (E) is irrelevant.

5. **E** If "no test has no easy questions," then all tests have at least one question. Thus (A), (B), (C), and (D) are all true. But a test could have all easy questions.

6. **C** "Considerate" (B) and "knowledgeable" (D) both roughly fit the meaning of the passage, but "considerate" carries too many other connotations, and "knowledgeable" is not idiomatic.

7. **A** This is the only statement that is consistent with the information in sentence 4.

8. **D** Arnold's wincing during his knee examination is a specific instance supporting the statement that his disability was apparent.

9. **C** "Failure to be prompt" is a phrase which simply repeats the meaning of the term "tardiness." Nothing new is added to the sentence.

10. **B** The consequences of raising geraniums is a hypothetical situation—an event that is being "imagined," that has not actually occurred.

11. **E** The author states that the present programs are at best weak and hopefully won't fail as they have in the past.

12. **D** The statement that "Hopefully, they won't fail as they have in the past" tells us that our government is *not* trying a new approach to end inflation. (A) is close, but the passage states that foreign oil is "high-priced," not "overpriced." "High-priced" tells us the relative cost, not the actual comparative value.

13. **E** The author clearly states that the major factor in this trend is our dependence on oil from foreign countries.

14. **A** Three possibilities exist:
    (a) You read *Weight-Off* magazine, are fat, and do not eat chocolate.
    (b) You are fat, eat chocolate, but do not read *Weight-Off* magazine.
    (c) You eat chocolate, are not fat, and do not read *Weight-Off* magazine.

Thus,
(A) is inconsistent by (a) and (b). (B) is not inconsistent if (b) and (c) are void of people. (C) is not inconsistent if (c) is void of people. (D) and (E) are not inconsistent by (c) and (a).

15. **B**   Dave felt that Jerry implied that no one except Jerry's wife cooks fantastic meals.

16. **D**   "Acquainting" people with subjects is synonymous with educating them.

17. **C**   Because the author speaks of general, rather than specific, relationships between men and knowledge, he is most likely to be a philosopher.

18. **C**   (a) Joe talks to Henry implies that Mike talks to Joe.
(b) Henry does not talk to Dave implies that Mike does not talk to Joe.
Thus,
(A) is true based on (a). (C) is false based on (b). (D) is true based on (b). (B) is based on (a) and (E) on (b). (Technically, if x implies y, then "not y" implies "not x."

19. **A**   X's new realization is expressed in his final sentence: "We must know all the characteristics of men, and that Socrates has all of them, before we can be sure." The "characteristics of men" are what is implied by the generalization "man," in "Socrates is a man." Therefore, deductive thinking is simply reminding ourselves of the particular specifics implied by generalizations.

20. **D**   Symbolically, A is necessary to have B (a good telescope to see moons of Neptune). You do not have B (can't see moons with my telescope). Therefore, you cannot have A (a good telescope). (D) is the only choice that follows this line of reasoning. Symbolically, A is necessary to have B (knowing area of circle to find circumference). You do not have B (can't figure out circumference). Therefore, you cannot have A (area of circle).

21. **D**   Extensive psychological research would most likely give the information that the author discusses. (E) limits the research to clinical psychologists and to recent findings.

22. **B**   "Conscious behavior eventually becomes habit" is indirectly stated in the last sentence. (A) is a close answer, but that absolute word "all" is inconsistent with the words "can become" in the last sentence. This does not imply that they *must* become unconscious behavior.

23. **B**   The given advice would be strengthened by the assurance that such measures are effective. Each of the other choices either weakens the advice, or addresses only a portion of the paragraph.

24. **B**   The disease under discussion is termed "it," and thus its identity is unclear. The other choices either are not applicable to the second sentence or refer to terms that require no further definition.

25. **E**   (E) weakens the argument that young people have abundant time. The other choices are only tangentially relevant to the argument.

26. **D**   The passage says that worrying about writing unfortunately keeps one from writing at all; (D) summarizes this viewpoint. (B) and (C) are irrelevant notions; (A) contradicts the author's implied support for writing theorists; and (E) is an unreasonable, unsupported conclusion.

SECTION II

Passage 1

1. **C** The chief purpose of the Sixth Amendment was to assure the assistance of counsel in criminal cases. The guarantee to the right to self-representation was not the chief purpose of the amendment though the amendment has been used to support it.

2. **A** The phrase refers to the end of the second paragraph. The author regards the waiving of the right to counsel as a choice, which should not be seen as a guarantee of the right of self-representation.

3. **A** The phrase *"in propria persona"* means "in his own person," "by himself," or "by herself."

4. **B** If the Court had believed a fair trial was impossible without the assistance of counsel, it would not have allowed self-representation.

5. **C** The passage emphasizes the importance of warning a defendant of the risks of self-representation.

6. **D** Though true, the tradition of self-representation is not a valid objection to the practice. In fact, it might be cited as an argument in favor of self-representing defendants.

7. **E** The last paragraphs of the passage indicate the major reservations of the author.

Passage 2

8. **A** Aristotle's democracy had the poor "promoting their selfish interests." (D) may be considered, but must be eliminated because no clear relationship exists between "selfish interests" and the *purity* of one's needs.

9. **C** By mentioning small countries in which pure democracy is viable, the author implies that large countries cannot administer pure democracy, but he does not detail the difficulties of direct representation on a large scale. Each of the other choices is explicitly mentioned in the paragraph.

10. **C** After explaining Aristotle's theory, the author compares it to later conceptions. This overall purpose implies the praise of Aristotle's foresight (D), but the passage as a whole informs much more than it praises.

11. **B** The common welfare is an "underlying assumption" of modern democracy, says the author, one that "probably will result" (paragraph 3).

12. **C** A presumption is the taking of something for granted. By citing Aristotle only, the author seems to presume his singular relevance to modern democracy. (B) and (D) are not matters taken for granted, and (A) and (E) are irrelevant to the passage.

13. **E** The author's stress on how "democracy" has changed since Aristotle's time helps us to eliminate (B) and (C). (A) and (D) are neither expressed nor implied. (E) summarizes the belief that motivates the whole discussion.

Passage 3

14. **B** The first sentence of the third paragraph discusses the influence of the Industrial Revolution in the western European manufacturing belt.

15. **B** With the common knowledge that the USSR and the United States are military rivals (knowledge stressed in the final sentence of the passage), we may conclude that strategic considerations are military ones. Each of the other choices is either not related to a *strategic* consideration or not related to the issue of *location*.

16. **E** Choice (E), "motivators of," is closest to the meaning of "spurs to" in this context.

17. **D** Although North America, Europe, and the Soviet Union are compared during the course of the passage, (A) is not best because it does not specify the nature of the comparison, and is therefore too vague. (D) is both comprehensive and precise.

18. **C** This is stated explicitly in the fourth paragraph. (A), (B), and (D) are contradicted in the passage, and (E) is illogical.

19. **C** The advantages are listed in paragraph 2, and climate is not one of them.

20. **A** Although each of the other choices is touched upon in the passage, the overall survey is geographical.

Passage 4

21. **C** The theories of Carlyle and Wells are treated with respect, so (E) should be eliminated. (D) is also incorrect, because the evidence given is incomplete and tentative, not conclusive. (A) and (B) are irrelevant to the purpose of the passage, which is well described by (C).

22. **B** Since Wells's style is more modern than Carlyle's, and since Wells imagines extraterrestrial life while Carlyle merely wonders about it, we may conclude that Wells is a more modern thinker than is Carlyle.

23. **D** This is defined in paragraph 2: "ETI (a fashionable new acronym for Extraterrestrial Intelligence)."

24. **B** The words, "intellects vast and cool and unsympathetic, regarded this earth with envious eyes . . ." suggest that earth was being scrutinized by superior aliens. The quotation also indicates that some sort of plan against us may be imminent ("they drew their plans against us"), but choice (C) is incorrect, as Wells does not necessarily imply an "intergalactic war."

25. **D** Paragraph 4 discusses the development of ETI and says that even planets which are similar to earth are not certain to develop life as advanced as we know it, perhaps not even life as "intelligent as a fish."

26. **A** Paragraph 2 states, "'Exobiology' has already been named even though its entire subject matter may not exist."

27. **A** The first sentence of paragraph 3 mentions both the 200 billion *other* suns in our galaxy and the billions of other galaxies outside our own. The following question, "Are there other planets?" refers directly to planets surrounding these suns and galaxies outside our own solar system.

Section III

Answers 1–6

UPPER-case letters denote colors given in the problem, and lower-case letters denote deduced colors.

1. **E**

	1	2	3	4	5	
	b/w	R	W	b	R	(flag)
	w/g	B	g	w	B	(pennant)

The 3rd pennant cannot be blue or white, so therefore it is green. The 4th flag cannot be white or red, so it must be blue. The 4th pennant cannot be green or blue, so it must be white. The 1st flag cannot be red, so it is either blue or white. The 1st pennant cannot be blue, so it must be green or white.

2. **C**

	1	2	3	4	5	
	R	w	r/b			(flag)
	g/w	B	g/w			(pennant)

(A) is clearly true. If the 5th flag is red, then the 3rd flag cannot be, since the 1st flag is red and we can have only two of any one color. Thus, (B) is true. If the 4th pennant is green, then the 3rd pennant must be white. But that does not determine the color of the 1st pennant. Thus, (C) is not necessarily true. (D) is the same as (A) and is also true. If the 4th pennant is green, this implies that the 3rd pennant must be white. If the 5th pennant is white, then the 1st pennant cannot be. Therefore (E) is true.

3. **D**

	1	2	3	4	5	
	W	r	W	r	b	(flag)
	g	B	g	B	w	(pennant)

The facts in this problem determine the complete configuration of flags and pennants. (D) is the one statement that is false.

4. **B**

	1	2	3	4	5	
	B	w	r	B		(flag)
		W	g			(pennant)

Statement (B) is true since the 1st pennant cannot be blue or white. Statement A is false since the 5th pennant could be blue or white. Statement (C) is false since it is white. Statements (D) and (E) are false since they could be white.

5. **A**

1	2	3	4	5	
R	W	r			(flag)
	g	B			(pennant)

If the 5th flag is white, then the 5th pennant must be green. Thus the 1st and 2nd pennants cannot be green and cannot be the same color, so one of them is blue. Therefore, (A) is true. All the other statements are false.

6. **C**

1	2	3	4	5		1	2	3	4	5
W	B	W	B	r	(flag)	B	W	B	W	r
g	W	B	W	B	(pennant)	g	B	W	B	W

Since blue and white are the two common colors between flags and pennants, the above are the only two arrangements possible. In both cases, the 5th flag is red and the 1st pennant is green.

Answers 7–13

7. **D**

1	2	3	4	5	6	7	8	9	10
E	E	E					M		M

If the 8th book is a math book, then the three English books must be in positions 1, 2, and 3, since they cannot be in positions 8, 9, and 10. Thus, the other math book is in position 10. The 4th book must be next to the English book in position 3.

8. **A**

1	2	3	4	5	6	7	8	9	10
M				P	P		E	E	E

If the 9th book is an English book, then so are the 8th and 10th books. Thus there is a math book in position 1. The science books must be in positions 2 and 3 *or* 3 and 4. This leaves only positions 4 and 7 for the other math book. Thus (A) is always true. (C) could be true, but does not have to be true. The 3rd poetry book could be in position 2.

9. **B**

1	2	3	4	5	6	7	8	9	10
M					S	S	E	E	E

If the 1st book is a math book, then the 8th, 9th, and 10th books must be the English books. If the 7th book is a science book, so must be the 6th book. This means that the other math book must be either the 3rd, the 4th, or the 5th book. The remainder of the books are poetry books, including the 2nd book.

10. **C**

1	2	3	4	5	6	7	8	9	10
M	P	P	M	S	S	P	E	E	E
				or					
E	E	E	M	S	S	P	P	P	M

If the 4th book is a math book and the 5th book is a science book, then the 6th book is also a science book. This leaves two possible arrangements for the remaining books, as shown above. Statement (C) is the only correct one.

11. **E**

1	2	3	4	5	6	7	8	9	10
E	E	E	P					P	M

or

| M | P | | | | | P | E | E | E |

The poetry books must be in positions 4 and 9 *or* 2 and 7, depending on whether the math book is in position 1 or 10. See diagrams above. For example, let us assume that the math book is the 10th book. In order for no two poetry books to be next to each other, the 4th and 9th books must be poetry books, with the 3rd poetry book in either position 6 or 7, depending on the positions of the science books. The same argument holds if the 1st book is a math book.

12. **C**

1	2	3	4	5	6	7	8	9	10
E	E	E	S	S	M	P	P	P	M

and

| M | P | P | P | M | S | S | E | E | E |

These are the two possible arrangements. We see that (A) is false, (B) could be false, (D) is false, and (E) could be false. Only (C) is always true.

13. **B**

1	2	3	4	5	6	7	8	9	10
E	E	E	M	S	S	P	P	P	M

and

| E | E | E | S | S | M | P | P | P | M |

These are the only two possible combinations; thus, (B) is the correct answer.

Answers 14–19

A simple chart, as follows, will help to answer the questions:

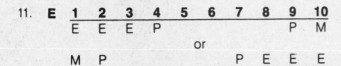

14. **C** From the chart we can see that a freshman can take everything except Latin (if he takes American History), or take everything except American History (if he takes Latin).

15. **A** In order to enroll in American History and the Sex Lab, a freshman must take Marriage/Family Relations plus Greek. Therefore, only (A) is true.

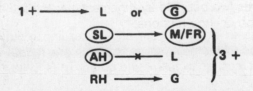

16. **C** If a freshman does not enroll in Greek, he can take only Latin, Sex Lab, and Marriage/Family Relations.

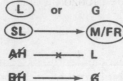

17. **E** If a freshman enrolls in Latin, his course load could consist of Latin, Greek, and Roman History; or it could consist of Latin, Sex Lab, and Marriage/Family Relations; or it could consist of Latin, Greek, and Marriage/Family Relations.

18. **B** If a freshman does not take Greek or American History, he must take Latin, and cannot take Roman History (because Roman History requires taking Greek). Therefore, the other two courses left for him to take are Sex Lab and Marriage/Family Relations.

19. **C** If a freshman enrolls in Latin, he may choose from any of the classes except American History. Thus, he may choose from Greek, Sex Lab, Marriage/Family Relations, and Roman History—a total of four.

Answers 20–24

Drawing a diagram, below, will help answer the questions.

	EVENTS				
	1	**2**	**3**	**4**	**5**
RED	G	—	G	—	G
BLUE	—	B/S	–	B/S	—
GREEN					
YELLOW					

Since the red team wins only 3 gold medals, it must win gold medals in events 1, 3, and 5, since no team wins gold medals in consecutive events. Also, note that since blue wins only two medals (neither of them gold), it must have won medals in events 2 and 4, so that it didn't fail to win a medal within two consecutive events. Be aware then that green and yellow, therefore, must each have won medals in all five events.

20. **C** If the green team wins only one gold medal, there remains only one gold medal, which the yellow team must win.

21. **B** Since three medals are given for each event, and, according to our diagram from the facts, red and blue already account for their total awards with one medal in each event, the other two medals in each event must go to yellow and green. Thus, yellow and green will each be awarded five medals.

22. **D** By completing the chart such that the yellow team wins five silver medals, we can see that green must win two gold and three bronze medals.

	1	2	3	4	5
RED	G	—	G	—	G
BLUE	—	B/S	—	B/S	—
GREEN					
YELLOW	S	S	S	S	S

23. **D** We know choices (A) and (B) are both true: both the green and yellow teams each must win five medals. Therefore (E) is also true. Choice (C) is true because three of the gold medals are already won by the red team; since blue doesn't win gold, if green wins one gold, yellow wins the remaining gold medal. Choice (D) is not true: if the green team wins only one silver medal, the yellow team must win at least two silver medals.

24. **C** If a fifth team enters all events and wins only three consecutive silver medals, it must win the silver in events 2, 3, and 4, so that it does not fail to win a medal within two consecutive events. Therefore our diagram would look like this:

	1	2	3	4	5
RED	G	—	G	—	G
BLUE	—	B	—	B	—
GREEN					
YELLOW					
ORANGE	—	S	S	S	—

Therefore, if yellow wins a gold in the 2nd event, green must win a medal in the 3rd event (since no team fails to win a medal within two consecutive events). Thus, green must win a bronze in the 3rd event.

Section IV

1. **D** This choice provides the most direct evidence of the effectiveness of the PUC consumer action. Each of the other choices is only tangentially related to the argument.

2. **D** This choice most seriously weakens the author's contention that the PUC acts in the public interest. (C) is a weaker choice, especially because "slightly" softens the statement.

3. **A** This choice parallels both the reasoning and the structure of the original. The original reasoning may be summarized as follows: most $X \rightarrow Y$; therefore $X \rightarrow Y$ (probably).

4. **C** The reasoning goes as follows: All good teachers are patient (rephrasing of the first statement); some good teachers (patient) are good administrators; therefore, some good administrators are patient. To use a term of degree other than *some* requires assumptions beyond the information given.

5. **B** Since good personnel relations of an organization, according to the passage, rely upon "mutual confidence, trust and good will," one of the causes of personnel difficulties would most certainly be the employees' not believing in the good faith of the organization.

6. **B** In the second sentence, the author implies that the lack of facilities is related to the lack of research mentioned in the first sentence. In any case, the passage reveals the author's concern with both research and assistance, and therefore agrees more fully with (B) than with (A), which mentions research only.

7. **D** Since some short people have red hair, and since anyone with red hair can't have brown eyes, (A) is true: there are short people who do not have brown eyes. Likewise, since there are some short people with red hair, and those red-haired people cannot have brown eyes, (B) is true: there are people without brown eyes who are short.
    Or, by using Venn diagrams, three groupings can be drawn that satisfy the given conditions:

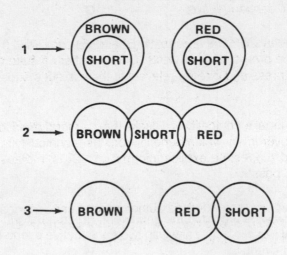

Notice that, based on alternative 3, (D) need not be true. (C) and (E) merely restate the given.

8. **E** The correct answer is "circular." The argument that what the Church says is true is ultimately based upon this same assertion.

9. **A** Kathy believes Mary to have meant that *only Italians* are great lovers. Therefore, Kathy takes issue with this and points out in her reply that there are non-Italians who are great lovers. (A), if replaced for Mary's statement, would make Kathy's reply a reasonable one.

10. **B** Only (B) addresses Dimple's assumption that Mrs. Wilson is the *only* applicant whose qualifications are ideal. Other choices are irrelevant to the *argument*, although some may be relevant to the implied situation.

11. **A** Only (A) addresses the substance of Dimple's argument.

12. **A** Greeley suggests that we are always comparing what we have with what we don't have. Therefore, (A) is correct. None of the other choices makes a *comparison*.

13. **D** The author of the argument avoids the issue of <u>quality</u>. The statement that stresses the incompleteness of the pro-hygienist position weakens it. (B) and (E) are irrelevant.

14. **D** The passage describes two types of obstacles to happiness: exterior forces and personal attitude. Both these factors are mentioned in (A), (B), (C), and (E). (D) requires the assumption that the two categories discussed by the author are the only categories.

15. **B** (A) may be eliminated because changing one's mind need not involve issues of right and wrong (in the moral sense that Eliot implies). (C) and (E) may be eliminated because they refute the underlying assumption of Eliot's words, that one can tell what is right. The passage does not address the issue of temptation (D).

16. **E** Without an implied or explicit definition of "civilized," the relevance of the examples is vague, at best. (A) and (D) are irrelevant considerations, and (B) and (C), although possibly relevant, do not address the most apparent weakness of the passage.

17. **B** (A) and (C) strengthen the argument. Although (D) and (E) partially weaken certain aspects of the argument, only (B) introduces a situation which suggests that freedom of the press may have harmful consequences.

18. **A** (B) and (C) are irrelevant to the argument. (D) and (E) contradict the implied assertion that a free press must be protected at all costs. Only (A) offers a statement both favorable to the concept of a free press and directly relevant to the subject discussed: the use of privileged information.

19. **E** By stating that "a legal technicality . . . ducks the . . . moral question," the author is implying that the federal government which benefits from the technicality is associated with dodging the issue. (A) and (B) restate explicit information; (C) is implausible; and (D) contradicts information in the passage.

20. **B** Private medical aid would render the author's argument unnecessary. (C), a choice worth considering, is not the best one because the author's focus is less on the aliens' needs than on the monetary burden borne by the counties.

21. **C** By documenting the rate at which the medical expense burden grows, the author could strengthen the argument that the situation he describes is indeed a burden.

22. **D** The passage talks about communes as failures. Therefore, the most logical completion must be a negative term consistent with failure. The only negative choice is (D).

23. **C** By linking Herb's ability with his "cousinhood," Herb is assuming that the latter determines the former; therefore, he is ignoring (C). (B) is irrelevant. (A) is too vague to be the best answer. (D) is inapplicable, because Keith uses "good" in a context that makes its meaning clear. Finally, (E) refers to contradictory information.

24. **E** In order to argue for the value of renewable prescriptions, the author must first assume that more medicine may be necessary, or, in other words, that the patient may suffer a relapse. Without the possibility of relapse, a call for more medicine that has already effected a cure ("worked effectively") is illogical.

25. **C** The passage consistently implies a difference between the past and the present, and (C) makes this contrast explicit. (B) contradicts the implication of the passage, while (A) and (D) narrow the focus unnecessarily, and (E) is irrelevant.

26. **D** This fact would strengthen the merely impressionistic evidence that lawsuits were less prevalent 40 years ago. It is the only choice dealing directly with the implied subject of the passage—lawsuits.

Section V

Passage 1

1. **B** Each of the other choices is too specific and/or not indicative of the *neutral* rather than argumentative *tone* of the passage.

2. **B** In the fourth paragraph, the author notes that after Congress had stopped enacting its reapportionment power, "serious malapportionment" problems ensued; the author thus implies that federal supervision is necessary. (C), (D), and (E) are issues on which the author does not imply an opinion.

3. **E** A clue to this answer occurs in paragraph 5, in which "malapportionment" is replaced by "the size and shape of electoral districts." Each of the other choices *may contribute* to malapportionment, but each is too specific to be the best choice.

4. **E** In the fifth paragraph we learn that the *voters* asked the Warren Court to rule on apportionment issues; therefore, we must assume that a ballot was taken that expressed the voters' opinions.

5. **A** Question (A) is answered in the first paragraph. (B), (C), (D), and (E) are issues, but not questions that are answered.

6. **B** Justice Frankfurter did not declare his opinion about reapportionment per se, but did declare that the Supreme Court should not address the issue; the Warren Court, on the other hand, did deliberate over the reapportionment issue. Therefore, we may conclude that Frankfurter was not a member of the Warren Court.

7. **A** The passage is a summary of events that occurred through the century, relative to apportionment. Each of the other choices has the author writing a passage calculated to persuade rather than to inform.

Passage 2

8. **B** Directly following the mention of a *roman policier*, we have a coordinate statement about detective stories; the indication is that a *roman policier* is a detective story. Also, note that *policier* suggests the English word "police." Altogether, it appears that a *roman policier* centers on the investigation of a crime.

9. **E** After enumerating the possible components of the plot of *Marienbad*, the author says, "You take your choice"; earlier he notes that "the spectator's work" becomes part of the "creation." (D) is possibly but not necessarily true.

10. **E** The first paragraph states that he "wants his readers to feel disappointed," and that their disappointment tells him he has been successful.

11. **C** In the second paragraph we are told that Robbe-Grillet's first novel contained descriptions stemming from his work as an agronomic (farming) engineer. (D) is probably true, but quite vague. (A) refers to an observation from childhood, but we are not told that he is *familiar* with the *habits* of the birds.

12. **B** The first and second sentence imply a connection between popularity and less cerebral (intellectual) work, and the only logical antecedent to "that" is the initial statement that Robbe-Grillet is less cerebral.

13. **C** Paragraph 2 begins abruptly with *LIFE*, and introduces biographical details apart from the preceding discussion of Robbe-Grillet's writing. (B), (D), and (E) do not describe stylistic features.

14. **E** In the mention of Sarraute and Butor at the beginning of the passage, the author declares only that they can be compared to Robbe-Grillet. All other choices require more information than is given.

Passage 3

15. **C** According to the first paragraph of the passage, the priority of business is to make the most money at the smallest cost.

16. **E** The passage specifically criticizes or implies criticism of the first four options; the author gives no indication of his disapproval of the legal system in this passage.

17. **E** The manufacturer is liable "only if the product . . . is defective and the particular defect is within those sought to be prevented by imposing the duty" (paragraph 2).

18. **C** The supporters of the restrictive view would keep the decisions about crashworthiness out of the court and in the hands of engineers. They would endorse (A), (B), (D), and (E).

19. **A** The two decisions reflect different philosophies. The issue is unsettled.

20. **B** As defined by the Eighth Circuit Court, the "second collision" is "of the passenger with the interior part of the automobile," with the windshield, for example.

21. **D** The expansive view is more likely to fix the blame on the manufacturer.

Passage 4

22. **D** Paragraph 2 explicitly states that the men and boys live in half the tent, and the women and girls live in the other half. (E) is also correct, but not as complete as (D).

23. **B** As commonly understood, sanctuary was shelter (within the church) for a criminal in flight. The other choices might be eliminated simply because they are not exclusively Medieval practices.

24. **D** The nomads, always on the move, comprise five percent of the populace; presumably, the rest have stationary residences (see paragraph 1).

25. **A** In paragraph 6, a parenthetical remark states that tribes are comprised of clans; this means, of course, that *several* clans make up *one* tribe. (D) is possible, but not verified in the passage.

26. **D** In paragraph 3 we are told, "He rarely eats meat."

27. **E** The passage consists of fact after fact, simply presented in plain language. The author is objective, and never presents information that seems, on the face of it, biased or controversial.

Chapter

Model Test Three

This chapter contains full-length Model Test Three. It is geared to the format of the LSAT, and it is complete with answers and explanations. It is equivalent to the LSAT in question structure, number of questions, level of difficulty, and time allotments. (The questions used are not taken directly from the LSAT, as those questions are copyrighted and may not be reproduced.)

Model Test Three should be taken under strict test conditions. The test ends with a 30-minute Writing Sample, which is not scored.

Section	Description	Number of Questions	Time Allowed
I	Reading Comprehension	27	35 minutes
II	Analytical Reasoning	24	35 minutes
III	Logical Reasoning	26	35 minutes
IV	Reading Comprehension	28	35 minutes
V	Logical Reasoning	25	35 minutes
	Writing Sample		30 minutes
TOTALS:		130	3 hours 25 minutes

Now please turn to the next page, remove your answer sheets, and begin Model Test Three.

ANSWER SHEET—MODEL TEST THREE
LAW SCHOOL ADMISSION TEST (LSAT)

Section I:
Reading Comprehension

1. Ⓐ Ⓑ Ⓒ Ⓓ Ⓔ
2. Ⓐ Ⓑ Ⓒ Ⓓ Ⓔ
3. Ⓐ Ⓑ Ⓒ Ⓓ Ⓔ
4. Ⓐ Ⓑ Ⓒ Ⓓ Ⓔ
5. Ⓐ Ⓑ Ⓒ Ⓓ Ⓔ
6. Ⓐ Ⓑ Ⓒ Ⓓ Ⓔ
7. Ⓐ Ⓑ Ⓒ Ⓓ Ⓔ
8. Ⓐ Ⓑ Ⓒ Ⓓ Ⓔ
9. Ⓐ Ⓑ Ⓒ Ⓓ Ⓔ
10. Ⓐ Ⓑ Ⓒ Ⓓ Ⓔ
11. Ⓐ Ⓑ Ⓒ Ⓓ Ⓔ
12. Ⓐ Ⓑ Ⓒ Ⓓ Ⓔ
13. Ⓐ Ⓑ Ⓒ Ⓓ Ⓔ
14. Ⓐ Ⓑ Ⓒ Ⓓ Ⓔ
15. Ⓐ Ⓑ Ⓒ Ⓓ Ⓔ
16. Ⓐ Ⓑ Ⓒ Ⓓ Ⓔ
17. Ⓐ Ⓑ Ⓒ Ⓓ Ⓔ
18. Ⓐ Ⓑ Ⓒ Ⓓ Ⓔ
19. Ⓐ Ⓑ Ⓒ Ⓓ Ⓔ
20. Ⓐ Ⓑ Ⓒ Ⓓ Ⓔ
21. Ⓐ Ⓑ Ⓒ Ⓓ Ⓔ
22. Ⓐ Ⓑ Ⓒ Ⓓ Ⓔ
23. Ⓐ Ⓑ Ⓒ Ⓓ Ⓔ
24. Ⓐ Ⓑ Ⓒ Ⓓ Ⓔ
25. Ⓐ Ⓑ Ⓒ Ⓓ Ⓔ
26. Ⓐ Ⓑ Ⓒ Ⓓ Ⓔ
27. Ⓐ Ⓑ Ⓒ Ⓓ Ⓔ

Section II:
Analytical Reasoning

1. Ⓐ Ⓑ Ⓒ Ⓓ Ⓔ
2. Ⓐ Ⓑ Ⓒ Ⓓ Ⓔ
3. Ⓐ Ⓑ Ⓒ Ⓓ Ⓔ
4. Ⓐ Ⓑ Ⓒ Ⓓ Ⓔ
5. Ⓐ Ⓑ Ⓒ Ⓓ Ⓔ
6. Ⓐ Ⓑ Ⓒ Ⓓ Ⓔ
7. Ⓐ Ⓑ Ⓒ Ⓓ Ⓔ
8. Ⓐ Ⓑ Ⓒ Ⓓ Ⓔ
9. Ⓐ Ⓑ Ⓒ Ⓓ Ⓔ
10. Ⓐ Ⓑ Ⓒ Ⓓ Ⓔ
11. Ⓐ Ⓑ Ⓒ Ⓓ Ⓔ
12. Ⓐ Ⓑ Ⓒ Ⓓ Ⓔ
13. Ⓐ Ⓑ Ⓒ Ⓓ Ⓔ
14. Ⓐ Ⓑ Ⓒ Ⓓ Ⓔ
15. Ⓐ Ⓑ Ⓒ Ⓓ Ⓔ
16. Ⓐ Ⓑ Ⓒ Ⓓ Ⓔ
17. Ⓐ Ⓑ Ⓒ Ⓓ Ⓔ
18. Ⓐ Ⓑ Ⓒ Ⓓ Ⓔ
19. Ⓐ Ⓑ Ⓒ Ⓓ Ⓔ
20. Ⓐ Ⓑ Ⓒ Ⓓ Ⓔ
21. Ⓐ Ⓑ Ⓒ Ⓓ Ⓔ
22. Ⓐ Ⓑ Ⓒ Ⓓ Ⓔ
23. Ⓐ Ⓑ Ⓒ Ⓓ Ⓔ
24. Ⓐ Ⓑ Ⓒ Ⓓ Ⓔ

Section III:
Logical Reasoning

1. Ⓐ Ⓑ Ⓒ Ⓓ Ⓔ
2. Ⓐ Ⓑ Ⓒ Ⓓ Ⓔ
3. Ⓐ Ⓑ Ⓒ Ⓓ Ⓔ
4. Ⓐ Ⓑ Ⓒ Ⓓ Ⓔ
5. Ⓐ Ⓑ Ⓒ Ⓓ Ⓔ
6. Ⓐ Ⓑ Ⓒ Ⓓ Ⓔ
7. Ⓐ Ⓑ Ⓒ Ⓓ Ⓔ
8. Ⓐ Ⓑ Ⓒ Ⓓ Ⓔ
9. Ⓐ Ⓑ Ⓒ Ⓓ Ⓔ
10. Ⓐ Ⓑ Ⓒ Ⓓ Ⓔ
11. Ⓐ Ⓑ Ⓒ Ⓓ Ⓔ
12. Ⓐ Ⓑ Ⓒ Ⓓ Ⓔ
13. Ⓐ Ⓑ Ⓒ Ⓓ Ⓔ
14. Ⓐ Ⓑ Ⓒ Ⓓ Ⓔ
15. Ⓐ Ⓑ Ⓒ Ⓓ Ⓔ
16. Ⓐ Ⓑ Ⓒ Ⓓ Ⓔ
17. Ⓐ Ⓑ Ⓒ Ⓓ Ⓔ
18. Ⓐ Ⓑ Ⓒ Ⓓ Ⓔ
19. Ⓐ Ⓑ Ⓒ Ⓓ Ⓔ
20. Ⓐ Ⓑ Ⓒ Ⓓ Ⓔ
21. Ⓐ Ⓑ Ⓒ Ⓓ Ⓔ
22. Ⓐ Ⓑ Ⓒ Ⓓ Ⓔ
23. Ⓐ Ⓑ Ⓒ Ⓓ Ⓔ
24. Ⓐ Ⓑ Ⓒ Ⓓ Ⓔ
25. Ⓐ Ⓑ Ⓒ Ⓓ Ⓔ
26. Ⓐ Ⓑ Ⓒ Ⓓ Ⓔ

ANSWER SHEET—MODEL TEST THREE
LAW SCHOOL ADMISSION TEST (LSAT)

Section IV:
Reading Comprehension

1. Ⓐ Ⓑ Ⓒ Ⓓ Ⓔ
2. Ⓐ Ⓑ Ⓒ Ⓓ Ⓔ
3. Ⓐ Ⓑ Ⓒ Ⓓ Ⓔ
4. Ⓐ Ⓑ Ⓒ Ⓓ Ⓔ
5. Ⓐ Ⓑ Ⓒ Ⓓ Ⓔ
6. Ⓐ Ⓑ Ⓒ Ⓓ Ⓔ
7. Ⓐ Ⓑ Ⓒ Ⓓ Ⓔ
8. Ⓐ Ⓑ Ⓒ Ⓓ Ⓔ
9. Ⓐ Ⓑ Ⓒ Ⓓ Ⓔ
10. Ⓐ Ⓑ Ⓒ Ⓓ Ⓔ
11. Ⓐ Ⓑ Ⓒ Ⓓ Ⓔ
12. Ⓐ Ⓑ Ⓒ Ⓓ Ⓔ
13. Ⓐ Ⓑ Ⓒ Ⓓ Ⓔ
14. Ⓐ Ⓑ Ⓒ Ⓓ Ⓔ
15. Ⓐ Ⓑ Ⓒ Ⓓ Ⓔ
16. Ⓐ Ⓑ Ⓒ Ⓓ Ⓔ
17. Ⓐ Ⓑ Ⓒ Ⓓ Ⓔ
18. Ⓐ Ⓑ Ⓒ Ⓓ Ⓔ
19. Ⓐ Ⓑ Ⓒ Ⓓ Ⓔ
20. Ⓐ Ⓑ Ⓒ Ⓓ Ⓔ
21. Ⓐ Ⓑ Ⓒ Ⓓ Ⓔ
22. Ⓐ Ⓑ Ⓒ Ⓓ Ⓔ
23. Ⓐ Ⓑ Ⓒ Ⓓ Ⓔ
24. Ⓐ Ⓑ Ⓒ Ⓓ Ⓔ
25. Ⓐ Ⓑ Ⓒ Ⓓ Ⓔ
26. Ⓐ Ⓑ Ⓒ Ⓓ Ⓔ
27. Ⓐ Ⓑ Ⓒ Ⓓ Ⓔ
28. Ⓐ Ⓑ Ⓒ Ⓓ Ⓔ

Section V:
Logical Reasoning

1. Ⓐ Ⓑ Ⓒ Ⓓ Ⓔ
2. Ⓐ Ⓑ Ⓒ Ⓓ Ⓔ
3. Ⓐ Ⓑ Ⓒ Ⓓ Ⓔ
4. Ⓐ Ⓑ Ⓒ Ⓓ Ⓔ
5. Ⓐ Ⓑ Ⓒ Ⓓ Ⓔ
6. Ⓐ Ⓑ Ⓒ Ⓓ Ⓔ
7. Ⓐ Ⓑ Ⓒ Ⓓ Ⓔ
8. Ⓐ Ⓑ Ⓒ Ⓓ Ⓔ
9. Ⓐ Ⓑ Ⓒ Ⓓ Ⓔ
10. Ⓐ Ⓑ Ⓒ Ⓓ Ⓔ
11. Ⓐ Ⓑ Ⓒ Ⓓ Ⓔ
12. Ⓐ Ⓑ Ⓒ Ⓓ Ⓔ
13. Ⓐ Ⓑ Ⓒ Ⓓ Ⓔ
14. Ⓐ Ⓑ Ⓒ Ⓓ Ⓔ
15. Ⓐ Ⓑ Ⓒ Ⓓ Ⓔ
16. Ⓐ Ⓑ Ⓒ Ⓓ Ⓔ
17. Ⓐ Ⓑ Ⓒ Ⓓ Ⓔ
18. Ⓐ Ⓑ Ⓒ Ⓓ Ⓔ
19. Ⓐ Ⓑ Ⓒ Ⓓ Ⓔ
20. Ⓐ Ⓑ Ⓒ Ⓓ Ⓔ
21. Ⓐ Ⓑ Ⓒ Ⓓ Ⓔ
22. Ⓐ Ⓑ Ⓒ Ⓓ Ⓔ
23. Ⓐ Ⓑ Ⓒ Ⓓ Ⓔ
24. Ⓐ Ⓑ Ⓒ Ⓓ Ⓔ
25. Ⓐ Ⓑ Ⓒ Ⓓ Ⓔ

SECTION I
READING COMPREHENSION

Time—35 Minutes
27 Questions

Directions:
Read the passages and answer the questions following each passage by blackening the appropriate space on the answer sheet. You may refer back to the passages when answering the questions. Answer all questions on the basis of what is stated or implied.

Passage 1

Federal preemption has historical origins in the United States Constitution. The preemption power is expressed in the Supremacy Clause of the Constitution and is used in a variety of contexts to affirm the primacy or preeminence of federal statutes and regulation over the states. The initial reason for preemption of state statutes or regulation under the Supremacy Clause of
(5) the Constitution is the potential for state enactments to either conflict directly with federal enactments or to otherwise frustrate federal objectives. To prevent a direct conflict, a federal statute or rule may expressly reserve from the states any jurisdiction over the matter described. The presence of an actual conflict is resolved by deferral to the federal power when preemption is express. Assuming the constitutionality of the federal statute, the inquiry is focused upon
(10) whether the preemption sought is within the scope of the statutory provision.

Where preemption is not expressly provided for, preemptive effect may nevertheless be implied by the language of the statute and the intent underlying its adoption. The test to determine if state regulation must give way to the federal enactment on constitutional grounds is whether "both regulations can be enforced without impairing the federal superintendence of the
(15) field. . . . A holding of federal exclusion of state law is inescapable and requires no inquiry into congressional design where compliance with both federal and state regulations is a physical impossibility for one engaged In Interstate commerce," or the state enactment "stands as an obstacle to the accomplishments and execution of the full purposes and objectives of Congress."
(20) Often when a federal agency regulates an industry pursuant to statute, the question of the extent of intended congressional preemption of state regulation arises. The congressional intent to preempt need not be express, but may be implicitly contained in the statute's structure and purpose. The stated purpose of the enactment is not conclusive, however, as to the implied intent to preempt. In the absence of explicit preemptive language, Congress' intent to supersede state
(25) law altogether may be inferred because "the scheme of federal regulation may be so pervasive as to make reasonable the inference that Congress left no room for the states to supplement it." A federal agency's rules and regulations "have no less preemptive effect than federal statutes." Thus, based upon agency determination of congressional intent, the scope of preemption may range from a total occupation of the field by federal regulation to partial preemption of limited
(30) impact.

Preemption analysis does not weigh the goals of state enactments versus the goals of federal enactments. Thus, whether or not it is desirable from a policy perspective for federal agencies to involve themselves in matters viewed by the states as overwhelmingly intrastate in nature, the agency's actions preempting state regulation will generally be upheld if it is pursuing a
(35) reasonable course, implicitly or explicitly delegated to it by federal statute.

A final implied preemption rationale accepted by the courts is that the matter sought to be preempted demands "exclusive federal regulation in order to achieve uniformity vital to national interests." This policy-based inquiry increasingly supports Federal Communications Commission decisions preempting state regulations that are found to frustrate the commission's pro-
(40) competitive telecommunications policies.

1. The title that best describes the contents of this passage is
    (A)   Legal Analysis of the Supremacy Claim
    (B)   The Constitution and States' Rights
    (C)   Legal Analysis of Federal Preemption
    (D)   The Congress and States' Rights
    (E)   Law and Preemption

2. Basic to the arguments of this passage is the assumption that
    (A)   the Constitution gives each state and the federal government equal powers
    (B)   the Constitution gives federal statutes priority over those of the states
    (C)   when Congress' intention is only implicit, the federal government does not necessarily have powers of preemption
    (D)   when Congress' intention is only implicit, the federal government has no powers of preemption
    (E)   when Congress' intention is only implicit, the federal government may have powers of preemption

3. According to the passage, the Supremacy Clause of the Constitution (lines 2–4) provides for the federal preemption of state statutes in order to
    (A)   frustrate federal objections
    (B)   encourage state enactments outside the scope of federal laws
    (C)   avoid redundancy in state and federal laws
    (D)   prevent state laws that contradict federal laws
    (E)   reserve exclusive federal jurisdictions

4. Assuming that city, state, and federal regulations can be enforced without conflict, federal preemption powers would
    (A)   give federal laws precedence over both state and city laws
    (B)   give federal laws precedence over state laws only
    (C)   give federal laws precedence over city laws only
    (D)   not solve the conflict of state and city laws
    (E)   be irrelevant

5. Compared to federal statutes, the regulations of a federal agency
    (A)   have equal preemptive effect
    (B)   have less preemptive effect
    (C)   have greater preemptive effect
    (D)   are less subject to questions of implied congressional intent
    (E)   are more subject to questions of implied congressional intent

6. If the Congress has delegated to a federal agency the regulatory authority over a specific practice, we can infer that the agency would NOT have preemptive power in cases
    (A)   involving that practice and a city ordinance
    (B)   where state and federal interests conflict
    (C)   involving that practice and a county ordinance
    (D)   involving that practice and a state law
    (E)   where the constitutionality of the federal agency is in question

7. Which of the following describes a situation in which the federal law would NOT have preemptive power?
    (A)   a situation where a federal law contradicting a state law implies, but does not specifically provide for preemption
    (B)   a situation where federal laws conflict with state laws on interstate commerce
    (C)   a situation where federal laws conflict with state laws on intrastate commerce
    (D)   a situation where federal laws are the same as state laws on interstate commerce
    (E)   a situation where a federal agency's rules conflict with those of a state agency

Passage 2

In the negotiation of tax treaties, developing nations, as a group, share two objectives somewhat at odds with those of developed-nation treaty partners. One such goal, attracting foreign investment, is in the broader context of foreign policy objectives. In the narrower realm of tax policy a common developing-country objective is to maximize the public capture of revenues
(5) from foreign investment activities.

Unfortunately for potential Third World treaty partners, this latter goal can conflict directly with the desires of both First World governments and individual investors. The preference of First World authorities for restricted source-based taxation is due to considerations of administrative feasibility. Such restrictions, though formally reciprocal, only produce equitable revenue effects
(10) when investment flows between treaty partners are relatively equal. However, when investment flows primarily in one direction, as it generally does from industrial to developing countries, the seemingly reciprocal source-based restrictions produce revenue sacrifices primarily by the state receiving most of the foreign investment and producing most of the income—namely, the developing country partner. The benefit is captured either by the taxpayer in the form of reduced
(15) excess credits, or by the treasury of the residence (First World) state as the taxpayer's domestically creditable foreign tax liabilities decrease. The potential public revenue gain to the residence state further bolsters the industrial nations' preference for restrictions on source-based taxation—at the direct expense of the treaty partner's revenue goals.

The United Nations Model Double Taxation Convention Between Developed and Developing
(20) Countries (the UN Model) represents one attempt to balance these considerations. In general, the UN document preserves greater source-based taxation than is typical in the industrial nations' treaties. This is done through provisions such as broader permanent establishment definitions and higher withholding-rate ceilings on dividend, interest, and royalty income.

If a developing country negotiates a favorable bargain in the face of a First World government's
(25) theoretical and pragmatic arguments, however, the problem of excess foreign tax credits, and the disincentive they represent to private investors, could remain. Indeed, the more taxing jurisdiction reserved to the source country by the treaty, the more likely the generation of excess credits will be. Thus, the overall maximization of tax revenues actually could require some restriction of at-source taxation. Though ascertaining the optimal revenue-producing balance is
(30) essentially an empirical issue, attaining what is perceived as the desired balance may be of central concern to treaty negotiators in developing countries.

The facilitation of foreign investment by tax treaties, whereas potentially serving the tax-policy goal of maximizing public revenue, also (or even instead) may serve broader economic objectives of developing countries. Foreign investments may be seen as essential sources of
(35) technical and managerial knowledge, capital, jobs, and foreign exchange. As such, the significance of foreign investments as an immediate source of public revenue could pale next to their longer-term "ripple effect" on development. In the negotiation of tax treaties, then, a developing country might be expected to ignore revenue goals and accept substantial limitations on source-based taxation, at least insofar as such limitations could be expected to
(40) encourage investment.

Frequently, however, Third World nations take a considerably more aggressive approach, seeking treaty terms that, in effect, provide subsidies to private investors at the expense of First World treaty partners. "Tax sparing" is one such potential measure. Tax sparing involves the residence state granting credits for foreign income taxes that would have been levied (or
(45) exemptions for income that would have been taxed at the source) but for tax holiday benefits granted by the source state. A more subtle method is "tax sharing," the concession by the residence state of still broader, or higher, source-based taxation than might be considered necessary to compensate for unequal investment and income flows. The United States has embraced neither concept. Traditionally, it has followed a strict policy of "capital export
(50) neutrality," providing no tax incentives for investment in the Third World through either the Internal Revenue Code or tax treaty provisions.

8. Normally, a developing country will negotiate a tax treaty for the purpose of
(A) attracting foreign workers
(B) decreasing tax revenues
(C) attracting international investment and reducing tax revenues
(D) attracting foreign investment and increasing tax revenues
(E) decreasing dependence on special interest local investors

9. We can infer that a reciprocal source-based taxation treaty between a First World and a developing nation will produce
(A) greater revenues for the First World nation
(B) greater revenues for the developing nation
(C) equal revenues for each country
(D) no revenues for either country
(E) losses to the economy of the First World nation

10. In negotiated treaties with developing countries, a First World country is likely to prefer
(A) unrestricted source-based taxation
(B) reciprocal restricted source-based taxation
(C) nonreciprocal source-based taxation
(D) equal investment flow between the partners
(E) limited investment flow between the partners

11. The United Nations Model Double Taxation Convention Between Developed and Developing Countries (the UN Model) mentioned in lines 19—20 is intended to
(A) reduce royalty income in developed and undeveloped countries
(B) provide higher withholding rates on income taxes
(C) equalize the investment flow between developed and developing nations
(D) equalize the foreign tax credits accumulated as a result of the treaty
(E) equalize the revenues from investment in undeveloped nations between developed and developing countries

12. In a treaty with a developing country that generates an excess of foreign tax credits, all of the following are likely EXCEPT
(A) the treaty will require some reduction of at-source taxation
(B) the treaty will discourage private investors
(C) the treaty will not produce what is perceived as the optimal revenue-producing balance
(D) the treaty will require some expansion of at-source taxation
(E) the excess of tax credits will be larger if the source country reserves more taxing jurisdiction

13. According to the passage, all of the following are potential advantages of foreign investment to developing countries EXCEPT
(A) increased managerial expertise
(B) increased capital
(C) increased availability of new materials
(D) increased foreign exchange
(E) increased employment

14. A developing country that did not insist upon immediate higher public revenues might be expected to
(A) deter foreign investment
(B) increase foreign investment
(C) avoid the "ripple effect"
(D) decrease employment
(E) decrease the availability of raw materials

15. "Tax sparing" and "tax sharing" are policies
   - (A)   that most developed countries employ
   - (B)   that are employed only by the United States
   - (C)   to encourage private investment
   - (D)   to encourage equal investment flow between trading partners
   - (E)   of "capital export neutrality"

Passage 3

As medical technology becomes more sophisticated, the resolution of guidelines for the termination of medical intervention becomes more imperative. The California legislature has recognized "that there exists considerable uncertainty in the medical and legal professions as to the legality of terminating the use or application of life-sustaining procedures where the patient

(5)   has voluntarily and in sound mind evidenced a desire that such procedures be withheld or withdrawn." The critical question is at which point during an individual's illness should he or she be allowed to refuse life-support treatment. Thus far, all statutes and prior decisions have limited patient and surrogate termination decisions to treatments artificially prolonging the moment of inevitable death, or where brain death has been established. In *Dority v. Superior Court,* for

(10)   example, the court held "that once brain death has been determined, by medical diagnosis under Health and Safety Code section 7180 or by judicial determination, no criminal or civil liability will result from disconnecting the life-support devices." Likewise, the right of an incurably and terminally ill patient to discontinue life-support treatment has generally been upheld, in *Eichner v. Dillon,* for example.

(15)   The Bartling case, however extended the right to terminate life-support equipment to an adult patient with serious illnesses that were probably incurable, but not terminal. This extension raises the possibility of overreaching. Specifically, patients and surrogate decision makers would be making decisions on the quality of life. Because patients in Mr. Bartling's position do not have a terminal illness, any decision to withhold or withdraw vital treatments assumes greater signifi-

(20)   cance. Although the decision, whether made by the patient or a surrogate, may relieve prolonged suffering, it can no longer be considered merely an acceleration of an inevitable and imminent death. The result has to be viewed as suicide or active euthanasia.

The difficulty in determining when a patient may authorize termination of life-support is further compounded by the conflict between the statutory definitions of murder and the scant decisional

(25)   law currently existing. According to California's Homicide Statute, a homicide is the killing of one human being by another human being. The Barber court noted that "the life-sustaining technology involved in this case is not traditional treatment in that it is not being used to directly cure or even address the pathological condition. It merely sustains biological functions in order to gain time to permit other processes to address the pathology." It then held that, as physicians

(30)   had no duty to continue full-time ineffective treatments, the disconnecting of the respirator merely hastened a natural death and thus, was not an unlawful killing. This, however, was merely conclusionary reasoning by the court. The facile finding that no duty existed allowed the court to conclude that no unlawful killing had occurred. There is precious little foundation that would allow physicians, or hospital and patients or their surrogates to proceed confident that their acts would

(35)   not be found unlawful by another court. The Barber court decision leaves unanswered under which circumstances health providers' actions or inactions will be found "merely to hasten a natural death."

16. The primary focus of the passage is upon
   - (A)   doctors' responsibilities in terminating life-support equipment
   - (B)   the technology of life-support equipment
   - (C)   the uncertainty in the laws governing the termination of life-support equipment
   - (D)   civil liability in cases involving the termination of life-support equipment
   - (E)   the termination of life-support in cases of terminal illness

17. With which of the following is the author of the passage likely to disagree?
  (A)   Euthanasia is neither justifiable nor excusable.
  (B)   All patients have a fundamental right to determine their medical care.
  (C)   The state has a responsibility to preserve life.
  (D)   There are some circumstances that justify the termination of life-support devices.
  (E)   Brain death may be determined by medical diagnosis or by judicial determination.

18. We can infer from the passage that the decision in the Bartling case
  (A)   permitted the termination of life-support equipment in the case of a patient who was not terminally ill
  (B)   permitted the termination of life-support devices in a brain dead patient
  (C)   permitted the termination of life-support equipment in the case of a terminally ill patient
  (D)   refused to allow the termination of life-support devices in a brain dead patient
  (E)   refused to allow the termination of life-support equipment in the case of a patient who was not terminally ill

19. According to the passage, the remarkable feature of the decision in the Bartling case is the
  (A)   extension of the right to terminate life-support to a patient incurably ill
  (B)   extension of the right to terminate life-support at the request of someone other than the patient
  (C)   refusal of the request to terminate life-support of a terminally ill patient
  (D)   extension of the right to terminate life-support to a patient not terminally ill
  (E)   court's indifference to the quality of life

20. According to the passage, which of the following is true of both *Dority* v. *Superior Court* (line 9) and *Eichner* v. *Dillon* (line 14)?
  (A)   Both involve brain death.
  (B)   In both, the termination of life-support systems was forbidden.
  (C)   In both, an inevitable and imminent death was accelerated.
  (D)   Both must be viewed either as suicide or as euthanasia.
  (E)   In both, the termination of life-support systems led to both civil and criminal liabilities.

21. If the principles of the decision of the Bartling court were applied to another case, which of the following situations might result?
  (A)   A brain-dead patient might be removed from life-support equipment.
  (B)   A child suffering great pain from a terminal disease might be removed from life-support equipment.
  (C)   An adult suffering great pain from a terminal disease might be removed from life-support equipment.
  (D)   An adult suffering great pain from a minor injury might be released from a hospital.
  (E)   An adult suffering great pain from an incurable disease might be removed from life-support equipment.

22. The author finds fault with the decision of the Barber court because
  (A)   the death was unlawful
  (B)   another court might find the death unlawful
  (C)   doctors cannot be allowed to hasten a natural death
  (D)   so few decisions in cases of this sort have been reached
  (E)   the termination of life-support merely hastened a natural death

Passage 4

It is deemed a necessity to understand clearly the nature of science in a time commonly known as the "scientific age." Of significance is the student's ability to see that biology, for example, is a science and to relate it to other sciences like chemistry or physics. While compartmentalizing knowledge into biology, chemistry, geology, or anthropology is a convenience, there is danger in that we can easily overlook how these seemingly unrelated fields actually complement one another.

The word *science* is heard so often in modern times that almost everybody has some notion of its meaning. On the other hand, its definition is difficult for many people. The meaning of the term is confused because many endeavors masquerading under the name of science do not have any valid connection with it. Therefore everyone should understand its import and objectives. Just to make the explanation as simple as possible, suppose science is defined as classified knowledge (facts). An example that adequately meets the requirements is astronomy. On the other hand, astrology, regardless of how sincerely it is believed by some, must be excluded since it is not based on fact.

Even in the true sciences distinguishing fact from fiction is not always easy. For this reason great care should be taken to distinguish between beliefs and truths. There is no danger as long as a clear difference is made between temporary and proved explanations. For example, hypotheses (tentative theories) and theories are attempts to explain natural phenomena. From these tentative positions the scientist continues to experiment and observe until they are proved or discredited. The exact status of any explanation should be clearly labeled to avoid confusion.

The objectives of science are primarily the discovery and the subsequent understanding of the unknown. Man cannot be satisfied with recognizing that secrets exist in nature or that questions are unanswerable; he must solve them. Toward that end specialists in the field of biology and related fields of interest are directing much of their time and energy. A beginning student should understand the motivation of science and acquire the spirit of inquiry. That kind of spirit, plus practice in the methods of science, should make a course more meaningful.

Actually, two basic approaches lead to the discovery of new information. One, aimed at satisfying curiosity, is referred to as *pure* science. The other is aimed at using knowledge for specific purposes—for instance, improving health, raising standards of living, or creating new consumer products. In this case knowledge is put to economic use. Such an approach is referred to as *applied* science.

Sometimes practical-minded people miss the point of pure science in thinking only of its immediate utilization for economic rewards. One can see that an extraordinary amount of knowledge about chemistry is necessary before one can possibly understand functions of protoplasm like respiration or photosynthesis. Chemists responsible for many of the discoveries could hardly have anticipated that their findings would one day result in applications of such a practical nature as those directly related to life and health. Furthermore, geneticists working on insects could not foresee all the possible applications of their findings to the improvement of plants and animals through selective breeding. The discovery of one bit of information opens the door to the discovery of another. Some discoveries seem so simple that one is amazed they were not made years ago; however, one should remember that the construction of the microscope had to precede the discovery of the cell, and a knowledge of the chemical nature of oxygen and carbon dioxide had to come before a breakthrough in the understanding of photosynthesis. The host of scientists dedicating their lives to pure science are not apologetic about ignoring the practical side of their discoveries; they know from experience that most knowledge is eventually applied. Probably one can safely say that even from a practical point of view all discoveries will eventually be used.

23. To define science, we may simply call it
    (A)   the complementation of unrelated fields
    (B)   the convergence of unrelated fields
    (C)   biology, chemistry, geology, physics, and anthropology
    (D)   biology, chemistry, geology, and anthropology
    (E)   classified knowledge

24. According to the passage, which of the following cannot be classified as a science?
  (A) phrenology   (B) astronomy   (C) astrology   (D) chemistry   (E) botany

25. Pure science, leading to the construction of a microscope,
  (A) may lead to antiscientific, "impure" results
  (B) necessarily precedes applied science, leading to the discovery of a cell
  (C) is not always pure
  (D) comes largely from the efforts of eccentric scientists
  (E) necessarily results from applied science and the discovery of a cell

26. A scientist interested in adding to our general knowledge about oxygen would probably call his approach
  (A) applied science   (B) beginning science   (C) agricultural science
  (D) pure science   (E) botanical science

27. The best title for this passage is
  (A) Manifestations and Relationships of Life
  (B) Biology and the Scientific Age
  (C) The Nature of Science and Scientists
  (D) Organisms and Their Environments
  (E) Changing Life

STOP

IF YOU FINISH BEFORE TIME IS UP, CHECK YOUR WORK ON THIS SECTION OF THE TEST ONLY. DO NOT GO ON TO THE NEXT SECTION OF THE TEST UNTIL TIME IS UP FOR THIS SECTION.

SECTION II
ANALYTICAL REASONING

Time—35 Minutes
24 Questions

Directions:
In this section you will be given groups of questions based on different sets of conditions. Drawing a simple diagram may be helpful in answering some of the questions. You are to choose the best answer and mark the corresponding space on your answer sheet.

Questions 1–7

The city of Buldonia can be very difficult to enter. A guard is assigned to each entrance road to make sure that those trying to enter have the necessary card.

To get into Buldonia you need a blue card.
To get a blue card you need a yellow ticket and a blue ticket.
To get a blue ticket you need a green hat or a yellow card.
You can trade a yellow card for either a blue ticket or a yellow ticket.
You can trade a red ticket for either a green hat or a yellow card.
You can trade a red card for a yellow ticket.

1. Which of the following will NOT get you into Buldonia?
(A)   a red ticket and a red card
(B)   a yellow ticket and a green hat
(C)   a blue ticket and a yellow card
(D)   a red card and a yellow ticket
(E)   a green hat and a red ticket

2. Which of the following will get you into Buldonia?
(A)   two green hats
(B)   two red tickets
(C)   a red card and a yellow ticket
(D)   a green hat and a blue ticket
(E)   two red cards

3. Which of the following, when used in combination with a yellow card, will NOT get you into Buldonia?
(A) green hat   (B) red card   (C) red ticket   (D) yellow ticket
(E) Any of these will get you in.

4. If you could trade a yellow hat for a green hat, then which of the following would NOT get you into Buldonia?
(A)   a yellow hat and a red card
(B)   a yellow hat and a red ticket
(C)   a yellow hat and a blue ticket
(D)   a yellow hat and a yellow card
(E)   a yellow hat and a yellow ticket

5. If the price of a blue card is two blue tickets and one yellow ticket, then which of the following will get you into Buldonia?
(A)   two red cards and a green hat
(B)   a red card, a yellow card, and a yellow ticket
(C)   three green hats
(D)   three red cards
(F)   three red tickets

6. If the price of a blue card is two yellow tickets and one blue ticket, then which of the following will NOT get you into Buldonia?
(A)   three red tickets
(B)   a red ticket and two green hats
(C)   three yellow cards
(D)   a red ticket, a red card, a yellow card
(E)   a green hat, a red card, a yellow card

7. If a green ticket will get you a yellow ticket, then which of the following will NOT get you into Buldonia?
(A)   a red ticket and a green ticket
(B)   a red card and a red ticket
(C)   a green ticket and a red card
(D)   a green hat and a red card
(E)   a yellow ticket and a red ticket

Questions 8–14

Seven students (George, Hal, Ken, Jon, Neil, Lynn, and Melanie) are playing a game involving play money.

The only bills used are play dollar bills.
No coins are used.
Jon has more bills than Lynn, Melanie, and Neil combined.
The total of Lynn's and Melanie's bills are equal to Neil's bills.
Melanie has more bills than Ken and George combined.
Hal has fewer bills than George.
Ken and George have the same number of bills.

8. Which of the following students has the most bills?
   (A) Ken   (B) George   (C) Jon   (D) Lynn   (E) Melanie

9. Which of the following students has the fewest bills?
   (A) Melanie   (B) Neil   (C) George   (D) Ken   (E) Hal

10. Which of the following must be true?
   (A)   Melanie has fewer bills than Ken.
   (B)   Neil has more bills than Lynn.
   (C)   Lynn has fewer bills than Melanie.
   (D)   Lynn has more bills than George.
   (E)   George has more bills than Melanie.

11. Assume that Ken is given one bill from Hal. Assume also that Melanie has more bills than Ken, George, and Lynn combined. If none of the students has the same number of bills, which of the following is a possible order from highest to lowest of students who have the most bills?
   (A)   Jon, Melanie, Lynn, Neil, Ken, George, Hal
   (B)   Jon, Neil, Melanie, Lynn, George, Ken, Hal
   (C)   Neil, Jon, Melanie, George, Ken, Hal, Lynn
   (D)   Jon, Neil, Ken, Melanie, George, Lynn, Hal
   (E)   Jon, Neil, Melanie, Ken, George, Hal, Lynn

12. Assume that Lynn does not have the same number of bills as Ken. Which of the following must be FALSE?
   (A)   Lynn has the same number of bills as Hal.
   (B)   Neil has twice as many bills as Melanie.
   (C)   George has more bills than Hal and Lynn combined.
   (D)   George does not have the same number of bills as Lynn.
   (E)   Jon has fewer than twice the number of Lynn's and Melanie's bills combined.

13. If Lynn and Melanie have the same number of bills, then which of the following must be FALSE?
   (A)   Neil has more bills than Melanie.
   (B)   Melanie has more bills than Ken, George, and Hal combined.
   (C)   George has fewer bills than Hal and Ken combined.
   (D)   Neil has fewer bills than Lynn, George, and Hal combined.
   (E)   Jon has more bills than Lynn, Ken, George, and Hal combined.

14. Assume that Tom decides to join the game. Assume also that he is given bills from the bank. If his total number of bills are more than Ken's and fewer than Lynn's, which of the following must be true?
   (A)   Melanie has fewer bills than Tom.
   (B)   Tom has fewer bills than George.
   (C)   Lynn has fewer bills than Melanie.
   (D)   Melanie and Lynn have the same number of bills.
   (E)   Lynn has more bills than Hal.

Questions 15–18

(1) Axel, Benty, and Carmen are sitting around a table. Each is a member of one of the following clubs: the YES Club, the NO club, and the MAYBE Club. Each belongs to a different club.
(2) A YES always tells the truth.
(3) A NO always tells a lie.
(4) A MAYBE, answering two or more questions, tells the truth and lies alternately; however, the first answer may be either a lie or the truth.
(5) Axel answered his first question: "I am a MAYBE."
(6) Axel answered his second question: "Benty is a YES."
(7) Axel answered his third question: "Carmen is a NO."

15. From statements (1), (2), (3), (4), and (5) it can be determined that
    (A)   Axel is telling the truth
    (B)   Axel is telling a lie
    (C)   Axel is not a YES
    (D)   Axel is not a NO
    (E)   Axel is not a MAYBE

16. If Benty were asked the question, "Who are you?," what would his reply be?
    (A)   I am a YES.
    (B)   I am a NO.
    (C)   I am a MAYBE.
    (D)   I am not a MAYBE.
    (E)   Any of the above are possible answers.

17. Which of the following must be true?
    (A)   Axel is not a NO.
    (B)   Carmen is not a YES.
    (C)   Axel is a YES.
    (D)   Benty is a NO.
    (E)   Carmen is a MAYBE.

18. If Carmen were asked the question about membership in the club, which of the following could be the response?
    (A)   Benty is a NO.
    (B)   Axel is a MAYBE.
    (C)   Benty is not a MAYBE.
    (D)   Axel is not a NO.
    (E)   I am not a MAYBE.

Questions 19–24

(1) Six people sat equally spaced around a circular table with six seats. Their first names were Albert, Beatrice, Clyde, Dexter, Eileen, and Frances. Their last names were Truckner, Upland, Williams, Xymer, Youngton, and Zipley (not necessarily in that order). They all faced toward the center of the table.
(2) Xymer sat two places to the left of Clyde.
(3) Frances sat two places to the right of Youngton.
(4) Williams sat on Albert's left, and Eileen sat on Albert's right.
(5) Dexter sat on Upland's right, and Truckner sat on Upland's left.
(6) Zipley sat directly across from Frances.
(7) There is one seat between Beatrice and Eileen.
(8) Dexter's last name is Williams.

19. Which of the following can be deduced from facts (1), (3), and (6)?
   (A)   Zipley sat directly across from Youngton.
   (B)   There are two seats between Frances and Zipley.
   (C)   Youngton sat on Zipley's left.
   (D)   Frances' last name is Trucker.
   (E)   Youngton's first name is Albert.

20. Which of the following CANNOT be deduced from facts (1), (4), (5), and (8)?
   (A)   Upland sat two places to the left of Albert.
   (B)   Eileen sat directly across from Upland.
   (C)   Truckner sat directly across from Albert.
   (D)   Truckner sat two places to the left of Eileen.
   (E)   Upland sat next to Williams.

21. What is Truckner's first name?
   (A) Albert   (B) Beatrice   (C) Clyde   (D) Dexter   (E) Eileen

22. Which of the following must be true?
   (A)   Zipley is Frances' last name.
   (B)   Williams sat two places to the right of Zipley.
   (C)   Frances sat directly across from Albert.
   (D)   Zipley sat next to Beatrice.
   (E)   Eileen's last name is Zipley.

23. Which of the following must be FALSE?
   (A)   Clyde sat directly across from Dexter.
   (B)   Eileen sat directly across from Frances.
   (C)   Clyde sat next to Eileen.
   (D)   Beatrice sat between Clyde and Frances.
   (E)   Clyde sat directly across from Albert.

24. What is Clyde's last name?
   (A) Truckner   (B) Upland   (C) Xymer   (D) Youngton   (E) Zipley

STOP

IF YOU FINISH BEFORE TIME IS UP, CHECK YOUR WORK ON THIS SECTION OF THE TEST ONLY.
DO NOT GO ON TO THE NEXT SECTION OF THE TEST UNTIL TIME IS UP FOR THIS SECTION.

SECTION III
LOGICAL REASONING

Time—35 Minutes
26 Questions

Directions:
In this section you will be given brief statements or passages and will be required to evaluate the reasoning involved. In some instances, more than one choice will appear to be a possible answer. You are to choose the *best* answer. Use common sense and reasonableness in making your selection; then mark the proper space on the answer sheet.

1. Recent studies show that reduction in the maximum speed limit from 65 mph to 55 mph substantially reduces the number of highway fatalities.

The preceding statement would be most weakened by establishing that
(A) most fatal car accidents occur at night
(B) most accidents occurring at speeds between 45 and 55 mph are nonfatal
(C) few fatal accidents involve only one vehicle
(D) prior to this reduction, 97 percent of fatal accidents occurred below 45 mph
(E) prior to the reduction, 97 percent of fatal accidents occurred between 55 and 65 mph

2. Board member Smith will vote for the busing of students if she is reelected to the board. If the busing of students is passed by the board, then Smith was not reelected to the board. Smith was reelected to the board.

Given the foregoing information, which of the following can be concluded?
(A) Smith assisted in the passage of student busing.
(B) The passage of busing carried Smith to a reelection victory.
(C) Smith voted against busing; however, it still passed.
(D) Busing was defeated despite Smith's vote in favor of it.
(E) Student busing was voted down by a majority of the board.

3. Daniel Webster said, "Falsehoods not only disagree with truths, but usually quarrel among themselves."

Which of these would follow from Webster's statement?
(A) Quarreling is endemic to American political life.
(B) Truth and falsehood can be distinguished from one another.
(C) Liars often quarrel with each other.
(D) Those who know the truth are normally silent.
(E) Truth and falsehood are emotional, rather than intellectual, phenomena.

4. A recording industry celebrity observed: "I am not a star because all my songs are hits; all my songs are hits because I am a star."

Which of the following most nearly parallels this reasoning?
(A) A college professor noted: "I am the final word in the classroom not because my judgment is always correct, but my judgment in the classroom is always correct because I am the instructor."
(B) A nurse observed: "I am not competent in my duties because I am a nurse, but I am competent in my duties because of my training in nursing."
(C) A dance instructor noted: "I am not the instructor because I know all there is about dance; rather I am an instructor because of my ability to teach dancing."
(D) A recording industry celebrity observed: "I am not wealthy because I am a star; I am wealthy because so many people buy my recordings."
(E) A recording industry celebrity observed: "I am not a star because my every song is enjoyed; I am a star because people pay to watch me perform."

5. The enzyme Doxin cannot be present if the bacterium *Entrox* is absent.

Given the foregoing condition, which of the following would NOT be true?
(A) *Entrox* may be present without the presence of Doxin.
(B) Doxin and *Entrox may be present together*.
(C) There may be a case in which neither Doxin nor *Entrox* is present.
(D) If Doxin is present, *Entrox* cannot be absent.
(E) Doxin may be present without *Entrox*.

6. If a speaker were highly credible, would an objectively irrelevant personal characteristic of the speaker influence the effectiveness of her communication? For example, if a Nobel prize-winning chemist were speaking on inorganic chemistry, would she induce a lesser change in the opinions of an audience if she were known to be a poor cook? Would the speaker's effectiveness be different if she were obese rather than trim, sloppy rather than neat, ugly rather than attractive?

By failing to consider irrelevant aspects of communicator credibility, studies in communication science have unknowingly implied that audiences are composed of individuals who are responsive only to objectively relevant aspects of a speaker.

Which of the following represent(s) assumptions upon which the foregoing passage is based?
(A) Audiences are composed of people who are responsive only to objectively relevant aspects of a communicator.
(B) Objectively irrelevant personal characteristics have a bearing on a speaker's effectiveness.
(C) Some characteristics of a communicator are of greater relevance than others.
(D) A trim speaker is likely to be more persuasive than an obese one.
(E) Irrelevant aspects of a communication have more effect on an audience than the content of a speech.

Questions 7–8 refer to the following passage.

I read with interest the statements of eminent archaeologists that the presence of a crude snare in an early Neolithic grave indicates that man of this period subsisted by snaring small mammals. I find this assertion open to question. How do I know the companions of the deceased did not toss the snare into the grave with the corpse because it had proved to be totally useless?

7. The author employs which of the following as a method of questioning the archaeologists' claims?
(A) evidence that contradicts the conclusion drawn by the archaeologists
(B) a doubtful tone about the motives of the archaeologists
(C) a body of knowledge inconsistent with that employed by the archaeologists
(D) an alternative to the conclusion drawn by the archaeologists
(E) the suggestion that archaeological studies are of little use

8. Which of the following best expresses the author's criticism of the archaeologists whose statements he questions?
(A) They have not subjected their conclusions to scientific verification.
(B) They have stressed one explanation and ignored others.
(C) They have drawn a conclusion that does not fit the evidence upon which it was based.
(D) They failed to employ proper scientific methods in arriving at their conclusion.
(E) They have based their conclusion on behaviors exhibited by more modern humans.

9. Semanticists point out that words and phrases often acquire connotations tinged with emotions. Such significances are attached because of the context, the history of the usage of the expression, or the background of the person reading or listening. Thus, "the hills of home" may evoke a feeling of nostalgia or a pleasant sensation; but "Bolshevik" may arouse derision or disgust in the minds of many people.

The term "progressive education" has gone through several stages in the connotative process. At one time progressive education was hailed as the harbinger of all that was wise and wholesome in classroom practice, such as the recognition of individual differences and the revolution against formalized dictatorial procedures. However, partly because of abuses on the fanatical fringe of the movement, many people began to associate progressive schools with frills, fads, and follies. What had been discovered and developed by Froebel in Germany, by Pestalozzi in Switzerland, by Montessori in Italy, and by men like Parker and Dewey in the United States was muddled in a melange of mockery and misunderstanding and submerged in satirical quips. As a result, many educators have recently avoided the expression and have chosen to call present educational practices "new" or "modern" rather than "progressive."

Which of the following would most seriously weaken the author's argument?
(A) In a recent poll of American voters, 76 percent responded that they would certainly not vote for the Progressive Labor Party.
(B) Open classrooms have recently fallen out of the educational limelight.
(C) New techniques in teaching cognitive skills, called "progressive learning," have recently met with widespread approval in middle class public schools.
(D) Parker and Dewey were well respected by academicians and educational theorists.
(E) Every new advance in education is first denounced as a "fad."

10. *Bill*: Professor Smith has been late for class almost every morning.
Dave: That can't be true; he was on time yesterday.

Dave apparently believes that Bill has said which of the following?
(A) Professor Smith is seldom late.
(B) Professor Smith does not enjoy teaching.
(C) Professor Smith has been late every day without exception.
(D) Professor Smith was late yesterday.
(E) Professor Smith informs Bill of his whereabouts.

11. Sunbathers do not usually spend much time in the shade. Shade prevails during most of June in La Jolla. It is June 14.

Which of the following conclusions would be logically defensible, based upon the foregoing premises?
(A) La Jolla is the site of frequent sunbathing.
(B) The sun is not shining today.
(C) There are sunbathers in La Jolla today.
(D) There may be sunbathers in La Jolla today.
(E) There are more sunbathers in La Jolla in July than in June.

12. Although American politicians disagree about many things, none of them disagrees with Wendell Willkie's assertion that "the Constitution does not provide for first- and second-class citizens."

Willkie's statement implies that
(A) the Constitution provides for third- and fourth-class citizens
(B) first-class citizens don't need to be provided for
(C) there is no such thing as a second-class citizen
(D) the Constitution makes no class distinctions
(E) no citizens can be first and second class simultaneously

13. Recently, psychologists have proposed that American productivity is dropping because workers spend much of their time creating excuses for their laziness instead of focusing on assigned tasks. Although such workers sometimes experience "good" days when they labor efficiently and productively, such days are rare, and wasted time is the rule.

Which of the following proverbs best summarizes the argument above?
(A) As ye sow, so shall ye reap.
(B) Don't count your chickens before they hatch.
(C) A stitch in time saves nine.
(D) He that is good for making excuses is seldom good for anything else.
(E) You can fool some of the people all of the time.

14. Nothing can come of nothing; nothing can go back to nothing.

Which of the following follows most logically from the above statement?
(A) Something can come out of something; something can go back to something.
(B) Something can come out of nothing; something can go back to nothing.
(C) Nothing can come out of something; nothing can go back to something.
(D) Something must come out of something; something must go back to something.
(E) Something must come out of something; nothing can go back to nothing.

15. The president has vowed in speeches across the country that there will be no increase in taxes and no reduction in defense; he has repeatedly challenged Congress to narrow the deficit through deeper spending cuts. Congressional critics have responded with labored comparisons between a bloated Pentagon and the nation's poor being lacerated by merciless budget cutters. In Democratic cloakrooms, laments about the "intolerable deficit" are code words for higher taxes.

Which of the following additions to the passage would make clear the author's position on the budget issue?
(A) Everyone agrees that the president's budget deficit of around 100 billion is highly undesirable, to say the least.
(B) Everyone agrees that the president's budget deficit is both undesirable and unavoidable.
(C) Everyone agrees that this will be a summer of hot debate in Congress over the president's budget proposal.
(D) Everyone agrees that the partisan disagreement over the president's budget proposal will be won by those who create the most persuasive terminology.
(E) Everyone agrees that the president's budget proposal is a product of careful, honest, but sometimes misguided analysis.

16. *The average wage in this plant comes to exactly $7.87 per working day.* In this statement *average* has the strict mathematical sense. It is the quotient obtained by dividing the sum of all wages for a given period by the product of the number of workers and the number of days in the period.

Which of the following is the most logical implication of the passage above?
(A) More workers in the plant earn $7.87 per day than those who do not earn $7.87 per day.
(B) Any particular worker in the plant receives $7.87 per day.
(C) There must be workers in the plant who earn far more than $7.87 per day.
(D) If some workers in the plant earn more than $7.87 per day, there must be others in the plant who earn less than $7.87 per day.
(E) There must be workers in the plant who earn exactly $7.87 per day.

17. *Magazine article*: Davy "Sugar" Jinkins is one of the finest boxers to have ever fought. Last week Davy announced his retirement from the ring, but not from the sport. Davy will continue in boxing as the trainer of "Boom Boom" Jones. With Jinkins handling him, we are sure that Boom Boom will become a title contender in no time.

The foregoing article is based upon all of the following assumptions EXCEPT
(A) boxers who have a good trainer can do well
(B) those who were good boxers can be fine trainers
(C) Jones is capable of being trained
(D) title contenders should be well trained
(E) Jinkins did well as a boxer

18.   Motivation implies action, but the motivated individual will pursue certain goals and avoid others. The types of goals pursued and avoided have been determined by a statistical study of the (18) ——————————————— and deterrents, satisfactions and dissatisfactions, and rewards and punishments described by a number of motivated individuals.

Which of the following represents the most likely completion of the foregoing passage?
(A) incentives   (B) discouragements   (C) rewards   (D) avoidances   (E) goals

19.   The stores are always crowded on holidays. The stores are not crowded; therefore, it must not be a holiday.

Which of the following most closely parallels the kind of reasoning used in the above sentences?
(A)   The stores are always crowded on Christmas. The stores are crowded; therefore, it must be Christmas.
(B)   Reptiles are present on a hot day in the desert. Reptiles are absent in this desert area; therefore, this cannot be a hot desert day.
(C)   There is a causal relationship between the occurrence of holidays and the number of people in stores.
(D)   The voting places are empty; therefore, it is not an election day.
(E)   The stores are always empty on Tuesdays. It is Tuesday; therefore, the stores will be empty.

Questions 20–21 refer to the following passage.

For one to be assured of success in politics, one must have a sound experiential background, be a polished orator, and possess great wealth. Should an individual lack any one of these attributes, he most certainly will be considered a dark horse in any campaign for public office. Should an individual be without any two of these attributes, he cannot win an election. If Nelson Nerd is to win the presidency, he must greatly improve his ability as a public speaker. His extraordinary wealth is not enough.

20. The author of the above passage appears to believe that
(A)   Nerd is the wealthiest candidate
(B)   Nerd is a sufficiently experienced politician
(C)   being a good public speaker alone can win one a high public office
(D)   if Nerd's public speaking improves, he will win in the presidency
(E)   Nerd is not a dark horse now

21. Which of the following would most weaken the speaker's claims?
(A)   Nerd is not the wealthiest candidate running for president.
(B)   The incumbent president had little relevant experience before coming into office and has always been a poor public speaker.
(C)   Of the individuals elected to public office, 0.001 percent have lacked either oratory skill, experience, or money.
(D)   Nerd failed in his last bid for the presidency.
(E)   The incumbent president, who is running for reelection, is as wealthy as Nerd.

22. Since this car is blue, it must not accelerate quickly.

The foregoing conclusion can be properly drawn if it is also known that
(A)   all red cars accelerate quickly
(B)   there are some slow blue cars
(C)   all blue cars may not accelerate slowly
(D)   all cars that accelerate quickly are red
(E)   all slow cars are red

Questions 23–24 refer to the following passage.

As almost everyone is painfully aware, the federal government has butted into almost every sector of human existence in recent years. But this manic intrusiveness isn't always the government's fault. Sometimes there is a compulsion to enlist Uncle Sam as a superbusybody.

23. Which of the following is one of the author's basic assumptions?
   (A) Most of his readers have suffered government intrusion.
   (B) All government intrusion is unwarranted.
   (C) Government intrusion is always government-initiated.
   (D) All memories of government intrusion are painful memories.
   (E) At no time has the federal government practiced nonintrusiveness.

24. Which of the following most nearly restates the final sentence?
   (A) Most of the time government is responsible for government intrusion.
   (B) Sometimes government does more than intrude; it compels intrusion.
   (C) Sometimes Uncle Sam himself enlists in the ranks of the intruders.
   (D) Sometimes Uncle Sam is compulsive rather than merely symbolic.
   (E) Sometimes the government itself is not responsible for government intrusion.

25. Those who dictate what we can and cannot see on television are guilty of falsely equating knowledge with action. They would have us believe that to view violent behavior is to commit it.

On the basis of the content of the above passage, we may infer that the author would believe which of the following?
   (A) Knowing how to manufacture nuclear weapons leads to nuclear war.
   (B) Those guilty of committing a crime were not necessarily influenced by an awareness that such crimes occurred.
   (C) Media censorship is based upon logical justification.
   (D) Know your enemy.
   (E) The truth shall set you free.

26. In 1975, the U.S. Supreme Court ruled that the federal government has exclusive rights to any oil and gas resources on the Atlantic Outer Shelf beyond the three-mile limit.

Which of the following must be true in order for this ruling to be logical?
   (A) The U.S. Supreme Court has met recently.
   (B) The Atlantic Outer Shelf may possibly contain oil and gas resources.
   (C) No oil and gas resources exist within the three-mile limit.
   (D) In 1977, the Court reversed this ruling.
   (E) Oil and gas on the Atlantic Shelf has not been explored for in the past three years.

STOP

IF YOU FINISH BEFORE TIME IS UP, CHECK YOUR WORK ON THIS SECTION OF THE TEST ONLY. DO NOT GO ON TO THE NEXT SECTION OF THE TEST UNTIL TIME IS UP FOR THIS SECTION.

SECTION IV
READING COMPREHENSION

Time—35 Minutes
28 Questions

Directions:
Read the passages and answer the questions following each passage by blackening the appropriate space on the answer sheet. You may refer back to the passages when answering the questions. Answer all questions on the basis of what is stated or implied.

Passage 1

Moviemakers have always been interested in politicians, and vice-versa. As early as 1912, Raoul Walsh followed Pancho Villa around, filming his ambushes and executions. Villa even delayed them by two to three hours so Walsh would have enough light to shoot the scenes.

In Russia, Sergei Eisenstein made several films at Stalin's request, including *Alexander Nevski* in 1938 and *Ivan the Terrible* in 1945, both of which made the new regime appear to be the heir of a glorious revolutionary tradition. In Germany, the "Mabuse" series from 1922 to 1933 sketched the portrait of a budding dictator, but when Goebbels as propaganda minister asked Fritz Lang to become the Third Reich's official film maker, Lang refused.

Hitler himself charged Leni Riefenstahl to film the Nazi rallies at Nuremberg in 1934. The result was *The Triumph of Will*, which took two years to make and included oceans of swastika flags, miles of military parades, stylized eagles, rolling drums, and an omnipresent Hitler whose profile stood out against the sky.

But the movies soon helped create a political style less stridently heroic and melodramatic than that inspired by the theater and opera. At the beginning, of course, early cinema techniques encouraged the leader to pantomime heavily with excessive gestures and expressions. The result was similar to expressionist theater. But it soon became clear that the cinema offered possibilities unknown on the stage; for example, the close-up, which abolished the distance between the actor and the audience and made exaggerated gestures unnecessary. With the actor's image enlarged on the screen, even a trembling of the lips or batting of the eyelids would be magnified.

When the talkies appeared, the theatrical delivery of lines was no longer the rule. A conversational tone—even a whisper—was easily heard by the audience, making actors adopt a more natural style.

Political leaders have adapted their style to this evolution of the dramatic arts. The hero leader necessarily has a style more suited to the theater or silent movies and is less able to use the new tone required by cinema and television, which is more sober, allusive, and elliptical. In this sense, de Gaulle was of the theater generation while Giscard d'Estaing belongs to the cinema and television generation that understands the need for a more nuanced "stage presence."

Another result of the cinema has been to make actors more influential as models to imitate, since they are so much more visible. It was this that gave rise to the star system, which for a long time was virtually the basis of the movie industry.

In a sense, the era of the star system can be broken down into three phases, each corresponding to three main types of stars. Each offered different models to the audience—and to political leaders.

The first phase was from 1920 to 1932, when stars were inaccessible, marmoreal, and inimitable. These were the idols, surrounded by an aura of myth. In short, they were the cinema equivalent of the hero leader.

Then, during the 1930s and 1940s, the star became more human. He or she, though still shining brightly, was less exceptional, a bit more like the rest of us. The star became a model that could be imitated—like the charm leader.

The third phase was in the 1950s and 1960s, when stars became virtually the reflection of the spectator if not, indeed, his double. It became more difficult to imitate a star, since he or she was already like everyone else. This corresponded to the political Mr. Everyman.

1. Franklin Roosevelt's "Fireside Chats" (seemingly informal radio talks with his constituency) might have been mentioned in this passage as an example of the
(A) same mode of propaganda practiced by the Germans and Russians
(B) unpopularity of excessive theatricality during the 1930s and 1940s
(C) use of a new medium for political communications
(D) more natural style of presentation that developed in both movies and politics
(E) mastery of nuance

2. Overall, the passage develops a comparison between
(A) bandits and political leaders
(B) actors and politicians
(C) moviemakers and politicians
(D) Nazis and Communists
(E) de Gaulle and d'Estaing

3. The author's attitude toward the factualness of the two films mentioned that Eisenstein made for Stalin is
(A) enthusiastic   (B) satiric   (C) angry   (D) skeptical   (E) ambiguous

4. The author might agree that the exaggerated gestures in Hitler's speeches were influenced by
(A) the Führer's desire to outdo Russian propaganda
(B) Leni Riefenstahl's direction
(C) the style of movie heroes
(D) the dramatic style of the theater and opera
(E) Hitler's effort to stress profile features

5. Which of the following is the most appropriate title for this passage?
(A) The Movies Invade Politics
(B) The Waning of Expressionist Theater
(C) Propaganda as Entertainment
(D) Four Countries and Theatricality
(E) Government as Cinema

6. According to the passage, after 1932 both actors and politicians began to seem
(A) less like mirror images of each other
(B) less introverted
(C) more popular
(D) less unique
(E) more involved in each other's profession

7. By developing an analogy between the movies and politics, the author assumes which of the following?
(A) Public life is an art form.
(B) Movies about politics generate government policies.
(C) Before the advent of the movies, politics lacked character.
(D) Events in life can be imitations of art.
(E) Movies have been the most important influence on politics in recent history.

Passage 2

Taxonomy, the science of classifying and ordering organisms, has an undeserved reputation as a harmless, and mindless, activity of listing, cataloguing, and describing—consider the common idea of a birdwatcher, up at 5:30 in the morning with binoculars, short pants, and "life list" of every bird he has seen. Even among fellow scientists, taxonomy is often treated as "stamp collecting," while its practitioners are viewed much as the Biblical hyraxes—"a feeble folk that dwelleth among the rocks."

It was not always so. During the eighteenth and early nineteenth centuries, taxonomy was in the forefront of the sciences. The greatest biologists of Europe were professional taxonomists— Linnaeus, Cuvier, Lamarck. Darwin's major activity during the twenty years separating his Malthusian insights from the publication of his evolutionary theory was a three-volume work on the taxonomy of barnacles. Thomas Jefferson took time out from the affairs of state to publish one of the great taxonomic errors in the history of paleontology—he described a giant sloth claw as a lion three times the size of Africa's version. These heady days were marked by discovery as naturalists collected the fauna and flora of previously uncharted regions. They were also marked by the emergence of intellectual structure, as coherent classifications seemed to mirror the order of God's thought.

A Species of Eternity is an account of America's part in this great epoch of natural history. We often forget that 150 years ago much of our continent was as unknown and potentially hazard-ous as any place on earth. During the eighteenth century, when most naturalists denied the possibility of extinction, explorers expected to find mammoths and other formidable fossil creatures alive in the American West.

Kastner's theme is discovery and the American frontier. His book is a series of short biographies, chronologically arranged, of the dozen or so passionate, single-minded iconoclasts who fought the hostility of the wilderness, and often of urban literary people, to disclose the rich fauna and flora of America. For the most part, they worked alone, with small support from patrons or government. The Lewis and Clark expedition is the only official trip treated here—and its primary purpose was not natural history. We may now look upon tales of frontier toughness and perseverance as the necessary mythology of a nation too young to have real legends. But there is often a residue of truth in such tales, and Kastner's dozen are among the genuine pioneers.

In his stories about them they appear as eccentric, undaunted. Alexander Wilson walked from New England to Charleston peddling subscriptions to his *American Ornithology*. Thomas Nuttall seems dottily heroic—oblivious to danger, a Parsifal under a lucky star, vanquishing every Klingsor in the woods, he discovered some of the rarest, most beautiful, and most useful of American plants. We find J.J. Audubon lying and drinking his way across Europe but selling his beautiful pictures of birds to lords and kings. Charles Willson Peale, the great promoter of natural history, was snubbed as an old man and excluded from the ceremonies honoring Lafayette on his triumphal return to Philadelphia in 1824. While Peale stood as a spectator on the steps of Independence Hall Lafayette saw his old companion, rushed over to embrace him, and stood by him through all the official homages. John Lawson, captured by Tuscarora Indians, met the following fate according to an eyewitness: "They stuck him full of fine small splinters or torchwoods like hog's bristles and so set them gradually afire." David Douglas fell into a pit trap for wild cattle and was stomped to death by a bull.

8. This passage is largely a
   (A) description of the modern bias against taxonomy
   (B) comparison of Wilson to Kastner
   (C) book review
   (D) history of taxonomy
   (E) species of eternity

9. Parsifal and Klingsor were probably a
  (A) German taxonomist and his nemesis
  (B) man and a plant
  (C) taxonomist and a fauna
  (D) flora and a fauna
  (E) knight and a monster

10. As Jefferson showed, a flaw that the careful taxonomist should avoid is
  (A) presumption   (B) intellectualization   (C) foolhardiness   (D) mindless activity
  (E) cataloguing

11. Taxonomy was considered to be an important science from about
  (A) 1800 to 1930   (B) 1700 to 1830   (C) 1818 to 1918   (D) 1700 to 1800
  (E) 1700 to 1950

12. The last story in Kastner's book probably describes incidents that occurred
  (A) in the nineteenth century
  (B) recently in the American West
  (C) in 1824 in Philadelphia
  (D) when homesteading was not enforced
  (E) when fossil creatures were alive

13. The scope of Kastner's book does NOT include
  (A) Meriweather Lewis
  (B) Linnaeus and Cuvier
  (C) Charles Peale
  (D) the Tuscarora Indians
  (E) J.J. Audubon

Passage 3

Just as the members of the Inter-American Tropical Tuna Commission have subscribed to annual quotas on the tuna harvest, they are agreed that cooperation is essential in limiting the porpoise kill. The common interest is preservation of the tuna industry. And since modern fishing methods exploit the cozy relationship between the yellowfin tuna and the porpoise, according to a report presented at recent commission meetings in San Diego, California, "the fishery for tuna would . . . become less profitable" as the number of porpoises decreased. Tuna and porpoise are often found together at sea, and the fishermen have learned to cast their nets where they see the porpoises, using them to locate the tuna. The problem is that many porpoises die in the nets.

The commission deliberations acknowledged the environmental pressures that have led to strict regulation of U.S. tuna crews under federal law. Delegates also recognized that porpoise protection goals are relatively meaningless unless conservation procedures are adopted and followed on an international basis. Commission supervision of survey, observer, and research programs won general agreement at the eight-nation conference. The method and timetable for implementing the program, however, remain uncertain.

Thus the federal regulation that leaves U.S. crews at a disadvantage in the tuna-harvest competition remains a threat to the survival of the tuna fleet. Still, the commission meetings have focused on the workable solution. All vessels should be equipped with the best porpoise-saving gear devised; crews should be trained and motivated to save the porpoise; a system must be instituted to assure that rules are enforced.

Above all, the response must be international. Porpoise conservation could well be another element in an envisioned treaty that remains unhappily elusive at the continuing Law-of-the-Sea Conference in New York City.

The tuna industry interest in saving porpoises is bothersome to many who also want to "save the porpoise," but object to the industry motivation for doing so. For fishermen, saving the porpoise is valuable only because the porpoise leads them to tuna. For more compassionate souls, however, the porpoise is not just a tuna finder, but, more important, the sea creature that seems most "human." Fredson Delacourte, national chairman of the "People for Animals" drive, says this: "It is especially sad that these sea creatures, in spite of their keen intelligence, cannot outwit the tuna fishermen who, anxious to meet their annual quota, ensnare and destroy porpoises as well. But it is even sadder that the tuna industry is so intent upon using the porpoise so greedily." Mr. Delacourte praises the fishing industry for its plans to save the porpoises, at the same time that he wishes their motives were more altruistic. He insists that any "law of the sea" should be essentially a moral law rather than an economic one.

14. The primary purpose of this passage is to
    (A) resolve a controversy
    (B) discuss the protection of porpoises
    (C) praise the Law-of-the-Sea Conference
    (D) implement a program for new fishing techniques
    (E) create international cooperation

15. Fredson Delacourte and the tuna industry do NOT share which of the following?
    (A) a wish that international fishing crews cooperate
    (B) information about the tuna/porpoise relationship
    (C) a common interest in the porpoise/tuna relationship
    (D) a common desire to protect porpoises
    (E) a common motive for the preservation of porpoises

16. The author presents the information in this passage
    (A) cynically   (B) angrily   (C) objectively   (D) humorously   (E) indifferently

17. The author implies that the government and industry representatives concerned with porpoise conservation may lack which of the following?
    (A) knowledge   (B) influence   (C) greed   (D) compassion   (E) purpose

18. Fredson Delacourte would probably object to which of the following?
    (A) a reduced tuna quota
    (B) the use of animal fur for coats
    (C) an international treaty that requires porpoise conservation
    (D) the enforcement of rules for porpoise conservation
    (E) the regulation of the tuna industry

19. Which of the following is NOT described explicitly in the passage?
    (A) Fredson Delacourte's sentiments
    (B) the federal regulations that U.S. fishermen must obey
    (C) the items that won general agreement at the conference
    (D) the relationship between porpoise and yellowfin
    (E) the elements of a solution to the porpoise conservation problem

20. Which of the following questions is NOT answered by the passage?
    (A) Has the tuna industry finalized a law of the sea?
    (B) Are fishing regulations moral as well as economic issues?
    (C) Has the general public expressed interest in a moral law of the sea?
    (D) Does the porpoise have a value to fishermen?
    (E) Which sea creature seems most human to many non-fishermen?

Passage 4

   If, during a counseling session, the psychotherapist learns that his patient intends to harm someone, does he have the duty to warn the potential victim? The question became more than academic when Stanton Smolde brutally murdered Leticia Menaska on September 21, 1968, and several people, including his psychologist, had known for over a month that he planned to kill
(5) her. The Montana Supreme Court held the psychologist had the duty to warn Menaska's family or the police of his patient's threats revealed during treatment.

   The court held, over strenuous objections raised by the defendants and by the American Psychiatric Association as amicus curiae, that the facts gave rise to a duty to warn. "When a therapist determines, or pursuant to the standard of his profession should determine that his
(10) patient presents a serious threat of violence to another, he incurs a duty of due care." The court transformed a privilege protecting patient disclosures into a duty requiring the psychotherapist to warn either the potential victim or anyone likely to apprise the victim of the threat if he foresees it being carried out.

   As a general rule there is no duty to warn of the acts of third persons and consequently no
(15) liability for the resultant harm. However, there are exceptions. For example, a duty to warn arises when a special relationship exists between the injured person and the person aware of the danger or between the person making the threat and the person aware of the threat. In finding a duty, the court in Montana found persuasive the decision in a New York case. The Veterans Administration, under its work therapy program, placed a mental patient with known dangerous
(20) propensities on a privately owned farm. While the farmer was away, the patient killed the farmer's wife. Because no one at the Veterans Administration informed the husband of the patient's background, it was held liable.

   In the Menaska case, Dr. Reimer knew that Smolde intended to kill Leticia but neither he nor the hospital warned Leticia or her family of the threats. However, did Dr. Reimer or the hospital have
(25) the right to reveal to someone else information that Smolde had divulged confidentially during a treatment session? To be effective, the psychotherapist must be able to assure the patient that everything the patient reveals will not be revealed to anyone else. This special need has been recognized by the Montana legislature in the Montana Evidence Code and in the Landis-Short Act. The interpersonal relationship between a patient and his psychotherapist justifiably gives
(30) rise to an expectation of confidentiality. Without it, free dialogue will not develop.

   Today, however, the psychotherapist has been dubbed a "double agent" because in many instances he acts not only as a doctor treating a patient, but also as an agent of the court. For example, he must report incidents of child abuse that are divulged and testify against his patient in civil or criminal commitment proceedings. The list is so exhaustive that confidentiality is
(35) virtually nonexistent in many instances. If the patient were aware of his therapist's "double agent" role, suspicion would surely destroy all chances of ever developing free dialogue. In fact, there may be a point at which the therapist becomes, in effect, a police informant after gaining his patient's confidence.

   The "dangerous patient" exception of the Montana Evidence Code also creates problems for
(40) the psychotherapist because it allows him to disclose his patient's threats to persons and property if he has "reasonable cause to believe that the patient is dangerous." The code does not define what is meant by "reasonable cause to believe." The psychotherapist may have to seek legal advice in order to decide whether to breach the confidential relationship. He must not only weigh the probability of his patient's carrying out the threat against the possibility of nullifying all
(45) the benefits of treatment, but must also consider the nature of the damage threatened. Clearly if the patient threatens to blow up an office building during business hours the therapist has a duty to warn. But what if he threatens to vandalize his neighbor's garage? Where does he draw the line? Is there a monetary figure at which the exception becomes operational?

   Further, from several extensive studies, it is clear that psychotherapists cannot predict their
(50) patient's future course of conduct. If this is true, how can they be expected to know when they should warn? Warning the intended target of the patient may prevent harm to that particular person; but the patient, seeing that the trust he placed in his therapist had been breached, will no doubt never seek help again. His problem will still exist—possibly resulting in more victims.

21. Of the following, the author of this passage is most concerned with the well-being of the
  (A) psychiatric patient
  (B) potential victim of the attack
  (C) law enforcement agencies
  (D) Supreme Court of Montana
  (E) police informants

22. From its use in line 8, we can infer that "amicus curiae" means
  (A) a witness for the prosecution
  (B) an interested party called upon for advice
  (C) a careful friend
  (D) the plaintiff
  (E) the defendant

23. The task of the psychotherapist dealing with a potentially dangerous patient who has threatened a third person is made more difficult for all of the following reasons EXCEPT
  (A) he cannot be sure if the patient will act on his threat
  (B) the patient may feel betrayed if reported by the doctor
  (C) the court does not define "reasonable" in "reasonable cause to believe the patient is dangerous"
  (D) reporting the patient may undo all the benefits of his psychotherapy
  (E) the damage threatened by the patient may be very serious

24. In which of the following situations would the courts be likely to find that a person has a duty to warn a second person about the potentially dangerous actions of a third person?
  (A) when there is a special relationship between the person making the threat and the person threatened
  (B) when there is a special relationship between the person knowing of the threat and the person threatened
  (C) when the dangerous third person is unknown to the person threatened
  (D) when there is a special relationship between the person making the threat and the person aware of the threat
  (E) when none of the three persons have any special relationship to each other

25. The Montana Evidence Code requirement of disclosure of threats to persons and property "where there is reasonable cause to believe the patient is dangerous" is problematic because it is difficult to determine all of the following EXCEPT
  (A) what "reasonable cause" means
  (B) what "dangerous" means
  (C) what threat to property is dangerous
  (D) at what monetary figure the requirement of threats to property becomes optional
  (E) whether or not the warning will come in time

26. According to the passage, the Montana Evidence Code
  (A) guarantees the confidentiality of all communications between a psychiatrist and his patient
  (B) fails to recognize the need for confidential communications between a psychiatrist and his patient
  (C) questions the expectation of a confidential relationship between a therapist and patient
  (D) excepts dangerous patients from the assurance of confidentiality
  (E) is endorsed by almost all psychotherapists and their national associations

27. The description of the psychotherapist as a "double agent" is especially appropriate because
  (A) he is working for two different employees
  (B) he has two different jobs
  (C) whereas one person thinks the therapist is assisting him, the therapist is really assisting another
  (D) the worlds of law and psychotherapy are both related to espionage
  (E) he is divided in his sympathy

28. We can infer that the author of the passage is likely to agree with all of the following assertions EXCEPT
(A)   the Menaska decision puts the rights of the potential victim above those of the patient
(B)   the Menaska decision puts the rights of the potential victim above those of the psychotherapist
(C)   the Menaska decision forces the psychotherapist to become a double agent
(D)   the duty to warn someone in danger is not absolute if the danger is uncertain
(E)   by warning a potential victim, the doctor has protected his patient rather than betrayed him

STOP

IF YOU FINISH BEFORE TIME IS UP, CHECK YOUR WORK ON THIS SECTION OF THE TEST ONLY. DO NOT GO ON TO THE NEXT SECTION OF THE TEST UNTIL TIME IS UP FOR THIS SECTION.

SECTION V
LOGICAL REASONING

Time—35 Minutes
25 Questions

Directions:
In this section you will be given brief statements or passages and will be required to evaluate the reasoning involved. In some instances, more than one choice will appear to be a possible answer. You are to choose the *best* answer. Use common sense and reasonableness in making your selection; then mark the proper space on the answer sheet.

Questions 1–2 refer to the following passage.

By passing more and more regulations allegedly to protect the environment, the state is driving the manufacturing industry away. And when the employers leave, the workers will follow. The number of new no-growth or environmental rules passed each year is increasing by leaps and bounds. Rich environmentalists who think they are sympathetic to workers have no real sympathy for the blue-collar employees who are injured by their activities. One major manufacturer has been fined for failing to establish a car-pool plan. Another is accused of polluting the air with industrial emissions, although everyone knows that two thirds of the pollutants come from cars and trucks. No wonder the large manufacturers are moving to states with fewer restrictive laws. And as the manufacturers go, unemployment and the number of workers leaving the state will rise more rapidly than ever before.

1. The author's argument that strict environmental laws will eventually lead to loss of workers in the state will be most weakened if it can be shown that
   (A) so far, the number of manufacturers who have left the state is small
   (B) the unemployment rate has climbed steadily in the last three years
   (C) most workers who leave the state give as their reason for leaving the poor environmental quality
   (D) several other manufacturing states have strict environmental laws
   (E) rich environmentalists are more powerful in many other states

2. Which of the following is NOT an argument of this passage?
   (A) Environmentalists are responsible for depriving workers of their jobs.
   (B) When workers leave a state, it is a sign that manufacturers will follow.
   (C) A car-pool law should not be enforced, as cars and trucks are responsible for most air pollution.
   (D) Large manufacturers prefer states with fewer restrictions.
   (E) A rise in unemployment will lead to an increase in workers leaving the state.

3. This supermarket has the highest prices in town. I had to pay $3.00 per pound for hamburger today.

   Which of the following statements best expresses the main premise that underlies the author's conclusion?
   (A) Hamburger should cost less than $3.00 per pound.
   (B) No other supermarket charges as much as $3.00 per pound for hamburger.
   (C) All hamburger is of the same quality.
   (D) Prices for other items at this store are equally high.
   (E) Other supermarkets may charge less for hamburger, but more for other items.

4. Unlike most graduates of American high schools, all graduates of high schools in Bermuda have completed four years of advanced mathematics.

Which of the following, if true, would best explain the situation described above?
(A) Math anxiety is higher in the United States than in Bermuda.
(B) There are far more high schools and high school students in the United States than in Bermuda.
(C) More students in America take full-time jobs without completing high school.
(D) Math programs in American high schools are frequently understaffed.
(E) High Schools in Bermuda require four years of advanced mathematics for graduation.

5. Psychological novels are superior to novels of adventure. Immature readers prefer novels of adventure to novels with less action and greater psychological depth. The immature reader, who prefers James Bond's exploits to the subtleties of Henry James, can be identified easily by his choice of inferior reading matter.

A criticism of the logic of this argument would be likely to find fault with the author's
(A) presupposing the conclusion he wishes to prove
(B) failure to define "adventure" clearly
(C) failure to cite possible exceptions to this rule
(D) hasty generalization on the basis of a limited specific case
(E) inaccurate definitions of key terms

6. All mathematicians are physicists.
Some chemists are mathematicians.
Some physicists are biologists.
No biologists are chemists.

If all of these statements are true, which of the following statements must also be true?
(A) Some chemists are biologists.
(B) Some chemists are physicists.
(C) No mathematicians are biologists.
(D) All biologists are physicists.
(E) All physicists are mathematicians or biologists.

7. In professional athletics, the small number of record-setting performers in each thirty-year span is remarkably consistent. In hockey, for example, 5 percent of all the professional players were responsible for more than half of the new records, and 95 percent of the new records were set by only 8 percent of the players. Similar percentages were found in baseball, football, and basketball records, where the numbers of participants are much higher.

If the statements above are true, which of the following conclusions may be most reasonably inferred?
(A) An increase in the number of athletic teams playing hockey, football, or baseball would significantly increase the number of record-setting performances.
(B) Reducing the number of athletic teams playing hockey, football, or baseball would not necessarily cause a decrease in the number of record-setting performances.
(C) Record-setting performances would increase if the number of amateur teams were increased.
(D) Many record-setting performances are not recorded by statisticians.
(E) As records become higher with the passage of time, fewer and fewer records will be broken.

8. By refusing to ban smoking in restaurants, the city council has put the financial well-being of restaurant owners above the health of the citizens of this city. No doubt the council would support the restauranteurs if they decided to use asbestos tablecloths and to barbecue using radioactivity. These devices would be no more risky.

The author of this paragraph makes her case by arguing
(A) from experience
(B) from example
(C) by authority
(D) from observation
(E) from analogy

9. The GOP's attempt to win the South has, however indirectly, played on the racial anxiety of white voters. It has produced a vocabulary of civility to conceal their opposition to school integration ("forced busing") and affirmative action ("quotas"). And, to the horror of regular Republicans, the party's candidate for senator in Louisiana is a neo-Nazi and Ku Klux Klan alumnus. The ease with which this candidate has merged his bigotry with a respectable conservative social agenda is frightening. There is, however, a ray of hope. The candidate is supported by about 30 percent of the voters.

The passage above is structured to lead to which one of the following conclusions?
(A) If the candidate disavows his views, he will lose his support; but if he does not disavow them, he cannot gain any new supporters.
(B) And that 30 percent has grown from only 15 percent three weeks ago.
(C) We cannot predict now whether that percentage will increase or decrease before the election.
(D) Two opponents also have about 30 percent of voters with another 10 percent undecided.
(E) There is still a possibility that Louisiana, with its unmatched history of corrupt, demagogic, and ineffectual state politics, will support his candidacy.

Questions 10–11 refer to the following passage.

The gill-net is used to catch halibut and sea bass, but up to 72 percent of what it ensnares is not marketable and is thrown back dead. Gill-nets are often called "walls of death" because they entangle and painfully kill mammals such as dolphins, whales, and sea otters. To use the gill-net at sea is like strip mining or clear-cutting on land.

Powerful lobbyists representing the commercial fishing industry have prevented the legislature from passing a ban on the use of gill-nets within the three-mile limit. They claim that the banning of gill-nets will raise the price of fish. They also charge that the law would benefit rich sport fishermen who want the ocean for their yachts.

10. In the first paragraph, the case against gill-nets is made by using
(A) statistical analysis
(B) ambiguity and indirection
(C) biased definitions
(D) simile and metaphor
(E) understatement

11. Which of the following, if true, would support the argument in favor of a ban on gill-nets within the three-mile limit?
(A) Less than one percent of the fish sold in this country is imported from abroad.
(B) Gill-net users catch all but two percent of their fish within the three-mile limit.
(C) The halibut population has fallen to a near extinction level.
(D) There is a serious overpopulation of the coastal sea otter.
(E) Coastal sea otters have nearly destroyed the abalone beds along the coast.

12. According to the Supreme Court, the First Amendment does not protect "obscene" speech. To the "obscene," the Court explained, speech must appeal to a "prurient" interest, describe conduct in a way "patently offensive to contemporary community standards," and lack serious literary, artistic, or scientific value.

All of the following arguments can be used to question the validity of the Court's definition of "obscene" EXCEPT

(A) there is no certain way of knowing just what an "appeal" to "prurient interest" is
(B) the phrase "patently offensive" is impossible to define precisely
(C) no two communities are likely to have the same standards of decency
(D) most juries are incapable of determining what is "serious" artistic or literary value
(E) there is no writing that is without some "scientific value"

13. There are no edible fish in the streams of this county because there are no pesticide controls.

Which of the following assumptions must be made before the conclustion above can be reached?
(A) Edible fish cannot be found in areas where there are no pesticide controls.
(B) If there are pesticide controls, there will be many edible fish.
(C) Without adequate pesticide controls, the fish population will rapidly decline.
(D) If there are pesticide controls, there will be some edible fish.
(E) With pesticide controls, the fish population will rapidly increase.

14. For eighteen years, a state has had three conservative congressmen, all representing the agricultural counties in the northern parts of the state. It also has three liberal congressmen from the large capital city in the south. One of the two senators is a liberal from the south, and the other is a conservative from the north.

Which of the following can be inferred from this passage?
(A) Voters in the southern parts of the state will always vote liberal.
(B) Voters in the northern part of the state are likely to vote liberal in the next election.
(C) Voters in the state are influenced more by a candidate's political leanings than by where the candidate lives.
(D) The population of the three northern counties is about equal to the population of the capital city.
(E) The governor of the state is probably a liberal.

15. African-Americans have periodically raised the issue of reparations for injury and damage to Africans in America from slavery. The granting of reparations to Japanese-Americans has renewed the hope that the government will meet its moral obligation to address the claim of African-Americans. Free black labor helped to develop America, but slavery only injured African-Americans. The "freed" slaves were released into a hostile, racist, capitalistic society without land, capital, or any meaningful form of compensation. The oppression continued through terror, lynching, segregation, discrimination, and disenfranchisement.

Which sentence is the most logical conclusion of this passage?
(A) Historically, leaders from Frederick Douglass to Malcolm X have kept the issue of reparations alive.
(B) After World War II, West Germany paid reparations to the Jewish victims of the Holocaust.
(C) There can be no final reconciliation between African-Americans and the U.S. government until the just claim of reparations is recognized.
(D) Reparations in the form of cash, land, or government securities could be placed in a national development fund and used for the collective benefit of African-Americans.
(E) A small compensation bill was passed by Congress after the Civil War, but vetoed by President Andrew Johnson.

16. Over the last three decades, the President's party has lost an average of 22 House of Representatives seats and two Senate seats in the midterm elections. This year, with a popular Republican President in the White House, GOP strategists had hoped to pick up seats in the House and the Senate. But the polls show these expectations are unrealistic. This should be an election with results much like those of the recent past.

According to information in this passage, the election should
(A) produce large Republican gains in the House and the Senate
(B) produce about 25 new House and Senate seats for the Democrats
(C) result in virtually no change in the balance of Republican and Democratic members of the House
(D) produce small Republican gains in the House and even smaller gains in the Senate.
(E) produce two new Republican seats in the Senate

17. Ten percent of the state lottery winners interviewed by researchers of the paranormal have reported that they had visions or other signs instructing them to select the winning numbers. On the basis of these results, the researchers claim to have proved the existence of paranormal gifts.

Which of the following pieces of additional information would be most relevant in assessing the logical validity of the researcher's claim?
(A) the total sum of money these men and women win on the lottery
(B) the percentage of lottery players who win money
(C) the percentage of contestants interviewed who were not lottery winners
(D) the percentage of lottery players who had visions or signs but did not win money
(E) the amount of money the lottery winners spend each year on lottery tickets

18. By spraying with pesticides like malathion, we can eradicate dangerous pests like the fruit-fly. But malathion spraying also destroys the ladybug, the best natural predator of aphids. Areas that have been sprayed with malathion are now free of the fruit-fly, but infested with aphids. This is the price we must pay to protect our citrus crop.

The argument above assumes all of the following EXCEPT
(A) pesticide spraying is the only way to eradicate the fruit-fly
(B) the aphid infestation is caused by the lack of ladybugs
(C) a pesticide that would kill fruit-flies and spare ladybugs cannot be made
(D) the use of pesticides has disadvantages
(E) the aphid infestation could be prevented by introducing a natural predator other than the ladybug

19. The Superintendent of Education complains that the share of the total state budget for education has decreased in each of the last four years; he blames the fall-off on the steady rise in the cost of law enforcement. Organizations opposing increased spending on education point out that the amount of money the state has spent on education has increased by at least three million dollars in each of the last four years.

Which of the following, if true, best resolves the apparent contradiction in the passage above?
(A) The total state budget has increased more rapidly than the expenditure for education.
(B) Both the pro- and con-educational-spending spokesmen have failed to take inflation into account.
(C) Law-enforcement costs have not risen as rapidly as the Superintendent claims.
(D) Some educational expenses are not included in the state budget, but are paid by local taxes.
(E) School construction is paid for by funds from bonds, not by funds from the state budget.

20. How can I write any of the essays when there are so many essays to be written?

In terms of its logical structure, the remark above most closely resembles which of the following?
(A) How can he buy a new car when he is already deeply in debt?
(B) How can she increase her collection of books when it is already so large?
(C) How can he iron any of his shirts when he has so many shirts that need ironing?
(D) How can she visit London and Paris when she has not yet visited New York and Washington?
(E) How can they raise horses when they already raise so many cows?

21. Great playwrights do not develop in countries where there is no freedom of opinion. Repressive countries are likely to produce great satiric writers.

If both of these statements are true, which of the following is the most logical continuation?
(A) Therefore, countries with no restrictions on expression will produce great satiric playwrights.
(B) Therefore, great satirists in repressive countries will use forms other than the play.
(C) Therefore, playwrights in repressive countries will not write satire.
(D) Therefore, great satiric writers will not develop in countries where there is freedom of speech.
(E) Therefore, no great satire is likely to be written in dramatic forms.

22. Contrary to the expectations of the Canadian government, a majority of the Mohawk population in Quebec is calling for native sovereignty. The Mohawk separatists cite a written agreement from colonial times in which Great Britain recognized the Mohawks' separateness from Canada. Unfortunately, the various Mohawk factions, each with its own agenda, have made it difficult to reach lasting agreements. What satisfies one group displeases another. The bleak outlook is for _____ .

Which of the following most logically concludes this paragraph?
(A) continued struggle within the tribe and between the tribe and the Canadian government
(B) some kind of compromise which recognizes the rights of both the Indians and the government of Canada
(C) some sort of agreement among the divided groups within the Mohawk tribe
(D) the establishment of a separate Mohawk state with its sovereignty recognized by the Canadian government
(E) a decline in Mohawk militarism and a series of fence-mending conferences

23. A new law will require labels giving consumers more nutritional information on all prepackaged foods manufactured in the United States. Food sold by restaurants or grocers with annual sales of less than $500,000 will be exempt. The required labels will reveal the number of servings, the serving size, the number of calories per serving, and the amount of fat, cholesterol, sodium, and dietary fiber.

The effectiveness of the new labels in improving overall U.S. nutrition could be seriously questioned if which of the following were shown to be true?

(A) More than 80 percent of the food sold in this country is not prepackaged.
(B) More than 80 percent of the prepackaged food sold in this country is marketed by the eight major food corporations.
(C) The amount of money Americans spend on prepackaged foods for microwaving has more than tripled every year for the last five years, and the trend is expected to continue.
(D) An increasingly large number of consumers now read the nutritional information on food packages.
(E) Small retailers who manufacture packaged foods sell to only a tiny percentage of American food buyers.

24.   A year ago the presidential science advisor announced prematurely that the United States would reveal its plan for combatting global warming at the World Climate Conference in Geneva, Switzerland. Five European countries have already announced plans to make reductions in carbon dioxide emissions, and five others have committed themselves to goals of stabilizing their emissions. But the United States is still unprepared to announce targets or a schedule for reducing carbon dioxide emissions.

Which of the following sentences would provide the most logical continuation of this paragraph?
(A)   The Geneva Conference will be the last international meeting before negotiations on a global-warming convention begin next year.
(B)   The United States accounts for about 22 percent of the carbon dioxide pumped into the atmosphere, while the Soviet Union accounts for 18 percent.
(C)   By adopting renewable energy strategies that would permit stabilization of carbon dioxide emissions, the United States could save millions of dollars.
(D)   The British Prime Minister and top environmental officials of many nations will attend the conference in Geneva.
(E)   Anticipating a debate in which the Europeans will criticize the United States for failing to act, the administration is downplaying the importance of the conference.

25. There is increasing reason to believe that Americans are talking themselves into a recession. Consumers are becoming more and more pessimistic, and the index of consumer confidence has plunged to its lowest level in years. What bothers analysts is fear that consumer pessimism about the economy will lead to spending cuts and become a self-fulfilling prophecy, speeding the onset of a recession.

    Widespread predictions in the media of a coming recession may be one reason for the pessimistic attitudes of consumers. They may be bracing for a recession by cutting back on spending plans for new cars, vacations, and restaurant meals—the very behavior pattern that analysts say will intensify the slump. Real estate values have been in decline for a year and a half, and the stock market has declined for four months in a row. When the economy is on the ropes, waning consumer confidence can deliver the knock-out punch.

The argument in the passage above would be weakened if it were shown that
(A)   in the 1955 recession, the widespread concern over the President's health precipitated an economic downturn
(B)   although consumer spending in the last fiscal quarter was the same as last year's, most of that strength stemmed from unusual government military spending
(C)   the steady rise in car sales has continued, despite the phasing out of discount prices and low-interest car loans
(D)   the predicted recession after the steep fall in stock prices two years ago did not lead to recession
(E)   some consumers are more eager than ever to maintain the living standards they have enjoyed for the last two years.

STOP

END OF MULTIPLE-CHOICE EXAMINATION. IF YOU FINISH BEFORE TIME IS UP, CHECK YOUR WORK ON THIS SECTION ONLY. DO NOT GO BACK TO ANY OTHER SECTION OF THE EXAMINATION.

EXAMINATION

WRITING SAMPLE

Time—30 Minutes

Directions:
You have 30 minutes to write an essay in response to a given topic. Take a few minutes to plan your work before you begin writing. DO NOT WRITE ON A TOPIC OF YOUR OWN CHOICE. ESSAYS THAT DO NOT ADDRESS THE GIVEN TOPIC ARE UNACCEPTABLE.

The quality of your writing is more important than the length of your response or the content. Pay attention to organization, appropriate diction, and correct usage. You will not be expected to display any specialized knowledge in your response, nor will you be expected to write a "perfect" essay; law schools understand that you are writing under a time constraint, and will allow for the minor lapses in writing ability that might occur under this circumstance.

Only the lined area in your booklet will be reproduced for the law schools, so do not write outside this space. *Do not* skip lines or use wide margins. These precautions, along with careful planning and legible handwriting that is not unduly large, will keep you within the allowed space.

SAMPLE TOPIC:

The State Legislature has appropriated funds to build a new maximum security prison somewhere in Metropolis County. The prison is to house one hundred prisoners convicted of serious crimes and also the two hundred prisoners awaiting trial or being tried in Metropolis City. These prisoners are now held at the overcrowded and antiquated Metropolis City Jail. Two locations have been proposed.

As an aide to the state senator who represents Metropolis County, you have been asked to write an argument to be presented to the Legislature in support of one of the sites. Two considerations guide your decision:

● The state funds for building and maintaining the prison and for transporting the prisoners to the courts are limited.

● The senator is eager to increase his popular support in anticipation of the upcoming election.

The Metropolis City site is located ten minutes from the court buildings near the downtown district. This area of the city is densely populated and has a high, slowly declining, crime rate. Residents of the district strongly oppose the building of the prison in their neighborhood, especially since a number of prisoners have recently escaped from the old Metropolis City Jail. Art preservation groups also oppose the proposed location since it would require the destruction of two buildings with unique architectural features. The estimated cost for the land and the construction of the prison on the Metropolis City site is eight million dollars.

The Deer Valley site is located in the sparsely populated Metropolis County, seventy-five miles from the court buildings. Deer Valley is a small town in a depressed rural area. Many of the residents of Deer Valley favor the construction of the prison, since they believe it will bring new jobs to the area. The roads between Deer Valley and Metropolis are narrow, and in a winter when the rains or snows are heavy, they may be impassable. The cost of utilities in Deer Valley is about twice the cost of utilities in Metropolis City. The estimated building cost in Deer Valley is seven million dollars.

ANSWER KEY

Section I: Reading Comprehension	Section II: Analytical Reasoning	Section III: Logical Reasoning	Section IV: Reading Comprehension	Section V: Logical Reasoning
1. C	1. D	1. D	1. D	1. C
2. B	2. B	2. D	2. B	2. B
3. D	3. E	3. C	3. D	3. D
4. E	4. C	4. A	4. D	4. E
5. A	5. E	5. C	5. E	5. A
6. A	6. B	6. C	6. D	6. B
7. D	7. C	7. D	7. D	7. B
8. D	8. C	8. B	8. E	8. E
9. A	9. C	9. C	9. E	9. A
10. B	10. B	10. C	10. A	10. C
11. E	11. E	11. D	11. B	11. C
12. D	12. E	12. D	12. A	12. E
13. C	13. D	13. D	13. B	13. A
14. B	14. E	14. D	14. B	14. D
15. C	15. C	15. A	15. E	15. C
16. C	16. E	16. D	16. E	16. B
17. B	17. D	17. E	17. D	17. C
18. A	18. E	18. A	18. B	18. E
19. D	19. B	19. B	19. B	19. A
20. C	20. D	20. B	20. C	20. C
21. E	21. B	21. B	21. A	21. B
22. B	22. E	22. D	22. B	22. A
23. E	23. E	23. A	23. E	23. A
24. C	24. D	24. E	24. D	24. E
25. B		25. B	25. E	25. C
26. D		26. B	26. D	
27. C			27. C	
			28. E	

MODEL TEST ANALYSIS

Doing model exams and understanding the explanations afterwards are of course important in acquainting you with typical LSAT question types and successful approaches to the questions. However, another benefit of carefully analyzing these model tests is to understand the kinds of errors you are making and thus work to minimize them. For instance, if a very high percentage of your incorrect answers is due to "careless error" or "misread problem," then perhaps you are working much too fast and should slow your pace accordingly. If your incorrect answers are due primarily to "lack of knowledge," then a careful rereading and reworking of the appropriate question-type chapter may be in order. Or if you find that you aren't completing a large number of questions because of lack of time, you may need to either increase your speed or learn to use the "one-check, two-check" technique more effectively.

This kind of analysis of the model tests will enable you to identify your particular weaknesses and thus remedy them.

Model Test Three Analysis

Section	Total Number of Questions	Number Correct	Number Incorrect	Number Unanswered*
I: Reading Comprehension	27			
II: Analytical Reasoning	24			
III: Logical Reasoning	26			
IV: Reading Comprehension	28			
V: Logical Reasoning	25			
TOTALS:	130			

*At this stage in your preparation, you should not be leaving any blank answer spaces. At least fill in a guess, as there is no penalty for a wrong answer.

Reasons for Incorrect Answers

You may wish to evaluate the explanations before completing this chart.

Section	Total Number Incorrect	Lack of Knowledge	Misread Problem	Careless Error	Unanswered or Wrong Guess
I: Reading Comprehension					
II: Analytical Reasoning					
III: Logical Reasoning					
IV: Reading Comprehension					
V: Logical Reasoning					
TOTALS:					

EXPLANATIONS OF ANSWERS

Section I

Passage 1

1. **C** The subject in all five paragraphs of the passages is federal preemption. Though the passage touches on the subjects mentioned in the other answers, the focus throughout is federal preemption.

2. **B** The constitutionality of federal preemption is an essential assumption of the passage. Most of the other answers are either doubtful or untrue.

3. **D** The first paragraph cites the potential conflict of state and federal laws as an initial reason for the Supremacy Clause of the Constitution.

4. **E** If laws can be enforced without conflict, there is no need for preemption. One purpose of preemption is to avoid conflicts.

5. **A** The third paragraph asserts that a federal agency's rules "have no less preemptive effect than federal statutes."

6. **E** The regulatory authority of the federal agency would be equal to that of a federal law and so would have preemptive power over any other ordinance unless the federal statute were unconstitutional.

7. **D** Where the laws are the same, there is no conflict and preemption is irrelevant.

Passage 2

8. **D** According to the first paragraph, a developing country hopes to attract foreign investment and increase its revenues from taxation ("maximize the public capture of revenues").

9. **A** Unless the investment flow is equal in each direction, the First World nation from which the greater revenue is likely to come is more likely to benefit.

10. **B** According to the second paragraph, reciprocal source-based taxation produces revenue sacrifices by the state receiving most of the foreign investment, that is, the developing country.

11. **E** The so-called UN Model is intended to make the revenue gains between the two treaty partners more equal.

12. **D** Excess foreign tax credits are a disincentive to private investors. If the at -source taxation is reduced, there will be fewer excess foreign credits.

13. **C** The passage makes no reference to the availability of raw materials. The four other options are cited.

14. **B** A country that reduced its revenue expectations would be expected to increase foreign investment.

15. **C** These are policies subsidizing, and so encouraging, private investments.

Passage 3

16. **C** The first sentence suggests that guidelines for ending medical interventions are unresolved and the rest of the passage discusses the difficulties and uncertainties this issue raises.

17. **B** There is nothing in the passage to suggest that the author would disagree with (A), (C), (D), and (E). Both the second and third paragraphs suggest the writer is concerned when such a decision may result in suicide, euthanasia, or murder.

18. **A** The first sentence of the second paragraph points out that the patient in the Bartling case had illnesses "that were probably incurable, but not terminal."

19. **D** The case is important because it extended the right to terminate life-support systems to a patient who was not terminally ill.

20. **C** Both cases involved patients whose death was certain: in *Dority,* a patient already brain dead, and in *Eichner,* a terminally ill patient.

21. **E** The Bartling decision permitted a patient whose illness was not terminal to be removed from life-support equipment.

22. **B** The next to last sentence of the passage makes clear the author's quarrel with the Barber court decision: another court might easily decide differently and a charge of murder might result.

Passage 4

23. **E** Paragraph 2 says, ". . . suppose science is defined as classified knowledge."

24. **C** Paragraph 2 specifically excludes astrology as a science (last sentence).

25. **B** Paragraph 6 compares pure science to applied science, stating, "The discovery of one bit of information opens the door to the discovery of another."

26. **D** This example of pure science is mentioned in paragraph 6.

27. **C** Clearly, the passage is a general discussion of the characteristics of science and scientists. The other choices are science-related but deal with other, more specific aspects of science.

Section II

Answers 1–7

A diagram will help you to organize the information.

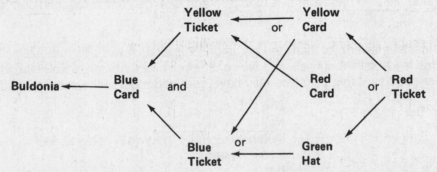

1. **D** From the diagram, a red card will get you a yellow ticket (which you already have), but you need a blue ticket with the yellow ticket to get a blue card to get into Buldonia. You have no way of getting a blue ticket.

2. **B**   Statement (B) is true since you could trade the two red cards for two yellow cards. With one yellow card you can get a yellow ticket, and with the other yellow card you can get a blue ticket. With a blue and yellow ticket, you can get a blue card, which gets you into Buldonia.

3. **E**   Since a yellow card will get you either a blue ticket or a yellow ticket, and each of (A)–(D) will get you either a blue ticket or a yellow ticket, the combination will get you into Buldonia.

4. **C**   A yellow hat gets you a green hat which gets you a blue ticket. Thus, you need a yellow ticket. Only (C) does not give you a yellow ticket.

5. **E**   Only (E) will get you two blue tickets and a yellow ticket. The other four choices do not give you two blue tickets.

6. **B**   Two green hats get you two blue tickets. We need two yellow tickets. Thus, (B) will get you into Buldonia.

7. **C**   A green ticket and a red card will each get you a yellow ticket. You have no way of getting a blue ticket.

Answers 8–14

From the information given, you could have made the following relationships:

$$J > L + M + N$$
$$N = L + M$$
$$M > K + G$$
$$G > H$$
$$K = G$$

8. **C**   From the diagram above, since Jon has more bills than Lynn, Melanie, and Neil combined and since Melanie has more bills than Ken and George combined, then Jon has the most bills.

9. **E**   Since Hal has fewer bills than George, and George has fewer bills than Melanie, and Melanie has fewer bills than Neil, and Neil has fewer bills than Jon, then Hal has the fewest number of bills. At this point you may have deduced most of the order of students:

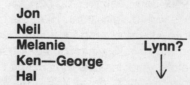

If you realized these relationships immediately from the initial conditions, you should have made this part of your first diagram.

10. **B** From the chart for the previous problem we see that only choice (B) must be true.

11. **E** Using this new information with the order chart, we have the following chart:

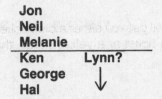

Jon
Neil
Melanie
Ken   Lynn?
George
Hal

You may have approached this problem by eliminating the incorrect choices.

12. **E** Since Neil has the same number of bills as Lynn and Melanie combined, and Jon has more bills than Lynn, Melanie, and Neil combined, therefore Jon has more bills than twice the number of Lynn's and Melanie's bills. Choice (E) is false.

13. **D** If Lynn and Melanie have the same number of bills, then Lynn has more bills than Ken and George combined. Since George has more bills than Hal and since Neil has the same number of bills as Lynn and Melanie combined, then Neil has more bills than Lynn, George, and Hal combined.

14. **E** If Tom has more bills than Ken and fewer than Lynn, the order of students would now be as follows:

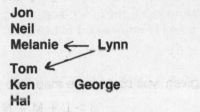

Jon
Neil
Melanie ← Lynn
Tom ←
Ken   George
Hal

Therefore, Lynn having more bills than Hal is the only one that must be true.

Answers 15–18

15. **C** If Axel were a YES, he would tell the truth and would say he was a YES. Since he said he was a MAYBE, he cannot be a YES.

16. **E** If Axel were a MAYBE, he would tell the truth and lie alternately. Since he said he was a MAYBE, his first response would be truthful. Thus, his third response must also be the truth. Thus, Carmen is a NO. His second response then has to be a lie. This means that Benty must be something other than a YES, which could not be possible since they all must belong to different clubs. Therefore, Axel is not a MAYBE. Since Axel is not a YES or a MAYBE, he must be a NO. Therefore, Benty is not a YES. This leaves the MAYBE as the only other alternative for Benty. Thus, Carmen is the YES. So Benty, being a MAYBE, could give a true or false answer to his question. Thus, any of the alternatives are possible.

17. **D** This follows from the above explanation.

18. **E** This follows from the above explanation.

	YES	NO	MAYBE
A		x	
B			x
C	x		

Answers 19–24

19. **B** From diagram 1 below we see that (B) is correct.

20. **D** From diagram 2, we see that only (D) is false. Truckner sat two places to the *right* (not left) of Eileen.

21. **B** From diagram 2 and fact 7, we see that Beatrice must be Truckner's first name, giving diagram 3.

22. **E** From diagram 3 and fact 6, the only place for Frances is between Beatrice and Dexter. Thus Upland's first name is Frances and Eileen's last name is Zipley.

23. **E** From figure 5, we see there is only one seat left for Clyde.

24. **D** Using either fact 2 or fact 3, we can complete the seating arrangement, as shown in diagram 6.

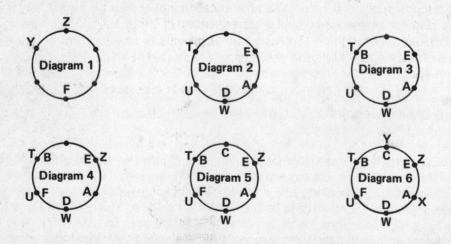

Section III

1. **D** If 97 percent of fatalities occurred *below 45 mph,* then a reduction in the maximum speed from 65 to 55 mph would have little impact, no more than a 3 percent reduction (if we assume that all other fatalities occurred between 55 and 65 mph). (A) and (C) are not relevant, (B) provides no conclusive data, and (E) *strengthens* the argument.

2. **D** The information states:
   1. If busing passes, then Smith was not reelected.
   2. Smith was reelected.
   Therefore, busing failed.
   3. If Smith is reelected she will vote for busing.
   4. Smith was reelected.
   Therefore, Smith voted for busing.

   (A) and (B) are wrong, because busing failed. (C) is wrong because Smith voted for busing. (E) is wrong because there are insufficient data to support it.

3. **C** Webster is stating that not only do lies disagree with truth, but they usually also disagree with other lies. Thus, it would follow that liars often quarrel with other liars.

4. **A** The given argument can be reduced to:
   is <u>not</u>   S (star)   because   H (hit)
     <u>is</u>   H   because   S

   (A) exhibits the structure closest to that of the given argument:
   is <u>not</u>   F (final word)   because   C (correct)
     <u>is</u>   C (correct)   because   F ("Instructor" is the final word.)

5. **E** *Setting aside the condition given* in the question, there are four possible states that could exist:

	Doxin	*Entrox*
1.	Present	Present
2.	Present	Absent
3.	Absent	Present
4.	Absent	Absent

   The condition contained in the question rules out state 2 only. (A) (state 3), (B) (state 1), and (C) (state 4) are true. (E) (state 2) is false.

6. **C** The discussion points out that (A) is an implication (rather than an assumption) of the studies. (B) is also not an assumption but is a restatement of the discussion's central issue. In order to consider speaker characteristics as either relevant or irrelevant, the author must assume that such a distinction exists; that assumption is expressed by (C). The passage does not assume a trim speaker will be "more persuasive" (D) or that irrelevant aspects are more influential than content (E), though it does suggest that these are issues worth examining.

7. **D** The final sentence of the passage offers an alternative explanation of the phenomenon introduced in the first sentence.

8. **B** The author, by offering an alternative explanation, stresses the scientists' unwillingness to consider such alternatives. (A), a choice worth considering, should be eliminated because the alternative suggested by the author is no more verifiable than the assertion he criticizes.

9. **C** The author argues that the term "progressive" is avoided by educators because of abuses in the progressive education movement, and that therefore, recently new, educational prac-

tices have avoided being tagged with the name "progressive." If choice (C) were true—that "progressive learning" has recently met with approval in middle class public schools—it would contradict the author's statement about the connotation of the word "progressive" and seriously weaken his argument.

10. **C** The misunderstanding arises from Dave's assumption that Bill has said *every* morning, not *almost* every morning. (D), although worth considering, is not best because it does not address the scope of Bill's remark.

11. **D** Because the first two statements are not absolute, we may conclude sunbathing is unlikely but still possible. There is no information in the passage to support (A), (B), (C), or (E).

12. **D** (A) and (B) are, by commonsense standards, implausible. (C) might be a valid statement, but it is not implied by Wilkie's assertion, which makes no distinction between first- and second-class citizens, and so implies (D).

13. **D** Although several of the choices mention or imply the virtue of productivity, only (D) links a decline in productivity with a reliance on excuses.

14. **D** If *nothing* produces only nothing, then the production of something *must* require something. (A) makes the production of something from something a possibility; however, the original statement implies that the something/something relationship is imperative.

15. **A** Only (A) makes an unqualified negative assessment; each of the other choices is either a neutral statement or one that attempts to balance positive and negative terms.

16. **D** The term *average* in the passage implies that if some workers earned more than $7.87 per day, others must have earned less. In choice (C) the words *far more than* make that choice not necessarily true.

17. **E** The magazine is sure that Jones will be a contender soon, and all that is offered to support this is the fact that Jinkins will train him. Therefore, (A) and (B) are the assumptions motivating the passage. (E) is not an assumption, but rather a statement made explicitly in the article.

18. **A** Note the relationship between the words in the pairs used in the concluding portion of the paragraph—they are sets of opposites, positive versus negative terms. The only choice that offers a positive/negative pairing of opposites is (A).

19. **B** The structure of question 19 may be simplified as follows:
C (crowded) <u>whenever</u> H (holiday)
<u>Not C</u>; therefore, <u>not H</u>

(B) is most nearly parallel to the relationships presented in the question:
R (reptiles) <u>whenever</u> D (hot desert day)
<u>Not R</u> (absent); therefore, not D.

20. **B** (A) is not a strong choice; the author indicates only that Nerd is *very* wealthy. The author does not compare Nerd's wealth to that of the other candidates. (C) contradicts the third sentence of the author's statement. Since the author tells us that Nerd has the necessary wealth and should acquire skill as a speaker, the author must believe that the third attribute (experience) is not an issue. In other words, the author believes that Nerd has satisfactory experience. The passage does not assert that an improvement in Nerd's public speaking will guarantee a win (D). Since Nerd has wealth and experience but inadequate speaking skills, he is a dark horse (E).

21. **B** (A) would not weaken the argument, since being wealthy, but not necessarily wealthiest, is all that is called for. (D) and (E) are consistent with the expressed or implied information in the argument. Although (C) is a possible answer choice, (B) is superior; it directly contradicts the author's assertions.

22. **D** The given statement tells us only that the car is blue. For us to be *assured* that it is slow we must know either that every blue car is slow *or* that no blue car accelerates quickly. (D) restricts quick acceleration to red cars.

23. **A** The argument obviously avoids absolute terms, relying instead on words such as "almost" and "sometimes." Therefore, it would seem consistent that a basic assumption would also avoid absolute terms; only (A) does so. In addition, (A) makes explicit the assumption underlying the first sentence of the passage.

24. **E** The second sentence diminishes the government's "fault," and the final sentence continues this idea; the only restatement that takes into account extragovernmental responsibility for intrusion is (E).

25. **B** The key phrase in the author's remarks is "*falsely* equating knowledge [viewing] with action [crime]." (A) is poor because it links knowledge with action. (C) is poor because the author indicates that those who dictate what we see (in other words, the censors) are guilty of drawing false (illogical) relationships. (D) and (E) are not relevant to the author's argument. (B) is consistent with the author's position that knowledge and action do not necessarily go hand in hand.

26. **B** A ruling on resources must at least presume the possibility that such resources exist; otherwise it is absurd. All other choices are irrelevant to the ruling.

Section IV

Passage 1

1. **D** A conversational tone is mentioned as part of the "natural style" that developed coincidentally with Roosevelt's administration in the 1930s (paragraph 5). Roosevelt's own radio "conversations" would seem to be examples of this natural style. (C) is an irrelevant point; (E) seems unrelated to the limitations of radio; (A) is not supported by a characterization of American politics as propaganda; (B) refers to theatricality, a characteristic largely unrelated to Roosevelt's chats.

2. **B** This is an explicit and repeated point.

3. **D** The author's skepticism is expressed when he says that the Russian films "made the new regime *appear* to be the heir of a glorious revolutionary tradition"; he calls into question the facts by labeling them as merely *apparent*.

4. **D** The author's persistent point, that the style of popular entertainment affects the style of politics, indicates this choice. He associates excessive gestures with early cinema and expressionist theater (paragraph 4); only (D) accounts for at least one of these media. (C) refers to the style of movie *heroes*, a style not necessarily associated with exaggerated gestures.

5. **E** All other choices are either inaccurate or too specific. The author's repeated comparison of politics and government to popular entertainment (mainly movies) indicates (E).

6. **D** We are told toward the end of the passage that during the 1930s and 1940s the isolated, idolized, one-of-a-kind stars became "more human" and could be imitated. The eventual result of their influence was "the political Mr. Everyman."

7. **D** The author must assume that art imitates life in order to argue that politics imitates phases in film history.

Passage 2

8. **C** Paragraph 3 begins commenting upon *A Species of Eternity*, and this commentary/review continues to the end of the passage.

9. **E** In paragraph 5, the author refers to Nuttall as "oblivious to danger." Implied then is a comparison between his bravery and that of a knight (Parsifal), who faces and vanquishes the danger of a monster (Klingsor).

10. **A** Paragraph 2 states that Jefferson mistakenly *presumed* "a giant sloth claw as a lion."

11. **B** Paragraph 2 says, "During the eighteenth and early nineteenth centuries, taxonomy was in the forefront of the sciences."

12. **A** Kastner's book is "chronologically arranged" (paragraph 4), so that the last story is probably not located in the early years of taxonomy—the eighteenth century. "The nineteenth century" is a probable answer. (B) and (C) are too specific, not directly supported by the passage.

13. **B** Kastner's book discusses the "American frontier," so foreign taxonomists are not within his scope.

Passage 3

14. **B** The passage is essentially neutral; the author does not take sides or suggest his own program or solution. "Discuss," the most neutral term of the five choices, signals (B) as the appropriate answer.

15. **E** Delacourte's motive is *moral*, and the industry's motive is *economic*; this difference is stressed in the final sentence of the passage.

16. **C** The author is *reporting* information without attempting to slant it subjectively. His impersonal tone should lead you to eliminate (A), (B), and (D), all of them suggesting personal involvement. However, the author is not indifferent (E) to the issue he describes; otherwise, he would not choose to discuss it so extensively.

17. **D** Without explicitly criticizing the tuna industry, the author does contrast fishermen with "compassionate souls" such as Delacourte (final paragraph).

18. **B** The chairman of a "People for Animals" drive would be certain to object to clothing produced through the destruction of animals. Delacourte would probably be in favor of the other choices.

19. **B** Although we are told that U.S. fishermen must conform to federal regulations, those regulations are not mentioned explicitly; we may *infer* that the regulations entail porpoise conservation.

20. **C** The passage gives answers to questions (A), (B), (D), and (E). The opinion of the general public is neither expressed nor implied in the passage.

Passage 4

21. **A** The author's sympathies are clearly with the psychotherapist and his patient. The harm the law may do to the patient's treatment is one of the author's central concerns.

22. **B** Literally, "a friend of the court," an amicus curiae is a person, often not a lawyer, called in to advise the court on a matter of concern to both.

23. **E** Each of the first four reasons are problems the doctor must face. If the damage the patient threatens is serious, the decision to inform is easier to make.

24. **D** The passage explicitly states the situations in the example in the third paragraph; they are exceptions to the general rule of there being no duty to warn of the acts of third persons.

25. **E** (A), (B), (C), and (D) are all problems the requirement raises, which the psychotherapist would have to decide. (E) is not an inherent difficulty in the language of the disclosure requirement.

26. **D** Though the code is enlightened in many ways, it makes an exception of the "dangerous patient" so "all communications cannot be confidential."

27. **C** The psychiatrist is not, as (A) claims, working for the state. His having to report what his patient regards as confidential does put the doctor in the position of the counterspy or double agent.

28. **E** The passage suggests the author's agreement with each of the first four statements. About the last, there is far less assurance. Such a case might exist, but the argument of this passage is on the other side.

Section V

1. **C** The passage argues that environmental restrictions will lead to losses of jobs and hence workers, but if workers are already leaving because the environmental quality is poor, the argument is seriously weakened.

2. **B** The passage makes no comment on workers leaving before a manufacturer. It argues that the loss of manufacturers leads to a loss of workers (E).

3. **D** The conclusion is a comment on the prices, not just on the price of hamburger. The speaker has inferred from the high price of hamburger that the prices of other items are also very high.

4. **E** Though choices (A), (B), (C), and (D) might contribute to increased study of math in Bermuda, (E) leaves no doubt. High schools in Bermuda require four years of advanced math for graduation; high schools in the United States do not.

5. **A** Though all of the choices are plausible here, (A) is the best choice. The first sentence asserts the conclusion ("superior"), and the second asserts a consequence ("immature . . . prefer"). The last repeats what has already been insisted upon.

6. **B** If all mathematicians are physicists and some chemists are mathematicians, those chemists are also physicists. Therefore, some chemists are physicists.

7. **B** The passage suggests that records are set only by rare, superior performers, and an increase or decrease in the number of participants would not significantly change the number of record-setting performances.

8. **E** The passage makes its point by analogy, comparing the dangers of smoking to the dangers of asbestos and radioactivity.

9. **A** The passage is clearly hostile to the racist candidate, and has found a "ray of hope." The conclusion should logically predict his defeat. Choice (A) also draws a conclusion related to the part of the paragraph that refers to "regular Republicans."

10. **D** The argument uses both simile ("like strip mining or clear-cutting") and metaphor ("walls of death").

11. **C** If the halibut population is endangered, the banning of gill-nets would improve the fish's chance for survival. If (A) and (B) are true, the fisheries' argument about the price rise has more merit. If (D) and (E) are true, the reduction of the sea otter population would be more defensible.

12. **E** Choices (A), (B), (C), and (D) are reasonable objections, but the argument that *no* writing is without some scientific value is an overstatement.

13. **A** The assumption is that where there are no pesticide controls, no edible fish can be found, not the reverse as in (B), (D), and (E).

14. **D** The results of the elections and the fact that there are three congressmen from the north and three from the south suggest that the populations are nearly equal. Choice (A) would be a likely choice if "always" were changed to "usually." Choice (B) is unlikely, and the passage gives us no reason either to believe in or to disbelieve (C) and (E).

15. **C** The passage makes it clear that the author regards the reparations claim as "just," for example, by the reference to the government's "moral obligation." This conclusion keeps the focus on the African-Americans, whose suffering is recounted in the two preceding sentences.

16. **B** If the results are like those of the "recent past," the total should approximate "an average of 22 House" and "2 Senate seats."

17. **D** The conclusion could be more reasonably assessed if we knew how often the paranormal signs had been false. The issue is not how many contestants win money or how much money they win. The issue is the paranormal aid.

18. **E** The words "this is the price we must pay" (that is, we must suffer aphid infestation because the rutabagas have been destroyed) indicated that the author makes all of the assumptions of (A), (B), (C), and (D). The idea of (E) may be true, but it is not an assumption of the passage.

19. **A** The apparent contradiction disappears if the total state budget has increased enough so that the *expenditure* on education has been raised by three million each year while at the same time the *percentage* spent on education is a smaller part of the whole budget.

20. **C** In each case, the verb ("iron" . . . "need ironing"; "write" . . . "to be written") is repeated, while the adjective ("many") modifies the repeated noun.

21. **B** The first statement asserts that great playwrights will not develop in repressive countries. Therefore, the great satirists which repressive countries will produce (the second statement) will not write plays.

22. **A** The details of the paragraph and the phrase "bleak outlook" suggest that a settlement is not likely.

23. **A** If the new labels will appear on less than 20 percent of the food sold, they will not be very effective.

24. **E** As the United States is still unwilling to act, its downplaying the conference is a predictable response. Though several of the other choices are plausible, none follows so clearly from what the paragraph has already said.

25. **C** If there has been a steady rise in car sales, consumers cannot be "cutting back on spending plans for new cars," as the predictions assert.

Chapter

9

Model Test Four

This chapter contains full-length Model Test Four. It is geared to the format of the LSAT, and it is complete with answers and explanations. It is equivalent to the LSAT in question structure, number of questions, level of difficulty, and time allotments. (The questions used are not taken directly from the LSAT, as those questions are copyrighted and may not be reproduced.)

Model Test Four should be taken under strict test conditions. The test ends with a 30-minute Writing Sample, which is not scored.

Section	Description	Number of Questions	Time Allowed
I	Analytical Reasoning	24	35 minutes
II	Logical Reasoning	26	35 minutes
III	Logical Reasoning	25	35 minutes
IV	Reading Comprehension	28	35 minutes
V	Analytical Reasoning	24	35 minutes
	Writing Sample		30 minutes
TOTALS:		127	3 hours 25 minutes

Now please turn to the next page, remove your answer sheets, and begin Model Test Four.

ANSWER SHEET—MODEL TEST FOUR
LAW SCHOOL ADMISSION TEST (LSAT)

Section I:
Analytical Reasoning

1. (A) (B) (C) (D) (E)
2. (A) (B) (C) (D) (E)
3. (A) (B) (C) (D) (E)
4. (A) (B) (C) (D) (E)
5. (A) (B) (C) (D) (E)
6. (A) (B) (C) (D) (E)
7. (A) (B) (C) (D) (E)
8. (A) (B) (C) (D) (E)
9. (A) (B) (C) (D) (E)
10. (A) (B) (C) (D) (E)
11. (A) (B) (C) (D) (E)
12. (A) (B) (C) (D) (E)
13. (A) (B) (C) (D) (E)
14. (A) (B) (C) (D) (E)
15. (A) (B) (C) (D) (E)
16. (A) (B) (C) (D) (E)
17. (A) (B) (C) (D) (E)
18. (A) (B) (C) (D) (E)
19. (A) (B) (C) (D) (E)
20. (A) (B) (C) (D) (E)
21. (A) (B) (C) (D) (E)
22. (A) (B) (C) (D) (E)
23. (A) (B) (C) (D) (E)
24. (A) (B) (C) (D) (E)

Section II:
Logical Reasoning

1. (A) (B) (C) (D) (E)
2. (A) (B) (C) (D) (E)
3. (A) (B) (C) (D) (E)
4. (A) (B) (C) (D) (E)
5. (A) (B) (C) (D) (E)
6. (A) (B) (C) (D) (E)
7. (A) (B) (C) (D) (E)
8. (A) (B) (C) (D) (E)
9. (A) (B) (C) (D) (E)
10. (A) (B) (C) (D) (E)
11. (A) (B) (C) (D) (E)
12. (A) (B) (C) (D) (E)
13. (A) (B) (C) (D) (E)
14. (A) (B) (C) (D) (E)
15. (A) (B) (C) (D) (E)
16. (A) (B) (C) (D) (E)
17. (A) (B) (C) (D) (E)
18. (A) (B) (C) (D) (E)
19. (A) (B) (C) (D) (E)
20. (A) (B) (C) (D) (E)
21. (A) (B) (C) (D) (E)
22. (A) (B) (C) (D) (E)
23. (A) (B) (C) (D) (E)
24. (A) (B) (C) (D) (E)
25. (A) (B) (C) (D) (E)
26. (A) (B) (C) (D) (E)

Section III:
Logical Reasoning

1. (A) (B) (C) (D) (E)
2. (A) (B) (C) (D) (E)
3. (A) (B) (C) (D) (E)
4. (A) (B) (C) (D) (E)
5. (A) (B) (C) (D) (E)
6. (A) (B) (C) (D) (E)
7. (A) (B) (C) (D) (E)
8. (A) (B) (C) (D) (E)
9. (A) (B) (C) (D) (E)
10. (A) (B) (C) (D) (E)
11. (A) (B) (C) (D) (E)
12. (A) (B) (C) (D) (E)
13. (A) (B) (C) (D) (E)
14. (A) (B) (C) (D) (E)
15. (A) (B) (C) (D) (E)
16. (A) (B) (C) (D) (E)
17. (A) (B) (C) (D) (E)
18. (A) (B) (C) (D) (E)
19. (A) (B) (C) (D) (E)
20. (A) (B) (C) (D) (E)
21. (A) (B) (C) (D) (E)
22. (A) (B) (C) (D) (E)
23. (A) (B) (C) (D) (E)
24. (A) (B) (C) (D) (E)
25. (A) (B) (C) (D) (E)

ANSWER SHEET—MODEL TEST FOUR
LAW SCHOOL ADMISSION TEST (LSAT)

Section IV:
Reading Comprehension

1. Ⓐ Ⓑ Ⓒ Ⓓ Ⓔ
2. Ⓐ Ⓑ Ⓒ Ⓓ Ⓔ
3. Ⓐ Ⓑ Ⓒ Ⓓ Ⓔ
4. Ⓐ Ⓑ Ⓒ Ⓓ Ⓔ
5. Ⓐ Ⓑ Ⓒ Ⓓ Ⓔ
6. Ⓐ Ⓑ Ⓒ Ⓓ Ⓔ
7. Ⓐ Ⓑ Ⓒ Ⓓ Ⓔ
8. Ⓐ Ⓑ Ⓒ Ⓓ Ⓔ
9. Ⓐ Ⓑ Ⓒ Ⓓ Ⓔ
10. Ⓐ Ⓑ Ⓒ Ⓓ Ⓔ
11. Ⓐ Ⓑ Ⓒ Ⓓ Ⓔ
12. Ⓐ Ⓑ Ⓒ Ⓓ Ⓔ
13. Ⓐ Ⓑ Ⓒ Ⓓ Ⓔ
14. Ⓐ Ⓑ Ⓒ Ⓓ Ⓔ
15. Ⓐ Ⓑ Ⓒ Ⓓ Ⓔ
16. Ⓐ Ⓑ Ⓒ Ⓓ Ⓔ
17. Ⓐ Ⓑ Ⓒ Ⓓ Ⓔ
18. Ⓐ Ⓑ Ⓒ Ⓓ Ⓔ
19. Ⓐ Ⓑ Ⓒ Ⓓ Ⓔ
20. Ⓐ Ⓑ Ⓒ Ⓓ Ⓔ
21. Ⓐ Ⓑ Ⓒ Ⓓ Ⓔ
22. Ⓐ Ⓑ Ⓒ Ⓓ Ⓔ
23. Ⓐ Ⓑ Ⓒ Ⓓ Ⓔ
24. Ⓐ Ⓑ Ⓒ Ⓓ Ⓔ
25. Ⓐ Ⓑ Ⓒ Ⓓ Ⓔ
26. Ⓐ Ⓑ Ⓒ Ⓓ Ⓔ
27. Ⓐ Ⓑ Ⓒ Ⓓ Ⓔ
28. Ⓐ Ⓑ Ⓒ Ⓓ Ⓔ

Section V:
Analytical Reasoning

1. Ⓐ Ⓑ Ⓒ Ⓓ Ⓔ
2. Ⓐ Ⓑ Ⓒ Ⓓ Ⓔ
3. Ⓐ Ⓑ Ⓒ Ⓓ Ⓔ
4. Ⓐ Ⓑ Ⓒ Ⓓ Ⓔ
5. Ⓐ Ⓑ Ⓒ Ⓓ Ⓔ
6. Ⓐ Ⓑ Ⓒ Ⓓ Ⓔ
7. Ⓐ Ⓑ Ⓒ Ⓓ Ⓔ
8. Ⓐ Ⓑ Ⓒ Ⓓ Ⓔ
9. Ⓐ Ⓑ Ⓒ Ⓓ Ⓔ
10. Ⓐ Ⓑ Ⓒ Ⓓ Ⓔ
11. Ⓐ Ⓑ Ⓒ Ⓓ Ⓔ
12. Ⓐ Ⓑ Ⓒ Ⓓ Ⓔ
13. Ⓐ Ⓑ Ⓒ Ⓓ Ⓔ
14. Ⓐ Ⓑ Ⓒ Ⓓ Ⓔ
15. Ⓐ Ⓑ Ⓒ Ⓓ Ⓔ
16. Ⓐ Ⓑ Ⓒ Ⓓ Ⓔ
17. Ⓐ Ⓑ Ⓒ Ⓓ Ⓔ
18. Ⓐ Ⓑ Ⓒ Ⓓ Ⓔ
19. Ⓐ Ⓑ Ⓒ Ⓓ Ⓔ
20. Ⓐ Ⓑ Ⓒ Ⓓ Ⓔ
21. Ⓐ Ⓑ Ⓒ Ⓓ Ⓔ
22. Ⓐ Ⓑ Ⓒ Ⓓ Ⓔ
23. Ⓐ Ⓑ Ⓒ Ⓓ Ⓔ
24. Ⓐ Ⓑ Ⓒ Ⓓ Ⓔ

SECTION I
ANALYTICAL REASONING

Time—35 Minutes
24 Questions

Directions:
In this section you will be given groups of questions based on different sets of conditions. Drawing a simple diagram may be helpful in answering some of the questions. You are to choose the best answer and mark the corresponding space on your answer sheet.

Questions 1–6

A committee is being selected from a pool of ten people. The men in the pool are A, B, G, and H. The women are C, D, E, F, I, and J. The Democrats are D, E, F, G, and H. The Republicans are A, B, C, I, and J.

The committee being formed must have six members. Not more than four members may come from the same political party.
At least two men must serve on the committee.
A will not serve on the same committee as H.
G will not serve on the same committee as D.
E will not serve on the same committee as J.

1. If four Democrats are selected, which of the following must be true?
   (A)   H may not be selected.
   (B)   B must be selected.
   (C)   A cannot be selected.
   (D)   G must be selected.
   (E)   D cannot be selected.

2. If B, G, H, and J are selected, which of the following must be true?
   (A)   E may be selected.
   (B)   A must be selected.
   (C)   C cannot be selected.
   (D)   If F is selected, then C is selected.
   (E)   If I is not selected then F must be selected.

3. If A and B cannot be selected, which of the following is true?
   (A)   J must be selected.
   (B)   C must be selected.
   (C)   G may not be selected.
   (D)   E cannot be selected.
   (E)   D must be selected.

4. If G and H cannot be selected and J must be selected, which of the following CANNOT be selected?
   (A) I and C   (B) I and D   (C) I and F   (D) C and D   (E) D and F

5. If H is not selected and both J and D are selected, which of the following must be selected?
   (A) B and C   (B) I and D   (C) I and F   (D) C and D   (E) A and F

6. If A, B, I, and J are selected, which of the following must be true?
   (A)   G must be selected.
   (B)   C can be selected.
   (C)   E can be selected.
   (D)   F must be selected.
   (E)   D cannot be selected.

Questions 7–12

A, B, C, D, and E are contestants in a talent show, and are ranked 1st through 5th with no ties.
Contestant A places ahead of contestant B.
Contestant C places 1st or last.
Contestant D places 1st or last.

7. If E finishes ahead of A, then which of the following must be true?

   (A) B finishes ahead of D.
   (B) B finishes 4th.
   (C) E finishes 3rd.
   (D) C finishes ahead of A.
   (E) C finishes 5th.

8. If C finishes ahead of B, then which of the following must be FALSE?
   (A) D is 5th.
   (B) E is 2nd.
   (C) B is 4th.
   (D) A finishes ahead of D.
   (E) A finishes 4th.

9. If B finishes ahead of E, then which of the following must be true?
   (A) A is 2nd.
   (B) B is 4th.
   (C) E finishes ahead of D.
   (D) C is 1st.
   (E) D is not 1st.

10. If C and B finish in consecutive positions, then which of the following must be true?

    (A) D finishes 1st.
    (B) E finishes ahead of A.
    (C) B finishes ahead of E.
    (D) C finishes 1st.
    (E) A finishes 2nd.

11. If a sixth contestant, F, places 4th, and B finishes behind F, then which of the following must be FALSE?
    (A) A and E finish consecutively.
    (B) A must place ahead of D.
    (C) B is 5th.
    (D) B and E do not finish consecutively.
    (E) B finishes behind D.

12. If E finishes 2nd and F, a sixth contestant, finishes next to C, then which of the following must be true?

    (A) F finishes ahead of B.
    (B) B finishes 4th.
    (C) A finishes ahead of D.
    (D) F finishes ahead of D.
    (E) C finishes 1st.

Questions 13–18

Along the coast of Zambatania there are four major cities, X, Y, Z, and Q. Each of these cities lies on a straight road that runs from east to west.

City X is 30 miles from city Y.
City Z is 40 miles from city Y.
City Q is 2 miles from city Z.

13. Which of the following could be true?
(A) City Z is 30 miles from city X.
(B) City Z is 40 miles from city X.
(C) City Z is 10 miles from city X.
(D) City Y is 50 miles from city Z.
(E) City Q is 80 miles from city Z.

14. All of the following could be true EXCEPT
(A) city Q is 38 miles from city Y
(B) city Q is 42 miles from city Y
(C) city Q is 68 miles from city X
(D) city Q is 8 miles from city X
(E) city Q is 38 miles from city X

15. If city Q is 12 miles from city X, then
(A) city Z is 70 miles from city X
(B) city Q is 38 miles from city Y
(C) city Q is 8 miles from city Y
(D) city Q is 18 miles from city Y
(E) city Z is 10 miles from city X

16. Each of the following is a possible order of cities along the coast road EXCEPT
(A) XYQZ
(B) XYZQ
(C) QZYX
(D) XQZY
(E) QZXY

17. If a traveler takes the coast road, beginning his trip at X and ending at Q, he must travel
(A) through city Y
(B) through both Y and Z
(C) through Z
(D) at least 10 miles
(E) at least 8 miles

18. If a fifth city, M, is located on the same straight coast road, and M is 5 miles from city Y, all of the following could be true EXCEPT
(A) M is 35 miles from city X
(B) M is 35 miles from city Z
(C) M is 45 miles from city Z
(D) M is 49 miles from city Q
(E) M is 47 miles from city Q

Questions 19–24

These facts are known about a large family:

Tony is John's father and Roy's son.
Roy's brother Mark has three daughters: Sue, Ann, and Shari.
Tony's wife, Debbie, and Shari's husband, Tom, are sister/brother.
Shari has only two children, sons Dave and Zak.
When Debbie married Tony, she gained two sisters-in-law, Trudy and Dawn.
Members of the family marry only once and never marry blood relatives.

19. Mark has at least how many nephews?
 (A) 0   (B) 1   (C) 2   (D) 3   (E) 4

20. If Dawn had any sons, they would be John's
 (A) brothers   (B) uncles   (C) nephews   (D) cousins   (E) grandsons

21. Which of the following must be true?
 (A)   Trudy is older than Zak.
 (B)   Tom is John's nephew.
 (C)   Mark is Tony's cousin.
 (D)   John's grandfather is Ann's uncle.
 (E)   John is older than Roy.

22. If Sue had as many children as Tony has sisters, then what is the fewest number of cousins that Dave could have?
 (A) 0   (B) 1   (C) 2   (D) 3   (E) 4

23. Mark is Zak's
 (A) brother   (B) grandfather   (C) uncle   (D) cousin   (E) nephew

24. From the information given, which of the following could be the total number of Dave's aunts?
 (A) 4   (B) 3   (C) 2   (D) 1   (E) 0

STOP

IF YOU FINISH BEFORE TIME IS UP, CHECK YOUR WORK ON THIS SECTION OF THE TEST ONLY.
DO NOT GO ON TO THE NEXT SECTION OF THE TEST UNTIL TIME IS UP FOR THIS SECTION.

SECTION II
LOGICAL REASONING

Time—35 Minutes
26 Questions

Directions:
In this section you will be given brief statements or passages and will be required to evaluate the reasoning involved. In some instances, more than one choice will appear to be a possible answer. You are to choose the *best* answer. Use common sense and reasonableness in making your selection; then mark the proper space on the answer sheet.

Questions 1–3 refer to the following passage.

It has long been apparent that the nation's violent crime problem is disproportionately a juvenile crime problem. Those under age 18 constitute a fifth of the population, but account for nearly half of the arrests for the seven major crimes on which the FBI maintains national statistics. The statistical trend lines suggest the problem is growing; the number of juveniles arrested for murder and aggravated assault rose 82 percent and 91 percent respectively from 1967 to 1976. Yet, under the laws of most states, courts are obliged to treat these young hard-core hoodlums as if they were little worse than wayward delinquents.

1. The author of this passage would argue that
   (A) crime has increased because of juveniles
   (B) young hard-core hoodlums account for nearly 50 percent of the seven major crimes
   (C) our legal system is biased in favor of hardened criminals
   (D) arrests for aggravated assault are growing more rapidly than those for murder
   (E) a fifth of our population is comprised of wayward delinquents

2. The author of this passage assumes all of the following EXCEPT
   (A) statistical trend lines are accurate predictors
   (B) 1967 to 1976 were not abnormal years
   (C) the laws of most states are consistent involving juveniles
   (D) the laws governing juvenile criminals are lenient in most states
   (E) the nation's nonviolent crime problem does not involve juveniles

3. This argument would be weakened most by pointing out that
   (A) the laws in each state are different concerning juveniles
   (B) the population has shifted to juveniles
   (C) there are eight major crimes
   (D) the FBI's national statistics are inaccurate
   (E) statistical trend lines are poor predictors

4. Some of Mike's chores take less than 1 hour to complete.
   Some of Mike's chores take more than 1 hour to complete.
   It will take Mike at least 2 hours to complete his chores.

   Which of the following additional conditions is necessary to make the third statement valid?
   (A) More chores take at least 1 hour to complete than take less than 1 hour to complete.
   (B) All chores, except one, take less than 1 hour to complete.
   (C) All chores, except one, take at least 1 hour to complete.
   (D) No chores take 1 hour to complete.
   (E) One chore takes more than 1 hour to complete.

5. Ten marbles are split among Juan, Maria, and Alvin. If Maria gives her marbles to Juan, then Juan will have more marbles than Alvin. Alternatively, if Alvin gives his marbles to Maria, then Maria will have more marbles than Juan.

Which of the following must be false?
(A) Maria has six marbles.
(B) Alvin has four marbles.
(C) Juan has six marbles.
(D) Maria has five marbles.
(E) Maria has seven marbles.

Questions 6–7 refer to the following statement.

Recent studies show that the height of the average American has increased 2 inches in the past 10 years, lending support to the view that modern foods stimulate growth.

6. The argument would be strengthened by pointing out that
(A) statistical studies were done on which foods were eaten
(B) modern foods are unhealthy
(C) all average heights are increasing
(D) comparisons have been studied in control groups
(E) there is no such thing as an average American

7. This argument would be weakened most by pointing out that
(A) statistics don't lie
(B) there are too many variables in this type of study
(C) the genetic background of the subjects was not investigated
(D) the sample group used was small
(E) some people's height decreased

Questions 8 and 9 refer to the following passage.

A glance at the five leading causes of death in 1900, 1910, and 1945, years representing in some measure the early and late practice of physicians still active, shows a significant trend. In 1900 these causes were (1) tuberculosis, (2) pneumonia, (3) enteritis, typhoid fever, and other acute intestinal diseases, (4) heart diseases, and (5) cerebral hemorrhage and thrombosis. Ten years later the only change was that heart disease had moved from fourth to first place, tuberculosis now being second, and pneumonia third. In 1945, however, the list had changed profoundly. Heart diseases were far out in front; cancer, which had come up from eighth place, was second; and cerebral hemorrhage and thrombosis, third. Fatal accidents, which had been well down the list, were now fourth, and nephritis was fifth. All of these are, of course, composites rather than single diseases, and it is significant that, except for accidents, they are characteristic of the advanced rather than the early or middle years of life.

8. Which of the following is the most logical conclusion from the passage above?
(A) A cure for cancer will be found within the decade.
(B) Many of the medical problems of today are problems of the gerontologist (specialist in medical problems of old age).
(C) Older persons are more accident-prone than are younger persons.
(D) Tuberculosis has been all but eliminated.
(E) Heart disease has never been a real threat to the aged.

9. Which of the following is not indicated by the passage?
(A) As one grows older he is more subject to disease.
(B) Pneumonia is no longer among the five most common causes of death.

(C) Compared to mortality rates for acute intestinal diseases, the mortality rate for cancer has increased.
(D) The incidence of heart disease has increased.
(E) Fatal accidents today claim more lives than ever.

10. Bitter it is, indeed, in human fate, when life's supreme temptation comes too late.

—*John Masefield*

Which of the following is neither implied nor expressed in the above quotation?
(A) the specific nature of the temptation
(B) the time of life during which the supreme temptation occurs
(C) the effect of the supreme temptation coming late in life
(D) the role of fate
(E) the importance of the temptation

Questions 11–12 refer to the following passage.

Within the unconscious realm of the mind, of which we are normally unaware, lie our basic drives and the coordination and control of our bodily functions and chemistry. This dark area of the mind constitutes about 90 percent of our mind and is responsible for about 95 percent of our behavior. We are dimly aware of its existence through our dreams, spontaneous recall of forgotten memories, and slips of speech.

11. Which of the following is implied in the passage?
(A) Ninety-five percent of our behavior is controlled by 90 percent of our mind.
(B) Five percent of our behavior is uncontrolled.
(C) Dreams, spontaneous recall, and slips of speech constitute about 90 percent of our behavior.
(D) The conscious mind controls our body chemistry.
(E) About ten percent of our mind controls five percent of our behavior.

12. The author of this passage assumes that
(A) all humans have the same bodily functions and chemical balance
(B) it is difficult to define the unconscious realm of the mind
(C) behavior modification could not take place in the conscious realm of the mind
(D) our basic drives and the coordination and control of our bodily functions take place in the same half of the brain
(E) a small part of our mind controls a small part of our behavior

13. All teachers like some of their students. No teacher likes all of his or her students.

If the statements are true, then all of the following must be true EXCEPT
(A) some teachers dislike some of their students
(B) all teachers dislike some of their students
(C) no teacher dislikes all of his or her students
(D) most teachers like most of their students
(E) no teacher likes all of his or her students

Questions 14–15 refer to the following passage.

There seems to be no way of accounting for the fundamental and widespread misunderstanding of the relation between language and thought unless the reason be the one quoted from Aristotle, that the mind is characteristically blind to things that are at once (14) ——————.
Be this as it may, the most important thing to know about language, regardless of any of its particular functions, is the principle of (15) ——————.

14. This sentence would be best completed by the words
- (A) logical and obscure
- (B) irrelevant and complex
- (C) linguistic and cerebral
- (D) important and obvious
- (E) simplistic and subjective

15. This sentence would be best completed by the word
- (A) ambiguity   (B) clarity   (C) unity   (D) logic   (E) communication

16. On-the-job training alone, of course, cannot solve the unemployment problem. The national economic recession is basically responsible for the recent surge in unemployment. The administration is pinning its chief hope for full employment on its program for revitalizing the economy.

Which of the following topics would most logically precede the passage above?
- (A) successful economic plans of the past
- (B) government policies preceding the administration
- (C) the motives of the administration
- (D) causes of the recession
- (E) opportunities for on-the-job training

17. On the one hand, "little white lies" are sinful; on the other hand, when we lie in order to save a friend from unnecessary pain, the "whiteness" of our lie becomes more apparent. Those who tell the whole truth all of the time are sure to leave misery in their wake.

The author makes which of the following arguments?
- (A) Lying is either sinful or virtuous.
- (B) Truthtellers are sure to be miserable.
- (C) Little white lies are the only justifiable lies.
- (D) It is good to lie in order to avoid hurting someone.
- (E) Pain is the result of truth.

18. Cleenup Soap will scour your pots and pans while it whitens your sink. You'll want Cleenup for all your clean-up chores, especially the hard jobs around the house.

The advertisement above implies that Cleenup Soap
- (A) is better than the rest
- (B) is the best soap for household clean-up chores
- (C) can be used for many cleaning jobs
- (D) is economically the best buy
- (E) can be used only for jobs around the house

19. *Landlord*: When are you going to pay last month's rent?
Renter: First, I've already paid it. Second, I don't owe you anything. Third, not until you fix the heater.

The weakness in the renter's response is best expressed by which of the following?
- (A) He contradicts himself.
- (B) He dislikes his landlord.
- (C) He assumes the landlord has a poor memory.
- (D) He repeats himself.
- (E) He makes no sense.

Questions 20–21 refer to the following passage.

It is a common belief that a thing is desirable because it is scarce and thereby has ostentation value. The notion that such a standard of value is an inescapable condition of settled social existence rests on one of two implicit assumptions. The first is that the attempt to educate the human race so that the desire to display one's possessions is not a significant feature of man's social behavior, is an infringement against personal freedom. The greatest obstacle to lucid discourse in these matters is the psychological antivaccinationist who uses the word freedom to signify the natural right of men and women to be unhappy and unhealthy through scientific ignorance instead of being healthy and happy through the knowledge which science confers. Haunted by a perpetual fear of the dark, the last lesson which man learns in the difficult process of growing up is "Ye shall know the truth, and the truth shall make you free." The professional economist who is too sophisticated to retreat into the obscurities of this curious conception of liberty may prefer to adopt the second assumption, that the truth does not and cannot make us free because the need for ostentation is a universal species characteristic, and all attempts to eradicate the unconscionable nuisance and discord which arise from overdeveloped craving for personal distinction artificially fostered by advertisement, propaganda and so-called good breeding are therefore destined to failure. It may be earnestly hoped that those who entertain this view have divine guidance. No rational basis for it will be found in textbooks of economics. Whatever can be said with any plausibility in the existing state of knowledge rests on the laboratory materials supplied by anthropology and social history.

20. According to the writer, the second assumption is
  (A) fostered by propaganda and so-called good breeding
  (B) basically opposite to the view of the psychological antivaccinationist
  (C) not so curious a conception of liberty as is the first assumption
  (D) unsubstantiated
  (E) a religious explanation of an economic phenomenon

21. The author's purpose in writing this paragraph is most probably to
  (A) denounce the psychological anti-vaccinationists
  (B) demonstrate that the question under discussion is an economic rather than a psychological problem
  (C) prove the maxim "Ye shall know the truth, and the truth shall make you free"
  (D) suggest that ostentation is not an inescapable phenomenon of settled social existence
  (E) prove the inability of economics to account for ostentation

22. You do not succeed unless you take a gamble. Gambling is foolish. Therefore, only fools succeed.

Which of the following would weaken the conclusion the most?
  (A) Most fools gamble.
  (B) Most fools do not succeed.
  (C) Some succeed without gambling.
  (D) Most successful gamblers are not foolish.
  (E) A fool and his money are soon parted.

23. Christopher Lasch is, in one sense, a modern-day Aesop. The ancient Greek philosopher once said, "Self-conceit may lead to self-destruction," and this warning is echoed by Lasch in his best-selling study, *The Culture of Narcissism.*

Which of the following excerpts from the above passage is least relevant to a comparison between Lasch and Aesop?
  (A) "warning is echoed"   (B) "ancient Greek philosopher"   (C) "modern-day Aesop"
  (D) "best-selling" (E) "in one sense"

24.   In the Soviet Union, it was a crime for anyone to offer religious instruction to a person under the age of 18. The overtly religious were systematically excluded from any higher education, or position of professional responsibility. By definition, every person holding official power was an atheist. And religious activists, most especially those who shared Dr. Graham's evangelical spirit, were prime candidates for the torment of life in the Gulag Archipelago.

Which of the following assumptions does the author of the above passage necessarily make about his readers?
(A)   They knew who Dr. Graham was.
(B)   They were enemies of the Soviet Union.
(C)   They were not religious activists.
(D)   They had been offered religious instruction.
(E)   They may have become evangelical themselves.

25.   There is something sinister about progress. Just look at the folks who cling to the past, and whom do you find?—friendly, neighborly types who respect traditional religious and moral values and who fear a machine age that will replace the leisurely back-fence conversation with instantaneous ''telephonatronics.''

With which of the following would the author be likely to agree?
(A)   Progress is our most important product.
(B)   We have nothing to fear except fear itself.
(C)   Lack of progress coincides with a migration from the cities.
(D)   The enemies of the future are always the very nicest people.
(E)   The best people own no machines.

26.   Far too often today, concern about nuclear weapons is focused exclusively on the superpowers. The issue of nuclear proliferation is, at best, considered secondary. Yet more and more nations are moving to the threshold of the nuclear club. The search for ways to curb nuclear proliferation deserves as much attention as the quest for arms control between the United States and the USSR.

Which of the following statements, if true, would weaken the argument above?
(A)   Nuclear proliferation is given more attention than human rights.
(B)   All nations, including the United States and the USSR, have promised not to abuse their nuclear technology.
(C)   An arms reduction by the United States and the USSR will result in an overall arms reduction by other countries.
(D)   Two adversary middle-Eastern countries have aimed nuclear missiles at each other.
(E)   Arms control in general has never before received as much attention as it has in this decade.

STOP

IF YOU FINISH BEFORE TIME IS UP, CHECK YOUR WORK ON THIS SECTION OF THE TEST ONLY. DO NOT GO ON TO THE NEXT SECTION OF THE TEST UNTIL TIME IS UP FOR THIS SECTION.

SECTION III
LOGICAL REASONING

Time—35 Minutes
25 Questions

Directions:
In this section you will be given brief statements or passages and will be required to evaluate the reasoning involved. In some instances, more than one choice will appear to be a possible answer. You are to choose the *best* answer. Use common sense and reasonableness in making your selection; then mark the proper space on the answer sheet.

1. There is no teddy bear that is not cuddly. Only a cuddly toy is safe for children.

   If the statements above are true, which of the following conclusions can be drawn?
   (A) Only some teddy bears are safe for children.
   (B) Only teddy bears are safe for children.
   (C) Any toy that is safe for children is cuddly.
   (D) Any toy that is safe for children is a teddy bear.
   (E) All cuddly toys are safe for children.

2. Industrial nations have agreed to a global ban on dumping industrial waste at sea. About 80 percent of all ocean pollution is generated on land, with 10 percent coming from industrial wastes disposed of by ships at sea, and the rest thrown or discharged from routine operation of ocean-going vessels. The measure calls for phasing out all industrial waste dumping at sea by 1995. Spokesmen for the environmental group Greenpeace praised the resolution, but _____ .

   Which of the following is the most logical conclusion of the passage above?
   (A) expressed grave concern about the 10 percent of the wastes that are not accounted for
   (B) expressed grave concern about the pollution generated on land
   (C) expressed a hope that the 1995 date could be extended to the year 2000
   (D) expressed concern about the pollution generated by nonindustrial nations
   (E) expressed concern about the decline in the ocean mammal population

3. The band always practices on Tuesday afternoons when the weather is good. The band is not practicing this afternoon.

   Which of the following can be logically deduced from the premises above?
   (A) Therefore, the weather is not good.
   (B) Therefore, today must be Wednesday.
   (C) Therefore, the band will practice tomorrow if the weather is good.
   (D) Therefore, if today's weather is bad, today must be Tuesday.
   (E) Therefore, if the weather is good, today cannot be Tuesday.

4. With the end of the cold war, many Americans see an end to the nightmare fear of nuclear destruction. But for antinuclear activists the threat has merely changed its form. Hardly any nuclear weapons have been destroyed, and new and more dangerous weapons are still being developed. If the threat of an American-Soviet showdown has declined, the danger in other quarters has increased. Compared with the weapons we have now, the Hiroshima bomb was far more powerful.

   The logic of the paragraph would be most improved by the elimination of which of its five sentences?
   (A) the first ("With the end . . .")
   (B) the second ("But for antinuclear . . .")
   (C) the third ("Hardly any nuclear . . .")
   (D) the fourth ("If the threat . . .")
   (E) the fifth ("Compared with the . . .")

Questions 5–7 refer to the following passage.

The dire shortage of rental housing in the city is the result of our unfair, strict rent-control laws. As long as we have rent control, no new rental units will be built, because they offer no chance of profit to landlords. But if rent controls are eliminated, new apartments will eventually be built, and when there is no longer a shortage of rental units, rents will no longer go up.

5. All of the following are assumptions of the author of the passage EXCEPT
   (A) the motive for building new housing is expectation of profit
   (B) the only builders of new housing are private companies
   (C) the reason no new rental housing is being built is rent control
   (D) if rent controls are eliminated, apartment construction will be inhibited by other factors
   (E) at the present level, rents are unfairly low

6. Which of the following, if true, would support the argument of this passage?
   (A) There is a shortage of low-cost housing.
   (B) There is no shortage of high-cost rental housing.
   (C) The population of the city declines steadily each year.
   (D) A city nearby with no rent control has a shortage of low-cost rental housing.
   (E) Fewer rental units were built this year in a city nearby with no rent control than were built here.

7. Which of the following is not a plausible solution to the housing-shortage problem as the passage presents it?
   (A) Some, but not all, of the rent controls could be gradually phased out.
   (B) Newly constructed rental units could be exempted from rent controls, without removing other controls.
   (C) Government agencies could finance the construction of low-cost housing.
   (D) State bonds could finance the cost of low-cost housing.
   (E) More rental units could be converted into condominiums.

8. For the sixth year in a row, the average score for males taking the mathematics section of a nationally administered examination for high school seniors was ten points higher than the average score for females. Both males and females had taken twenty or more full-year academic classes in high school, and the socioeconomic background of the test takers was virtually the same. This result shows clearly the bias of the test in favor of males.

The argument of this passage would be weakened if which of the following were shown to be true?
   (A) Regardless of gender, the higher a student's grades are in high school, the higher his or her scores on nationally administered examinations are likely to be.
   (B) The highest scoring performers on the exam were students who had taken four or more years of mathematics courses.
   (C) The highest scoring ethnic group on the examination was Asian-Americans.
   (D) While 40 percent of the female test takers had studied computer programming, only 38 percent of the male test takers had.
   (E) Females taking the test had completed an average of 1.3 fewer mathematics and natural science classes than males.

9.   All vegetables for sale in this market are low in calories; therefore this market sells only low-calorie vegetables.

Which of the following is most like the argument above?
(A)   All the classes in this catalog offer three units of credit; therefore all three-unit courses are listed in this catalog.
(B)   All graduates of this high school have completed four science courses; therefore all graduates know chemistry, biology, and physics well.
(C)   All the machines in this factory are powered by electricity; therefore this factory uses only electrically powered machines.
(D)   All the players on this football team exercise for three hours daily; therefore all football players should exercise for three hours each day.
(E)   All the articles in this magazine were written by women; therefore the editors of this magazine must all be female.

10.   If members of the City Council vote to impose a surtax on gasoline to raise money for the new railway system, they will certainly be voted out of office in the June election by the unified action of voters in the western precincts, who argue that the system will not be of use to them. The following year, when construction of the system is complete, the support of voters in the eastern precincts will be so great that only Council members who voted for the railway will certainly be elected at that time.

To assure continued election to the City Council, a member would have to
(A)   vote against the gasoline surtax
(B)   find an alternate way of financing the railway
(C)   appeal to the voters in the eastern precincts in the June election
(D)   support the gasoline surtax, but oppose the construction of the railway
(E)   oppose both the gasoline tax and the construction of the railway

Questions 11–12 refer to the following passage.

The new clean-air legislation is going to cost a great deal of money. Industry and consumers will share costs that are predicted to run to ten billion dollars a year by 1995, and twenty billion ten years later. Electric bills in the Midwest are likely to increase by 20 percent. Gasoline will cost 10 cents per gallon more to refine. Car costs will increase by more than $100 a car. And cleaner air will not show as a productivity gain for the economy. Small companies that cannot pass added costs on to their customers will be especially hard pressed.

For very good reasons, the American public has decided that clean air is worth the high price. The pollution control industry, of course, will get a big boost. So will makers of catalytic converters and ethanol products, as well as many specialized engineering firms. The implementation of the clean air legislation may lead to the commercial development of wind or solar-generated electricity, new power sources for trains, and nonpolluting cars. Good public policy may become good business.

11.   The passage as a whole is structured to lead to which one of the following conclusions?
(A)   The costs of implementing the new clean-air legislation will be enormous.
(B)   The clean-air legislation will so improve public health that the large costs are a good investment.
(C)   The high cost of cleaning the air may be accompanied by the development of new business opportunities.
(D)   The implementation of the clean-air act will lead to large rises in the cost of electricity, gasoline, and automobiles.
(E)   Regardless of the cost, it is essential to put an end to air pollution.

12. Which of the following best describes the organization of the argument of this passage?
  (A) The passage deals with specific details in the first paragraph and with general principles in the second.
  (B) The passage deals with economic issues in the first paragraph and social issues in the second.
  (C) The passage presents the liabilities of the legislation in the first paragraph and some possible benefits in the second.
  (D) The passage evaluates the legislation in the first paragraph in a way which the second paragraph contradicts.
  (E) The passage uses examples and analogies in the first paragraph, while the second paragraph uses only examples.

Questions 13–14 refer to the following statements.

Assume that the following statements are true:

  (1) Left-handed people never live in apartments.
  (2) People who live in apartments are always suspicious.
  (3) People who don't live in apartments are always thin.

13. If David is left-handed, which of the following cannot be true?
  (A) David does not live in an apartment.
  (B) David is not suspicious.
  (C) David is thin.
  (D) David is suspicious.
  (E) David is not thin.

14. If Jane is left-handed, all of the following could be true EXCEPT
  (A) Jane is not suspicious
  (B) Jane is suspicious
  (C) Jane is thin
  (D) Jane does not live in an apartment
  (E) Jane lives in an apartment

15. Chemists studying the lithium level in water supplies of ten Texas cities have correlated those levels with the incidence of crime. They have found that communities with no lithium in the drinking water have consistently higher rates of suicides, homicides, violent crimes, and drug abuse than cities with naturally high levels of lithium in the drinking water. A second study of prison inmates has shown that violent offenders have lower levels of lithium in their bodies than do nonviolent offenders. Lithium is now used to treat manic depressive illness.

Which of the following can be inferred from the passage above?
  (A) The suicide rate and level of violent crime could probably be reduced by increasing lithium levels in the water supply.
  (B) No two different scientific studies can prove exactly the same thing.
  (C) There is a need to repeat similar studies in other parts of the country.
  (D) The crime rate of a city can be predicted by examining the lithium levels in its water supply.
  (E) The suicide rate will probably be lower in cities with a high rate of drug abuse and violent crime.

16.   The use of referendums or initiatives on the state ballot allows the electorate to make decisions about important issues such as the environment, taxes, education, and crime. It exposes the electorate to a deluge of communication that is cynical and manipulative. Negative techniques in initiative campaigns are often used by candidates in the election that follows.

The reasoning in the passage above is flawed because the passage
(A)   does not give examples of issues that can be decided by initiative
(B)   presents inconsistent judgments on initiatives.
(C)   deals only with state, not national, elections
(D)   fails to discriminate between initiatives and referendums
(E)   regards advertising in elections negatively

17. *Dave:* According to my doctor, by adding high-fiber foods to your diet, you can help your weight-loss program.
Jane: That's not true. My sister eats some high-fiber foods, and she is seriously overweight.

Dave can best counter Jane's assertion by pointing out that
(A)   it has not yet been scientifically proved that adding high-fiber foods to the diet will cause weight loss
(B)   Jane's sister may be avoiding high-fiber foods, although Jane doesn't know this
(C)   Jane's sister is the exception that proves the rule
(D)   other components of Jane's sister's diet may be the cause of her being overweight
(E)   the metabolism of every human being is unique

18.   Let me say at once that I believe all the UFOs that people claim to have seen or visited are either figments of the imagination or explainable phenomena. I disagree with the UFO believers' charge that unbelievers are close minded and so self-centered that we cannot imagine a civilization more scientifically advanced than ours. Why do all the aliens turn out to look like oddly formed humans? Why do UFOs always appear in the sticks, rather than, say, in New York City or on the White House lawn? Why do these aliens never stick around long enough to be interviewed on television? Why don't they kidnap the president of MIT or Cal. Tech. instead of some tobacco farmer from rural Carolina?

The author of this passage makes his point chiefly by
(A)   drawing an analogy
(B)   disputing evidence cited by those with an opposing view
(C)   using personal experience to derive a general principle
(D)   basing a conclusion upon a specific case
(E)   showing that the opposition's argument is based upon a contradiction

19.   There are two basic clothing styles designed today for children. One is pseudo-Victorian, imitations of the clothes that Lewis Carroll's Alice might have worn. The other is a miniature version of the clothes the parents are now wearing. These may include cocktail dresses or fake mink coats, rock-star clothes, and leather anything, together with the new lines of children's perfumes and cosmetics. On the basis of this evidence, I infer two types of parents. One hopes to shield the child from contemporary reality. The other wants children to reflect what the parents have become, a mirror for themselves.

All of the following are true of the evidence the author of this passage cites EXCEPT
(A)   it is based on observation
(B)   it supports the author's conclusions
(C)   it may not be the only evidence to support the author's conclusions
(D)   it is used to support ideas that assume that childrens' clothes express adults' hopes
(E)   it is irrelevant to the conclusions the author reaches

20. *Jane:* All New Yorkers are rude.
Jack: No. I know many people from Pittsburgh who are very impolite.

Jack's answer reveals that he has interpreted Jane's statement to mean that
(A) rudeness can be restricted to a single city
(B) New Yorkers are worse than people who live in other cities
(C) only New Yorkers are rude
(D) New Yorkers are likely to be more rude than people from anywhere else
(E) degrees of rudeness can be measured

Questions 21–22 refer to the following passage.

A large National Science Foundation grant was recently awarded to Florida State University. The money will fund a center to study high-energy magnetism. Competing for the grant was MIT, which, according to the NSF review panels, had the better physicists. But the state of Florida pledged financial and political support that won it the award. Defenders of the award point out that, though the government would appear to get the best value by investing in the best institution, by diversifying the locations of its awards, the NSF has created new centers of research of world-class standing.

The real reason is a fundamental shift in the way we spend money on science. For years the primary reason scientists got money was for national security. But nowadays economic development is a primary cause. Consequently, politics is becoming more important than dispassionate peer reviews. The state with more than 25 percent of the members of the National Academy of Sciences gets just over 10 percent of the science funds, because its congressional delegation is splintered. The economic benefits are, at best, unpredictable. The benefits to science are even more doubtful.

21. Which of the following, if true, would support the awarding of the grant to Florida?
(A) The NSF has already awarded a large number of grants to Florida State University.
(B) The NSF has already awarded a large number of grants in the South.
(C) The science review panels described the physics department at Florida State as adequate.
(D) The University of Texas, once a mediocre research institution, has with government support become a world-class center of scientific research.
(E) The physics department at MIT is universally regarded as the best in the country.

22. Which of the following, if true, would weaken the argument of the second paragraph?
(A) The area around Los Alamos, a recipient of huge government funding, has not developed in the last 30 years.
(B) The development of the Silicon Valley in California is due chiefly to its climate and quality of life.
(C) Economic development of an area depends chiefly on an infrastructure of entrepreneurial faculty and venture capital.
(D) The proximity of the National Institutes of Health has made Montgomery, Maryland, a center of biotechnology entrepreneurialism.
(E) The unity of a congressional delegation profoundly influences its effectiveness in pork-barrel competition.

23. Every time I am beaten at golf, I become short-tempered, and I curse at anyone who makes me short-tempered.

Which of the following can be logically concluded about the speaker of the passage above?
(A) He curses anyone who beats him at golf.
(B) Everyone whom he curses makes him short-tempered.
(C) People whom he beats at golf are not cursed at.
(D) Every time he curses he has been beaten at golf.
(E) He does not curse when he is not short-tempered.

Questions 24–25 refer to the following passage.

The mayor's attempt to ban smoking in the restaurants in the city was irresponsible. Everyone knows that smoking is unhealthy for the smoker and for the people near him. We know that traffic, smog, pesticides, and overeating are bad for us. Shall we ban all cars from the city? After all, it's not the nondriver's fault that so many others are addicted to the automobile.

Fortunately the City Council voted against the mayor's proposed smoking ban. The councilors realized that banning smoking in city restaurants would result in patrons' going to the suburbs. Though many councilors, like the mayor, are nonsmokers, they unselfishly voted to protect the livelihood of thousands of restaurant owners and workers.

24. The author makes his criticism of the mayor chiefly by
(A)   drawing an analogy
(B)   ridiculing his logic
(C)   questioning his assumptions
(D)   defining his areas of disagreement
(E)   exposing his contradictions

25. Which of the following, if true, would tend to weaken the author's argument?
(A)   Studies of the danger of second-hand cigarette smoke are still inconclusive.
(B)   Cigarette manufacturers are large contributors to the campaign funds of the mayor.
(C)   Profits of restaurants with separate smoking and nonsmoking areas have increased.
(D)   Restaurants in cities that have banned smoking report no decline in their profits.
(E)   Some of the city council members are nonsmokers.

STOP

IF YOU FINISH BEFORE TIME IS UP, CHECK YOUR WORK ON THIS SECTION OF THE TEST ONLY. DO NOT GO ON TO THE NEXT SECTION OF THE TEST UNTIL TIME IS UP FOR THIS SECTION.

SECTION IV
READING COMPREHENSION

Time—35 Minutes
28 Questions

Directions:
Read the passages and answer the questions following each passage by blackening the appropriate space on the answer sheet. You may refer back to the passages when answering the questions. Answer all questions on the basis of what is stated or implied.

Passage 1

There are many dictionary definitions of "existentialism"; each carries some degree of truth. These will not be discussed, nor will they be analyzed since that process would involve several volumes. However, central to each definition is the assertion that existentialism is a theory or statement about the nature of man's existence. There is entire agreement about that point. Errors come from accompanying statements that scientific or idealistic approaches are not adequate in defining or understanding existentialism.

Let us understand clearly that no theory of any kind of human existence can be defined in terms solely those of a scientific or idealistic process. Definition, as must be true of any other process, must be a matter of total personality. As such, existentialism must involve the viewpoints of thinking, feeling, and sensing. Second, existentialism, overall, and existentialism, as reflected specifically in any behavioral account of its operation—is subject to the scientific detection of its operation through any one of several modern psychological approaches. Different emotive states carry their principles into operation through certain unique linguistic structures, both macroscopic and microscopic. Those operating in an "existential way" can be identified as uniquely different from the other theories of human existence.

Existentialism is one of a limited number of views of man's nature, central to which is his existence. The other views are that man's nature is one that falls into one of the following categories: an operational balance among the elements of thought, feeling, and sensation—classicism, an imbalance weighted in favor of the world of volitions (feeling, emotions, and will) over the world of mind and senses—romanticism, an imbalance among the categories of head, heart, and hand in favor of thought—rationalism, an imbalance resulting from choosing the world of materiality—the world of the senses and things, over the claims of spirit and thought—naturalism.

Then existentialism is a view of human existence, and, as such, finds itself in the class with classicism, romanticism, rationalism, and naturalism. Obviously, for each individual, the meanings of each view must be carried by words which have ranges of meaning. If we can find one of the views which differs from all other views in accepting a range of meaning, then the view can be defined at least from a semantic point of view. Whether one is a romanticist, a rationalist, a classicist, or one in the grim hold of naturalism, he accepts words describing each as holding the same range of meanings for all views, even including that of existentialism. He accepts the range of meanings describing each one, although he selects from the range according to his unique viewpoint. However, since the existentialist denies that he can be bound to the external control of any range of meanings, including those of words, he can be defined as uniquely different from his *philosophers*. Here, the definition, and an effective one, is on semantical grounds. He creates his own range of meanings of words; if they approach those used in the other philosophies of man's existence, they do so only accidentally. The existentialist deliberately—and unconsciously sometimes—rejects traditional ranges of meaning in his own language environment. Quite often he does so through using the words in an opposite sense. We could rest on this linguistic view, and do so safely, did we so desire. However, we can also define existentialism in the light of a historical uniqueness.

1. The author does not imply that a full definition of existentialism should be
   (A) pithy   (B) prolix   (C) many-faceted   (D) difficult   (E) complex

2. Despite all the different definitions of existentialism, one central point around which they all cohere says that
   (A) there is no central point
   (B) existentialism is the essence of existence
   (C) existentialism tries to explain the nature of human existence
   (D) existentialism tries to define the nature of human nature
   (E) existential theorists are tending toward universal agreement

3. The existentialist is different from other philosophers because he
   (A) rejects definitions
   (B) embraces all theories
   (C) makes a pact with his existence
   (D) is uniquely grim
   (E) is more astute than the others

4. According to the passage, several existentialists would be likely to define "reality" in
   (A) two ways   (B) strange ways   (C) similar ways
   (D) unseemly ways   (E) several ways

5. Each dictionary definition of existentialism is, at best,
   (A) partial   (B) equivocal   (C) abstract   (D) redundant   (E) in error

6. The best title for this passage would be:
   (A) Modern Philosophy and Its Complexities
   (B) Existence vs. Essence
   (C) Where the Dictionary Goes Wrong
   (D) Is Existentialism Definable?
   (E) Words Do Not Have Meanings

7. According to the passage, which of the following is not an alternative view to existentialism?
   (A) classicism   (B) romanticism   (C) rationalism   (D) naturalism   (E) dogmatism

8. The existentialist's use of words may often be

(A) lucid   (B) partial   (C) contradictory   (D) precise   (E) obscure

Passage 2

Under very early common law, all felonies were punishable by death. The perpetrators of the felony were hanged whether or not a homicide had been committed during the felony. Later, however, most felonies were declared to be noncapital offenses. The common law courts, in need of a deterrent to the use of deadly force in the course of these noncapital felonies, developed the "felony-murder rule."

In 1535, there appeared probably the first formal statement of the rule in Lord Dacre's case: "Any killing by one in the commission of a felony is guilty of murder." The killing was a murder whether intentional or unintentional, accidental or mistaken. The usual requirement of malice was eliminated and the only criminal intent necessary was the intent to commit the particular underlying felony. All participants in the felony were guilty of murder—actual killer and nonkiller confederates.

Proponents of the rule argued that it was justified because the felon demonstrated a lack of concern for human life by the commission of a violent and dangerous felony; that the crime was murder either because of a conclusive presumption of malice or simply by force of statutory definition.

Opponents of the rule are numerous and vocal in severe and sweeping criticism. They describe the rule as a highly artificial concept and "an enigma wrapped in a riddle." They are quick to point out that the rule has been abandoned in England where it originated, abolished in India, severely restricted in Canada and a number of other commonwealth countries, is unknown in continental Europe, and abandoned in Michigan. In reality, the real strength of the opponents' criticism stems from the bizarre and oft times unfair results achieved when the felony-murder rule is applied mechanically. Defendants have been convicted under the rule where:

(1) the killing was purely accidental;
(2) participants in the felony had forbidden their associate to kill;
(3) the killing took place after the felony during the later flight from the scene;
(4) one third party killed another (police officer killed a citizen or vice versa);
(5) a victim died of a heart attack 15–20 minutes after the robbery was over;
(6) the person killed was an accomplice in the felony.

Intelligentsia attacks have come from all directions with basically the same demand—re-evaluate and abandon the archaic legal fiction; restrict and limit vicarious criminal liability; prosecute killers for murder, not nonkillers; increase punishment for the underlying felony as a real deterrent; and initiate legislative modifications.

The courts have not been quick to hold certain applications of the felony-murder rule unconstitutional. Rather, they have taken a long, hard look at the modern legislative decisions, the jury verdicts, and the attitude of society as a whole in making these decisions. The California legislature, which is known to be one of the leading jurisdictions, is in a trend of holding a criminal defendant liable only for his personal conduct. The logical result of this would be the abandonment of the felony-murder rule. The criminal defendant could still be convicted of murder under a reckless disregard or other theory, however, this would require some showing of his personal intent to kill. This may be more difficult to prove than the mere inference from the intent to commit the underlying felony, but clearly to submit one to this most grave of penalties should require more than the mere intent to commit the underlying felony.

With the unstable history of the felony-murder rule, including its abandonment by many jurisdictions in this country, as well as the asserted trend toward abandonment in one of this country's leading jurisdictions, the felony-murder rule is dying a slow but certain death.

9. Which of the following best states the central idea of the passage?
(A) The felony-murder rule should be abolished.
(B) California is about to abandon the felony-murder rule.
(C) The felony-murder rule can be unfair.
(D) The felony-murder rule should be abolished by the Supreme Court of the United States.
(E) There are strong arguments to be made both for and against the felony-murder rule.

10. The felony-murder rule was developed in order to
(A) deter felonies
(B) deter murders
(C) deter deadly force in felonies
(D) return death for death
(E) extend the definition of murder to any malicious act resulting in death

11. Arguments in favor of the felony-murder rule may include which of the following?
(A) We can infer that anyone undertaking a violent felony does so maliciously.
(B) We can infer that anyone undertaking a dangerous felony demonstrates an indifference to human life.
(C) If the punishment for the use of deadly force whether intended or not is the same, criminals will be less likely to use deadly force.
(D) Because a life has been taken, the crime is murder by force of statutory definition.
(E) The victim of murder may be an accomplice of the felon.

12. According to the passage, opponents of the felony-murder rule have raised all of the following objections to the statute EXCEPT
(A) the felony-murder rule results in murder prosecutions of defendants who have not committed murder
(B) the felony-murder rule is an archaic law based upon a legal fiction
(C) the felony-murder rule is based upon a presumption of malice even if the death is wholly accidental
(D) the felony-murder rule deters the use of deadly force in noncapital felonies
(E) the felony-murder rule assigns a criminal liability vicariously

13. In which of the following situations would the defendant be liable to the charge of murder under the felony-murder rule?
(A) In escaping from an unsuccessful attempt to rob a bank, the defendant crashes his car, killing an innocent pedestrian in another city.
(B) A bank security officer, pursuing the defendant after a robbery, falls down a flight of stairs and suffers serious permanent brain and spinal cord injuries.
(C) The driver of the escape car, who has not entered the bank, crashes the car, killing the armed gunman who committed the robbery.
(D) A bank teller, locked safely in the bank vault by the robber, has a stroke and dies.
(E) The driver of a stolen car forces another car off the road, killing a passenger.

14. According to the passage, the decline of support for the felony-murder rule is indicated by the abandoning of the rule in all of the following locations EXCEPT
(A) continental Europe
(B) Michigan
(C) India
(D) England
(E) California

15. The author believes that the felony-murder rule is
(A) unconstitutional
(B) bizarre and unfair
(C) supported by several hundred years of sound legal tradition

(D)   an unfair equating of intent to commit a felony with intent to commit murder
(E)   a serviceable rule unfairly attacked by the "intelligentsia"

Passage 3

The Constitution of the United States protects both property rights and freedom of speech. At times these rights conflict. Resolution then requires a determination as to the type of property involved. If the property is private and not open to the general public, the owner may absolutely deny the exercise of the right of free speech thereon. On the other hand, if public land is at issue, the First Amendment protections of expression are applicable. However, the exercise of free speech thereon is not absolute. Rather it is necessary to determine the appropriateness of the forum. This requires that consideration be given to a number of factors including: character and normal use of the property, the extent to which it is open to the public, and the number and types of persons who frequent it. If the forum is clearly public or clearly private, the resolution of the greater of rights is relatively straightforward.

In the area of quasi-public property, balancing these rights has produced a dilemma. This is the situation when a private owner permits the general public to use his property. When persons seek to use the land for passing out handbills or picketing, how is a conflict between property rights and freedom of expression resolved? There have been several cases decided by the United States Supreme Court, notably in 1945, 1967, and 1976.

In 1967, the Court concluded that constitutional safeguards were inapplicable because the shopping center was not the equivalent of a municipality. Action by the private owner does not constitute state action and the First Amendment affords no protection from private conduct. If the shopping center is equivalent to a municipality, then the exercise of free speech is protected without regard to the content of expression.

The Court's conclusions in 1967 that the shopping center owner had not performed the "full spectrum of municipal power" is difficult to justify in light of the nature and role of shopping centers in America. There are instances where entire districts have been replaced by the downtown shopping mall. For many Americans, the mall is replacing the old corner drugstore, the city park, and Main Street as the core of the community.

The Court did not weigh property rights against free speech. It was held that the constitutional protection of free speech from state action had no application to the facts of that case. Thus, prohibition of handbilling and picketing has not yet occurred. It is suggested that case law and social principles be applied to ensure that freedom of expression remains viable.

From 1967 through to 1976, the Court has overlooked important language in the decision of 1945, namely:

> Ownership does not mean absolute dominion. The more an owner, for his advantage, opens up his property for use by the public in general, the more do his rights become circumscribed by the statutory and constitutional rights of those who use it.

The precept that a private property owner surrenders his rights in proportion to the extent to which he opens up his property to the public is not new. In 1675, Lord Chief Justice Hale wrote that when private property is "affected with a public interest, it ceases to be private." Throughout the development of Anglo-American law, the individual has never possessed absolute dominion over property. Land becomes clothed with a public interest when the owner devotes his property to a use in which the public has an interest. The chairman of the board of the company that launched the Wilde Lake Shopping Center in Columbia, Maryland said:

> The only real purpose and justification of any of these centers is to serve the people in the area—not the merchants, not the architects, not the developers. The success or failure of a regional shopping center will be measured by what it does for the people it seeks to serve.

These doctrines should be applied when accommodation must be made between a shopping center owner's private property rights and the public's right to free expression. It is hoped that when the Court is asked to balance these conflicting rights it will keep in mind what Justice Black said in 1945: "When we balance the Constitutional rights of owners of property against those of the people to enjoy (First Amendment) freedom(s) . . . we remain mindful of the fact that the latter occupy a preferred position."

16. In which of the following cases would the owner of the property probably be most free to restrict the freedom of speech?
    (A) an amusement park attended by five million people each year owned by a multinational company
    (B) a small grocery store owned by a husband and wife
    (C) an enclosed shopping mall owned by a single woman
    (D) a fenced public garden and park owned by a small town
    (E) an eight-unit residential apartment building owned by a large real estate company

17. A conflict between property rights and freedom of speech might arise in all of the following situations, EXCEPT
    (A) protesters carrying signs outside a cinema in an enclosed shopping mall
    (B) a disgruntled employee passing out leaflets in front of a hairdresser's salon
    (C) a religious order soliciting funds and converts in the swimming pool area of a condominium
    (D) a candidate for mayor handing out flyers in front of his opponent's headquarters
    (E) environmentalists carrying signs at the entrance to an oil refinery

18. According to the passage, an owner's freedom to deny freedom of speech on his property is determined by all of the following EXCEPT
    (A) whether or not the land is open to the public
    (B) the nature of and the usual use of the property
    (C) the type of person who frequents the land
    (D) the nature of character of the owner
    (E) how many people use the property

19. According to the passage, the author believes most shopping malls in America
    (A) are the functional equivalents of municipalities
    (B) have a right to prohibit the distribution of advertising handbills
    (C) have a right to prohibit the distribution of religious printed matter
    (D) have a right to determine what handbills may or may not be distributed
    (E) are more important than the city halls

20. Picketing and handbill distribution in shopping malls have not yet been prohibited despite the Supreme Court decision in 1967, because the Court found
    (A) in favor of the picketers
    (B) in favor of the mall owners
    (C) that free speech was not a relevant issue
    (D) that free speech was properly denied
    (E) that the constitutional guarantees of free speech outweighed rights of ownership

21. According to the passage, the idea that a property owner's rights decline as the property is more used by the general public
    (A) is peculiar to recent Supreme Court decisions
    (B) is attested to by a three-hundred-year-old opinion
    (C) conflicts with the idea that property affected with a public interest ceases to be private
    (D) is in accord with the idea that ownership confers absolute dominion
    (E) is now universally accepted in Great Britain and in Canada

22. All other things being equal, the courts must favor
    (A) First Amendment rights over property rights
    (B) Fourth Amendment rights over property rights
    (C) property rights over First Amendment rights
    (D) property rights and First Amendment rights equally
    (E) property rights and Fourth Amendment rights equally

Passage 4

The American, though he dresses like an Englishman, and eats roast beef with a silver fork—or sometimes with a steel knife—as does an Englishman, is not like an Englishman in his mind, in his aspirations, in his tastes, or in his politics. In his mind he is quicker, more universally intelligent, more ambitious of general knowledge, less indulgent of stupidity and ignorance in others, harder, sharper, brighter with the surface brightness of steel, than is an Englishman; but he is more brittle, less enduring, less malleable, and I think less capable of impressions. The mind of the Englishman has more imagination, but that of the American more incision. The American is a great observer, but he observes things material rather than things social or picturesque. He is a constant and ready speculator; but all speculations, even those which come of philosophy, are with him more or less material. In his aspirations the American is more constant than an Englishman—or I should rather say he is more constant in aspiring. Every citizen of the United States intends to do something. Every one thinks himself capable of some effort. But in his aspirations he is more limited than an Englishman. The ambitious American never soars so high as the ambitious Englishman. He does not even see up to so great a height; and when he has raised himself somewhat above the crowd becomes sooner dizzy with his own altitude. An American of mark, though always anxious to show his mark, is always fearful of a fall. In his tastes the American imitates the Frenchman. Who shall dare to say that he is wrong, seeing that in general matters of design and luxury the French have won for themselves the foremost name? I will not say that the American is wrong, but I cannot avoid thinking that he is so. I detest what is called French taste; but the world is against me. When I complained to a landlord of a hotel out in the West that his furniture was useless; that I could not write at a marble table whose outside rim was curved into fantastic shapes; that a gold clock in my bedroom which did not go would give me no aid in washing myself; that a heavy, immovable curtain shut out the light; and that *papier-maché* chairs with small fluffy velvet seats were bad to sit on—he answered me completely by telling me that his house had been furnished not in accordance with the taste of England, but with that of France. I acknowledged the rebuke, gave up my pursuits of literature and cleanliness, and hurried out of the house as quickly as I could. All America is now furnishing itself by the rules which guided that hotel-keeper. I do not merely allude to actual household furniture—to chairs, tables, and detestable gilt clocks. The taste of America is become French in its conversation, French is its comforts and French in its discomforts, French in its eating, and French in its dress, French in its manners, and will become French in its art. There are those who will say that English taste is taking the same direction. I do not think so. I strongly hope that it is not so. And, therefore, I say that an Englishman and an American differ in their tastes.

23. The primary purpose of this passage is to
    (A) explain America to a foreign audience
    (B) recount the travels of an Englishman in America
    (C) compare and contrast Englishmen and Americans
    (D) insult the French
    (E) argue that Englishmen are better than Americans

24. The author believes that, although Americans are "constant" in their aspirations, they are also
    (A) cautious   (B) dizzy   (C) speculative   (D) incapable   (E) unimaginative

25. Relative to the popularity of French taste, the author believes that he constitutes
    (A) an advocacy
    (B) a minority
    (C) a new viewpoint
    (D) a moral alternative
    (E) a majority

26. Of the four contrasting characteristics that the author mentions in the first sentence, the one he says no more about is
(A) mind   (B) aspirations   (C) tastes   (D) politics   (E) eating style

27. The author claims that America is becoming "French in its comforts and French in its discomforts." The comforts resulting from French taste are
(A) marble tables
(B) gilt clocks
(C) porcelain wash basins
(D) heavy curtains
(E) not mentioned

28. From the last four sentences, we may infer that the English and the Americans will continue to differ in taste as long as
(A) English furniture retains its utilitarian character
(B) the English stay out of America
(C) Englishmen continue to pursue "literature and cleanliness"
(D) English taste does not move closer to French taste
(E) the French populate America

STOP

IF YOU FINISH BEFORE TIME IS UP, CHECK YOUR WORK ON THIS SECTION OF THE TEST ONLY. DO NOT GO ON TO THE NEXT SECTION OF THE TEST UNTIL TIME IS UP FOR THIS SECTION.

SECTION V
ANALYTICAL REASONING

Time—35 Minutes
24 Questions

Directions:

In this section you will be given groups of questions based on different sets of conditions. Drawing a simple diagram may be helpful in answering some of the questions. You are to choose the best answer and mark the corresponding space on your answer sheet.

Questions 1–7

Kelly, Clyde, Roland, Fred, and Harriet are a lawyer, an accountant, a doctor, a police officer, and a cab driver, not necessarily in that order.

(1)   Kelly is not the doctor or the accountant.
(2)   If Fred is the accountant, then Kelly is the doctor.
(3)   Roland is not the police officer.
(4)   If Clyde is the doctor, then Harriet is the lawyer.
(5)   If Harriet is the cab driver, then Kelly is not the police officer.
(6)   Harriet is the cab driver.

1. If the accountant, the doctor, and the police officer meet for lunch, which three people get together?
  (A)   Kelly, Fred, and Clyde
  (B)   Roland, Fred, and Kelly
  (C)   Roland, Clyde, and Kelly
  (D)   Roland, Fred, and Clyde
  (E)   Harriet, Roland, and Fred

2. Which of the following is true about Clyde?
  (A)   He is the accountant.
  (B)   He could be the lawyer.
  (C)   He is not the doctor.
  (D)   He is the police officer.
  (E)   He could be the cab driver.

3. If Roland is the doctor, then Clyde is the
  (A)   police officer
  (B)   accountant
  (C)   lawyer
  (D)   cab driver
  (E)   doctor

4. If Clyde is NOT the accountant, then
  (A)   Fred is the police officer
  (B)   Clyde is the lawyer
  (C)   Roland is the doctor
  (D)   Roland is not the accountant
  (E)   Fred is the doctor

5. If Fred is the police officer, then
  (A)   Roland could be the doctor
  (B)   Roland must be the accountant
  (C)   Clyde must be the accountant
  (D)   Clyde could be the lawyer
  (E)   Clyde must be the doctor

6. The doctor could be
- (A)   Kelly or Fred
- (B)   Roland or Clyde
- (C)   Fred or Clyde
- (D)   Kelly or Roland
- (E)   Roland or Fred

7. If the cab driver picks up the lawyer and the accountant, which three people could be in the cab?
- (A)   Harriet, Roland, and Clyde
- (B)   Kelly, Fred, and Harriet
- (C)   Clyde, Harriet, and Fred
- (D)   Harriet, Roland, and Kelly
- (E)   Roland, Fred, and Harriet

Questions 8–14

Eleven people stand single file in a straight line. There are four women, three men, two boys and two girls.

The children are all next to each other.
Three of the women stand next to each other at one end of the line.
No man stands next to another man.

8. If a child is in the sixth place, which of the following must be true?
- (A)   A woman is in the first place.
- (B)   A woman is in the second place.
- (C)   A woman is in the seventh place.
- (D)   A woman is in the eighth place.
- (E)   A woman is in the ninth place.

9. Which of the following must be true?
- (A)   A woman is either first or third.
- (B)   A woman is either second or tenth.
- (C)   A woman is either sixth or seventh.
- (D)   A woman is fourth.
- (E)   A woman is seventh.

10. All of the following must be true EXCEPT
- (A)   if a man is first, a woman is last
- (B)   if a child is second, a man is sixth
- (C)   if a child is sixth, a woman is tenth
- (D)   if a man is fourth, a child is eighth
- (E)   if a woman is third, a man is sixth

11. If a girl is second and a boy is third, which of the following must be true?
- (A)   The two boys are next to each other.
- (B)   The two boys are not next to each other.
- (C)   The two girls are not next to men.
- (D)   The two girls are not next to each other.
- (E)   A boy is next to a woman.

12. If a boy is eighth, which of the following could be true?
- (A)   A woman is last and a girl is sixth.
- (B)   A man is fourth and ninth.
- (C)   A woman is sixth and a girl is ninth.
- (D)   A man is sixth and a woman is tenth.
- (E)   A man is last and a girl is tenth.

13. If a man is fourth, a woman must be
- (A) first and fifth
- (B) second and tenth
- (C) first and second
- (D) first and tenth
- (E) second and fifth

14. If each man is next to at least one woman, which of the following must be true?
- (A) A man is first.
- (B) A woman is second.
- (C) A woman is third.
- (D) A child is fourth.
- (E) A man is eighth.

Questions 15–20

The math club at Union Junior High School consists of three boys—Bill, Clem, and Drew, and four girls—Ann, Ellen, Fran, and Gina. While doing a math project involving measurement, the members arrive at the following information:

- (1) Bill is taller than Ann.
- (2) Drew is shorter than Bill.
- (3) Clem is taller than Drew, but shorter than Ann.
- (4) Ellen is taller than Clem, but shorter than Bill.
- (5) Fran is taller than Ellen.
- (6) Gina is shorter than Ann.

15. If Ann is 5 feet tall, then which of the following could NOT be true?
- (A) Fran is 4 feet 10 inches tall.
- (B) Ellen is 5 feet 10 inches tall.
- (C) Drew is 5 feet 10 inches tall.
- (D) Clem is 4 feet 10 inches tall.
- (E) Gina is 4 feet 10 inches tall.

16. Which of the following could NOT be true?
- (A) Drew is shorter than Ann.
- (B) Ellen is 4 feet tall.
- (C) Bill is taller than Fran.
- (D) Fran is shorter than Clem.
- (E) Drew is 4 feet tall.

17. If Ellen is taller than Ann, then which of the following must be true about Fran?
- (A) Fran is shorter than Gina.
- (B) Fran is taller than Ann.
- (C) Fran is shorter than Clem.
- (D) Fran is taller than Bill.
- (E) Fran is the tallest.

18. Which statement about the math club members is redundant and repeats information obtainable from the other statements?
(A) (1)   (B) (2)   (C) (3)   (D) (4)   (E) (5)

19. If Hank joins the group, and if he is shorter than Gina, then which of the following must be true?
- (A) Hank is taller than Drew.
- (B) Clem is shorter than Hank.
- (C) Hank is shorter than Ellen.
- (D) Hank is taller than Ann.
- (E) Bill is taller than Hank.

20. If Fran and Ann are the same height, then which of the following must be true?
(A)   Gina is taller than Ellen.
(B)   Ann is taller than Ellen.
(C)   Gina is taller than Fran.
(D)   Gina and Ellen are the same height.
(E)   Fran is taller than Bill.

Questions 21–24

A researcher is experimenting with breeding four different groups of minks: A, B, C, and D. The researcher's initial results are consistent and indicate the following:

If a male and female from the same group breed, all of the offspring are from that group.

If a male and female from different groups breed, the male offspring is always from the same group as the male parent, but the female offspring is not always from the same group as the female parent.

The offspring of a group must be members of either the father's or mother's group.

The offspring of a male C and a female B is never a C.

The offspring of a male A and a female C must be a female C.

The offspring of a male B and a female C must be a female C.

A's and B's will not breed together.

C's and D's will not breed together.

A female D will only breed with a male A.

21. The first-generation offspring of a female C could breed with all of the members of which of the following groups EXCEPT
(A)   A, B   (B) A, C   (C) A, D   (D) B, C   (E) A, B, C

22. If the second-generation offspring of a male A is a male A, then the initial male parent could NOT have bred with
(A)   the offspring of a female A
(B)   a second-generation offspring of a female D
(C)   the offspring of a female C
(D)   a second-generation offspring of a female A
(E)   a female D

23. The first-generation female offspring of a male C and a female B may breed with any of the following EXCEPT
(A)   a male C   (B) the second-generation offspring of a female A
(C)   the first-generation offspring of a female D   (D) a male D   (E) a male A

24. If a male A and a female D breed, which of the following must be true?
(A)   The first-generation offspring is a C.
(B)   The second-generation male offspring of a male A is an A.
(C)   The first-generation offspring is a B.
(D)   The second-generation female offspring is a B.
(E)   The second-generation male offspring is a D.

STOP

END OF MULTIPLE-CHOICE EXAMINATION. IF YOU FINISH BEFORE TIME IS UP, CHECK YOUR WORK ON THIS SECTION ONLY. DO NOT GO BACK TO ANY OTHER SECTION OF THE EXAMINATION.

EXAMINATION

WRITING SAMPLE

Time—30 Minutes

Directions:
You have 30 minutes to write an essay in response to a given topic. Take a few minutes to plan your work before you begin writing. DO NOT WRITE ON A TOPIC OF YOUR OWN CHOICE. ESSAYS THAT DO NOT ADDRESS THE GIVEN TOPIC ARE UNACCEPTABLE.

The quality of your writing is more important than the length of your response or the content. Pay attention to organization, appropriate diction, and correct usage. You will not be expected to display any specialized knowledge in your response, nor will you be expected to write a "perfect" essay; law schools understand that you are writing under a time constraint, and will allow for the minor lapses in writing ability that might occur under this circumstance.

Only the lined area in your booklet will be reproduced for the law schools, so do not write outside this space. *Do not* skip lines or use wide margins. These precautions, along with careful planning and legible handwriting that is not unduly large, will keep you within the allowed space.

SAMPLE TOPIC:

Read the following descriptions of Basil and Nottingham, two finalists for the position of curator at the Museum of Modern Art. *Then, in the space provided, write an argument for hiring either Basil or Nottingham.* The following criteria are relevant to your decision:
- The curator must acquire valuable artworks, design their display, and maintain museum security.
- Acquiring artworks will often require international travel and a talent for negotiating with collectors worldwide.

BASIL was educated at Oxford University, where he studied foreign cultures and languages in preparation for a career in the British diplomatic corps. A sizable family inheritance has allowed him to purchase, over the years, one of the world's largest and most valuable collections of Renaissance sculpture. Those visiting his home marvel at the unobtrusiveness of the sculptures on display there; a London art critic recently noted that "each sculpture seems an integral part of the room in which it is placed." Not one piece of Basil's personal collection has ever been stolen, even though he is often away on foreign travel, and his country home is not equipped with burglar alarms.

NOTTINGHAM'S family moved from England to Italy, where his father took a post with the Vatican security force, when Nottingham was only a child. Although he was surrounded by great works by the traditional masters, Nottingham became more interested in experimental artwork—especially painting—and while studying modern art at the University of Rome, he began painting surrealistic landscapes that quickly gained public attention. In the twelve years since his graduation, Nottingham has been recognized as a productive and controversial artist, one whose abstract paintings are representative of the fragmentation and confusion of modern life. Galleries throughout Italy show Nottingham's paintings often, with the artist himself personally supervising every showing.

ANSWER KEY

Section I: Analytical Reasoning	Section II: Logical Reasoning	Section III: Logical Reasoning	Section IV: Reading Comprehension	Section V: Analytical Reasoning
1. C	1. B	1. C	1. A	1. D
2. E	2. E	2. B	2. A	2. C
3. B	3. D	3. E	3. A	3. B
4. A	4. A	4. E	4. A	4. E
5. E	5. C	5. D	5. A	5. C
6. D	6. D	6. A	6. D	6. E
7. B	7. B	7. A	7. E	7. D
8. E	8. B	8. E	8. C	8. B
9. A	9. A	9. C	9. A	9. B
10. A	10. A	10. B	10. C	10. E
11. B	11. E	11. C	11. E	11. D
12. B	12. E	12. C	12. D	12. E
13. C	13. D	13. E	13. B	13. C
14. E	14. D	14. E	14. E	14. B
15. E	15. A	15. A	15. D	15. C
16. D	16. E	16. B	16. E	16. D
17. E	17. D	17. D	17. C	17. B
18. D	18. C	18. B	18. D	18. B
19. B	19. A	19. E	19. A	19. E
20. D	20. D	20. C	20. C	20. B
21. D	21. D	21. D	21. B	21. C
22. D	22. C	22. D	22. A	22. C
23. B	23. D	23. A	23. C	23. E
24. B	24. A	24. A	24. A	24. B
	25. D	25. D	25. B	
	26. C		26. D	
			27. E	
			28. D	

MODEL TEST ANALYSIS

Doing model exams and understanding the explanations afterwards are of course important in acquainting you with typical LSAT question types and successful approaches to the questions. However, another benefit of carefully analyzing these model tests is to understand the kinds of errors you are making and thus work to minimize them. For instance, if a very high percentage of your incorrect answers is due to "careless error" or "misread problem," then perhaps you are working much too fast and should slow your pace accordingly. If your incorrect answers are due primarily to "lack of knowledge," then a careful rereading and reworking of the appropriate question-type chapter may be in order. Or if you find that you aren't completing a large number of questions because of lack of time, you may need to either increase your speed or learn to use the "one-check, two-check" technique more effectively.

This kind of analysis of the model tests will enable you to identify your particular weaknesses and thus remedy them.

Model Test Four Analysis

Section	Total Number of Questions	Number Correct	Number Incorrect	Number Unanswered*
I: Analytical Reasoning	24			
II: Logical Reasoning	26			
III: Logical Reasoning	25			
IV: Reading Comprehension	28			
V: Analytical Reasoning	24			
TOTALS:	127			

*At this stage in your preparation, you should not be leaving any blank answer spaces. At least fill in a guess, as there is no penalty for a wrong answer.

Reasons for Incorrect Answers

You may wish to evaluate the explanations before completing this chart.

Section	Total Number Incorrect	Lack of Knowledge	Misread Problem	Careless Error	Unanswered or Wrong Guess
I: Analytical Reasoning					
II: Logical Reasoning					
III: Logical Reasoning					
IV: Reading Comprehension					
V: Analytical Reasoning					
TOTALS:					

EXPLANATIONS OF ANSWERS

Section I

Answers 1–6

You could have come up with the following diagram:

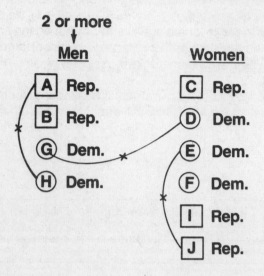

We will use the following more formal chart to actually show you the possibilities for each question:

	—Men—			—Women—					
—Rep.—	Dem.			—Dem.—			—Rep.—		
B	A	H	G	D	F	E	J	I	C
Question 1.	?	n	y	y	n	y	y	n		
	y	n	y	n	y	y	y	n		
Question 2.	y	n	y	y	n		n	y		
Question 3.	n	n	y	y	n	y	?	?	y	y
Question 4.	y	y	n	n	y	y	n	y		
Question 5.	y	y	n	n	y	y	n	y		
Question 6.	y	y	n		y	n	y	y	y	n

1. **C** There are five Democrats. D and G cannot serve at the same time. Thus H, E, and F must be selected. If H is selected, A cannot be selected. If D is selected and G is not, then B must be selected since there must be two men on the committee. But if G is selected and D is not, then B does not have to be selected.

2. **E** If H is selected then A is not. If G is selected then D is not. If J is selected then E is not. This leaves F, I, and C to fill the other two slots on the committee. If I is not selected, then the other two must be.

3. **B** If A and B cannot be selected, then G and H must be selected since there must be two men on the committee. If G is selected then D cannot be selected. This leaves F, E, J, I, and C to fill the remaining four slots. Since E and J cannot both be selected, the other three must be selected. E or J must be selected, but we do not know which one.

4. **A** If G and H cannot be selected, then A and B must be selected since there must be at least two men on the committee. If J is selected, then E cannot be selected. This leaves D, F, I, and C to fill the other three slots on the committee. Both I and C cannot be selected since this would make five Republicans on the committee.

5. **E** If J is selected then E is not. If D is selected then G is not. Therefore both A and B must be selected since there must be two men on the committee. This leaves F, I, and C to fill the other two slots. Both I and C cannot be selected since that would place five Republicans on the committee. This means only one of them can be selected. This forces F to be selected.

6. **D** If A is selected then H is not. If J is selected then E is not. C cannot be selected since that would make five Republicans on the committee. This leaves G, D, and F to fill the other two slots. Since G and D cannot both be selected, F must be selected.

Answers 7–12

Note: UPPER-case letters denote fixed positions. Lower-case letters denote various possibilities.

7. **B**

1	2	3	4	5
c/d	E	A	B	d/c

Since E, A, and B cannot be 1st or 5th, their places are fixed. Thus, only (B) is true.

8. **E**

1	2	3	4	5
C	e	a	b	D
	a	e	b	
	a	b	e	

(A) is always true. (B) could be true. (C) could be true. (D) is always true. (E) can't be true. Thus the answer is (E), because if A finishes 4th, B would have to finish 5th.

9. **A**

1	2	3	4	5
c/d	A	B	E	d/c

Since B finishes ahead of E, we have A, B, and E in fixed positions. Since we do not know the positions of C and D, (C), (D), and (E) are false. (B) is false, since B is 3rd and not 4th. (A) is true.

10. **A**

1	2	3	4	5
D	a/e	e/a	B	C

Since A finishes ahead of B, B cannot finish 2nd. Thus, B must finish 4th, C finishes 5th, and D finishes 1st.

11. **B**

1	2	3	4	5	6
c/d	a/e	e/a	F	B	d/c

(A), (C), and (D) are all true from observation. (B) is false since we cannot determine the exact positions of C and D. (E) could be false.

12. **B**

1	2	3	4	5	6
D	E	A	B	F	C

This is the only arrangement that is possible based on the facts. From this arrangement, we see that B finishes 4th.

Answers 13–18

Drawing the simple diagram below will help answer the questions.

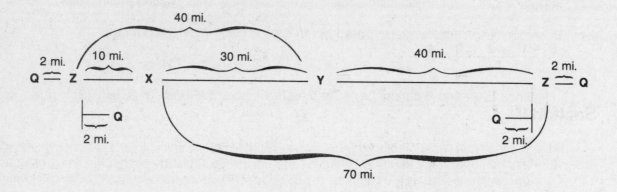

13. **C** Since Z is 40 miles from Y, and X is 30 miles from Y, Z could be 10 miles from X (left side of diagram).

14. **E** Q may be either 38 or 42 miles from Y, and either 68 or 8 miles from X. City Q may not be 38 miles from city X.

15. **E** If city Q is 12 miles from X, Q must be situated at the extreme left side of the diagram above. Therefore Z must be 10 miles from city X.

16. **D** XQZY may not be a possible order because Q may not come between X and Y.

17. **E** If a traveler begins at X and ends at Q, he may possibly only travel 8 miles, directly to Q without passing through any other city.

18. **D** By adding M 5 miles on either side of Y, all of the choices could be true, with the exception of D.

Answers 19–24

The following drawing shows the relationships:

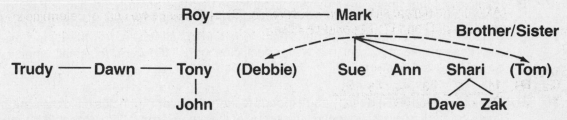

19. **B** We see that Tony is Mark's nephew. We do not know of any more.

20. **D** Since Dawn and Tony are brother and sister, their children are cousins.

21. **D** John's grandfather Roy is Ann's uncle. No relationship in age between Trudy and Zak has been shown. Since Debbie and Tom are brother and sister, John is Tom's nephew.

22. **D** If Sue has two children, then Dave could have three cousins: Sue's two children (1st cousins) and John (2nd cousin).

23. **B** Since Zak is Shari's son, and Shari is Mark's daughter, Mark is Zak's grandfather.

24. **B** From the information given, Dave has three aunts; Ann, Sue, and Debbie.

Section II

1. **B** The passage states, "Those under…18…account for nearly half of the arrests for the seven major crimes….Yet…courts are obliged to treat these young hard-core hoodlums…" (A) is a close answer; however, the author is not pointing out that crime has increased, but that violent crime has become more disproportionate.

2. **E** All of the following except (E) are assumed by the author. He would not rely on statistical trend lines if they were not accurate predictors (A). If the years from 1967 to 1976 were abnormal years, his statistics would be suspect (B). He finally makes a statement grouping the laws in most states as handling juveniles in the same manner and leniently (C) and (D). He does not address juveniles and nonviolent crime (E).

3. **D** If the FBI's national statistics are inaccurate, then violent juvenile crime may not be disproportionate, thus nullifying the argument. (E) is a close answer, as this would also weaken the argument, but not as significantly as (D).

4. **A** If "chores" is plural and "more" takes at least an hour to complete, there must be at least two one-hour chores.

5. **C** If Juan ends up with more marbles than Alvin, that means that Alvin must have less than five marbles. If Maria can end up with more marbles than Juan, then Juan must also have less than five marbles. We do not know how many marbles Maria has. Thus, (C) is false.

6. **D** (B) and (E) weaken the argument, (A) repeats the argument, and (C) makes no sense, since "average height" is a *single* composite of all heights.

7. **B** Pointing out that "there are too many variables in this type of study" weakens the argument tremendously, because isolating the reason for the growth increase now becomes very difficult. Thus, we could not deduce that modern foods stimulate growth. (D) is close, as it also weakens the argument, but it isn't specific enough. If (D) were "*too* small," then it would be an excellent answer.

8. **B** The information in (B) directly corresponds to the "significant" conclusion in the paragraph's final sentence. (A) is beyond the time scope of the paragraph; (C) is untenable because the final sentence states that accidents are not characteristic of advanced years. There is no evidence in the paragraph which supports (D) or (E).

9. **A** All of the statements except (A) are solidly supported by a comparison of the "cause lists" for 1900, 1910, and 1945. (A) is a conclusion that may be true, but it is not an issue the paragraph raises.

10. **A** We are not provided with an implicit or explicit clue to what the temptation is, but we are told that it occurs late (B), has a bitter effect (C), is caused by fate (D), and is "supremely" important (E).

11. **E** The passage states that 90 percent of our mind controls 95 percent of our behavior, thus implying that the other 10 percent of our mind controls 5 percent of our behavior. The passage does not state or imply that "dreams, spontaneous recall, and slips of speech constitute about 90 percent of our behavior."

12. **E** The passage states that 90 percent of our mind controls 95 percent of our behavior; therefore, a small part of our mind controls a small part of our behavior, as the other 10 percent of our mind must control 5 percent of our behavior.

13. **D** The passage makes no comment on the majority of a teacher's students.

14. **D** (B), "irrelevant," and (E), "simplistic," are inconsistent with the implied importance of the statement. (C) does not advance the argument; it merely supplies obvious synonyms for language and thought. (A) is self-contradictory; something is not likely to be at once logical *and* obscure.

15. **A** Since the passage is all about the unsolved misunderstanding of the relation between language and thought, its subject remains, of course, ambiguous.

16. **E** The passage begins with a sentence about the value of on-the-job training, but leaves that topic rather than developing it. The implication of this first sentence is that on-the-job training has just been discussed, thus allowing a transition to consequent topics.

17. **D** This choice summarizes the argument of the paragraph. (A) contradicts the "two-sidedness" of lying that the author explains; (B) and (E) are unsupported conclusions; and (C) is an overstatement because it employs "only."

18. **C** Neither (A) nor (B) is implied, because no comparison is made with other brands of soap. Nor is (D) correct because there is no implication regarding what is economically the best value or price. And though the advertisement states that Cleenup is good for household jobs, it doesn't infer that household chores are its only range. That Cleenup Soap may be used for scouring pots and pans, whitening the sink, and performing other household chores indicates that it can be used for many cleaning jobs (C).

19. **A** The renter's third statement contradicts his second statement.

20. **D** The notion that "the need for ostentation is a universal species characteristic" has "no rational basis." According to the professional economist, "the craving for personal distinction" is fostered by propaganda and so-called good breeding (A) and its effects cannot be eradicated. The writer does not imply that the economist's assumption is fostered by the same influences.

21. **D** The author sets out to demonstrate this thesis by attacking the validity of the two assumptions made by those who oppose his view and who believe ostentation is either a natural right or an unavoidable impulse in man.

22. **C** (C) is the correct choice, since it contradicts the original statement. (A), (D), and (E) are obviously incorrect; they do not have anything to do with the problem. (B) would tend to strengthen the argument.

23. **D** The fact that Lasch's book is a best-seller has nothing to do with his similarity to Aesop, at least not in the context of this passage. Each of the other choices reinforces or clarifies the comparison.

24. **A** Dr. Graham is not given a full name, and we are not told anything beyond the mention of his evangelical spirit. Therefore, we must conclude that the author is writing to an audience already familiar with the identity and significance of Dr. Graham. Each of the other choices is a possible but not necessary underlying assumption.

25. **D** The author stresses the nice qualities of "folks who cling to the past" (in other words, "the enemies of the future") (A) contradicts the author's viewpoint, and the other choices provide irrelevant or unsubstantiated conclusions.

26. **C** This choice ties reduced nuclear proliferation to arms reduction by the United States and the USSR, thus weakening the author's argument that proliferation and arms control are separate issues. (D) strengthens the argument. (A), (B), and (E) are tangential if not irrelevant.

Section III

1. **C** Be sure not to confuse "Only a…" with "All…." If only a cuddly toy is safe, any toy that is safe must be cuddly.

2. **B** The connective "but" alerts the reader to a contrast, an expression of disapproval. Option (C) is illogical, and (D) and (E) are issues that the passage has not touched upon. Between (A) and (B), (B) is the more likely since the pollution generated on land is 80 percent of the total.

3. **E** (A) is not necessarily true; it could be Wednesday. (B) is not necessarily true; the weather could be bad or it could be Thursday. (C) would be true only if it is Monday, of which we cannot be certain. (D) does not follow; it could be any day. If the band practices in good weather on Tuesdays and the weather is good and the band is not practicing, it cannot be Tuesday.

4. **E** The last sentence, unlike the rest of the paragraph, suggests that the nuclear threat was greater in the past.

5. **D** The passage argues that new construction will flourish if rent controls are abolished. All of the other choices are assumptions the author makes.

6. **A** A shortage of low-cost housing supports the author's claim of a "dire shortage," but (B) does not. If the population is declining (C), the housing shortage should diminish. (D) and (E) contradict the argument that rent control causes the housing shortage or the lack of building new units.

7. **E** (A), (B), (C), and (D) are plausible, but to convert more rental units to condominiums would only increase the shortage of available units for rent.

8. **E** If the women taking the tests had studied less math and science, the disparity in grades would be more likely to be due to this difference than to a bias of the test.

9. **C** The pattern is "all the 1 in this 2 are 3; therefore this 2 uses only 3, 1."

10. **B** The situation described makes it impossible for a councilman to continue to be elected. Only by finding an alternative way of funding the railway could a politician avoid defeat.

11. **C** The first paragraph describes the costs, while the second discusses some possible benefits for businesses.

12. **C** The "liabilities" of the legislation are the high costs enumerated in paragraph 1; the "benefits" are those described in the second paragraph.

13. **E** David does not live in an apartment, may or may not be suspicious, and must be thin.

14. **E** Like David, Jane does not live in an apartment, may or may not be suspicious, and is thin.

15. **A** The results of the two different studies both point to the possibility suggested in choice (A).

16. **B** The first sentence presents a benefit of the initiative process, while the second and third sentences criticize initiative campaigns.

17. **D** Dave has not presented high-fiber foods as a cause of weight loss in themselves, but Jane has assumed that he has.

18. **B** The series of questions is based upon the reports of those who claim to have seen UFOs or their inhabitants.

19. **E** The evidence that this author cites *is* relevant to the conclusions. Although this may not be the only evidence to support the author's conclusions, the author is using the observations as a basis for the conclusions. (E) states that the evidence is irrelevant to the conclusions. Thus (E) is false. Choices (A), (B), (C), and (D) are all true with regard to the evidence given.

20. **C** Jack has confused "all" and "only." Compare question 1.

21. **D** If by awarding grants to a wider range of universities the NSF is able to develop new world-class research institutions, there is good reason to do so.

22. **D** The second paragraph questions the economic benefits of the politicization of the awards, but this example supports the case for economic development as a consequence of science centers.

23. **A** (A) follows logically, but we cannot know certainly from the passage if (B), (C), (D), and (E) are true or false.

24. **A** The passage compares banning smoking and banning cars.

25. **D** If restaurants in cities that have banned smoking have not lost money, health reasons would appear to prevail, as the economic arguments no longer apply.

Section IV

Passage 1

1. **A** A definition of existentialism cannot be pithy (short, brief) because the process of full definition "would involve several volumes" (paragraph 1).

2. **C** Paragraph 1 states, "Central to each definition is the assertion that existentialism is a theory or statement about the nature of man's existence."

3. **A** According to paragraph 4, "The existentialist deliberately…rejects traditional ranges of meaning."

4. **E** In paragraph 4, the writer claims that each existentialist creates his own range of meanings of words.

5. **A** Paragraph 1 states that each dictionary definition of existentialism "carries some degree of truth."

6. **D** The passage as a whole deals with problems and approaches to defining existentialism. (A) is too general; (B), (C), and (E) are too specific.

7. **E** Paragraph 3 lists all the terms except (E) as alternatives.

8. **C** According to paragraph 4, the existentialist rejects traditional meanings of words and often "uses words in an opposite sense."

Passage 2

9. **A** The passage makes the author's support of the abandonment of the felony-murder rule. Options (B) and (C) are true but are not the central idea of the passage. The passage makes no recommendations on Supreme Court actions.

10. **C** The best answer here is to deter the use of deadly force in felonies.

11. **E** Each of choices (A), (B), (C), and (D) can be cited to support the felony murder rule.

12. **D** All of the arguments except (D), which supports the rule, have been made against the felony-murder rule.

13. **B** Because death does not occur in (B), the felony-murder rule would not apply. It could be used in the other cases.

14. **E** The next-to-last paragraph makes clear that California has not yet wholly abandoned the rule.

15. **D** The author uses "bizarre and unfair" to describe the results often achieved by the law, but not to describe the law itself. In the final sentence of the next-to-last paragraph he explicitly objects to the equating of the intent to commit murder with "the mere intent to commit the underlying felony."

Passage 3

16. **E**   Each of the first four cases is public or quasi-public land. The last is private, not likely to be open to the general public and therefore the owner may deny free speech on the property.

17. **C**   In this instance, the property is clearly private; in the other cases, it is not always clear whether the property is public or private.

18. **D**   The nature or character of the owner of the property is not a factor mentioned by the passage. All of the four other options are alluded to in the opening paragraphs of the passage.

19. **A**   The author quarrels with the Supreme Court's finding and argues that the decision "is difficult to justify" and that the mall is rapidly becoming "the core of the community."

20. **C**   So long as the Court finds that a shopping center is not the equivalent of a municipality, the issue of free speech is not relevant in that the owner's actions are private conduct.

21. **B**   The passage cites Lord Chief Justice Hale's remarks of 1675. (C) and (D) are false and the passage does not discuss current practice in Canada and Great Britain (E).

22. **A**   The passage concludes with Justice Black's remarks on the "preferred position" of First Amendment freedoms.

Passage 4

23. **C**   Although the passage discusses French taste to an extent, this is done only to further expand and clarify the overall comparison between Englishmen and Americans. The author does not really argue that Englishmen are better than Americans (E); he mentions the good and bad points of both nationalities.

24. **A**   When the author talks of American aspirations, he notes that Americans are always "fearful of a fall." When he calls aspiring Americans "dizzy" (B), he is speaking metaphorically rather than literally.

25. **B**   The author explicitly "detests" French taste, but notes that "the world is against me."

26. **D**   The passage ends with a discussion of taste, the third of four contrasting characteristics introduced. Politics is not discussed. Each of the other choices is a characteristic mentioned in the passage.

27. **E**   Each of the other choices in the passage is associated with a *discomfort* of French taste.

28. **D**   In this final section, the author justifies his assertion that the English and Americans differ in tastes by stressing that English taste is not taking the "direction" of American taste, that is, closer to French taste. (C) is a characteristic mentioned at an earlier point in the passage.

Section V

Answers 1–7

From the information given, the following chart may be drawn to help you to answer the questions:

	L	A	Dr.	P.O.	C.D.
Kelly	√	X	X	X	X
Clyde	X		X		X
Roland	X			X	X
Fred	X	X			X
Harriet	X	X	X	X	√

Note the following: In statement (2), since Kelly is *not* the doctor [see statement (1)], then Fred cannot be the accountant. And in statement (4), since Harriet is not the lawyer [see statement (6)], then Clyde cannot be the doctor.

1. **D** From our chart we can see that the only persons left to be the accountant, the doctor, and the police officer are Clyde, Roland, and Fred.

2. **C** From the chart we can see that Clyde is not the lawyer, the doctor, or the cab driver.

3. **B** If Roland is the doctor, then from our chart we can see that Fred must be the police officer, and thus Clyde must be the accountant.

4. **E** If Clyde is not the accountant, he must be the police officer. Therefore Fred must be the doctor, leaving Roland to be the accountant.

5. **C** If Fred is the police officer, then Clyde must be the accountant.

6. **E** The doctor could be either Roland or Fred.

7. **D** If the cab driver, the lawyer, and the accountant are in the cab, then Harriet (cab driver) and Kelly (lawyer) are definitely in the cab. Since the accountant is either Clyde or Roland, then either of them *could* possibly be also in the cab. Thus, the answer is Harriet, Roland, and Kelly.

Answers 8–14

Drawing a simple diagram will help answer the questions. Note, however, that there are several possible diagrams. First, since three of the women are together at one end of the line, these women could be at either the beginning or the end:

W	W	W								
1	2	3	4	5	6	7	8	9	10	11
								W	W	W

Then note that, since a man never stands next to another man, there can only be two possible arrangements of men for each of the above arrangements of women:

W	W	W	M	W/C	M/C	C/C	C/C	C/M	C/W	M
1	2	3	4	5	6	7	8	9	10	11
M	W/C	M/C	C/C	C/C	C/M	C/W	M	W	W	W

Now the questions are more easily answered.

8. **B** Note that if a child is in the sixth place (the middle four possible arrangements) then a woman must be in the second place.

9. **B** Since the rules state that three of the women stand next to each other at one end of the line, then a woman must be either second or tenth (second to last).

10. **E** All of the choices must be true except choice (E). If a woman is third, a child could be sixth, as in the second arrangement.

11. **D** If a girl is second and a boy is third, it can only be the fourth arrangement (the bottom arrangement) because that is the only time children are in the second and third positions. Since the other two children are in the fourth and fifth positions, the two girls cannot be next to each other.

12. **E** If a boy is eighth, we may consider both the first and second arrangements. Therefore, a man could be last (in fact, he must be last) and a girl could be tenth.

13. **C** If a man is fourth, we may consider the first and second arrangements. Therefore, women *must* be in the first and second positions.

14. **B** If each man is next to at least one woman, we may rule out the first and fourth arrangements. Therefore, considering the other two arrangements, only that a woman is second must necessarily be true.

Answers 15–20

15. **C** First we draw a diagram to show the height comparisons:

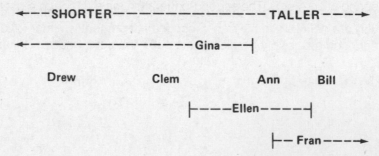

We see Drew is shorter than Ann. Therefore, (C) is false. Also, Fran and Ellen COULD be taller or shorter than Ann.

16. **D** Since Fran is taller than Ellen and Ellen is taller than Clem, Fran is taller than Clem.

17. **B** Since Fran is taller than Ellen, and if Ellen is taller than Ann, then Fran must be taller than Ann.

18. **B** From statement (3) Drew is shorter than Ann. From statement (1) Ann is shorter than Bill. It follows that Drew is shorter than Bill.

19. **E** (A), (B), (C), and (D) are false by inspecting the chart. Only (E) can be deduced.

20. **B** Since Fran is taller than Ellen, Ann must also be taller than Ellen. Since Gina is shorter than Ann, Gina must be shorter than Fran too. No relationship has been established between Gina and Ellen. Since Ann is shorter than Bill, Fran is shorter than Bill.

Answers 21–24

From the information given, you could have constructed a simple connection diagram as follows:

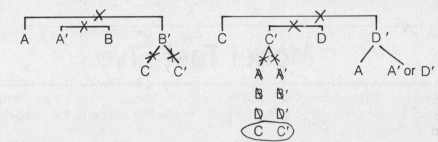

Letters with primes (such as A′) denote females. Letters without primes denote males.

21. **C** From the diagram, the first-generation offspring of a female C must be a C. A C cannot breed with a D.

22. **C** From the information given, the male parent must be an A. The offspring of a female C is a C, therefore the male parent of a male A could not have bred with a female C.

23. **E** From the diagram, the first-generation female offspring of a male C and a female B must be a B, because she can't be a C. A female C cannot breed with a male A.

24. **B** From the diagram, if a male A and a female D breed, then the male offspring is an A and the female offspring is an A or D. The second-generation male offspring must therefore be an A.

Chapter

10

Model Test Five

This chapter contains full-length Model Test Five. It is geared to the format of the LSAT, and it is complete with answers and explanations. It is equivalent to the LSAT in question structure, number of questions, level of difficulty, and time allotments. (The questions used are not taken directly from the LSAT, as those questions are copyrighted and may not be reproduced.)

Model Test Five should be taken under strict test conditions. The test ends with a 30-minute Writing Sample, which is not scored.

Section	Description	Number of Questions	Time Allowed
I	Analytical Reasoning	24	35 minutes
II	Reading Comprehension	26	35 minutes
III	Logical Reasoning	26	35 minutes
IV	Analytical Reasoning	24	35 minutes
V	Logical Reasoning	25	35 minutes
	Writing Sample		30 minutes
TOTALS:		125	3 hours 25 minutes

Now please turn to the next page, remove your answer sheets, and begin Model Test Five.

ANSWER SHEET—MODEL TEST FIVE
LAW SCHOOL ADMISSION TEST (LSAT)

Section I:
Analytical Reasoning

1. Ⓐ Ⓑ Ⓒ Ⓓ Ⓔ
2. Ⓐ Ⓑ Ⓒ Ⓓ Ⓔ
3. Ⓐ Ⓑ Ⓒ Ⓓ Ⓔ
4. Ⓐ Ⓑ Ⓒ Ⓓ Ⓔ
5. Ⓐ Ⓑ Ⓒ Ⓓ Ⓔ
6. Ⓐ Ⓑ Ⓒ Ⓓ Ⓔ
7. Ⓐ Ⓑ Ⓒ Ⓓ Ⓔ
8. Ⓐ Ⓑ Ⓒ Ⓓ Ⓔ
9. Ⓐ Ⓑ Ⓒ Ⓓ Ⓔ
10. Ⓐ Ⓑ Ⓒ Ⓓ Ⓔ
11. Ⓐ Ⓑ Ⓒ Ⓓ Ⓔ
12. Ⓐ Ⓑ Ⓒ Ⓓ Ⓔ
13. Ⓐ Ⓑ Ⓒ Ⓓ Ⓔ
14. Ⓐ Ⓑ Ⓒ Ⓓ Ⓔ
15. Ⓐ Ⓑ Ⓒ Ⓓ Ⓔ
16. Ⓐ Ⓑ Ⓒ Ⓓ Ⓔ
17. Ⓐ Ⓑ Ⓒ Ⓓ Ⓔ
18. Ⓐ Ⓑ Ⓒ Ⓓ Ⓔ
19. Ⓐ Ⓑ Ⓒ Ⓓ Ⓔ
20. Ⓐ Ⓑ Ⓒ Ⓓ Ⓔ
21. Ⓐ Ⓓ Ⓒ Ⓓ Ⓔ
22. Ⓐ Ⓑ Ⓒ Ⓓ Ⓔ
23. Ⓐ Ⓑ Ⓒ Ⓓ Ⓔ
24. Ⓐ Ⓑ Ⓒ Ⓓ Ⓔ

Section II:
Reading Comprehension

1. Ⓐ Ⓑ Ⓒ Ⓓ Ⓔ
2. Ⓐ Ⓑ Ⓒ Ⓓ Ⓔ
3. Ⓐ Ⓑ Ⓒ Ⓓ Ⓔ
4. Ⓐ Ⓑ Ⓒ Ⓓ Ⓔ
5. Ⓐ Ⓑ Ⓒ Ⓓ Ⓔ
6. Ⓐ Ⓑ Ⓒ Ⓓ Ⓔ
7. Ⓐ Ⓑ Ⓒ Ⓓ Ⓔ
8. Ⓐ Ⓑ Ⓒ Ⓓ Ⓔ
9. Ⓐ Ⓑ Ⓒ Ⓓ Ⓔ
10. Ⓐ Ⓑ Ⓒ Ⓓ Ⓔ
11. Ⓐ Ⓑ Ⓒ Ⓓ Ⓔ
12. Ⓐ Ⓑ Ⓒ Ⓓ Ⓔ
13. Ⓐ Ⓑ Ⓒ Ⓓ Ⓔ
14. Ⓐ Ⓑ Ⓒ Ⓓ Ⓔ
15. Ⓐ Ⓑ Ⓒ Ⓓ Ⓔ
16. Ⓐ Ⓑ Ⓒ Ⓓ Ⓔ
17. Ⓐ Ⓑ Ⓒ Ⓓ Ⓔ
18. Ⓐ Ⓑ Ⓒ Ⓓ Ⓔ
19. Ⓐ Ⓑ Ⓒ Ⓓ Ⓔ
20. Ⓐ Ⓑ Ⓒ Ⓓ Ⓔ
21. Ⓐ Ⓑ Ⓒ Ⓓ Ⓔ
22. Ⓐ Ⓑ Ⓒ Ⓓ Ⓔ
23. Ⓐ Ⓑ Ⓒ Ⓓ Ⓔ
24. Ⓐ Ⓑ Ⓒ Ⓓ Ⓔ
25. Ⓐ Ⓑ Ⓒ Ⓓ Ⓔ
26. Ⓐ Ⓑ Ⓒ Ⓓ Ⓔ

Section III:
Logical Reasoning

1. Ⓐ Ⓑ Ⓒ Ⓓ Ⓔ
2. Ⓐ Ⓑ Ⓒ Ⓓ Ⓔ
3. Ⓐ Ⓑ Ⓒ Ⓓ Ⓔ
4. Ⓐ Ⓑ Ⓒ Ⓓ Ⓔ
5. Ⓐ Ⓑ Ⓒ Ⓓ Ⓔ
6. Ⓐ Ⓑ Ⓒ Ⓓ Ⓔ
7. Ⓐ Ⓑ Ⓒ Ⓓ Ⓔ
8. Ⓐ Ⓑ Ⓒ Ⓓ Ⓔ
9. Ⓐ Ⓑ Ⓒ Ⓓ Ⓔ
10. Ⓐ Ⓑ Ⓒ Ⓓ Ⓔ
11. Ⓐ Ⓑ Ⓒ Ⓓ Ⓔ
12. Ⓐ Ⓑ Ⓒ Ⓓ Ⓔ
13. Ⓐ Ⓑ Ⓒ Ⓓ Ⓔ
14. Ⓐ Ⓑ Ⓒ Ⓓ Ⓔ
15. Ⓐ Ⓑ Ⓒ Ⓓ Ⓔ
16. Ⓐ Ⓑ Ⓒ Ⓓ Ⓔ
17. Ⓐ Ⓑ Ⓒ Ⓓ Ⓔ
18. Ⓐ Ⓑ Ⓒ Ⓓ Ⓔ
19. Ⓐ Ⓑ Ⓒ Ⓓ Ⓔ
20. Ⓐ Ⓑ Ⓒ Ⓓ Ⓔ
21. Ⓐ Ⓑ Ⓒ Ⓓ Ⓔ
22. Ⓐ Ⓑ Ⓒ Ⓓ Ⓔ
23. Ⓐ Ⓑ Ⓒ Ⓓ Ⓔ
24. Ⓐ Ⓑ Ⓒ Ⓓ Ⓔ
25. Ⓐ Ⓑ Ⓒ Ⓓ Ⓔ
26. Ⓐ Ⓑ Ⓒ Ⓓ Ⓔ

ANSWER SHEET—MODEL TEST FIVE
LAW SCHOOL ADMISSION TEST (LSAT)

Section IV:
Analytical Reasoning

1. Ⓐ Ⓑ Ⓒ Ⓓ Ⓔ
2. Ⓐ Ⓑ Ⓒ Ⓓ Ⓔ
3. Ⓐ Ⓑ Ⓒ Ⓓ Ⓔ
4. Ⓐ Ⓑ Ⓒ Ⓓ Ⓔ
5. Ⓐ Ⓑ Ⓒ Ⓓ Ⓔ
6. Ⓐ Ⓑ Ⓒ Ⓓ Ⓔ
7. Ⓐ Ⓑ Ⓒ Ⓓ Ⓔ
8. Ⓐ Ⓑ Ⓒ Ⓓ Ⓔ
9. Ⓐ Ⓑ Ⓒ Ⓓ Ⓔ
10. Ⓐ Ⓑ Ⓒ Ⓓ Ⓔ
11. Ⓐ Ⓑ Ⓒ Ⓓ Ⓔ
12. Ⓐ Ⓑ Ⓒ Ⓓ Ⓔ
13. Ⓐ Ⓑ Ⓒ Ⓓ Ⓔ
14. Ⓐ Ⓑ Ⓒ Ⓓ Ⓔ
15. Ⓐ Ⓑ Ⓒ Ⓓ Ⓔ
16. Ⓐ Ⓑ Ⓒ Ⓓ Ⓔ
17. Ⓐ Ⓑ Ⓒ Ⓓ Ⓔ
18. Ⓐ Ⓑ Ⓒ Ⓓ Ⓔ
19. Ⓐ Ⓑ Ⓒ Ⓓ Ⓔ
20. Ⓐ Ⓑ Ⓒ Ⓓ Ⓔ
21. Ⓐ Ⓑ Ⓒ Ⓓ Ⓔ
22. Ⓐ Ⓑ Ⓒ Ⓓ Ⓔ
23. Ⓐ Ⓑ Ⓒ Ⓓ Ⓔ
24. Ⓐ Ⓑ Ⓒ Ⓓ Ⓔ

Section V:
Logical Reasoning

1. Ⓐ Ⓑ Ⓒ Ⓓ Ⓔ
2. Ⓐ Ⓑ Ⓒ Ⓓ Ⓔ
3. Ⓐ Ⓑ Ⓒ Ⓓ Ⓔ
4. Ⓐ Ⓑ Ⓒ Ⓓ Ⓔ
5. Ⓐ Ⓑ Ⓒ Ⓓ Ⓔ
6. Ⓐ Ⓑ Ⓒ Ⓓ Ⓔ
7. Ⓐ Ⓑ Ⓒ Ⓓ Ⓔ
8. Ⓐ Ⓑ Ⓒ Ⓓ Ⓔ
9. Ⓐ Ⓑ Ⓒ Ⓓ Ⓔ
10. Ⓐ Ⓑ Ⓒ Ⓓ Ⓔ
11. Ⓐ Ⓑ Ⓒ Ⓓ Ⓔ
12. Ⓐ Ⓑ Ⓒ Ⓓ Ⓔ
13. Ⓐ Ⓑ Ⓒ Ⓓ Ⓔ
14. Ⓐ Ⓑ Ⓒ Ⓓ Ⓔ
15. Ⓐ Ⓑ Ⓒ Ⓓ Ⓔ
16. Ⓐ Ⓑ Ⓒ Ⓓ Ⓔ
17. Ⓐ Ⓑ Ⓒ Ⓓ Ⓔ
18. Ⓐ Ⓑ Ⓒ Ⓓ Ⓔ
19. Ⓐ Ⓑ Ⓒ Ⓓ Ⓔ
20. Ⓐ Ⓑ Ⓒ Ⓓ Ⓔ
21. Ⓐ Ⓑ Ⓒ Ⓓ Ⓔ
22. Ⓐ Ⓑ Ⓒ Ⓓ Ⓔ
23. Ⓐ Ⓑ Ⓒ Ⓓ Ⓔ
24. Ⓐ Ⓑ Ⓒ Ⓓ Ⓔ
25. Ⓐ Ⓑ Ⓒ Ⓓ Ⓔ

SECTION I
ANALYTICAL REASONING

Directions:
In this section you will be given groups of questions based on different sets of conditions. Drawing a simple diagram may be helpful in answering some of the questions. You are to choose the best answer and mark the corresponding space on your answer sheet.

Questions 1–6

The Westlake Baseball All-Star team is lined up in a single row for a picture. The nine All-Stars consist of players from five different teams. There are three Panthers, two Badgers, two Rockets, one Cobra and one Viking. The positions in the picture are numbered left to right from 1 through 9.

The Viking is not next to a Rocket.
The two Rockets are separated by exactly three other players.
The three Panthers are located in not more than 5 consecutive positions in the line.
The Cobra is between the two Rockets.
The two Badgers are next to each other in line.

1. If the Viking is not between the two Rockets, and a Rocket is next to a Badger, then what position is NOT possible for the Cobra?
   - (A) 2
   - (B) 4
   - (C) 7
   - (D) 8
   - (E) 9

2. If the Viking is between the two Rockets and a Panther is first in line, then which of the following must be true?
   - (A) A Panther is 3rd in line.
   - (B) The Viking is 6th in line.
   - (C) The Cobra is 6th in line.
   - (D) A Badger is 7th in line.
   - (E) The Viking is 3rd in line.

3. If a Rocket is in position 2, how many possible positions are there for the Viking?
   - (A) 1   (B) 2   (C) 3   (D) 4   (E) 5

4. If the Viking is in position 3 and the Cobra is in position 8, then all of the following must be true EXCEPT that
   - (A) a Rocket is in position 5
   - (B) a Badger is in position 6
   - (C) a Panther is in position 4
   - (D) a Rocket is in position 9
   - (E) a Panther is next to the Viking

5. If the Viking is next to the Cobra, which of the following is false?
   - (A) The Viking is in an odd-numbered position.
   - (B) The three Panthers are not in consecutive positions.
   - (C) The Cobra is in an even-numbered position.
   - (D) A Badger is either first or last in line.
   - (E) A Badger is next to a Viking.

6. If a Badger is next to the Cobra, which of the following must be true?
   - (A) A Panther is in position 4.
   - (B) A Badger is in position 6.
   - (C) The Cobra is in position 2 or 8.
   - (D) A Badger is in position 3 or 7.
   - (E) A Rocket is in position 4 or 6.

Questions 7–12

Three men, A, B, and C, and three women, X, Y, and Z, are seated equally spaced around a round table.

X is C's sister.
B is Z's husband.
Y is A's mother.
B is sitting next to X.
A is sitting next to Y.
Z is sitting directly across from Y.

7. Which of the following could be true?
(A)   C sits next to X.
(B)   Z sits next to A.
(C)   Y sits next to B.
(D)   C sits next to Y.
(E)   B sits next to A.

8. If B sits next to his wife, who does C sit directly across from?
(A) A   (B) B   (C) X   (D) Y   (E) Z

9. If C sits directly across from his sister, which of the following must be true?
(A)   C sits next to X.
(B)   X sits next to A's mother.
(C)   A sits next to C's sister.
(D)   Y sits next to Z's husband.
(E)   Z sits next to X.

10. Which of the following must be true?
(A)   Y sits next to C.
(B)   X sits next to Z.
(C)   B sits next to Y.
(D)   A sits next to C.
(E)   B sits next to Z.

11. If X does not sit directly across from her brother, then C sits directly across from whom?
(A) A   (B) B   (C) X   (D) Y   (E) Z

12. How many women have a man sitting to their left?
(A) 0   (B) 1   (C) 2   (D) 3   (E) 4

Questions 13–18

Ron, Sharon, and Tom share an office and equipment. Their secretaries are, not necessarily respectively, Fran, George, and Hilda. In the office, there are three computers: a Comstar, a Doufast, and an Excellocalc. The three programs that run on the computers are a spreadsheet, database, and word processing program.

Not all three computers can run all three programs.

A program can only be run on one computer at a time.

Ron and Sharon do their own word processing, but have their secretaries do the spreadsheets and databases.

George won't use the Excellocalc.

Hilda uses only the Doufast.

The Doufast cannot run the database program.

Fran will not use the Comstar.

The Comstar cannot run the word processing program.

13. Which computer(s) could Sharon use for her own work?
(A) Comstar only
(B) Doufast only
(C) Excellocalc only
(D) Doufast or Excellocalc
(E) Comstar or Doufast

14. Which computer(s) can George use for word processing?
(A) Comstar
(B) Doufast
(C) Excellocalc
(D) Doufast or Excellocalc
(E) Comstar or Doufast

15. Which of the following must be true?
(A) Sharon does not use the Doufast.
(B) Fran won't use the database program.
(C) Ron does not use the Comstar.
(D) Hilda won't use the spreadsheet program.
(E) George does not use the Doufast.

16. If Tom's secretary uses the Comstar, which program(s) could they be using?
(A) word processing
(B) spreadsheet
(C) word processing or spreadsheet
(D) spreadsheet or database
(E) word processing or database

17. If George is Tom's secretary, which of the following must be true?
(A) Ron's secretary cannot use the Doufast.
(B) Sharon's secretary cannot use the Comstar.
(C) Ron's secretary cannot use the Excellocalc.
(D) Sharon's secretary cannot use the Excellocalc.
(E) Tom's secretary cannot use the Doufast.

18. If the Doufast is upgraded so it can run the database program and Tom's secretary will only use the Excellocalc, which of the following must be true?
(A) Hilda can use the Comstar.
(B) Fran is Tom's secretary.
(C) Ron's secretary can use the Excellocalc.
(D) The Doufast cannot run the spreadsheet program.
(E) Hilda won't use the Doufast.

Questions 19–24

The following information is known about a family:

Tom's son, Phil, has one son, Rich, and one daughter, Sonia.
Rich's maternal grandmother, Martha, has one sister, Cynthia, and one brother, Dave.
Sonia's paternal grandmother is named Doris.

19. It can be determined from the information given that one of Phil's parents is
(A) Dave   (B) Martha   (C) Sonia   (D) Doris   (E) Cynthia

20. How is Dave related to Phil's wife?
(A) brother   (B) father   (C) uncle   (D) son   (E) cousin

21. If Alice is Phil's wife, then which of the following is the proper relationship between Doris and Alice?
(A) Alice and Doris are sisters.
(B) Alice and Doris are cousins.
(C) Doris is the mother-in-law of Alice.
(D) Alice is the mother-in-law of Doris.
(E) Doris is the sister-in-law of Alice.

22. If Cynthia has a son, Wilson, Dave's father would be Wilson's
(A) uncle   (B) grandfather   (C) father   (D) cousin   (E) brother

23. If Phil has two brothers, Ted and John, how is Ted related to Sonia?
(A) grandson   (B) uncle   (C) cousin
(D) paternal grandfather   (E) maternal grandfather

24. Suppose Phil's wife is named Alice, and Alice's mother is married to Edgar. If Edgar has twin sisters, Helen and Hilda, then from the information given, the total number of aunts and uncles that Alice would have is
(A) 1   (B) 2   (C) 3   (D) 4   (E) 5

STOP

IF YOU FINISH BEFORE TIME IS UP, CHECK YOUR WORK ON THIS SECTION OF THE TEST ONLY.
DO NOT GO ON TO THE NEXT SECTION OF THE TEST UNTIL TIME IS UP FOR THIS SECTION.

SECTION II
READING COMPREHENSION

Directions:
Read the passages and answer the questions following each passage by blackening the appropriate space on the answer sheet. You may refer back to the passages when answering the questions. Answer all questions on the basis of what is stated or implied.

Passage 1

Literary periods are slippery concepts. When dates are established and cultural developments are outlined, predecessors and successors have a way of making them dissolve. One discovers that the Romantic Period in English literature so comfortably introduced as extending from 1800 to 1830 has a long Pre-Romantic development and that it really isn't over yet. The same thing is true of American literary history, perhaps more so. But if there is one date that seems to make a decisive cut in the continuity of twentieth-century America, it is probably the stock market crash at the end of October 1929. By 1930 reassessment was forced on the American consciousness.

The Twenties have a character of their own, an individualized and particularized decade for which there has come to be felt considerable nostalgia among the older generation. Clear memories can hardly regard these years as the good old days (this was the era of prohibition and gangsters), but one of the blessings of the human condition is the tendency to forget unpleasantness and remember what one chooses to remember. Perhaps even the Sixties will become a happy recollection in the twenty-first century.

Three major designations arose in the Twenties to define the Twenties as a cultural phenomenon: the Jazz Age, the Lost Generation, and the Wasteland—all with significant literary associations. Of them all the Jazz Age, as represented best in F. Scott Fitzgerald's fiction, was most clearly cut off by the stock market collapse and the ensuing depression. It is the period of the Twenties alone. But the Lost Generation (as proclaimed in the double epigraph from *Ecclesiastes* and Gertrude Stein in the 1926 *The Sun Also Rises*—"You are all a lost generation."—Gertrude Stein in conversation) continued to be lost in the Thirties. The uprootedness and disillusionment of the post-World War I fiction writers, many of whom had participated in that war and perhaps particularly of the Paris expatriate group including Hemingway, Elliot Paul, Henry Miller, and others, pursued them into the depression and beyond. The third term, the Wasteland, established by T. S. Eliot in his 1922 poem, had perhaps an even longer life; it has come to represent an age extending from the Twenties to 1945 and may indeed suggest the central features of the landscape of this larger period. The Wasteland poets, including Ezra Pound, Eliot himself, and possibly William Carlos Williams, Archibald MacLeish, and e. e. cummings, although many of them had written distinctive poetry even before 1920 and certainly before 1930, continued to develop and sharpen both their verse and their ideas into the Thirties and Forties. The Wasteland runs into and disappears in the Age of Anxiety.

This is one reason for the inclusion of such American writers as Gertrude Stein, Ezra Pound, T. S. Eliot, Williams, cummings, and Hemingway in the post-1930 Canon rather than in the pre-1930 one. They had all certainly made a mark in the literary world before 1930, but they were ahead of their time and made a larger and deeper mark after that date. This is true even for Gertrude Stein, who had only sixteen more years to live and who had begun her serious writing in the first decade of the twentieth century with *Things as They Are* (originally *Quod Erat Demonstrandum*) and *Three Lives* (1909). *Tender Buttons*, among her stylistically most radical work, appeared in 1914, and even *Four Saints in Three Acts* had been written and published in *transition* by 1929. But although she had been read and sought out by other writers like Sherwood Anderson and Hemingway, her initial impact on the public, even the most literate portion of it, probably did not come until the Thirties (and production of the Stein-Virgil Thomson opera, *Four Saints in Three Acts*) when people began to make fun of "A rose is a rose is a rose is a rose is" (often misquoting the lovely verse from *The World is Round*, a book for children) and the phrase from *Four Saints*, "Pigeons on the grass, alas." Gertrude Stein was always avant-garde and probably still is. Although T. S. Eliot became the most important single literary influence on Hart Crane, whose major creative period was over by 1930, again his greatest impact on a more general public had hardly begun. That half or third of his creative effort in verse drama did not get under way until the mid-Thirties.

It is in this fashion that American literature approaches the period which begins in 1930, trailing clouds of several impulses—some would say glory—as it comes. Realism and naturalism are by this time established as dominant modes, but antirealistic frames of reference like expressionism, surrealism, psychology, and religious ideology are also operative.

1. When the author says in the third paragraph, "It is the period of the Twenties alone," he probably means that
   (A) the Jazz Age was a phenomenon of the Twenties only
   (B) he will discuss the 1920s only
   (C) "it" is a synonym for "period"
   (D) the stock market crash and the depression occurred in the 1920s
   (E) the 1920s alone constituted a cultural phenomenon

2. At the beginning of paragraph 4, the term "Canon" probably means
   (A) canyon in the Wasteland
   (B) literary weaponry
   (C) catalogue
   (D) a list of saints
   (E) partnership

3. We may conclude that the author regards the 1960s as
   (A) a worse decade than the 1920s
   (B) a replica of the 1920s
   (C) a happy recollection
   (D) not the best of times
   (E) a political and artistic disaster

4. The author's extensive attention to Gertrude Stein is intended to stress that
   (A) she wrote much before her death in 1946
   (B) although many of her major works preceded 1930, her fame reached its height after 1930
   (C) she was a versatile writer, even in her youth
   (D) she lived until the age of 46
   (E) she was not a public figure

5. In view of the author's skepticism in the first paragraph about the strict demarcation of literary and historical periods, he would probably agree with which of the following statements about the stock market crash?
   (A) Economics did not impinge upon the Romantic Age.
   (B) The stock market crash affected economic history but not literary history.
   (C) The crash was the focus of a series of events that both preceded it and followed it.
   (D) The crash was not a welcome phenomenon.
   (E) The crash motivated a wave of new poems and novels.

6. According to the author, the literature of the 1930s was dominated by
   (A) no particular mode or frame of reference
   (B) realism
   (C) impressionism

(D) expressionism
(E) surrealism

7. In the final sentence of paragraph 3, the term "the Wasteland" is used
(A) malignantly   (B) sloppily   (C) ambiguously   (D) literally   (E) figuratively

Passage 2

From this day natural philosophy, and particularly chemistry, in the most comprehensive sense of the word, became nearly my sole occupation. I read with ardour those works so full of genius and discrimination, which modern enquirers have written on these subjects. I attended the lectures, and cultivated the acquaintance of the men of science at the university.

My application was at first fluctuating and uncertain; it gained strength as I proceeded, and soon became so ardent and eager, that the stars often disappeared in the light of morning whilst I was yet engaged in my laboratory. As I applied so closely, it may be easily conceived that my progress was rapid.

. . . One of the phenomena which had peculiarly attracted my attention was the structure of the human frame, and, indeed, any animal endued with life. Whence, I often asked myself, did the principle of life proceed? It was a bold question, and one which has never been considered as a mystery; yet with how many things are we on the brink of becoming acquainted, if cowardice or carelessness did not restrain our enquiries. I revolved these circumstances in my mind, and determined thenceforth to apply myself more particularly to those branches of natural philosophy which relate to physiology. Unless I had been animated by an almost supernatural enthusiasm, my application to this study would have been irksome, and almost intolerable. To examine the causes of life, we must observe the natural decay and corruption of the human body. In my education my father had taken the greatest precautions that my mind should be impressed with no supernatural horrors. I do not ever remember to have trembled at a tale of superstition, or to have feared the apparition of a spirit. Darkness had no effect upon my fancy; and a churchyard was to me merely the receptacle of bodies deprived of life, which, from being the seat of beauty and strength, had become food for the worm. Now I was led to examine the cause and progress of this decay, and forced to spend days and nights in vaults and charnel houses. My attention was fixed upon every object the most insupportable to the delicacy of the human feelings. I saw how the fine form of man was degraded and wasted; I beheld the corruption of death succeed to the blooming cheek of life; I saw how the worm inherited the wonders of the eye and brain. I paused, examining and analyzing all the minutiae of causation, as exemplified in the change from life to death, and death to life, until from the midst of this darkness a sudden light broke in upon me—a light so brilliant and wondrous, yet so simple, that while I became dizzy with the immensity of the prospect which it illustrated, I was surprised, that among so many men of genius who had directed their enquiries towards the same science, I alone should be reserved to discover so astonishing a secret.

8. In paragraph 3, the statement "I saw how the worm inherited the wonders of the eye and brain" is a figurative expression of which of the following literal statements?
(A) I watched a despicable relative inherit wonderful things.
(B) I saw worms become more clear-sighted and intelligent.
(C) I saw men humiliated and executed.
(D) I studied the organs of sight and intellect in corpses.
(E) I saw the ways in which death caused blindness and mental illness.

9. We may infer that the two academic subjects which contributed most to the narrator's final discovery were
(A) natural philosophy and the occult
(B) chemistry and physiology
(C) life and death
(D) courage and care
(E) psychology and religion

10. From the preceding details, we may conclude that the astonishing discovery which the narrator makes is related to
(A) his sensitivity to human feelings
(B) contact with the spirit world
(C) overcoming his fear of superstition
(D) the principle of life
(E) beauty and strength

11. The passage is written in the style of a
(A) scientific treatise   (B) personal journal   (C) soliloquy   (D) confession   (E) drama

12. By stressing that he does not acknowledge or fear "supernatural horrors" (paragraph 3) the narrator implies that he practices
(A) obedience to his father
(B) a systematic devotion to the occult
(C) the analysis of nocturnal phenomena
(D) scientific objectivity
(E) natural philosophy

13. In the second paragraph, the narrator is using "application" to mean
(A) experiments that affect the stars themselves
(B) attendance at lectures
(C) study of chemistry
(D) insomnia
(E) checklist of chemical reactions

Passage 3

The term "wrongful life" refers to a lawsuit in which the child alleges that he or she should not have been born. Actions for wrongful life have consistently failed as a result of public policy considerations and damage considerations. Specifically, two main reasons have traditionally been given for denial of such a cause of action. The first reason is that a legal right not to be born
(5)   is alien to a state's policy to preserve and protect human life. The second reason is that damages are unascertainable because such would require the legal system to consider the abstract issue of being versus nonbeing.

The esoteric controversy of being versus nonbeing, that has long been the basic rationale used by courts to deny recovery for wrongful life, now appears to have been relegated to
(10) philosophers. There now seems to be a judicial realization that not all who live experience a joyous life, and that to deny a claim for wrongful life is as unjust as a denial for wrongful death.

As to damages, there appears to be a realization by courts that they can be determined with the same inherent inaccuracies and weaknesses as in other tort actions. Courts seem to not be deterred from awarding damages because the amount given would be speculative. They seem
(15) to agree that speculation is involved in most tort suits where damages are awarded, and that a cause of action so fundamental to society's existence should not be deemed not proper to be examined in courts of justice because damages are difficult to determine.

As a result of these changes, courts are now holding that it is not against public policy nor too formidable to determine damages. Based on such decisions, it now appears that if certain
(20) criteria are met, an infant plaintiff has a cause of action for wrongful life if:

1. The infant sustained severe observable or measurable physical and mental impairments;
2. The injury sustained by the infant resulted from the direct action or negligence of the defendant and was not a mere circumstance of birth;
(25) 3. Had the defendant used reasonable care, the injury would not have occurred and the infant would either have not been born, or would not have been born defective; and
4. The damages are readily ascertainable based upon medical expenses, pain and suffering, and shortened life span.

(30)   One caveat to be kept in mind with respect to wrongful life suits is that the enumerated standards indicated that only an infant can bring such a suit. In cases where the parents bring the suit, they should expect to be denied recovery routinely, on the theory that they are suing for their own injuries under the umbrella of wrongful life.

(35)   One of the most recent wrongful life cases was a California case judged in 1980. The infant plaintiff inherited Tay-Sachs disease from her parents who were negligently advised by the defendant that they were not carriers of the disorder. The infant plaintiff is mentally retarded and has gross physical deformities. The plaintiff sought compensation from the defendant resulting from her birth on the allegation that if the defendant had used due care, she would not have been born and thus subject to a multitude of physical and mental impairments as well as a shortened life span.

(40)   The Superior Court of Los Angeles County sustained the defendant's demurrer to the plaintiff's cause of action and refused to allow the plaintiff leave to amend. The plaintiff appealed and the holding was reversed by the Court of Appeals, Second District, which held that a wrongful injury had occurred and was amenable to judicial review. The case is still under review by the California Supreme Court, and as of yet no decision has been rendered by the court.

(45)   An affirmative ruling by the California Supreme Court will have a profound impact on the legal system and the medical and allied professions. Such a holding will induce medical professionals to expand their knowledge and revise their tendency to attribute certain potentially preventable birth defects to providence or fate.

14. The acceptance of the validity of wrongful life actions implies an acceptance of
   (A)   a legal right not to be born
   (B)   a legal right to be born
   (C)   a state's duty to protect and preserve all human life
   (D)   the idea that being and non-being are identical
   (E)   the waiving of claims for damage to the unborn

15. Wrongful life actions are based on the supposition that
   (A)   it is better to be alive and suffer than not be alive at all
   (B)   the controversy of being and nonbeing has been resolved by philosophers
   (C)   abortion is not a reasonable alternative to birth defects
   (D)   wrongful life damages cannot be determined
   (E)   no life may be preferable to impaired life

16. An infant plaintiff would appear to have a cause of action for wrongful life if all of the following conditions are met EXCEPT
   (A)   the damages based upon medical expenses, pain and suffering, and abbreviated life span are ascertainable
   (B)   the infant suffers grave observable physical impairment
   (C)   the infant's impairment is a circumstance of birth
   (D)   the defendant could have prevented the infant's being born with these defects by exercising reasonable care
   (E)   the infant suffers grave observable mental impairment

17. According to the passage, the parents of an infant gravely impaired by the negligence of a physican whose proper care could have prevented the child's injuries at birth
   (A)   may not be plaintiffs in a wrongful life action against the physician
   (B)   may not be plaintiffs in a malpractice action against the physician
   (C)   may expect a suit brought by the infant to be routinely dismissed
   (D)   may sue for their own injuries under the umbrella of wrongful life
   (E)   may be co-plaintiffs with an infant in wrongful life actions

18. From their use in lines 40–41, we can infer that the terms (1) "demurrer" and (2) "leave to amend" mean
   (A)   (1) delay (2) a period in which to reapply
   (B)   (1) plea for dismissal (2) permission to revise
   (C)   (1) disagreement or argument (2) departure

(D) (1) contest (2) bequest to emend
(E) (1) objection (2) absence from court

19. We can infer from the passage that at the time the article was written
  (A) the decision of the California Supreme Court in the California case was in favor of the plaintiff
  (B) the decision of the California Supreme Court in the California case was in favor of the defendant
  (C) the decision of the California Supreme Court in the California case had not been published
  (D) there had been a very large number of wrongful life actions won by the plaintiffs
  (E) there had been a few wrongful life actions won by the parents of impaired children

20. The larger incidence of wrongful life actions in recent years is probably chiefly a consequence of the
  (A) rise in medical malpractice actions
  (B) rise in the number of legal actions
  (C) rise in the number of doctors and lawyers
  (D) increased sophistication of prenatal diagnostic tests
  (E) increased number of births outside of hospitals

Passage 4

Naturalism differs from realism in several aspects, none of which is clear-cut and definitive. It tends to be more doctrinaire in its exposition of pseudoscientific principles, it is less interested in character and more in the conflict of social forces, and it is concerned to a greater extent with the sordid, the shocking, and the depressing sides of existence. By these criteria, however, there are naturalistic elements in Dostoevsky; and Galsworthy, Hemingway, and Scott Fitzgerald demonstrate many qualities of typical realists. Some further suggested qualities of literary naturalism are as follows:

(a) Naturalism is scientific or pseudoscientific in its approach; it attempts to treat human beings as biological pawns rather than agents of free will. The author does not attempt to judge his characters or to comment on their actions; he merely inserts them into a crucial situation and then pretends to stand back and watch them with the impassivity of the scientists. Although Zola applied this principle with some success, it has generally remained a synthetic theory and has only infrequently been applied to actual literary works.

(b) The naturalist attempts to make literature into a document of society. He writes "novel cycles" purporting to cover every aspect of modern life, or creates characters who are personifications of various social classes. Many naturalists gather copious data from actual life and include it in their literary works: they write novels around specific occupations such as railroading or textile manufacturing in which they utilize technical details of the trade for story-interest. This aspect of naturalism represents an attempt to remove literature from the realm of the fine arts into the field of the social sciences.

(c) Because of the above-described documentary nature of naturalism, the technique often involves the conscious suppression of the poetic elements in literature. The prose style is flat, objective, and bare of imagery; it includes copious details and explanations, and is wary of highly literary metaphors. Like the pseudoscientific dogma described in (a) above, this quality is often more theoretical than practical. The best naturalists are those who do not totally abandon the literary traditions of the past. On the other hand some naturalists are merely writers lacking in the poetic instinct; they avoid a highly literary prose because they have little feeling for style and imagery. Others like Hardy are essentially poets who achieve highly poetic effects in their prose.

(d) Naturalistic literature tends to be concerned with the less elegant aspects of life; its typical settings are the slum, the sweatshop, the factory, or the farm. Where the romantic author selects the most pleasant and idealistic elements in his experience, the naturalistic author often seems positively drawn toward the brutal, the sordid, the cruel, and the degraded. This tendency is in part a reaction against earlier literature, especially against the sentimentalism of the Dumas school where vice is invariably made to appear romantic. The real motivating forces in a naturalistic novel are not religion, hope, or human idealism; they are alcohol, filth, disease, and the human instinct toward bestiality. It will be seen immediately that there are important exceptions to this principle. Galsworthy's scenes are middle-class, and Scott Fitzgerald prefers to do his slumming at the Ritz.

21. The passage implies that one reason for calling naturalism "pseudoscientific" rather than "scientific" is that
(A) a scientist would acknowledge the existence of free will
(B) Zola's theory has been infrequently applied
(C) biological pawns are not amenable to study
(D) Zola did not meet with total success
(E) the author's scientific perspective is a pretense

22. In paragraph (c), the author turns from description to
(A) documentary (B) evaluation (C) praise (D) disdain (E) naturalism

23. A naturalist suppressing highly literary metaphors might avoid which of the following?
(A) The sunset was full of reds and yellows.
(B) His nemesis was iron-willed.
(C) The community regarded Frank as a tower of strength.
(D) The President describes the period of military laxity as a "window of vulnerability."
(E) Marriage is a sad, sober beverage.

24. The passage suggests that the naturalist behaves most like a scientist when he
(A) gathers details from life
(B) transforms fact into fiction
(C) de-emphasizes the importance of character
(D) writes history or biography rather than actual literary works
(E) restricts his subject matter

25. In the first paragraph the author is careful not to make
(A) suggestions
(B) absolute pronouncements
(C) any useful distinctions between naturalism and realism
(D) his examples too noteworthy
(E) any references to arts other than literature

26. We may infer that the naturalist novel is unlikely to contain
(A) a rural setting
(B) an acknowledgment of human woes
(C) a romantic hero
(D) a social crisis
(E) an urban setting

STOP

IF YOU FINISH BEFORE TIME IS UP, CHECK YOUR WORK ON THIS SECTION OF THE TEST ONLY. DO NOT GO ON TO THE NEXT SECTION OF THE TEST UNTIL TIME IS UP FOR THIS SECTION.

SECTION III
LOGICAL REASONING

Time—35 Minutes
26 Questions

Directions:
In this section you will be given brief statements or passages and will be required to evaluate the reasoning involved. In some instances, more than one choice will appear to be a possible answer. You are to choose the *best* answer. Use common sense and reasonableness in making your selection; then mark the proper space on the answer sheet.

Questions 1–2

Some scientists believe that legal standards for pesticide residues are seriously flawed and were established without adequate health and safety data for produce. Because of the media attention to this issue, it should be no surprise that opinion polls say pesticide residue now tops the list of consumer food worries, beating out cholesterol and calories.

1. Which of the following would be the most logical completion of the passage above?
   (A)   So produce safety has now become the latest battleground in the supermarket wars.
   (B)   Farm workers should be concerned with residue standards.
   (C)   But consumers should not be worried; opinion polls are often misleading.
   (D)   And it is possible that cholesterol standards have been improperly established.
   (E)   Media attention to any issue seems to bring unwanted attention and distort the facts.

2. It would be reasonable to conclude from the passage above that
   (A)   scientists have been protesting pesticide residue levels for many years
   (B)   recommended cholesterol and calorie levels should also be researched
   (C)   cholesterol and calories had been the major concern of consumers
   (D)   many legal standards are seriously flawed
   (E)   most scientists believe that the legal standards for pesticide residue have been adequately researched

3.   The Capital City Q's and the Pretoria P's are two boys' clubs that enter a blink-blunk tournament. Blink-blunk is a new game in which each team scores 3 points for a blink and 1 point for a blunk. Neither team scored a blunk in period 1 or 2, and no blinks were scored by either team in period 3 or 4. There are four periods in a blink-blunk game, and the scoring was as follows:

Team	Period				Total
	1	2	3	4	
Q's	6	3	3	1	13
P's	3	3	5	3	14

From the information given, it can be concluded that the
   (A)   P's and Q's were never tied during the game
   (B)   P's scored the last point of the game
   (C)   Q's scored the last point of the game
   (D)   Q's scored more blinks than the P's did
   (E)   Q's scored more blunks than the P's did

4. *Tom:*   Sometimes products that are needed by the consumer just don't seem to sell well.
   Stan: That's probably because the product is always sold out.
   Tom: That's ridiculous! How can something that doesn't sell well be sold out!

It can be assumed from Tom's reply that he believes that Stan
(A) thinks that all products that are in stock don't sell well
(B) feels that products need to sell well to be sold out
(C) knows that products that are in demand are always kept in stock
(D) knows more about consumers than Tom
(E) is using faulty logic

5. Scientists are continually making technological breakthroughs such as developing laser technology. Yet they have not been able to cure the common cold. Once scientists had the proper financial backing from the government, they immediately proceeded to develop laser technology. The proper funding seemed to make all the difference. When our government allocates the necessary financial resources, our scientists will find a cure for the common cold.

In the passage above, the author does all of the following EXCEPT
(A) fail to consider the significant differences between finding a cure for the common cold and the development of laser technology
(B) explain that there is no significant distinction between developing laser technology and curing the common cold
(C) intimate that the government has not found a cure for the common cold because the government has not allocated sufficient funds to do so
(D) imply that the government has not found a cure for the common cold because there is less desire to do so than there was to develop laser technology
(E) present an analogy between developing laser technology and finding a cure for the common cold

Questions 6–7

Numerous medical studies have been published that associate health risks with the consumption of caffeine. Yet many Americans continue to consume coffee in huge quantities.

6. Which of the following conclusions does NOT logically follow from the sentences alone?
(A) Therefore, for these Americans, the benefits of coffee apparently outweigh the risks.
(B) Therefore, many Americans may not be aware of the medical studies.
(C) Therefore, some Americans may not accept the studies' conclusions.
(D) Therefore, some Americans continue to risk their health.
(E) Therefore, the amount of caffeine consumed should be determined by the size of the individual.

7. Which of the following statements would NOT weaken the point of the first sentence?
(A) Most of the medical studies published are based on faulty research.
(B) Many doctors feel that caffeine has many benefits.
(C) Medical research has improved over the past few years.
(D) As a rule, coffee drinkers live longer than those who do not drink coffee.
(E) Ingestion of foods high in caffeine has been shown to hasten the healing of broken bones.

Questions 8–9

Hundreds of new self-help books, audio tapes, and video tapes, have been pushed onto the market in the last decade. These self-help methods generally reflect a positive, optimistic approach to modern problems and challenges and are usually based on current research in psychology. The purpose of many of the authors is to offer help to a needy society. Unfortunately, some of those involved in producing self-help materials see the trend and are only in it for the "quick buck."

8. Which of the following can be inferred from the statements in the passage above?
   (A)   An increasing percentage of self-help authors are only in the market for the "quick buck."
   (B)   Most of the self-help authors don't care about their product's profits.
   (C)   Profits are not the only goal of many self-help authors.
   (D)   The trend of self-help authors is toward the "quick buck."
   (E)   Self-help authors are positive and optimisitic about the sale of their products.

9. Which of the following statements about the producers of self-help materials is the most logical continuation of the passage above?
   (A)   Their products exhibit the same quality of care and workmanship as the majority of self-help products.
   (B)   Moreover, their optimism extends not only to the sale of their items, but also to the effectiveness of solving their customers' problems.
   (C)   Their involvement includes a close and careful supervision of their excellent self-help products.
   (D)   Their products tend to be hastily manufactured and display a disregard for the needs of the consumer.
   (E)   Their heartfelt concerns about a needy society may someday be realized.

10.   Operation of nuclear reactor-driven power plants does not adversely affect small-game hunting within nearby public ranges. The Fertile Crescent Nuclear Facility began operating this year, and the number of squirrels caught nearby set a five-season high.

All of the following statements, if true, are valid objections to the foregoing argument EXCEPT
   (A)   radiation from such reactors renders certain species of rodents sterile
   (B)   radiation from such reactors reduces the mortality rate among immature squirrels
   (C)   factors having nothing to do with the well-being of squirrels may have a marked impact on the number of animals taken in a given season
   (D)   radioactivity emanating from power plant reactors interferes with the growth of various forms of vegetation consumed by squirrels
   (E)   squirrels are only one of numerous species of small game that may be affected by the presence of a nuclear reactor

11.   Williams will be elected to the Retirement Fund Board, and since he will, so will Johnson. In addition, if Johnson and Smith are both elected, then Davidson will be elected. If Davidson is elected, then he will be accused of embezzling retirement funds, found guilty, and sentenced to ten years in prison. Therefore, Davidson will be found guilty of embezzling retirement funds and will be sentenced to ten years in prison.

Which of the following additional premises must be included among those in the passage above in order for the conclusion to be a logical one?
   (A)   Davidson will be elected to the board.
   (B)   Smith will be elected to the board.
   (C)   Johnson will be elected to the board.
   (D)   Williams will be elected to the board.
   (E)   Davidson will embezzle funds.

Questions 12–13

The Federal Safety Commission recently released its study regarding motorbike safety. The study showed some useful statistics. The most noteworthy is that when motorbike operators wearing helmets have accidents, there is a 20 percent chance that they will be seriously injured. However, when motorbike operators who are not wearing helmets have accidents, the chance that they will be seriously injured is 40 percent.

12. From the information above, which of the following is the best conclusion?
    (A) Many more motorbike operators do not wear helmets than do wear helmets.
    (B) A motorbike operator not wearing a helmet has a greater chance of having an accident than does an operator who is wearing a helmet.
    (C) A motorbike operator not wearing a helmet has a greater chance of having a serious, personal-injury accident than does an operator who wears a helmet.
    (D) If a motorbike operator does not wear a helmet, there is a 40 percent chance that the operator will have an accident.
    (E) If a motorbike operator has an accident while not wearing a helmet, the chances are greater that the operator will be seriously injured than if the operator had an accident while wearing a helmet.

13. Which of the following statements must be true in order to conclude that the number of helmeted motorbike operators seriously injured in accidents is greater than the number of nonhelmeted operators seriously injured in accidents?
    (A) Three times as many motorbike operators wear helmets as do not wear helmets.
    (B) Half as many motorbike operators do not wear helmets as do wear helmets.
    (C) There are twice as many accidents involving motorbike operators who were not wearing helmets as there are accidents involving operators who were wearing helmets.
    (D) There are four times as many accidents involving motorbike operators wearing helmets as there are accidents involving motorbike operators who are not wearing helmets.
    (E) Three times as many motorbike operators wear helmets as do not wear helmets.

14. All commercial buildings constructed within the city of Philadelphia after 1987 have automatic sprinkler systems, and all commercial buildings constructed within the county of Philadelphia after that date have hallway smoke alarms. The city of Philadelphia is within the county of Philadelphia and must abide by all county rules and ordinances.

    If the Consolidated Corporation is a commercial business, and if its office building has smoke alarms in all hallways, but does not have an automatic sprinkler system, which of the following must be true?
    (A) Consolidated's office building is not located in the city of Philadelphia.
    (B) If Consolidated's office building was constructed in 1988, it is not situated in the city of Philadelphia.
    (C) If Consolidated's office building was erected prior to 1987, it is located in the city of Philadelphia.
    (D) Consolidated's office building was built prior to 1987; it was constructed in the city of Philadelphia.
    (E) If Consolidated's office building was built prior to 1987, it was constructed in the city of Philadelphia.

15. A Broadway show is a greater theatrical pleasure than a high school play because people with a great appreciation of theater invariably select Broadway shows over high school plays. One can identify these people who appreciate theater by their preferences for Broadway shows.

In logically critiquing the statements above, one would most probably point out that the author
(A) contradicts his own reasoning
(B) does not cite any authority in theatrical matters
(C) presupposes the point he intends to establish
(D) draws a generalization from specific evidence
(E) does not distinguish between Broadway and high school theatrical performances

16. Mr. Miko is very good at the sport of Jodo. Therefore, Mr. Miko is a good sport.

The author of the argument above relies upon which of the following to arrive at a conclusion?
(A) purposely overestimating Mr. Miko's ability in Jodo
(B) generalizing from a particular example
(C) establishing a specific case based upon a general occurrence
(D) establishing a causal relationship
(E) assuming a similarity of meaning between "good at the sport" and "good sport"

17. All Certified Public Accountants are required to have a specified minimal number of hours of auditing experience. Roger, a recent college graduate, has passed all of the required exams and completed all of the necessary course work, but has no auditing experience. Therefore, Roger is not a Certified Public Accountant.

If the information above regarding Roger's auditing experience is not true and Roger has recently started a job as an auditor, the most that could be logically inferred from the passage is that Roger
(A) does not intend to become a Certified Public Accountant
(B) is eligible to become a Certified Public Accountant
(C) will probably become a Certified Public Accountant
(D) would be an excellent Certified Public Accountant
(E) is not qualified to become a Certified Public Accountant

18. The greatest danger to a society ruled by a monarchy is the increasing bureaucratization of the ruling process. As the bureaucracy becomes more entrenched, it becomes less responsive to both the ruler and the ruled. There is a threshold beyond which the result is governance by technocracy.

It can be inferred from the foregoing that the author believes that
(A) bureaucracy should be curbed
(B) monarchy is doomed
(C) bureaucracies are more efficient than monarchies
(D) bureaucrats are hostile to those they serve
(E) bureaucracy is a superior form of governance

19. In a recent poll, 93 percent of the 5000 randomly chosen military personnel favored the use of capital punishment. Therefore, it follows that approximately 93 percent of all military personnel favor capital punishment. From this information, it follows that military personnel are more likely to be in favor of capital punishment than people who are not members of the military.

It can be concluded from the statements above that the author most likely makes which of the following assumptions?
(A) Everyone who is not a member of the military does not favor capital punishment.
(B) Everyone who is a member of the military favors capital punishment.
(C) More than 93 percent of those people not in the military favor capital punishment.
(D) Less than 93 percent of those people not in the military favor capital punishment.
(E) There are more people who are not in the military than people who are in the military.

20. The number of foreign-born students enrolled in the college district increased from 5 percent to 15 percent between 1985 and 1988. Mr. Wong was a member of the district college board between 1985 and 1988. Board member Wong's reelection will bring another rise in the number of foreign students.

Which of the following statements, if true, would most strengthen the argument above?
(A) Mr. Wong himself is foreign born.
(B) Mr. Wong served on the college board from 1982 to 1983.
(C) Mr. Wong believes that a college education should be available to all.
(D) Board member Wong is the head of the board committee that plays an important role in setting district college admissions policy.
(E) The percentage of students who are foreign-born is less than the percentage of students who are not foreign-born.

Questions 21–22

Within the population of artists, there is not always an even distribution of artistic talent. Recent surveys have indicated that the most productive 5 percent of the artistic community create over half of the artwork sold by that community. As a matter of fact, 15 percent of that community's members creates in excess of 90 percent of the community's sold works.

21. Which of the following conclusions may be most reasonably inferred from the statements above?
(A) Overall, the creative output of the artistic community is far less than what it should be.
(B) A significant number of artists sell their creations.
(C) Reducing the number of artists would not necessarily cause a decrease in the quantity of artwork sold by the artistic community.
(D) Eighty-five percent of the members of the artistic community never sell their work.
(E) An increase in financial support for the arts would result in a needed increase in the creative output of the artistic community.

22. Which of the following most effectively calls into question the reasoning in this passage?
(A) Historically, art undergoes significant changes in "style" from one generation to the next.
(B) Many talented people are not artists.
(C) Artistic talent is an ambiguous characteristic that may not be measured in terms of sales.
(D) Many artists who try to sell their work are unsuccessful because they lack talent.
(E) Most major artists do not achieve high sales until after their deaths.

23.   Given that police cars always have a loud siren and flashing lights, and the vehicle following me has a loud siren and flashing lights, it follows that the vehicle following me is a police car.

All of the following statements might reasonably be used to challenge the soundness of the argument used EXCEPT
(A)   ambulances have loud sirens and flashing lights
(B)   automobiles used by the fire department have loud sirens and flashing lights
(C)   given that ostriches have feathers and are flightless, it follows that my featherless and flightless penguin is an ostrich
(D)   given that oysters have shells and are found in the sea, it follows that a lobster is an oyster
(E)   police cars sometimes do not use their sirens

24.   The rural community of Potsville has a low crime rate. Urban Los Angeles has a high crime rate. Shady Junction, a small agricultural community, has a high rate of criminal activity. The city of Washington, D.C., has a low rate of criminal activity.

Which of the following most closely expresses the main point in the passage above?
(A)   Urban communities generally have higher crime rates.
(B)   Crime is rampant in all communities.
(C)   Rural communities generally have higher crime rates.
(D)   Crime is not solely an urban nor a rural phenomenon.
(E)   Urban crime is more violent than rural crime.

25.   Hitting a baseball is certainly one of the most difficult feats in sports. Even the greatest hitters of all time have only been able to hit safely once for every three times at bat. In other words, even great hitters in baseball fail more often than they succeed.

All of the following would logically complete this paragraph EXCEPT
(A)   therefore, one does not have to succeed more than fail, to be successful as a hitter in baseball
(B)   therefore, success is relative to the situation in life
(C)   therefore, one should not give up if one fails on the first try
(D)   therefore, without having failed one cannot succeed
(E)   therefore, baseball can teach us useful lessons

26.   Robert was concerned that he could not find the Maximinima TQ 1000 video camera in stock anywhere. While speaking with him yesterday he explained, "Last month, I finally ordered the Maximinima TQ 1000, the most advanced, state-of-the-art video camera model that has been introduced in years. The Maximinima must be a reliable camera because everybody wants to buy one. With ultra-small size, the Maximinima focuses beautifully, even when the subject is moving."

Which of the following statements, if true, would weaken Robert's assessment of his camera's reliability?

(A)   The Maximinima is not reliable because its small size has nothing to do with how well it focuses.

(B)   The Maximinima is not reliable because no one knows if a camera purchased last month will still work after a year.

(C)   The Maximinima is not reliable merely because it focuses well on moving subjects.

(D)   The Maximinima is not reliable merely because everyone wants to buy one.

(E)   The Maximinima is not reliable because it focuses poorly on stationary subjects.

STOP

IF YOU FINISH BEFORE TIME IS UP, CHECK YOUR WORK ON THIS SECTION OF THE TEST ONLY. DO NOT GO ON TO THE NEXT SECTION OF THE TEST UNTIL TIME IS UP FOR THIS SECTION.

SECTION IV
ANALYTICAL REASONING

Time—35 Minutes
24 Questions

Directions:
In this section you will be given groups of questions based on different sets of conditions. Drawing a simple diagram may be helpful in answering some of the questions. You are to choose the best answer and mark the corresponding space on your answer sheet.

Questions 1–5

(1) Six people are seated around a circular table. There are no empty seats. Each person is wearing a colored shirt and a colored hat.

(2) Three people are wearing red shirts, two are wearing blue shirts, and one is wearing a green shirt.

(3) Two people are wearing blue hats, two are wearing red hats, and two are wearing green hats.

(4) One person is wearing a matching hat and shirt.

(5) No two people with the same color hats are sitting next to each other.

(6) No two people with the same color shirts are sitting next to each other.

(7) The one person who is wearing the green shirt is sitting between and next to the two people wearing the blue hats.

(8) The two people wearing the blue shirts are wearing the green hats.

1. Which of the following statements must be true?
   (A)   A green hat is worn by a person in a red shirt.
   (B)   A blue hat is worn by a person in a blue shirt.
   (C)   Both blue hats are worn by people in red shirts.
   (D)   The person wearing a matching shirt and hat is wearing blue.
   (E)   The person wearing the green shirt is wearing a blue hat.

2. If the green shirt should turn red, then how many of the above conditions would NO LONGER be true?
   (A) 1   (B) 2   (C) 3   (D) 4   (E) 5

3. If the two blue shirts turned green, then which of the following must be true?
   (A)   Two people would be wearing matching shirts and hats.
   (B)   Except for those wearing blue hats, everyone is wearing matching shirts and hats.
   (C)   Red and green shirts would alternate around the table.
   (D)   A person with a green hat is sitting between two people with blue hats.
   (E)   A person with a red shirt is sitting between two people with blue hats.

4. If each person passed his hat two people to the left, how many people would end up with the same color hat they started with?
   (A) one   (B) two   (C) three   (D) four   (E) five

5. If each person passed his hat three people to the right, then which of the following would be false?
   (A)   Three people would now be wearing matching shirts and hats.
   (B)   No one wearing a red shirt would be wearing a blue hat.
   (C)   The two people wearing green hats would be wearing red shirts.
   (D)   No one wearing a red hat would be wearing a blue shirt.
   (E)   No one wearing a blue hat is wearing a blue shirt.

Questions 6–11

A new bank has decided to stay open only on weekends—all day Saturday and Sunday—and no other days. The bank has hired two managers (U and V), four tellers (W, X, Y, and Z), and two operations officers (S and T), for a total of exactly eight full-time employees. No part-time employees are hired. Each employee works a complete day when working.

A manager must be on duty each day.
The managers cannot work on the same day.
At least two tellers must be working on the same day.
W and X will not work on the same day.
S and Z will only work on Saturday.
No employee can work on consecutive days, but each employee must work on Saturday or Sunday.

6. Which of the following could be false?
   (A)   If U works on Saturday, then V works on Sunday.
   (B)   If X works on Saturday, then W works on Sunday.
   (C)   T can work either day.
   (D)   If W works on Saturday and Y works on Sunday, then X works on Sunday.
   (E)   If U works on Sunday, then X works on Saturday.

7. Which of the following is an acceptable group of employees that could work on Saturday?
   (A)   ZWYST   (B)   UVWYZS   (C)   VWXZT   (D)   UZST   (E)   VWZS

8. What is the greatest number of employees that can work on Saturday?
   (A) 2   (B) 3   (C) 4   (D) 5   (E) 6

9. If W works on Sunday, then which of the following must be true?
   (A)   X works on Saturday.
   (B)   Y works on Saturday.
   (C)   T works on Sunday.
   (D)   Z works on Sunday.
   (E)   U works on Saturday.

10. Which of the following must be true?
   (A)   T always works the same day as Y.
   (B)   S never works the same day as U.
   (C)   Z never works the same day as X.
   (D)   If W works on Sunday, then Y always works on Saturday.
   (E)   Only two tellers work on Saturday.

11. Which of the following is a complete and accurate list of the employees who have the possibility of working on Sunday?
   (A)   UWYZ   (B)   UWYS   (C)   UVWXT   (D)   UVWXYT   (E)   UVWXYTS

Questions 12–16

Flit Flies, which can mate on the day they are born, are insects capable of quick reproduction. Therefore, they are commonly used in laboratory experiments.

   (1)   Flit Flies mate only if three of four conditions are met: the presence of *agar-agar* (1) in a *petri dish* (2) at *78° temperature* (3) at *normal barometric pressure* (4).
   (2)   There is a 5-day interval from the time when Flit Flies mate to the birth of the offspring, during which time the Flit Flies may continue to mate.
   (3)   Flit Flies mate only once within any 24-hour period.
   (4)   Flit Flies are placed in a petri dish on June 1.

12. If a second generation of Flit Flies is born, then which of the following must be true?
  (A) If agar-agar is present, then the temperature is 78 degrees.
  (B) If normal barometric pressure, then the temperature is 76 degrees.
  (C) If agar-agar is present, then there is normal barometric pressure.
  (D) If there is normal barometric pressure, then agar-agar was present.
  (E) If the temperature was 76 degrees, then agar-agar was present.

13. From June 1 to June 4, if agar-agar is present at 78° at normal barometric pressure, then which of the following must be true?
  (A) The Flit Flies will mate.
  (B) The Flit Flies will mate twice in one day.
  (C) Offspring will not appear.
  (D) The Flit Flies will not mate once daily.
  (E) Offspring will mate.

14. If a third generation of Flit Flies appears on June 15, which of the following must be true?
  (A) The first generation didn't begin mating until after June 5.
  (B) The second generation didn't begin mating until after June 5.
  (C) The second generation didn't begin mating until after June 10.
  (D) The first generation didn't begin mating until after June 10.
  (E) The fourth generation will begin to appear on June 20.

15. If a second set of second-generation Flit Flies appears on June 13, all of the following could be true EXCEPT
  (A) a first set of second-generation Flit Flies appeared on June 7
  (B) a first set of third-generation Flit Flies appears on June 13
  (C) the petri dish contained agar-agar at 78° temperature
  (D) a first set of third-generation Flit Flies appeared on June 9
  (E) a first set of second-generation Flit Flies mated on June 8

16. If suddenly Flit Flies are discovered to be dangerous to produce, what steps must the governor take to eliminate the Flit Fly population?
  (A) The governor must destroy all petri dishes and destroy all first generation Flit Flies.
  (B) The governor must maintain the temperature at 82 degrees and destroy all second generation Flit Flies.
  (C) The governor must destroy all first and second generation Flit Flies and confiscate all agar-agar.
  (D) The governor must combine first and second generation Flit Flies and confiscate all agar-agar.
  (E) The governor must confiscate all agar-agar and destroy all petri dishes.

Questions 17–24

Crimes against people, habitation, society, or property may be divided into two types: felonies and misdemeanors. Felonies are the more serious crimes, punishable by death, or forfeiture of property and/or freedom for an extended period of time.

(1) Murder, manslaughter, rape, robbery, and kidnapping are felonies against people.
(2) Burglary and arson are crimes involving habitation, and are of the same level.
(3) Assault and battery are crimes against people that are not felonies.
(4) Crimes involving property are larceny, embezzlement, forgery, and the receiving of stolen goods; only one of these is always a felony.
(5) Embezzlement and larceny are the only crimes that can be either a felony or misdemeanor, depending on severity.
(6) Burglary and robbery are the same level of crime, but receiving stolen goods is not.
(7) Adultery, incest, bigamy, and prostitution are moral offenses, only two of which are felonies.
(8) Adultery and prostitution are not the same level as arson, but incest and bigamy are the same level as forgery.

Using only the statements above and common sense reasoning, answer the following questions.

17. Which of the following must be felonies?
(A)　rape and larceny
(B)　arson and larceny
(C)　rape and arson
(D)　rape and embezzlement
(E)　larceny and embezzlement

18. How many crimes can be classified as either felonies or misdemeanors?
(A) one　　(B) two　　(C) three　　(D) four　　(E) five

19. Which of the following could be misdemeanors?
(A)　embezzlement, prostitution, and receiving stolen property
(B)　larceny, forgery, and adultery
(C)　prostitution, larceny, and murder
(D)　burglary, embezzlement, and receiving stolen property
(E)　bigamy, incest, and adultery

20. If all felonious crimes against people were punishable by death, then
(A)　arson and burglary would not be punishable by death
(B)　murder, rape, manslaughter, robbery and kidnapping would be punishable by death
(C)　assault and battery would be punishable by death
(D)　some of the felonious crimes against people would be punishable by loss of freedom
(E)　arson, assault, and rape would be punishable by death

21. The most frequently committed crimes are
(A)　crimes against people
(B)　crimes against habitation
(C)　crimes against society
(D)　crimes against property
(E)　not determinable by these statements

22. Which of the following can be deduced from the statements and must be true?
(A)　Burglary is a misdemeanor.
(B)　Larceny is a misdemeanor.
(C)　Assault is a felony.
(D)　Receiving stolen property is the same level of crime as adultery.
(E)　Incest is a misdemeanor.

23. If indecent exposure is a crime against society, then what must it be?
(A)　a misdemeanor
(B)　a crime against people
(C)　punishable by forfeiture of property
(D)　a felony
(E)　cannot be determined

24. According to statements 1–8, there are
   (A) more felonies than misdemeanors committed each year
   (B) seven sorts of crimes against people
   (C) no two crimes that can be committed at the same time
   (D) three sorts of moral offenses that are felonies
   (E) less than two crimes that can be felonies or misdemeanors

STOP

IF YOU FINISH BEFORE TIME IS UP, CHECK YOUR WORK ON THIS SECTION OF THE TEST ONLY.
DO NOT GO ON TO THE NEXT SECTION OF THE TEST UNTIL TIME IS UP FOR THIS SECTION.

SECTION V
LOGICAL REASONING

Time—35 Minutes
25 Questions

Directions:
In this section you will be given brief statements or passages and will be required to evaluate the reasoning involved. In some instances, more than one choice will appear to be a possible answer. You are to choose the *best* answer. Use common sense and reasonableness in making your selection; then mark the proper space on the answer sheet.

1. The health-care and lost-productivity costs of smoking exceed 15 billion dollars a year. Despite the evidence linking smoking to a number of fatal diseases, 30 percent of the American population still smokes. If we were to tax cigarettes at the high rates imposed in Canada or Great Britain, we could raise badly needed tax money, and greatly reduce the health-care and lost-productivity costs of smoking.

   The argument of the passage would be most weakened if which of the following were shown to be true?
   (A) Taxes on cigarettes fall more heavily upon the poor than upon the rich.
   (B) Only 15 percent of the population of Canada smokes cigarettes.
   (C) The number of smokers in Canada did not decline when the high taxes on cigarettes were imposed.
   (D) About 25 percent of the population of Great Britain smokes tobacco.
   (E) Taxes on alcoholic beverages in Canada and Great Britain are lower than similar taxes in the United States.

2. *Jane:* I haven't found anyone in the English class who agrees with the professor's interpretation of this poem.
   Dave: No, you're wrong. The three students who got A's on the paper must have agreed with the professor's reading.

   Dave's reply shows that he has interpreted Jane's comment to imply which of the following?
   (A) Jane has consulted all of the students in the English class.
   (B) Jane has not consulted any of the students who agree with the professor.
   (C) Some students who say they disagree with the professor may change their minds.
   (D) Jane has not consulted all of the students in the English class.
   (E) Some students who say they agree with the professor do not, in fact, believe in his interpretation.

Questions 3–4 refer to the following passage.

"You deserve the freedom to choose any doctor and to have no more medical bills. These benefits can be yours when you join Red Shield and go to your choice of one of five thousand Red Shield preferred physicians."

3. This advertisement presupposes as part of its argument that the reader
   (A) wishes to choose what doctor she will go to
   (B) does not belong to a health maintenance program
   (C) belongs to a program which allows the choice of a doctor
   (D) pays no medical bills
   (E) wishes to reduce her annual medical expenses

4. Which single word in the advertisement leads to a logical inconsistency to its claim?
- (A) deserve
- (B) freedom
- (C) any
- (D) choice
- (E) preferred

5. With its large community of conservative former colonists from Algeria and an equally conservative retiree population, Nice is France's only large city sympathetic to the far-right-wing politics of Jean Le Pen. Jacque Medecin, the mayor of Nice for twenty-five years, has said he agrees with 99 percent of Le Pen's ideas, which include hostility to immigration, Arabs, and Jews. Conservatives have been shocked by Medecin's sudden flight to South America with two of his party allies, presumably to avoid prosecution for massive looting of public funds. Medecin claims he is the victim of a Socialist plot.

Which of the following is most clearly suggested by the information in this passage?
- (A) Some right-wing politicians may be guilty of dishonesty.
- (B) Some right-wing politicians may deplore racism.
- (C) The young are naturally more conservative than the elderly.
- (D) Conservatives are likely to be the victims of Socialist plots.
- (E) Not all conservatives support the ideas of Jean Le Pen.

6. If Jack were a first baseman for the New York Mets, he would be rich. He is not a first baseman, since he is not rich.

The conclusion above is unsound because the author does not consider the possibility that Jack could be
- (A) a rich third baseman
- (B) a first baseman for another team
- (C) rich for some other reason
- (D) a guard for the Boston Celtics
- (E) a second baseman for the New York Mets

7. All Italian greyhounds are graceful and fast, but some are nervous. Graceful and fast greyhounds are slender, but nervous greyhounds are unpredictable.

If the statements are true, all of the following must be true EXCEPT
- (A) all Italian greyhounds are slender
- (B) some greyhounds are nervous
- (C) no Italian greyhounds are slow
- (D) no Italian greyhounds are predictable
- (E) all Italian greyhounds are graceful

8. Researchers have shown that females of a certain species of fish are more attracted to the male of the species when males are fitted with a plastic, swordlike extension of the ends of their tails. The artificial fin makes the males resemble the males of a different species, the swordtail. For some time biologists have wondered how traits like the swordlike tail of the swordtail arise. Do males evolve traits that females later prefer? Or do the traits and preference evolve together? Or do the females have the preference first, and the males evolve to respond to it? The results of the experiment suggest that _____.

Which of the following is the most logical conclusion of the paragraph?
- (A) we still cannot reach even a tentative answer to these questions.
- (B) the female's preference arose first and the males adapted to it.
- (C) the males' development must come first, and evolutionary pressure causes the females to respond.

    (D)   the females' and the males' traits and preferences must arise at the same time.

    (E)   the whole notion of evolutionary development must be in error.

9. Doctors are becoming wary of herbal teas and similar preparations. Many herbs sold in health-food stores or even supermarkets may be toxic. Sales of herbal products are nearly half a billion dollars yearly. And though the majority of herbal products are probably safe, at least twenty-five commonly sold herbs can cause cardiac, gastrointestinal, or nervous system diseases. Some herbs that have been used for thousands of years are neither safe nor effective. The prevailing myth that herbs are "natural" and therefore can do no harm is false. Too few commonly available herbs have been rigorously tested. The same requirements that apply to new drugs should also apply to herbal remedies.

The author of this passage would probably agree with which of the following statements?

    (A)   Whole herbs are more effective than their isolated active constituents.

    (B)   Natural or organic herbs are superior to synthetic drugs.

    (C)   Harmful plants like cocaine, opium, tobacco, or marijuana should not be regarded as herbs.

    (D)   Herbs should be classified as foods, not drugs.

    (E)   Herbs are to be avoided by pregnant or nursing women.

10. When we examine the diets of men of the same age and similar background, we see that the smaller the amount of fiber in the diet, the greater the incidence of colon cancer. Therefore, fiber in the diet probably prevents cancer of the colon.

Which of the following uses reasoning that most closely parallels the reasoning in the argument above?

    (A)   Studies show that a second child in a family learns to speak at an earlier age than the first child, and also at an earlier age than a third child. Therefore, the second-born child must be more intelligent.

    (B)   Researchers have shown that shoppers with shopping lists spend less money in supermarkets than shoppers without lists. The same study reported that men are more likely to buy luxury or unnecessary foods than women. Therefore, a woman with a shopping list is likely to spend less in a supermarket than a man without a shopping list.

    (C)   When one hundred rats are placed in a small cage, a certain percentage will become cannibalistic, and the smaller the cage, the higher the percentage of cannibalism. Over-crowding, therefore, is probably the cause.

    (D)   Two out of three automobile accidents happen within two miles of the driver's home. Therefore, drivers must be overconfident and more careless when driving on a familiar road.

    (E)   In certain wilderness areas, more forest fires are caused by acts of nature, such as lightning, than by human acts. But the closer a forest is to a city, the more likely it is that a fire will be caused by human beings. Therefore, the number of fire watchers must be higher nearer urban areas.

Questions 11–12 refer to the following passage.

    The Yoruba faith considers animal sacrifice during religious ceremonies a source of spiritual power and purity. In Yoruba ceremonies, farm animals, usually chickens, are sacrificed and then consumed. The city has passed an ordinance which forbids any animal sacrifice, and the religious group has challenged the law and vowed to continue the practice. The attorney for the Yorubas argues that denial of the ritual is like forbidding Christians to take communion.

    The ban on animal sacrifice was passed in response to complaints about animal remains found in trash containers. Officials attributed the remains to Satanists and to Caribbean and South American communities practicing Santeria, an African animist religion. The Yorubas have pointed out that the remains cannot have come from their ceremonies, where the animal is consumed, and that their animals are killed according to state codes.

11. Which of the following conclusions should be drawn from the passage above?
   (A) This case will be decided in favor of the Yorubas.
   (B) This case will be decided in favor of the city ordinance.
   (C) If the Yorubas win, the case for animal sacrifice by believers in Santeria will be weakened.
   (D) Animal-rights activists are likely to support the Yorubas in this case.
   (E) A decision in this case will offend against either religious freedom or animal rights.

12. All of the following arguments might be used in defense of the regulation prohibiting animal sacrifices EXCEPT
   (A) even if the Yorubas kill animals humanely, the law is necessary to prevent inhumane killing by other sects
   (B) scientific studies have shown that animals feel pain as intensely as humans
   (C) not all religious beliefs—polygamy, for example—are tolerated in the United States
   (D) animal sacrifices have been a part of religious ceremonies for thousands of years
   (E) the sight of animal sacrifice may be traumatic to children

13. After installing an expensive computer-operated drip irrigation system designed to measure moisture and to save up to 20 percent of water usage, Jackson Orchards discovered that its water bill for the month of September was 10 percent higher than last September's bill, before the new system was in use. Jackson Orchards demanded a refund from the irrigation systems company.

   Jackson Orchards' demand would be more convincing if which of the following were true?
   (A) The rates charged by the water company were virtually unchanged.
   (B) It could demonstrate that the irrigation system was functioning as it should.
   (C) The acreage under cultivation was slightly smaller this September than last.
   (D) September a year ago was noteworthy for its heavy rains.
   (E) None of the farms nearby had any change in their water bills from one September to the other.

Questions 14–15 refer to the following passage.

Investors in the bonds of Washington Savings Bank have lost all the money that they invested. Therefore, no savings bank should be permitted to sell new bonds without careful governmental supervision.

14. Which of the following is an assumption made in the argument above?
   (A) Government insurance does not cover the losses of investors in bonds issued by banks.
   (B) The investors should have been warned by the bank of the possibility of default on the bonds.
   (C) The government will have to make up the losses suffered by the bankrupt savings and loan companies.
   (D) If the bonds of one bank are in default, the bonds of all banks are likely to be in default.
   (E) Government supervision of the Washington Bank could have prevented its issuing bonds that became worthless.

15. Which of the following arguments most closely resembles the argument above?
   (A) Children exposed to second-hand tobacco smoke in the home are more likely to develop respiratory diseases. Therefore, parents should reduce their smoking in the home.
   (B) Twelve percent of fatal traffic accidents are caused by drivers over 75 years old. Therefore, drivers over 75 should be permitted to drive only after careful state examination.
   (C) Three widely sold brands of herbal tea have been found to contain comfrey, an herb that can be toxic with repeated ingestion. Therefore, these brands of herbal tea should be removed from grocery shelves.
   (D) Two members of the state legislature have pleaded guilty to charges of bribery. Therefore, the laws against bribery must be strengthened.
   (E) A child who does not want to attend school will not do good work in the classroom. Therefore, special classes should be established for weakly motivated students.

16. By reading the advertisements in the real estate section of the newspaper, anyone can see that there are far more condominiums for sale than duplex apartment buildings or single-family homes. Builders are beginning to recognize that there is a shortage of homes in the median price range.

Which of the following would best conclude the passage above?
(A)   We should soon see a decline in the high price of condominiums.
(B)   Real estate agents are concerned about the lack of movement in the apartment market.
(C)   New housing construction will probably concentrate on medium-priced duplex and single-family buildings.
(D)   The price of real estate will probably decline if the area is perceived to be overbuilt.
(E)   Next year, the number of unsold condominiums should be even larger.

17. The results of the election in Texas show that women can campaign negatively in order to survive mud-slinging primaries, and can win when the opposing party picks a fool as its condidate. But they cannot expect people to vote for them just because they are women. Incumbents still have a huge advantage, and an overwhelming percentage of incumbents are men.

Which of the following is the most logical conclusion of this paragraph?
(A)   So women are still unlikely to win a large number of elective offices.
(B)   Therefore, the number of women elected to national and state offices should increase regularly.
(C)   If all the women voters supported women candidates, women in office would outnumber men.
(D)   Therefore the re-election of office holders should decline in the near future.
(E)   So the number of mud-slinging campaigns may be expected to increase.

18. All Japanese gardens inspire contemplation, because they are filled with beautiful plantings.

Of the following, which is the missing premise in the statement above?
(A)   All Japanese gardens are beautiful.
(B)   Only gardens that inspire contemplation are filled with beautiful plantings.
(C)   Beautiful gardens contain beautiful plantings.
(D)   Beautiful plantings inspire contemplation.
(E)   Only beautiful plantings inspire contemplation.

Questions 19–20 refer to the following passage.

Children are not afraid of math and science. They approach these subjects full of questions. For parents who can answer these questions, the danger is explaining too much and preventing the children from learning for themselves and experiencing the pleasures of discovery. Most of us often find ourselves unable to answer such questions as "Why is the sky blue?" What we should do is praise children for their curiosity, and then help them learn where to look for answers. Most libraries stock books geared to introducing math and science to children.

What is most important, however, is the attitude of the adults toward learning. At the turn of the century, it was often the children of Jewish immigrants who excelled in science. Now it is often the Asian children who excel. Both groups have a tradition of respecting education. Obviously children who hear teachers and education praised at home will perform differently in school from children whose parents denigrate education. The attitudes of parents toward education are more important than how much they themselves know.

19. The author of the passage would probably disapprove of
(A)   parents who feel inadequate or embarrassed because they cannot answer their children's questions
(B)   children whose knowledge of math and science is greater than that of their parents
(C)   parents who respond to children's questions with irritation
(D)   immigrant parents with an imperfect knowledge of English
(E)   teaching math and science in elementary schools

20. Which of the following, if true, would provide the most serious challenge to the argument of this passage?
(A) Studies show that the earliest appearance of math anxiety is normally in junior high school age students.
(B) Most children are introduced to science by television rather than by reading.
(C) Asian-Americans had the highest average score on the mathematics section of the Scholastic Aptitude Test this year.
(D) The number of males who major in mathematics and science is much greater than the number of females.
(E) Jewish and Asian parents are more likely to criticize elementary and secondary schools than parents in other ethnic groups.

21. Photography is an art because it imposes form upon the chaos of the natural world.

The statement above assumes which of the following?
(A) Whatever is photographed is art.
(B) Painting is an art superior to photography.
(C) Art is the expression of human life.
(D) Whatever has form is an art.
(E) The natural world is artistic.

Questions 22–23 refer to the following passage.

Should the Forest Service post more warning signs in the areas visited by the public? Advocates say putting up signs would protect the agency from lawsuits and would be easy to do. The Forest Service argues that, by putting up a sign, the agency provides a potential litigant with evidence, if the sign has been removed. Also, almost any location in the wilderness might be dangerous, so the number of signs would equal that of trees. The problem, according to Forest Service spokesmen, is a public unprepared for the woods. People come wearing sandals and shorts, without a map, water, or sunglasses.

22. Which of the following explains the paradox of using as evidence a sign that has been removed?
(A) If the sign had never been placed in the forest, the visitor would be unaware of the danger.
(B) By putting up a sign, the Forest Service gives notice of a hazard.
(C) Whether or not a victim of an accident has seen a warning sign will be difficult to assess.
(D) The sign could be placed at the entrance to the forest; then it would not be stolen.
(E) Not all visitors to the forests understand English, so the signs would have to be in several languages.

23. The case against the Forest Service would be most strengthened if which of the following were true?
(A) The Forest Service has only five permanent employees per thousand square miles of forest.
(B) More than 40 percent of the visitors to the forests are non-English speaking.
(C) The Forest Service keeps no records of accidents, but private records indicate that fatalities in California forests average fifty per year.
(D) A high percentage of the accidents in national forests are caused by sudden changes in the weather.
(E) Studies show that 75 percent of park visitors will follow a rule or warning when they understand it.

24. Banning the sale of aerosol spray paints in this city will result in huge losses for paint manufacturers. Not all graffiti are painted with spray paints, and the aerosols' damage to the air is 100 times less than the harm done by automobile exhausts. Therefore the sale of spray paints should not be banned.

Which of the following, if true, would most seriously weaken the argument in the passage above?
(A) The cost of graffiti removal outweighs the projected losses of paint manufacturers.
(B) Industrial air pollution is also 100 times greater than pollution caused by aerosols.

(C) The quality of the air in the city has improved steadily in the last four years.
(D) Many serious art critics regard graffiti as a legitimate, artistically significant form of self-expression.
(E) The banning of spray paints may be the first step in a series of repressive city incursions on personal freedoms.

25. All continents have mountain ranges with mountains that are dangerous to climb. Therefore all the world's mountain ranges have mountains dangerous to climbers.

Which of the following most closely parallels the reasoning in the passage above?
(A) Every bird is warm blooded. Therefore every flying animal is warm blooded.
(B) All the geology books in the library circulate. Therefore all the library books about geology must circulate.
(C) Every atom is made up of electrons. Therefore all things must contain electrons.
(D) Every number is either odd or even. Therefore half of the numbers are odd.
(E) All the television channels on this set are in Spanish. Therefore all the television channels in this city must be in Spanish.

STOP

END OF MULTIPLE-CHOICE EXAMINATION. IF YOU FINISH BEFORE TIME IS UP, CHECK YOUR WORK ON THIS SECTION ONLY. DO NOT GO BACK TO ANY OTHER SECTION OF THE EXAMINATION.

EXAMINATION

WRITING SAMPLE

Time—30 Minutes

Directions:
You have 30 minutes to write an essay in response to a given topic. Take a few minutes to plan your work before you begin writing. DO NOT WRITE ON A TOPIC OF YOUR OWN CHOICE. ESSAYS THAT DO NOT ADDRESS THE GIVEN TOPIC ARE UNACCEPTABLE.

The quality of your writing is more important than the length of your response or the content. Pay attention to organization, appropriate diction, and correct usage. You will not be expected to display any specialized knowledge in your response, nor will you be expected to write a "perfect" essay; law schools understand that you are writing under a time constraint, and will allow for the minor lapses in writing ability that might occur under this circumstance.

Only the lined area in your booklet will be reproduced for the law schools, so do not write outside this space. *Do not* skip lines or use wide margins. These precautions, along with careful planning and legible handwriting that is not unduly large, will keep you within the allowed space.

SAMPLE TOPIC

Dolores is a single parent of twelve-year-old twins who attend a private school on scholarship. The head of the purchasing department of a large company located in downtown St. George, Dolores has recently sold the small house she owned in the city and must decide whether to purchase a condominium in the attractively redeveloped harbor area of the city or a house in the suburbs. *In the space provided, write an argument supporting one of the two choices*. The following factors should be taken into consideration:

- Dolores's doctor has urged her to spend more time on her two relaxing hobbies—gardening and bicycling.
- Dolores must significantly increase her yearly savings in order to provide for the twins' college education.

The suburban house that Dolores is considering is sixteen miles from her office. Dolores does not own a car. The house has a large yard and garden. The town is quiet and traffic-free, with stable property values. After making the down payment with the money from the sale of the house she has sold, Dolores will have tax and interest costs of $600 per month. Because the winters in St. George are severe, her yearly heating costs will be an additional $2,000 per year.

The harborfront condominium is located two miles from Dolores's workplace, and the city has bicycle lanes on all of its streets. The down payment on the condominium is equal to that of the house in the suburbs, but the apartment is smaller and has only a small brick patio for outdoor living. Dolores's tenancy costs, including her tax and interest payments would be $700 per month. Property values in the harbor area of the city have risen sharply in the recent past, but have fallen slightly this year.

ANSWER KEY

Section I: Analytical Reasoning	**Section II:** Reading Comprehension	**Section III:** Logical Reasoning	**Section IV:** Analytical Reasoning	**Section V:** Logical Reasoning
1. E	1. A	1. A	1. C	1. C
2. C	2. C	2. C	2. D	2. A
3. A	3. D	3. D	3. C	3. A
4. B	4. B	4. E	4. B	4. C
5. E	5. C	5. B	5. E	5. A
6. D	6. B	6. E	6. E	6. B
7. C	7. E	7. C	7. E	7. D
8. C	8. D	8. C	8. D	8. B
9. B	9. B	9. D	9. A	9. E
10. D	10. D	10. B	10. E	10. C
11. B	11. B	11. B	11. D	11. E
12. C	12. D	12. E	12. E	12. D
13. D	13. C	13. D	13. C	13. D
14. B	14. A	14. B	14. B	14. E
15. C	15. E	15. C	15. D	15. B
16. D	16. C	16. E	16. E	16. C
17. B	17. A	17. C	17. C	17. A
18. B	18. B	18. A	18. B	18. D
19. D	19. C	19. D	19. A	19. C
20. C	20. D	20. D	20. B	20. E
21. C	21. E	21. C	21. E	21. D
22. B	22. B	22. C	22. D	22. B
23. B	23. E	23. E	23. E	23. C
24. D	24. A	24. D	24. B	24. A
	25. B	25. D		25. B
	26. C	26. D		

MODEL TEST ANALYSIS

Doing model exams and understanding the explanations afterwards are of course important in acquainting you with typical LSAT question types and successful approaches to the questions. However, another benefit of carefully analyzing these model tests is to understand the kinds of errors you are making and thus work to minimize them. For instance, if a very high percentage of your incorrect answers is due to "careless error" or "misread problem," then perhaps you are working much too fast and should slow your pace accordingly. If your incorrect answers are due primarily to "lack of knowledge," then a careful rereading and reworking of the appropriate question-type chapter may be in order. Or if you find that you aren't completing a large number of questions because of lack of time, you may need to either increase your speed or learn to use the "one-check, two-check" technique more .effectively.

This kind of analysis of the model tests will enable you to identify your particular weaknesses and thus remedy them.

Model Test Five Analysis

Section	Total Number of Questions	Number Correct	Number Incorrect	Number Unanswered*
I: Analytical Reasoning	24			
II: Reading Comprehension	26			
III: Logical Reasoning	26			
IV: Analytical Reasoning	24			
V: Logical Reasoning	25			
TOTALS:	125			

*At this stage in your preparation, you should not be leaving any blank answer spaces. At least fill in a guess, as there is no penalty for a wrong answer.

Reasons for Incorrect Answers

You may wish to evaluate the explanations before completing this chart.

Section	Total Number Incorrect	Lack of Knowledge	Misread Problem	Careless Error	Unanswered or Wrong Guess
I: Analytical Reasoning					
II: Reading Comprehension					
III: Logical Reasoning					
IV: Analytical Reasoning					
V: Logical Reasoning					
TOTALS:					

EXPLANATIONS OF ANSWERS

Section I

Answers 1–6

The following notations may be helpful:

3 P	P P P (5 places or less)
2 B	BB
2 R	R R
1 C	R ? C ? R
1 V	V —✳— R

1. **E** Since the Cobra must be between the two Rockets, it cannot be on an end.

1	2	3	4	5	6	7	8	9	
V	B	B	R				R	P	5,6,7
B	B	R				R	P	V	4,5,6
R	C	B	B	R					2

2. **C** From the information added in the question, you could have constructed the following:

1	2	3	4	5	6	7	8	9
P	P	R	P	V	C	R	B	B

If the Viking is between the two Rockets along with the Cobra, the remaining slot must be a Panther. Thus, this is the only possible arrangement of the players.

3. **A** You could have tried these:

1	2	3	4	5	6	7	8	9	
	R		V		R				(not valid)
	R				R		V		(not valid)
	R				R			V	

With a Rocket in position 2, and therefore 6, there seem to be three possible positions for the Viking, as illustrated above. BUT, the first two are not valid, since after putting in the Badgers, the Panthers would be spread over more than 5 consecutive positions. Thus, the third arrangement is the only possible one.

4. **B** You could have constructed the following:

1	2	3	4	5	6	7	8	9
		V		R			C	R

This is the only possible arrangement of the players. The Badgers can be in either 6 and 7, or 1 and 2. Thus, B could be true, but it could be false. The other choices must be true.

5. **E** From the information given, you could have set up these possibilities:

1	2	3	4	5	6	7	8	9
B	B	P	P	R	P	V	C	R
P	P	R	P	V	C	R	B	B

and the reverse of these two

R	C	V	P	R	P	P	B	B
B	B	R	C	V	P	R	P	P

These are the only arrangements possible.

6. **D** You could have constructed the following:

1	2	3	4	5	6	7	8	9
V	P	P	P	R	B	B	C	R
				R	C	B	B	R

The Viking may be in 1, 2, or 3.

These arrangements may be reversed, left to right. One of the Badgers must be in position 7 or 3, making (D) the correct answer. Since the Panthers cannot be split on either side of the Rockets and are not between the Rockets, the Panthers and the Vikings must occupy the four positions on one end of the line or the other. Thus, there must be a Rocket in positions 5 and 9 or in positions 1 and 5.

Answers 7–12

You could have constructed the following diagrams:

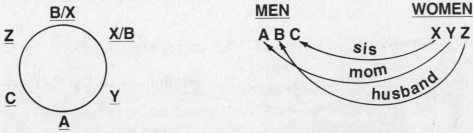

7. **C** From the diagram, we see that Y could sit next to B, depending on the positions of X and B. Thus, (C) could be true. All the other possibilities are always false.

8. **C** If B sits next to Z, then the arrangement is illustrated by those letters to the left of the /. Therefore C sits across from X.

9. **B** If C sits across from X, the arrangement is illustrated by those letters to the left of the "/". Thus, X sits next to Y, making (B) true. From the diagram, we see that the other four statements are false.

10. **D** From the diagram, we see that A must sit next to C. The other choices are either always false or sometimes false.

11. **B** If X does not sit across from her brother, then the arrangement is illustrated by those letters to the right of the /. Therefore, C sits across from B.

12. **C** At the table, since there are two of the women sitting next to each other, one of them always has a man to her left. The other woman also has a man to her left. Thus, 2 is the correct number.

Answers 13–18

The following charts prove helpful in organizing the data:

	SS	WP	DB		Com	Dou	Ex		Com	Dou	Ex
R		y		F	n			WP	n		
S		y		G			n	SS			
T				H	n	y	n	DB		n	

13. **D** Since Sharon only does her own word processing, she cannot use the Comstar, since it is not used for word processing. The other two are available.

14. **B** The Comstar is not available for word processing. George cannot use the Excellocalc at all. Thus, only the Doufast can be used.

15. **C** Since Ron only does word processing, and the Comstar is not available for word processing, this statement must be true.

16. **D** If Tom's secretary uses the Comstar, they must be using either database or spreadsheet programs, since the Comstar is not available for word processing.

17. **B** If George is Tom's secretary, then Sharon's secretary must be either Fran or Hilda. Neither Fran nor Hilda uses the Comstar. Thus (B) must be true.

18. **B** Since Tom's secretary will only use the Excellocalc, she must be Fran, thus (B) is true. Based on the diagram, the other four statements are false.

Answers 19–24

From the information given, you could have constructed the following family tree:

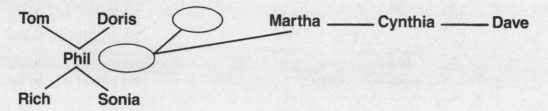

19. **D** From the chart, since Sonia's paternal grandmother is Doris, then Doris is Phil's mother.

20. **C** From the chart, since Martha is Rich's maternal grandmother, she must be Phil's wife's mother. So Martha's brother is Phil's wife's uncle.

21. **C** Since Alice is married to Phil, then Phil's mother, Doris, is the mother-in-law of Alice.

22. **B** The additional information would give us this chart:

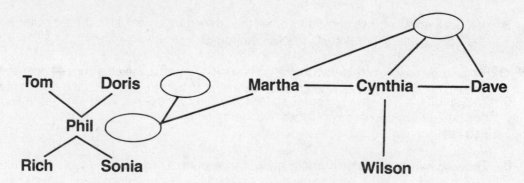

Since Dave's father is also Cynthia's father, then he would be Wilson's grandfather.

23. **B** Since Sonia is Phil's daughter, then Phil's brother would be her uncle.

24. **D** If Edgar has two sisters, and if Martha has one brother and one sister, then Alice has a total of 4 aunts and uncles.

Section II

Passage 1

1. **A** In the preceding sentence of the third paragraph, the author states that the Jazz Age ended with the 1929 depression, thus stressing that it was a phenomenon of the 1920s only. Recognizing that "it" stands for "Jazz Age," and refers to the preceding sentence, you must choose (A).

2. **C** The sentence indicates that the "Canon" consists of a group of writers and their works; the only choice that suggests a group or collection is (C).

3. **D** The 1960s are mentioned at the end of the second paragraph, just after the author has noted the human tendency to "forget unpleasantness." The '60s may become a happy recollection, we are told, but not until the twenty-first century. This speculation suggests that the author presently regards the '60s as an unhappy time that may be recalled more pleasantly after the passage of a few decades.

4. **B** The long assessment of Gertrude Stein in paragraph 4 follows the author's statement that she is one who made a deep impact after 1930, although many of her works were written before 1930. She, along with others, was "ahead of her time." (A), (C), and (D) are all true, but state subordinate facts rather than stressed points.

5. **C** Although the author acknowledges the importance of the stock market crash as an event that makes a "decisive cut" in literary history, he also stresses, "When dates are established, . . . predecessors and successors have a way of making them dissolve," thus suggesting that the crash cannot be isolated as a demarcation point without accounting for the events that led up to it and followed it. (D) and (E) are supported by the passage, but irrelevant to this particular question.

6. **B** In the final paragraph of the passage, the author states that in the 1930s "realism and naturalism are by this time established as dominant modes."

7. **E** Earlier in the third paragraph, we are told that the Wasteland "represents" a view of the '20s, '30s, and '40s. Therefore, the term does not literally describe an actual wasteland (D), but rather stands for a point of view that artists held about this era; it is a *figurative* term.

Passage 2

8. **D** The statement follows the narrator's admission that he is spending time in "vaults and charnel houses," that is, studying corpses. "Wonders of the eye and brain," explicitly refers to sight and intellect. Only (D) mentions corpses.

9. **B** The narrator stresses his interest in chemistry in the first sentence, and later stresses his interest in physiology. He also mentions anatomy, but that subject is not offered as a choice. (A), (C), and (D) are not *academic* subjects.

10. **D** The central question that motivates the narrator's research is "Whence . . . did the principle of life proceed?"

11. **B** The narration of personal experiences is appropriate in a personal journal. A "soliloquy" is a dramatic mode in which a character speaks privately, without acknowledging an audience.

12. **D** The narrator's comment on his lack of superstition immediately precedes his scientific investigation of the dead and thus verifies the objectivity of that investigation. His lack of superstition was, admittedly, influenced by his father, but is not described as a species of obedience (A).

13. **C** The first paragraph introduces the narrator's interest in chemistry, and the second paragraph describes "application . . . in my laboratory," clearly the further pursuit of scientific (chemical) study.

Passage 3

14. **A** A wrongful life action is based upon a belief in a right not to live, upon the belief that to deny a claim for wrongful life is as unjust as to deny a claim for wrongful death.

15. **E** A wrongful life action assumes that no life is preferable to the impaired life the plaintiff must endure.

16. **C** The relevant conditions are listed in the fourth paragraph of the passage. The point is that the impairments are *not* mere circumstances of birth, but preventable injuries.

17. **A** The passage says nothing about malpractice actions. If the parents are plaintiffs, the suit is likely to fail, but if the plaintiff is the infant, the case may be heard.

18. **B** It is clear from the paragraph as a whole that the first action was decided in favor of the defendant, but that the action of the Superior Court was reversed by the Court of Appeals.

19. **C** The passage cites no example of a plaintiff's winning a wrongful life case. If they existed, we can assume the author would discuss these actions rather than an indeterminate and incomplete case.

20. **D** Given the insistence on negligence prior to the birth or at birth and on the possibility of the defects being avoided or the birth not taking place in the criteria for damage in wrongful life actions, it is clear that medical advances that permit so much more knowledge of the fetus must play a large part in the incidence and the disposition of wrongful life actions.

Passage 4

21. **E** Paragraph (a) tells us that the author only "pretends" to watch with the "impassivity of the scientists."

22. **B** Halfway through paragraph (c), the author begins generalizing about the "best naturalists," distinguishing them from "mere" naturalists. This section is a mixture of both praise and disdain.

23. **E** Each of the other choices is either factual or a commonplace expression not regarded as literary, or a quite nonliterary use of metaphor (D). (E) compares marriage to a beverage and produces an unusual, highly subjective metaphor that departs from the dispassionate objectivity of the most conservative naturalism.

24. **A** Paragraph (b), which aligns naturalism with social science, stresses the writer's attention to "data from actual life." (C) is generally true of naturalism, but deemphasized character does not receive so close a comparison with scientific research.

25. **B** Note the author's emphasis that differences between realism and naturalism are not "clearcut and definitive," and his enumeration of tendencies rather than unquestionable facts. He does not refer to arts other than literature (E), but this is not because he is "careful" not to, but simply because he excludes the subject. His lack of absolutism, however, comes across through careful wording.

26. **C** Throughout the passage the author stresses the "real life" quality of naturalism. In the final paragraph he explicitly distinguishes between the "romantic" author and the "naturalistic" one, and enumerates factors mentioned in (A), (B), (D), and (E) as aspects of naturalism.

Section III

1. **A** Because the passage mentions produce safety and opinion polls, and then leads to a list of consumer food worries, it follows that this could be the latest supermarket battleground.

2. **C** Because the last sentence in the paragraph says "now tops the list of . . . beating out cholesterol and calories," one could reasonably conclude that these last two items were major concerns of consumers.

3. **D** If neither team scored a blunk in period 1 or 2, then in those two periods the Q's must have scored *3 blinks* and the P's must have scored *2 blinks*. Since no more blinks were scored in period 3 or 4, the Q's scored more blinks than the P's, 3 to 2.

4. **E** Tom's reply shows a disbelief in what he has just heard. Stan's statement doesn't logically follow.

5. **B** The author's argument, that if we can develop laser technology we can cure the common cold, assumes little or no significant distinction between the two challenges. The author, however, does not address this important point.

6. **E** Choice (E) brings in the "size of the individual," which is not an issue in the passage.

7. **C** Statements (A), (B), (D), and (E) would all weaken the claim of the first sentence, but (C) would not.

8. **C** Because the passage states that "the purpose of many of the authors is to offer help to a needy society," it can therefore be inferred that profits are not the *only* goal of many of the authors. Choice (A), an "*increasing* percentage," is not substantiated by the passage.

9. **D** This choice continues the idea that those only in the self-help business for the "quick buck" care little about the needs of the customer. Note the word "hastily" supports the notion of "quick buck."

10. **B** Reducing the mortality rate among squirrels would result in an increase in the squirrel (small game) population. (B) is the only answer that does not point out an ill effect of the reactor—(A), (D)—or a weakness in the argument presented—(C), (E).

11. **B** In order for the conclusion ("Therefore, Davidson will be found guilty . . .") to logically follow, Johnson *and* Smith must be elected for Davidson to be elected. Thereafter Davidson can be accused and found guilty. Therefore II, "Smith will be elected to the board," must be included in the passage.

12. **E** The only conclusion that can be drawn is that, given an accident, a motorbike operator has less chance for serious injury when wearing a helmet than when not wearing a helmet. Note that there is no relationship given between wearing a helmet and the chance of having an accident.

13. **D** If there are four times as many accidents involving motorbike operators wearing helmets as there are accidents involving operators who are not wearing helmets, and if there is 20 percent chance of serious injury to the former and 40 percent chance to the latter, then helmeted operators will be seriously injured more often (2 out of 10, but 4 times as many, compared to 4 out of 10).

14. **B** If the Consolidated building was constructed in 1988 in the city of Philadelphia, then it would have sprinkler systems. Therefore, it must not be situated in the city of Philadelphia.

15. **C** The author argues that a Broadway show is a greater theatrical experience than a high school play because more people with a greater appreciation elect to attend Broadway shows. This is called circular reasoning, or presupposing a point one later establishes.

16. **E** The author of this argument does not see the difference between "good at the sport" and "good sport."

17. **C** Because it appears that Roger has all of the necessary requirements except auditing experience, when he gains the proper auditing experience he will probably become a Certified Public Accountant.

18. **A** (B) is inappropriate because the argument speaks only of a "danger" and a "threshold beyond which" the monarchy is lost. (C) and (E) are completely contrary to the argument. (D) is inappropriate because the argument does not address bureaucrats or suggest any hostility. (A) is the proper choice because the argument clearly presents bureaucracy as a threat to monarchy.

19. **D** To conclude, based upon the poll, that military personnel favor capital punishment more often than nonmilitary personnel, one must assume that less than 93 percent of the nonmilitary personnel favor capital punishment.

20. **D** That Mr. Wong's committee plays an important role in setting district admissions policy would be a major factor determining the admissions policies from 1985 to 1988. Because there is no reason to doubt that those policies would not continue with Mr. Wong's reelection, (D) is the best answer.

21. **C** Reducing the number of artists would not necessarily decrease the amount of artwork sold, if that reduced number consisted only of artists who never sell their work.

22. **C** Because the author defines "artistic talent" as the number of works sold, an argument challenging that definition must weaken the author's argument.

23. **E** Each of statements (A), (E), and (C) presents additional examples challenging the soundness of the argument. (A) and (B) each introduce the argument that a police car may not be the only vehicle with a loud siren and flashing lights, and that another type of vehicle may exist with those qualities. (C) used birds to suggest that two qualities may be shared by several different items (in this case, ostriches and penguins), much like the police cars and other types of vehicles. (D) uses the same strategy. (E) may be true, but it does not undermine the statement.

24. **D** The passage points out that crime rates can be high or low in rural or urban communities.

25. **D** (A), (B), (C), or (E) are logical conclusions but (D), though it may be true, does not follow from this passage.

26. **D** Robert states that the Maximinima TQ 1000 must be a reliable camera because everyone wants to buy one. Only choice (D) directly addresses this dubious cause-effect statement.

Section IV

Answers 1–5

From the statements we can construct a chart as follows, using statements 2, 3, and 8:

HATS:				G	G	
SHIRTS:	R	R	R	B	B	G

Now, from statement 7 we know that the person wearing the green shirt is not wearing a blue hat. Therefore, we get:

HATS:		B	B	G	G	
SHIRTS:	R	R	R	B	B	G

which leaves the two red hats to complete the chart:

HATS:	R	B	B	G	G	R
SHIRTS:	R	R	R	B	B	G

Now, placing the people around the table, using first statement 7 and then statement 6, gives:

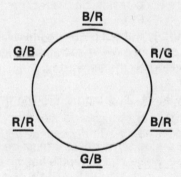

Now all the questions can be easily answered.

1. **C** Only (C) is true.

2. **D** If the green shirt should suddenly turn red, then statements 2, 4, 6, and 7 would no longer be true.

3. **C** If the two blue shirts turned green, then red and green shirts would alternate around the table, thus (C) is true. From the diagram, the other four are false.

4. **B** One of the two people who started with a green hat would still have a green hat, and one of the two people who started with a blue hat would still have a blue hat.

5. **E** The two people wearing blue hats would both be wearing blue shirts, thus (E) is false. All of the other statements are true.

Answers 6–11

From the information given, you may have constructed a simple grouping display of information similar to this:

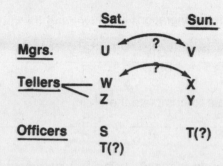

Another possible display might look like this:

	Sat.	**Sun.**
Mgrs.	U ⟷?	V
Tellers	W ⟷?	X
	Z	Y
Officers	S	T(?)
	T(?)	

6. **E** From the original information, a manager must be on duty each day and the managers cannot work on the same day. Therefore (A) must be true. (E) does not have to be true, since U's schedule has no bearing on X's schedule. Since W and X will not work on the same day, (B) must also be true. There is no restriction placed on T.

7. **E** V, W, Z, S can work on Saturday without breaking any of the conditions given. Choice (A) is missing a manager. Choice (B) has two managers working on the same day. Choices (C) and (D) have W and X working on the same day.

8. **D** Five employees, U or V, X or W, Z, S, and T are the greatest number to work on Saturday.

9. **A** Since W and X will not work on the same day, (A) must be true. (B) is false since Y must work on Sunday. (C) could be true. Since W's schedule has no effect on Z and U, (D) and (E) may be true or false.

10. **E** Since no employee can work on consecutive days, and there are four tellers, then two must work on Saturday.

11. **D** U, V, W, X, Y, Z, and T have the possibility of working on Sunday; S and Z do not.

Answers 12–16

12. **E** If a second generation of Flit Flies is born, then at least three of the four conditions necessary for Flit Flies to mate must be met, namely, the presence of *agar-agar* in a *petri dish* at 78° and at *normal barometric pressure*. Since statement 4 fulfills one condition (petri dish), then only one of the other remaining three conditions may be deleted (but not necessarily has to be).

13. **C** Since three of the conditions are met (agar-agar, petri dish, and 78°), then conditions are sufficient for Flit Flies to mate, but they don't necessarily have to. Thus we eliminate (A). (B) is blatantly incorrect, as it is against the rules. (C) is correct, since 5 days must intervene between mating and birth of the offspring. (D) could be true, but not necessarily must be. And (E) must be incorrect because offspring will not have appeared by June 4.

14. **B** No matter when a third generation appears, a second generation cannot start mating until 5 days after the beginning of the experiment, since 5 days must intervene before the second generation offspring are born. (E) may not be true since more than one of the breeding conditions may not be met.

15. **D** The earliest a second generation could have appeared would be on June 6 (June 1 + 5 days); thus, the earliest a third generation could appear would be June 11 (June 6 + 5 days). Therefore, a third generation could not have appeared on June 9.

16. **E** Simply destroying first-generation Flit Flies will not solve the problem, as the second or third or fourth generation may continue to reproduce. If, however, the governor eliminates two of the four necessary conditions for Flit Fly reproduction, then the species will not be able to reproduce and will, in fact, become extinct.

Answers 17–24

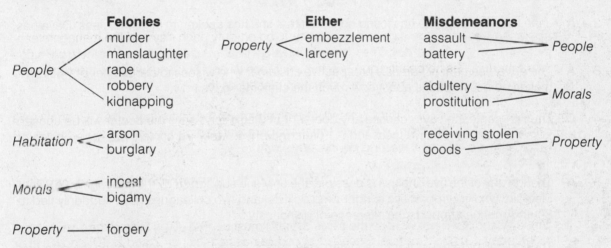

A COMMON MISTAKE IS TO *OVERCHART,* THAT IS, TO MAKE YOUR CHART TOO COMPLEX OR TOO COMPLETE, AND NOT HAVE ENOUGH TIME FOR THE QUESTIONS. KEEP YOUR CHART SIMPLE AND EASY TO READ.

17. **C** Rape and arson must be felonies, according to the chart. If we refer to the statements, statement 1 tells us that rape is a felony; statement 6 tells us that burglary and robbery are the same level of crime—therefore, by statement 1, burglary is a felony; and statement 2 tells us that arson and burglary are the same level—thus arson is also a felony.

18. **B** Embezzlement and larceny are the only two crimes that are stated (statement 5) as having the possibility of being one or the other.

19. **A** The chart shows that embezzlement, prostitution, and receiving stolen goods could be misdemeanors. If we do not use the chart: embezzlement (statement 5) could be a misdemeanor; prostitution, not being the same level as arson (statement 8), must be a misdemeanor (arson was deduced as a felony in question 16); and receiving stolen goods must be a misdemeanor (statement 6), as it is also not the same level as arson.

20. **B** If all felonious crimes against people were punishable by death, then murder, rape, manslaughter, robbery, and kidnapping would be punishable by death, because they are felonious crimes against people (statement 1 or chart).

21. **E** The most abundant crimes are not determinable by these statements. They never refer to the number of crimes.

22. **D** That burglary is a felony and that receiving stolen property is the same level as adultery can be deduced, using the chart.

23. **E** Cannot be determined. None of the choices *must* be true.

24. **B** According to the statements, there are seven sorts of crimes against people. This can be seen in the chart.

Section V

1. **C** Though choice (A) may be true, it does not weaken the argument. However, if higher taxes do not reduce the number of smokers, as was the case in Canada, the proposed reductions in health care and lost productivity will not materialize.

2. **A** Jane has said only she has found none, not that she has spoken to all of the class. Dave has misunderstood.

3. **A** The advertisement assumes a prospective customer who wishes to choose her physician. It makes no assumptions about how much the customer pays now.

4. **C** The first sentence says "choose any doctor," but the second says the doctor will be chosen from the company's "five thousand . . . preferred physicians"—a choice, but not a choice of "any" doctor.

5. **A** Though any of the five choices is possible, the only one supported by the passage is (A). That Medicin, who is sympathetic to right-wing politics, and two colleagues have suddenly fled to South America supports the inference of dishonesty.

6. **B** The logical conclusion from the statements is that, since Jack is not rich, he is not a first baseman for the New York Mets, not that he is not a first baseman. He could be a first baseman for some other team and not be rich.

7. **D** All Italian greyhounds are graceful and fast (C), (E), and graceful and fast greyhounds are slender, so all Italian greyhounds are slender (A). If some graceful and fast Italian greyhounds are nervous, then some greyhounds are nervous (B).

8. **B** In this experiment, the female's preference must already have been present before the artificial fins were added to the males. The evolution of the males presumably has not yet caught up to the female predisposition.

9. **E** The author would probably disagree with choices (A), (B), (C), and (D), but endorse the precaution of (E).

10. **C** The reasoning pattern is as follows: the smaller the *x*, the greater the *y*. Therefore the absence of *x* probably causes *y*.

11. **E** From the information given, it is not clear how the case will be decided. But any decision will violate the religious rights of the Yorubas or the "rights" of animals.

12. **D** (A), (B), (C), and (E) would support the prohibition, but (D) would oppose it with a historical precedent.

13. **D** If there were heavy rains a year ago, the orchards would use less water and water bills would be lower than normal.

14. **E** The argument assumes that "careful governmental supervision" can prevent default.

15. **B** In each case, the first sentence presents an unhappy event. The second argues for careful oversight (in question 14, "governmental supervision"; here, "state examination").

16. **C** The correct response is based on information from both sentences: the relative scarcity of duplex and single-family homes for sale in the first, the shortage of median-priced homes in the second.

17. **A** If incumbents have an advantage and incumbents are chiefly men, women can win a large number of offices only by unseating the advantaged incumbents—an unlikely event.

18. **D** The logic of the statement is that beautiful plantings inspire contemplation; therefore Japanese gardens, which are filled with beautiful plantings, inspire contemplation.

19. **C** The author would disapprove of parents who discouraged intellectual curiosity in children.

20. **E** The author cites Jewish and Asian parents as examples of those who respect education rather than criticize it.

21. **D** The assumption here is that form is essential to art. Presumably some photographs will not have a formal quality to qualify them as art.

22. **B** The putting up of a warning sign is an admission that a hazard exists. This fact can be used against the Forest Service if the sign has been removed and not replaced.

23. **C** If the number of fatalities in one state is so high, the need for warning signs is underlined.

24. **A** Only choice (A) makes specific use of the details of the argument. Choices (C) and (D) would strengthen the case against banning spray paints.

25. **B** In the passage, "All continents" = "the world," and "mountains . . . dangerous to climb" = "mountains dangerous to climbers." In the correct answer, "All the geology books" = "all . . . books about geology," and "circulate" = "circulate."

Chapter

11

Model Test Six

This chapter contains full-length Model Test Six. It is geared to the format of the LSAT, and it is complete with answers and explanations. It is equivalent to the LSAT in question structure, number of questions, level of difficulty, and time allotments. (The questions used are not taken directly from the LSAT, as those questions are copyrighted and may not be reproduced.)

Model Test Six should be taken under strict test conditions. The test ends with a 30-minute Writing Sample which is not scored.

Section	Description	Number of Questions	Time Allowed
I	Logical Reasoning	25	35 minutes
II	Reading Comprehension	28	35 minutes
III	Logical Reasoning	25	35 minutes
IV	Analytical Reasoning	23	35 minutes
V	Reading Comprehension	28	35 minutes
	Writing Sample		30 minutes
TOTALS:		129	3 hours 25 minutes

Now please turn to the next page, remove your answer sheets, and begin Model Test Six.

ANSWER SHEET—MODEL TEST SIX
LAW SCHOOL ADMISSION TEST (LSAT)

Section I:
Logical Reasoning

1. Ⓐ Ⓑ Ⓒ Ⓓ Ⓔ
2. Ⓐ Ⓑ Ⓒ Ⓓ Ⓔ
3. Ⓐ Ⓑ Ⓒ Ⓓ Ⓔ
4. Ⓐ Ⓑ Ⓒ Ⓓ Ⓔ
5. Ⓐ Ⓑ Ⓒ Ⓓ Ⓔ
6. Ⓐ Ⓑ Ⓒ Ⓓ Ⓔ
7. Ⓐ Ⓑ Ⓒ Ⓓ Ⓔ
8. Ⓐ Ⓑ Ⓒ Ⓓ Ⓔ
9. Ⓐ Ⓑ Ⓒ Ⓓ Ⓔ
10. Ⓐ Ⓑ Ⓒ Ⓓ Ⓔ
11. Ⓐ Ⓑ Ⓒ Ⓓ Ⓔ
12. Ⓐ Ⓑ Ⓒ Ⓓ Ⓔ
13. Ⓐ Ⓑ Ⓒ Ⓓ Ⓔ
14. Ⓐ Ⓑ Ⓒ Ⓓ Ⓔ
15. Ⓐ Ⓑ Ⓒ Ⓓ Ⓔ
16. Ⓐ Ⓑ Ⓒ Ⓓ Ⓔ
17. Ⓐ Ⓑ Ⓒ Ⓓ Ⓔ
18. Ⓐ Ⓑ Ⓒ Ⓓ Ⓔ
19. Ⓐ Ⓑ Ⓒ Ⓓ Ⓔ
20. Ⓐ Ⓑ Ⓒ Ⓓ Ⓔ
21. Ⓐ Ⓑ Ⓒ Ⓓ Ⓔ
22. Ⓐ Ⓑ Ⓒ Ⓓ Ⓔ
23. Ⓐ Ⓑ Ⓒ Ⓓ Ⓔ
24. Ⓐ Ⓑ Ⓒ Ⓓ Ⓔ
25. Ⓐ Ⓑ Ⓒ Ⓓ Ⓔ

Section II:
Reading Comprehension

1. Ⓐ Ⓑ Ⓒ Ⓓ Ⓔ
2. Ⓐ Ⓑ Ⓒ Ⓓ Ⓔ
3. Ⓐ Ⓑ Ⓒ Ⓓ Ⓔ
4. Ⓐ Ⓑ Ⓒ Ⓓ Ⓔ
5. Ⓐ Ⓑ Ⓒ Ⓓ Ⓔ
6. Ⓐ Ⓑ Ⓒ Ⓓ Ⓔ
7. Ⓐ Ⓑ Ⓒ Ⓓ Ⓔ
8. Ⓐ Ⓑ Ⓒ Ⓓ Ⓔ
9. Ⓐ Ⓑ Ⓒ Ⓓ Ⓔ
10. Ⓐ Ⓑ Ⓒ Ⓓ Ⓔ
11. Ⓐ Ⓑ Ⓒ Ⓓ Ⓔ
12. Ⓐ Ⓑ Ⓒ Ⓓ Ⓔ
13. Ⓐ Ⓑ Ⓒ Ⓓ Ⓔ
14. Ⓐ Ⓑ Ⓒ Ⓓ Ⓔ
15. Ⓐ Ⓑ Ⓒ Ⓓ Ⓔ
16. Ⓐ Ⓑ Ⓒ Ⓓ Ⓔ
17. Ⓐ Ⓑ Ⓒ Ⓓ Ⓔ
18. Ⓐ Ⓑ Ⓒ Ⓓ Ⓔ
19. Ⓐ Ⓑ Ⓒ Ⓓ Ⓔ
20. Ⓐ Ⓓ Ⓒ Ⓓ Ⓔ
21. Ⓐ Ⓑ Ⓒ Ⓓ Ⓔ
22. Ⓐ Ⓑ Ⓒ Ⓓ Ⓔ
23. Ⓐ Ⓑ Ⓒ Ⓓ Ⓔ
24. Ⓐ Ⓑ Ⓒ Ⓓ Ⓔ
25. Ⓐ Ⓑ Ⓒ Ⓓ Ⓔ
26. Ⓐ Ⓑ Ⓒ Ⓓ Ⓔ
27. Ⓐ Ⓑ Ⓒ Ⓓ Ⓔ
28. Ⓐ Ⓑ Ⓒ Ⓓ Ⓔ

Section III:
Logical Reasoning

1. Ⓐ Ⓑ Ⓒ Ⓓ Ⓔ
2. Ⓐ Ⓑ Ⓒ Ⓓ Ⓔ
3. Ⓐ Ⓑ Ⓒ Ⓓ Ⓔ
4. Ⓐ Ⓑ Ⓒ Ⓓ Ⓔ
5. Ⓐ Ⓑ Ⓒ Ⓓ Ⓔ
6. Ⓐ Ⓑ Ⓒ Ⓓ Ⓔ
7. Ⓐ Ⓑ Ⓒ Ⓓ Ⓔ
8. Ⓐ Ⓑ Ⓒ Ⓓ Ⓔ
9. Ⓐ Ⓑ Ⓒ Ⓓ Ⓔ
10. Ⓐ Ⓑ Ⓒ Ⓓ Ⓔ
11. Ⓐ Ⓑ Ⓒ Ⓓ Ⓔ
12. Ⓐ Ⓑ Ⓒ Ⓓ Ⓔ
13. Ⓐ Ⓑ Ⓒ Ⓓ Ⓔ
14. Ⓐ Ⓑ Ⓒ Ⓓ Ⓔ
15. Ⓐ Ⓑ Ⓒ Ⓓ Ⓔ
16. Ⓐ Ⓑ Ⓒ Ⓓ Ⓔ
17. Ⓐ Ⓑ Ⓒ Ⓓ Ⓔ
18. Ⓐ Ⓑ Ⓒ Ⓓ Ⓔ
19. Ⓐ Ⓑ Ⓒ Ⓓ Ⓔ
20. Ⓐ Ⓑ Ⓒ Ⓓ Ⓔ
21. Ⓐ Ⓑ Ⓒ Ⓓ Ⓔ
22. Ⓐ Ⓑ Ⓒ Ⓓ Ⓔ
23. Ⓐ Ⓑ Ⓒ Ⓓ Ⓔ
24. Ⓐ Ⓑ Ⓒ Ⓓ Ⓔ
25. Ⓐ Ⓑ Ⓒ Ⓓ Ⓔ

ANSWER SHEET—MODEL TEST SIX
LAW SCHOOL ADMISSION TEST (LSAT

Section IV:
Analytical Reasoning

1. Ⓐ Ⓑ Ⓒ Ⓓ Ⓔ
2. Ⓐ Ⓑ Ⓒ Ⓓ Ⓔ
3. Ⓐ Ⓑ Ⓒ Ⓓ Ⓔ
4. Ⓐ Ⓑ Ⓒ Ⓓ Ⓔ
5. Ⓐ Ⓑ Ⓒ Ⓓ Ⓔ
6. Ⓐ Ⓑ Ⓒ Ⓓ Ⓔ
7. Ⓐ Ⓑ Ⓒ Ⓓ Ⓔ
8. Ⓐ Ⓑ Ⓒ Ⓓ Ⓔ
9. Ⓐ Ⓑ Ⓒ Ⓓ Ⓔ
10. Ⓐ Ⓑ Ⓒ Ⓓ Ⓔ
11. Ⓐ Ⓑ Ⓒ Ⓓ Ⓔ
12. Ⓐ Ⓑ Ⓒ Ⓓ Ⓔ
13. Ⓐ Ⓑ Ⓒ Ⓓ Ⓔ
14. Ⓐ Ⓑ Ⓒ Ⓓ Ⓔ
15. Ⓐ Ⓑ Ⓒ Ⓓ Ⓔ
16. Ⓐ Ⓑ Ⓒ Ⓓ Ⓔ
17. Ⓐ Ⓑ Ⓒ Ⓓ Ⓔ
18. Ⓐ Ⓑ Ⓒ Ⓓ Ⓔ
19. Ⓐ Ⓑ Ⓒ Ⓓ Ⓔ
20. Ⓐ Ⓑ Ⓒ Ⓓ Ⓔ
21. Ⓐ Ⓑ Ⓒ Ⓓ Ⓔ
22. Ⓐ Ⓑ Ⓒ Ⓓ Ⓔ
23. Ⓐ Ⓑ Ⓒ Ⓓ Ⓔ

Section V:
Reading Comprehension

1. Ⓐ Ⓑ Ⓒ Ⓓ Ⓔ
2. Ⓐ Ⓑ Ⓒ Ⓓ Ⓔ
3. Ⓐ Ⓑ Ⓒ Ⓓ Ⓔ
4. Ⓐ Ⓑ Ⓒ Ⓓ Ⓔ
5. Ⓐ Ⓑ Ⓒ Ⓓ Ⓔ
6. Ⓐ Ⓑ Ⓒ Ⓓ Ⓔ
7. Ⓐ Ⓑ Ⓒ Ⓓ Ⓔ
8. Ⓐ Ⓑ Ⓒ Ⓓ Ⓔ
9. Ⓐ Ⓑ Ⓒ Ⓓ Ⓔ
10. Ⓐ Ⓑ Ⓒ Ⓓ Ⓔ
11. Ⓐ Ⓑ Ⓒ Ⓓ Ⓔ
12. Ⓐ Ⓑ Ⓒ Ⓓ Ⓔ
13. Ⓐ Ⓑ Ⓒ Ⓓ Ⓔ
14. Ⓐ Ⓑ Ⓒ Ⓓ Ⓔ
15. Ⓐ Ⓑ Ⓒ Ⓓ Ⓔ
16. Ⓐ Ⓑ Ⓒ Ⓓ Ⓔ
17. Ⓐ Ⓑ Ⓒ Ⓓ Ⓔ
18. Ⓐ Ⓑ Ⓒ Ⓓ Ⓔ
19. Ⓐ Ⓑ Ⓒ Ⓓ Ⓔ
20. Ⓐ Ⓑ Ⓒ Ⓓ Ⓔ
21. Ⓐ Ⓑ Ⓒ Ⓓ Ⓔ
22. Ⓐ Ⓑ Ⓒ Ⓓ Ⓔ
23. Ⓐ Ⓑ Ⓒ Ⓓ Ⓔ
24. Ⓐ Ⓑ Ⓒ Ⓓ Ⓔ
25. Ⓐ Ⓑ Ⓒ Ⓓ Ⓔ
26. Ⓐ Ⓑ Ⓒ Ⓓ Ⓔ
27. Ⓐ Ⓑ Ⓒ Ⓓ Ⓔ
28. Ⓐ Ⓑ Ⓒ Ⓓ Ⓔ

SECTION I
LOGICAL REASONING

Time—35 Minutes
25 Questions

Directions:
In this section you will be given brief statements or passages and will be required to evaluate the reasoning involved. In some instances, more than one choice will appear to be a possible answer. You are to choose the *best* answer. Use common sense and reasonableness in making your selection; then mark the proper space on the answer sheet.

1. The President's party normally loses seats in the House of Representatives and none in the Senate in the years when there is no presidential election. Johnson lost 47 House seats in 1966, and Nixon lost 12 House seats in 1970. Since the end of World War II, the average loss in the House is 24 seats. In 1990, the Republicans lost only 12 House seats, and so the Congressional election may be regarded as a Republican victory.

   The conclusion of this argument is called into doubt by all of the following EXCEPT
   (A) the Republicans lost an above-average number of seats in the Senate
   (B) the Republicans held fewer seats in the House than usual before the elections
   (C) the Republican House losses in this election, added to losses in the House in the presidential election two years before, give them fewer seats than at almost any time since 1946
   (D) there were only two Republican Senate seats up for reelection and the Democrats won both
   (E) the voter turnout across the country this year was smaller than normal

2. A kindergarten teacher from Solana Beach has won an award for teaching geography. She had her class write to friends or relatives in as many states as possible, and posted the replies on a large classroom map. Her students learned the lessons well. In a competition to locate the states on a blank map, they easily defeated a team from San Marcos High School. The prize was a large collection of materials for teaching geography.

   Which of the following is the most logical concluding sentence for this passage?
   (A) These prize materials didn't include workbooks.
   (B) Needless to say, these materials are probably more needed at the high school.
   (C) It is not surprising that Americans are less likely than Europeans to know much about geography.
   (D) Many American educators are concerned about our lack of geographical knowledge.
   (E) The kindergarten students located all fifty states without an error.

3. When Mr. Smith attempted to buy the fish of the day at his local supermarket, he discovered there was none left. The store manager explained that the fish of the day had already been sold out.

   The store manager's explanation is an example of
   (A) failure to generalize from a specific case
   (B) euphemism
   (C) rephrasing but not explaining a problem
   (D) attempting to change the grounds of an argument
   (E) using evidence not relevant to a conclusion.

Questions 4–5 refer to the following passage.

The makers of Volvo have spent more than $100,000 for advertisements that apologize for fakery in an earlier ad that showed a reinforced Volvo surviving punishment that destroyed other makes of cars. But the greater cost to the Swedish car company will be the loss of public trust. Company officials say only that one ad is at fault. But prospective customers may be wondering, "If one ad can't be trusted, how about all the others?"

Volvo is not the only advertiser caught trying to hoodwink the public. Every year dozens of fake advertisers are exposed by consumer advocates, Better Business Bureaus, or even the Federal Trade Commission. A cola comparison ad was dropped from television recently when its test results were found unconvincing. The deer in a Canadian travel ad came from a petting zoo. In fact, the history of advertising is a long, nasty story of ads that deceive. Only 8 percent of the consumers responding to a recent survey said they were confident that advertising is truthful.

4. Which of the following best describes the structure of the argument in this passage?
  (A) It moves from the general to the specific.
  (B) It replies to anticipated objections of the other side.
  (C) It argues from inconsistent points of view.
  (D) It relies heavily on the use of analogy.
  (E) It moves from a specific example to a conclusion.

5. Which of the following, if true, would best support the argument of the passage?
  (A) Advertisers, or their agencies, insist that hardly any ads are deceptive.
  (B) The Federal Trade Commission says that every time they forbid a deceptive practice, advertisers find a new way around it.
  (C) The National Advertising Division is a watchdog of advertising for the Better Business Bureau.
  (D) The number of convictions on charges of using the mails to defraud declined slightly in the last three years.
  (E) Advertisers are now using thirty-minute "informercials" that combine entertainment and commercial messages.

6. Agriculture presents the biggest problem at the world trade negotiations. Developed nations must agree to reduce farm subsidies and supports as a *quid pro quo* for developing nations to agree to new rules on services and investments. But the European Community has dragged its feet on the farm subsidy issue for years. Germany and France are especially reluctant to agree to any reduction in farm subsidies, no doubt, in part, because the German chancellor faces an election next month. And the European ban on virtually all American meat imports (on the basis of "health inspection standards") is not encouraging.

We can infer from the passage above that
  (A) the United States does not support the reduction of farm subsidies
  (B) farmers in Germany are a large voting constituency
  (C) farm supports and subsidies are common in developing countries
  (D) European bans on American meat are based on the known health dangers of American products
  (E) French politicians would support the reduction in farm subsidies if they did not face election campaigns

7. According to a leading conservative African-American commentator, preferential admissions policies have not been helpful to African-American students. Their college dropout rate is about 70 percent. What is really needed, he suggests, is an improved public school system. The call for an "ethnic" curriculum comes at a cost to more basic learning. Meanwhile the white middle class that can afford private schools is leaving the public schools, and asking for government help to pay the bills for private education.

Which of the following statements, if true, could offer the strongest refutation of the argument in the passage above?
  (A) The college dropout rate overall is 35 percent.
  (B) The call for an "ethnic" curriculum comes not only from African-Americans, but also from Latinos, Asian-Americans, and Native Americans.

(C)   Test scores show that the public schools in California have made slow but steady progress in the past four years.

(D)   The worker shortage in the years ahead is expected to encompass both blue-collar and white-collar workers.

(E)   The society that we construct gives us the education that we deserve.

8. (1) Super Bowl tickets this year will each cost $150, $25 more than last year, and $50 more than the year before. (2) National Football League spokesmen have pointed out that for $150 the fan will receive a full afternoon's entertainment, four quarters of football, and a half-time show, while people recently paid $1000 for a world-championship boxing match that lasted only seven minutes. (3) Hotel and food prices on the Super Bowl weekend are expected to rise by about 25 percent. (4) The National Football League expects the price rise to continue until the public is no longer stupid enough to pay whatever price is asked. (5) In 1995, the cost per ticket will be $250.

The author's attitude to the price of Super Bowl tickets is made clear first in the
(A)   first sentence of the paragraph
(B)   second sentence of the paragraph
(C)   third sentence of the paragraph
(D)   fourth sentence of the paragraph
(E)   fifth sentence of the paragraph

9. *Brian:*   "Evolutionists begin by assuming that science excludes the possibility of a creator."
Darrell: "No. Evolutionists attempt to explain the origin of species, not the origin of life."

If Darrell's is the correct view of evolutionary thought, the evolutionists
(A)   will not explain where matter came from
(B)   would support a view in which the development of life forms is divinely controlled
(C)   will support a belief that all the animals were saved by Noah
(D)   will deny the existence of the supernatural
(E)   will favor Christianity over any of the religions of the East

Questions 10–11 refer to the following passage.

An embargo on the importation of Mexican tuna was recently overturned in an appeals court decision. Environmentalists had won the ban as part of an effort to stop fishing practices that kill dolphins swimming near tuna schools. The decision comes at a time when the administration is trying to adopt a free-trade agreement with Mexico. The government contends that Mexican fishermen have curtailed the dolphin deaths, while the environmentalists charge the government's statistics are inadequate and misleading. The Mexican government claims it has reduced the dolphin kill by 70 percent in recent years. Neither the Mexican nor the U.S. commerce departments would connect the embargo to the talks on a free-trade agreement between the two companies.

10. The paragraph implies that
(A)   the embargo and the free-trade agreement are connected
(B)   the Mexican fisheries have not reduced the number of dolphins killed
(C)   the environmentalists had succeeded in having Mexican tuna imported into the United States
(D)   the government's statistical support of U.S. tuna fishermen is inadequate
(E)   the courts will decide in favor of the environmentalists on this issue

11. From the information presented in the passage, an impartial reader should
(A)   take sides with the environmentalists
(B)   take sides with the U.S. and Mexican governments
(C)   be unable to determine which side is right
(D)   regard the disagreement as one that can never be settled
(E)   regard the disagreement as inappropriate for legal dispute

12. An American defense of a Persian Gulf country is based, not on self-interested protection of our oil source, but on moral principles that do not permit us to tolerate the invasion of an innocent nation. The Iraqi invasion of Kuwait is just such an action; and if the only Kuwaiti export were tennis balls, we would still defend the country against aggression.

The argument of this paragraph can be described as all of the following EXCEPT
(A) the offering of a moral rather than a materialistic reason for American actions
(B) a condemnation of Iraq as an aggressor
(C) a defense against an accusation of acting on self-interested motives
(D) concealing what is an act of aggression under the guise of a nonaggressive act
(E) using an analogy to support its main point

13. Because the presentation of mothers in the novels of Jane Austen is unflattering and even hostile, many readers have concluded that Jane Austen's attitude to her own mother was disapproving.

Which of the following, if true, would best support the conclusion above?
(A) The hostile comments about mothers are spoken by characters in the novels of whom the author clearly disapproves.
(B) Jane Austen's presentation of fathers in her novels is equally unflattering.
(C) What an author says in a work of fiction does not necessarily reflect the author's beliefs.
(D) The unfavorable attitude toward mothers is reflected in the ironic comments of the narrator of the novels as well as in the dialogue.
(E) The attitude toward mothers in novels by other writers written in the same period is also disapproving.

Questions 14–15 refer to the following passage.

That a record album was made by unnamed studio musicians rather than by the singers whose names appear on the cover is bad enough. The larger embarrassment to the record industry is that the record was chosen for special honor as the best of the year. The album sold nearly eight million copies, a triumph of marketing since the songs themselves are mediocre and the performances equally pedestrian. Why, then, did it win an award? Because _____ .

14. Which of the following most logically completes the paragraph?
(A) the voters for the awards are sophisticated musicians
(B) all awards for excellence in the arts are folly
(C) in determining awards sales figures are more important than the quality of the product
(D) the record company was unaware of the deceptions
(E) the record industry is made up of performing artists and business people

15. Which of the following, if true, would most greatly weaken the argument of the passage?
(A) Last year's winner of record of the year sold fewer than 200,000 copies.
(B) The record company was aware that the singers advertised on the album cover had not made the recording.
(C) Sales of records are now influenced more by television than by radio publicity.
(D) Not all of the workers in the record industry voted for this year's award.
(E) Some reviewers praised the performers and others praised the songs on this year's award-winning album.

16. A Supreme Court decision ruled that a state employee of 61, who retired because of Alzheimer's disease but was barred from disability benefits, was not protected under the Age Discrimination in Employment Act (ADEA). The court limited the application of the act to wages, hiring, and dismissals, not to employee benefits. A proposed new law restoring protection of employee benefits to older workers has been criticized by the President as imposing unfair burdens upon business, and he has threatened to veto it if it is enacted. The American Association of Retired Persons has _____ .

Which of the following best completes the last sentence in the passage above?
(A) criticized the proposed new law as likely to raise the cost of business operations
(B) refused to take a stand on the Supreme Court's decision
(C) supported the Supreme Court's decision as a reasonable interpretation of the ADEA
(D) thrown its support behind the new law, and will lobby for an override of the President's veto
(E) expressed concern that passage of the new law might lead to a reduction in Medicare benefits

17. Anyone can become a financial planner. All you have to do is put up a sign advertising financial planning services, give advice to anyone who asks for it, and collect a fee. Legally, all an "investment advisor" has to do is register with the Securities and Exchange Commission and fill out an information form. Many financial planners lack skill or training, and give bad advice that injures their clients. Some are downright dishonest and either encourage investments in financial products for which the planner receives a fee ("self-dealing"), or run up large fees for unnecessary services, or actually steal from clients.

Which of the following is the author's main point in this paragraph?
(A) There is insufficient regulation of financial planners.
(B) Some financial planners are dishonest.
(C) To become a financial planner, one must register with the Securities and Exchange Commission.
(D) There should be a required degree and examination for all financial planners.
(E) There are good and bad financial planners, and an investor should choose with care.

18. Suzanne discovers that she can play two or three strenuous sets of tennis if she eats a light breakfast and no lunch, but only one set if she has a full meal at either time. She concludes that eating lightly improves her stamina.

Which of the following most closely resembles the reasoning in the passage above?
(A) David is told that by reducing the fat in his diet he may feel more vigorous in the mornings, but will be more fatigued in the evenings.
(B) Arlene practices golf an hour a day more than Marge and regularly scores better. Arlene concludes that the extra practice makes her the better golfer.
(C) Jean's lawyer tells her that, if she pays her taxes in quarterly payments, she need not pay withholding taxes. She agrees to do so.
(D) Rats that are fed at nine and twelve each day gain more weight than rats that are fed the same total amount of food at a single midafternoon feeding. They also live longer than the rats fed once a day.
(E) Arthur believes that by taking a multivitamin and a vitamin C tablet each day he can reduce the number of colds he has each winter.

Questions 19–20 refer to the following passage.

There is rust between the tines of this fork. This diner must buy cheap utensils. The fork cannot be made of stainless steel.

19. Which of the following is the best expression of an unstated premise that underlies the reasoning in this passage?
(A) If a diner uses cheap tableware, it will probably save money.
(B) If a utensil is made of stainless steel, it will not rust.
(C) It a utensil is cheap, it will rust quickly.
(D) If there is rust between the tines of a fork, the diner using it must buy cheap tableware.
(E) Nothing that is not made of stainless steel will not rust.

20. Which of the following could the author logically use to strengthen the argument's conclusion?
(A) Restaurants should not use cheap tableware.
(B) No rusted utensil I have found is made of stainless steel.
(C) Every rusted fork on this table is a cheap utensil.
(D) Cheap utensils are often stolen.
(E) Rusted silverware can be replaced cheaply.

21. Middle-aged American actresses, regardless of their skill, are not trusted to guarantee the box-office success of a film. The audience always wants younger women. While men may be in their forties or fifties, the audiences will not accept women of that age in romantic roles. Middle-aged men often play love scenes with actresses younger than their daughters, while an actress over forty plays a spinster or a nun. Our culture is youth oriented, but with a double standard.

Which of the following, if true, would most seriously weaken the argument of the passage above?
(A) The largest grossing romantic movie of this year starred a 28-year-old man and a 23-year-old woman.
(B) The most sought-after American actress is paid about 60 percent of the salary of her male co-star.
(C) In European films, actresses continue to appear in romantic roles when they are in their thirties.
(D) The screenplays of two out of three of the year's most successful films were written by women.
(E) The successful film "White Palace" is the love story of an older woman from a blue-collar background and a younger, upper-middle-class man.

22. Arthur's explanation of the budget deficit must be the best one because he is the only economist with a Ph.D. who answered the question.

The author of the argument above assumes that
(A) anyone who has a Ph.D. cannot be wrong
(B) any economist who has a Ph.D. is right about economic issues
(C) an economist with a Ph.D. is a better judge of an economic matter than others
(D) an economist with a Ph.D. is a better judge than other economists
(E) any economist with a Ph.D. will usually give the best answer to a question

Questions 23–24 refer to the following passage.

According to conservative grammarians, "hopefully" is a perfectly good English word. It is an adverb, that is, a word used to modify an adjective, verb, or other adverb, and it means "in a hopeful manner." "My horse will win the race," he remarked hopefully. However, the word is not a parenthetical expression that means "I hope," as in "Hopefully, my horse will win the race," he said.

23. The author's argument in this passage includes all of the following EXCEPT
(A) providing an example
(B) explaining the misuse of a word
(C) explaining the proper use of a word
(D) defining a term
(E) drawing an analogy

24. According to the argument of this paragraph, in which of the following is the word ''hopefully'' used correctly?
   (A)   Despite the score of the game after the first half, the coach hopefully encouraged his players.
   (B)   If we can keep the other team from scoring in the third quarter, hopefully we will score in the fourth.
   (C)   Hopefully, the other team will begin to make more mistakes, and we can still win this game.
   (D)   This year my income taxes, hopefully, will be lower than they were last year.
   (E)   Hopefully, the rain will not start until after we reach home.

25. More than ever before, American TV viewers are watching cable television programs. About 60 percent of American homes are now equipped with cable, and about one quarter of the programs watched are cable programs. Yet some cable networks are already losing their very small share of the audience. They are losing viewers to other cable channels, despite the continuing growth in cable's audience share.

The apparent contradiction of this passage can be explained by the fact that
   (A)   overall, fewer people are watching any television, network or cable
   (B)   the monthly fees for cable television deter potential viewers from subscribing to cable channels
   (C)   video rentals have become increasingly popular and have reduced the number of cable television watchers
   (D)   only 15 percent of the television shows Americans watch are cable programs, while 85 percent are still network programs
   (E)   the number of cable channels is increasing more rapidly than the cable television share of the audience

STOP

IF YOU FINISH BEFORE TIME IS UP, CHECK YOUR WORK ON THIS SECTION OF THE TEST ONLY. DO NOT GO ON TO THE NEXT SECTION OF THE TEST UNTIL TIME IS UP FOR THIS SECTION.

SECTION II
READING COMPREHENSION

Time—35 Minutes
28 Questions

Directions:
Read the passages and answer the questions following each passage by blackening the appropriate space on the answer sheet. You may refer back to the passages when answering the questions. Answer all questions on the basis of what is stated or implied.

Passage 1

In the fall of 1946, President Truman asked for a comprehensive study of Soviet-American relations, which he knew would be the central problem of American foreign policy. The result was an important state paper prepared through the secretary of state, the secretary of war, the attorney general, the secretary of the navy, Fleet Admiral Leahy (who had been Roosevelt's chief military adviser), the joint chiefs of staff, Ambassador Edwin W. Pauley (in charge of negotiating postwar reparations), the director of central intelligence, and other persons with special knowledge of foreign affairs. The document was imposing in its scope and depth, comprising nearly a hundred thousand words and divided into an introduction and six sections. It dealt with Soviet foreign policy, Soviet-American agreements, Soviet violations of its agreements with the U.S., conflicting views on reparations, Soviet activities affecting American security, and U.S. policy toward the Soviet Union.

This study Truman asked for was drafted on the premise that only through an accurate understanding of the Soviet Union would the U.S. be able to make and carry out policies that would reestablish international order and protect the U.S. at all times. The key, according to the study, was to realize that Moscow's leaders adhered to the Marxian theory of ultimate destruction of capitalist states by communist states but that they sought to postpone the inevitable conflict while they strengthened and prepared the Soviet Union for its clash with the Western democracies. The study said Moscow's main concern regarding the other nations of Western Europe was to prevent the formation of a Western bloc. It noted, too, that Red Army troops and Russian planes in combat readiness outnumbered American units opposite them in Germany, Austria, and Korea in overwhelming strength, placing U.S. forces literally at the mercy of the Soviet government.

1. The passage associates President Truman with
   (A) peace with honor
   (B) anti-Communist sentiment
   (C) the long-standing Cold War
   (D) Western imperialism
   (E) sympathy for U.S. forces

2. The author's attitude toward Truman seems to be
   (A) supportive   (B) skeptical   (C) cynical   (D) worshipful   (E) hostile

3. Evidence in the passage allows us to conclude that the study described in this passage was notable for its
   (A) far-reaching effects
   (B) controversial wording

(C)   literary quality
(D)   objectivity
(E)   completeness

4. The passage implies that U.S. forces in 1946 needed to
(A)   engage in a new sort of training
(B)   increase
(C)   come home
(D)   confront Soviet forces
(E)   retrain

5. The state paper described in this passage did not deal with
(A)   agreements between the U.S.S.R. and the U.S.A.
(B)   those Russian activities relevant to U.S. security
(C)   the Truman policy of containment
(D)   the respective views of the United States and the USSR concerning reparations
(E)   the foreign policy of the Russians

6. A Russian government official might argue that "accurate" (paragraph 2, line 1) is an imprecise term because
(A)   accuracy is an unattainable goal
(B)   Truman never visited Russia
(C)   the anti-Soviet conclusions in the study were biased
(D)   Communism is not concerned with accuracy
(E)   English is an imprecise language

7. The branch of government not participating in the preparation of the described document was
(A)   the legislative
(B)   the judicial
(C)   both the legislative and the judicial
(D)   not stated or implied
(E)   the executive

Passage 2

Yesterday's announcement that Monarch Steel plans to close three mills, thereby eliminating three hundred jobs, came as a surprise. Things have been going badly at Monarch for some time now, and this latest news bears out what we all have suspected for some time now—that the situation isn't improving.

The net effect is that three hundred more people will soon be added to the approximately seven hundred already on layoff. The culprit, according to a Monarch spokesperson, is the increasing influx of low-cost foreign steel into the United States and increased labor and material costs.

The situation at Monarch makes all too clear an economic fact of life that we in the United States seem reluctant to accept: that our country is no longer an economic "island unto itself." No longer can we go about merrily doing as we please, living lavishly with no care for tomorrow, relying on the economic strength and abundant wealth of the United States to carry us.

There was a point in time—and it wasn't so long ago—when the wealth of our country was so great that we were virtually self-contained. We could overcome any obstacle, surmount any problem, because as a nation we were, quite simply, very rich.

But that time has now passed, and while our country is a little less rich, the rest of the world, generally speaking, is a little more rich. Now, other countries have improved technology and production methods, and are capable of manufacturing numerous products more cheaply than we do. Unfortunately, steel is one of those products.

Another fact of economic life which must be accepted if we are to continue to prosper is that the day when everyone "bought American" is over, just as the day when everyone shopped exclusively with his or her local community merchants is over. Say what we will, people nowadays go where the prices are best and the quality greatest; it is a truism that holds for the local housewife as well as for giant manufacturing concerns.

While we may condemn others for not buying American-made products, how many of us drive foreign cars, own foreign televisions, or any of the hundreds of other foreign products which have proliferated in our markets? The simple truth is that we all want the best quality and performance at the lowest possible price, and the vendor who offers them is the one who gets our dollar.

Before any significant progress can be made in solving the problem of foreign imports, both management and labor are going to have to accept these economic facts and act accordingly. Once they recognize that they must compete not only with other U.S. industries engaged in a similar activity, but also with those same type industries in other countries, they can begin to develop a strategy for competing.

Perhaps management, labor, and stockholders will all discover that they must accept a little less and lower their expectations in order to get back into the economic mainstream, but it's a small price to pay when compared with the alternative: annihilation.

The problems at Monarch aren't going to go away quickly, though, and in the near term we can only hope that the displaced workers can be put back on the payroll somewhere else. According to one company spokesman, the chances of the three mills being reopened are "nonexistent," so if the three hundred workers can't be placed in other jobs, the community loses, the company loses, but, worst of all, the former employees lose.

8. According to the author, the U.S. economy is suffering from
   (A) overactive exuberance
   (B) being less rich than the rest of the world
   (C) economic annihilation
   (D) complacent isolationism
   (E) having three mills too many

9. A reason for the closure of three steel mills is
   (A) Monarch's authoritarian policy
   (B) the appealing cost of foreign steel
   (C) too many workers who "bought American"
   (D) a rift between management and labor
   (E) too many displaced workers on the payroll

10. The truism with which the author agrees is that
    (A) consumers favor low prices and high quality
    (B) the vendor is the one who gets our dollar
    (C) the local housewife holds with giant manufacturing concerns
    (D) the alternative to lowered expectations is economic annihilation
    (E) the chances of the three mills being reopened are nonexistent

11. No so long ago, according to the author,
    (A) the proliferation of foreign products was inevitable
    (B) some strategy for competing was not necessary
    (C) a net loss of a thousand workers would not be tolerated
    (D) steel was not in demand in this country
    (E) the United States was wealthier than it is today

12. The author implies that American consumers who chastise the buyers of foreign goods are
    (A) insensitive   (B) tightfisted   (C) largely members of management   (D) traitorous
    (E) hypocritical

13. Faced with a definition of *laissez-faire* economics, the author of this passage would probably
  (A) modify it
  (B) approve it
  (C) sanction it
  (D) misunderstand it
  (E) annihilate it

14. The layoffs at Monarch Steel
  (A) came as no surprise
  (B) continued a discouraging trend
  (C) reversed an encouraging trend
  (D) portend starvation for many families
  (E) are strictly temporary

Passage 3

Recently in Florida, there have been attempts to eliminate pornography bookstores and theaters under the authority of local public nuisance ordinances. Testing the validity of this procedure, the state supreme court held that municipalities could forbid the sale of explicitly obscene materials, but to close down the stores and movie houses without a hearing is an
(5) impermissible prior restraint.

Today what is considered a public nuisance is defined by statute in all jurisdictions. Generally these statutes are broadly construed as to encompass those activities that would have been public nuisances at common law. They are enforced through the police power of the states to protect the public health, safety, and general welfare. Once an activity has been judged to be a
(10) public nuisance, the state may suppress the activity by forbidding it, or by closing down the establishment carrying on the proscribed activity.

The United States Supreme Court, in 1977, recognized that establishments selling and exhibiting obscene materials are injurious to the public morals and that the state has the power to regulate such establishments in order to protect the public. Armed with this decision, local
(15) prosecutors hoped to take advantage of the relative ease with which a civil action can be used to abate a public nuisance. For example, in civil proceedings, the plaintiff prosecutor only needs to prove his allegation that the material in question is obscene, and therefore a public nuisance, by a preponderance of the evidence, rather than beyond a reasonable doubt as is required in criminal proceedings. Furthermore, obtaining an injunction, even though a temporary one, will
(20) halt the display of the questioned material at least until the trial takes place. Also, whenever an equitable remedy, such as an injunction, is sought, a jury is not required as a matter of right. This is significant because only one person, the judge, must be convinced that the material is obscene, and the job is made easier if the judge is one who adheres to a broad definition of obscenity.

(25) These substantive and procedural advantages account for the increase in civil nuisance actions to abate the distribution of pornography by closing down establishments that sell sexually explicit material. However such attempts are limited by the First Amendment prohibition against prior restraints. Inherent in that amendment's provision for freedom of the press is the aim to avoid "previous restraints of publication" by eliminating any requirement of printing approval by state
(30) authorities. In keeping with this principle, state and federal courts have held that adult bookstores and theaters may be abated as a public nuisance only after all the material sold or exhibited has been determined to be obscene.

In Florida, the state supreme court ruled that a business could be prohibited from selling or exhibiting material if it consists of specifically named books, magazines, or movies previously
(35) judicially determined to be obscene, but the business could not be closed unless and until all the material sold or shown there was judged to be obscene. It reasoned that closing bookstores or theaters, even temporarily, before all the material is determined to be obscene is in effect to forbid the sale or exhibition of constitutionally protected books, magazines, or films, as well as potentially obscene matter. This, the court called an "impermissible prior restraint in violation of

(40) the First and Fourteenth Amendments."
        Although adult bookstores and theaters cannot be closed by using public nuisance actions, zoning ordinances may be used to regulate their location. The restrictions could permit such establishments anywhere within the city limits provided certain conditions are met. Such an ordinance was enacted by the city of Detroit and it was upheld by the United States Supreme
(45) Court. The ordinance prohibited adult bookstores, adult motion picture theaters, and adult mini-theaters within five hundred feet from a residential dwelling or rooming unit.
        A zoning ordinance similar to that employed by Detroit has two advantages over public nuisance statutes. The need for an obscenity hearing is eliminated and the type of material that would subject the establishment to the zoning restriction is defined according to what is depicted—not whether
(50) what is depicted is found to be obscene. Also, the danger of a prior restraint is avoided because the sale or exhibition of specified materials is not totally prohibited. Instead, it is restricted to certain areas of the city.

15. Which of the following titles best summarizes the content of the passage?
(A) Pornography and Zoning
(B) Using Nuisance Ordinances to Control Pornography
(C) Using Zoning Ordinances to Control Pornography
(D) The Prohibition of Using Nuisance Ordinances to Control Pornography
(E) Legal Arguments for Using Nuisance Ordinances to Control Pornography

16. All of the following might be cited as examples of public nuisance EXCEPT
(A) a pickpocket
(B) a pig farm in a residential district
(C) a malicious billboard
(D) a poker parlor
(E) a leaking factory afterburner

17. According to the passage, the First Amendment seeks to
(A) guarantee the freedom of the press to publish whatever it found appropriate
(B) guarantee the citizens' right to read according to the dictates of conscience
(C) assure state or federal approval of matter before it is printed
(D) avoid state or federal approval of matter before it is printed
(E) protect publishers of so-called obscene materials

18. The advantages of using public nuisance statutes to close a pornographic bookshop would include all of the following EXCEPT
(A) a burden to prove obscenity only by a preponderance of the evidence
(B) the halting of display if an injunction is obtained
(C) the possibility of avoiding a jury in the injunction request
(D) the need to convince only one person of the obscenity of the material
(E) the closing of a bookstore may precede the determining that the material on sale is obscene

19. According to the passage, the effect of the Supreme Court's 1977 decision (line 12) was to
(A) make it possible for prosecutors to use public nuisance laws against establishments exhibiting obscene materials
(B) increase the number of civil prosecutions of pornographic exhibitors
(C) decrease the number of prosecutions against pornographic exhibitors
(D) greatly increase the number of successful closings of pornographic theaters and bookstores
(E) greatly decrease the number of successful closings of pornographic theaters and bookstores

20. The appeal of an establishment that has exhibited demonstrably obscene material in the past and has been closed after prosecution for public nuisance would
    (A) probably be upheld at all levels
    (B) probably be upheld but only if the federal court also found the material obscene
    (C) result in permission to open under more liberal public nuisance statutes
    (D) probably result in permission to open until all currently displayed materials were found to be obscene
    (E) probably be upheld on the grounds that the exhibition of obscenity is injurious to public morals

21. It is likely to be difficult to close an adult bookshop using public nuisance ordinances because the bookshop
    (A) may change its location
    (B) may close voluntarily
    (C) is permitted to remain open until all the material sold or exhibited has been found to be obscene
    (D) cannot change its books
    (E) can be prohibited from selling specifcally named books previously judicially determined to be obscene

22. The advantage of controlling adult theaters and bookstores by zoning regulations rather than by nuisance ordinances is that zoning ordinances
    (A) are less costly to enforce
    (B) are supported by a greater portion of the public
    (C) are not likely to be reversed for impermissible prior restraint
    (D) are more easily amended than public nuisance laws
    (E) can be used to prohibit theaters and bookstores within a thousand feet of someone's home

Passage 4

Mary Hamilton, a twenty-eight year-old black field secretary for the Congress of Racial Equality (CORE), participated in a demonstration in Gadsden, Alabama, in 1963. White police officers arrested her, along with fellow demonstrators. Believing their arrests to be unlawful, the group petitioned the Circuit Court of Etowah County for release on a writ of habeas corpus (unlawful imprisonment). The hearing on the petition was held on June 25, before Judge Cunningham, a white judge, assisted by white court clerks and bailiffs.

Black attorneys Charles Conley and Norman Amaker represented the petitioners and white Solicitor Rayburn spoke for the state. Mr. Rayburn followed the southern establishment practice of addressing each black witness by his or her first name, despite objections from the opposing counsel.

When Mary Hamilton completed her direct testimony, Solicitor Rayburn began his cross-examination by asking, "What is your name, please?"

"Miss Mary Hamilton."

"Mary, . . . who were you arrested by?"

"My name is Miss Hamilton. Please address me correctly," she said.

"Who were you arrested by, Mary?" the solicitor asked again, deliberately.

"I will not answer a question—" she began, and Attorney Amaker interjected, "The witness's name is Miss Hamilton."

"— your question until I am addressed correctly," she finished.

"Answer the question," Judge Cunningham ordered.

Miss Hamilton would not be intimidated. "I will not answer them unless I am addressed correctly."

"You are in contempt of court," ruled the judge.

"Your Honor—your Honor—" Attorney Conley began, but the judge paid no attention.

"You are in contempt of this court," he went on, "and you are sentenced to five days in jail and a fifty-dollar fine."

Miss Hamilton was taken to jail then and there, and served the five days. Since she did not intend to pay the fine, and therefore would be subject to another twenty days in jail, she was allowed out on bond to appeal the contempt conviction.

On July 25, she petitioned the Alabama Supreme Court to review the contempt citation on two grounds. Her lawyers contended that the solicitor's manner of addressing black witnesses violated the equal protection clause of the Fourteenth Amendment. Finding no cases on this point, they relied on logic, history, and etiquette. They rejected the state's reliance on Emily Post and Amy Vanderbilt because their books did not discuss the use of first names in a racial situation. They also reminded the court that Miss Hamilton's contempt conviction violated the due process clause because she was summarily sentenced without even being given a trial—an opportunity to present a defense to the charge. (Remember the Red Queen in *Alice in Wonderland*—"sentence first, trial afterward"?)

The Alabama Supreme Court found, however, that "the question was a lawful one and the witness invoked no valid legal exemption to support her refusal to answer it. The record conclusively shows that petitioner's name is Mary Hamilton, not Miss Mary Hamilton. Many witnesses are addressed by various titles, but one's own name is an acceptable appellation at law. . . . In the cross-examination of witnesses, a wide latitude is allowed resting in the sound discretion of the trial court and unless the discretion is grossly abused, the ruling of the court will not be overturned. . . . We hold that the trial court did not abuse its discretion and the record supports the summary punishment inflicted."

The NAACP Legal Defense and Educational Fund then took the case up to the United States Supreme Court for review. The defense lawyers relied on long-standing principles governing the conduct of prosecuting attorneys: as quasi-judicial officers of the court they are under a duty not to prejudice a party's case through overzealous prosecution or to detract from the impartiality of courtroom atmosphere. The defense presented historical and sociological proof that the forms of address used by Solicitor Rayburn were a distinct part of a "racial caste system" that deprived black citizens of equal protection of the laws. They also quoted from novels by Richard Wright, James Baldwin, and Lillian Smith.

The United States Supreme Court handed down a summary decision the same day. Six justices joined in an order reversing Miss Hamilton's contempt citation.

23. By objecting to being addressed by her first name, Mary Hamilton implies that such an address is
    (A) illegal
    (B) not appropriate in a southern court
    (C) incorrect and demeaning
    (D) defamatory and criminal
    (E) unfortunate

24. By alluding to *Alice in Wonderland*, the author seems to brand the judge as
    (A) a literary artifact
    (B) an absurd tyrant
    (C) childish
    (D) an intimidating legislator
    (E) an insensitive official

25. We must presume that the author of this passage was either present at the trial or
    (A) given a brief summary of the outcome
    (B) able to secure a transcript of the court proceedings
    (C) able to secure a paraphrase of the court proceedings
    (D) consulted with the judge
    (E) consulted with Mary Hamilton

26. The question raised but left unanswered in this passage is which of the following?
(A) Is impartiality possible?
(B) What did the U.S. Supreme Court decide?
(C) Is Mary Hamilton still politically active?
(D) Can a court ruling be made without precedent?
(E) Are Emily Post and Amy Vanderbilt recognized authorities?

27. By stressing that the judge and the court staff were white, the author implies which of the following questions?
(A) Was the court biased against Mary Hamilton?
(B) Should the legal profession in Alabama be integrated?
(C) Should Mary Hamilton have been tried in another court?
(D) Is the race of judges less crucial today?
(E) Is the race of the judge more important than that of the arresting officers?

28. The author suggests that the judge's response to Miss Hamilton was an effort to
(A) intimidate the witness
(B) demonstrate that only the judge should be formally addressed
(C) cut short the cross examination
(D) elicit an answer that would help decide the case
(E) offer a popular ruling

STOP

IF YOU FINISH BEFORE TIME IS UP, CHECK YOUR WORK ON THIS SECTION OF THE TEST ONLY.
DO NOT GO ON TO THE NEXT SECTION OF THE TEST UNTIL TIME IS UP FOR THIS SECTION.

SECTION III
LOGICAL REASONING

Time—35 Minutes
25 Questions

Directions:

In this section you will be given brief statements or passages and will be required to evaluate the reasoning involved. In some instances, more than one choice will appear to be a possible answer. You are to choose the *best* answer. Use common sense and reasonableness in making your selection; then mark the proper space on the answer sheet.

1. The use of polystyrene for packaging fast food is, fortunately, on the way out. But Carol Wilson has complained in a letter to the editor that paper containers do not keep foods warm or greaseless. She reasons that, because the rocks in landfills biodegrade slowly, we should not worry if plastic cups and hamburger boxes are slow too. And with all the mountain ranges in America, she goes on, there can be no shortage of landfills.

   The author's case against Carol Wilson's letter can be strengthened by pointing out all of the following EXCEPT
   - (A) many areas of the country have no mountain ranges
   - (B) the use of mountain ranges for landfills would make them unavailable for other uses
   - (C) Carol Wilson's letter to the editor is a tongue-in-cheek parody of antienvironmentalism
   - (D) the manufacture of Styrofoam containers releases chemicals that deplete the ozone layer
   - (E) plastics are manufactured from petroleum products, the supply of which is limited

2. A light rain has fallen on the Concord Turnpike. Seventy-five percent of the 400 yearly traffic accidents on this turnpike take place when the road is wet. Furthermore, two-car collisions are most likely to take place at the evening rush hour between 5 and 6 o'clock in the winter. It is now 5 PM, in January.

   In addition to the information above, which of the following would be most useful for determining the probability that there will be a two-car collision on the Concord Turnpike in the next hour?
   - (A) the percentage of traffic accidents that take place on other roads under the same circumstances
   - (B) the percentage of wet-road traffic accidents on the turnpike that are two-car collisions
   - (C) the percentage of evening-rush-hour, winter-traffic accidents that take place on the turnpike when the road is wet
   - (D) the percentage of rush-hour, winter-traffic-accidents that take place when the road is not wet
   - (E) the number of cars involved in traffic accidents on the highways in the month of January

3. If you were allowed to enter the United States after 1965, you must have had a polio shot.

   The statement above can be logically deduced from which of the following?
   - (A) Only if a person were allowed to enter the United States after 1965 could he have had a polio shot.
   - (B) No one permitted to enter the United States before 1965 had a polio shot.
   - (C) All people allowed to enter the United States after 1965 have had polio shots.
   - (D) Before 1965, a polio shot was not required for entry to the United States.
   - (E) All polio shots have been administered after 1965.

Questions 4–5 refer to the following passage.

A recession is not always bad news for everyone. During hard times, people spend money on repairing broken possessions rather than on buying new ones. Repair services from shoe cobblers to computer technicians are already reporting an increase in business. An increase in repairs can offset a drop in the sales of new items for appliance stores that handle both new sales and repairs.

But there may not be a recession right now. This time of year is usually a busy time in repair shops. And people may be holding onto their money because they fear a recession, not because one is here already. But one businessman claims his sales are always a sure sign. When repairs account for more than 60 percent of his business, the economy is in bad shape.

4. We can infer from the information in the passage
   (A) that a recession is bad news for most businesses
   (B) that the business of repair shops is likely to thrive in times of economic prosperity
   (C) a recession is now in progress
   (D) that, if repair services report an increase in business, there is certainly no recession
   (E) that, during a recession, consumers are likely to spend more money

5. The most logical final sentence of the second paragraph would
   (A) conclude there is no recession
   (B) conclude there is a recession
   (C) conclude that we do not yet know whether or not there is a recession
   (D) reveal the percentage of repair sales of the businessman
   (E) disagree with the businessman's reasoning

6. All of Fedmart's customers pay by using Fedmart charge accounts. Only if the O'Haras pay by Fedmart charge will they buy garden tools or rose bushes, but not both and not anything else.

   If the O'Haras bought rose bushes, which of the following must be true?
   (A) The O'Haras bought garden tools.
   (B) The O'Haras paid by charge account.
   (C) The O'Haras paid in cash.
   (D) The O'Haras have no charge accounts.
   (E) The O'Haras also bought rose food.

7. In three years, six whales have died at Sea World, including three killer whales. Officials maintain that five of the six died of diseases that could have taken their lives in the wild. The deaths may affect the breeding of killer whales as the Sea World parks have twelve females, but just one male. Since the lone male is not related to any of the females, there is no genetic reason why he cannot mate with them all. The parks have produced five healthy captive-born babies. Breeding is necessary since Sea World's economic success depends on killer whales, and no federal permits to capture the whales have been issued for some time.

   Which of the following, if true, would tend to support the argument that the parks are not depleting the killer whale population?
   (A) The transportation of killer whales from one park to another presents a threat to their health.
   (B) In the wild, killer whales live longer than killer whales in theme parks.
   (C) Three of the killer whales born in captivity died within a year.
   (D) Killer whales in captivity are less fertile than those in the wild.
   (E) Killer whales in theme parks are protected against diseases common in the wild.

8. When asked if they would prefer to add ten points to their IQ's or three inches to their height, most American men preferred to be taller, while most American women chose the gain in intelligence.

   All of the following may be logically inferred from this statement EXCEPT
   (A) to be taller is more important to most men than to most women
   (B) to be taller is more important to most men than to be more intelligent
   (C) to be taller is not as important to most women as to be more intelligent
   (D) to be less intelligent is less important to most men than to be taller
   (E) to be taller is more important to most men than to be more intelligent is to most women

Questions 9–10 refer to the following passage.

Contrary to popular Western beliefs, the Islamic religion does not forbid women to participate in economic and political life. The Koran has never excluded women from access to education, public office, or employment. The blame lies with social custom and conservative leaders in the male-dominated societies of the Arab world. And despite the prejudices against women in public life, a small number of women have had some success. In Turkey, a woman serves in a Cabinet position, and for a time Benazir Bhutto was Prime Minister of Pakistan.

9. The author of this passage makes her points by using all of the following EXCEPT
   (A) citing a specific case in support of her opinion
   (B) disputing evidence cited by the opposition
   (C) alluding to a popular misconception
   (D) pointing to specific causes of injustice
   (E) referring to spiritual authority.

10. If true, which of the following would not weaken the author's argument that Arab women can succeed in politics?
   (A) Benazir Bhutto's political power was due more to her being a member of a powerful family than to her gender.
   (B) There are no women in positions of leadership in the Persian Gulf states.
   (C) The female Cabinet member in Turkey is a self-made politician from a modest background.
   (D) Moslem voters in India always strongly opposed Indira Gandhi.
   (E) There are no females in positions of political power in Syria or Iraq.

11. Twenty-five years ago, the poor in America were disproportionately old and female. Now the greater part of those living below the poverty level are young, including children. Women, however, still suffer more than men. The older Americans have taken matters into their hands and promoted legislation that protects them. Laws like Proposition 13 in California and rent controls in New York were intended to allow the elderly to keep their homes after they had retired. But the laws also keep housing out of the reach of younger people with growing families. And now a Republican assemblyman is proposing that senior citizens with no children in the public schools should be exempted from school taxes.

Using the same line of reasoning as the Republican assemblyman, it could be argued that
   (A) the young have a greater need of a tax break than the old
   (B) the greater part of the tax burden already falls upon younger taxpayers
   (C) younger taxpayers should be exempted from taxes that support medical payments to the elderly
   (D) the tax burden should fall more heavily on men than on women
   (E) laws like Proposition 13 and rent controls should be overturned

12. A computer analysis of 180,000 drivers shows that women are generally safer drivers than men. Sixteen-year-old girls get fewer traffic tickets than sixteen-year-old boys, and women tend to have fewer accidents at all age levels except at 18, where the sexes are alike and worse than at any other age.

The results of the analysis would be strengthened if all of the following could be shown EXCEPT that
   (A) the survey considered how many miles per week both the men and the women drive
   (B) equal numbers of men and women were studied
   (C) the survey considered drivers in both rural and urban situations
   (D) the survey considered drivers of automobiles of similar types
   (E) statistics of eighteen-year-old male drivers were compared to those of females of other ages

13. Does anyone need to be told about the corrupting influence of money on government? The latest revelation comes from internal campaign documents showing that aides and commissioners

appointed by the mayor have raised more than a million dollars for her re-election war chest. Much of that money came from business people with contracts with the city. One cannot help asking if there was a *quid pro quo* (something for something).

To make matters worse, these same aides and commissioners were out raising funds on city time, not on their weekends. Unless the voters enact some ethics laws to prohibit officials from activities like these, the practices will continue. And, if anything that has been done is already illegal, the city attorney should prosecute to recover the public resources that have been lost.

All of the following are implied but not explicitly stated by the passage EXCEPT

(A) business people have contributed to the mayor's campaign funds in order to secure city contracts

(B) the unethical actions of the aides and commissioners are not prohibited by law

(C) if the mayor wins reelection, she will owe favors to business contributors

(D) city aides and commissioners have been fundraising for the mayor rather than doing the jobs for which they are paid

(E) the awarding of city contracts is influenced by the mayor and her staff

Questions 14–15 refer to the following passage.

A survey at an eastern state university suggests that most of the large impersonal universities are plagued by dishonest students. A poll of 230 students revealed that 78 percent of them cheated at one time or another and 33 percent admitted cheating regularly. The techniques included copying from other students' exams, using cheat sheets, plagiarizing papers, and stealing tests in advance. Members of fraternities and sororities were more likely to cheat than nonmembers, and the worst offenders were students majoring in economics. That economics majors were the most likely to cheat raised the question whether such dishonesty was "anticipatory socialization for modern American business life."

The motives for cheating were diverse. Competition for entrance into graduate school was the most often cited, but sheer laziness and a preference for partying over studying were common. More than half of the students said their cheating was motivated by a desire for revenge against indifferent professors, large lecture classes, and professors too lazy to make up new examinations each year.

14. The quotation that concludes the first paragraph of the passage implies that

(A) cheating is commonplace in American business

(B) economics majors are likely to have to cheat to achieve the grades necessary for admission to American business schools

(C) American businesspeople anticipate very active social lives

(D) economics majors who cheat as undergraduates will not be accepted by the American business community

(E) American businesspeople would question the charge that economics majors are more likely to cheat

15. From the information in the second paragraph we can infer all of the following EXCEPT

(A) there is less cheating in classes with small enrollments

(B) premedical and prelaw students are more likely to cheat than students who do not plan on a graduate education

(C) there will probably be less cheating in the class of a professor who is diligent, well prepared, and well liked by students than in the class of a less able teacher

(D) both teachers and students may be lazy

(E) most professors use the same examinations year after year

16. Unlike historians elsewhere, Russian textbook writers cannot revise or rewrite the history books now in print, which are seriously distorted. For more than sixty years, history textbooks have been used to indoctrinate Russian school children, and have contained only statements that supported the views of the leaders in power. But there are now no censors waiting to cut out any offending truth, and historians must start almost from scratch.

In many ways, the old history was easier to write. New historians must separate the truth from the lies, evasions, and half-truths of the books in print. Many sources are still unavailable. Newspapers and magazines are constantly reporting revised versions of history, and every month a famous figure from the past may be rehabilitated or vilified. After a lifetime of caution and self-censorship, historians discover that writing history as it really happened requires a whole new way of thinking.

The author of the passage believes all of the following EXCEPT
(A) Russian historians wrote inaccurate and untrustworthy accounts of historical events
(B) historians in Europe and the United States do not have to deal with many of the problems facing contemporary Russian historians
(C) a Russian history book written in 1950 would reflect the views of the people in power at that time
(D) we now know that Russian men of the past will be reevaluated and rehabilitated
(E) historians of the last sixty years in Russia were subject to self-censorship and state censorship

17. The average value of a share of stock on the American Stock Exchange has increased by 20 percent in the last year. Therefore the value of the shares of bank stocks listed on the American Stock Exchange cannot have gone down in the same period of time.

The reasoning in the passage above is parallel to the reasoning in which of the following?
(A) The costs of transcontinental flights have declined in each of the last three years. Therefore the cost of railway fare from New York to San Francisco cannot have remained unchanged.
(B) American troops are no longer stationed at airforce bases in Great Britain. Therefore American troops are no longer stationed at bases in Europe.
(C) The price of fruits and vegetables has decreased slightly for each of the last six months. Therefore the cost of Winesap and Granny Smith apples cannot have risen in the last two quarters.
(D) Americans watch more television each week than Europeans. Therefore, Americans watch more television each year than Europeans.
(E) The price of unleaded gasoline has remained unchanged for six months. Therefore, the price of leaded gasoline and heating oil cannot have changed for six months.

18. The Hemlock Society advocates the legalization of euthanasia in the United States. Its founder, Derek Humphry, believes that, when two doctors have verified that a patient's condition is terminal, the patient should be permitted to put an end to life. In 1984, Holland sanctioned euthanasia by doctors when requested by patients. A physician's-aid-in-dying bill will shortly be voted on in the state of Washington, and the state Medical Association has already opposed the proposal.

All of the following supporting arguments would be reasonable for doctors to use to oppose the passage of the bill described in this paragraph EXCEPT
(A) it is possible that the two doctors making the terminal diagnosis would be wrong
(B) if the bill fails to pass, a doctor who assisted in a suicide could be charged with murder
(C) it is inappropriate for doctors to be participants in the intentional death of a patient
(D) it is possible that a patient who has elected euthanasia will have a change of mind
(E) it is possible that a new cure for a disease believed to be terminal may be found

Questions 19–20 refer to the following passage.

About two thirds of the eligible voters did not cast ballots in the recent election in which all of the members of the House of Representatives were chosen. Once again, the United States placed near the bottom in the scale of eligible voters participating in a national election. All over the country, politicians, educators, and newspaper columnists are expressing horror at the low voter turnout. Because the rich or well-to-do are more likely to vote than the poor, are the poor being disenfranchised? Because older people are more likely to vote than young ones, do the elderly have an unfair influence? The answers to these and questions like them are very surprising.

19. If the electorate was only one third of the total of eligible voters and this third was an accurate cross section of the whole electorate, the election results would
   (A) reflect the will of the whole voting population
   (B) unfairly prevent two thirds of the potential voters from expressing their preference
   (C) probably represent the preference of rich or well-to-do voters
   (D) probably represent the preference of young rather than older voters
   (E) determine the winners of all 100 Senate seats

20. The concern of those who deplore the large number of nonvoters would probably be lessened by all of the following, if true, EXCEPT
   (A) Switzerland, generally regarded as one of the best governed countries in the world, has an even lower percentage of voter turnout than the United States
   (B) two different polls in 1988 found that the nonvoters preferred President Bush over Michael Dukakis by exactly the same margin as the voters
   (C) the demographic differences between voters and nonvoters are narrowing each year because voters in all economic groups have stopped going to the polls
   (D) the same percentage of Asian, Hispanic, African-American, and white voters failed to vote
   (E) of voters over 60, ten percent failed to vote, while ten percent of the voters between 18 and 28 voted in the 1988 election

21. *Jane:* I can't afford not to pay a gardener and a maid each ten dollars an hour to take care of my lawn and to do my housework.

   Of the following, the most logical interpretation of Jane's comment is that
   (A) Jane's time is worth more than ten dollars an hour
   (B) Jane is compulsively neat
   (C) Jane is indifferent to how much money she spends each week
   (D) most gardeners and maids earn much more than ten dollars an hour
   (E) Jane has no sympathy for the working class

22. Every year about 100,000 fewer fishing licenses are sold in California, so the state is now short of funds to protect wildlife and restock the streams and lakes. The decline in fishing is blamed on drought, pollution, and development. Five years of drought have dried up many trout streams, but the decline in angling began before the drought. Diversion of water supplies to farmers has caused major damage. To reach streams, city dwellers have to travel on overcrowded roads, and even the mountain air may be choked with smog. Once-quiet lakes are now crowded with water-skiers and the shores are lined with condominiums. Tackle shops must now sell video games to survive. Programs that manage and protect fish habitats will have one million dollars less this year, and one fifth of the staff biologists will lose their jobs.

   All of the following can be inferred from the information above EXCEPT
   (A) the habitats of fish have declined because of human encroachment on wild areas
   (B) a primary cause of the decline in fishing in California is the increase in population
   (C) as the number of fishermen declines, the quality of the fish habitats can be expected to decline

(D) a primary cause of the decline in fishing in California is the high cost of fishing licenses

(E) if current trends continue, the number of fish in California lakes and streams will decline

23. All investors are well dressed and are asked to the dance. Some investors do not tango.

Which of the following can be validly concluded from these statements?
(A) All the well-dressed are asked to the dance.
(B) Some of the well-dressed are asked to the dance.
(C) All those who do not tango are asked to the dance.
(D) None but investors are asked to the dance.
(E) Most of those asked to the dance do not tango.

Questions 24–25 refer to the following arguments.

(A) I pay $100 each year to insure myself against uninsured motorists who pay nothing. I am therefore paying for both their insurance and for mine.

(B) David will travel only by car or train since he is afraid of both ships and planes. Because of his fear of plane crashes and shipwrecks, he is able to travel only by train or by car.

(C) The mayor's Oversight Commission has exonerated the city police department of the wrongful death of a drug dealer. This is no surprise, since the mayor and the police chief have always been in collusion.

(D) Caffeine does not keep people awake. There are some people who, when they think they are drinking decaffeinated coffee but are really drinking coffee with caffeine, sleep as well as when they have drunk decaffeinated coffee that they believe contains caffeine.

(E) Air bags can prevent 90 percent of the fatalities in traffic accidents. Therefore, all older cars should be retrofitted with air bags.

24. Which of the arguments above is directed against the proponent of a claim rather than against the claim itself?

25. Which of the arguments above attempts to refute a generalization by means of exceptional cases?

STOP

IF YOU FINISH BEFORE TIME IS UP, CHECK YOUR WORK ON THIS SECTION OF THE TEST ONLY. DO NOT GO ON TO THE NEXT SECTION OF THE TEST UNTIL TIME IS UP FOR THIS SECTION.

SECTION IV
ANALYTICAL REASONING

Time—35 Minutes
23 Questions

Directions:
In this section you will be given groups of questions based on different sets of conditions. Drawing a simple diagram may be helpful in answering some of the questions. You are to choose the best answer and mark the corresponding space on your answer sheet.

Questions 1–5

(1) Six friends—three boys (Tom, Fred, and Simon) and three girls (Jan, Lynn, and Enola)—are going to the movies.
(2) All six sit in the same row, which has only six seats.
(3) No friends of the same sex sit next to each other.
(4) Tom will not sit next to Lynn.
(5) Fred has friends on each side of him.
(6) Lynn sits between Fred and Simon, and next to each of them.
(7) Enola sits in the first seat and Simon sits in the last seat.

1. It can be deduced from statements (1), (2), and (7) that
(A) Lynn sits next to Simon
(B) Simon does not sit next to Tom
(C) Fred sits between two friends
(D) Jan sits next to Enola
(E) Enola does not sit next to Jan

2. It can be deduced from statements (1), (2), (6), and (7) that
(A) Fred sits next to Jan
(B) Tom doesn't sit next to Simon
(C) Tom sits next to Enola
(D) Jan sits next to Fred
(E) Fred sits between Jan and Lynn

3. Which of the following statements must be true?
(A) Enola sits between Tom and Fred.
(B) Fred sits between Jan and Lynn, but not next to either one.
(C) Tom sits next to Enola, and next to Jan.
(D) Lynn sits next to Fred, but not Simon.
(E) Jan sits between Tom and Simon, and next to each.

4. Which of the following must be FALSE?
(A) Tom sits next to Jan.
(B) Enola sits next to only one friend.
(C) Lynn sits next to Tom.
(D) Fred sits next to Lynn.
(E) Lynn sits between Enola and Simon.

5. The friends could sit in which order?
(A) Enola, Tom, Jan, Fred, Lynn, Simon
(B) Enola, Fred, Jan, Tom, Lynn, Simon
(C) Simon, Lynn, Tom, Jan, Fred, Enola
(D) Simon, Tom, Lynn, Fred, Jan, Enola
(E) Fred, Lynn, Simon, Enola, Tom, Jan

Questions 6–12

All A's, B's, and C's are D's.
All B's are A's.
All E's are B's.
All A's are G's.
No C's are B's.
Some, but not all, C's are A's.

6. From the conditions given above, which of the following statements must be true?
(A)   All A's are E's.
(B)   All G's are D's.
(C)   Some but not all E's are A's.
(D)   Some C's are G's.
(E)   All C's are G's.

7. Which of the following statements must be FALSE?
(A)   All A's are D's.
(B)   All E's are A's.
(C)   All G's are D's.
(D)   No E's are C's.
(E)   Some C's are B's.

8. If all D's are G's, then
(A)   all C's are G's
(B)   all G's are C's
(C)   all C's are A's
(D)   all A's are C's
(E)   all D's are B's

9. If Q is within C, then Q must also be within
(A) A   (B) B   (C) G   (D) D   (E) E

10. Which of the following statements involving G's is true?
(A)   If all C's are A's, then all G's are A's.
(B)   All G's are D's.
(C)   G's and B's have nothing in common.
(D)   Some C's that are not G's are A's.
(E)   Some G's may not be D's.

11. If all J's are B's, then all J's must be
(A)   A's and C's
(B)   A's and D's
(C)   A's and E's
(D)   C's and E's
(E)   C's and D's

12. If all D's are M's, then all of the following must be M's EXCEPT
(A)   C's
(B)   A's
(C)   G's
(D)   B's
(E)   E's

Questions 13–18

An interior designer is choosing colors for six items in a room. These six items are carpet, drapes, two chairs, and two sofas. The possible colors to choose from are light green, dark green, blue, and yellow. The following restrictions apply to the choices:

Not more than two of the six items are the same color, that is, no color may be used more than twice.

Blue may not be used for the carpet.

Not more than one chair may be blue.

If the drapes are light green, then one of the sofas must be light green and one of the chairs must be dark green.

Both chairs may not be yellow, but either one could be.

If the carpet is yellow, then neither of the sofas can be dark green.

13. If one chair is yellow and the drapes are light green, which of the following must be true?
(A) If the carpet is yellow, one sofa is blue.
(B) If the carpet is dark green, one sofa is dark green.
(C) Only one item is light green.
(D) Two items are dark green.
(E) The carpet cannot be dark green.

14. If one sofa is yellow, the drapes are yellow and the carpet is a different color than either sofa, then what is NOT a possible color combination for the two chairs?
(A) blue and dark green
(B) light green and dark green
(C) blue and light green
(D) blue and yellow
(E) light green and light green

15. If the carpet cannot be light green and both chairs are dark green, then which of the following must be true?
(A) One of the sofas must be yellow.
(B) One of the sofas must be dark green.
(C) The two sofas could be the same color.
(D) The carpet may be blue.
(E) If the carpet is yellow, the drapes must be blue.

16. If the carpet and drapes are the same color, which of the following CANNOT be true?
(A) Both sofas may be blue.
(B) Both chairs may be light green.
(C) Both sofas may be yellow.
(D) Both sofas may be dark green.
(E) Both chairs may be dark green.

17. If the two chairs and two sofas are the same color combination pairs, then which of the following could NOT be that color combination?
(A) blue and yellow
(B) light green and yellow
(C) dark green and yellow
(D) light green and dark green
(E) dark green and blue

18. If dark green is not used, which of the following must be true?
- (A) The sofas are not yellow.
- (B) The drapes are not blue.
- (C) The carpet is not light green.
- (D) The carpet is not yellow.
- (E) The drapes are not light green.

Questions 19–23

Tom Alvarez has two married sisters, Olivia Sanford, Yolanda Jimenez and one unmarried sister, Carmen Alvarez. He also has two sons, Dan and Edward, but no daughters.
Olivia Sanford and her husband Frank have one son, Victor, and one daughter, Joy.
Yolanda Jimenez and her husband Ruben have two daughters, Susan and Martha.
Tom's wife, Ida, has only one brother, Arthur, and no sisters.
Tom and Ida have no children or siblings other than those listed above.
Tom's father, Gilbert, is the only living grandparent of Dan and Edward.

19. If Gilbert has a sister, she must be
- (A) Dan's grandmother
- (B) Martha's cousin
- (C) Susan's aunt
- (D) Carmen's aunt
- (E) Arthur's mother

20. If Susan marries and has one child, Bernie, which of the following must be FALSE?
- (A) Tom is Bernie's granduncle.
- (B) Carmen is Bernie's grandaunt.
- (C) Ruben is Bernie's grandfather.
- (D) Frank is Bernie's granduncle.
- (E) Dan is Bernie's uncle.

21. Ruben is Edward's
- (A) cousin
- (B) uncle
- (C) nephew
- (D) granduncle
- (E) stepfather

22. Which of the following must be true?
- (A) Dan has three male cousins.
- (B) Martha has two female cousins.
- (C) Joy has one uncle.
- (D) Susan has only one living grandparent.
- (E) Edward has one male cousin.

23. What relationship is Joy to Gilbert?
- (A) niece
- (B) first cousin
- (C) daughter
- (D) granddaughter
- (E) grandnephew

STOP

IF YOU FINISH BEFORE TIME IS UP, CHECK YOUR WORK ON THIS SECTION OF THE TEST ONLY.
DO NOT GO ON TO THE NEXT SECTION OF THE TEST UNTIL TIME IS UP FOR THIS SECTION.

SECTION V
READING COMPREHENSION

Time—35 Minutes
28 Questions

Directions:
Read the passages and answer the questions following each passage by blackening the appropriate space on the answer sheet. You may refer back to the passages when answering the questions. Answer all questions on the basis of what is stated or implied.

Passage 1

Seventy-five years after the death of Louis XIV, the French Revolution enlarged considerably the dimensions of the government show, organizing mass demonstrations with grandiose staging. The national holiday on July 14, 1790, attracted 200,000 people to the Champs de Mars. There were Memorial Day on August 26, 1792, to honor those who died on August 10, Unity of the Republic Day and the solemn funeral for Marat in 1793, and the Feast of the Supreme Being on June 8, 1794, organized by the painter David, "grand master of holidays of the Republic."

Robespierre held the main role as president of the Convention. While choirs intoned a specially composed hymn entitled "Father of the Universe, Supreme Intelligence," he lighted the flame before a statue of Atheism. Then, marching at the head of the column of members of the Convention, with each member carrying a bouquet of flowers and ears of wheat, he proceeded from the Tuileries Gardens to the Champs de Mars, where a symbolic hillock topped with the Tree of Freedom had been erected.

The objective of these vast liturgical assemblies? To strike the public imagination mobilize it and involve it in a collective ritual. Later, mass demonstrations in Red Square or Tienanmen Square would be held for the same reason. Participation in such rituals has become an act of allegiance to official beliefs.

Other regimes, like fascism or Nazism, aim not only at raising the consciousness of the people, but at creating a "mass psychology" by using gigantic demonstrations, whether in Rome or in the stadium at Nuremberg.

Here, following Durkheim's theory, the demonstration has the double aspect of ceremony-spectacle and diversion. It is diversion also in the sense of diverting attention away from true problems and realities. The public lives in a surrealistic atmosphere of festivals and games, like plebians during the Roman empire.

Other political systems also mix show business and politics in a minor way. American elections are the occasion for confetti, parades, and majorettes, and each national political convention has a show business style orchestra. At the Democratic National Convention in 1976, Peter Duchin's orchestra, perched on the bleachers behind the official rostrum, played the traditional hymn, "Happy Days Are Here Again." At the Republican National Convention, Manny Harmon's orchestra, presented by former actor and senator George Murphy, played "God Bless America." Mrs. Betty Ford, presented to the public by Cary Grant, even danced the bump with Tony Orlando.

For that matter, political rallies are often held in places generally reserved for shows or sports events like Madison Square Garden in New York, where the Democratic Convention was held, or the Walnut Street Theater in Philadelphia, where the first Ford-Carter debate was held.

So it can be seen that politics does have its play function. Indeed, we often speak of the "political game," as if politics also constituted entertainment, amusement, recreation.

And, as with a show, we speak of the "public" to designate the people. Some refer to what they consider to be the public's taste for theatricalization, arguing that politics must use star system techniques to save it from the public's lack of interest, to adapt it to "mass culture."

From the moment when the television viewer can choose between his president, a film, and a variety show, the president has to become an entertainer to compete effectively with show business professionals and keep his popularity rating. In short, to compete with stars, political stars have to use their methods and personalize their "performances."

1. The author of this passage would agree that
(A)   Durkheim's theory is unrelated to the alignment of politics with show business
(B)   the "surrealistic atmosphere of festivals and games" occurred only in Ancient Rome
(C)   politics consistently stresses serious public problems
(D)   the theatricality of present-day politics has no historical precedent
(E)   a show-business atmosphere has pervaded the politics of democratic as well as totalitarian regimes

2. The primary purpose of this passage is to
(A)   compare Ancient Rome to modern America
(B)   argue that show business and politics have converged throughout history
(C)   show that politics diverts attention from real problems
(D)   establish Robespierre as the first political "star"
(E)   demonstrate that television has sustained the politician as celebrity

3. Which of the following is the most appropriate substitute for "liturgical assemblies" (paragraph 3)?
(A)   political circuses
(B)   political conventions
(C)   spectacles of worship
(D)   human dramas
(E)   religious holidays

4. The author's attitude toward politicians who are deliberately entertaining would most likely be
(A) sympathetic   (B) skeptical   (C) supportive   (D) unconcerned   (E) hostile

5. The author implies that citizens who are attracted by entertaining politicians are
(A)   too obedient
(B)   not facing reality
(C)   television addicts
(D)   not interested in politics
(E)   victims of a totalitarian regime

6. The author strengthens his argument through the use of which of the following techniques?
(A)   the acknowledgement that he might be mistaken
(B)   a profusion of references to experts
(C)   a profusion of historical facts
(D)   an appeal to the "official beliefs" of his readers
(E)   the use of specialized terminology

7. Which of the following would be an additional example of the sort of politics the author describes?
(A)   Ronald Reagan's speaking at the Academy Awards
(B)   Nancy Reagan's preference for the color red
(C)   Edward Kennedy's New England accent
(D)   Rich Little's impersonation of Richard Nixon
(E)   Richard Nixon's purchase of a Park Avenue penthouse

Passage 2

On October 30, 1973, a Tuesday afternoon around two o'clock, radio station WBAI, N.Y., N.Y., owned and operated by the Pacifica Foundation, was conducting a general discussion of contemporary society's attitude toward language as part of its regular programming. The WBAI host played a segment of the album, "George Carlin, Occupation: Foole," a twelve-minute comedy routine entitled "Filthy Words" in which Carlin related his thoughts about "the words you couldn't say on the public . . . airwaves." He proceeded to list and repeat numerous times a number of colloquial expressions for sexual and excretory activities and organs.

In response, the Federal Communications Commission (FCC) issued a regulation restricting the broadcast of "indecent" language to certain hours of the day. On review of the commission's order, the United States Court of Appeals reversed; later, the United States Supreme Court reversed. (Thus, the Supreme Court reversed the court of appeals' reversal.)

The Pacifica decision signals a trend by the United States Supreme Court away from the more liberal approach to obscenity or indecency expressed previously in other decisions. Arguably the Court senses that the American public desires more stringent controls concerning the regulation of what has admittedly been a continuing trend of liberalization and freedom in various forms of expression. It can hardly be denied that the proliferation of so-called dirty books and films has, to date, reached almost a saturation point.

However, the Pacifica case deals specifically with the mere use of certain "taboo" words. The rationale asserted in regard to protecting innocent children from exposure to such words does seem, at first blush, to be highly commendable. But a serious question that must be considered is whether the government, in the embodiment of the FCC, should be allowed to decide what is proper language for children to be allowed to hear, or rather should the decision be left to the discretion of parents.

One must not forget that the real point of Mr. Carlin's routine was to illustrate the absurdity of many people's attitude in regard to the use of these particular words. Indeed, it is quite conceivable that many open-minded parents would not object to their children being exposed to Carlin's monologue in hope that their children might acquire a more objective and realistic attitude toward these supposedly "filthy" words.

The concept of channeling such language to a time of day when children are less likely to be in the listening audience would very likely be interpreted by children as reinforcing the notion that these words are in fact somehow dangerous and would no doubt pique their curiosity. It is not difficult to imagine children surreptitiously listening in to a late broadcast in order to hear what all the furor is about and then proudly displaying their new found vocabulary to their friends.

What the Supreme Court seems to be doing by making this ruling is to reaffirm the notion that these words are, indeed, something dangerous, which can somehow warp the supple minds of our youth. This attitude appears to be much less rational than that of George Carlin who was attempting to put in a more realistic perspective the use of, and reaction to, this kind of language.

One must not lose sight of the fact that this case represents a suppression of perhaps our most cherished freedom, the freedom of speech. It is difficult to conceive how the suppression of speech can be rationalized in this particular context. The Supreme Court does not acknowledge the irrefutable fact that children are bound to be exposed to "dirty words" in a myriad of ways other than through the public airwaves. The language used by Carlin in his monologue is far from uncommon in the playgrounds, and in many instances, the homes of America's children.

Ironically, the FCC has repeatedly refused to impose sanctions on the depiction of violence on the public airways, but has been continually vigilant in attempting to guard against the use of "indecent" or "obscene" language. This puzzling attitude seems to convey the most troublesome message that it is all right for our children to be exposed to and influenced by a seemingly never-ending barrage of graphic and gratuitous violence, but heaven forbid if they should hear a few so-called "dirty words."

8. At the present, the Federal Communications Commission regulation on the use of "indecent" language has been
   (A) referred to Congress
   (B) disallowed by two courts
   (C) upheld by the court of appeals but not by the Supreme Court

(D)   upheld by the court of appeals but reinstated by the Supreme Court
(E)   disallowed by the court of appeals but reinstated by the Supreme Court

9. According to the Supreme Court decision, a radio station would
(A)   be allowed to broadcast the reading of a James Joyce novel, which included some of the taboo words, at an hour when children would be likely to listen
(B)   not be allowed to broadcast the reading of a D. H. Lawrence novel, which included some of the taboo words, at any hour
(C)   not be allowed to broadcast the reading of a James Joyce novel, which included some of the taboo words, at any hour
(D)   be allowed to broadcast the George Carlin routine at an hour when children are not likely to be listening
(E)   be allowed to broadcast the George Carlin routine at any hour

10. We can infer from the passage that the author's attitude to the use of taboo words on radio is unlike that of
(A)   George Carlin
(B)   the majority of the court of appeals
(C)   the majority of the Supreme Court
(D)   radio station WBAI
(E)   the Pacifica Foundation

11. The author argues that restricting taboo language to odd hours of the broadcast day is likely to
(A)   increase the number of children listening at those hours
(B)   make this language appear more enticing to children
(C)   increase the number of adults listening at these hours
(D)   cut children off from contact with many great works of literature in English
(E)   cut adults off from contact with many great works of literature in English

12. We can infer from the passage that the author would agree with the Supreme Court majority about
(A)   the recent dramatic rise in the number of obscene films
(B)   the absurdity of many people's attitudes to the taboo words
(C)   the need to protect innocent children from exposure to "filth"
(D)   the meaning of freedom of speech
(E)   the indecency of the violence on the public airwaves

13. The author argues that the Supreme Court's decision reveals
(A)   that Carlin's belief in the danger of certain words is correct
(B)   an irrational fear of the power of language to corrupt
(C)   a move to more liberal attitudes on censorship
(D)   an indifference to serious sexually oriented literature
(E)   a shrewd understanding of adolescent behavior

14. Basic to the author's argument in the passage is the assumption that
(A)   the "filthy" words are harmless
(B)   there should be no restriction on what is broadcast on public airwaves
(C)   the number of "dirty" books and films has reached a saturation point
(D)   what children should be permitted to hear should be determined by children
(E)   forbidden fruits are more alluring because they are forbidden

Passage 3

In a sense, no intelligent person in his lifetime can entirely escape at least some informal speculation. In the form of a dilemma, Aristotle presented this truth in the fragment of one of his lost treatises, *Protreptikos:* "You say one must philosophize. Then you must philosophize. You say one should not philosophize. Then to prove your contention you must philosophize. In any case you must philosophize." To abandon philosophy altogether is itself a philosophical decision. In spite of some incurious or inept minds, the human intellect is naturally philosophical; it has a quenchless thirst for knowledge, not merely for data but for their explorations, justifications, and proofs; it tries to grasp its findings in an ultimate understanding of reality. Man's search is always for truth; he even proves truth by truth. In a popular sense, every thinking person is philosophizing.

Philosophy in the strict, technical sense, however, is quite different from the popular use of the term. The philosophizing of the common man is superficial, vague, haphazard, unconscious, uncritical, and subjective; but philosophy in the strict sense is a conscious, precise, critical, objective, and systematic study of all things.

Etymologically, the term "philosophy" derives from two Greek words: *philia* ("love") and *sophia* ("wisdom"). According to Cicero and Diogenes Laërtius, the term "philosophy" goes back to Pythagoras, one of the Seven Wise Men of ancient Greece, who allegedly repudiated the arrogant name of "sage" (*sophos*) by which contemporary thinkers had designated themselves. Pythagoras claimed, "No man, but only God, is wise"; since the goal of perfect wisdom is beyond the attainment of mortal men, he wanted to be called a *philosophos*, a "lover of wisdom."

Originally the term *sophia* designated the carpenter's art, the art of making pontoons, the art of navigation and guessing riddles. Later it meant talent in poetry and excellence in any art, music in particular. In ancient Greece a wise man was a person characterized by common sense or by great skill and outstanding performance in any art. Not until the time of Aristotle, though, did the term "philosophy" assume a technical meaning, distinguishing it from the other branches of learning.

Wisdom in the strict sense, as an intellectual virtue, is the certain and evident knowledge of all things through the ultimate reasons, principles, and causes. Philosophy, then, the loving quest for wisdom, is, according to its essential definition, the supreme science of all things through the ultimate reasons, principles, and causes acquired by means of natural human reason.

Science in general is universal, certain, evidenced, and systematized knowledge of things through their causes. Scientific knowledge is organized according to the intrinsic principles proper to its subject, thus making demonstrable its conclusions. Science does not desire a mere enumeration of facts, since the phenomena of nature are not isolated and independent; it seeks rather to discover the laws behind these facts in order to explain them and arrange them into a comprehensive system of knowledge. Philosophy goes beyond this purpose; it unites the findings of the various sciences into the highest system possible to the human intellect. Philosophy is not to be identified with any of the special sciences either singly or together; it is the unification and systematization of all important knowledge within the realm of reason. Philosophy is a universal science in the sense that it investigates and inquires into everything: knowledge itself and its methods, being in general, particular types of being both inanimate and animate, finite beings, and the Infinite Being. Its universal character, however, must not be understood in the sense that it is the sole science of mankind, absorbing all the special sciences, being merely their supreme synthesis. Philosophy is the supreme science, for it is not content with just the intermediate principles of truth, but also studies things in their ultimate aspects. It is preoccupied with the totalization of knowledge; it integrates the multiplicity of reality into a total and fundamental unity.

The main objects of philosophy, those that best indicate its meaning, are speculation and criticism. Concerning speculation, philosophy looks upon things from the broadest possible perspective; as for criticism, it has the twofold role of questioning and judging everything that pertains either to the foundations or to the superstructure of human thinking. [It is interesting to note that the English word "speculation" comes from the Latin verb *specere* ("to see"), but its immediate origin is in the noun *specula,* indicating a "watch tower" or, metonymically, a "hill." Just as one can see the wide horizon from a tower or a hilltop, so he obtains through philosophy a broad view of reality.] In short, philosophy is the science of beings in search of their ultimate reasons, causes, and principles.

As a science of beings, philosophy is concerned with everything that is or becomes or is known. Whereas the special sciences are looking for the proximate causes of things, philosophy searches for the ultimate explanations and causes of being.

15. Which of the following occupations was not associated with the term for wisdom by the ancient Greeks who preceded Aristotle?
(A) fortune-telling   (B) navigation   (C) making pontoons   (D) guessing riddles
(E) carpentry

16. According to the passage, one cannot escape philosophizing, because
(A) Aristotle could not
(B) antiphilosophy is superficial and vague
(C) to decide not to philosophize is itself a philosophical decision
(D) all human beings are intelligent during their lifetimes
(E) one is obliged to pursue the systematic study of all things.

17. The author of this passage would probably call philosophy
(A) the province of the Greeks
(B) one of the best of the practical arts
(C) an essential definition
(D) a supreme study, encompassing all things
(E) an indeterminate but highly rewarding pursuit

18. *Philosophos* is derived from which of the following sources?
(A) Greek   (B) Phythagoras   (C) Cicero   (D) Diogenes   (E) etymology

19. The main point of the sixth paragraph is emphasized in the last paragraph through which of the following processes?
(A) subtlety   (B) repetition   (C) deduction   (D) induction   (E) elimination

20. The "desire" of philosophy, according to the passage, is to
(A) systematize and enumerate causal phenomena
(B) make intrinsic properties demonstrable
(C) create universal tenets
(D) synthesize all knowledge
(E) publish the immediate principles of truth

21. According to the passage, the very fact that man thinks means that he is
(A) following in the tradition of the ancient Greeks
(B) tending toward a strict philosophical practice
(C) an informal philosopher
(D) a sage
(E) beyond the attainment of perfect wisdom

Passage 4

The United States Supreme Court has defined a presumption to be "an inference as to the existence of a fact not actually known, arising from its usual connection with another which is known." Jones explains a presumption as "an inference required by a rule of law to be drawn as to the existence of one fact from the existence of another established basic fact or combination of facts."

(5)   Specifically, an inference is the application of logic to support certain deductions drawn from relevant evidence. A fact or proposition is inferred by the process of reasoning wherein a logical conclusion is drawn from a given premise. Whereas a presumption is a conclusion that a rule of law directs shall be

made from proof of certain facts, an inference is a deduction that human experience teaches may be drawn from proof of other facts.

(10)   Primarily presumptions have developed independent of statutes. For example, judges gradually developed the rule independent of statutes that, if seven years elapse after a traveler has crossed the high seas without being heard from a presumption arises that he is dead. The several hundred presumptions normally grow out of the collective experience of observing certain repetitive and consistent factual situations arising from underlying, basic patterns of other facts.

(15)   As presumptions relate to criminal procedure, the only question is whether the presumption violates the United States Constitution. The Supreme Court has ruled on the extent to which presumptions can be employed in the criminal trial. In a civil trial, presumptions can come into play at two different stages: first, upon a motion for a directed verdict (where the judge directs the jury how to vote); second, upon introduction of evidence that contradicts the presumed fact and thereby ultimately sends the case to

(20)   the jury.

All authorities agree that a favorable presumption, by itself, will defeat a motion for a directed verdict made by the opposing party. Similarly, it is widely accepted that a lack of evidence to rebut the presumption mandates a directed verdict for the proponent thereof. A third situation exists when a presumption enters a case and contradicting evidence is introduced in rebuttal thereof. At this pivotal

(25)   point difficult procedural questions arise. The prevailing solution to this problem is sometimes called the Thayer Rule or the "bursting bubble theory." It states that when opposing evidence comes into a case, the presumption, having served its purpose, is no longer operative, and the issue is then determined on the evidence just as though no presumption had shifted the burden of producing evidence as to the presumed fact. Once rebuttal evidence is produced by the opposing party, the "presumption is spent

(30)   and disappears." In a majority of states this view has survived numerous challenges. The Thayer Rule has been severely criticized. The basic objection lies in the observation that the reasons for a presumption do not disappear with the introduction of a minimal amount of rebuttal evidence. Although public policy may back up the proponent of a presumption, his antagonist can seize the offensive simply by offering a few contrary facts. The proponent's only recourse is argument to the jury that the

(35)   probative force of the basic facts that he has proven satisfy his burden of proof.

22. Which of the following is an example of a presumption as defined by Jones in lines 3–4?

(A)   Because her father and mother have red hair and blue eyes, the baby will have red hair and blue eyes.
(B)   Because a six-year-old child is incapable of forming a criminal intent, he or she cannot commit a felony.
(C)   In times of economic depression, lawyers' fees decline.
(D)   Because the expected guest has not telephoned to explain his lateness, he must be unavoidably delayed.
(E)   A change in the law can act to preserve the stability of society in general.

23. According to the passage, all of the following describe a presumption EXCEPT
(A)   a conclusion made from proof of certain facts
(B)   an inference as to the existence of a fact not actually known
(C)   an inference about the existence of one fact drawn from the existence of another established fact
(D)   a legally accepted inference based on certain consistent factual situations
(E)   a deduction that human experience teaches may be drawn from proof of other facts

24. According to the passage, the sources of presumptions are primarily
(A)   statutes and regulations
(B)   social pressures
(C)   manners and conventions
(D)   observation and experience
(E)   public rules of law

25. All of the following statements about a presumption are true EXCEPT
   (A)   a presumption cannot be used to settle an apparently unanswerable question
   (B)   a motion for a directed verdict can be defeated by a favorable presumption in a civil case
   (C)   constitutionality is the only question to be raised about presumption in a criminal case
   (D)   normally, an unrefuted presumption will mandate a directed verdict for its proponent
   (E)   presumption may enter a civil case at two different stages

26. All of the following questions are relevant to a decision about the applicability of the Thayer Rule, EXCEPT
   (A)   In what state is the trial taking place?
   (B)   Is it a civil or a criminal case?
   (C)   Do new facts contradict a presumption?
   (D)   How effective is the reasoning that lies behind the presumption?
   (E)   Is a presumption part of the case?

27. Which of the following will NOT occur in most civil cases, when evidence contrary to a presumption is introduced?
   (A)   The court may invoke the Thayer Rule.
   (B)   The presumption is nullified.
   (C)   The reasons behind the presumption may no longer satisfy the burden of proof.
   (D)   The "bursting bubble theory" may be used.
   (E)   Any motion for a directed verdict made by the opposing party will be defeated.

28. The attitude of the author of the passage of the Thayer Rule can be described as one of
   (A)   unqualified approval
   (B)   qualified approval
   (C)   disapproval
   (D)   indifference
   (E)   ambivalence

STOP

END OF MULTIPLE-CHOICE EXAMINATION. IF YOU FINISH BEFORE TIME IS UP, CHECK YOUR WORK ON THIS SECTION ONLY. DO NOT GO BACK TO ANY OTHER SECTION OF THE EXAMINATION.

EXAMINATION

WRITING SAMPLE

Time—30 Minutes

Directions:
You have 30 minutes to write an essay in response to a given topic. Take a few minutes to plan your work before you begin writing. DO NOT WRITE ON A TOPIC OF YOUR OWN CHOICE. ESSAYS THAT DO NOT ADDRESS THE GIVEN TOPIC ARE UNACCEPTABLE.

The quality of your writing is more important than the length of your response or the content. Pay attention to organization, appropriate diction, and correct usage. You will not be expected to display any specialized knowledge in your response, nor will you be expected to write a "perfect" essay; law schools understand that you are writing under a time constraint, and will allow for the minor lapses in writing ability that might occur under this circumstance.

Only the lined area in your booklet will be reproduced for the law schools, so do not write outside this space. *Do not* skip lines or use wide margins. These precautions, along with careful planning and legible handwriting that is not unduly large, will keep you within the allowed space.

SAMPLE TOPIC

Ralph DeCinces is considering two job offers. Write an argument favoring one offer or the other, taking into account the following factors:

- Ralph has just finished an undergraduate degree in economics and wants to use his knowledge in government service to create programs that reduce inflation and poverty.
- Ralph is interested in running for public office after he gains some practical experience with the machinery of government.

The State Office of Budget and Management has offered Ralph a position as liaison to the Senate Finance Committee. The liaison must be present at all Finance Committee meetings but may only participate when called upon by a Senator. The liaison must be prepared with information from his office that is relevant to the Committee's deliberations and must supply that information from a nonpartisan perspective. In private, informal meetings, Committee members sometimes try to influence the liaison to slant his information in a partisan way. The liaison reviews all Finance legislation before it is discussed by the Committee, in order to be prepared with necessary data.

Wilson County has offered Ralph the position of County Manager. For the last fifteen years, Wilson County has suffered the highest percentage of citizens living in poverty, a situation that has contributed to widespread voter apathy. The County Manager proposes a budget to the County Board of Supervisors each year and administers the County Budget that finally wins approval. Once a budget is approved, the Manager has complete authority to monitor the spending of County funds and must be especially alert to the misuse of funds by any County agency. The former County Manager left his position after an unsuccessful attempt to stop officials in the Public Housing Office from awarding unreasonably lucrative contracts to a local building contractor.

ANSWER KEY

Section I: Logical Reasoning	Section II: Reading Comprehension	Section III: Logical Reasoning	Section IV: Analytical Reasoning	Section V: Reading Comprehension
1. E	1. B	1. C	1. C	1. E
2. B	2. A	2. B	2. B	2. B
3. C	3. E	3. C	3. C	3. C
4. E	4. B	4. A	4. C	4. B
5. B	5. C	5. D	5. A	5. B
6. B	6. C	6. B	6. D	6. C
7. C	7. D	7. E	7. E	7. A
8. D	8. D	8. E	8. A	8. E
9. A	9. B	9. B	9. D	9. D
10. A	10. A	10. C	10. E	10. C
11. C	11. E	11. C	11. B	11. B
12. D	12. E	12. E	12. C	12. A
13. D	13. A	13. D	13. A	13. B
14. C	14. B	14. A	14. D	14. A
15. A	15. D	15. E	15. C	15. A
16. D	16. A	16. D	16. D	16. C
17. A	17. D	17. C	17. D	17. D
18. B	18. E	18. B	18. E	18. A
19. B	19. B	19. A	19. D	19. B
20. B	20. D	20. E	20. E	20. D
21. E	21. C	21. A	21. B	21. C
22. C	22. C	22. D	22. E	22. B
23. E	23. C	23. B	23. D	23. E
24. A	24. B	24. C		24. D
25. E	25. B	25. D		25. A
	26. B			26. D
	27. A			27. E
	28. A			28. C

MODEL TEST ANALYSIS

Doing model exams and understanding the explanations afterwards are of course important in acquainting you with typical LSAT question types and successful approaches to the questions. However, another benefit of carefully analyzing these model tests is to understand the kinds of errors you are making and thus work to minimize them. For instance, if a very high percentage of your incorrect answers is due to "careless error" or "misread problem," then perhaps you are working much too fast and should slow your pace accordingly. If your incorrect answers are due primarily to "lack of knowledge," then a careful rereading and reworking of the appropriate question-type chapter may be in order. Or if you find that you aren't completing a large number of questions because of lack of time, you may need to either increase your speed or learn to use the "one-check, two-check" technique more effectively.

This kind of analysis of the model tests will enable you to identify your particular weaknesses and thus remedy them.

Model Test Six Analysis

Section	Total Number of Questions	Number Correct	Number Incorrect	Number Unanswered*
I: Logical Reasoning	25			
II: Reading Comprehension	28			
III: Logical Reasoning	25			
IV: Analytical Reasoning	23			
V: Reading Comprehension	28			
TOTALS:	129			

*At this stage in your preparation, you should not be leaving any blank answer spaces. At least fill in a guess, as there is no penalty for a wrong answer.

Reasons for Incorrect Answers

You may wish to evaluate the explanations before completing this chart.

Section	Total Number Incorrect	Lack of Knowledge	Misread Problem	Careless Error	Unanswered or Wrong Guess
I: Logical Reasoning					
II: Reading Comprehension					
III: Logical Reasoning					
IV: Analytical Reasoning					
V: Reading Comprehension					
TOTALS:					

EXPLANATIONS OF ANSWERS

Section I

1. **E**   (A), (B), (C), and (D) would call a Republican "victory" into question. In regard to (B), if the party held fewer seats than usual before the election, there would be fewer to lose and each seat lost would represent a higher percentage of the total. That fewer people voted would not undermine the claim to a victory.

2. **B**   The subject of the paragraph has been the kindergarten class and its surprising win over a high school class. (C) and (D) introduce new issues.

3. **C**   Phrases like "none left" and "sold out" state the problem but do not explain it.

4. **E**   The first paragraph is concerned specifically with the deceptive Volvo ad, and the second with fake advertising and consumer distrust in general.

5. **B**   The Federal Trade Commission is, presumably, an objective commentator, and this comment is a grave indictment of advertising.

6. **B**   That the Americans are not cited as opposing the move incumbent on developed nations and that they are victims of a questionable European practice suggest that the United States supports the reduction of subsidies. If the German chancellor hesitates to act and faces an upcoming election, we can infer his eagerness not to offend a large voting constituency of farmers. The quotation around "health inspection standards" and the tone of the passage suggest that the author believes this reason for excluding American products is bogus. We have no information on French politicians to infer (E).

7. **C**   The passage calls for an improved public school system and suggests the public schools are in decline. But the California test results cited here contradict this view.

8. **D**   The passage appears to be a dispassionate account of the rise in prices except for the fourth sentence, where the reference to the public's stupidity reveals the author's disapproval of the rising cost of tickets.

9. **A**   Darrell asserts that evolutionists do not explain the origin ("where matter came from") of life, and so take no stand on a creator.

10. **A**   The passage never explicitly connects the trade agreement and the embargo, but it twice mentions the trade agreement. The effect is to imply a connection.

11. **C**   The passage makes points favorable to both sides of this question making it very hard to determine a right side and a wrong side.

12. **D**   The argument cites "moral principles" and uses the tennis ball analogy to make its point.

13. **D**   Choices (A), (C), and (E) would not support the conclusion. Though the narrator is not Jane Austen, the narrator is probably closer to the author than any character in the novels.

14. **C**   The paragraph has already revealed the large sales of the record and the skilled marketing of an inferior product.

15. **A**   The point of the paragraph is that awards are based on sales. Choice (A) would contradict this idea.

16. **D**   A support group for retired persons would logically support a law intended to benefit retired workers.

17. **A** Though choices (B), (C), (D), and (E) are relevant, the purpose of the paragraph as a whole is to call attention to the lack of regulation of financial planners.

18. **B** The original uses a discovery based upon a personal experience. Choices (A), (C), and (D) do not follow this pattern. Choice (E) has no clear cause-and-effect relationship.

19. **B** The reasoning is as follows: this fork is rusted/it cannot be made of stainless steel. The unstated premise between those parts is that, if a utensil is made of stainless steel, it will not rust.

20. **B** (B) would support the conclusion from personal experience. (A), (C), (D), and (E) do not refer to the conclusion of the passage.

21. **E** The film described in choice (E) contradicts the argument of the paragraph.

22. **C** The author assumes the superiority of the explanation of (1) an economist, (2) with a Ph.D., (3) on the budget deficit, but does not assume that the explanation is right. Choice (D) does not specify the subject judged.

23. **E** No analogy is used here, but all the other four choices are employed.

24. **A** Only in (A) is "hopefully" used as an adverb (modifying "encouraged"), meaning "in a hopeful way."

25. **E** The apparent contradiction is resolved if the number of cable channels dividing the audience is growing more rapidly than the cable share, as a whole, of the audience.

Section II

Passage 1

1. **B** (A) and (E) are implied in the passage: "Peace with honor" is implicitly related to two of the desired goals—"international order" and the protection of the United States; "sympathy for U.S. forces" is implied by the final sentence, which says that U.S. forces are outnumbered. However, the *best* answer is (B) because anti-Communist sentiment is explicitly described and associated with the overall conclusions of the passage.

2. **A** The terms describing the state paper are positive; it is called "important" and "imposing"; such terms imply praise of Truman, who is responsible for the project. (D) is unsupported by extensive and extremely positive remarks. The passage expresses or implies no negative judgments, so (B), (C), and (E) should be eliminated.

3. **E** In the first paragraph we are told, "The document was imposing in its scope and depth," and we are given details supporting this idea. A possible choice, (D), may be eliminated because the conclusions of the study are clearly subjective—anti-Soviet in sentiment.

4. **B** The final sentence stresses that U.S. forces are outnumbered, thus implying the value of an increase; otherwise, they are "literally at the mercy of the Soviet government."

5. **C** All other choices are mentioned in the passage. The Truman containment policy is a real historical phenomenon, but is not mentioned or implied in the passage.

6. **C** The "understanding" of the Soviets that is described in this passage is one that cites no positive qualities, and characterizes the Russians as threatening enemies. A Russian would certainly not accept such a characterization as accurate.

7. **D** Many people were involved in the drafting of the document, including "other persons with special knowledge of foreign affairs"; such persons could be affiliated with any or no branch of government.

Passage 2

8. **D** The author says that "our country is no longer an economic 'island unto itself'" and later urges business to develop strategies for competing with foreign concerns; in other words, our country can no longer sit back, disregarding the rest of the economic world, and grow rich.

9. **B** This answer is stated explicitly in the second paragraph: "The culprit . . . is the increasing influx of low-cost foreign steel." There are other reasons for the steel mill closure, but the question asks only for *a* reason.

10. **A** Only this choice is explicitly called a "truism" in the passage (paragraph 6).

11. **E** This choice is stated explicitly in paragraph 4. None of the other choices is mentioned or implied in the paragraph.

12. **E** In paragraph 7 the point is made that, although "we may condemn others for not buying American-made products, how many of us drive foreign cars . . ."; in other words, how many of us are hypocrites! However, the passage does not condemn such foreign buying by implying that it is "traitorous" (D). Nor does it even go so far as to label price-conscious U.S. consumers as "tightfisted" (B).

13. **A** *Laissez-faire* economics advocates noninterference; it recommends that industries do as they please without government regulation. This author would probably modify *laissez-faire*, for although he does not explicitly advocate government interference, he does prescribe change, saying that we can no longer go about "doing as we please." (B) and (C) are synonymous, and inconsistent with the author's opinion, (D) is inconsistent with his obvious knowledge of economics, and (E) implies a sort of anger not present in the passage.

14. **B** Paragraphs 1 and 2 demonstrate that layoffs have been going on at Monarch "for some time now."

Passage 3

15. **D** Because the point of most of the passage is the objection by higher courts to the use of nuisance ordinance against pornography, option (D) most accurately suggests the content of the passage.

16. **A** Public nuisance is usually anything that is injurious to health, indecent or offensive, or obstructive to free passage. A pickpocket would be prosecuted under other laws.

17. **D** The passage speaks of the First Amendment's "aim to avoid previous restraints" by eliminating states' approval of printed matter.

18. **E** According to the third paragraph, (A), (B), (C), and (D) are advantageous. (E) is untrue.

19. **B** The immediate effect of the 1977 decision was to increase the number of civil nuisance actions. But these actions were to be reversed on appeal.

20. **D** The fourth and fifth paragraphs suggest that the nuisance laws cannot be used until all currently displayed materials have been found to be obscene.

21. **C** (A) and (B) would result in removal of the store. (D) is untrue; (E) is true but does not logically support the question.

22. **C** The advantage of zoning ordinances is they avoid the problems of prior restraint violations that impair the effectiveness of nuisance regulations.

Passage 4

23. **C** Miss Hamilton's statement, "Please address me correctly" implies that she has been incorrectly addressed. Her later petition indicates the implication of her objection; she cites "equal protection" and "etiquette" in her favor. Both are related to the "demeaning" quality of her court experience.

24. **B** The Red Queen in *Alice* is an absurd tyrant, as you should realize by recognizing that "sentence first, trial afterward" is both absurd and tyrannical.

25. **B** The author's ability to *quote* the court participants indicates that he was either at the hearing or privy to a direct transcript.

26. **B** Only (B) is a question that is both raised and not answered in the passage. Other choices are either questions that are answered or questions that are never raised.

27. **A** (C) is irrelevant to the race of *this* judge and staff; (B) refers to the legal profession in general rather than the officers of the court in particular; (D) should be eliminated because the present racial situation is not addressed; and (E) should be eliminated because the race of the arresting officers is never mentioned.

28. **A** In the midst of recounting the court dialogue, the author says, "Miss Hamilton would not be intimidated," thus suggesting the judge's purpose.

Section III

1. **C** Choices (A), (B), (D), and (E) are all points *against* the argument of the letter. If the letter is ironic, however, there would be no need to make a case against it.

2. **B** The issue is the likelihood of a two-car collision, not simply a traffic accident. Only (B) provides information about two-car collisions.

3. **C** Only (C)—"all…have had"—will lead to the conclusion in the statement. The best way to answer questions of this type is to formulate a correct answer before reading the choices given on the test.

4. **A** The correct answer is implied in the first paragraph: "not always bad news," but usually. (B), (D), and (E) are untrue.

5. **D** The paragraph questions whether or not a recession is in progress. It then introduces a businessman who claims to know the answer, but the paragraph breaks off before giving it. The logical last sentence would reveal what the repair percentage tells us about the possible recession.

6. **B** If they bought rose bushes, they did not buy garden tools or anything else; if they bought roses, they paid by charge account.

7. **E** (E) would help preserve the whales, but (A), (B), (C), and (D), if true, would not.

8. **E** The information in the passage does not compare the degrees of importance to men and to women of height and intelligence. Therefore, though (A), (B), (C), and (D) are logical, (E) is impossible to infer.

9. **B** The passage identifies an opposition, but it does not cite and dispute the evidence proposed by the other side. It does use all the other four techniques.

10. **C** If (C) is true, it shows a woman who has succeeded on her own. (A), (B), (C), and (D) weaken the author's case.

11. **C** The assemblyman's line of reasoning is that a constituency which does not directly benefit from a tax should not have to pay it. By this line of reasoning, younger taxpayers should not have to pay taxes that benefit the old.

12. **E** Choices (A), (B), (C), and (D) present useful definitions of aspects of the survey. In the case of (E), we already know that, at 18, male and female drivers are alike, and worse than at any other age.

13. **D** (A), (B), (C), and (E) are implied but not explicitly stated in the passage. We are not able to infer whether or not the aides have been doing their jobs.

14. **A** The quotation wryly suggests that the dishonesty among economics majors is practice for what they will be doing in business.

15. **E** (A), (B), (C), and (D) are reasonable inferences. We cannot know if "most" professors reuse examinations.

16. **D** The passage says "every month a famous figure from the past may be rehabilitated or vilified."

17. **C** The Winesap and Granny Smith apples of the second sentence in III are fruits, while the first sentence refers to fruits and vegetables. Similarly the passage refers to bank stocks listed on the American Exchange in the second sentence, and to the American Exchange in general in the first.

18. **B** (B) is not a reasonable or convincing argument against the bill. Presumably the doctor would not act until after the bill had passed.

19. **A** If the voting third accurately reflected the will of the nonvoting two thirds, the election results would reflect the will of the whole population. The whole Senate is not elected in the same year.

20. **E** (A), (B), (C), and (D) suggest the low voter turnout does not greatly affect the political power of certain groups or the election results. (E) suggests the old have a far larger block of voters than the young.

21. **A** By saying "I can't afford," Jane indicates that the hiring of a maid and a gardener is a financially prudent decision.

22. **D** There is nothing in the passage that would suggest that the cost of a fishing license is too high. (A), (B), (C), and (E) can be inferred; note that the first sentence links the sale of fishing licenses with funds for environmental improvement.

23. **B** If all investors are well dressed and all investors are asked to the dance, some of those asked to the dance must be well dressed. There may be others who are well dressed but are not investors who are not asked to the dance.

24. **C** The argument in (C) is directed against the mayor's Oversight Commission, the mayor, and the police chief, not against the issue of the wrongful death.

25. **D** The argument attempts to refute the generalization that caffeine causes sleeplessness by referring to cases where this effect has not occurred.

Section IV

Answers 1–5

1. **C** From statements (1), (2), and (7) we can deduce only that Fred must sit between two people because the end seats are already taken.

2. **B** From statements (1), (2), (6), and (7) we can construct the following chart:

$$\underline{\quad E \quad}\ \underline{\qquad\quad}\ \underline{\qquad\quad}\ \underline{\quad F \quad}\ \underline{\quad L \quad}\ \underline{\quad S \quad}$$

We now know that Tom cannot sit next to Simon because Lynn already occupies that seat.

3. **C** From all the information given, the following chart can be constructed:

$$\underline{\quad E \quad}\ \underline{\quad T \quad}\ \underline{\quad J \quad}\ \underline{\quad F \quad}\ \underline{\quad L \quad}\ \underline{\quad S \quad}$$

Thus, Tom sits next to Enola and next to Jan.

4. **C** From the chart we can see that Lynn sits next to Fred and Simon, not next to Tom. Note that (E) is still true ("Lynn sits between Enola and Simon") even though Lynn doesn't necessarily sit next to them.

5. **A** From the information given, the friends could sit only in this order: Enola, Tom, Jan, Fred, Lynn, Simon.

Answers 6–12

The following Venn diagram may be constructed from the information to help you answer the questions:

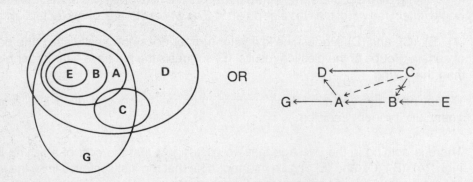

Note that the circles indicate all the possibilities that may exist.

6. **D** If some C's are A's, and all A's are G's (from statements 6 and 4), then logically some C's are G's. Since all E's are B's, and all B's are A's, then all E's are G's.

7. **E** Since statement 5 tells us no C's are B's, then "some C's are B's" must be false. Note that (C) *may* be false, but not necessarily *must* be false.

8. **A** If all D's are G's, then from statement 1 we can conclude that all A's, B's, and C's are also G's. Thus (A) is true. From the diagram, the others are false.

9. **D** Since all C's are D's (statement 1), then, if Q is within C, Q must also be within D.

10. **E** There is no statement that tells us about G's. Therefore, we can conclude only that (E) is true since it to says nothing specific about the G's. The rest of the statements are false.

11. **B** If all J's are B's, then all J's must lie within A's and D's.

12. **C** If all D's are M's, then all C's and all A's are M's, since all C's and all A's are D's.

Answers 13–18

From the information given we could have constructed the following chart:

Carpet	Drapes	Sofa	Sofa	Chair	Chair
b					b
		?Y	or		?Y

13. **A** If one chair is yellow, and the drapes are light green, then one of the sofas must be light green and one of the chairs must be dark green. Your chart would look like this:

Carpet	Drapes	Sofa	Sofa	Chair	Chair
	LG	LG		Y	DG

If the carpet is yellow then the sofas cannot be dark green. They also cannot be light green or yellow since we have used two of each color. Thus, one sofa must be blue.

14. **D** Since we already have two yellows, (D) is not possible.

15. **C** The chart would now look like this:

Carpet	Drapes	Sofa	Sofa	Chair	Chair
Y	Y	B?	B?	DG	DG

Since the carpet cannot be light green and cannot be blue or dark green, it must be yellow. This does not affect the color of the sofas. It is possible that both sofas are the same color.

16. **D** If the carpet and drapes are the same color, then they cannot be blue or light green. If they were light green, this would force a sofa to be light green also, making three items light green. This leaves yellow and dark green for the carpet and drapes. If the carpet is yellow, the sofas cannot be dark green. If the carpet and drapes are dark green, then no other item can be dark green. Thus the sofas cannot be dark green.

17. **D** If the chair-sofa combinations were light green and dark green, this would force the carpet to be yellow. If the carpet is yellow, then the sofas cannot be dark green. Thus, (D) is false.

18. **E** If the drapes were light green, then one of the chairs must be dark green. Thus choice (E) is the answer.

Answers 19–23

From the information given, you could have made the following diagram:

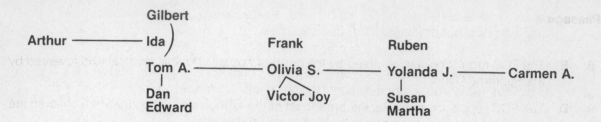

19. **D** From the diagram, since Gilbert is Carmen's grandfather, then his sister would be Carmen's aunt.

20. **E** From the diagram, since Dan and Susan are cousins, Dan couldn't be Bernie's uncle. All of the other choices are true.

21. **B** From the diagram, since Yolanda is Edward's aunt, then Ruben is Edward's uncle.

22. **E** From the diagram, Victor has one male cousin; this is the only statement that must be true.

23. **D** From the diagram, since Olivia is Gilbert's daughter, then Joy must be his granddaughter.

Section V

Passage 1

1. **E** The passage mentions diverse forms of government, from totalitarian Rome to modern American democracy, in each instance stressing the theatrical nature of political assemblies. The other choices are explicitly contradicted in the passage.

2. **B** Each of the other choices describes a subsidiary point of the passage. In general, the passage demonstrates that, in many governments at many times, politics has been a theatrical enterprise.

3. **C** The author uses "spectacle" at other points in the passage to describe the same sort of assembly he mentions here; we can call the "liturgical assembly" a "spectacle of worship," because the definition of "liturgical" is "connected with public worship."

4. **B** Although the author does not overtly and angrily criticize politics-as-show-business, he certainly calls into question through his descripitons of theatrical frivolity the worth of a politician who is "entertaining." If it seemed to you that the author was objective and neutral, your only possible choice would be (D), "unconcerned," which certainly contradicts the author's detailed interest in the phenomenon he describes.

5. **B** In the fifth paragraph, the author says that the diversion of political entertainment takes attention "away from true problems and realities."

6. **C** Each of the other choices may be eliminated easily, and it is quite obvious that historical facts occur repeatedly throughout the passage.

7. **A** Only (A) is an example of a politician taking part in show business; this example stresses the convergence of politics and show business that is the subject of the whole passage.

Passage 2

8. **E** The FCC regulation was reversed by the court of appeals but this reversal was reversed by the Supreme Court.

9. **D** The FCC regulation prohibits the broadcast of the taboo words at hours when children are likely to be listening, but permits them at some other hours.

10. **C** The author believes that words are not likely to corrupt, the view of George Carlin, the Court of Appeals, and probably of radio station WBAI, and the Pacifica Foundation, which broadcast George Carlin's record. The Supreme Court reversed the decision of the Court of Appeals.

11. **B** The passage suggests the possibility of children being more curious about the words if they are used only at times late at night. The passage makes no mention of literature and no predictions about increased listenership.

12. **A** The author comments explicitly on the number of obscene films. The Court would not endorse option (B) and we can make no inferences about the Court's view of violence.

13. **B** The author refers to the Court's view of language as "much less rational than that of George Carlin."

14. **A** Though the author might agree with options (C) and (E) the assumption that is the basis of his argument in the passage is that the words are harmless.

Passage 3

15. **A** Paragraph 4 mentions (B), (C), (D), and (E) as the arts designated by the term for wisdom.

16. **C** The correct answer is a paraphrase of the quotation from Aristotle in paragraph 1.

17. **D** Paragraph 6 states, "Philosophy is the supreme science...preoccupied with the totalization of knowledge."

18. **A** *Philosophos* was chosen as a label by Pythagoras, but the word was *derived* from Greek (*philia* + *sophia*).

19. **B** The last paragraph mainly defines philosophy and does so through repetition of the sixth-paragraph definition in different words: "Philosophy is a universal science...it is the sole science of mankind...Philosophy is the supreme science."

20. **D** Unlike the "desire" of science, philosophy works toward the "unification and systematization of all important knowledge" (paragraph 6).

21. **C** Paragraph 1 states, "In a popular sense, every thinking person is philosophizing." Such informal, popular philosophizing is opposed to "philosophy in the strict, technical sense" (paragraph 2).

Passage 4

22. **B** Jones's definition refers to the inference required by a rule of law not to just any logical inference. Though some of the other options are sensible inferences, only (B) is a presumption in the legal sense of the term.

23. **E** The definition of "presumption" can be found in the first and second paragraph. Definition (E) is of an "inference," the final line of the first paragraph.

24. **D** According to the passage, presumptions grow from the "collective experience of observing . . . factual situations arising from underlying, basic patterns of other facts."

25. **A** There is nothing in the passage about the use of presumption to decide unanswerable questions. In fact, presumptions are so used, for example, to decide the order of death when two members of a family die simultaneously. Options (B), (C), (D), and (E) all appear in the text of the fifth paragraph.

26. **D** All of the questions except (D) are relevant. The Thayer Rule is applied when evidence against a presumption enters a case. How effective the reasoning behind the presumption may be is of no matter.

27. **E** (A), (B), (C), and (D) are all possible, as described in the third paragraph. (E) refers to a "favorable presumption."

28. **C** The author's comments on the severe criticism the Thayer Rule has received and his phrase "simply by offering a few contrary facts" suggest strongly his disapproval.

PART FOUR

FINAL TOUCHES
Reviewing the Important Techniques

Chapter
12

A Summary of Strategies

DIRECTIONS AND STRATEGIES

GENERAL TIPS

- Use the "one-check, two-check" system, doing the easier questions first, and saving the time-consuming and difficult questions for later.
- Don't leave any blank answer spaces. At least guess on your unanswered questions.
- Eliminate unreasonable or irrelevant answers immediately, marking them out on your question booklet.
- Highlight key words and phrases by marking right in your question booklet. Use the margins to draw diagrams, set up charts, and so on.
- Mark "T" and "F" (for "True" and "False") alongside the Roman numeral statements in "multiple-multiple-choice" questions. Often these will allow you to immediately eliminate incorrect answer choices. This type of question has not appeared recently.
- Watch out for the common mistake—the MISREAD.
- Spend some extra time reviewing Logical Reasoning problems. Remember, Logical Reasoning will comprise two of the four scored sections of your exam.

REVIEW OF LSAT AREAS

Reading Comprehension

Directions:
Read the passages and answer the questions following each passage by blackening the appropriate space on the answer sheet. You may refer to the passages when answering the questions.

Strategies:
- Skim the questions first, marking key words and phrases. (Don't read the answer choices.)
- Skim the passage (optional). Read and mark the first sentence of each paragraph.
- Read actively, marking the passage. In particular, look for answer spots, repeat spots, intuition spots.
- Answer the questions. Skip if necessary. Eliminate weak choices. Don't "read into" the passage.

Analytical Reasoning

Directions:
In this section you will be given groups of questions based on different sets of conditions. Drawing a simple diagram may be helpful in answering some of the questions. You are to choose the best answer and mark the corresponding space on your answer sheet.

Strategies:
- No formal logic is required.
- Make simple charts or diagrams.
- Fill in as much of the diagram as possible, but don't worry if you cannot complete it.
- Look for the framework of the diagram that would be most effective.
- Apply evidence in both directions, that is, also use what you know is *not* true.
- Use question marks for information that is variable.
- Sometimes looking at the questions can tip off the framework of the diagram that would be most helpful.
- Sometimes no standard chart will apply. Then simply pull out information or use simple notes.

Logical Reasoning

Directions:
In this section you will be given brief statements or passages and will be required to evaluate the reasoning involved. In some instances, more than one choice will appear to be a possible answer. You are to choose the *best* answer. Use common sense and reasonableness in making your selection; then mark the proper space on the answer sheet.

Strategies:
- Read the question first; then go back and read the argument or statement. This will give insight into what is going to be asked.
- Watch for items in the answer choices that are irrelevant or not addressed in the given information. Eliminate these immediately.
- Notice the overall tone of the question: Positive or negative? Agreeing with and strengthening the author's argument or criticizing and weakening the statement?
- Watch for important words: *some, all, none, only, one, few, no, could, must, each, except.*

Writing Sample

Directions:

You have 30 minutes to write an essay in response to a given topic. Take a few minutes to plan your work before you begin writing. DO NOT WRITE ON A TOPIC OF YOUR OWN CHOICE. ESSAYS THAT DO NOT ADDRESS THE GIVEN TOPIC ARE UNACCEPTABLE.

The quality of your writing is more important than the length of your response or the content. Pay attention to organization, appropriate diction, and correct usage. You will not be expected to display any specialized knowledge in your response, nor will you be expected to write a "perfect" essay; law schools understand that you are writing under a time constraint, and will allow for the minor lapses in writing ability that might occur under this circumstance.

Only the lined area in your booklet will be reproduced for the law schools, so do not write outside this space. *Do not* skip lines or use wide margins. These precautions, along with careful planning and legible handwriting that is not unduly large, will keep you within the allowed space.

Strategies:
- Read statements and biographies or descriptions at least twice, actively.
- Choose your candidate or item.
- Outline your essay.
- Start with a direction. Your first sentence should serve a purpose.
- Support your argument with examples or other specifics.
- Do *not* write a closing paragraph that simply repeats what you have already said.
- Write legibly. Write clearly. Write naturally.
- Proofread and edit your essay.

A FINAL CHECKLIST

A Few Days before the Test
- Review the test directions and strategies for each area.
- Become familiar with the test site; visit it if necessary.
- Follow your normal daily routine; don't make drastic changes.

The Night before the Test
- Review briefly, but don't cram.
- Get a normal night's sleep; don't go to bed too early or too late.

On the Day of the Test
- Eat a high-protein breakfast, unless you never eat breakfast.
- Arrive on time, equipped with three or four sharpened No. 2 pencils, a good eraser, proper identification, your admission ticket, and a watch.
- Dress comfortably. (You may wish to dress in "layers" so that you can add or remove a sweater or jacket if the room temperature changes.)
- Read the test directions carefully.
- Use the "one-check, two-check" system.
- Read *actively*.
- In Reading Comprehension and Logical Reasoning, remember to look at all choices before marking your answer.
- In Analytical Reasoning, be aware that you may not always need to review all of the choices before marking your answer.
- Before you leave a problem, be sure to take a guess. Try to make it an educated guess by eliminating some choices.
- If there are only a few minutes left for a section, fill in the remaining problems with guesses before time is called.
- Remember: look for problems that you CAN DO and SHOULD GET RIGHT, and DON'T GET STUCK on any one problem.

PART FIVE

ABOUT THE LAW SCHOOLS AND LAW PRACTICE

Chapter

13

Law Schools at a Glance

The table on the following pages presents pertinent facts about the 176 law schools offering the J.D. that are approved by the American Bar Association.

The information in the Law Schools at a Glance table is self-explanatory.

In several categories of the table, a bullet (•) is used to indicate a "yes" answer; if the box remains blank, a "no" answer is indicated. The Time Offered, Joint Degree Program, Graduate Law Degree Program, and Matriculation Calendar (Matric Cal) categories all use this system. Thus, the first entry in the table, American University, is shown to schedule classes during the day and in the evening, to offer joint degree and graduate law degree programs, and normally to allow students to begin studies only in the fall.

Most law schools operate on a semester basis, and information on credits needed for the J.D. is in terms of semester hours. For schools operating on a quarter system, the abbreviation qh (for quarter hour) is included. Similarly, part-time tuition is presented on a semester-hour basis, unless the notation qh appears.

The number of volumes in the library generally includes microform volume-equivalents as well as hard-copy volumes. The figures for full-time tuition refer to annual charges.

If a category of the table does not apply to a school, the abbreviation not appl (for not applicable) appears; if information was not available, the space was left blank.

INSTITUTION	TIME OFFERED: DAY	EVENING	PROGRAMS: CREDITS NEEDED FOR J.D.	CREDITS FOR REQUIRED COURSES	JOINT DEGREE PROGRAM	GRADUATE LAW DEGREE PROGRAM	ENROLLMENT: FULL-TIME	PART-TIME	AVERAGE AGE AT MATRICULATION	PERCENT WOMEN	PERCENT MINORITY	ATTRITION RATE	FACULTY: FULL-TIME	PART-TIME	LIBRARY: NUMBER OF VOLUMES	MATRIC CALL: FALL	WINTER	SPRING	SUMMER	TUITION IN-STATE (F/T)	IN-STATE (P/T)	OUT-OF-STATE (F/T)	OUT-OF-STATE (P/T)
American University (Washington College of Law)	●	●	86	34	●	●	809	233	23	50	16		40	70	300,000	●				$15,634	$11,001	$15,634	$11,001
Arizona State University	●		87	40	●		506		28	45	26	4	33	7	212,662	●				$764		$3,467	
Baylor University	●	●	120 hours		●		440		24	39	9	3	22	17	172,197	●		●	●	$5,694			
Boston College	●		85	38	●		850		25	49	19	1	42	30	3,000,000	●				$15,570		$15,570	
Boston University	●		84	33	●	●	1333	187	23	46	18	5	54		252,934	●				$15,950		$15,950	
Bridgeport School of Law at Quinnipiac College	●	●	86	53			547	188	26	33	8	1	33	28	230,000	●		●		$12,480	$520/hr	$12,480	$520/hr
Brooklyn Law School	●	●	86	34	●		1059	395	24	42	15	3	66	43	383,000	●				$14,500	$10,900	$14,500	$10,900
California Western School of Law	●		89	43	●	●	818		26	41	15	16	42	19	113,257	●			●	$13,150		$13,150	$10,900
Campbell University (Norman Adrian Wiggins School of Law)	●		90 hours	70 hours			319			41	3		14	19	144,205	●				$9,500		$9,500	
Capital University	●	●	85 sem.	48 sem.	●		344	301	27	36	5	11	28	17	198,000	●		●		$8,804	$336/hr	$8,804	$336/hr
Case Western Reserve University	●		88	33	●		684	14	25	44	9	1	40	71	241,607	●				$14,800	$48/hr	$14,800	$48/hr
Catholic University of America (Columbus School of Law)	●	●	84	33			672	267	23	46	15	4	37	18	164,500	●				$15,600	$11,200	$15,600	$11,200
Catholic University of Puerto Rico	●	●	94	82	●	●	170	165	24	21		11	14		135,000	●				$9,120	$145/hr	$9,120	$145/hr
City University of New York (School of Law at Queens College)	●		92	70			431	5	29	52	33	5	34	21	160,000	●				$4,321		$6,800	

School																					
Cleveland State University (Cleveland-Marshall College of Law)	•	•	87	36 plus 11 †	•	646	•	419	27	44	13	2	42	25	337,420	•		$4,512	$3,480	$9,024	$6,960
College of William and Mary (Marshall-Wythe School of Law)	•	•	90	41	•	562	•		24	45	13	2	32	24	278,000	•	•	$4,296		$11,016	
Columbia University	•	•	83	32	•	1008	•		24	40	23		63	20	680,000	•	•	$17,606			
Cornell University	•	•	84	32	•	574	•		24	41	22	1	31	26	375,000	•		$17,000		$17,000	$17,000
Creighton University	•	•	94	39	•	581	•	12	25	40	7	9	27	24	150,000	•		$10,100	$340/hr	$10,100	$340/hr
De Paul University	•	•	86	37	•	675	•	240	24	41	10	5	44	36	280,000	•		$12,308	$437/hr		
Detroit College of Law	•	•	85 sem. hrs.	58 sem. hr.	•	349	•	349	27	40	10	15	24	30	182,000	•	•	$10,500	$7,900	$10,500	$7,900
Dickinson School of Law	•	•	88	41	•	538	•	3	24	47	7	5	25	32	285,000	•		$10,500	$700/hr		
District of Columbia School of Law	•	•	85	56	•	242	•		29	47	50	15	21	8	115,000	•		$2,851		$9,105	
Drake University	•	•	90	48 to 50	•	533	•	20	23	42	9	8	25	32	148,432	•	•	$11,600	$390/hr		
Duke University	•	•	89	30	•	639	•	2	23	39	15	2	32	45	414,401	•	•	$16,400		$16,400	
Duquesne University	•	•	86	64	•	302	•	341	27	46	6	2	22	30	174,730	•		$8,754	$6,594	$8,754	$6,594
Emory University	•	•	88 hours	39 hours	•	679	•		23	42	9	4	41	51	209,348	•		$15,250		$15,250	
Florida State University	•	•	88	38-39	•	608	•		28	44	22	6	41		300,000	•		$2,933		$9,500	
Fordham University	•	•	83	45	•	1000	•	446	40		17	7	49	127	408,646	•		$15,100	$11,325	$15,100	$11,325
Franklin Pierce Law Center	•	•	84	39	•	374	•		27	44			17	19	121,736	•		$10,680			
George Mason University	•	•	87	42	•	401	•	355	28	42	16	4	29	24	250,000	•		$4,872	$174/hr	$15,372	$549/hr
George Washington University (The National Law Center)	•	•	84	42	•	1121	•	305	23	42	17	3	73		415,000	•		$16,450	$11,760	$16,450	$11,760
Georgetown University	•	•	83	31	•	1798	•	482	27	46	24	3	85	83	661,095	•		$16,650	$11,970		
Georgia State University	•	•	90	45	•	339	•	270	27	47	18	13	28	26	120,310	•		$2,272	$1,420	$6,848	$4,280
Golden Gate University	•	•	86	62	•	373	•	224	25	48	20	25	18	26	200,000	•	•	$12,239	$8,919		

Institution	Time Offered: Day	Time Offered: Evening	Programs: Credits Needed for J.D.	Programs: Credits for Required Courses	Programs: Joint Degree Program	Programs: Graduate Law Degree Program	Enrollment: Full-Time	Enrollment: Part-Time	Avg Age at Matriculation	Percent Women	Percent Minority	Attrition Rate	Faculty Full-Time	Faculty Part-Time	Library: Number of Volumes	Matric Call: Fall	Matric Call: Winter	Matric Call: Spring	Matric Call: Summer	Tuition In-State (F/T)	Tuition In-State (P/T)	Tuition Out-of-State (F/T)	Tuition Out-of-State (P/T)
Gonzaga University	●		90	52	●		510	29	27	32	6	11	23	12	177,000	●				$10,500	$350/hr	$10,500	$350/hr
Hamline University	●	●	88	33	●		578		27	46	9	2	24	21	200,000	●				$10,980		$10,950	
Harvard University	●		84 hours	42 hours	●	●	1773		24	36	17	1	65	50	1,400,000	●				$16,000		$16,000	
Hofstra University	●		85	39	●		823		23	40	16	4	39	19	350,000	●				$13,290		$13,290	
Howard University	●		88		●		372			57	85	12	20		180,000	●				$8,346			
Illinois Institute of Technology (ITT Chicago-Kent College of Law)	●	●	90	42	●		660	323	26	43	10	3	47	30	403,000	●	●			$10,760	$7,420	$10,760	$7,420
Indiana University/Bloomington	●		86	36	●	●	620	15	24	38	12	2	31	9	304,414	●				$3,581	$116/hr	$9,850	$318/hr
Indiana University-Purdue University	●	●	85	52	●	●	528	324	26	44	9		39	15	400,000	●				$3,581	$2,310	$9,850	$6,355
Inter-American University of Puerto Rico	●	●	90	70	●		330	337		45		5	24	33	119,000	●				$165/hr	$165/hr	$165/hr	$165/hr
John Marshal Law School	●	●	90	52	●	●	759	458	25	35	12	5	45	78	270,000	●			●	$12,150	$7,290	$12,150	$7,290
Lewis and Clark College (Northwestern School of Law)	●	●	86	34-39	●	●	479	242	27	43	13	10	30	23	310,000	●				$12,015	$8,240	$12,015	$8,240
Louisiana State University (Paul M. Hebert Law Center)	●		97	36	●	●	798			36	7		36	32	373,731	●				$3,534		$7,734	
Loyola Marymount University	●	●	87	42	●		985	299	24	45	22	5	51	43	332,749	●				$14,016	$9,372		
Loyola University of Chicago	●	●	86	40	●	●	511	208	25	53	14	5	37	149	131,467	●				$11,600	$8,700	$11,600	$8,700

School																					
Loyola University-New Orleans	•	•	90	70	•	•	581	199	23	45	14	17	30	20	220,000	•		$12,710	$8,610	$12,710	$8,610
Marquette University	•	•	90 sem.	55 sem.	•	•	488		25	44	7	2	29	15	185,000	•		$10,480	$410/hr		
Memphis State University (Cecil C. Humphreys School of Law)	•	•	96	56	•	•	382	37	27	46	10		20	30	230,400	•		$2,416	$105/hr	$6,006	$261/hr
Mercer University (Walter F. George School of Law)	•	•	88	50	•	•	428	2	26	37	11	7	26	17	135,969	•		$11,700		$11,700	
Mississippi College	•	•	88 sem.	53	•	•	383		25	32	10		16	7	203,000	•		$8,700			
New England School of Law	•	•	84	42	•	•	643	514	22	41	3	8	36	58	230,000	•		$9,250	$6,940	$9,250	$6,940
New York Law School	•	•	86	29	•	•	850	457	26	45	11	5	49	88	330,000	•	•	$13,784	$10,338	$13,784	$10,338
New York University	•	•	82		•	•			27	47	18		80	65	825,000	•		$17,910		$17,910	
North Carolina Central University	•	•	88	65	•	•	229	73	25	51	44	20	20	13	150,000	•	•	$1,133	$621	$7,471	$4,737
Northeastern University	•	•	99	47	•	•	557		25	62	23	1	32	26	158,000	•		$15,000	$15,000	$313/hr	
Northern Illinois University	•	•			•	•	296		27	39	15	15	18	6	150,000	•		$3,031		$4,982	
Northern Kentucky University (Salmon P. Chase College of Law)	•	•	90	62	•	•	241	195	27	46	6	6	17	33	123,490	•	•	$2,770	$116/hr	$7,810	$326/hr
Northwestern University	•	•	86	38	•	•										•		$16,386			
Nova University (Shepard Broad Law Center)	•	•	84	31	•	•	744	15	26	44	18	14	35	38	244,532	•		$13,036	$550/hr	$13,036	$550/hr
Ohio Northern University (Claude W. Pettit College of Law)	•	•	87	54	•	•	450		26	29	8	20	27	14	171,659	•		$14,530		$14,530	
Ohio State University	•	•	84	31	•	•	640		22	45	18	3	41	12	558,000	•		$4,204		$10,364	
Oklahoma City University	•	•	90	43	•	•	429	242	27	35	7	8	26	31	198,000	•		$9,300	$7,500	$9,300	$7,500
Pace University	•	•	90	43	•	•	499	356	24	43	10	10	53	48	250,000	•		$14,576	$10,844		
Pepperdine University	•	•	88	57	•	•	650		24	39	10	10			215,000	•		$15,760			
Regent University School of Law	•	•	132 qtrs.	90 qtrs.	•	•	300		23	27	4	10 to 15	12	2	190,000	•		$9,000		$9,000	

Institution	Day	Evening	Credits Needed for J.D.	Credits for Required Courses	Joint Degree Program	Graduate Law Degree Program	Enrollment Full-Time	Enrollment Part-Time	Average Age at Matriculation	Percent Women	Percent Minority	Attrition Rate	Faculty Full-Time	Faculty Part-Time	Library Number of Volumes	Matric Fall	Matric Winter	Matric Spring	Matric Summer	Tuition In-State (F/T)	Tuition In-State (P/T)	Tuition Out-of-State (F/T)	Tuition Out-of-State (P/T)
Rutgers University–Camden	●	●	84	28	●		640	164	25	44	20	4	36	29	362,552	●				$5,794	$240/hr	$8,882	$370/hr
Rutgers University—Newark	●	●	84	31 to 32	●		595	252	29	42	28	6	42	46	388,053	●				$2,897	$240/hr	$4,441	$370/hr
Saint John's University	●	●	84	60	●		822	363	26	42		10	50	30	216,391	●			●	$12,690	$10,340	$12,690	$10,340
Saint Louis University	●	●	88 sem.	36 sem.	●	●	615	215	27	39	7	2	34	4	300,000	●				$9,600	$7,800	$9,600	$7,800
St. Mary's University	●		90	46	●		718			43	15	3	35	34	270,000	●				$11,250		$11,250	
St. Thomas University	●		90	47	●		454		27	35	25	3	25	24	190,000	●				$11,200		$11,200	
Samford University (Cumberland School of Law)	●		90	53	●		633			38	5	2	31	23	201,000	●				$11,600			
Santa Clara University	●	●	86	45	●		720	201	23	47	26	5	32	13	192,914	●				$13,054	$452/hr	$13,054	$452/hr
Seton Hall University	●	●	85	46	●		871	831	26	46	20	3	41	81	191,377	●				$14,400	$10,560	$14,400	$10,560
South Texas College of Law	●	●	90	41	●		828	573	29	41	10	9	55	24	149,238	●			●	$9,300	$5,890	$9,300	$5,890
Southern Illinois University/ Carbondale	●		90	46	●	●	307		28	39	11	5	25	5	281,281	●				$2,244	$93/hr	$6,732	$281/hr
Southern Methodist University	●		90	43	●		759		26	45	22	5	40	8	352,000	●				$15,500		$15,500	
Southern University and A & M College	●	●	96	76			336		28	38	54	10	19	8	182,982	●				$2,084		$3,884	
Southwestern University	●	●	87 sem.	54	●		787	369	27	47	19		42	31	198,058	●				$13,560	$8,588		

School																				
Stanford University	•	86	32-34	•	•	568		25	44	40	1	43	23	343,260	•		$16,722			
State University of New York at Buffalo	•	80 to 85	28 to 30	•	•	773		24	47	19	2	37	22	277,043	•		$4,200		$8,850	
Stetson University	•	86 hours	45	•	•	606	11	28	50	15	2	32	65	187,173	•	•	$11,990			
Suffolk University	•	84 cr. hr.	58	•	•	961	696	27	50	9	3	56	62	250,000	•		$11,990	$8,992	$11,990	$8,992
Syracuse University	•	86	50	•	•	783	15	25	40	19		38		164,338	•		$14,980	$652/hr		
Temple University	•	83	34	•	•	917	369	26	45	16	2	55	126	418,438	•		$6,486	$5,188	$11,978	$9,582
Texas Southern University (Thurgood Marshall School of Law)	•	90	70	•	•	570		27	39	93	15	31	16	200,000	•		$3,000		$5,700	
Texas Tech University	•	90	54	•	•	620		25	36	13	15	30	6	180,848	•		$3,200		$5,900	
Thomas M. Cooley Law School	•	90	72	•	•	110	1433	28	30	8	30	40	100	263,000	•	•	$10,500	$350/hr	$10,500	$350/hr
Touro College (Jacob D. Fuchsberg Law Center)	•	87	44 to 46	•	•	514	311	25	43	14	4	38	16	239,000	•	•	$12,270	$9,930	$12,270	$9,930
Tulane University	•	88	31	•	•	942		24	39	21	5	53	39	400,000	•				$15,750	
Union University (Albany Law School)	•	87	32	•	•	811	18	24	9	45	9	38	38	189,027	•		$14,500			
University of Akron	•	87	43	•	•	379	221	23	39	11	11	34	29	210,000	•		$3,651	$2,191	$6,610	$3,966
University of Alabama	•	90 sem.	43	•	•	551	15	23	36		2	28	23	216,492	•		$2,644		$5,508	
University of Arizona	•	85	39	•	•	455		27	47	21	2	31	22	300,000	•		$1,362		$5,484	
University of Arkansas	•	90	50	•	•	412		28	34	5		28	4	200,000	•		$2,560	$103/hr	$2,820	$220/hr
University of Arkansas at Little Rock	•	87	50	•	•	272	120	27	45	6	11	21	21	135,714	•		$2,324	$2,152	$4,914	$4,637
University of Baltimore	•	90	52	•	•	597	513	26	47	17	9	43	48	236,637	•		$5,382	$208/hr	$9,154	$337/hr
University of California (Hastings College of the Law)	•	88		•	•	1282		24	48	25		60	54	502,000	•		$3,161		$10,860	
University of California at Berkeley (Boalt Hall)	•	81	30	•	•	805		24	44	34	2	74	47	680,000	•		$3,205		$10,904	
University of California Davis	•	88		•	•	488		26	48	23	4	29	8	247,407	•		$3,058		$10,757	

Institution	Day	Evening	Credits Needed for J.D.	Credits for Required Courses	Joint Degree Program	Graduate Law Degree Program	Enrollment Full-Time	Enrollment Part-Time	Avg. Age at Matriculation	Percent Women	Percent Minority	Attrition Rate	Faculty Full-Time	Faculty Part-Time	Library Number of Volumes	Matric Fall	Matric Winter	Matric Spring	Matric Summer	Tuition In-State (F/T)	Tuition In-State (P/T)	Tuition Out-of-State (F/T)	Tuition Out-of-State (P/T)
University of California/Los Angeles	●		87	35	●	●	941		25	39	37	9	71	21	411,917	●				$3,323		$11,022	
University of Chicago	●		140	49	●	●	540			38	8		39	7	500,000	●				$16,980		$16,980	
University of Cincinnati	●		88	34	●		394		26	45	13	1	26	50	227,096	●				$4,425		$9,084	
University of Colorado	●	●	89	41	●		490		27	49	19	6	31	4	197,182	●				$3,528		$10,530	
University of Connecticut	●	●	86	40	●	●	442	228	25	50	14		43	44	350,000	●				$6,280	$4,599	$13,246	$9,702
University of Dayton	●	●	87	36	●		492		25	37	8	12	29	29	200,000	●				$10,970		$10,970	
University of Denver	●	●	90	47	●	●	748	279	27	44	11	4	40	23	244,072	●				$13,609	$8,780	$13,609	$8,780
University of Detroit Mercy	●	●	86	45	●	●	583	212	26	44	6	9	27	32	222,000	●				$355/hr			
University of Florida	●		86	32	●	●	1152		24	38	6	2	69	17	502,503	●			●	$2,701		$8,605	
University of Georgia	●		88	33	●	●	629		24	35	9	5	35	2	426,707	●				$2,122		$6,360	
University of Hawaii-Manoa (The William S. Richardson School of Law)			89	42	●	●	236		27	43	70	10	14	5	102,000	●				$2,010		$6,230	
University of Houston	●	●	88	35	●	●	966	285	25	47	16	7	52	56	218,696	●				$3,500		$6,080	
University of Idaho	●		88	33	●	●	315		27	31	1	1	17		137,458	●		●		$1,736		$2,510	
University of Illinois	●		90	39	●	●	655		24	35	16	1	32	18	491,495	●				$3,776		$10,608	

School																						
University of Iowa	•	•	90	35	•	•	701		25	46	22	8	45	6	514,636	•	•		$2,518		$8,006	
University of Kansas	•	•	90	43-45	•	•	564		24	41	11	4	29	10	300,000	•	•		$2,006		$5,720	
University of Kentucky	•	•	90	34	•	•	446		22	44	5	8	22	20	312,814	•	•	•	$2,600		$7,700	
University of Louisville	•	•	90		•	•	383	116	27	43	8		25	18	220,000	•	•		$2,660	$2,448	$7,700	$7,068
University of Maryland	•	•	84	42	•	•	611	256	26	51	24	10			280,000	•	•		$5,382	$207/hr	$9,848	$368/hr
University of Miami	•	•	88	73	•	•	1151	183	26	40	21	5	54	73	359,726	•	•		$14,150	$10,610	$14,150	$10,610
University of Michigan	•	•	83	31	•	•	1202		25	39	19	1	72	23	722,737	•	•	•	$8,890		$16,864	
University of Minnesota	•	•	88 sem hours	30	•	•	810		25	44	16	2	42		519,236	•	•		$5,120		$10,240	
University of Mississippi	•	•	90	54-57	•	•	498	4	24	35	8	9	22	9	132,000	•	•	•	$2,571		$4,033	
University of Missouri-Columbia	•	•	89 hours	53 hours	•	•	440		24	36	11	1	27	7	201,200	•	•		$4,731		$9,325	
University of Missouri-Kansas City	•	•	90	57	•	•	489	2	27	39	7	10	28	1	169,741	•	•		$4,906		$9,461	
University of Montana	•	•	90	72	•	•	228		30	41	5	11	14	12	115,074	•	•		$2,982		$5,433	
University of Nebraska	•	•	96	45	•	•	457	2	26	38	7	5	24	23	170,583	•	•		$3,012	$74/hr	$6,936	$191/hr
University of New Mexico	•	•	86	33	•	•	326		29	54	29	5	28	27	300,000	•	•		$2,010		$6,810	
University of North Carolina at Chapel Hill	•	•	86	33	•	•	696		23	45	14	3	35	4	350,000	•	•		$1,314		$8,676	
University of North Dakota	•	•	90	76	•	•			24	37	17	14	15	25	200,000	•	•		$2,566		$6,358	
University of Notre Dame	•	•	90	63	•	•	535		25	37	12	4	35	8	320,000	•	•		$14,095		$14,095	
University of Oklahoma	•	•	90	40	•	•	687		25	42	12	4	32	8	173,859	•	•		$2,665		$7,915	
University of Oregon	•	•	85	33	•	•	446		27	36	13	4	19	15	262,835	•	•		$5,018		$9,446	
University of Pennsylvania	•	•	93 1/2	36	•	•	751	1	22	41	14		41	43	425,000	•	•		$15,066	$753/hr	$15,066	$753/hr
University of Pittsburgh	•	•	88	40	•	•	726		25	47	8	2	35	25	230,000	•	•		$8,410		$12,910	

Institution	Day	Evening	Credits Needed for J.D.	Credits for Required Courses	Joint Degree Program	Graduate Law Degree Program	Enrollment Full-Time	Enrollment Part-Time	Average Age at Matriculation	Percent Women	Percent Minority	Attrition Rate	Faculty Full-Time	Faculty Part-Time	Library Number of Volumes	Fall	Winter	Spring	Summer	In-State (F/T)	In-State (P/T)	Out-of-State (F/T)	Out-of-State (P/T)
University of Puerto Rico	●	●	92	70	●		329	194	23	49		10	41	18	131,000	●				$1,350	$45/hr	$3,000	
University of Puget Sound	●	●	90	45	●	●	761	164	28	49	12	6	37	20	280,984	●				$11,400	$380/hr	$11,400	$380/hr
University of Richmond (The T.C. Williams School of Law)	●		86	38	●		454	5	25	47	14	3	23	26	203,005	●		●		$11,995	$590/hr	$11,995	$590/hr
University of San Diego	●	●	85	52	●	●	786	317	23	43	16	10	60	55	289,676	●				$13,200	$9,355	$13,200	$9,355
University of San Francisco	●		86	48	●	●	550	150	25	51	19	9	30	53	230,000	●				$13,610	$488/hr		
University of South Carolina	●		91	46	●		793		25	40	3	4	43	26	330,000	●				$3,900		$8,290	
University of South Dakota	●		90	45	●		224		26	34	3	3	18	2	140,495	●				$62/hr		$122/hr	
University of Southern California	●		88		●	●	612		24	39	24	1	48	23	237,633	●				$17,430		$17,430	
University of Southern Maine	●		89	41	●		269	1	27	46	7	3	16	2	260,000	●				$5,160	$172/hr	$10,320	$344/hr
University of Tennessee	●		89	45	●		466			41	11		33	22	313,378	●				$2,228		$5,818	
University of Texas at Austin	●		86	38 to 39	●	●	1558	385	24	43	21	1	56	45	700,000	●				$2,700		$5,400	
University of the Pacific (McGeorge School of Law)	●	●	88	62	●	●	845		25	43	12	8	58	35	355,871	●				$13,426	$7,952	$13,426	$7,952
University of Toledo	●	●	87	42	●		402	203		40	10	8	35	20	250,000	●				$4,353	$137/hr	$8,435	$137/hr
University of Tulsa	●	●	88	42	●		446	233	26	33	6	8	30	15	260,000	●				$10,500	$7,350	$10,500	$7,350

School		Yr			Enroll	%								Volumes						
University of Utah	•	88	40	•	382	5	27	37	13	2	27	30	•	185,000	•		$2,843		$6,476	
University of Virginia	•	86	27	•	1137			40	13	2	52	40	•	650,000	•		$4,802		$11,482	
University of Washington	•	135 qtrs.		•	464		25	47	30	2	40		•	426,000	•		$3,387		$8,472	
University of Wisconsin-Madison	•	90	35	•	805	59	25	45	11	2	60		•	377,000	•		$3,479	$145/hr	$9,499	$396/hr
University of Wyoming	•	88	52	•	219		28	42	7	8	15	19	•	167,316	•		$1,554		$4,358	
Valparaiso University	•	90	49	•	460	34	24	40	8	3	23	36	•	203,470	•		$10,900	$400/hr	$10,900	$400/hr
Vanderbilt University	•	88	34	•	540		27	39	18	2	34	23	•	207,887	•		$15,800		$15,800	
Vermont Law School	•	84	44	•	484		25	41	4	8	30		•	156,600	•		$12,970		$12,970	
Villanova University	•	86	32	•	653			48	7	2	40	21	•	367,000	•		$12,000		$12,000	
Wake Forest University	•	89		•	462		24	43	8	5	32	32	•	222,642	•		$11,650		$11,650	
Washburn University	•	90	34	•	444		26	40	16	8	26		•	237,090	•		$4,620	$196/hr	$5,880	$196/hr
Washington University in St. Louis	•	86	38	•	670	14	26	42	12	7	38	48	•	460,000	•				$15,950	
Washington and Lee University	•	85	38	•	385	30	25	40	14	1	32	11	•	282,019	•		$12,050		$12,050	
Wayne State University	•	86		•		38	27	50	17	3			•	390,000	•		$4,958	$165/hr	$10,875	$363/hr
West Virginia University	•	90 cr. hr.	49	•	405		26	41	8	5	23	39	•	155,219	•		$1,946	$81/hr	$5,256	$265/hr
Western New England College	•	88	45	•	531		26	50	7	12	29	10	•	265,000	•		$9,975	$7,480		
Whittier College	•	87	39	•	478		26	40	18	4	28	85	•	190,000	•	•	$13,324	$10,223		
Widener University	•	87		•			26	40	5		81	15	•	400,000	•	•	$11,215	$8,328	$11,215	$8,328
Willamette University	•	88	37	•	477		26	33	10	1	19	34	•	126,394	•		$11,450	$381/hr	$11,450	$381/hr
William Mitchell College of Law	•	88 sem 52 sem hrs		•	1100		25	42	8	2	33	30	•	200,000	•		$10,260	$7,450	$10,260	$7,450
Yale University	•	82	19	•	605		24	42	20		59		•	710,000	•	•	$17,610	$17,610	$17,610	
Yeshiva University (Benjamin N. Cardozo School of Law)	•	84	33	•	960		23	43	9	2	52	34	•	320,000	•	•	$14,300	$14,300	$14,300	

Chapter

14

Your Chances of Law School Admission

A PROFILE OF RECENT FIRST-YEAR LAW STUDENTS

The following table presents basic admissions statistics for all 176 law schools that are approved by the American Bar Association and offer the J.D. The information, which has been carefully compiled, is for a recent first-year class. By comparing your GPA and LSAT percentile with those of a first-year class at a school, and by noting the number of applicants accepted in relation to the number who applied, you will get an idea of your chance of admission to the school. You should also keep in mind that many law schools have special admissions policies, which give special consideration to students with unusual backgrounds whose GPA and LSAT scores are lower than those preferred.

A blank space on the table indicates that the information was not available.

478

A PROFILE OF RECENT FIRST-YEAR LAW STUDENTS

LAW SCHOOL	ACADEMIC STATISTICS			ADMISSIONS STATISTICS		
	Approx. Median LSAT Score Percentile of Enrolled Students	Approx. Lowest LSAT Score Percentile of Accepted Students	Median GPA (4.0 scale) of Enrolled Students	Total Applicants	Applicants Accepted	Applicants Enrolled
American University (Washington College of Law)	83		3.2	6328	1439	370
Arizona State University	82		3.4	2064	465	189
Baylor University	83	41.8	3.6	981	189	66
Boston College	90		3.4	6257	945	289
Boston University	89.7		3.4	5943	1744	444
Bridgeport School of Law at Quinnipiac College	66.1		2.9	2600	900	200
Brigham Young University (J. Reuben Clark Law School)	86.5	18.6	3.5	610	240	151
Brooklyn Law School	83	37.3	3.2	4055	1393	471
California Western School of Law	70	33	3.1	3516	1011	261
Campbell University (Norman Adrian Wiggins School of Law)	36		3.2	752	173	116
Capital University	56		3.2	1200	425	264
Case Western Reserve University	84		3.4	2201	637	225
Catholic University of America (Columbus School of Law)	79.6	16.1	3.2	3415	870	296
Catholic University of Puerto Rico	2.3		2.9	234	167	127
City University of New York (School of Law at Queens College)	37.3		3.0	1100	362	156
Cleveland State University (Cleveland-Marshall College of Law)	58	8	3.1	2152	673	320
College of William and Mary (Marshall-Wythe School of Law)	92.3	28.8	3.3	3386	636	208
Columbia University	96.1		3.5	6136	997	341
Cornell University	94.5	50	3.6	4500		190
Creighton University	66	33	3.2	1605	474	201
De Paul University	80		3.3	2667	900	337
Detroit College of Law	46.5		3.0	961	518	285
Dickinson School of Law	70	6.7	3.3	2326	557	178
District of Columbia School of Law	32.9	5.4	2.8	584	174	102

LAW SCHOOL	ACADEMIC STATISTICS			ADMISSIONS STATISTICS		
	Approx. Median LSAT Score Percentile of Enrolled Students	Approx. Lowest LSAT Score Percentile of Accepted Students	Median GPA (4.0 scale) of Enrolled Students	Total Applicants	Applicants Accepted	Applicants Enrolled
Drake University	66.1		3.2	1208	420	194
Duke University	96.1		3.7	4345	810	200
Duquesne University	75		3.4			204
Emory University	89.7		3.4	3600	880	219
Florida State University	75.2	4.4	3.4	1796	435	192
Fordham University	90	12	3.3	5083	1058	458
Franklin Pierce Law Center	61.2	9.7	3.0	1885	390	127
George Mason University	89.7	50	3.4	3680	497	163
George Washington University (The National Law Center)	92	30	3.5	8232	1734	465
Georgetown University	94.5	21.6	3.5	9400	2013	650
Georgia State University	75.2	18.6	3.1	2233	402	187
Golden Gate University	70	32.9	3.1	1247		208
Gonzaga University	56	51.3	3.1	1251	544	214
Hamline University	70	8.1	3.1	1471	525	199
Harvard University				8500		540
Hofstra University	39	18	3.2	3384	943	295
Howard University	56	30	2.8	1410	325	148
Illinois Institute of Technology (ITT Chicago-Kent College of Law)	66.1		3.1	1800		328
Indiana University/Bloomington	86	16	3.4	2171	530	207
Indiana University-Purdue University	75.2	37.3	3.4	1258	447	259
Inter-American University of Puerto Rico			2.8	757	320	187
John Marshal Law School	79.6		3.0	1934	729	306
Lewis and Clark College (Northwestern School of Law)	86	21	3.2	2321	695	227
Louisiana State University (Paul M. Hebert Law Center)	70	18.6	3.1	1292	527	301
Loyola Marymount University	87	28	3.2	4198	1007	420
Loyola University of Chicago	84	40	3.3	3075	701	228

A PROFILE OF RECENT FIRST-YEAR LAW STUDENTS

LAW SCHOOL	ACADEMIC STATISTICS			ADMISSIONS STATISTICS		
	Approx. Median LSAT Score Percentile of Enrolled Students	Approx. Lowest LSAT Score Percentile of Accepted Students	Median GPA (4.0 scale) of Enrolled Students	Total Applicants	Applicants Accepted	Applicants Enrolled
Loyola University-New Orleans	64		3.1	1904	639	274
Marquette University	70	20	3.2	800	360	170
Memphis State University (Cecil C. Humphreys School of Law)	68	13	3.1	1416	327	163
Mercer University (Walter F. George School of Law)	70		3.1	1630	320	143
Mississippi College	56	21.6	3.0	1085	357	160
New England School of Law	66.1	14	3.1	4368	1084	347
New York Law School	70		3.1	3517		405
New York University	96.1		3.6	7803	1264	401
North Carolina Central University	28.8	8.1		576	244	146
Northeastern University	80		3.3	3188	733	202
Northern Illinois University	75.2		3.0	1323	294	106
Northern Kentucky University (Salmon P. Chase College of Law)	56	11.6	3.2	983	250	160
Northwestern University				4704	728	201
Nova University (Shepard Broad Law Center)	54	4	2.9	3143	650	286
Ohio Northern University (Claude W. Pettit College of Law)	68	40	2.8	1805	480	165
Ohio State University	87	21	3.6	2099	517	230
Oklahoma City University	48	8	2.9	1223	543	237
Pace University	83		3.2	3100	270	
Pepperdine University	79.6		3.2	2641	900	266
Regent University School of Law	151*	137*	3.0	498	189	130
Rutgers University-Camden	83	13.7	3.1	2659	677	260
Rutgers University--Newark	86.5	8.1	3.4	3379	635	249
Saint John's University	36	21	3.3	3708	835	301
Saint Louis University	70		3.1	1600	561	250
St. Mary's University	72	17	3.0	1800	647	261

LAW SCHOOL	ACADEMIC STATISTICS			ADMISSIONS STATISTICS		
	Approx. Median LSAT Score Percentile of Enrolled Students	Approx. Lowest LSAT Score Percentile of Accepted Students	Median GPA (4.0 scale) of Enrolled Students	Total Applicants	Applicants Accepted	Applicants Enrolled
St. Thomas University	51.3		2.9	1752	379	171
Samford University (Cumberland School of Law)	70		3.1	1502		226
Santa Clara University	79.6		3.3	4002		283
Seton Hall University	66.1	11.6	3.3	3046	885	439
South Texas College of Law	71		3.0	1760	700	399
Southern Illinois University/Carbondale	66.1		3.2	1013	337	123
Southern Methodist University	80	16	3.2	2150	685	250
Southern University and A & M College	24.9	9.7	2.6	812	165	129
Southwestern University	61.2	28	3.2	3341	1213	459
Stanford University	96.1		3.7	6006	471	180
State University of New York at Buffalo	38		3.4	1885	558	247
Stetson University	70	32.9	3.3	2777	570	238
Suffolk University	79.6		3.2	3800		500
Syracuse University	72	20	3.2	3110	950	282
Temple University	66.1	16.1	3.3	3989	1061	420
Texas Southern University (Thurgood Marshall School of Law)	21.6	4.4	2.7	1375	417	258
Texas Tech University	75.2	18.6	3.3	1755	493	220
Thomas M. Cooley Law School	32.9		2.8	2081	1709	1038
Touro College (Jacob D. Fuchsberg Law Center)	51.3		3.1	2085	723	290
Tulane University	86.5	21.6	3.3	3100	1000	338
Union University (Albany Law School)	75.2	16.1	3.3	2434	854	281
University of Akron	61.2	9.7	3.1	2013	535	210
University of Alabama	75.2		3.4	1116	349	203
University of Arizona	83	21.6	3.3	1612	404	151
University of Arkansas				700		162
University of Arkansas at Little Rock	58	8	3.2	772	276	137

LAW SCHOOL	ACADEMIC STATISTICS			ADMISSIONS STATISTICS		
	Approx. Median LSAT Score Percentile of Enrolled Students	Approx. Lowest LSAT Score Percentile of Acceptd Students	Median GPA (4.0 scale) of Enrolled Students	Total Applicants	Applicants Accepted	Applicants Enrolled
University of Baltimore	66.1	13	3.2	2873	759	340
University of California (Hastings College of the Law)	92		3.4	3568	995	459
University of California at Berkeley (Boalt Hall)	96.1	41.8	3.8	6528	741	204
University of California Davis	93	40	3.4	4092	675	158
University of California/ Los Angeles	89.7	41.8	3.5	7268	1026	312
University of Chicago	96.1		3.7	2700		176
University of Cincinnati	86.5	28.8	3.4	1481	345	122
University of Colorado	92.3	32.9	3.3	2700	480	165
University of Connecticut	86.5		3.3	2428	397	207
University of Dayton	70	4.4	3.2	2802	575	186
University of Denver	78		3.1	2529	913	336
University of Detroit Mercy	66.1	41.8	3.1	1300	497	304
University of Florida	89.7	56	3.5	2200	750	400
University of Georgia	89.7	24.9	3.3	2375	454	215
University of Hawaii-Manoa (William S. Richardson School of Law)	86.5	70	3.4	650	130	80
University of Houston	86.5	24.9	3.3	3345	874	372
University of Idaho	60		3.1	1008	234	125
University of Illinois	89.7	28.8	4.4	2265	554	222
University of Iowa	83		3.6	1795	414	224
University of Kansas	79.6	25	3.4	1097	378	221
University of Kentucky	80	21*	3.3	1160	311	159
University of Louisville	66.1	21.6	3.2	1383	410	195
University of Maryland	83		3.0	3136	762	262
University of Miami	70	10	3.2	3149	1176	459
University of Michigan	97.4	35	3.7	6666	940	361
University of Minnesota	41	28.8	3.6	2424	657	270

LAW SCHOOL	ACADEMIC STATISTICS			ADMISSIONS STATISTICS		
	Approx. Median LSAT Score Percentile of Enrolled Students	Approx. Lowest LSAT Score Percentile of Accepted Students	Median GPA (4.0 scale) of Enrolled Students	Total Applicants	Applicants Accepted	Applicants Enrolled
University of Mississippi	61.2		3.3	1602	348	190
University of Missouri-Columbia	79.6	28.8	3.4	1376	380	144
University of Missouri-Kansas City	66.1	51.3	3.4	1221	416	167
University of Montana	66.1		3.1	447	141	74
University of Nebraska	63		3.3	908	344	160
University of New Mexico	70		3.2	1054		110
University of North Carolina at Chapel Hill	89.7	32.9	3.5	3290	570	235
University of North Dakota	46.5		3.1	269	170	81
University of Notre Dame	83		3.4	2700		170
University of Oklahoma	56	28	3.3	913	352	237
University of Oregon	86.5	56	3.2	2046	401	119
University of Pennsylvania	94.5		3.6	4496	1107	289
University of Pittsburgh	83	21.6	3.3	2077	638	262
University of Puerto Rico	32.9		3.3	461	165	147
University of Puget Sound	80	50	3.3	1724	619	286
University of Richmond (T.C. Williams School of Law)	39		3.0	2108	436	160
University of San Diego			3.3	4202	1070	334
University of San Francisco			3.3	3500		
University of South Carolina	75.2		3.5	1943	414	248
University of South Dakota	60	30	3.3	700	189	79
University of Southern California	94.5	44*	3.4	4010	755	186
University of Southern Maine	75.2	20	3.4	1154	208	92
University of Tennessee	70		3.4	1222	340	160
University of Texas at Austin	92.3	41.8	3.5	4000	900	508
University of the Pacific (McGeorge School of Law)	70		3.2	2875	1157	461
University of Toledo	70		3.1	923	478	206
University of Tulsa	33		3.0	830	454	238

A PROFILE OF RECENT FIRST-YEAR LAW STUDENTS

LAW SCHOOL	ACADEMIC STATISTICS			ADMISSIONS STATISTICS		
	Approx. Median LSAT Score Percentile of Enrolled Students	Approx. Lowest LSAT Score Percentile of Accepted Students	Median GPA (4.0 scale) of Enrolled Students	Total Applicants	Applicants Accepted	Applicants Enrolled
University of Utah	87	25	3.5	1000	280	129
University of Virginia	43	20	3.6	5887	953	381
University of Washington	93		3.5	2400	450	161
University of Wisconsin-Madison	40		3.4	2653	690	285
University of Wyoming	66.1	35	3.4	778	171	84
Valparaiso University	66.1		3.2	1079	420	168
Vanderbilt University	92.3		3.6	2500		185
Vermont Law School	70	32.9	3.0	2166	617	175
Villanova University	86.5		3.4	2124	667	233
Wake Forest University	83	13.7	3.3	2207	423	160
Washburn University	61		3.2	901	311	152
Washington University in St. Louis	82	30	3.3	1882	749	219
Washington and Lee University	89.7	18.6	3.3	2348	368	120
Wayne State University	75.2		3.3	1324	480	237
West Virginia University	70		3.2	1085	314	168
Western New England College	61.2	8.1	3.1	2397	698	267
Whittier College	66.1		2.9	2421	687	211
Widener University				1677	714	204
Willamette University	36		3.2	1046		165
William Mitchell College of Law	66.1	3.6	3.1	1100	600	330
Yale University	97	79	3.8	5381	407	183
Yeshiva University (Benjamin N. Cardozo School of Law)	83		3.2	2566	931	356

ANALYZING YOUR LSAT SCORE: A BROAD RANGE SCORE APPROXIMATOR

The chart that follows is designed to give you a general approximation of the number of questions you need to get right to fall into a general score range and percentile rank on your LSAT. It should help you see if you are in the "ballpark" of the score you need. This range approximator is *not* designed to give you an exact score or to predict your LSAT score. The actual LSAT will have questions that are similar to the ones encountered in this book, but some questions may be either easier or more difficult. The variance in difficulty levels and testing conditions can affect your score range.

Obtaining Your Approximate Score Range

Although the LSAT uses a very precise formula to convert raw scores to scaled scores, for the purpose of this broad range approximation simply total the number of questions you answered correctly. Next divide the total number of correct answers by the total number of questions on the sample test. This will give you the percent correct. Now look at the following chart to see the approximate percent you need to get right to get into your score range. Remember, on the actual test one of the sections is experimental and, therefore, doesn't count toward your score.

Approximate Scaled Score Range	Approx. % of Correct Answers Necessary	Approx. Score Percentile for 91-92 Testtakers (Est. % below)
171–180	93% and up	98–99.9
161–170	79%–92%	86–97
151–160	62%–78%	52–83
141–150	44%–61%	17–48
131–140	30%–43%	3–15
121–130	20%–29%	0–2

On the actual LSAT, the percent of correct answers to get certain scores will vary slightly from test to test, depending on number of problems and level of difficulty of that particular exam.

An average score is approximately 151.

If you are not in the range that you wish to achieve, check the approximate percent of correct answers that you need to achieve that range. Carefully analyze the types of errors you are making and continue practicing and analyzing. Remember, in trying to approximate a score range, you must take the complete sample test under strict time and test conditions.